CAESAR: POLITICIAN AND STATESMAN

MATTHIAS GELZER

CAESAR

POLITICIAN AND STATESMAN

Translated by Peter Needham

HARVARD UNIVERSITY PRESS
CAMBRIDGE, MASSACHUSETTS

CONTENTS

Map (Inside back cover)

THE ROMAN EMPIRE AT THE TIME OF CAESAR

PUBLISHER'S NOTE

THANKS are due to Mr. Peter Needham for translating this book. Thanks too are due to Professor E. Badian for the most valuable contribution of his scholarship and for devoting generous expense of care and time to seeing the book through the press.

Professor Gelzer has made certain corrections of fact and agreed to the addition of a few references. Professor Badian has also supervised the preparation of an analytical index of personal names for this edition. Miss Susan Williams has throughout afforded him valuable assistance.

INTRODUCTION TO THE SIXTH EDITION

Pour être un grand homme, il faut savoir profiter de
toute sa fortune (F. de la Rochefoucauld, Maxim 343).

THE first edition of this book was published by the Deutsche
Verlagsanstalt in 1921. I summoned up the courage to start
on it in 1917 when I learned that Erich Marks and Karl
Alexander von Müller intended to publish a series of monographs
entitled 'Masters of Politics'. When they accepted my offer
to undertake the volume on Caesar I wrote it during the period
1918–20. Since as a result of the war the series could not be produced
on the scale originally intended—in its place there appeared in 1921
the omnibus volume 'Meister der Politik, eine weltgeschichtliche
Reihe von Bildnissen', with a second edition in three volumes
in 1923—the publishers agreed to print my book as a separate work.
As I said in the introduction, I attempted thereby 'on the basis of a
conscientious evaluation of the sources to give the educated public
a lively picture of the complete political career of one of the great
statesmen of the past'. I started with the assumption that the writing
of history helps us to learn from the past, and continued: 'The
contemplation of great political situations where the working of
cause and effect can be discerned gives an insight into political
events and a standard whereby they may be judged. With this in
mind I regard it as most important that all available details should be
recorded.' In the year 1940 the publishing firm of D. W. Callwey
invited me to undertake a revision, and in this form the fifth and
most recent edition of the work appeared in 1943. Since this had
long been unavailable, and frequent inquiries could not be satisfied,
the publishing house of Franz Steiner kindly offered to bring out a
sixth edition. I am particularly grateful to them because, on their
own initiative, they have made it possible for me on this occasion
to substantiate and justify my account by means of notes.

I have been constantly working on the sources for the history
of the late Roman republic for nearly half a century. In addition to
Caesar, his opponents Cicero, Pompey, Cato and Brutus have
engaged my attention. In particular, I have tried to understand the
working of the society in which they played their parts. I first

developed my ideas on this subject in 1912 in my little book on the nobility of the Roman republic. With the fearful experiences of recent decades my views have changed and deepened. Much has been written about Caesar. The appearance of despotic rulers of quite a different stamp has not always been favourable to the judgment passed on him. A fresh study of the sources has, on the whole, convinced me of the correctness of my interpretation. I have therefore only changed the narrative in so far as recent research has led me to make factual alterations. Accordingly, I ask the reader not to look for bibliographical completeness in the notes. They are intended to show how I interpret the sources. No one knows better than I myself how much I owe to my predecessors and fellow scholars.

MATTHIAS GELZER

Frankfurt-on-Main
    October 1959

INTRODUCTION TO THE TRANSLATION

Now that the translation of my *Caesar* has been completed, I have the pleasant duty of expressing my sincere thanks to the Publisher, for making it possible.

MATTHIAS GELZER

Frankfurt-on-Main
    10th April 1966

CHAPTER ONE

THE POLITICAL WORLD

Two distinct qualities characterize a statesman. One is a quick grasp of and prompt reaction to the circumstances with which he is faced: this can serve the needs of the moment by allowing him to take account of existing trends with a clear head. The second, and nobler, is creative political ability, which can lead the statesman's contemporaries in new directions and itself create new circumstances.

Caesar had both these qualities. It must be admitted that he lived in an age that had need of them. For some time before his birth on July 13, 100 B.C.,[1] the foundations of the Roman Republic had been severely shaken by a series of crises. Suppression of the symptoms was not enough: the question was whether means could be found to remove the roots of the disease. Our immediate task is to consider how it was that things could come to such a pass.

Since the expulsion of the kings, governmental authority had been exercised by the magistrates, in particular by the two consuls. These

---

[1] The year of his birth is stated by Suet. *Caes.* 88; App. *b.c.* 2, 620; with less precision Vell. 2, 41, 2; Plut. *Caes.* 69, 1. The day can be deduced from Dio 47, 18, 6. Macrob. *Sat.* 1, 12, 34; *Fasti Amit.* (*Inscr. It.* 13, 2, 188, 9); *Fasti Ant.* (ibid., 208) give July 12, since in 42 B.C. the celebrations were brought forward by a day because of the games in honour of Apollo, which took place on July 13 (Groebe, *RE*, 10, 186, cf. *Inscr. It.* 13, 2, 482). Mommsen, *R.G.* 3, 16, 1 (English translation Vol. 4 (1866), pp. 15 ff.) opted for 102 as the year of birth. In *RStR* 1³, 568, n. 2; 569, 2, he concluded from Cic. *Brut.* 323; *off.* 2, 59; *leg. agr.* 2, 3; *Phil.* 5, 48, that after Sulla forty-two was the minimum age for the consulship. Caesar became consul in 59, at the age of forty. For this reason Karl Nipperdey, *Die leges annales* (Leipzig 1865; *Abh. der k. sächs. Ges. d. Wiss.* 5), 57, declared Mommsen's interpretation mistaken. In support of Mommsen's dating, see T. Rice Holmes, *The Roman Republic* (1923), 1, 436–42. Another solution is put forward by Lily Ross Taylor, *Greece and Rome*, 4 (1957), 12; 17, on the basis of an unpublished thesis by Helen E. Russell. According to Suet. *Caes.* 2, Caesar was decorated with the *corona civica* in the year 80; according to Liv. 23, 23, 6, after the battle of Cannae those *qui civicam coronam accepissent* became members of the Senate. On the strength of this, the conjecture is made that Sulla followed the same practice when he reconstructed the Senate, and that preferential treatment in standing for office was connected with it. Thus Cicero (*Phil.* 5, 52) proposes '*uti L. Egnatuleio triennium ante legitimum tempus magistratus petere, capere, gerere liceat*'. On this see also Nipperdey, op. cit., 53. Although he (op. cit., 4) questions the view that a special dispensation was granted to Caesar, Cicero's motion—of which we happen to hear by mere chance—suggests that such exceptions were nothing unusual. On Sulla's *lex annalis* see E. Gabba, *Athenaeum* 29 (1951), 263, 3. E. Badian, *JRS* 49 (1959), 88 ff. (=*Studies in Greek and Roman History* (1964), 140 ff.), argues that patricians were allowed to stand for the praetorship and the consulate (but not the quaestorship, which Caesar in fact held at the legal age two years earlier than plebeians.

1

magistrates were elected annually by the whole people according to
a system weighted in favour of the well-to-do middle class. Accordingly one might also have expected members of this class to fill the
magistracies. In fact the results of the elections usually favoured the
aristocracy. For a century only patricians were elected. But even
these early patricians already possessed the same remarkable political
instinct, which continued to distinguish the Roman aristocracy: they
fought obstinately to maintain their position, but knew how to
choose the right moment to make concessions and so to keep their
power. Thus from the beginning of the fourth century they allowed
prominent plebeians to reach the consular tribunate, and from the
middle of the century the consulship. This does not mean that the
magistracy became more democratic, only that the existing governing class was broadened to include a wider circle.

Even among the patricians those families which had once produced
a consul already formed an upper class, the nobility.[1] The patrician
nobiles were now joined by plebeians and henceforth the *nobiles* as
a whole (i.e. the descendants of the ex-consuls) formed the most
distinguished section of the Roman aristocracy. We find members
of these families reaching the consulship most frequently and so
maintaining a dominant position in the politics of the Roman state.

The reason for the striking phenomenon that assemblies dominated by the middle class always preferred to elect members of the
aristocracy as their leaders is to be found in the mutual dependence of
the stronger and weaker elements in Roman society. In the old days
the patricians were the full citizens, while the other inhabitants of
the city and the country districts belonging to Rome were their
'clients' (bondsmen) and enjoyed the protection of patrician patrons.
Patron and client were bound by a relationship of reciprocal good
faith. With the growth of the Roman Commonwealth there also
developed alongside the patricians a body of citizens—the plebs—
equal before the law, but without full political rights. In order to
live in security, plebeians also entrusted themselves as clients to the
protection of patricians: in their case, however, there was no longer
any question of bondage. The original clients were gradually
absorbed into the free plebs in historical times. Henceforth the
number of rich and powerful people in this section of the population increased: they no longer needed patrician patrons, but in fact

---

[1] M Gelzer, *Die Nobilität der römischen Republik* (1912), 22 ff. (= *Kl. Schr.* 1 (1962), 39 ff.);
H. Strasburger, *RE*, 17, 785; Ronald Syme, *The Roman Revolution* (1939), 10 ff.; Lily Ross
Taylor, *Party Politics in the Age of Caesar* (1949), 3; 186.

demanded political equality with the full citizens. In particular this was the aim of noblemen who moved to Rome from foreign communities. In the course of a long struggle they won the right of admission to the offices of state as well as to a majority of the priesthoods. In addition certain special plebeian rights were recognized: the plebeian officials became magistrates of the state and decrees of the plebeian assembly came to be recognized as equivalent to decrees of the whole people.

However, as we have observed, the chief significance of these achievements was that powerful plebeians entered the ranks of the ruling families. Their principal means to this end was that they took upon themselves, as plebeian patrons, the interests of the weaker members of their own class, who were often dependent on them economically: in this way they secured for themselves the necessary electoral following. As soon as the patrons had reached their goal, they began to use their positions of authority to further the interests of their clients. This very fact that they had clients of their own did more than anything else to make them the social equals of the patricians. Indeed, the power of the nobility rested on the patron-client relationship with its purpose of mutual advancement. The patron represented his client in court; as a magistrate he secured advantages for him, as a senator he championed his interests. The client for his part above all had the duty of working for his patron at elections, and in general of voting according to his instructions. The more clients a patron controlled, the greater his political influence. Coalitions with other patrons were the stuff of politics. This relationship was called 'friendship' (*amicitia*). Since its purpose was to fight a political opponent, we also find its converse, enmity (*inimicitiae*) or a state of feud. The reader who has grasped these relationships will understand why it was that the nobility always set the tone at the elections, and why as a rule only nobles were elected, or such as enjoyed the favour of influential circles of the nobility.

The rule of the nobility found particular expression in the authority of the Senate. The Senate was originally a body of experienced men, to whose advice first the kings and later the magistrates would listen, but without being bound by it. It goes without saying that from time immemorial the most distinguished citizens formed its membership. It became the practice under the Republic for the censors compiling the lists of senators always to consider first the claims of ex-magistrates. The Senate was only allowed to express its opinion when consulted. The consulting magistrate would call on members strictly in order of seniority: consulars, praetorians, aedilicians, tribunicians and quaestorians.[1] What eventually materialized as the result of a vote was a *senatus consultum* or senatorial 'advice'. The decisive votes were, as a rule, cast by the consulars, who as 'the chief men of the state' (*principes civitatis*) were recognized as holding a special position. We have already considered the manner in which the consulship was filled, and so it will be clear that here too the voice of the nobility was decisive. The line taken by the remaining senators was for the most part determined by their 'friendship' or 'enmity' to the controlling *principes*.

As the Roman Commonwealth annexed more and more territory, the importance of the Senate grew enormously. For two consuls, who were changed annually, could not possibly manage by themselves the affairs of an empire that embraced all Italy and soon had to take account of the whole Mediterranean world. Since the third century *senatus consulta*, which had not originally been binding, had gradually acquired the force of directives to the magistrates, including the tribunes of the people. As a result the Senate emerged as the actual governing body, whose decisions had to be implemented by the magistrates. Legally, of course, they could have ignored them. But what sort of position in the Senate would such a man hold after his year of office? Who would help him if the tribunes called him to account before the popular court?

So despite the fact that, in the matter of elections and voting in the assembly, Roman citizens enjoyed limited democratic rights, the Roman system of government was a pronounced oligarchy. The ruling class was the senatorial order, socially a group of large landowners. In accordance with their aristocratic concepts, the notion of pay for public service was foreign to the Romans of the Republic. Only men with a sufficient private income could become magistrates and senators. As early as 220 it was expressly laid down that senators and their sons might only invest their capital in land. The object of this law was to separate politics from business interests, but it also served to distinguish the senatorial class socially. The leadership of this circle was admitted to belong to the nobility.

With this oligarchy the Romans won their Empire and survived the gravest military crises. Since 287, when the government had finally recognized the special privileges of the plebeians, the Roman

---

[1] [Tr. note: These were men whose highest office had been, respectively, the consulship, the praetorship, the aedileship, the tribunate and the quaestorship.]

people had remained staunchly loyal to it, although it expected the greatest efforts from them under pressure of war. The Roman people, with whom the politicians had to reckon at the polls, were the small farmers, who were allied to the senators by a common economic interest. The establishment of control over Italy meant the acquisition of land for Roman citizens, and, thanks to the different uses to which the newly-conquered territory was put, both small and great could be satisfied by the establishment of settlements and colonies, or through the purchase or lease of public land. The struggles of internal politics took place within the ranks of the oligarchy and often arose from personal opposition between the *principes*: political issues were always inseparable from personal ones. The senators also showed themselves true Romans in that they naïvely took for granted that they could use their dominant position to further their own interests and those of their class. On the other hand, the political instinct which characterized the Roman people was developed in that distinguished assembly into a statecraft that ruled the world.

However, in the course of the second century, although on the surface Rome seemed to be becoming more and more powerful through progressive annexation of overseas provinces, the oligarchy showed itself incompetent to deal with the problems of governing the Empire. Let us review the primitive state of the constitution as it then was. The following magistrates were elected annually: two consuls, six praetors, four aediles, eight quaestors, ten tribunes of the people. Of these, two praetors, two quaestors and all the tribunes and aediles were required to fill posts in Rome, and only twelve men were available for war and provincial administration. Consequently magistracies had often to be prolonged for a further period of years. All political decisions concerning administrative measures in Rome, Italy and the provinces, as well as negotiations with foreign powers and allied and subject communities, were arrived at after involved discussion in the Senate.

The nobility were past masters at keeping the reins of government in their own hands: hardly a movement that could anywhere have endangered their supremacy escaped their constant watchfulness. But, according to custom, the Senate only concerned itself with matters which had been referred to it, and could never become a body which would completely reshape the traditional scheme of things. On the contrary, it was characteristic of the oligarchy to

obstruct the rise of powerful individuals, who might have felt themselves called to such deeds. The fall of the elder Scipio Africanus in
the year 184 was the clearest danger-signal. As a result, Roman
control of the provinces continued to be confined to measures
ensuring military security. These were regarded by the inhabitants
as foreign oppression and a deprivation of their former freedom. To
be sure, the Romans showed themselves masters at splitting their
subjects by discriminatory treatment and at avoiding general up-
risings. However, since the middle of the second century, thoughtful
senators had no doubt that beneath the surface of the Empire a crisis
was festering. Terrorization was the motive for the destruction of
Carthage, Corinth and Numantia. Nevertheless, while, from the
year 90 onward, Italy was experiencing the horrors of civil war,
Mithridates, king of Pontus, arose as leader of the East, and again
jeopardized all that Rome had firmly occupied in that area. And
when after a decade of fratricidal bloodshed Italy appeared to have
calmed down, war broke out anew in Spain. This was the political
world in which Caesar grew up.

Particularly in view of his later career, it is worth stressing that
the original cause of this crisis was the formation of the Empire
with the consequent growth of political tasks for which the machinery of the Roman state had not been constructed. Its greatest
achievement was the political unification of Italy, as seen in the
middle of the third century B.C. In its constitutional aspect the
organization was called 'the Romans and their allies': on one side
there was the Roman Commonwealth (res publica populi Romani),
the largest in Italy in area and population; on the other, 150 communities with similar constitutions, which were subordinated to
Rome in foreign relations and were bound by treaties to supply her
with troops, while enjoying internal autonomy. Among their allies
the Romans gave preferential treatment to the Latins. Originally
these were the communities in Latium, such as Tibur and Praeneste,
which stood closest to Rome because of their common language.
To these must be added the 'Latin colonies', which were of far
greater importance: they were new communities founded by the
Romans after their victorious campaigns in all districts of Italy as
supports for their supremacy, and were settled both by citizens and
by reliable allies. This system was simple, but, managed with skill
and dexterity, it allowed the Romans to make use in war of the
military resources of the whole of Italy, while keeping their own
political institutions within traditional limits.

The growth of any great power naturally incurs the hostility of the older great powers. Before the rise of Rome, Carthage had united the Phoenician cities of the western Mediterranean under her leadership, and had absorbed into her Empire the greater part of the large islands off the coast of Italy. Of Sicily, only the eastern part had remained independent, and here Rome was now faced with the question whether she could also allow Carthage to establish herself in Messana, the bridgehead facing the south of Italy. Rome's answer was negative, and the First Punic War broke out: after twenty-three years of indecisive warfare Carthage lost the three islands and Rome acquired her first 'provinces'. In these areas, in contrast to her policy in Italy, Rome regarded herself as the legal successor of Carthage: accordingly she transferred the government of Sicily and Sardinia (including Corsica) to magistrates henceforth annually appointed for the purpose. *Provincia* means the sphere of office of a Roman magistrate, in which he exercised his power of command (*imperium*): this applied equally in the military, judicial and administrative sphere. This form of administration, which was new to Rome, was primarily intended to turn to economic advantage, by the imposition of various taxes, territories that had been won at the cost of such great sacrifices in lives and property.

But Carthage was not yet ready to abdicate from her position as a great power, and sought to find in Spain a substitute for what she had lost. For this purpose fate provided her with a leader of genius in Hannibal, as great a general as he was a statesman, who was determined to risk a new and decisive struggle. After he had succeeded in carrying the war to Italy and had inflicted three crushing defeats on the Romans, it really looked as if he was going to achieve his object. But then, when they had been forced on to the defensive and were fighting for their very existence, the Romans, under the leadership of their nobility, showed all the toughness and powers of resistance of which their massive political system was capable. With the enemy in their own country, they unflinchingly continued the war both in Spain and Sicily. When Philip V of Macedon joined Hannibal's side and the struggle more and more assumed the dimensions of an ancient world war, they succeeded in holding their new enemy in check with the help of allies found in the east, until he consented to a separate peace in 205. Meanwhile they had produced in Publius Cornelius Scipio a general of the same calibre as Hannibal, who drove the Carthaginians out of Spain, crossed over to Africa and finally defeated Hannibal himself. As a fruit of victory Spain fell to Rome in the peace of 201.

This time the humiliation of Carthage was final. But if Rome's predominance in the west was now indisputable, this had immediate repercussions in the east—although the Romans failed to appreciate their full extent—and all the more so because they had already involved themselves in eastern politics through the Macedonian War. If, almost as a matter of course, a fresh contest with Philip followed as early as 200, although this was at the request of the king of Pergamum and the Republic of Rhodes, who called for Roman help against the expansion of the Antigonid Philip in the Aegean, the Romans were glad of this opportunity to take vengeance for his treacherous attack during the recent war. However, Philip's defeat was soon followed by a collision with the Seleucid Antiochus III, ruler of Asia, who was determined to resist Rome's expansion towards the east. This war brought her as far as Asia Minor, and her victory at Magnesia (189) removed this opponent too from the list of great powers, with the result that the hegemony of the Mediterranean world was now *de facto* in Rome's hands.

The earlier empires of antiquity had been the creation of great rulers. On the other hand, when the Roman Senate decided on war against Hannibal, it had no inkling of the tremendous consequences that would come out of its decision. In particular, no one could have foreseen that the collapse of the two great Hellenistic powers would follow so soon on the defeat of Carthage. So Roman policy suddenly found itself faced with a completely new set of problems. The vast area from Spain to Syria had to be watched continuously. Moreover, Spain had not yet really been conquered and the final reduction of the Celtic peoples of northern Italy still required considerable military efforts. For these reasons the Senate resorted to a political system in the east, which spared the Roman state the burden of new provinces. The world of Hellenistic states which had been freed from the pressure of the great powers, that is to say, the Greek states and federations as well as the kingdoms of Asia Minor, were to remain independent. Of course, the balance of power was fixed by Rome with the express intention of preventing any state from predominating, and so endangering Rome.

In the long run, however, this system proved a failure because it required continual Roman intervention, which restricted the development of political life among those it affected and consequently produced growing discontent. In view of this situation Rome found herself forced, two decades later, to put an end to the Macedonian kingdom once and for all, and in 146 she finally took over Macedonia and Greece as a province. The same year saw the destruction of Carthage also, and her territory became the province of Africa.

If the Senate's steps along the path to a provincial Empire were hesitant, this was because it correctly recognized that, as a result, the traditional framework of the Republic was being destroyed. That was so not only because of the numerical insufficiency of the existing magistrates and the difficulty of supervising them in the exercise of their offices in distant provinces, but also, and more particularly, because, in order to protect and control the provinces, it became necessary to keep troops permanently under arms. Hitherto Roman armies had been citizen levies, which were only called up for the duration of a war. Since the Roman soldier had to provide his equipment from his own means, these were formed from citizens resident on the land, i.e. mainly from small farmers, who could not with impunity be removed from their farms for years at a time. It was above all the prolonged wars in distant Spain that exposed this difficulty, which as early as the middle of the second century led to occasional resistance to the levy. And then Gaius Marius[1] found a way out of this threatening emergency. In 107 he had been entrusted as consul with the conduct of the war against the Numidian king, Jugurtha, and had filled the gaps in his army with volunteers from the mass of citizens without property or livelihood. Then, after his victorious return, he was elected to the consulship continuously from 104 to 100 in order to save Italy from invasion by the Cimbri and Teutones. This gave him a great opportunity to consolidate the new army organization in grand style. Although Roman citizens remained liable for military service as before, in the provinces standing armies of enlisted professional soldiers took the place of the militia.[2] This was a development with far-reaching social and political consequences. For the emergence of the soldier committed to serve for as long as he was fit for service immediately faced the state with the problem of providing for the veteran.[3]

---

[1] Sall. *Iug.* 86, 2–3; Plut. *Mar.* 9, 1. E. Gabba, *Athenaeum* 27 (1949), 181ff. shows that Marius brought to its conclusion a development recognizable since the Hannibalic War. By gradually lowering the census required for liability to military service, the levy could be made to apply more widely (Pol. 6, 19, 2). Marius disregarded the census requirement altogether.

[2] *voluntarius miles* (Tac. *ann.* 4, 4, 2; *Dig.* 49, 16, 4, 10); cf. E. Gabba, *Athenaeum* 29 (1951), 180 ff.

[3] A comprehensive list of modern literature on this topic is to be found in E. Gabba, op. cit., pp. 221 ff.

B

According to Roman concepts this was, in the first instance, a question of providing him with land. The generals were faced with the duty of championing this claim, but at the same time they gained a new and imposing *clientela*. As a result the figure of the victorious general acquired political power of unprecedented dimensions, and it is clear that the greatest danger for the oligarchy lay in the increased power that could now be won by individuals in this way.

Of course, contemporaries did not immediately grasp the decisive significance of this shift in the internal bases of power. It was fully realized only when the slow-burning crisis flared up in revolution and civil war. This further development soon followed. When the Senate had once abandoned its reservations, the provincial Empire was further extended. In 133 the last king of Pergamum bequeathed his kingdom—henceforward the province of Asia—to the Roman people; in 118, after repeated campaigns against the Celts beyond the Alps, the overland route to Spain was established by the creation of Further Gaul; in 103 Rome gained a footing in Cilicia to combat the pirate menace. A magistrate (praetor, proconsul or propraetor) was sent to each province to combine in one person the functions of military governor, chief justice and head of the civil administration; but, in accordance with the normal practice, he was generally replaced after a year. To these men, and above all to their often quite shameless avarice, the subjects were handed over almost without protection. Characteristically, as early as 149, through the agency of a well-intentioned tribune of the people, an extraordinary court was constituted, to give the provincials a legal means of suing governors for the restoration of money that had been wrongfully taken from them. Nevertheless, Roman provincial administration soon acquired a bad name, confirmed by the economic decline of the territories under her rule. In addition to a fixed tribute, tithes and customs duty were also levied. The collection of these items of variable revenue was left to companies of tax-farmers (*publicani*). Their profit came from actually collecting more from the provinces than they had contracted to deliver to the Treasury.[1] Accordingly they used all manner of underhand devices to squeeze out as much as they could. For the most part the governors let them have their way: even if they had no personal interest in this exploitation, they were unwilling to alienate the financial world with its electoral influence— it was principally the equestrian class which now applied itself to

[1] Cf. M. Rostovtzeff, *The Social and Economic History of the Hellenistic World* (1941), 2, 817; 965 ff.; 3, 1524 f.; 1567 ff.

this profitable business. This dependence became even more evident from 122: from that year the juries of the court which passed judgment on accused governors were drawn exclusively from the knights. As a result Roman provincial government only succeeded in making itself hated and piled up the revolutionary tinder that was ignited by the spark of the Italian Civil War.

The Roman state itself suffered the greatest damage from the demoralizing repercussions of the new imperialist policy on the social conditions of Italy. As a result of the wars in the east with their booty and compulsory reparations, together with the recurring revenues from the provinces, prodigious fortunes flowed into Rome. In addition, cheap labour in the form of tens of thousands of prisoners of war filled the slave markets. Under these circumstances the economy of Rome, which hitherto had been purely agrarian, now assumed strong capitalist tendencies. From the start these new possibilities were put to good use by the rich and enterprising, by senators and knights—the broad class of prosperous landowners who served on horseback in war and used this distinction to raise themselves above the rest of the citizen body. Land was bought up, and soon large estates appeared all over Italy, manned by slave gangs and devoted to the cultivation of olives, vines and fruit. Other land not suitable for these purposes served as pasture for cattle. In consequence numerous smallholdings disappeared. Their dispossessed inhabitants moved to the towns and, in particular, to Rome itself, and there tried to keep body and soul together by casual work and service as clients. Besides, the number of small farmers had already shrunk seriously during the Hannibalic War and this class then had to bear the brunt of the wars that followed. Although the Senate tried to help with an active policy of colonization, the ruthless expansion of large estates elsewhere more than counteracted the success of such measures. The gap between rich and poor increased rapidly. As already mentioned, the knights found a lucrative field of activity not only in a system of agriculture directed at maximum profits, but also in the lease of public contracts. At the same time the ruling nobility was also transformed into a downright plutocracy, which at elections and popular votes now had to reckon chiefly with a steadily increasing group of impoverished city-dwellers. In these conditions it was inevitable that the old client-patron relationships were gradually corrupted. Altogether the changed political and economic circumstances and the eager adoption of Hellenistic civilization shattered the moral standards of old Rome to an alarming degree.

In the political sphere, the decline in population fit to bear arms was particularly striking, because it directly threatened the newly-won *imperium populi Romani* in the provinces. So long as Rome wished to retain the militia system, there was only one remedy, the restoration of the class of small farmers, whose inexhaustible ranks had won the Republic its past victories. But to achieve this aim, land in Italy was needed for their settlement. In the age of the wars for the hegemony of Italy, when it was Rome's practice to punish her defeated enemies by annexation of territory on a large scale, there had never been any lack of land. Now, however, as a result of the economic developments which have been described, there was no more available. Such a design could only be implemented by an attack on existing property arrangements, which would be diametrically opposed to the plutocratic tendencies of the time and, as an attempt at implementation soon showed, would inflame passions to the pitch of revolution.

While others appreciated this danger and had misgivings over such a policy, in 133 Tiberius Sempronius Gracchus, an offshoot of one of the most eminent noble families of the day and the grandson of Scipio Africanus, had the courage to use his position as tribune of the people to come forward with a bill for the relief of want on a large scale. It proposed to distribute to settlers some of the occupied *ager publicus*, public land, occupation of which had hitherto been left uncontrolled. This proposal touched the interests of the large landowners at their most tender point, and it soon became apparent that a majority of the Senate would not support it. Tiberius joined battle with the oligarchy. His weapon was the tribunician veto, which he used to cripple the entire business of state. When his colleague Octavius followed the wishes of the occupiers and vetoed the bill, Tiberius had him removed from his post by the plebeian assembly and so carried the day. After this first act of violence there was no going back for him. He wished—again illegally—to stand a second time for the tribunate of the following year, and intended to bring in new legislation, which would divide the knights, as well as the common people, from the senatorial oligarchy. But, on the day of the elections, he was killed by his opponents as a revolutionary. The fall of this high-principled man showed with terrible clarity the extent of Rome's decline. Her ruling class was unable to cope with a problem, the importance and urgency of which could hardly fail to be recognized by all; yet the wound it had inflicted on itself was the most grievous of all, since the enemy it had killed had been one of its finest members. Office and precedence had long been fiercely contested, but none of that could stand comparison with the hatred that greeted the tribune's attempt on this occasion. The man who incited the senators to bloodshed was Tiberius' own cousin, the *pontifex maximus* Publius Scipio Nasica, and no one pronounced a harsher judgment on the dead man than his brother-in-law, Publius Scipio Aemilianus, the younger Africanus. This was understandable. To these men the recovery of the *ager publicus* with the approval of the popular assembly seemed a damnable assault on the sacred structure of state and society. But such a purely negative attitude was insufficient for the pressing needs of the moment. Once the sluice gates had been opened, the flood of the revolutionary movement could no longer be halted.

The political ideas of Tiberius Gracchus did not perish with him. They lived on in the circle of his friends. In particular his brother Gaius soon took up his work with greater effect. Politicians with new ideas now appeared, opposing the senatorial politicians of the old school. These were also members of the Senate—according to Roman notions it would have been unthinkable for them not to be—but in opposition to the senatorial policy, steeped in class prejudice as it was, they wished to serve the interests of the people, and, by means of repeated appeals to the popular assembly, to break the rule of a Senate incapable of producing timely reforms. As a result they acquired the name of *populares*. Their opponents, as defenders of the traditional rule of the nobility and the security of property, called themselves *boni* or *optimates*. It is characteristic of Roman conditions that both these names were applied only to the politicians and never to their supporters, whom each side called upon for help in the struggle for votes in the popular assembly.[1] If from now on one speaks of two parties at Rome, the point at issue between them was whether political decisions should continue to be made by the Senate, or whether, as had always been constitutionally possible, they should be transferred to a greater extent to the popular assembly. Accordingly, 'populares' would be most appropriately rendered by 'demagogues'.

If these leaders were to attain their ends, they had to follow the plans of Tiberius Gracchus in setting large sections of the people with votes in the assemblies against their established rulers.

[1] H. Strasburger, *RE*, 18, 783.

Accordingly, in 125, they unleashed a campaign of agitation for the granting of citizenship to all the Italian allies. Next Gaius Gracchus showed remarkable talent in inflaming all centres of dissatisfaction: he renewed his brother's agrarian legislation, promoted new colonies, modified the hardships of military service, adopted the cause of the ill-treated allies, supplied the urban populace with cheap corn, gave the knights a share in the administration of justice and let them have the tax-farming rights in the recently-acquired province of Asia. But the blow which hurt the Senate most was the bill of Manius Acilius Glabrio,[1] referred to above, which provided that knights instead of senators were to form the juries in the court dealing with cases of extortion brought against Roman magistrates. This made the knights a powerful factor in politics, with a very effective means of bringing pressure to bear on the Senate, of which they made ruthless use in the furtherance of their business interests. In the event, the original intention of removing culpable magistrates from the all too lenient jurisdiction of their peers was not infrequently distorted into the other extreme by party bias—a development not unwelcome to the authors of the new order, since it served to widen the breach between the two higher orders.

In this way the *populares* sought to achieve a majority in the popular assembly. With this support they intended to replace the Senate and to govern the state from the Forum. In constitutional form, the magistrates were no longer to receive their instructions from the Senate, but to become the servants of the sovereign people. In actual fact, this idea represented an unrealistic piece of play-acting. The decisions of the Roman people in the capital normally expressed the will of only a small fraction of the Roman citizen-body scattered all over Italy and the Empire. Further, the people who counted most were the citizens resident in the city; at that time this meant the impoverished *plebs urbana*, dependent on the generosity of the rich. So from the start the *populares* were less concerned that the government should follow the popular will than that the demagogues' plans should have the authority of the people. The system, as conceived by Gaius Gracchus, suffered from the internal contradiction that he wished to govern the Empire in a manner

[1] Fragments of the law in *CIL* 1[2], 583; Bruns, *Fontes iuris Romani*[7], No. 10; Riccobono, *Fontes iuris Romani anteiustiniani*[2], No. 7. The name of its author does not survive, but is deduced from Cic. *Verr.* 1, 51, taken with ps.-Asconius on 2, 1, 26. I do not think that G. Tibiletti (*Athenaeum* 31 (1953), 33 ff.) has disproved this conclusion. Cf. *Gnomon* 25 (1953), 319; Broughton, *MRR*, 1, 519, n. 4.

appropriate to a city state with limited territory and, at the same time, to extend Roman citizenship to the whole of Italy and even, by the establishment of colonies, to the provinces. However, the immediate cause of the failure of his ventures is to be found in the irreconcilable conflict between the different interests he had summoned to join battle against the government of the oligarchy: paupers and capitalists, citizens and non-citizens, could not permanently be harnessed together before his political chariot. In particular, the wedge he wished to drive between the senatorial and equestrian capitalists proved ineffective. When he passed to open revolution, senators and knights united with one accord behind the government and crushed this movement as they had the first.

But in this way the weighty political problems, over which these battles were fought, were no more disposed of than were the popular politicians. The daily blunders made and abuses practised by the oligarchy provided the opposition with weapons enough, and again split the senators and knights.

Another strong popular attack was mounted in the year 103, led by the tribune of the people Lucius Appuleius Saturninus. Its prospects of success were increased by the alliance of Saturninus with the war-hero Gaius Marius. Marius had gone further than anyone before him in riding rough-shod over the claims of the nobility. He came of municipal equestrian stock, a land-owning family from the town of Arpinum, which was situated in Roman territory, and he was the first of his family to reach the Senate, a *homo novus*, as such men were known in senatorial circles. By his own merits and through his distinguished connections he rose as high as the praetorship, and by his marriage to Julia, the sister of Caesar's father, he established ties of relationship with the aristocracy. But for the nobility it was inconceivable that such a man should aspire even to the consulship. The highest magistracy had to be reserved for senators' sons and, as far as possible, for members of the nobility. Yet Marius overcame all obstacles and in 107 was elected to the consulship, mainly through the help of the equites, from whose ranks he had sprung. The people had particular confidence in him in times of acute military crisis, and in the period from 104 he filled the consulship another five times. We have already recorded the important changes he made in the Roman army during his long command. His abilities were far more military than political. But after his glorious victories over the Teutones and Cimbri, the time had come to fulfil the promises he had given in order to enlist men with no property. In 103 the skilful demagogue had already offered welcome help with a bill to establish settlements. In the year 100 he carried a bill of far wider application, albeit by force and against the combined opposition of all property-owners and the urban proletariat. Renewed and more vicious acts of violence at the consular elections in December gave the senatorial government the opportunity for armed intervention for which it had been looking. On this occasion, as before, it found support in the usually hostile knights. Similarly the consul Marius kept to the path of duty and did everything to crush the revolution: the irresponsible behaviour of the *populares* had gone too far for his liking. Of course, he had not intended the death of his 'popular' friends in the process. As a result of it, he lost all political influence for the time being: not even the bill providing for his veterans was carried in its intended form.

As was always the case, this optimate victory brought the good elements in the popular reform movement to a standstill. On the other hand, the struggle between senators and knights revived more bitterly than before. The knights ever more brazenly exploited their monopoly of the important jury courts to further their own interests. Every senator who as provincial governor did not allow Roman financiers a free hand had to reckon with an eventual prosecution and certain condemnation. But the greatest sufferers from this state of affairs were the exploited provinces. For the moment, however, their injuries were outweighed by the ever more menacing problem of the allies. Ever since the time of the Gracchi, the claim of the allied communities of Italy for recognition of their political equality with the hegemonial power had been as ardently canvassed by the popular party as it had been rejected by the optimates. Once again the Senate did not make concessions in time, and the year 90 saw the outbreak of the terrible Social War. Rome was forced to grant her citizenship to all the communities south of the Po, and in terms of constitutional law these became municipalities. The territory of the Roman Commonwealth now embraced the entire peninsula. The idea that the whole citizen-body should share in the business of government, as envisaged in the constitution, became more and more illusory, since this participation could only take place in the popular assemblies at Rome.

Hardly had the danger of this war been exorcised, when another great *popularis*, Publius Sulpicius Rufus, tribune of the people for 88, launched a new and powerful offensive against the oligarchic nobility. The Senate was to receive an influx of members from the equestrian order. Further, he wished to do away with the ungenerous provision whereby the new citizens were allotted to only 8 of the 35 electoral districts and so, according to the prevailing voting system, were never able to make their votes felt, and to remove the restriction of freedmen to the 4 urban districts. These measures were designed to win him the necessary support. Finally, he shrewdly turned the reputation of Marius, now an old man, to his own advantage by promising that he would pass a popular decree to get him the command of the war against Mithridates, which the Senate had already assigned to the consul Sulla.

These bills were put to the vote and passed; but Sulla had the audacity to march on Rome with his army; he had Marius and Sulpicius outlawed, declared their new laws invalid, and passed others instead, designed to protect the oligarchy. Of these the most important was the law which forbade tribunes of the people to bring proposals before the plebs without prior approval by the Senate. Yet he was unable to prevent the 'popular' patrician, Lucius Cornelius Cinna, from succeeding him in the consulship for 87 and reviving the plans of the murdered Sulpicius. Sulla avoided prosecution by taking his army off to the Mithridatic War. In Rome Cinna's colleague Gnaeus Octavius, representing the old citizens, successfully opposed the violence of the *populares* with violence, and finally had Cinna deposed from the consulship and outlawed. But Cinna escaped, and was skilful enough to raise forces from all over Italy to oppose the existing government: he won over one of the Roman armies, which was still in the field against the Italian rebels, and speedily increased his strength with contingents from the communities of new citizens and by the manumission of slaves. Marius hurried to his side and recruited volunteers. They could now besiege Rome. Cinna made peace with the last Samnites still under arms on terms even then refused by the Senate. All attempts by the government to relieve the city failed, and it realized that there was no alternative to capitulation.

For the first time victory in battle had gone to the *populares*: it was now up to them to show what they wanted and what they could do. The wild murders and plundering that took place in Rome may be accepted as an inevitable accompaniment of their victory, although Marius was doubtless primarily concerned with vengeance on his personal enemies. Sulla's thorough-going laws were, of course, repealed. But the 'popular' government, which lasted until the year 82, can point to no positive achievement in the constitutional field. One significant departure was the fact that, for a start, Cinna declared himself and Marius consuls for 86 without consulting the popular assembly; after the death of Marius he took Lucius Valerius Flaccus as his colleague, and at the end of 86, in the same unconstitutional manner, he appointed himself and Gnaeus Papirius Carbo as consuls for the two following years. For this was the road which avoided the fatal yearly change of office, and led to a stable and stronger governmental power. The pioneer work in this direction had been done by Gnaeus Pompeius Strabo, consul in 89 and father of a son (Pompey) whose fame was to exceed his own. After the capture of Asculum he had remained at the head of his army against the will of the Senate, and in 87 wished to make use of the embarrassment of the legitimate government to extort from them the consulship for 86, when he unexpectedly fell victim to an epidemic. Although this attempt came to nothing, it served notice— as Cinna's imitation shows—of a new era of revolution after the unsuccessful efforts of the *populares*. In future the leaders of this revolution were no longer satisfied with the services of unreliable clients at the polls, but, in the struggle for power, employed their victorious armies, which expected booty and a livelihood from their generals. The immediate result of this development was merely that from now on party strife could at any time turn into civil war. Another result of the victory of the revolutionaries was that the previous pre-eminence of the nobility in the Senate was destroyed. Admittedly Cinna, Flaccus and Carbo, as well as Lucius Cornelius Scipio, consul in 83, and Marcus Junius Brutus, tribune of the people in that year, were themselves members of the nobility, but the old system by which the nobles claimed the exclusive right to decide who might reach the consulship was broken. Those of the old *principes* who escaped with their lives were forced into exile, and the Senate House was filled with new men from the equestrian order. There was no question of an improvement in the system of government, necessary though that was: rather, it was a case of a new class forcing its way into the Senate, determined to enjoy the benefits traditionally to be derived from governing the Empire. An odd man of the calibre of Quintus Sertorius may have had his path to a responsible post eased; but, in general, these new men— they included Gaius Verres—inspired anything but confidence. The notorious greed of the Romans was even more in evidence among the knights, the capitalist bourgeoisie, than among the nobles. Accordingly, when Sulla and his friends restored the old power of the nobility, this was widely welcomed as a deliverance.

Gaius Julius Caesar was thirteen years old when his uncle Gaius Marius entered Rome at Cinna's side at the end of 87, and was immediately drawn into the maelstrom of events as a result of his family connections.

The Julii were one of the original patrician families, but one that had so far left little mark upon history. The consul of 157 was not one of Caesar's ancestors. His father was praetor, perhaps in 92, then proconsul of Asia, and died at Pisae in 85 without having reached the consulship.[1] Possibly Sextus Caesar, consul in 91, who died in 90, was this man's brother. Of Caesar's grandfather we know only that he was married to a Marcia of the family of the Marcii Reges.[2] His mother, Aurelia, was also a plebeian noble by birth. She was related to—probably a cousin of—the three brothers named Aurelius Cotta, who were consuls in 75, 74 and 65. The eldest of these, Gaius, one of the best orators of his time, was brought back to political life by Sulla. Tradition ranks Aurelia with Cornelia, the mother of the Gracchi, on account of the fine upbringing she gave her son. She lived until the year 54.[3] But the fact that, for the time being, mattered most, was that Marius had married the sister of Caesar's father.

Among the victims of the revolution was the venerable *flamen Dialis*, the priest of Jupiter, Lucius Cornelius Merula, who had had the temerity to fill the consulship rendered vacant by the deposition of Cinna. This priesthood made special demands on its holder in

---

[1] His *elogium* is given in *Inscr. It.* 13, 3, p. 53, no. 75a. A second copy was found in 1925 in the Forum of Augustus, and was interpreted by T. Robert S. Broughton, *AJA* 52 (1948), 324 ff. (See *Inscr. It.* 13, 3, p. 13, no. 7). He argues—against Münzer (*Hermes* 71 (1936), 226, n. 4) that Caesar was *decemvir agris dandis adtribuendis iudicandis* before his quaestorship, and in this capacity led a colony to the island of Cercina in the Lesser Syrtis, presumably either in 103, or—more probably—in 100, on the strength of a colonization law of Appuleius Saturninus, which provided for the veterans of Marius. Since he died at Pisae, it may perhaps be conjectured that he was one of the *legati* appointed in 85 by the consuls Cinna and Carbo, to raise troops against Sulla in Italy, to collect money and to lay in reserve stocks of corn (App. *b.c.* 1,348; Liv. *per.* 83; *Hermes* 63 (1928), 136). For an inscription in honour of the proconsul at Delos, see Dessau, *ILS*, 7272. His death is mentioned in Pliny, *n.h.* 7, 181; Suet. *Caes.* 1, 1; cf. Münzer, *RE*, 10, 185, No. 130. For Sex. Caesar see ibid., 476, No. 151. For the family tree, see 184; Broughton, *MRR*, 2, 17, with note, p. 19, n. 2 and p. 645, supplementing 1, 575.

[2] Suet. *Caes.* 6, 1; Münzer, *RE*, 14, 1601, No. 113.

[3] Suet. *Caes.* 1, 2; 26, 1; 74, 2; Plut. *Caes.* 9, 3; Tac. *dial.* 28, 6. On her relationship to the three consuls, see F. Münzer, *Röm. Adelsparteien und Adelsfamilien* (1920), 324–5, with the family tree on p. 327. On C. Aurelius Cotta, see Klebs, *RE*, 2, 2482, No. 96; E. Badian, *Historia* 6 (1957), 322, n. 31.

respect both of civil and sacral law; among other things, patrician birth was required, and that was why the victors considered Julia's nephew for this office. Since Marius died on January 13 in 86, they were clearly in a hurry over this, possibly for religious reasons. For Merula had not waited to go through the farce of being condemned to death by a popular court, but after depositing his priest's cap in the temple of Capitoline Jove and cursing Cinna and his followers, had opened his veins himself.[1] The boy for whom these plans were made was of course unable to take up the office, and so nothing happened until 84, perhaps in connection with the according of the *toga virilis*. Since the man chosen to be *flamen Dialis* had to marry a patrician, he was forced to break off his engagement to a daugher of a rich equestrian family and to wed Cornelia, daughter of the consul Cinna.[2] Despite the fact that towards the end of the year his father-in-law was assassinated by mutinous soldiers,[3] I am inclined to think that this connection significantly strengthened the impulses which were afterwards to make Caesar follow so distinctly 'popular' a line. The traditional account of Cinna with its optimate bias simply dismisses him as a tyrant.[4] But, since he had begun by reviving the policy of Sulpicius Rufus in favour of the new citizens,[5] we may include him among the *populares*, who protested against the failure of the optimates to understand what was required by the times. Caesar took no part in the civil war which broke out anew on Sulla's return in 83, while his cousin Marius had himself unconstitutionally elected to the consulship for 82[6] despite his mother Julia's disapproval.[7]

But when Sulla won his decisive victory before Rome on November 1, 82, and proceeded to declare invalid all the enactments of the revolutionary government, Caesar's expectation of a post of high honour disappeared. Otherwise he remained unharmed,

---

[1] Vell. 2, 43, 1; App. *b.c.* 1, 342; Vell. 2, 22, 2; Val. Max. 9, 12, 5; Flor. 2, 9, 16.

[2] Suet. *Caes.* 1, 1. L. R. Taylor (*ClPh* 36 (1941), 115 f.) has proved that he was not installed, for, according to Tac. *ann.* 3, 58, 2, and Cass. Dio 54, 36, 1, no successor to Merula was appointed until 10 B.C.

[3] App. *b.c.* 1, 357.

[4] Cic. *Phil.* 1, 34; 2, 108; *Brut.* 227; Sall. *hist.* 1, 64; Vell. 2, 23, 2; Val. Max. 6, 9, 6; Tac. *ann.* 1, 1, 1; Plut. *Caes.* 1, 1; *Sull.* 22, 1.

[5] Cic. *Phil.* 8, 7; Vell. 2, 20, 2; App. *b.c.* 1, 287; Dio, frag. 102, 8. On Sulpicius, see Münzer, *RE*, 4A, 847; on Cinna, *RE*, 4, 1283.

[6] Münzer, *RE*, 14, 1813.

[7] Sall. *hist.* 1, 35. L. R. Taylor (*Greece and Rome*, 4 (1957), 12) conjectures that Caesar kept himself in the background in view of his future priesthood.

Sulla only insisted that he should divorce Cinna's daughter. Presumably he, like Pompeius,[1] was to contract an alliance that suited the dictator. But he resolutely rejected this sign of goodwill, although his wife forfeited her dowry and all claim to outstanding legacies from her family.[2] This was an exceedingly dangerous piece of audacity, and he soon thought it wiser to go into hiding in the Sabine country. But even so, he was captured by a Sullan patrol and forced to buy his life from its leader at the cost of 12,000 denarii. He was eventually rescued from the life of a wretched fugitive—rendered even less tolerable by malaria—by the intercession of his noble relatives at the court of the all-powerful dictator. In addition to the Vestal Virgins, Mamercus Aemilius Lepidus, later consul for the year 77, and his mother's cousin Gaius Aurelius Cotta, later consul of 75, pleaded for him. Sulla granted their request and jokingly warned them to beware of the ill-clad boy. There were, he said, many Mariuses in him.[3]

We cannot tell how far the young Caesar was personally involved in the premature attempt to secure for him the dignity of the priesthood. It was an office hedged with old-fashioned obligations, which would have blocked his path to a great political career. Thus the *flamen Dialis* was forbidden to mount a horse, to see troops under arms, or to spend more than two consecutive nights outside Rome.[4] Probably he at first did not worry much about this, and later he would surely have found a way round these obstacles. We certainly see the authentic Caesar in his brave resistance to Sulla's demand. Cornelia remained his wife until her death in 69. About 76 she bore him his daughter Julia.[5]

Making a resolute break, Caesar left Rome to become a soldier. As a senator's son he naturally became an officer immediately, and joined the staff of the propraetor of Asia, Marcus Minucius Thermus. The latter was then engaged upon the subjugation of

[1] Plut. *Sull.* 33, 4; *Pomp.* 9, 2. Vell. 2, 41, 2 adds M. Pupius Piso as one who complied with an order to divorce his wife.

[2] Suet. *Caes.* 1, 2; Plut. *Caes.* 1, 1. Plut. *Caes.* 1, 3, stating that Caesar had applied for a priesthood, is a misunderstanding. See H. Strasburger, *Caesars Eintritt in die Geschichte* (1938), 80; L. R. Taylor, *ClPh* 36, 116.

[3] Suet. *Caes.* 1, 2–3; Plut. *Caes.* 5, 1–7; *Schol. Gronov.* on Cic. *Lig.* 12. On their relationship, Münzer, *R. Adelsp.* 313; Strasburger, op. cit., 82, 88.

[4] G. Wissowa, *Rel. u. Kult. d. Röm.*[2], 505.

[5] Suet. *Caes.* 1, 1; 6, 1; Plut. *Caes.* 5, 7. 83 is usually taken as the year of Julia's birth: Münzer *RE*, 10, 894. But since she did not become engaged until 59 (Suet. *Caes.* 21; Plut. *Caes.* 14, 7; *Pomp.* 47, 10; App. *b.c.* 2, 50), I prefer the later date; daughters of such distinguished houses were usually married before they were twenty-four (Münzer, *R. Adelsp.* 106).

Mytilene, the last Greek state still unwilling to abandon the cause of Mithridates. Caesar received instructions to bring up part of the fleet of Nicomedes IV from Bithynia. There he was welcomed with signal honours and known throughout the country as the king's guest. At the same time he was also looking after the business interests of one of his freedmen.[1] In the year 80, he took part in the successful attack on Mytilene and was decorated by the commander with the civic crown for conspicuous bravery.[2] Then, in 78, when the proconsul Publius Servilius Vatia began the war against the Cilician pirates, Caesar continued his military training in his camp.[3] But he never neglected the political scene in Rome and was aware that after Sulla's abdication some *populares* were planning a new insurrection; and on hearing news of the great man's death, he at once set out for Rome. But the ex-Sullan, Marcus Aemilius Lepidus, who was then consul and leader of the movement, did not inspire much confidence in him, in spite of urgent appeals for his participation in the revolt. Accordingly he was untouched by its total collapse.[3]

In 77 he prosecuted, on charges of extortion, a leading Sullan, Gnaeus Cornelius Dolabella (the consul of 81, who had returned from Macedonia to a triumph) thus following a path to a political

[1] Suet. *Caes.* 2. For Nicomedes IV Philopator, see Geyer, *RE*, 17, 497, No. 6; Rostovtzeff, *Soc. and Ec. Hist. Hell. World*, II, 827; III, 1529, note 104. Caesar's participation in the life of the court gave rise to obscene jokes, later interminably repeated (Suet. *Caes.* 22, 2; 49, 1–3). They recur in the indecent songs sung by the soldiers at his triumph in 46 (Suet. *Caes.* 49, 4). On that occasion Caesar had protested vigorously and swore that the whole story was false (Dio 43, 20, 4).

[2] Suet. *Caes.* 2. The *corona civica* was an oak wreath, which might be worn by the recipient on all festive occasions. When a holder of this high decoration appeared at the public games, all the spectators, including senators, rose from their seats. He was allowed to sit next to the senators. He was released from civic duties, as were his father and grandfather. The *corona civica* was awarded only to those who had saved the lives of comrades in battle (Polyb. 6, 39, 6; Plin. *n.h.* 16, 11–14). The famous jurist Masurius Sabinus, a contemporary of the Emperor Tiberius (W. Kunkel, *Herkunft und soziale Stellung d. röm. Juristen* (1952), 119), gave the following definition (Gell. *n.A.* 5, 6, 13): *civicam coronam tum dari solitam, cum is, qui civem servaverat, eodem tempore etiam hostem occiderat neque locum in ea pugna reliquerat.* See Fiebiger, *RE*, 4, 1634; *vacatio munerum*, Mommsen, *RStR*, 3³, 224. Caesar later commented with malicious irony on the usefulness of officers and candidates for commissions from the senatorial and equestrian class (*b.G.* 1, 39, 2–5). This makes all the more noteworthy the seriousness with which he took his own service, and the way in which he made his mark by both bravery and extraordinary military efficiency. On p. 1, n. 1 (above) attention was drawn to the conjecture that in the case of senators' sons this high military decoration was connected with preferential treatment in the *cursus honorum*. Finally, one must not forget that Minucius Thermus was a Sullan (Münzer, *RE*, 15, 1966, No. 64), which shows how one should regard Sulla's pardoning of Caesar.

[3] Suet. *Caes.* 3.

career that had become increasingly common in the last half century. He was very well equipped to do so, since he had received an excellent education from his tutor, the freedman Marcus Antonius Gnipho, who had himself been educated in Alexandria and was a master of both Greek and Latin rhetoric.[1] Dolabella, of course, had the benefit of the services of the two leading defence counsel of the day,[2] Gaius Cotta (Caesar's cousin) and Quintus Hortensius, and was acquitted.[3] Nevertheless Caesar worked up his speeches into an imposing document, which survived as a literary masterpiece and won for its author, despite his defeat in court, a reputation as one of Rome's leading orators.[4] His Greek clients did not lose confidence in him and, in the following year, entrusted him with the case against the notorious Sullan, Gaius Antonius, who as *legatus* in the Mithridatic War had shamelessly plundered Greece. Caesar tackled the matter with such skill that Antonius appealed for, and caused a scandal by receiving, tribunician protection against the indictment.[5]

In the year 75 Caesar travelled to the East again, this time to round off his oratorical education at Rhodes by attending the lectures of the rhetorician Apollonius Molon.[6] *En route* he fell into the hands of Cilician pirates near the islet of Pharmacussa, south of Miletus. The campaigns of Servilius Isauricus had failed to get to the roots of this evil, and now, with the war against Sertorius in Spain at its height and the strength of the Roman Empire diminished by the bloody civil wars in Italy, an operation of sufficient scale could not be mounted. When the pirates demanded a ransom of 50 talents (300,000 denarii) for their distinguished captive, Caesar placed the responsibility for his misfortune on the inadequate coastal

[1] Suet. *gramm. et rhet.* 7.

[2] Suet. *Caes.* 4, 1; 55, 1; Plut. *Caes.* 4, 1; Münzer, *RE*, 4, 1297, No. 134; Caes. frag. (ed. Kübler), 1897, p. 135.

[3] Val. Max. 8, 9, 3 wrongly gives L. Cotta. Hortensius is given by ps.-Ascon. on Cic. *div. in Caec.* 24; cf. Cic. *Brut.* 317, according to which Cicero was present in the audience.

[4] Cic. *Brut.* 261; Vell. 2, 43, 3; Tac. *dial.* 34, 7; Plut. *Caes.* 3, 2.

[5] Plut. *Caes.* 4, 2–4; Ascon. on Cic. *tog. cand.* frag. 2 (Schoell); Q. Cic. *comm. pet.* 7. C. Antonius (Klebs, *RE*, 1, 2757, No. 19) was later Cicero's colleague as consul in 63. He was expelled from the Senate by the censors of 70, but returned on his election as tribune for 68 (Dessau, *ILS*, 38, 1); on the date of his tribunate, see L. R. Taylor, *ClPh* 36, 121, n. 32; Broughton, *MRR*, 2, 141, n. 8. M. Lucullus, the praetor of 76 mentioned by Plutarch, was, according to Asconius, *praetor peregrinus*. If so it was either a civil action or Lucullus (exceptionally) acted as *praetor repetundarum*. Plutarch's account contains misunderstandings.

[6] Suet. *Caes.* 4, 1; Plut. *Caes.* 3, 1 (chronologically inaccurate; see Strasburger, *Caesars Eintritt*, 9). On Apollonius, Brzoska, *RE*, 2, 141, No. 85. Cicero had already taken lessons from him at Rome (*Brut.* 312) and in 78 did so again at Rhodes (*Brut.* 316).

police maintained by the communities on the coast of Asia Minor[1] and forced them to raise the sum. They had to be grateful to him for at least making the pirates, on payment of the ransom money, furnish hostages to the cities for their future good behaviour. As soon as he was released, he undertook the policing of the seas. At the head of a squadron raised by the communities, he brought the pirates to battle, captured several of their vessels and took numerous prisoners. To decide their fate, he paid a personal visit to the governor of Asia Minor, Marcus Juncus, who was then engaged in settling Bithynia—bequeathed to Rome by the will of its last king—as a province. When he failed to give instructions for their execution, but wished rather to sell them for the benefit of the treasury, Caesar returned at top speed to Pergamum, where they were held in custody, and had them crucified on his own initiative.[2]

As he refused to recognize the will of Nicomedes IV, Mithridates, in 74, opened hostilities against the Romans for the third time, relying on support from Sertorius. Caesar had just arrived in Rhodes when he learned that a detachment of the king's forces had broken into the province of Asia. He immediately crossed over to the mainland, took over command of the local militia and expelled the enemy.[3] Our sources stress that Caesar took action against the pirates entirely on his own initiative. Nor did he receive the authority of the proconsul on this occasion.[4] This is evidence of his limitless audacity and self-confidence, but it also shows the provincial administration of the time in a strange light. Still, it is worth noting that Cicero, in his work On the State, approves of such initiative when 'the freedom of Roman citizens' was at stake.[5] It was perfectly natural that a holder of the corona civica should act as Caesar did on the outbreak of the Mithridatic War.

In the year 74 the Senate once again decided to take action against the pirate menace, and the task of cleaning up the Mediterranean was entrusted to the praetor Marcus Antonius.[6] It appears that Caesar

---

[1] Cf. Cic. Flacc. 27.

[2] Suet. Caes. 4, 1–2; 74, 1; Plut. Caes. 1, 8—2, 7; Vell. 2. 42, 1–3; Val. Max. 6, 9, 15; Polyaen. strat. 8, 23, 1. The adventure lent itself to embellishment. On Juncus, see Münzer, RE, 10, 954, No. 4.   [3] Suet. Caes. 4, 2.

[4] Vell. 2, 42, 2–3: contracta classe et privatus et tumultuaria invectus in eum locum . . .

[5] Cic. rep. 2, 46, of the first consul L. Brutus: 'primus in hac civitate docuit in conservanda civium libertate esse privatum neminem'; and Augustus begins his Res Gestae with the words: 'annos undeviginti natus exercitum privato consilio et privata impensa comparavi, per quem rem publicam a dominatione factionis oppressam in libertatem vindicavi'.

[6] Vell. 2, 31, 2; Klebs, RE, 1, 2594, No. 29; Broughton, MRR, 2, 101. He is the brother of C. Antonius and father of the later triumvir.

was assigned to his staff; for in an inscription from the Laconian port of Gytheum, we find, among the names of other junior officers, a *legatus* called Gaius Julius, who in 73 was given lodging by two resident Roman citizens.[1] This visit fits in well with our other evidence, according to which he was co-opted into the college of *pontifices* in 73 on the death of his cousin, the consular Gaius Cotta, and it was on receipt of this news that he started his return journey from Rhodes. To escape the attentions of the pirates he crossed the Adriatic in a small boat, accompanied only by two friends and ten slaves.[2]

We should pay special attention to this co-option. If Caesar was taking the place of Gaius Cotta, it is reasonable to suppose that his mother Aurelia played a part in the business. Perhaps the original proposal came from Mamercus Aemilius Lepidus Livianus, who in 81 had helped to secure Caesar's pardon, and it evidently met with no opposition from the remaining optimate members of the college, such as Servilius Isauricus, Quintus Lutatius Catulus and Marcus Terentius Lucullus. The *pontifex maximus*, Quintus Metellus Pius, was conducting operations against Sertorius in Spain. We see that Caesar's attack on Dolabella was of no significance, and may conjecture that Servilius Isauricus was pleased with the achievements of his former lieutenant. The nobility accepted him as one of themselves.[3]

Looking back at Caesar's life to date, we find that he already knew how to exploit his talents to the full. Although he had been disappointed in his hopes of a career on the side of the beneficiaries of

---

[1] Dittenberger, *Syll.*[3] 748, 22; Broughton *MRR*, 2, 113; L.R. Taylor, *Greece and Rome*, 4 (1957), 13. Since, apart from an obscure Catilinarian (Sall. *Cat.* 27, 1), we know of no other C. Julius, this will refer to Caesar. *Legati* are normally senators. Did Caesar's *corona civica* make this exception possible? In Nep. *Att.* 6, 4 we read that in 61 Q. Cicero wanted to offer a position as *legatus* to his brother-in-law Atticus. But the accuracy of such a designation in a Greek popular decree is questionable. At any rate, it seems a reasonable conjecture that Caesar's assumption of command was retrospectively recognized in Rome.

[2] Vell. 43, 1–2; based on good tradition, according to Strasburger, *Caesars Eintritt*, 84. If the journey was successful, one can understand that Caesar thought of repeating the venture in 49. See below, p. 228.

[3] The assessment of the co-option is the work of L. R. Taylor, *ClPh* 36, 117–120. In the list of *pontifices* in Macrob. *Sat.* 3, 13, 11, M. Aemilius Lepidus is mentioned. But, as L. R. Taylor (*AJPh* 63 (1942), 342) ingeniously recognized by a comparison with the list in Cic. *har. resp.* 12, M. Aemilius did not enter the college until after 63. Therefore 'M.' is to be emended to 'Mam.'. According to Val. Max. 7, 7, 6, Mamercus may have become *princeps senatus* in 70 (Taylor, op. cit., 393, 22; Münzer, *R. Adelsp.*, 312–313). Broughton, *MRR*, 2, 114 agrees with L. R. Taylor. She also conjectures (op. cit., 403, n. 59) that Servilia (Münzer, *RE*, 2A, 1817, No. 101) may have won her cousin Catulus (*RE*, 2A, 1817, No. 98) for Caesar; cf. Plut. *Caes.* 7, 2.

C

the revolution, he was clever enough to maintain, through a difficult period, the political position he had taken up, and so could always count on the support of those with 'popular' tendencies. On the other hand he fully benefited by the considerable advantages of his distinguished birth. This is not to say that contemporaries already caught glimpses of his future greatness. The nobility was only too rich in young men of his type, who, while ambitious and pleasure-loving, were efficient in war and seriously concerned to master the rhetorical education essential for a senator. Still, the young Pontifex was already a respected orator and, as a dashing officer, had not only shown bravery, but also given some indication of the way in which he was later to intervene in the corrupt provincial administration.

CHAPTER TWO

EARLY POLITICAL CAREER

SULLA, despite his great ability as an officer, diplomat, general and statesman, proved too much of an epicurean to hold on for life to the dictatorship which he had obtained. The very functions of a 'dictatorship for the drawing up of laws and ordering of the State', which he had assigned to himself, show that he had never entertained any such idea. He was also very well aware that he had won his victory as the champion of the nobility. His camp in Greece had been the place where the refugees had gathered, and it was for this reason that, after his landing in Italy, all those elements flocked to him which embodied the old relationship of the nobility to their protégés (clients of every kind, even whole communities). Thus, in addition to his veterans he was able to put three armies into the field in the north, under the command of Gnaeus Pompeius, Quintus Metellus Pius and Marcus Lucullus. This was why he used his unlimited powers to strengthen the oligarchy, whose rule before the revolution had been based on custom, by constitutional legislation. Since the Roman constitution was not based on written law, except for some points of detail, it lacked system and unity. In particular, the functions of the tribunate of the people—originally a revolutionary institution—had not been rigidly defined vis-à-vis the other authorities. The significance of this first became evident through the activities of the *populares*: constitutionally it was not clear in whose hands the power of government lay. Sulla had already put an end to this uncertainty during his consulship, when he made tribunician proposals dependent on the approval of the Senate. He now further tied the hands of the tribunate by fresh enactments, of which we need only mention the one that forbade an ex-tribune to stand for any curule office: in future such a man could become neither praetor nor consul.

The equestrian order had formed the core of the popular party in the civil war. Now its ranks were not only terribly thinned by the proscriptions, but it was also deprived of its uncommonly important special political privilege, that of providing the juries for the criminal courts. These juries now again became a senatorial monopoly. At the same time, by an extension of these courts, Sulla made a clean sweep of the old popular jurisdiction, and, in this field too, made senatorial government a reality. One of the biggest flaws in the constitution was that it still clung to the forms of a city-state, when the participation of all the citizens in state business had long since become an impossibility. Although Sulla did not abolish the popular assemblies he made sure that they could no longer be used as vehicles of anti-senatorial policy—and it was a fact that they could not even be regarded as representative of the people.

Through precise regulation of the official career and of administrative spheres both within and outside Italy, he wished, as far as possible, to secure the equality of all senators and to make the Senate into a capable instrument of government. This hope, in particular, turned out to be an illusion. The body, whose membership had been raised to about 600,[1] proved unable to cope with the problems of governing the Empire. Their equality consisted mainly in the fact that each member watched carefully to see that no other secured greater advantages than himself, while he personally lost no opportunity for profit. Even more than before, politics degenerated into the unceasing activity of factions. In the face of the selfishness of men who felt their possessions secure, feelings of responsibility for the Empire as a whole were hardly allowed to develop.

A man of nobler aims than those which satisfied the average senator was obliged to look around for other means. The arrangements for the administration of the provinces were quite inadequate. Thanks to the system of mutual connivance, this sphere offered the proconsuls and propraetors, even more than before, a more or less legitimate opportunity to make or restore their fortunes. On the other hand, a man who took a broader view of the interests of the state was faced with difficulties, since the oligarchy was reluctant to entrust extraordinary power to any of its members. The experiences of Caesar described above shed a sufficient light on the consequent confusion in the Empire.

These faults first crippled the effectiveness of the Sullan constitution and eventually conditioned the further development of the Roman state. Caesar's attitude to them, when he returned to political life in 73, was influenced partly by his popular connections, but more particularly by his own abilities. As we have already remarked, there was nothing to prevent him from following a normal optimate career. Yet we find him engaged wherever there was an opportunity to clear the way for political activity in opposition to the oligarchic restrictions placed on its scope. The

---

[1] P. Willems, Le sénat de la république romaine (1878), 1, 405.

immediate aim of a man who thought on these lines was naturally the restoration of the old tribunate of the people. As early as 75 Caesar's cousin, Gaius Cotta, as consul, had brought in a bill by which ex-tribunes were again allowed to stand for the curule offices; in 73 the tribune Gaius Licinius Macer continued the struggle and found enthusiastic support in Caesar.[1] In this year too he was elected, for 72, to one of the twenty-four military tribunates, annually filled by popular vote—a fact probably mentioned by our sources only because this was the first post assigned him by the people.[2] We can do no more than wonder whether, as military tribune, he had to take part in the Slave War. Perhaps we hear nothing of this because there was nothing special to relate. He himself later praises the victory over Spartacus as a triumph for Roman *constantia*.[3]

No doubt the speech which he delivered against Marcus Juncus in an extortion case brought by the Bithynians belongs to this period. From a surviving fragment we see that he justified this prosecution as a duty to his former host, Nicomedes, and his clients in that area. But, after his own experience of this proconsul, we may conjecture that he was not reluctant to take the case.[4] The next occasion on which we hear of him is in the year 70, after the consuls Pompey and Crassus had freed the tribunate of the people from all restrictions. Acting in the spirit of Pompey, the tribune Plautius brought a bill before the people granting a complete amnesty to the followers of Lepidus and Sertorius. Caesar recommended its acceptance in a speech which was also published, and again emphasized that it was a duty particularly incumbent upon him to work for the recall of his brother-in-law Lucius Cinna.[5]

[1] Suet. *Caes.* 5. Speech of Licinius Macer in Sall. *hist.* 3, 48, explained by me in Haas's edition of Sallust (1953), p. 135. Cf. Strasburger, *Caesars Eintritt*, 93.

[2] Suet. *Caes.* 5; Plut. *Caes.* 5, 1; Mommsen, *RStR* 2³, 576; Strasburger, *Caesars Eintritt*, 85. Broughton, for no apparent reason, places the post in the year 71.

[3] Caes. *b.G.* 1, 40, 5: *factum etiam nuper in Italia servili tumultu, quos tamen* (sc. *servos*) *aliquid usus ac disciplina quam a nobis accepissent sublevarent, ex quo iudicari posse, quantum haberet in se boni constantia, propterea quod, quos aliquamdiu inermes sine causa timuissent, hos postea armatos ac victores superassent.*

[4] Gell. *n.A.* 5, 13, 6; Caes. frag. (Kübler), p. 139. The fragments were thus explained by H. Dahlmann, *Hermes* 73 (1938), 341 ff.

[5] Suet. *Caes.* 5; Gell. *n.A.* 13, 3, 5; Caes. frag. (Kübler), p. 136; Dio 44, 47, 4. In my discussion of the first consulship of Pompey (*Abh. Berlin* (1943), 1, 8, n. 3), I wrongly placed the popular decree in the year 72. Since then I have been convinced by L. R. Taylor (*ClPh* 36, 121, 32) and Broughton (*MRR*, 2, 128) who opt for 70. In my view the decisive point is that in this year a bill establishing colonies for the veterans of Metellus Pius and Pompey was also passed, the implementation of which had to be postponed through lack of funds (Dio 38, 5, 1). It was taken up again in 60 by the tribune Flavius, on which Cicero (*Att.* 1, 18, 6) comments: '*agraria autem promulgata est a Flavio sane levis, eadem fere quae fuit Plotia.*'

However, it would be false to imagine that in these years political ambition was Caesar's sole interest. His contemporaries saw him rather as a man possessed by a wild extravagance, a prey to expensive tastes which grossly exceeded his means. The rumour was circulating that his debts were approaching eight million denarii. In optimate circles it was expected that he would come to a bad end, and he was not regarded as a serious political opponent! Some details are known. He built himself an expensive country house on Lake Nemi, but not finding it completely to his taste, immediately had it pulled down again. He was also a passionate art collector and paid fabulous sums for choice slaves. Finally, not the least expensive item in his budget will have been the gallant adventures of which the *chronique scandaleuse* of the upper classes could tell so much. For example, as late as 59 it was said that he bought Servilia, the mother of his future murderer Brutus, a pearl costing 1½ million denarii.[1]

At this time the centre of gravity of Roman politics lay in the provinces. Contrary to its principles, the Senate was forced time after time to resort to extraordinary commands. As against Lepidus in 78, so in 77 Gnaeus Pompeius, twenty-nine years old, was entrusted with a proconsular command against Sertorius, which made him the equal of Quintus Metellus Pius, the regular proconsul in Further Spain. Pompey was the most successful of all the Sullans. Although he was only a knight, the dictator had hailed him as Imperator (the honorific title of a victorious general) and Magnus ('the Great'), and later had also allowed him to hold a triumph. Pompey, treading in his father's footsteps, made no secret of the fact that the Senate must continue to recognize his special position. In the year 74, the praetor Marcus Antonius received a command against the pirates over all the coasts of the Mediterranean; immediately afterwards, the consul Lucius Licinius Lucullus was appointed to the command against Mithridates with *imperium* (magisterial power of command) over the two provinces of Cilicia and Asia;

---

[1] Plut. *Caes.* 4, 5–6; 5–8; Suet. *Caes.* 46; 47; 50, 1–2. Plutarch's information is confirmed by Strasburger's research into Cicero's utterances (*Caesars Eintritt*, 45 ff., especially 50–52 and 89). On p. 46 he argues that the incident reported in Suet. *Caes.* 49, 3, in which Caesar intervened in the Senate on behalf of Nysa, the daughter of Nicomedes IV, and Cicero replied with an insulting reference to Caesar's relations with the king, should be dated as early as the seventies. But Caesar was not yet a senator at that time, and so we may rather agree with Münzer (*RE*, 17, 1630, No. 7) that Caesar as consul designate in 60 may have spoken in the debate on the new organization of the provinces of Asia Minor. An interruption of this kind by Cicero is in fact very unlikely. Strasburger attributes it to Tiro's collection of Cicero's *ioci* (Macr. *Sat.* 2, 1, 12). Among these there were no doubt many examples of *esprit d'escalier*.

finally proconsular *imperium* was given to Marcus Crassus, a praetorian, in order to put down the slave revolt in Italy.

Since Sulla had shown what political ventures a man in a commanding military position could embark upon, the guardians of strict oligarchy viewed all such steps with justified apprehension. In 71 Crassus and Pompey, at the head of their victorious armies, won themselves the consulship for the following year by military blackmail. After their election the two former Sullans restored the tribunate to its previous position and, in the same year, the praetor Lucius Aurelius Cotta (also a cousin of Caesar's mother) passed a new law about the composition of the jury courts. This provided that the juries should be formed equally from senators, knights and *tribuni aerarii* (a lower census qualification than that required for the equestrian order: they thus needed a minimum qualification of less than 100,000 denarii). In this way the two main pillars of the Sullan constitution were broken, and this led to an evil period of anarchy and confusion. Of the traditional popular programme only the catchwords were left now: the sovereign rights of the people represented the driving wheel of the vast machine used by all opponents of the optimate oligarchy in their unceasing attempts to hasten its fall.

Caesar naturally welcomed this development, but, since he was not yet a senator, could only play a subordinate part in these important happenings. According to the Sullan order, election to the quaestorship brought with it membership of the Senate. Caesar held this office in 69.[1] Soon after he had entered upon it, he delivered the funeral oration over Marius' widow and, dwelling on her ancestry both on her father's and on her mother's side, gave full vent to the pride which he felt in his birth: 'On her mother's side my father's sister Julia was descended from kings; her father traced his lineage back to the immortal gods. From Ancus Marcius came the Marcii Reges, which was her mother's name, and from Venus the Julii, the stock to which our family belongs. So her ancestry contains the honour due to kings, who are most powerful among men, and the sanctity of the gods, in whose power kings themselves lie.' Yet effigies of Marius, father and son, were carried in the funeral procession, in defiance of Sulla's prohibition, and were greeted with enthusiasm by the public. Soon afterwards his wife, Cornelia, also died. It had not previously been the custom to honour young

---

[1] L. R. Taylor (*ClPh* 36, 124) argues for this date. She is followed by Broughton, *MRR*, 2, 132.

women with a public oration, but Caesar had no qualms about setting a precedent, and his moving words met with great approval.[1] Those that have survived seem strangely prophetic of the last years of his own life, although his peers will have found them boastful and on a level with the rest of his extravagant behaviour. But the 'people' in Rome no doubt approved.

As quaestor he was assigned to the propraetor of Further Spain,[2] and as his representative administered justice on a section of the circuit, finding many opportunities to lay the provincials under obligation to himself. But suddenly he was seized by the ambition for quicker advancement. In 68 he left the province before the governor and made his way to Transpadane Gaul. The grant of Roman citizenship by virtue of the laws of 90 and 89 went only as far as the Po. North of the river it applied only to the two Latin colonies of Cremona and Aquileia. In 89 the remaining Gallic townships had been combined by the consul Gnaeus Pompeius Strabo into a number of urban communities, and these received the rights enjoyed by the former Latin colonies, the most important of which was that tenure of a local magistracy conferred Roman citizenship.[3] In recent decades Romanization had made progress in this area, and the inhabitants resented the fact that they were less privileged than their neighbours south of the Po. The oligarchy, however, was opposed to any further extension of the citizenship. Accordingly unrest was rife, and Caesar, entirely in the spirit of the old *populares*, hurried to seize this opportunity, visited the communities and hoped for an armed uprising. At this time the Senate had available two legions destined for Cilicia, for the Mithridatic War, and it held them back in Italy until things in the north had quietened down again.[4] From this unsuccessful attempt we can see that at the age of thirty-two Caesar was a bold gambler and one ready to play for high stakes early in the game. Furthermore, by his passionate support for the Transpadanes he laid the foundations of a condition of patronage that was to have considerable consequences.

---

[1] Suet. *Caes.* 6, 1; Plut. *Caes.* 5, 2–5.

[2] Suet. *Caes.* 7, 1; Plut. *Caes.* 5, 6; Vell. 2, 43, 3; Caes. *bell. Hisp.* 42, 1. I agree with Strasburger (op. cit., 95) that the anecdotes placed here by Suetonius and Dio (37, 52, 2) are wrongly dated.

[3] Ascon. on Cic. *Pis.* frag. 9; Gelzer, *Vom römischen Staat* (1943), 2, 70.

[4] Suet. *Caes.* 8. The legions were those of the consul of 68, Q. Marcius Rex; see Dio 36, 2, 2; 15, 1; 17, 2; Dessau, *ILS*, 868; Gelzer, *RE*, 13, 400; *contra* Münzer, *RE*, 14, 1584; L. R. Taylor, op. cit., 123, n. 39; Broughton, *MRR*, 2, 137.

On his return to Rome he married Pompeia. Since her father was the son of Quintus Pompeius Rufus, consul in 88, and her mother Sulla's daughter, she was the granddaughter of the two consuls who in 88 had so emphatically reduced the power of the tribunate.[1] Clearly memories of this sort did not count with Caesar. Since 67, as a quaestorian, he had attended meetings of the Senate. As a result of the failure of Antonius, the activity of the pirates had got out of hand to such an extent that only a special military effort could deal with them. The tribune Aulus Gabinius now put forward a proposal for the creation of an extraordinary command with authority unprecedented in Roman history. All knew that this was intended for Pompey. The entire Senate followed the lead of the respected head of the Optimates, Quintus Catulus, and rejected the plan: only Caesar, from the lowest ranks of the senatorial hierarchy, had the impudence to support it. However little he liked Pompey's new elevation, he was left with no alternative if he wished to make his way as a *popularis*.[2] Next he was elected curator of the Via Appia, a position in which good administration could easily win gratitude from many quarters. Despite his chronic indebtedness he made significant contributions from his own means and established himself still further in popular favour.[3]

Meanwhile there had been important changes on the great political stage. Even before the appointment of Pompey, Lucius Lucullus, despite his great services, had been deprived of his command through the agency of Gabinius. Since he had put an end to the draining of the province of Asia by the unspeakable greed of Roman financiers, he was pursued by the hatred of the equestrian order until finally their ceaseless agitation succeeded in bringing about the fall of this outstanding member of the nobility. Like Metellus Pius, to whom Rome was indebted, even more than to Pompey, for dealing with the war against Sertorius, Lucullus was a sincere supporter of the Sullan system of an optimate oligarchy. But it was the tragic weakness of this form of government that it could not bear outstanding personalities. The optimate cliques, dominated by pompous busybodies, dropped the most important man in the régime of the nobility, while he himself was above allying himself

---

[1] Suet. *Caes.* 6, 2; Plut. *Caes.* 5, 7. She was not related to the family of Cn. Pompeius Magnus. See Strasburger, op. cit., 135.

[2] Plut. *Pomp.* 25, 8; Strasburger, op. cit., 101. On the war against the pirates, see Gelzer, *Pompeius*[2] (1959), 71 ff.

[3] Plut. *Caes.* 5, 9. Mommsen, *RStR*, 2³, 669 does not mention this evidence. Cf. Dessau, *ILS*, 5800 and Broughton, *MRR*, 2, 141, n. 8.

with the *populares*. The intention was to conclude the Mithridatic
War through the regular proconsuls. But in 66 they had still not
come to grips with their task, and meanwhile the initiative had
slipped out of the hands of the senatorial leaders.[1]

The war against the pirates allowed Pompey's talents to shine in
the best and brightest light: by well-planned organization he was
able to concentrate his far superior forces and to strike annihilating
blows. By the end of 67, not only had the pirates disappeared from
the Mediterranean, but a large number of these restless raiders was
being sent out to settle in deserted Greek towns, to live decent,
respectable lives. All the circumstances conspired to prove Pompey
the fit successor to Lucullus—which was his burning desire. Ordinary
people in Rome were enthusiastic for the hero who had assured
them their daily bread. The capitalists were alarmed to see that
since the blocking of Lucullus the war had again been carried into
the Roman provinces, and all their state-holdings were again in
jeopardy. Pompey himself was available for new commissions.

At the beginning of 66 the tribune Gaius Manilius proposed to
extend Pompey's command to the conduct of the Mithridatic
War and to grant him the right of declaring war, concluding peace
and making treaties. In a word, the settlement of the whole eastern
question was put in his hands. Since the restoration of the tribunate,
the Senate could no longer withstand the strength of such a movement. The senatorial leaders, Catulus and Hortensius, were fighting
for a lost cause: on this occasion four consulars of their own persuasion, including men of note such as Publius Servilius Isauricus
and Gaius Scribonius Curio, swam with the tide.

Political opportunities of a kind which Sulla had won for himself
as an outlaw in civil war were now placed in Pompey's lap by public
authority. Those who did not wish to be crushed by the foreseeable
new order had to humour their future master. Caesar was faced with
this bitter necessity. But, since it had to be, he was not content
to be a mere time-server; rather, he became an enthusiastic supporter
of the bill,[2] rivalled only by the praetor of this year, Marcus Tullius
Cicero. He too could not act otherwise, if he ever wished to see the
great wish of his life fulfilled, for, despite his equestrian birth, he was
aiming at the consulship on the strength of his oratory. Although
sincerely impressed by the glorious past of noble rule, under the
existing senatorial régime he could not as a new man hope for the

[1] Gelzer, *RE*, 13, 404.
[2] Dio 36, 43, 2–3; Gelzer, *Pompeius*[2], 80; on Cicero, *RE* 7A, 855.

consulship. In the eyes of these high and mighty gentlemen he could count himself lucky that they had let him rise as far as the praetorship.

Up to the year 62 Pompey had done all that was expected of him as a soldier and organizer. Until his return at the beginning of 61, Rome had to be content with rumours about the political conclusions he intended to draw from his position.[1] As a result, political life was conducted in a climate of frightful suspense. Any politician who thought himself destined for a big role had to act before a stronger man deprived him of his freedom. On the surface it was business as usual, but the initiated knew that they were living on top of a volcano, whose eruption would cause incalculable devastation. The atmosphere was oppressive.

It is hardly possible to paint too gloomy a picture of the moral decline of the Roman people at this time. The old Roman morality, like the old religion, had been rough and unbending, but a sense of justice had worked as a moderating influence on the brutal egoism,[2] which was Rome's national characteristic. World dominion undermined the solid ground from which Rome had drawn her finest elements. In particular the growing infiltration of things Greek could only have a disintegrating effect. For it was only the high-minded and independent people—a small fraction in any society—who could adopt what was good and of eternal value in the spiritual life of the Greeks. The coarse sensuality of the Romans was more likely to be impressed with other sides of an over-ripe culture, its frivolity and luxury, its pleasures and vices. The Roman in the East, who became accustomed to the political corruption and unscrupulous money-making of the Greeks, and who might see every day that they could most easily and profitably be handled with brutality, must have had his old concepts of honesty blurred. Greek rhetoric permeated the judicial and political oratory of the Forum. *Optimates* and *populares* competed to corrupt the populace of Rome. In Rome at the end of the second century, as had long been the case in Greece, everything was to be had for money, and this applied to the highest as to the lowest in the land.[3] Those in positions of power exploited it ruthlessly, and not only the big men involved in provincial administration: the businessmen, headed by the tax-farming companies and their employees, were every bit as bad. Loyalty and

---

[1] Cf. Gelzer, *Pompeius*[2], 112 ff.
[2] Cato in the Rhodian speech, *ap.* Gell. *n.A.*, 6, 3, 37; Vell. 2, 27, 1.
[3] Polyb. 18, 35, 2; 31, 25, 3; 6, 57, 6; cf. *Gnomon* 29 (1957), 407.

trust were only valid in so far as they served a man's own interests. Family life was, to a large extent, shattered. Cicero's forensic speeches give us a terrible insight into what was going on not only in Rome, but also in the municipalities. Similarly the client-patron relationship and that of political friendship, socially so important, increasingly became mere business connections. The fabulous fortunes which flowed into Rome continually drove luxury to new excesses. It was smart to take part in these. In the course of a few youthful years huge fortunes were squandered. But however high his debts mounted, a senator's son could console himself with the thought that a political career would repay him all with interest.

From 90 onwards this demoralized world was faced with one economic crisis after another. The Social War seriously disrupted the Italian economy and brought business to a halt.[1] In 88 the massacre of Italians in Asia Minor ordered by Mithridates cost not only 80,000 lives, but vast amounts of capital.[2] In the revolutionary period that followed the victorious knights acquired the nickname of 'money-bags'.[3] The 1,600 Roman knights who fell victims to Sulla's proscriptions were the answer to their exploitation of this favourable turn of events.[4] Once again property conditions were completely altered. The Sullans bought the confiscated estates at bargain prices and in addition 120,000 veterans were settled in Italian communities.[5] The enormous gains on the one side were matched by the distress and poverty of the refugees on the other. A large part of those who suddenly found themselves rich squandered their treasures just as rapidly. The lesson drawn from this succession of ghastly upheavals by all those impoverished and in debt was that there was hope that the wheel of fortune would soon turn once more, bringing to the top what was then depressed.[6] So, in

---

[1] Oros. 5, 18, 27; App. *Mithr.* 84; *b.c.* 1, 234; Liv. *per.* 74; Val. Max. 9, 7, 4.

[2] Memnon (*FgrHist* 434), 22, 9. Plut. *Sull.* 24, 7 actually mentions 150,000. Cf. Cic. *imp. Cn. Pomp.* 7, 19; *Flacc.* 60; 61.

[3] Ascon. on Cic. *tog. cand.* frag. 17 (Schoell).

[4] App. *b.c.* 1, 442; Flor. 2, 9, 25.

[5] App. *b.c.* 1, 489.

[6] Cic. *Cat.* 2, 19, 20; Sall. *Cat.* 16, 4; 20, 14; 39, 4. In the introduction to his masterly dialogue *de oratore* (1, 1) Cicero beautifully describes how he would have liked to live *in optima re publica* (he is thinking of the time before 133), when senators *eum vitae cursum tenere potuerunt, ut vel in negotio sine periculo vel in otio cum dignitate esse possent.* Instead of which (3) *prima aetate incidimus in ipsam perturbationem disciplinae veteris, et consulatu devenimus in medium rerum omnium certamen atque discrimen, et hoc tempus omne post consulatum* (Cicero is writing in the year 55) *obiecimus iis fluctibus, qui per nos a communi peste depulsi in nosmet ipsos redundarunt.* Sallust (*Cat.* 38, 1–39, 4) gives a sketch of the years 70–63.

the prevailing moral atmosphere of Rome, all that was unclean, ranging from unprincipled frivolity to complete lack of scruples, had the upper hand to a depressing degree. Especially in the political world, where one was in permanent contact with this kind of behaviour, only a very few could keep themselves completely free of contamination. We must bear all this in mind, as events develop in the following years, in order to save ourselves from erroneous judgments.

For the year 65 Caesar had been elected curule aedile. The aedileship was a purely urban magistracy: its function was police control of market trade and generally the supervision of public order in the streets and squares, including the care of the temples and public buildings; and it carried the right to impose fines on transgressors.[1] But what made the post desirable, as a rung on the ladder of a senatorial career, was the additional duty of holding the games which were celebrated on public holidays. Money from the treasury was authorized for this purpose;[2] but it had long been recognized by candidates for higher offices that the best way to endear themselves to the electorate was to stage more magnificent games at their own expense. One can imagine how Caesar used this opportunity. The curule aediles—there were also two plebeian aediles whose duties included other games—were responsible for organizing the seven days of games in April in honour of the mother-goddess Cybele (*ludi Megalenses*)[3] and the fifteen days[4] of the Roman games in September (in honour of Jupiter Capitolinus).

Caesar's colleague was Marcus Calpurnius Bibulus, a man of integrity, though a loyal supporter of the optimate system, and, as he was to discover even more painfully as consul in 59, no match for Caesar. As he humorously remarked on that occasion, 'During his aedileship he had fared like Pollux, just as the temple of the Dioscuri in the Forum is only referred to as the temple of Castor, so the combined generosity of himself and Caesar was attributed to Caesar alone.' Special extra items ensured that only the latter was mentioned. But he put Bibulus still further in the shade by using his year of office, despite his debts, to honour the memory of his father, who had died twenty years earlier, with gladiatorial games of unparalleled splendour. The custom of honouring the dead in this way originated with the Etruscans. The gladiators were trained in barracks of their own, and it was not so long ago that Spartacus

[1] Mommsen, *RStR*, 2³, 476, 492, 499, 505, 507.　　[2] Habel, *RE Suppl.* 5, 619.
[3] G. Wissowa, *Rel. u. Kult. d. Röm.*², 318.　　[4] Cic. *Verr.* 1, 31.

had escaped from such an institution.[1] So it is not surprising that
the Senate heard with alarm of Caesar's preparations. Although a
limit was fixed, 320 pairs appeared, their armour and weapons
glittering with silver.[2] Not content with this, one night Caesar had
the memorials of Marius' victories, which had been dismantled by
Sulla, re-erected in the Forum. The common people were delighted,
but the guardians of the optimate tradition felt that this demagogic
behaviour was becoming dangerous, and their leader, Lutatius
Catulus, said in the Senate: 'Caesar is no longer trying to undermine
the Republic: he is using battering-rams now.' But the accused's
reply was clever enough to lay the storm.[3] Unfortunately we are
not told what he said, but may conjecture that he took the line
that it was time to bury old enmities and again recognize the
permanent services rendered by the old war-hero. Over and over
again Caesar revealed a special talent for putting his opponents
in the wrong and making them appear as absurd fanatics. We must
not overlook the fact that by this time there was only a limited
circle of unrepentant Sullans:[4] it would be wrong to imagine
that among the nobility Caesar's was a lone voice.[5]

Caesar's aedileship was by no means the most alarming event
of a year which began with an unsuccessful *coup d'état*. Publius
Autronius and Publius Sulla, the consuls elect for 65, had been
condemned for electoral corruption, and their places were taken
by their successful fellow candidates and accusers, Lucius Aurelius
Cotta (cousin of Caesar's mother) and Lucius Manlius Torquatus.
In alliance with Lucius Sergius Catilina, the condemned men

---

[1] Plut. *Crass*. 8, 2.

[2] Suet. *Caes*. 10, 1; Plut. *Caes*. 5, 9; Dio 37, 8; Plin. *n.h*. 33, 53; Schneider, *RE Suppl*. 3, 763.

[3] Suet. *Caes*. 11; Plut. *Caes*. 6; Vell. 2, 43, 3.

[4] In this year the trial of C. Cornelius, tribune of 67, for high treason took place. He was defended by Cicero, whose speeches are known to us only through the commentary of Asconius. The prosecution was launched by the same optimate circle, but Cornelius was acquitted by a large majority. I attempted to describe the complicated circumstances in *RE*, 7A, 860–862.

[5] R. Syme, *Rom. Rev.*, 68–70. In Rome's 'high society' everyone knew everyone else; we happen to possess a delightful account of a banquet given just at this time by the *pontifex maximus* Q. Metellus Pius in honour of a newly inducted *flamen Martialis*. Unfortunately the list of *pontifices* who were present is incomplete in the manuscript, but we learn that Caesar and Catulus participated, and Metellus also was among these optimates (Macrob. *Sat*. 3, 13, 10–12). The list was completed by L. R. Taylor in *AJPh* 63 (1942), 400 ff. and *Transactions of the American Philological Association* 73 (1942), 13, n. 25; 15, n. 31. Strasburger's idea (*HZ* 175 (1953), 233) that Caesar's enmity towards the leaders of the nobility was based on resentment against Sulla which he had never overcome seems wrong to me. If this were the case, he would surely not have married Sulla's granddaughter.

wished to become consuls in spite of all and over the dead bodies of their rivals. But the assassinations planned for January 1 failed, as did the attempt to repeat the performance on February 5. The consuls wanted a senatorial decree authorizing the suppression of the plot, but discussion of this was prevented by a tribunician veto.[1] Thus in 62 Cicero could maintain that he had heard nothing of the matter at the time.[2]

We must concern ourselves with this obscure affair, because well-documented sources[3] report that Caesar was involved in this 'conspiracy': in the confusion Crassus was to have seized the dictatorship with Caesar as his *magister equitum*. As far as Caesar is concerned, it is clear from the evidence quoted in the notes that this accusation first appeared in the political pamphleteering, dictated entirely by malice, of the year 59, the year of Caesar's consulate; the edicts of Bibulus and speeches by the consular Gaius Scribonius Curio are mentioned. A convincing refutation is that Cicero in his pamphlet *De consiliis suis* (=*About his Plans*), which was written at this time, but, on his instructions, not published until after his death, mentions only Crassus in connection with this business.[4] In fact, it is highly improbable that Caesar would have lent himself to plans aiming at the murder of his cousin Cotta. This makes his wanting to be *magister equitum* a malicious invention, and with it the dictatorship of Crassus; although the latter's behaviour encouraged men to think that he was promoting the prevailing unrest.[5]

Like Pompey a former partisan of Sulla, Crassus also had the ambition to win for himself a position of power independent of the

---

[1] Sall. *Cat.* 18, 5; Cic. *Cat.* 1, 15; Cic. *Mur.* 81; Dio 36, 44, 3–5.

[2] Cic. *Sull.* 11–13; 81.

[3] Suet. *Caes.* 9, 1–3.

[4] This decisive point was recognized by H. Strasburger, *Caesars Eintritt*, 108. The passage from Cicero's lost pamphlet is in Ascon. on Cic. *tog. cand.* frag. 1 (Schoell); *HRF*, p. 209, frag. 2. For the date, see Cic. *Att.* 2, 6, 2; 14, 17, 6; Dio 39, 10, 3; Plut. *Crass.* 13, 4; cf. *RE*, 7A, 909. In the earlier editions of this book and in *RE*, 2A, 1696–1697; 13, 309; 7A, 859, I believed in Caesar's involvement since I failed to appreciate Asconius correctly. The sentence quoted by Suet. *Caes.* 9, 2 from a letter of Cicero to Axius (Klebs, *RE*, 2, 2633, No. 4) could also belong to this period: '*Caesarem in consulatu confirmasse regnum, de quo aedilis cogitarat*'. *Regnum* and *rex* are used like the Greek τυραννίς and since the time of the Gracchi had been in vogue as defamatory catchwords. They were even applied to Cicero because of his execution of the Catilinarians (Cic. *Sull.* 21; 22; 48). In Plut. *Caes.* 6, 3 we read that the optimates called out that Caesar τυραννίδα πολιτεύεσθαι because he was restoring the memorials of Marius. This will also be what the passage in Cicero's correspondence refers to (Strasburger, op. cit., 108). On Tanusius Geminus and Actorius Naso, the authorities named by Suetonius in *Caes.* 9, 2–3, see Strasburger, op. cit., 26, 34, 108.

[5] Sall. *Cat.* 19, 1; Ascon. on Cic. *tog. cand.* frag. 1, cf. Suet. *Caes.* 9, 3; Plut. *Crass.* 34, 27; *RE*, 13, 299.

optimate oligarchy. Increasing his wealth by skilful and often un-scrupulous methods, he had become the richest man in Rome.[1] 'A man whose income was insufficient to support an army could never become a leading statesman'—that was the sort of thing he was heard to say.[2] Despite his victory over Spartacus his military reputa-tion lagged far behind that of Pompey, who had since then con-ducted the wars against the pirates and Mithridates. But at all costs Crassus was determined to remain at the top. In 65 he secured election to the censorship and had great hopes of this office. First, in compiling the roll of citizens he wished to include the Trans-padanes (which would have brought him a large new *clientela*), and even more promising was his intention to make Egypt into a province. For this purpose he relied on an alleged will of Ptolemy XI Alexander II, who, established as king by Sulla in 80, had been murdered after nineteen days. Both proposals met with such deter-mined opposition from his colleague Catulus that the normal censorial duties could not be carried out. Crassus preferred that they should both resign. One of their successors elected for 64 was Lucius Cotta, but they too were crippled by tribunician vetoes in the exercise of their functions.[3]

We also learn that, during the argument over the Egyptian legacy, Caesar hoped that in the following year he would receive an extraordinary command by popular decree to execute the will.[4] Nothing came of this because the optimates spoiled the manœuvre with the will. I do not regard this as a sufficient reason for expunging this episode from Caesar's life.[5]   The plan to enfranchise the

---

[1] Plut. *Crass.* 2, 4–7; *RE*, 13, 299.

[2] Cic. *off.* 1, 25: *qui in re publica princeps vellet esse.* It is hardly possible to give an adequate translation of the concept *princeps*; Wickert (*RE*, 22, 2037) says, 'only a man recognized by public opinion as such is a *princeps*'. On Crassus, see ibid., 2024, No. 56. For other interpreta-tions of Crassus' saying, see *RE*, 13, 300.

[3] Dio 37, 9, 3–4; Plut. *Crass.* 13, 1–2. On the king's will, see App. *b.c.* 1, 476–477; Por-phyry, *Chronicle* (*FgrHist* 260, F 2), 11. Cicero delivered his speech *de rege Alexandrino* against the annexation of Egypt. (The king referred to is Ptolemy XII Neos Dionysos, with the nickname Auletes—the *aulos* player—, who had been on the throne since the year 80. The *aulos* is the familiar ancient wind instrument that sounded like the modern oboe, although classical scholars and archaeologists persist in translating it as 'flute'.) Cicero's speech is known only through *Schol. Bob.* (For the fragments see Schoell, p. 457—wrongly dating them to the year 56.) Cicero referred back to the matter in 63 (*leg. agr.* 1, 1; 2, 41–44; cf. *RE*, 7A, 862; H. Volkmann, *Kleopatra* (1953), 34—English translation, (1958), p. 51).

[4] Suet. *Caes.* 11. As Strasburger (op. cit., 113), among others, remarks, Suetonius in his account also refers to events which belong to 59 and 57.

[5] This is also the view of T. Rice Holmes, *The Roman Republic* (1923), 1, 227. Strasburger (op. cit., 114) is of the opinion that an aedilician could not have dared to aim so high. But Caesar had been an unusual aedile!

Transpadanes lends support to the view that at this time there was an alliance between Caesar and Crassus, and it would indeed have been remarkable had they not stood together against their common foe Catulus.[1] In this contest Caesar was already gaining the upper hand by virtue of his victory in the Senate. To think of an extraordinary command was certainly audacious, but not surprising in Caesar, who had twice supported the grant of such powers to Pompey. It is a pity that we do not have the speeches he delivered at this time, but the very fact of their delivery shows the extent of his interest in the problem. We can have little doubt that Caesar felt himself as capable as Pompey had been when at the age of twenty-nine he received such a command for the war against Sertorius.

The next year began just as stormily. Lucius Sergius Catilina was a candidate for the consulship of 63; in this he was financed by Crassus —in league with Caesar, as Cicero was convinced.[2] Of course they expected something in return. Crassus always had his eyes on Pompey. If Caesar joined forces with him, we need not suppose that it was a one-sided connection; rather that in such a combination he saw possibilities of a great future for himself. He was therefore prepared to put up with the vile Gaius Antonius as Catiline's partner. But they went to such lengths in their canvassing that the optimates bestirred themselves and helped the *homo novus* Cicero to victory—the man who shortly before the elections had blasted the criminal past of his two rival candidates in a brilliant speech before the Senate.[3]

There was a piquant sequel. In this same year, 64,[4] the quaestorship was held by Marcus Porcius Cato, the great-grandson of the famous censor and a man who had already made a name for himself by his strength of character and penetrating study of Stoic philosophy. The usual practice for the beginners who held this post because it was prescribed by the law regulating the official career was to rely on their subordinates in all matters concerning the office. Cato, however, had conscientiously prepared himself, and struck at this lax routine like a thunderbolt.[5] Since 72 there had been a law providing for the collection of the money, payment of which had been

---

[1] Plut. *Crass.* 7, 6.   [2] Ascon. on Cic. *tog. cand., argum.* and frag. 1.
[3] Sall. *Cat.* 23, 5; Plut. *Cic.* 11, 2; App. *b.c.* 2, 5; *RE*, 7A, 863–864.
[4] Broughton, *MRR*, 2, 165, n. 5. Previously, 65 had been assumed as the date because Plut. *Cat. Min.* 16, 6 refers to Catulus as censor. This is probably a misunderstanding of *censorius*.   [5] Plut. *Cat. Min.* 16, 2–10.

D

remitted by Sulla to his favourites in the sale of the property of the proscribed. But nothing happened[1] until Cato put an end to this financial laxity.[2] Going further, he applied this law to the recipients of blood money (12,000 denarii) and treated them as criminals. As a result an attempt was made to bring them to court on a charge of murder.[3] According to the Sullan settlement there were seven jury courts competent to deal with the various crimes.[4] These were conducted by praetors. In view of the number of murder cases, it became necessary to co-opt aedilicians to preside over this court in particular.[5] In the course of this year Caesar found himself as one of these *quaesitores* or *iudices quaestionis*.[6] Since Sulla, in his edict authorizing the proscriptions, had provided that the proscribed might be killed with impunity, it was questionable whether prosecutions of this kind were legally admissible. Caesar decided that they were—understandably, in view of his own experiences during the reign of terror. A number of prominent Sullans were then condemned, among them Lucius Luscius, an ex-centurion with an alleged fortune of 10 million sesterces, and Lucius Bellienus, Catiline's uncle. But when Lucius Lucceius, a praetorian who had close connections with Pompey and an orator of note, went so far as to prosecute Catiline himself, the unsuccessful consular candidate, the latter was acquitted, despite the fact that he made a habit of boasting of his disgraceful deeds.[7]

The president of the court had no part in the verdict of the jury. But it was clear that powerful influences had been brought to bear in order to keep Catiline alive politically. He again became a candidate for the consulship. Pompey was reporting great successes in the East. All minds were filled with anxious thoughts of the future: the consul Cicero was approaching a troubled year of office.

When the new tribunes took up office on December 10, 64, one of them, Publius Servilius Rullus, brought forward a comprehensive agrarian law. This was nothing but an attempt on a large scale by Crassus and Caesar to secure for themselves a powerful

[1] Sall. *hist.* 4, 1; Ascon. on Cic. *Corn.* 1, frag. 34; cf. *RE*, 7A, 857.
[2] Plut. *Cat. Min.* 17, 2.   [3] Plut. *Cat. Min.* 17, 5–7.
[4] Mommsen, *Röm. Strafr.*, 203.   [5] Mommsen, ibid., 206.
[6] Mommsen, ibid., 183, 3; 615; 629.
[7] Suet. *Caes.* 11; Ascon. on Cic. *tog. cand.* frag. 21; Dio 37, 10, 1–3; Cic. *Att.* 1, 16, 9; *Sull.* 83; *Pis.* 95; *Lig.* 12. Strasburger (op. cit., 118) wishes to infer from the false statement in *Schol. Gronov.* on Cic. *Lig.* 12 that Caesar acted as prosecutor. Perhaps Suet. *Caes.* 74, 1 is relevant in this context: he reports that Caesar did not allow any action to be taken against the head-hunter from whom he bought his life.

extraordinary position.[1] The proposal combined far-seeing political and social aims with downright power politics.

The city of Rome was to be relieved of its vast citizen proletariat, men who vegetated in idleness on the scraps which the political struggles of their noble rulers provided for them.[2] Many thousands were to be settled in Italy on splendid allotments. The territory contemplated was in the first instance the Campanian public land, the last cultivated land which remained public property after the settlements and distributions of the previous decades, and the regular income from which formed the basis of the state's budget.[3] But there was not nearly enough of it. Further land had to be purchased. It was laid down that all sales should be voluntary, and to reassure the Sullan settlers, their property was expressly guaranteed.[4] This seemed to be the road to a peaceful solution of a social problem, the settlement of which was very much in the public interest.

But the execution of these provisions was put in the hands of a commission of ten, with powers that exceeded all that had gone before. These officials received praetorian power for five years and were not responsible to anybody. Each was assigned a staff of twenty knights and numerous clerks.[5] It was proposed that the money

---

[1] Cicero's three surviving speeches *de lege agraria* are the main source. According to *Att.* 2, 1, 3 there were four in the edition of 60. The beginning of the first, which Cicero delivered in the Senate on January 1, 63, is lost. See further Cic. *Pis.* 4; Plut. *Cic.* 12, 2–3; Dio 37, 25, 4. Cicero no more mentions Crassus and Caesar here than in *tog. cand.* frag. 1, where Asconius gets his information from *de consiliis suis*. But he leaves no doubt that Rullus is a pawn in the hands of important *populares* (1, 22, 23 and 27; 2, 6, 7, 15, 23, 25 and 98) who aim to secure for themselves powers (*extraordinaria imperia*, 2, 8) characterized as *regna* (2, 15, 24, 29, 32 and 35). These are the same men as those who wished to gain control of Egypt in 65 (2, 44; 1, 1; 2, 41–44). Further, they are described as the sort of people who regard *iudiciorum perturbationes, rerum iudicatarum infirmationes, restitutio damnatorum* as 'Popular' policy (2, 10). Justinus Klass (*Cicero und Caesar, ein Beitrag zur Aufhellung ihrer gegenseitigen Beziehungen* (Berlin, 1939), 28), recognized particularly in *restitutio damnatorum* a certain allusion to Caesar, who had spoken for the *lex Plotia de reditu Lepidanorum* in 70, and was now supporting a tribune's proposal to restore the *ius honorum* to the sons of the proscribed (Vell. 2, 43, 4). According to Plut. *Cic.* 12, 2; Dio 37, 25, 3; 44, 47, 4, this *rogatio* was approximately contemporaneous with that of Rullus. Cicero repulsed this attempt too with his speech *de proscriptorum filiis* (*Att.* 2, 1, 3; *Pis.* 4: from these passages it appears not to have been delivered until after the *pro Rabirio*). Quintilian, 11, 1, 85 summarizes it in the sentence: '*ita legibus Syllae cohaerere statum civitatis affirmat, ut his solutis stare ipsa non possit*'; Cicero himself in *Pis.* 4: '*ego adulescentis bonos et fortis, sed usos ea condicione fortunae ut, si essent magistratus adepti, rei publicae statum convolsuri viderentur, meis inimicitiis, nulla senatus mala gratia comitiorum ratione privavi*'. Thus, *pace* Strasburger (*Caesars Eintritt*, 115), one is not 'left to make intuitive judgments'.

[2] *leg. agr.* 2, 70.   [3] 1, 22; 2, 34, 75, 76, 80, 83, 96.
[4] 2, 68; 3, 6.   [5] 2, 32.

needed to buy the land should be raised by selling state domains
or increasing their yields. This was not very relevant to Italy, but
vast tracts of the provinces came within the scope of the provision.[1]
In addition, the commissioners were given judicial authority to
determine which land belonged to the state and which was private
property. It was even left to them to decide whether or not to
annex Egypt on the strength of the late king's will: this was not
stated explicitly, but the bill could be interpreted in such a way.
Mention was actually made of the royal estates of Mithridates,
whose kingdom had just been conquered by Pompey.[2] A further
section dealt with the booty won by magistrates on military campaigns: in particular, arrears in payment were to be handed over
to the commission. This was directed primarily against Faustus
Sulla, the dictator's son, and was in the spirit of the criminal charges
brought against the Sullans, which were mentioned above. Pompey
was expressly excluded from this provision. As far as he was concerned, it was enough that he was deprived of the opportunity to
provide his veterans with land. The settlements planned in Italy had
a further military and political importance in that the people whose
livelihoods depended on the agrarian law could, if need be, form an
army to oppose the returning general.[3]

The provisions for the appointment of the commissioners openly
sought as far as possible to ensure the election of particular persons.
It was proposed that the same procedure be adopted as was used
for the election of the *pontifex maximus*. In this case, for religious
reasons, only 17 of the 35 electoral districts participated, and so
9 districts formed a decisive majority. Translated into real political
terms this meant that a candidate had only to concern himself
with the votes of 9 tribes.[4]

Had this proposal been accepted, Crassus and Caesar would
have been in a very powerful position, which, if handled skilfully,
might have allowed them to by-pass the Senate and establish a
power to counter-balance that of Pompey.[5] But it was Cicero's first
achievement as consul to lay bare these intentions so effectively that
in 63 he succeeded, despite the opposition of his colleague Gaius
Antonius, in repelling this attack on the very foundations of the state.
This fresh reverse must have been painful to the two *populares*, but,
on this occasion too, they had kept themselves sufficiently in the
shadows not to feel the full force of the blow. Caesar's activity

[1] 2, 39.   [2] 1, 13.   [3] 1, 17; 2, 75, 99.
[4] 2, 17–22.   [5] 2, 25, 50, 54.

continued unabated. In a case of *repetundae* (the procedure for the recovery of money extorted from his subjects by a Roman magistrate), he attacked Gaius Calpurnius Piso (consul of 67), a former proconsul of Gaul and an uncompromising optimate, with the greatest bitterness for the unjust execution of a Transpadane. The consular had Cicero's oratory to thank for his acquittal, but remembered Caesar's with burning hatred.[1] Caesar next showed the same ardour in defending a Numidian nobleman, whom the king Hiempsal claimed as a tributary vassal. Carried away by enthusiasm for his cause, he seized the prince Juba, who was representing his father, by the beard. The case was lost, but Caesar protected his client from the consequences by hiding him in his house and smuggling him out in his own litter when he left for Spain in 61.[2] In both cases he proved himself a model patron, who fulfilled the obligations imposed by his trust fearlessly and devotedly. This was a point of great importance for a Roman's political reputation: time after time we find Caesar showing a sure moral sense when politics required.

Apart from Rullus his main collaborator was the tribune Titus Labienus. He came from Picenum where Pompey had a large *clientela*, which he had inherited from his father.[3] Presumably Caesar knew him from the time they had served together under Servilius Isauricus, and it is worth noting that he had by no means committed himself to Crassus' policy of hostility to Pompey. In pursuing their fight against the Sullan oligarchy they selected as their next target the old senator Gaius Rabirius, a staunch friend of the optimates. He was accused of a crime against the state, in that, in the year 100, he had killed Saturninus, a sacrosanct tribune of the people, after the consul Marius had promised him protection on behalf of the community. But the case was not brought before the regular Sullan court; rather, as *populares*, they had recourse to a quite outdated procedure, by which judgment rested, in the first instance, with two officials specially appointed to deal with high treason; the condemned man could then appeal to the popular assembly. Caesar himself was nominated as one of the judges by a praetor— not a *popularis* at all—and the lot fell on him to give judgment. He pronounced the death sentence. The result of the appeal before the

---

[1] Sall. *Cat.* 49, 2; Cic. *Flacc.* 98.

[2] Suet. *Caes.* 71; Cic. *leg. agr.* 2, 59. At all events, the Numidian Masintha turned to Caesar as the nephew of C. Marius (*b. Afr.* 32, 3; 56, 3). One can understand why King Juba was Caesar's bitter enemy in the Civil War.

[3] Cic. *Rab. perd.* 21; cf. Münzer, *RE*, 12, 260; R. Syme, *Rom. Rev.*, 31, 6.

popular assembly in the Campus Martius was in doubt, when
Rabirius was saved by the praetor and augur Quintus Metellus
Celer, who made use of one of the devices for which constitutional
law, with its meticulous preservation of every ancient practice,
offered many pretexts. He had the flag on the Janiculum hill lowered.
In ancient times, when Rome was surrounded by hostile neighbours,
this meant that the guard had moved off, the assembly was no longer
secure and consequently it was a signal to adjourn. On this occasion,
too, the assembly broke up. The Senate, led by the consul Cicero,
now intervened in favour of the accused. Labienus agreed to take
up the case again in the form of a prosecution for high treason
conducted by a tribune before the plebs, with the threatened penalty
reduced to a fine. This time Hortensius and Cicero conducted the
defence: an easy matter, since the name of the slave who had received
his freedom as a reward for killing Saturninus was known; and
Rabirius was acquitted.[1] A frivolous game had been played with
the old man's life for political reasons in order to disparage one of
the great days of senatorial government. The same political trend
is to be seen in a tribunician proposal to restore to the sons of the
proscribed the right to stand for office. This naturally had Caesar's
support, but it too was defeated by Cicero. From the point of view of
the senatorial government, the admission of these elements, thirsting
for revenge, could only worsen the situation.[2]

On the other hand Labienus with his colleague Titus Ampius
carried a bill which allowed Pompey, in recognition of his outstanding services, to wear a special robe of honour on festive occasions,
a distinction of which he was to make hardly any use. Caesar, who
not so long ago had put up Rullus against Pompey, characteristically supported the bill with the greatest zeal. Labienus' next bill
was concerned with the restoration of popular election to the
priesthoods (for the colleges of *pontifices*, *augures* and *quindecemviri
sacris faciundis*), which Sulla had abolished in favour of co-option.[3]

Much of the credit for its success also went to Caesar and created
the atmosphere for his own election as *pontifex maximus*. This, the
highest religious honour in the Roman state, had previously always
gone to most respected consulars. Its last holder, for instance, had

---

[1] Suet. *Caes.* 12; Dio 37, 26–28. The main source is Cicero's speech *pro Rabirio perduel-
lionis reo*. This was delivered at the second trial; Labienus' proposal is a *multae inrogatio* (8).
The case for my interpretation is fully argued in *RE*, 7A, 870–872, and follows Mommsen,
Röm. Strafr., 588, 1. See L. Lange, *Röm. Altert.*, 3, 241.

[2] P. 43, n. 1, above.

[3] Dio 37, 21, 4; 37, 1; Vell. 2, 40, 4.

been Quintus Metellus Pius, one of the most distinguished of Sulla's supporters. This gives us some idea of the audacity of Caesar, who was still only a candidate for the praetorship, in aiming so high. His opponents were the illustrious *principes*, Quintus Lutatius Catulus and Publius Servilius Isauricus. In view of his position Catulus was the obvious successor. But as Caesar's prospects were equally good, thanks to the enormous sums he had spent in bribing the electorate, and as he was in debt on a vast scale, Catulus attempted to persuade him to withdraw voluntarily by a large financial offer. But Caesar only arranged fresh loans and increased his bribes to the voters. On the day of the election he told his mother that now he could only come home victorious . . . or not at all. In the event, he scored so brilliant a victory that even in his rivals' voting districts he secured more votes than they did in all seventeen put together.[1]

Meanwhile Catiline was a candidate for the consulship. Initially his prospects were not unfavourable. One of the consuls, Gaius Antonius, was on his side; some of the tribunes were already following his line and working for a cancellation of debts;[2] no doubt he was in touch with Crassus and Caesar. But, as had happened before, this danger brought together the propertied classes, in particular the senatorial and equestrian orders. This 'Concord of the Orders' remained a life-long source of pride for the consul Cicero, the leader of the party of law and order.[3] Faced with this opposition Catiline had little hope left of attaining his object by constitutional means and prepared to win the consulship by force.

This enterprise had an incomparably broader base than that of January 1, 65, since Catiline wished to carry out his great revolution before Pompey was in a position to hinder him.[4] A considerable number of senators, men faced with bankruptcy, who had gambled away or wasted their fortunes, were in alliance with him. These were the officers of the revolution: their army was formed, on the one hand, of the unfortunates who had lost everything at Sulla's hands, and, on the other, of their equally unfortunate successors, Sullans who had immediately squandered their possessions.[5]   These

---

[1] Suet. *Caes.* 13; Plut. *Caes.* 7, 1–4; Dio 37, 37, 1–3; Sall. *Cat.* 49, 2; Vell. 2, 43, 3; cf. Münzer, *RE*, 13, 2091.

[2] Dio 37, 25, 4.

[3] H. Strasburger, *Concordia ordinum* (Dissert. Frankfurt 1931), 39 ff., 71; Cic. *Att.* 1, 17, 9; 18, 3; cf. *RE*, 7A, 890.

[4] The course of the 'Catilinarian conspiracy', with all the evidence, is discussed in *RE*, 7A, 873–890. See Cic. *Cat.* 2, 11; Sall. *Cat.* 16, 5; Plut. *Cic.* 10, 2.

[5] Cic. *Cat.* 2, 17–23.

elements were particularly numerous in Etruria, but were also in evidence in Bruttium, Apulia, Picenum and Gaul.[1] Finally they could always count on the rabble in Rome. This strong and radical revolutionary movement naturally no longer represented in any way the political aims of Crassus.[2]

In a conspiracy of this size traitors could not be excluded and for some time Cicero had been kept informed of developments.[3] But, in view of the plentiful sympathy for the conspirators existing in the Senate, he was unable to secure the passing of an effectual decree. Even if, in public, all expressed horror at Cicero's revelations, there was a group of senators who held that these should not be believed or that the misguided should be taught the error of their ways by friendliness and kindness.[4] We may assume that Caesar was among these. But in spite of these difficulties Cicero successfully maintained law and order, and Decimus Silanus and Lucius Murena were elected consuls instead of Catiline. On the other hand Caesar secured the praetorship without difficulty—as always in his career. Cicero had frustrated Catiline's plan by calling up a strong body of armed followers.[5]

Catiline, however, had no intention of vacating the field; rather, he began to enrol volunteers. These preliminaries to the creation of a revolutionary army lasted until the end of October. The revolution was to start in Etruria on October 27; on the next day fire-raising was to sow confusion among the citizens at Rome and the leading personalities in the government were to be murdered.[6] But as early as the night of October 20/21 Crassus passed on to Cicero an anonymous letter betraying these intentions; on the next day the consul reported this and other information to the Senate, and the Senate finally invested the consuls with dictatorial authority to take all necessary steps in Rome and Italy to secure the safety of the state.[7] On October 27 the insurrection broke out in Etruria, but the assassinations could not be carried out on the next day: on October 30 the Senate declared a state of war.[8] Thereupon Catiline issued fresh

[1] Cic. *Cat.* 2, 6; Sall. *Cat.* 27, 1; 30, 2; 42, 1.
[2] Sall. *Cat.* 48, 5; Plut. *Cic.* 15, 1–3; Dio 37, 31 and 1.
[3] Sall. *Cat.* 23, 1–4 (wrongly dated to the year 64); 26, 3.
[4] Cic. *Cat.* 1, 30; 2, 3; 14; *Mur.* 51; Dio 37, 29, 3.
[5] Plut. *Cic.* 14, 8; Cic. *Mur.* 52; Sall. *Cat.* 26, 4; Suet. *Caes.* 14, 1.
[6] Cic. *Cat.* 1, 7.
[7] Plut. *Cic.* 15, 1–3; Cic. *Cat.* 1, 4; 7; Sall. *Cat.* 29, 2; Dio 37, 31, 1–2.
[8] Sall. *Cat.* 30, 3.

orders and early on the morning of November 7[1] another attempt was made to murder Cicero, who immediately summoned the Senate, only to find a considerable number of senators still protecting Catiline. Accordingly Cicero was satisfied with driving his dangerous foe from the city with his first speech against Catiline. When it was confirmed on about November 15 that Catiline had joined his army in Etruria, the Senate declared him a public enemy and expressly ordered the consuls to hold levies.

But it was not until the beginning of December that the conspirators in the city laid themselves open to attack: they committed themselves in writing to some envoys from the Allobroges on the subject of a rebellion in Transalpine Gaul and were betrayed by these to the consul. Five of the leading Catilinarians were at once arrested. Faced with these documents at the meeting on December 3 the Senate could not help but sanction Cicero's conduct and order the arrest of four more culprits. To be sure, only the original five were in custody and these were handed over, under open arrest, to five senators,[2] among them Crassus and Caesar,[3] who were anxious to demonstrate their loyalty. Cicero and the other magistrates concerned were showered with praise, and Cicero personally honoured with a thanksgiving. With all this Caesar agreed.[4] Meanwhile the irreconcilable opponents of the two outstanding *populares* did not let themselves be deceived by this attitude. During the session on December 4 a witness appeared who alleged that he had been entrusted with a message from Crassus to Catiline. This was diametrically opposed to the policy of Cicero, who, while he had no doubt that Crassus and Caesar had been privy to the plot, now wished to keep them on his side. Accordingly it was on his motion that the Senate decided to reject the information. Similarly Quintus Catulus and Gaius Piso made great efforts to throw suspicion on the heavily indebted Caesar and reproached Cicero with protecting him. They regarded this as an excellent opportunity to make a clean sweep of the popular leaders, while Cicero strained every nerve to isolate Catiline and his crew from the serious politicians.[5]

---

[1] Date in Asconius on Cic. *Pis.* 4; cf. *RE*, 7A, 877; see also Cic. *Cat.* 1, 10; Sall. *Cat.* 28, 2–3.

[2] Cic. *Cat.* 3, 14; Sall. *Cat.* 43–47; 50, 4.

[3] Sall. *Cat.* 47, 4.

[4] The proposal was made by Caesar's cousin, L. Aurelius Cotta, and the whole Senate agreed (Cic. *Phil.* 2, 13; *Pis.* 6).

[5] Sall. *Cat.* 48, 4–49, 3; Plut. *Caes.* 7, 5; 8, 4; Plut. *Cic.* 20, 6–7; App. *b.c.* 2, 20.

On December 5 the Senate was to decide the fate of the arrested Catilinarians. While Crassus chose not to attend this session,[1] Caesar put in an appearance and was perfectly at his ease. Cicero opened the proceedings with a report on the situation, but at once let it appear what he regarded as the right course of action. In the debate, according to the usual practice, he first called on the two consuls designate. Of these Decimus Junius Silanus declared that the Catilinarians deserved 'the ultimate penalty'.[2] This was generally understood to mean 'the death penalty', and his colleague and the fourteen consulars who were present concurred.[3] After the consulars it was the turn of Caesar, as praetor designate, to speak. In a long speech he justified the following proposal: the convicted Catilinarians were to be handed over for custody to the strongest municipalities, which were to be selected by Cicero. These were to be responsible for keeping them closely guarded: should a prisoner escape, this was to be regarded as a hostile act against Rome on the part of the community. The Senate would regard as a public enemy any magistrate, who at a future date tried to raise their case either before the Senate or before the people. The property of the men thus condemned was to be confiscated.[4]

In this way he rejected any idea of an association between himself and these criminals, who in his judgment had deserved the heaviest punishment. As he explained in his speech, he did not dispute the right of the consul to carry out the death sentence by virtue of his dictatorial authority. He had not denied this right at the trial of Rabirius, nor did he later attack as unconstitutional the decree that was directed against himself in 49.[5] In his historical work Sallust makes him describe the conspirators as 'murderers of the commonwealth' against whose execution no objection could be raised on the

[1] Cic. *Cat.* 4, 10: *video de istis, qui se populares haberi volunt, abesse non neminem, ne de capite videlicet civium Romanorum sententiam ferat; is et nudius tertius* (December 3) *in custodiam cives Romanos dedit et supplicationem mihi decrevit et indices hesterno die* (December 4) *maximis praemiis affecit. Iam hoc nemini dubium est, qui reo custodiam, quaesitori gratulationem, indici praemium decrevit, quid de tota re et causa iudicarit. At vero C. Caesar intelligit* etc. Cicero's remarks about *non nemo* are identical with those in *leg. agr.* (see above, p. 43, n. 1). Of course we are here concerned with the edition of 60. Sallust reports in *Cat.* 48, 9 how as quaestor in 55 he witnessed Crassus' burst of rage against Cicero in the Senate on the ground that Cicero exposed him on December 4 (*RE*, 7A, 952).
[2] Plut. *Cic.* 20, 4; *Cat. Min.* 22, 4. In Latin it presumably read *ultima poena*.
[3] Cic. *Cat.* 4, 7; Sall. *Cat.* 50, 4; Cic. *Att.* 12, 21, 1.
[4] Cic. *Cat.* 4, 7–8; 10; Sall. *Cat.* 51, 43; Plut. *Cat. Min.* 22, 5; Dio 37, 36, 1–2.
[5] Cic. *Rab. perd.* 28; Caes. *b.c.* 1, 7, 5.

grounds of constitutional propriety. Sallust himself likewise recognizes the legality of such a senatorial decree.[1]

Caesar rather stressed that life imprisonment, as suggested by himself, was actually a more severe penalty, since death was no punishment at all, but either a natural necessity or rest from toil and misery. More particularly, as he said, his proposal was dictated by considerations of political prudence. To carry out an execution on the strength of the decree conferring authority on the consuls was a measure dictated by an extreme emergency: it ran contrary to the generally recognized legal principles existing among the Roman people, which had been confirmed in a number of recent laws. He was thinking of the law sponsored by Gaius Gracchus in 123, which provided that a magistrate who had put Roman citizens to death without trial should be brought before the popular court and outlawed, and that, generally, no decision should be made about the life of a Roman citizen except by the People, nor should anyone be put to death without a regular trial and sentence. Caesar, who recognized the legality of the *senatus consultum ultimum*, could not make a formal appeal to this law, since it was just this measure that suspended its working. Cicero in his reply scored a further point, when he asserted that criminals of this kind had forfeited their citizenship. But Caesar emphasized that the death penalty desired by Silanus was inconsistent with Roman practice; this was a new kind of punishment. He did not dispute the right to introduce a change of this sort, but claimed that there was now no good reason for going outside the framework of the existing laws, and criticized the illogicality of Silanus in not proposing the flogging of the guilty before their execution; by this omission he was recognizing the continued validity of the Lex Porcia which forbade the flogging of citizens. Further, he was dissatisfied that the method which had been adopted should rob the guilty of the opportunity, guaranteed by the laws on criminal procedure, of avoiding the death sentence by voluntary exile. Finally, his main argument against execution was that the carrying out of the death sentence on men of such eminence would attract enormous attention. It would look as if the Senate was giving free rein to its passions—that such a thing had never occurred before was, he declared, a tribute to Roman statesmanship—and the people would be left only with the impression of their

[1] Sall. *Cat.* 51, 25; 55, 6.

dreadful end, while their crime would be completely forgotten.[1] Each member of the audience could work out for himself how the matter would be treated later by popular agitators, since in the sphere of the *contiones* (meetings of the people summoned to hear magisterial pronouncements) any description of the granting of dictatorial authority by the Senate as unconstitutional still raised immense applause.

These were Caesar's reasons for proposing the harshest of all penalties, yet one that was to some extent in accord with the legislation designed to protect the Roman citizen from magisterial abuses. His speech was a masterpiece without parallel. At a meeting where passions ran high, he used the language of reflection and objectivity, defended the principles of the *populares*, yet remained personally unassailable, while Crassus avoided the session. He did not contest the earlier proposals as illegal but as inexpedient. On the other hand, he had done all that was possible at that moment to save the prisoners, since in the prevailing political circumstances a senatorial decree forbidding further discussion of the matter for all time would by no means have sealed their fate.

In its immediate purpose of terrifying the senators with the inevitable consequences of the execution the speech was to a high degree successful. The remaining praetors designate, including Quintus Cicero,[2] the consul's brother, supported Caesar. Then the praetorian Tiberius Claudius Nero[3] proposed that they should fix a date for a fresh discussion under military protection. Marcus Cicero thought any postponement dangerous: in order to secure a decision on December 5, he interrupted the debate and again gave the senators an impressive account of the situation in a speech, which he published in the year 60 as the Fourth Catilinarian.[4] Then he started a new inquiry beginning again with Silanus who, impressed by Caesar's speech, now declared that by 'the ultimate penalty' he had meant only imprisonment. Of the consulars, only Catulus spoke against Caesar's new proposal,[5] and the rest of the senators agreed with Caesar until it came to the turn of the tribune designate, Marcus Porcius Cato, whom we have already met as quaestor. This unique man was in all respects the antithesis of Caesar. The moral principles

---

[1] Caesar's speech: Cic. *Cat.* 4, 7–10; Sall. *Cat.* 51. A comparison between the speech composed by Sallust and the details given by Cicero allows us to assume that Sallust also kept to the oral tradition.

[2] Suet. *Caes.* 14, 2. [3] Sall. *Cat.* 50, 4; App. *b.c.* 2, 19; cf. *RE*, 7A, 888.

[4] Cic. *Cat.* 4, 6. [5] Plut. *Cic.* 21, 4; *Caes.* 8, 1.

of Stoicism, which he had adopted through deep inward conviction, guided his conduct in all circumstances. In his private and political life he was always the same.

On this occasion he started with unsparing criticism of his brother-in-law Silanus for his pathetic change of front. But the main force of his passionate speech was directed against Caesar, whom he accused of destroying the state while he talked speciously of the common good and humanity, and of terrifying the Senate with arguments the consequences of which he himself ought to fear. When he should be glad to escape scot-free himself, he had the presumption to try and save their common enemies from punishment. He had no pity for his own city, but sounded a lament for these vile malefactors whose execution would free the state from grave danger. Finally Cato proposed that the death penalty should be carried out against the self-confessed criminals according to the ancestral usage which also involved the confiscation of their property.[1]

These inflammatory words swept with them all who followed him. Cicero now wished to put the proposals of Caesar and Cato to the vote. Caesar made one further attempt to soften Cato's motion by suggesting that separate votes should be taken on the death penalty and confiscation. This met with strong opposition. Caesar appealed to the tribunes, but they gave him no help. There was nearly a riot as the knights, summoned to protect the Senate, forced their way towards him with their swords, and it was only under the consul's protection that he could leave the Temple of Concord, where the Senate was meeting. But after his departure Cicero put Cato's proposal to the vote without mentioning confiscation of property.[2] It was accepted in this form, and the five traitors were executed immediately.[3]

After their victory the feelings of the party of law and order towards Caesar were exceedingly hostile and, for this reason, he kept away from meetings of the Senate until the end of the year.[4]

[1] On Cato's speech, see Plut. *Cat. Min.* 23, 1–2. Plutarch's biography is based on that by Cato's friend Munatius Rufus (37, 1; *HRF*, p. 243). According to Plut. *Cat. Min.* 23, 3 it was the only speech that was recorded, since Cicero had it taken down during the meeting. Sallust's version (*Cat.* 52), apart from the proposal in s. 36, serves only to give a character sketch of Cato in contrast to Caesar. Cf. Cic. *Sest.* 61; 63; *Att.* 12, 21, 1.

[2] Plut. *Cic.* 21, 5; *Caes.* 8, 2–4; Sall. *Cat.* 49, 4 (chronologically wrong).

[3] Plut. *Cic.* 22, 1–4; Sall. *Cat.* 55, 2–6; App. *b.c.* 2, 21–22; Dio 37, 36, 3.

[4] Suet. *Caes.* 14, 2; Plut. *Caes.* 8, 5; probably a confusion with what is related in Suet *Caes.* 16, 2.

It was one of his most important characteristics that he did not waste his energies on political skirmishing. He left no doubt that he approved of the year's popular attacks. In the case of the *rogatio agraria* of Rullus he personally remained in the background, and, if he gave public support to other tribunician activities, we may imagine that his conduct was similar to that of December 5, in that in *contiones* called by tribunes he recommended their proposals with studied objectivity. He had no longer to prove himself a *popularis*. As to his popularity with the *plebs*, he had secured that by other means, sufficiently proclaimed by his indebtedness. Yet no one had the courage to charge him with *ambitus*.[1]

In his published speech Cicero treats him with marked respect: true, he had entered on 'the popular path' and was 'dear and pleasing' to the people, but, faithful to the demands of his rank (*dignitas*)— Cicero was thinking of the *pontifex maximus*—and the traditions of his ancestors, his proposal vouched for his sense of political responsibility and made clear the difference between a demagogue and a man with an appreciation of the real interests of the people; and yet even so 'gentle and forbearing' a man proposed a very harsh penalty.[2] Cicero does not hesitate to state openly that this course would be less dangerous to himself, but adds that the Senate should think only of the public interest.[3]

This assessment certainly did not belong to a draft of the speech made immediately after December 5, 63. It comes rather from an edition, on which Cicero was working in June, 60; in the same letter, in which he promises to send it to Atticus, he says that he hopes soon to see Caesar, who was then on his way back from Spain, and optimistically expects to be able to exercise a modifying influence on his policies in the event of his election to the consulship.[4] But, when this came about, in 59, in his unpublished pamphlet *de consiliis suis*,[5] he named Crassus and Caesar as the instigators of the Catilinarian troubles and always maintained this conviction. Yet as early as 63 he knew very well that they only wished to make use of Catiline and dropped him as soon as his wild plans for social revolution became notorious, and on December 5 he was certainly well aware of Caesar's political ability. Those who did not know him particularly well may have had difficulty in deciding on the evidence of his behaviour to date whether he was more than a

[1] Mommsen, *Röm. Strafr.*, 869 ff.   [2] Cic. *Cat.* 4, 9–10.
[3] Cic. *Cat.* 4, 9; 24.   [4] Cic. *Att.* 2, 1, 3; 6; 9.
[5] Plut. *Crass.* 13, 4; *Cic.* 20, 7, cf. p. 39, n. 4, above.

talented outsider with a strong inclination for adventure.[1] It looked
as if there was no room for him in a political world dominated by
the optimates and the ever-victorious general Pompey. The real
optimates, with the insight of hatred, recognized him for what he
was before Cicero did, but they made a mistake in crudely placing
him in the same category as Catiline.

For the time being he could quietly let events take their course.
For when the new tribunes entered office on December 10, two of
them immediately began to agitate against the death sentences of
December 5, just as Caesar had foretold. On the last day of the year,
when Cicero wished to take his leave with a speech to the citizens,
one of them, Quintus Metellus Nepos, interposed his veto, and only
allowed him to swear the customary oath that he had conscientiously
observed the laws.[2]

On January 1 the new praetor supplied the populace with an
unexpected sensation. While the new consuls were assuming office
on the Capitol, he published a proposal whereby the commission for
the rebuilding of the temple of Capitoline Jove, which had been
entrusted to Quintus Lutatius Catulus by the Senate in 78, should be
cancelled and transferred to another. He justified this in a *contio*
and allowed Catulus to speak on his own behalf, but insulted him
by forbidding him to mount the rostrum. The temple had been
burnt down in 83. After his victory Sulla had at first taken on the
work of reconstruction himself. The temple was consecrated in 69,
but the building was not yet complete. This could be interpreted as a
piece of optimate dawdling, and Caesar demanded from Catulus
an account of his expenditure, not without hinting at misappropria-
tion. However, Catulus' friends came hurrying from the celebrations on the Capitol: since it looked as if they were going to break up
the assembly, Caesar put an end to the *contio* and the whole business.
The obvious conclusion to be drawn is that Caesar's intention was
only to inflict a grievous humiliation on the old gentleman who
had wanted to destroy him as a Catilinarian.[3] The public was

---

[1] Here we may recall the anecdote in Plut. *Cat. Min.* 24, 1–3 reporting that Caesar was
handed a note during one of the senatorial meetings. Cato suspected that it came from a
Catilinarian and demanded that it should be read out. Instead Caesar handed it to him, and
it proved to be a *billet-doux* from Cato's step-sister Servilia, the wife of the consul designate
D. Junius Silanus!

[2] Dio 37, 38; Cic. *fam.* 5, 2, 6–7; cf. *RE*, 7A, 892.

[3] Thus Suet. *Caes.* 15; Dio reports that Pompey was to be elected in place of Catulus. But
Suetonius seems right: the election was to be a further act (Cic. *Att.* 2, 24, 3). The burning of
the temple: Tac. *hist.* 3, 72. Date of consecration: Phlegon of Tralles, *FgrHist* 257, F 12, 11.
Inscriptions of Catulus in the *Tabularium*: Dessau, *ILS* 35, 35a; cf. Münzer, *RE*, 13, 2088–2089.

concerned with matters of greater moment. All waited in suspense for Pompey. Would he return as a second Sulla? A strengthening of the optimate government was the last thing to be expected from the restorer of the tribunes' powers, whose present authority rested on popular decrees. The possibility of a clash beside which Catiline's enterprise would be a mere storm in a tea-cup could not be excluded. As things stood, Caesar could only join Pompey, since he had broken his links with the optimates, and the popularity he enjoyed was an insufficient basis for an independent position between the groups. Even Crassus, who was then much stronger than he, could not maintain such a position and went away on a journey.[1]

It was well known that Metellus Nepos, who since 67 had served under Pompey as a *legatus*, had returned to Rome in order to look after his general's interests as tribune. His action against Cicero conformed to the popular line to which Caesar had referred on December 5, and it is understandable that Caesar now offered his services for a manœuvre designed to secure for Pompey another overwhelming position on his return. Since Catiline was still in the field, a popular decree was to entrust Pompey with the task of restoring order in Italy with his army. In fact Catiline was destroyed in February by the forces commissioned by the Senate. Perhaps Nepos had taken this possibility into account, since his brother Celer, as proconsul of Cisalpine Gaul, was taking part in the operations against the Catilinarians. For this reason we may well believe the report that he was preparing another popular decree allowing Pompey to stand for the consulship of 61 in his absence.[2] We must bear in mind that Caesar would be able to justify these proposals on grounds of expediency.[3] But once again it was Cato who fiercely denounced them as covert attacks on the optimate republic and gave notice of veto.

Trouble was, therefore, to be expected at the voting, and Nepos supplied a troop of gladiators and other stalwarts to meet all emergencies. On the day of the vote, as soon as he had taken his place on the steps of the temple of Castor together with the praetor Caesar, Cato and his colleague Quintus Minucius Thermus appeared in order to exercise their veto, and both seated themselves between Metellus and Caesar. When they forbade the usual reading of the bill, Metellus unleashed his men. Cato's companions fled, but he held out beneath a hail of stones and cudgel-blows, until the consul

[1] Plut. *Pomp.* 43, 2; Cic. *Flacc.* 32.   [2] *Schol. Bob.* on Cic. *Sest.* 62.
[3] Plut. *Cat. Min.* 26, 3.

Lucius Licinius Murena appeared and led him into the temple in order to save him from a worse fate. Metellus now wished to proceed with the vote, but his opponents had gathered so many yelling supporters in the meanwhile that he abandoned the attempt.[1]

On the same day the Senate reacted to these scandalous goings-on by conferring on the consuls dictatorial authority for the protection of the community, forbidding any further exercise of their functions to Metellus and Caesar, the two seditious magistrates, and declaring public enemies any who demanded the punishment of those responsible for the execution of the Catilinarians.[2] On this occasion too Caesar had the audacity to justify Metellus and himself in a speech.[3] Unfortunately we do not know what he said, but from his subsequent behaviour during his consulship we may conclude that as a *popularis* he had no qualms about combating with violence optimate obstruction, which made use of the veto to rob the popular assembly of the right to express its will. For his own part he was determined to ignore the prohibition forbidding him to continue his functions. Metellus, however, admitted defeat and in high dudgeon left for Asia Minor to report to Pompey.[4] Caesar, too, noticed that the consuls intended to use their authority against him and now thought it wiser to come to heel. He dismissed his lictors, removed his purple-edged toga and retired to his house.[5] After two days the picture changed. A mob demanded his restoration with such vehemence that the Senate was hastily summoned. But Caesar calmed the excitement of the crowd; for his correctness he was fetched to the Senate and thanked, while the decree directed against him was lifted.[6] There can be no doubt that he showed very great skill in thus making people forget the embarrassing fact that he had taken part in an affray in which a sacrosanct tribune of the people

[1] Plutarch's full account in *Cat. Min.* 26, 2—28, 5 goes back to Munatius Rufus, who as Cato's companion (27. 6) had witnessed all this himself. Cf. Cic. *Sest.* 62; Dio 37, 43, 1–3; Suet. *Caes.* 16, 1.

[2] Dio 37, 42, 3; 43, 3; Suet. *Caes.* 16, 1.

[3] Suetonius (*Caes.* 55, 3) says that he had read the speech *pro Metello*, or *quam scripsit Metello*, as it was called in some copies. He describes the second title as erroneous, since Caesar spoke in person, and adds that in Augustus' opinion it was a transcript produced by shorthand writers, not a speech published by Caesar himself. Cf. F. Lossmann, *Hermes* 85 (1957), 52. On transcripts of *contiones* by P. Sestius, see Cic. *Vat.* 3.

[4] Plut. *Cat. Min.* 29, 1–4; Dio 37, 43, 4. Cic. *fam.* 5, 2, 9 answers the complaint of Metellus Celer (5, 1, 1).

[5] In the year 48 Caesar approved of a similar measure on the part of the Senate (*b.c.* 3, 21, 3).

[6] Suet. *Caes.* 16, 1–2; Dio 37, 44, 2.

E

had been mishandled. By restraining the 'people' from violence, as on December 5, he again showed himself as the *popularis* who refused to conform to the generally accepted image of this catchword, and the moderate optimates did well to give him credit for this.[1]

He was concerned with the recognition of his *dignitas*, the position due to him in public life: on this we have his own testimony, 'his dignity had always come before everything else; he held it dearer than his life'.[2] The violence of his reaction, if touched on this point, was soon to show itself. After the destruction of Catiline near Pistoria in February 62, the victorious party proceeded to render the surviving conspirators harmless by judicial condemnation. As well as Quintus Curius, who had already betrayed the plot before October 21, 63, the Roman knight Lucius Vettius, another member of the conspiracy, turned informer. This man produced a whole list of the guilty, and gave notice that there were more to come. Among others whom he named to Novius Niger, the president of the court dealing with crimes of violence, was Caesar, and he promised to produce in evidence a hand-written letter to Catiline. Curius confirmed this denunciation in the Senate, and referred to information he had received directly from Catiline. Caesar denied the accusation before the Senate in the sharpest terms, successfully invoked Cicero as a witness in his defence, in that he had spontaneously passed information to the consul, and succeeded in preventing payment of the hoped-for informer's reward to Curius. Against Vettius, however, he employed his powers of *coercitio* (the Roman magistrate's right to secure obedience by measures of coercion): he ordered Vettius' punishment through the destruction of part of his property. His furniture was plundered, while he himself was beaten up in front of the rostrum, and thrown into prison. Caesar also had Novius imprisoned because he had given permission for a case against a higher-ranking magistrate to be heard in his court. Drastic action of this kind may create an unfavourable impression in our eyes, but Caesar was keeping within his legal

---

[1] Cf. Cic. *fam.* 5, 2, 9. According to Plut. *Cat. Min.* 29, 3–4 Cato also opposed the intention to depose Metellus in the Senate 'in order not to provoke Pompey': the φρόνιμοι approved of this.

[2] Suet. *Caes.* 16, 2: *multitudinem . . . operam sibi in adserenda dignitate tumultuosius pollicentem conpescuit.* Caes. *b.c.* 1, 9, 2: *sibi semper primam fuisse dignitatem vitaque potiorem.* When Suetonius describes the *multitudo* as *sponte et ultro confluentem*, this may give rise to doubts; but it is not impossible that a demonstrative suspension of the administration of justice should lead to a popular uproar. A somewhat similar case in Plut. *Caes.* 8, 5. (See p. 53, n. 4, above.)

rights. All Romans had to admit that he was only protecting his magisterial dignity.[1] We do not hear of anyone daring to attack him hereafter.

But at the end of the year he found himself unpleasantly involved in the sacrilege of Publius Clodius Pulcher,[2] a notorious representative of Rome's younger set, who saw in their noble descent and the political career which this guaranteed, above all a never-ending opportunity for limitless enjoyment. Clodius first served as an officer in the army of his brother-in-law Lucius Lucullus. Dissatisfied with the position to which he had been assigned, in 67 he assumed a leading role in the great mutiny which brought Lucullus' triumphant progress to such an inglorious conclusion. On his return he unsuccessfully prosecuted Catiline on a charge of extortion: however, it was not clear whether he took the case seriously. Meanwhile in 63 he served with enthusiasm in the equestrian guard raised by Cicero. The worst rumours were circulating about his private life. Lucullus categorically affirmed that he had had incestuous relations with his (Lucullus') former wife Clodia.[3] In the year 62 he turned his attention to Caesar's wife Pompeia. He was then quaestor designate, and was to assume office on December 5. Shortly before this, the festival of the Bona Dea (the women's goddess), gave him a chance to approach Pompeia. This celebration, to which only women were admitted, used to take place in the house of a magistrate with the characteristically Roman power of command (*imperium*). This year the house of the praetor and supreme pontiff Caesar was chosen. Clodius slipped in dressed as a woman, but was recognized and only escaped with the help of a female slave. With characteristic sureness

---

[1] Mommsen, *RStR*, 1³, 153; 160, 2; Suet. *Caes.* 17. Dio 37, 41 does not mention Caesar in connection with the denunciations of Vettius; in 37, 43 he also omits the collaboration with Metellus Nepos. Either there was nothing about it in Dio's annalistic source or Dio has not reproduced it. I see no reason for doubting Suetonius' version on this ground, as does Strasburger (*Caesars Eintritt*, 124). On the denunciation Suet. *Caes.* 17, 2 says: '*id vero Caesar nullo modo tolerandum existimans*'. We find a good parallel in Cicero's speech in defence of P. Cornelius Sulla, which was delivered at this time. The prosecutor L. Manlius Torquatus had accused Cicero of falsifying the records of what the Allobroges had said on December 3, 63; to which Cicero replied (46): '*nisi tibi aliquem modum tute constitueris, coges oblitum me nostrae amicitiae habere rationem meae dignitatis. Nemo umquam me tenuissima suspicione perstrinxit quem non perverterim ac perfregerim.*' The only difference is that in defence of his *dignitas* Cicero only pulverized his traducer with words, whereas Caesar as the holder of *imperium* could mount a more powerful attack. Sall. *ad Caes.* 2, 2, 4: *in praetura inimicorum arma inermis disiecit.*

[2] Fröhlich, *RE*, 4, 82 ff., No. 48.

[3] Cic. *Mil.* 73; cf. Münzer, *RE*, 4, 107, No. 67.

of touch Caesar immediately sent Pompeia a message divorcing her.[1]

In the event the scandal grew into a big political incident. For months Roman politics revolved round the question whether or not Clodius could be brought to trial before a special court. He had a large circle of friends who found their amusement in thoroughly annoying the guardians of religion and morality, against whom there was already considerable ill-feeling in the ranks of the defeated Catilinarians. He therefore enlisted an armed bodyguard and began to play the champion of the depressed popular cause. Eventually, however, and despite all these intrigues, the bill setting up a special court was passed, but in a form favourable to the accused, and at the last moment Crassus also lent him financial support, with the result that he was able to buy thirty-one of the jurors, while only twenty-five pronounced him guilty.[2] Caesar had already left for his province, but previously had shown remarkable restraint in a matter that touched him so nearly. Asked the actual reason for divorcing his wife, he replied, 'Because in my opinion members of my household must be as free of suspicion as of crime'.[3]

His behaviour is again very remarkable. He divorced his wife, because as a statesman in the grand style he did not wish to find himself in the ridiculous position of a deceived husband. But as soon as the scandal became a political issue, he found the people who might be of use to him politically on the side of Clodius.

Cicero's attitude was just the reverse. Originally he had no personal reason to get particularly excited. But when Clodius began to attack the leaders of the Senate such as Lucullus, Hortensius, Gaius Piso and the consul Messalla in his *contiones*, he did not spare Cicero either, who since his victory 'in the garb of peace' felt himself the equal of Pompey, made fun of his frequent declarations

---

[1] Cic. *Att.* 1, 12, 3; 13, 3, '*uxori Caesarem nuntium remisisse*' means that Caesar sent the declaration of divorce by a messenger (not in writing). P. Jörs-W. Kunkel, *R. Privatrecht* 177, 3; Plut. *Caes.* 9, 1–10, 11; Cic. *in P. Clod. et C. Cur.*, frag. 28, with *Schol. Bob.* On the Bona Dea, G. Wissowa, *Rel. u. Kult. d. Röm.*[2], 216 ff.

[2] Cic. *Att.* 1, 16, 5; ; *in P. Clod.* frag. 27.

[3] Strasburger, *Caesars Eintritt*, 111, n. 55, rightly remarks (against Suet. *Caes.* 74, 2; Plut. *Caes.* 10, 8) that Caesar did not appear as a witness in the trial, which took place in May, since he had already left for his province. But from Cic. *Att.* 1, 13, 3 and *Schol. Bob., argum.* to Cic. *in P. Clod.* (in mentioning the SC of January 61, *accedebat huc etiam praeiudicium quoddam C. Caesaris ipsius pontificis, qui uxorem suam ilico repudiavit*) it may be concluded that Caesar's remark was made in the Senate. According to Cicero the college of *pontifices* had passed the verdict that for a man to force his way in *nefas esse*. It would have been remarkable if no one had asked Caesar's opinion. Caesar's answer need not therefore be 'fictitious', as Strasburger says (p. 135).

during the Catilinarian troubles that 'he had information' and stirred up feeling against the act of violence committed under his leadership. This touched Cicero on the raw, and he did not take long to retaliate. While Clodius maintained in court that he was in Interamna at the time in question, Cicero gave evidence that Clodius had paid him a visit on that day. As a result of the verdict he saw the whole policy of his consulship, the victory of the united 'men of goodwill' over the 'wicked' breaking down, and used every opportunity to fight the new Catiline in jest and in earnest. On May 15, 61, he succeeded in striking Clodius dumb with his biting sarcasm, but at the same time made an enemy who knew how to make the next nine years of his life as unpleasant as possible.[1]

Because of the Clodius case the allotment of propraetorian provinces had been delayed until March.[2] When lots were cast, Caesar obtained Further Spain, where he had already served as quaestor, and left immediately without waiting for the senatorial decree granting money for his governorship. Rome was becoming too hot for him; for when property values came to be calculated, his debts allegedly amounted to 25 million denarii.[3] His creditors wished to use the interval between his praetorship and propraetorship, when he would again be a private citizen, to sue for the debts and threatened to hinder his departure by distraint upon his governmental equipment. In this emergency Crassus helped him to an agreement by giving security for about 5 million denarii.[4] Clearly our sources here depend on rumours which we cannot verify. But Crassus' aid will be historical and shows that he was still counting on Caesar's support.

In Further Spain Caesar made full use of the possibilities which a province offered to a Roman statesman. His next object was to reach the consulship in the year 59, the earliest date at which this was constitutionally possible. Although the actual powers of this senior magistracy had been considerably reduced in the course of time, it still gave entry to the circle of the real *principes civitatis*, and even a *homo novus*, such as Cicero, had recently shown to what uses it could be put in the hands of a skilful politician. In order to start his canvass in a commanding position, he was eager to return home to a triumph. He knew that the Lusitanian part of the province

[1] Cic. *Att.* 1, 14, 5; 16, 3–11; *Schol. Bob., argum.*, to Cic. *in P. Clod.*; cf. *RE*, 7A, 896–899.
[2] Cic. *Att.* 1, 13, 5; 15, 1. [3] App. *b.c.* 2, 26.
[4] Suet. *Caes.* 18, 1; Plut. *Caes.* 11, 1–3; *Crass.* 7, 6.

was infested with bandits, and gave this as the official explanation for his premature departure,[1] but in this way also avoided senatorial interference with his plans. On his arrival he again, as a general, showed himself the dashing officer of his youth, immediately enlisted ten new cohorts to reinforce the twenty already under arms[2] and ordered the bandits, who were occupying the Herminius range south of the Duero, to settle in the plain and there to follow peaceful callings. Their refusal gave him the victories for which he hoped. When some of the fugitives established themselves on an island off the west coast and his first attempt to secure a landing with rafts failed, he called up ships from Gades and forced their surrender.

Then he sailed with the squadron to Brigantium,[3] a city of the Callaici on the north coast, whose inhabitants, terrified by the unusual spectacle, also submitted. His army hailed him as Imperator, and the rich booty allowed him to some extent to repair his shattered fortune, but he did not forget to let his brave soldiers have their share, and also sent considerable sums to the treasury in Rome.[4] His opponents, of course, had stories to tell that he had on several occasions had cities plundered which offered him no resistance, and that he had accepted immoderate presents from grateful subjects.[5] But no one dared to charge him with extortion: on the contrary, the Senate granted him a triumph, and his hopes were splendidly fulfilled. Unfortunately we do not know the circumstances under which the decree was passed, but can form an impression of the style of his military despatches from Caesar's commentaries on the Gallic Wars. His skill in letting his achievements speak for themselves—after all they were always the glorious deeds of Roman soldiers—is as fresh and alive today as on the day when the words were first written. How much less could the senators avoid their spell! Even malevolent optimates had to admit that this campaign had pacified areas that had hardly been touched previously

---

[1] Suet. *Caes*. 18, 1. 54, 1 gives him the title *pro consule*. See Dio 37, 52, 1–2.

[2] Plut. *Caes*. 12, 1.

[3] Dio 37, 52, 3–53, 4; Plut. *Caes*. 12, 1; Suet. *Caes*. 54, 1. Brigantium, called Brigantia in Orosius 1, 2, 71; modern Betanzos, Hübner, *RE*, 3, 847.

[4] Plut. *Caes*. 12, 4; App. *b.c.* 2, 27; H. Vogel, *SavZ* 66 (1948), 413 ff. has shown against Mommsen, *RStR*, 1³, 242 (according to whom *praeda* and *manubiae* (the proceeds from the sale of booty) 'had always to be used in the public interest') that it was not considered illegal for the general in distributing the booty to his soldiers to provide for himself as well, so long as the booty had not been transferred to the Treasury. In particular he adduces Plut. *Mar*. 31, 4; 34, 6; 45, 12, and also the late annalists used by Livy and Dionysius of Halicarnassus who are also sound evidence for the last century of the Republic.

[5] Suet. *Caes*. 54, 1. Dio's account is also malicious. Cf. Catull. 29, 19.

and that this was necessary for the prosperous development of the province.[1]

In using the term 'optimate' as a convenient abbreviation, we must keep reminding ourselves not to imagine a modern parliamentary party. With the *principes* of the Senate it was a point of honour to exercise an independent judgment. They were perfectly ready to protect and increase the honour and greatness of the state, as their ancestors had done,[2] but this goodwill only operated within the boundaries of the traditional interests of the optimate class: it was not in evidence when they felt their predominance threatened.

During the winter Caesar applied himself with equal skill to civil administration. Some communities were still suffering under the reparations imposed by Metellus Pius during the war against Sertorius. He asked the Senate that these should be lifted. Numerous other complaints reached the Senate through his agency, and many communities and individuals found in him an active patron.[3] In this he was assisted by Lucius Cornelius Balbus, a Roman knight and native of Gades, one of his most loyal followers, with whom he had become acquainted during his quaestorship and whom in 61 he had nominated as his adjutant (*praefectus fabrum*). Like Lucullus in Asia Minor, he issued an order for the cancellation of debts, but one which was considerably more favourable to the creditors— mostly Roman knights. These secured a legal right to two-thirds of their debtors' income until the debt was paid off, whereas Lucullus had granted them only a quarter.[4] In Spain we already have the complete Caesar of the Gallic War. He conducted affairs like a born general and ruler, but never lost himself in this activity on the periphery of the Empire: what mattered was always its effect on Rome.

Even before his successor relieved him, he arrived outside Rome at the beginning of June 60 to begin his canvass for the consulship.[5] It was accompanied by promising preparations for his triumph, which were made outside the city, because a triumphant

---

[1] Plut. *Caes.* 12, 1; App. *b.c.* 2, 28.

[2] Cic. *leg.* 3, 40: *est enim ipse senator is, cuius non ad auctorem referatur animus, sed qui per se ipse spectari velit.* Cf. *Historia* 1 (1950), 640.

[3] *b. Hisp.* 42, 1–2; Caes. *b.c.* 2, 18, 5–6; 20, 2.

[4] Cic. *Balb.* 43; 63. Among other tasks, the *praefectus fabrum* looked after the *manubiae* so long as they were within the general's control, Plin. *n.h.* 36, 48; Plut. *Caes.* 12, 3; *Luc.* 20, 3; Vogel, op. cit., 407; *RE*, 13,394; M. Rostovtzeff, *The Social and Economic History of the Hellenistic World*, 954, 1563, n. 28.

[5] Cic. *Att.* 2, 1, 9; App. *b.c.* 2, 28.

magistrate lost his *imperium* on the day on which he crossed its sacred boundary, the *pomerium*.[1] This clause in the constitution was an annoying obstacle for Caesar, since in 63 it had been laid down that a candidate for the consulship must appear in Rome in person.[2] Polling day had already been announced and, since there was no time to hold the triumph beforehand, Caesar asked the Senate to free him from this regulation. The majority were inclined to give him permission, but the matter was urgent. Thus Cato, Caesar's harshest opponent, succeeded in frustrating the necessary decree by speaking for so long that the meeting had to be adjourned as darkness fell.[3]

Caesar again showed himself a purposeful statesman: he crossed the *pomerium*, and thereby waived his claim to a triumph.

Marcus Calpurnius Bibulus was another candidate. After their aedileship he had also been Caesar's colleague as praetor and was an embittered enemy. But as early as December 61 Caesar's candidature looked so promising that Lucius Lucceius, a praetorian who was not yet a member of the nobility, began to form hopes that, if he made an electoral compact with Caesar, he might squeeze his way into the consulship in place of the respected Bibulus.[4] Bibulus on the other hand counted rather on bringing the wealthy Lucceius over to his side. As soon as Caesar had arrived on the scene and surveyed the situation, he formed an electoral compact with Lucceius, the friend of Pompey.[5] Cicero, who had also attached himself to Pompey, flattered himself that he exercised no small influence on him, and also imagined that he could make Caesar a 'better' politician.[6] In the electoral compact (*coitio*) it was laid down that Lucceius, since he controlled no political following of his own worth mentioning, should distribute the electoral cash among the constituencies in both their names. This sounded so brilliant an arrangement that Bibulus was unable to counter it. Since Caesar's election was certain, Bibulus' friends concentrated all their efforts on at least getting an uncongenial colleague through. They contributed to a

---

[1] Mommsen, *RStR*, 1³, 66 ff., 128 ff., 638; H. Siber, *Röm. Verfassungsrecht* (1952), 205 ff.

[2] Cic. *leg. agr.* 2, 24 (January 63: it was not in existence then). L. Lange, R. *Altertümer*, 3, 263, conjectures that it was a clause in the *lex Tullia Antonia de ambitu* of 63; cf. Cic. *Mur.* 3; 5; 47; 67; *Schol. Bob.* on Cic. *Planc.* 83; *Sest.* 133; *Vat.* 37; *Sull.* 17. G. Rotondi, *Leges publicae pop. Rom.* (1912), 379.

[3] Suet. *Caes.* 18, 2; Plut. *Caes.* 13, 1–2; *Cat. Min.* 31, 2–5; App. *b.c.* 2, 28–30; Dio 37, 54, 1.

[4] Cic. *Att.* 1, 17, 11; 14, 7.   [5] Suet. *Caes.* 19, 1.

[6] Cic. *Att.* 2, 1, 6; see above, p. 54.

common electoral fund, and, on this occasion, even Cato approved since it was done in the public interest.[1] Further, in order to render Caesar's election as harmless as possible, they managed to carry a senatorial decree, which gave the future consuls of 59, on conclusion of their year of office in Rome, the ludicrous task of demarcating 'the forests and woodland paths' belonging to the state.[2] On polling day Caesar and Bibulus were elected consuls.

This was the situation with which Caesar was now faced. After six years of victorious campaigning, without parallel even by Roman standards, Pompey had landed at Brundisium early in 61 with a considerable part of his army. The Mediterranean had been swept clear of the pirate plague, Asia Minor lay at his feet, Mithridates was dead. In the north the Roman army had pushed forward into the Caucasus; in the south, Syria from the Euphrates to the frontiers of Egypt had been incorporated in the Roman Empire. On his arrival he immediately dismissed his soldiers to their home-towns without waiting for a senatorial or popular decree. Already among ancient historians it occasioned much surprise that he did not use his armed power to establish a military monarchy.[3] But this judgment seems only to spring from a retrospective evaluation. There is no authority for it in Cicero's letters of the period. On any reasonable calculation, Pompey had no need of a *coup d'état*. He had every reason to regard himself as the first man in Rome, the *princeps* of the *principes*.[4] While still in Asia Minor he had rewarded his soldiers royally. Most of them naturally longed for their release, and he had no reason to deny them this favour, since a Roman statesman's power depended on the number of votes he could control through his followers. Here Pompey could rely on his veterans, particularly as he promised to provide them with

---

[1] Suet. *Caes.* 19, 1.

[2] According to a law of C. Gracchus the Senate had to decide on the provinces of the future consuls before their election, and its decision could not be vetoed. Cic. *prov. cons.* 3; 17; 36; 37; *dom.* 24; 61; *fam.* 1, 7, 10; Sall. *Iug.* 27, 3. Suet. *Caes.* 19, 2: *opera ab optimatibus data est, ut provincia futuris consulibus minimi negotii, id est silvae callesque, decernerentur.* P. Willems, *Le sénat de la rép. rom.* (1883), 2, 576, 5, regards *id est silvae callesque* as a gloss by an ignorant grammarian. J. P. V. D. Balsdon, *JRS* 29 (1939), 182, holds that Italy is meant. But Ed. Meyer's *Caesars Mon.*, 57, 6, did well to adduce Tac. *ann.* 4, 27, 2 about a quaestor in A.D. 24 'cui provincia vetere ex more calles evenerant.' Likewise J. van Ooteghem, *Pompée le Grand* (1954), 321, 1; 470. Cic. *Vat.* 12 (*aquaria provincia*); cf. Mommsen, *RStR*, 2³, 573, 3.

[3] Vell. 2, 40, 3; Dio 37, 20, 5; 50, 6; Plut. *Pomp.* 43, 1; App. *Mithr.* 567.

[4] Cic. *p. red. ad Quir.* 16 (in 57): *vir omnium qui sunt, fuerunt, erunt, virtute sapientia gloria princeps.*

land on a grand scale. Should it become necessary, even as a private citizen, he could at any time raise an army. In the year 50 he still lived under the illusion that he had only to stamp on the ground for soldiers to flock to him in large numbers.[1]

At the beginning of February 61 he arrived in Rome.[2] Here he refused all further honours to avoid giving any cause of offence and was content with a special privilege allowing him to postpone his triumph. This he celebrated on the last two days of September with a splendour appropriate to his achievements.[3] He waited until the following magisterial year (60) to draw the political conclusions for his position at Rome. For the time being he was satisfied that one of his most loyal subordinate commanders, Lucius Afranius, had been elected to the consulship for that year, albeit by gross bribery of the voters.[4]

However, when the two demands which were to form the basis of permanent supremacy in the state were placed on the Senate's agenda, it became apparent that he had underestimated the oligarchy's powers of resistance to such a claim.[5] One was concerned with the ratification of the regulations he had made for provinces and communities in the newly won areas, the other with the provision of land for his veterans. The first proposal was opposed in particular by Lucius Lucullus, who demanded that each regulation should be discussed separately and that the Senate should especially reserve its judgment in cases where Pompey had departed from the arrangements made by Lucullus in Asia Minor. He was supported by one of the consuls, Quintus Metellus Celer, the half-brother of Pompey's recently divorced wife Mucia,[6] by Quintus Metellus Creticus, the ex-consul of 69, who like Lucullus had been deeply

---

[1] Plut. *Pomp.* 57, 9; 60, 7; *Caes.* 33, 5; App. *b.c.* 2, 146.

[2] Cic. *Att.* 1, 14, 1.

[3] Plin. *n.h.* 7, 98; Plut. *Pomp.* 45, 1.

[4] Cic. *Att.* 1, 16, 12; Plut. *Pomp.* 44, 4–6; *Cat. Min.* 30, 7.

[5] Dio 37, 49–50. Further evidence in my *Pompeius²* (1959), 126–129; van Ooteghem, op. cit., 290–298.

[6] Cic. *fam.* 5, 2, 6; Dio 37, 49, 3. She was the daughter of the famous jurist Q. Mucius Scaevola (Ascon. *argum.* to Cic. *Scaur.*). Her mother must have been previously married to Q. Caecilius Metellus Nepos, consul in 97 (*RE*, 3, 1216, No. 95). But perhaps (thus Fluss, *RE*, 16, 449, No. 28) *soror* is to be understood as cousin. Pompey divorced her in 62 (Cic. *Att.* 1, 12, 3). In 55 the consular C. Scribonius Curio published an invective against Caesar in dialogue form (Cic. *Brut.* 218–219) where an affair with Caesar is given as the ground for the divorce; Pompey is said to have described Caesar, with a groan, as his 'Aegisthus' (Suet. *Caes.* 50, 1). See Münzer, *RE*, 2A, 866. How far such invective might go can be seen from Cicero's *in Pisonem*. Cf. *RE*, 7A, 954–955; Strasburger, *Caesars Eintritt*, 38.

humiliated by Pompey's great command, as well as by Marcus Cato and Marcus Crassus. The provision for the veterans fared no better in the Senate, and, faced with a combination of so many influential opponents, the consul Afranius, who had little experience of senatorial tactics, proved a failure.[1]

As early as January Pompey employed the tribune Flavius to introduce a comprehensive bill for the distribution of land in the interests of his soldiers. In order to secure its passage, provision was also made for the granting of land to other needy citizens. However, despite the fact that it certainly kept within the bounds of what was politically and socially necessary,[2] the bill was opposed by the Senate led by the usual *principes*. It was the oligarchy's misfortune that its policy was determined primarily by the personal interests of its leading members. Thus men of ability and sense fought this bill on the ground that it was designed to give fresh power to Pompey. Of the people who mattered, only Cicero supported Pompey and he, too, was moved by personal reasons, since he hoped that Pompey would protect him from harassment by Clodius.

As the agitation on behalf of the bill continued, the consul Celer laid all manner of difficulties in the tribune's path, until the latter angrily led him off to prison in June 60.[3] Here he refused the help of the other tribunes, but calmly summoned the Senate to meet in the prison. Flavius now seated himself in the doorway to bar the senators' entrance, while the consul countered by having an opening broken in the wall. In this remarkable drama public sympathy lay with the intrepid Celer, and Pompey told the tribune to call a halt. The opposition had now completely won over the people, and consequently Pompey let the whole proposal drop.

From these proceedings Caesar could see that, despite a brilliant victory at the polls, his opponents were quite capable of crippling him as well by clever tactics. They had already made a start with the decree on the consular provinces for the year 58. Caesar's name, like that of Pompey, spelled a danger against which the splinter

---

[1] His earlier magisterial career is unknown. Broughton, *MRR*, 2, 130, n. 5, conjectures that he was praetor in 71. From 75 and again from 66 he spent years as *legatus* to Pompey. On Cicero's sarcastic description of him as *Auli filius (Att.* 1, 18, 5; 20, 5; 2, 3, 1) see van Ooteghem, op. cit., 291. According to Dio 37, 49, 3 he was better as a dancer than as a politician.

[2] Cic. *Att.* 1, 18, 6; 19, 4. It was modelled on the *rogatio Plotia* of 70, for which there had been insufficient funds at the time (Dio 38, 5, 1–2). E.g. Gabba, *La Parola del Passato* 13 (1950), 66 ff.; Broughton, *MRR*, 2, 128; van Ooteghem, op. cit., 294, n. 3; see above, p. 29, n. 5.

[3] Cic. *Att.* 2, 1, 8.

groups of the oligarchy always combined. As he could not cope alone with the united strength of the friends and clients that stood behind them, Caesar also had to have allies if he wished to be able to defy the oligarchy. The obvious men were Gnaeus Pompeius and Marcus Crassus, who had long regarded themselves as superior, or at least equal, to the oligarchy and controlled large followings.[1] For many years Caesar had made it his aim to be on friendly terms with both of them. The difficulty was that just at that time Crassus was going along with the oligarchy through hatred of Pompey.[2] To realize the plans which he had in mind for his consulship, Caesar needed reliable support, not just occasional help. For this reason it was essential that he should reconcile the old enemies Pompey and Crassus. In December 60 he had come to an agreement with Pompey. At that time Cornelius Balbus, Caesar's confidential agent, whom he appointed as his personal adjutant (*praefectus fabrum*) for 59 as previously in 61,[3] appeared at the house of Cicero, Pompey's most distinguished follower, and told him that Caesar was also counting on his support during his consulship, in particular over the agrarian law with which he proposed to start his programme; Caesar would seek his and Pompey's advice in all matters and aimed at reconciling Pompey with Crassus. Cicero, however, was unable to commit himself to a firm answer, since he believed he owed it to his past career—the real importance of which he exaggerated—not to sacrifice his independence to his security.[4]

However, the agreement with Crassus was concluded a little later. The three men bound themselves by a solemn promise to take no political action of which one of the three disapproved.[5] From this negative formula we can sense the great effort it took to overcome the distrust between Pompey and Crassus; and we shall probably not go far wrong if we attribute the wording of the formula to the resourceful brain of Caesar. The strength of the three confederates was quite uneven: Pompey was much stronger than Crassus, and Caesar still a beginner compared with either of them, but as consul the tactical initiative rested with him and, since he was also vastly their superior intellectually and in political skill, the

---

[1] Dio 37, 54, 3 describes them as τὰς ἑταιρείας ἔχοντας; cf. 57, 2.
[2] App. *b.c.* 2, 32. But he had no qualms about opposing them if it was to his advantage (Cic. *Att.* 1, 17, 9).
[3] Cic. *Balb.* 63.
[4] Cic. *Att.* 2, 3, 3-4.
[5] Suet. *Caes.* 19, 2; Liv. *per.* 103: *conspiratio inter tres civitatis principes.*

actual leadership fell to him.[1] Now his career of defiance of the *leges annales* caught up with Pompey. Spoiled by his good fortune from his youth upwards, he despised the normal activities of the senator in the Curia and Forum, and so never learned how to further his own interests there; accordingly, now that the great military problems of the Empire appeared to be settled, he saw himself forced to adopt a waiting role. Caesar's case was quite different: he had worked his way up by the regular route, and knew a way out of all the difficulties that were piled up against him.

Doubtless the programme for the year of Caesar's consulship was then at once agreed, at least in principle; for its implementation the three greatest patrons of Rome made available their combined followings, with which they could hope to control magistrates, Senate and popular assembly. For the time being the firmness of the bargain that had been struck remained a close secret—Crassus probably did not join the alliance until the beginning of the year 59. For the rest Caesar sought to engage practically everybody whom he found ready to join him. Such a one was the then praetor Publius Cornelius Lentulus Spinther, for whom Caesar procured a place in the college of pontiffs and Cisalpine Spain as a province for 59 and 58.[2]

It was of the greatest importance that Caesar should secure the services of some tribunes. Of those who assumed office on December 10, 60, he chose Publius Vatinius, an ambitious politician from the Sabine town of Reate, as his particular helper.[3] The latter demanded such sums for his services that even Caesar was astounded and later summed up this connection with the words, 'In his tribunate Vatinius did nothing gratis.'[4] Of the praetors, Quintus Fufius Calenus stood closest to Caesar: during the Clodius case he had already distinguished himself as a clever popular tribune. At the beginning of his year of office Vatinius produced a series of bills, including one about the composition of the jury courts, and warned the Senate that he had absolutely no intention of taking notice of

---

[1] Vell. 2, 44, 2 on Crassus: *ut quem principatum solus adsequi non poterat, auctoritate Pompei, viribus teneret Caesaris.* Flor. 2, 13, 10: *C. Caesar eloquentia et spiritu, ecce iam et consulatu, adlevabatur; Pompeius tamen inter utrumque eminebat. Sic igitur Caesare dignitatem comparare, Crasso augere, Pompeio retinere cupientibus omnibusque pariter potentiae cupidis de invadenda re publica facile convenit.* Asinius Pollio began his history of the Civil War with the year 60, according to Hor. c. 2, 1, 1: *Motum ex Metello consule civicum bellique causas* etc.

[2] Caes. *b.c.* 1, 22, 4.

[3] Cic. *Vat.* 13 ff., 16; cf. Gundel, *RE*, 8A, 495 ff.

[4] Cic. *Vat.* 38 (cf. 29); *Sest.* 114.

oligarchic obstruction by means of alleged omens, which was growing more and more systematic. Of his colleagues Gaius Alfius supported him.[1] This prelude gives us some idea how bitterly laden with hatred was the political atmosphere, and of the tensions that had to be released in the next consular year.

[1] Cic. *Vat.* 38 with *Schol. Bob.*

CHAPTER THREE

THE CONSULSHIP

ON January 1, 59, Caesar and Bibulus assumed office. Relations between these two distinguished men were avowedly hostile as each had the worst expectations of the other.[1] But behind their personal feud there now stood contrasts of much graver import, questions concerning the fate of the Roman Empire. No one appreciated this better than Caesar. Yet at the first meeting of the Senate he succeeded with consummate ease in glossing over the difficulties. He spoke fine words, 'that the consuls must be reconciled for the good of the state and that, although he took a "popular" line in politics, he intended to act only in agreement with the Senate'.[2] It was customary for each of the consuls in turn to take precedence for a month at a time: in the past this had been indicated by the fact that only the presiding magistrate held the *fasces*. Caesar now emphasized the correctness of his attitude towards Bibulus by ostentatious recognition of this cycle. When Bibulus, who had been returned second in the elections, came to have the *fasces* in February, Caesar made his lictors walk behind instead of in front of him. Likewise his regulation that a record of the daily proceedings of the Senate and popular assemblies should be regularly compiled and published, which created a kind of official gazette, appeared as a manifestation of his loyalty.[3] On particular occasions this had already been done before. Thus in 63 Cicero had had the depositions of the envoys of the Allobroges and Cato's speech against the Catilinarians distributed throughout Italy.[4] Doubtless Caesar hoped by this means to strengthen his position in the fight against the oligarchs' subterfuges.

His next measures were concerned with the plans of Pompey, which had been frustrated in the previous year, the provision of land for the veterans and the ratification of the arrangements in the East.

---

[1] On *inimicitiae* see Cic. *Flacc.* 2; *Rab. Post.* 19; *prov. cons.* 20–25; 47; *Sest.* 72; *Vat.* 28: *sumptis inimicitiis.*

[2] Dio. 38, 1, 1–2; App. *b.c.* 2, 34. That Caesar was in earnest can be seen from his attempt to win Cicero for his plans in December 60.

[3] Suet. *Caes.* 20, 1; Mommsen, *RStR*, 1³, 40, 1; L. R. Taylor and T. R. S. Broughton, *Mem. Amer. Acad. Rome* 19 (1949), 5.

[4] Cic. *Sull.* 41; Plut. *Cat. Min.* 23, 3.

Already in the year 60 he had been preparing public opinion for a new agrarian law.[1] The proposals of Rullus in 63 and Flavius in 60 had been defeated, although no man of sense could overlook that socially a state of emergency existed and was calling urgently for relief. Rome was overcrowded with impoverished idlers, while broad tracts of Italy lay uncultivated.[2] Caesar now removed a number of points that had given offence in the two earlier drafts: all land belonging to the state in Italy was to be made available for distribution with the exception of the important Campanian domain (*ager publicus* on lease).[3] The commission in charge of the distribution was only to acquire further land when it was voluntarily offered for sale, and then it should not be bought at an arbitrary price, but at the valuation set on it at the last census.[4] All existing tenure of property was recognized without inquiry into its legal basis, in order to avoid any disquiet among property-owners.[5] The cost of the purchases was to be defrayed from Pompey's booty and the provincial revenues newly made available by him.[6] The property granted to the colonists was to be inalienable for twenty years.[7] As the commission of ten proposed by Rullus had appeared so suspicious at the time, provision was now made for a commission of twenty with Caesar expressly excluded. In addition a committee of five, presumably intended as an inner board of management, is mentioned.[8]

Caesar read out the proposal in the Senate and declared himself ready to make any improvements suggested. To their great annoyance his opponents were unable to raise any material objections; they only saw the danger that threatened them from the powerful following Caesar would win by this measure. The senators who were called upon to speak attempted to put off the vote. Only when it came to Cato's turn did he demand that no change at all be made in existing conditions, and, as he had done before, he prolonged his speech until sunset in order to force an adjournment without a decision. Thereupon on the strength of his power of *coercitio* Caesar ordered one of his official servants to take the recalcitrant senator

---

[1] Cic. *Att.* 2, 3, 3. [2] Dio 38, 1, 3 f. [3] Ibid.
[4] Ibid. [5] Cic. *fam.* 13, 4, 2. [6] Dio. 38, 1, 5; Cic. *dom.* 23.
[7] App. *b.c.* 3, 5; 24.
[8] Dio 38, 1, 6–7; Cic. *Att.* 2, 6, 2; 7, 3 and 4; *prov. cons.* 41; *Att.* 9, 2a, 1. There is epigraphic evidence for M. Valerius Messalla (cos. 61) as a member of the board of five: *Vvir a(gris) d(andis) a(ssignandis) i(udicandis)* (*ILS* 46); Lange, *R.A.*, 3, 280; L. R. Taylor, 'Caesar's agrarian legislation and his municipal policy', in *Studies in Roman Economic History in Honor of A. C. Johnson*, 69; H. Schaeffer, *RE*, 8A, 2585.

off to prison. Cato offered no resistance, but a majority of the Senate followed him, among them Marcus Petreius, the conqueror of Catiline. Caesar raged at him and asked why he was leaving the meeting early, only to receive the reply, 'because he preferred Cato's company in prison to Caesar's in the Senate'. As soon as Caesar saw that he had been beating the air, he released Cato before he became a martyr, but told the Senate that he now saw himself forced to bring the bill before the Assembly without a senatorial decree, and adjourned the meeting.[1]

In the meetings of the popular assembly prior to the vote, the so-called *contiones*, Caesar employed the same tactics against the optimates. He publicly invited his colleague Bibulus to say if he had any criticisms to make of the bill. He again had nothing to offer, except that he was not going to allow any innovations to be made during his consulship. Then Caesar pleaded with Bibulus and called on the people to help him, since, as he said, all depended on Bibulus, until the latter was inept enough to shout haughtily, 'You are not going to get the law this year—not even if you all want it'.[2] Next Caesar led Pompey to the rostrum, and he had no difficulty in showing that the Senate majority was acting against its better judgment. For eleven years previously the Senate had promised land to his and Metellus Pius' veterans of the Sertorian War, but the decree could not be carried out at the time for lack of money.[3] Now, thanks to his successful campaigns, funds were available in abundance, and all who had served under his colours must now have their rights. When Caesar asked him whether he would lend his support against the opponents of the bill, Pompey replied, 'If anyone dares to draw his sword, I shall take up my shield as well'. Crassus spoke after him to the same effect.[4]

The result of the vote could not be in doubt, particularly as Pompey called his veterans to Rome.[5] In order to prevent meetings of the *comitia*, Bibulus and three optimate tribunes were now watching the heavens daily. To make doubly sure he also revived a manoeuvre which Sulla had used as consul in the year 88.[6] Without

---

[1] Dio 38, 2, 1–3, 3; Gell. *n. A.* 4, 10, 8 from C. Ateius Capito (died A.D. 22) *de officio senatorio*; Jörs, *RE*, 2, 1904, No. 8.

[2] Dio 38, 4, 1–3.

[3] Dio 38, 5, 1–2. The reference is to the *rogatio Plotia* of 70, see above p. 67, n. 2.

[4] Dio 38, 5, 3–5; Plut. *Caes.* 14, 2–6; *Pomp.* 47, 5–8.

[5] Plut. *Pomp.* 48, 1; Dio 38, 6, 2; Cic. *Vat.* 5: *num armatis hominibus templum tenuerit?*

[6] App. *b.c.* 1, 244; Mommsen, *RStR*, 1³, 82, n. 3; 2³, 136, n. 2. In 3³, 1058, n. 2, he dismisses the evidence of Appian in view of Plut. *Sull.* 8, 6. I do not find this convincing.

F

more ado he declared all remaining *dies comitiales* to be holidays, in accordance with the consular right of fixing the date for the celebration of movable feasts.[1] Caesar took no notice and prepared for the vote, even sending his followers to occupy the Forum during the night. The senatorial majority gathered at Bibulus' house and decided that he should exercise his veto against his colleague.[2] On the next day Bibulus successfully reached the temple of Castor, from the steps of which Caesar was addressing the people. However, when he mounted the steps himself and began to interrupt his colleague, he was showered with filth and then attacked by Vatinius and the armed men held in readiness. Eventually the consul and his companions, among them the loyal tribunes and Cato, were forced to flee, after being beaten up and wounded. His lictors had their *fasces* smashed.[3]

In this way Caesar's agrarian law was passed by the people. On the next day Bibulus reported the matter to the Senate in the hope that a state of war would be declared and dictatorial authority granted to him. However, no one had the courage to make the relevant proposal.[4] The law in its final form included the clause invented by the popular tribune Appuleius Saturninus in the year 100[5] by which all senators had within a stated period to swear an oath to abide by it. Once again men such as Metellus Celer and Cato tried at least to avoid this, until at the eleventh hour Cicero persuaded them to give way by pointing out that they would be committing political suicide.[6] Finally the committee of twenty was elected. Its leadership naturally went to Pompey and Crassus. Of the other members Marcus Atius Balbus, Caesar's brother-in-law and grandfather of Augustus, and Marcus Terentius Varro, the famous universal historian, deserve mention.[7]

The battle over the agrarian law may have been prolonged into March. But other laws of which we have knowledge also belong to the same period.[8]

---

[1] Dio 38, 6, 1; J. Bleicken, *Hermes* 85 (1957), 471, n. 2.

[2] App. *b.c.* 2, 37.

[3] Dio 38, 6, 1–3; Suet. *Caes.* 20, 1; Plut. *Pomp.* 48, 2–3; *Cat. Min.* 32, 3–4; *Luc.* 42, 6; App. *b.c.* 2, 38–41; Cic. *Att.* 2, 16, 2 (of Pompey): *agrariam legem sibi placuisse, potuerit intercedi necne nihil ad se pertinere*; *Vat.* 5: *num consuli vim attulerit, . . . num intercessorem vi deiecerit?*; cf. 15; 22.

[4] Plut. *Mar.* 29, 2; App. *b.c.* 1, 131; Flor. 2, 4, 2; cf. *Gnomon* 12 (1936), 104.

[5] Suet. *Caes.* 20, 1; Dio 38, 6, 4.

[6] Plut. *Cat. Min.* 32, 5–9; Dio 38, 7, 1–2; Cic. *Att.* 2, 5, 1.

[7] Dio 38, 1, 7; Suet. *Aug.* 4, 1; Cic. *Att.* 2, 12, 1; Varro *r.r.* 1, 2, 10; Plin. *n.h.* 7, 176; Broughton, *MRR*, 2, 191.

[8] For the dating of Cic. *Att.* 2, 4–7, of April and May 59, see *Hermes* 63 (1928), 114 ff.

First there was a matter which had occupied the Senate since the year 61, an application by the tax-farming companies, which had taken over the revenue of the province of Asia, for a reduction in the sum for which they had contracted. Although it was supported by Crassus as their patron, after a delay of several months, in the middle of 60, it received a negative answer, mainly as the result of Cato's efforts.[1] Caesar now brought this affair also before the people and had no difficulty in securing remission of a third of the debt, but afterwards gave the financiers a public warning not to bid so high in future.[2] Incidentally Caesar, just as much as Crassus, had a personal interest in tax-farming companies and probably gained a direct advantage from these proceedings. We hear that he paid off Vatinius, among others, with share certificates which stood particularly high at that time.[3] Of greater importance was the political advantage which came from having the equestrian order under obligation to him.

Furthermore, Pompey's settlement in the East was now ratified by law without arousing opposition.[4] When Lucullus—presumably in a *contio*—tried to speak against it, Caesar threatened him with judicial punishment for his own failure, whereupon he is alleged to have fallen at Caesar's feet and begged for mercy.[5] Pompey had made agreements mainly with the allied kings and free communities. Accordingly numerous treaties between these states and the Roman people were concluded as a consequence of the general law. Caesar left the final arrangements about these treaties to Vatinius, thus bypassing the Senate—a proceeding flagrantly contrary to tradition and one which, as his opponents affirmed, brought great loss to the treasury, since those areas remained free from tribute.[6]

[1] Cic. *Att.* 1, 17, 9; 18, 7; 2, 1, 8; Q. *fr.* 1, 1, 33; *Planc.* 34.

[2] Cic. *Att.* 2, 16, 2; *Planc.* 35 with *Schol. Bob.* on 31 and 35; Suet. *Caes.* 20, 3; Dio 38, 7, 4; App. *b.c.* 2, 47–48; 5, 19; Val. Max. 2, 10, 7: here, as in Suet. *Caes.* 20, 4, it is reported that on this occasion Caesar had Cato taken off to prison for obstruction; this is contrary to Dio 38, 3, 2, which I have followed.

[3] Cic. *Vat.* 29: *eripuerisne partis illo tempore carissimas partim a Caesare, partim a publicanis?* On the *partes* of the *adfines* (Liv. 43, 16, 2) of the companies undertaking public contracts, see L. Mitteis, *R. Privatr.*, 1, 413; Gaius, *instit.* 3, 150; Jörs-Kunkel, *R. Privatr.*, § 151, 3; Cic. *Rab. Post.* 4.

[4] Dio 38, 7, 5; Plut. *Pomp.* 48, 4; App. *b.c.* 2, 46; Vell. 2, 44, 2.

[5] Suet. *Caes.* 20, 4: *Lucio Lucullo liberius resistenti tantum calumniarum metum iniecit, ut ad genua ultro sibi acciderit.* Plut. *Luc.* 42, 6 reports this opposition in connection with the agrarian law. But Lucullus was in fact interested in the other law.

[6] Cic. *Vat.* 29: *fecerisne foedera tribunus plebis cum civitatibus, cum regibus, cum tetrarchis, erogarisne pecunias ex aerario tuis legibus?* *Att.* 2, 9, 1 (of Caesar and Vatinius): *qui regna, qui praedia tetrarchis, qui immanis pecunias paucis dederunt* and *fam.* 1, 9, 7: *de donatione regnorum.* Of the tetrarchs we may think of the Galatian Deiotarus: *b. Alex.* 68, 1: *contra quem Caesar* (in 47), *cum plurima sua commemorasset officia quae consul ei decretis publicis tribuisset* . . .

Connected with this was the decision reached on the Egyptian question in which Caesar had been interested since 65. At that time he urged the annexation of the kingdom on the basis of the alleged will of Ptolemy XI Alexander II. The then king Ptolemy XII Neos Dionysos, nicknamed Auletes ('the Oboist'), was still trying in 59 to obtain official recognition from Rome. When Pompey was fighting in Judaea in the year 63, he took over the maintenance of 8,000 knights and so publicly won himself a legal title.[1] But even more effective were the sums of money which flowed into the pockets of Roman politicians. For this purpose the king borrowed vast sums from Roman financiers such as Gaius Rabirius Postumus.[2] Since his efforts were rewarded in the year 59, we need not discredit the rumour that Caesar and Pompey received about 6,000 talents (36 million denarii).[3] As far as the credibility of the size of the king's payments is concerned, we have something to go by in that Aulus Gabinius was condemned in 54 for accepting 60 million denarii from him.[4] At all events Caesar brought the king's case before Senate and People and, in contrast with his previous attitude, made an alliance with him.[5] Of course political considerations were decisive in producing this change of front. In 65 and 63 the annexation of Egypt would have been a welcome task for Caesar. By now he must already have been nursing other plans for the proconsulship, which he wished to win for himself in defiance of the senatorial decree of the previous year.

During these troubled weeks of sharp political conflict, there occurred in March[6] the trial of Gaius Antonius, Cicero's colleague in the year 63. Here too there was a curious change of roles. Apparently because in 63 he had not fulfilled the hopes set on him by Caesar and Crassus, they now dropped him and backed his prosecution on a charge of misconduct in his province of Macedonia.[7]

---

[1] Plin. *n.h.* 33, 136.   [2] Cic. *Rab. Post.* 4.   [3] Suet. *Caes.* 54, 3.

[4] Cic. *Rab. Post.* 21; 30; *Schol. Bob.* on Cic. *Planc.* 86. The king himself denied that he had bribed Gabinius (Cic. *Rab. Post.* 34): *recitabatur identidem Pompei testimonium regem ad se scripsisse nullam pecuniam Gabinio nisi in rem militarem datam.* The point at issue was the restoration of the king in 55 by Gabinius, the proconsul of Syria; Cic. *Pis.* 48 : *se ipsum regi Alexandrino vendidit*; 49: *praebuit se mercennarium comitem regi Alexandrino*; Caes. *b.c.* 3, 103, 5; 110, 6; F. Vonder Mühll, *RE*, 7, 428.

[5] Caes. *b.c.* 3, 107, 2: *quod superiore consulatu* (59) *cum patre Ptolomaeo et lege et senatus consulto societas erat facta*; Cic. *Sest.* 57: *a senatu honorem istum consecutus*; *Rab. Post.* 6: *quicum foedus feriri in Capitolio viderat.*

[6] *Hermes* 63 (1928), 121.

[7] Cic. *Flacc.* 5, 95, according to which the trial was before the *repetundae* court. There is a fragment of the speech of the prosecutor M. Caelius Rufus in Quint. 4, 2, 123–124. See also Dio 38, 10, 1–3; *RE*, 7A, 907.

Cicero, on the other hand, took over his defence and, to his own misfortune, could not refrain from complaining about the sad state of the current political situation. The fatal words were spoken at midday; Caesar did not deign to reply to them, but three hours later Cicero's deadly enemy, Publius Clodius, was a plebeian.[1] Already in 60 Clodius had strained every nerve to secure this change of status in order to be able to stand for the tribunate, and during the consulship of his brother-in-law Metellus Celer (60) renounced his patrician status at a meeting of the plebs. But, as this ran counter to traditional practice, Celer refused to recognize its validity.[2] Such a change of *gens* by an adult citizen and head of a household required an examination of the circumstances by the college of pontiffs; when he had secured its agreement, he had to have himself adopted as another citizen's son before the *comitia curiata*, and the *curiae* had to give their approval.[3] At a hint from Caesar, the consul and *pontifex maximus*, all these restrictions disappeared. The formalities of *abrogatio* (the proceedings in the *comitia curiata*) were completed with unheard-of speed and nonchalance. Caesar deployed the thirty curial lictors,[4] Pompey appeared as augur and dealt with the auspices, and the plebeian Publius Fonteius, barely twenty years old, adopted Clodius, who was nearly twice his age, as his son, only to emancipate him immediately: for Clodius continued to bear his old name.[5]

Legally the procedure was invalid, because the intervals prescribed for a law—the agreement of the *curiae* represented a *lex curiata*—were not observed, because no regular pontifical decree was submitted, and finally because the auspices were not in order, since Bibulus was watching the heavens for omens at the time, as indeed he was every day.[6] The whole thing was meant as a warning to Cicero; it was not done out of love for Clodius, who was too self-willed to be of use as a catspaw. For the time being the men in

---

[1] Cic. *dom.* 41; Dio 38, 11, 2; Suet. *Caes.* 20, 4.

[2] Dio 37, 51, 1–2; Cic. *Att.* 1, 18, 4–5; *har. resp.* 45; *Cael.* 60. Clodius is described as Celer's cousin (*frater*) because Clodius' father, Ap. Claudius Pulcher, consul in 79, was married to Metella, the sister of Celer's father (Münzer, *RE*, 3, 1235, No. 135). Moreover, Celer had married his cousin Clodia (Münzer, *RE*, 4, 105, No. 66).

[3] Cic. *dom.* 34, 77; *Sest.* 16; Gell. *n.A.* 5, 19, 5–9; Mommsen, *RStR*, 3³, 38; 318.

[4] Cic. *leg. agr.* 2, 31.

[5] Cic. *dom.* 35–39; 77; 116; *har. resp.* 57; *Sest.* 15; *prov. cons.* 42; 45; *Att.* 2, 7, 2; 9, 1; 12, 1; 21, 4; 22, 2; 8, 3, 3; Dio 38, 12, 2; Suet. *Tib.* 2, 4.

[6] Cic. *dom.* 39: *negant fas esse agi cum populo, cum de caelo servatum sit*. On the *obnuntiatio*, see J. Bleicken, *Hermes* 85 (1957), 471.

power kept him on as tight a rein as possible. He was to go off as ambassador to Tigranes of Armenia, was not elected to the commission for the distribution of land, and Pompey made it clear to him from the start that, if he became tribune, he was not to use his position against Cicero.[1] As Cicero heard on April 19, this made Clodius fume with anger and threaten to cross over to the optimate camp as tribune.[2]

Gaius Antonius was found guilty and had to leave for exile in Cephallenia.[3] On the 'popular' side his fall was celebrated as vengeance for Catiline by the placing of wreaths on the latter's grave and by a banquet.[4]

The events and struggles leading up to the oath by which the senators bound themselves to observe the agrarian law form the first section of Caesar's consulship. The immediate objectives of the secret coalition had been achieved, and Pompey in particular could feel himself entirely satisfied. The opposition party had been overwhelmed. The clearest outward indication of this was that Bibulus withdrew to his house for the remaining eight months of his year of office,[5] after the Senate had not had the courage to grant him dictatorial authority by declaring a state of war.[6] Others followed suit. Cicero too retired to his estates, where he asked Atticus to keep him informed about the further course of events and hoped shortly for some consolation from a journey to Egypt.[7] What strikes a modern observer most in Caesar's conduct—this also appeared later in his military commentaries—is the masterly way in which he put his opponents morally in the wrong. His measures were concerned with urgent problems and were irreproachable in content. He showed himself ready to forget all previous quarrels and offered his hand to his enemies. Were they not wicked fools if they refused to take it? In fact, the opposition, as represented by Cato, was purely negative and only deserved to be ignored. All that can be said in favour of the optimates is that they could have no confidence in this consul. They knew too much about his past and felt too clearly that he was shaking at the foundations of their supremacy. A further point is that the Roman character was deeply conservative, and so their opposition found support in wide circles. However grotesque their

[1] Cic. *Att.* 2, 7, 2–3; 9, 1; 22, 2; *Sest.* 15.   [2] Cic. *Att.* 2, 12, 2.
[3] Strab. 10, 455; Cic. *Vat.* 28.   [4] Cic. *Flacc.* 95.
[5] Suet. *Caes.* 20, 1; Dio 38, 6, 5–6; Cic. *Vat.* 22; *fam.* 1, 9, 7; Vell. 2, 44, 5; Plut. *Caes.* 14, 9; *Pomp.* 48, 5; App. *b.c.* 2, 45.
[6] Suet. *Caes.* 20, 1; Dio 38, 6, 4.   [7] Cic. *Att.* 2, 4, 2; 5, 1; *Sest.* 63 (on M. Cato).

means of obstruction may seem to us, they kept touching upon what the Romans regarded as hallowed traditions, whose violation stirred uneasy feelings even among the enlightened.

Caesar, therefore, was by no means victorious. What had been achieved so far benefited the other two partners more than himself and consisted of a series of gross infringements of the constitution, for which he alone bore responsibility.[1] His popularity was waning. The continual protests of Bibulus against his ignominious expulsion from the Forum were not without effect, even though the joke[2] that men were now living under the consuls Julius and Caesar met with approval. For Bibulus was not idle. He accompanied his colleague's every step with biting edicts and pamphlets in which Caesar's past was ruthlessly exposed. On each occasion the public read and copied them with delight.[3] Gaius Scribonius Curio, the son of the consular and Cicero's young hopeful,[4] supported Bibulus vocally and won considerable approval thereby. The feeling of hostility towards the three despots also spread to the municipalities.[5] When Vatinius tried to take Bibulus from his house to prison, the other tribunes interposed their veto, and he abandoned the attempt.[6] Without doubt, all Caesar's acts to date were formally invalid as his opponents maintained; without doubt, he would be called to account for them at the end of his year of office, and this would mean his destruction unless he could defy these attacks from another position of superior power. For this reason, the most important question facing him was whether the triumvirate would continue to hold good when it came to carrying out his personal plans. It was well known that Pompey was uncomfortable about Caesar's acts of violence, since he was still susceptible to certain misgivings raised from the standpoint of the senatorial government.[7]

[1] Cic. *Att.* 2, 16, 2: Pompey said *se leges probare, actiones ipsum praestare debere*. In his invective against Vatinius of March 56, Cicero naturally sought to distinguish between the tribune and Caesar; *Vat.* 13; 15: *et quoniam hic locus est unus*—the disregarding of *obnuntiatio* — *quem tibi cum Caesare communem esse dicas, seiungam te ab illo, non solum rei publicae causa, verum etiam Caesaris, ne qua ex tua summa indignitate labes illius dignitati adspersa videatur*; 16: *seiunge te a consule*; 22; 29; 38; 30: the three partners are *summi viri*; 33: *clarissimi viri*. But a year later he was criticized by Piso (*Pis.* 75): *dixisti me cum iis confligere quos despicerem, non attingere eos qui plus possent, quibus iratus esse deberem*. On this, see *Pis.* 79.

[2] Dio 38, 8, 2; Suet. *Caes.* 20, 2 with the couplet
  Non Bibulo quiddam nuper sed Caesare factum est:
  Nam Bibulo fieri consule nil memini.

[3] Suet. *Caes.* 9, 2; 49, 2; Cic. *Att.* 2, 19, 2; 5, 20, 4; 6.

[4] Cic. *Att.* 2, 18, 1; 19, 3.   [5] Cic. *Att.* 2, 13, 2; 21, 1.

[6] Cic. *Vat.* 21–22: not quite clear, since Cicero is recalling incidents otherwise unknown.

[7] Cic. *Att.* 2, 14, 1; 16, 2; 7, 1.

At this time, therefore, Caesar's future depended on the firmness of Pompey, and in April he abruptly made up his mind to bind him by the strongest possible tie by giving him his only daughter in marriage. She was engaged to Quintus Servilius Caepio, an enthusiastic follower of Caesar, and within a few days of her marriage. Her bridegroom was now to console himself with Pompeia, the fiancée of Faustus Sulla.[1] This exchange is sufficient testimony for the political nature of the union. To underline its significance, from now on Caesar called on Pompey instead of Crassus to give his opinion first in the Senate.[2] Despite a difference in age of thirty years the marriage proved a success, and Caesar's hopes were completely fulfilled. Now the consuls for 58 could be chosen. Since Caesar was sure of Pompey, there was now nothing to stop him from rewarding Aulus Gabinius, who had deserved exceedingly well of his son-in-law, with one of the posts. As his colleague he selected Lucius Calpurnius Piso Caesoninus, whose daughter, Calpurnia, he married himself.[3]

The next blow which he now dealt was a fresh agrarian law. In the previous one he had respected his opponents' sensitivity where the Campanian domains were concerned, and provided chiefly for Pompey's veterans. But when it came to be carried out, the purchase of land took up much time, while Caesar was concerned that it should be effective immediately on a large scale. Thus already in April a tentative suggestion was made that the Campanian land should also be included, and now Caesar placed the proposal, which was recommended by Pompey, before the people.[4] Only Cato spoke against it in open session, whereupon Caesar again gave orders for his removal. This caused a great uproar as Cato continued to speak as he was walking away, and this new violation of civic freedom made a very painful impression. Since Cato himself made

[1] Suet. *Caes.* 21; Plut. *Caes.* 14, 7; *Pomp.* 47, 10; App. *b.c.* 2, 50; Dio 38, 9, 1; Cic. *Att.* 2, 17, 1 (the beginning of May 59): *ista repentina adfinitatis coniunctio.* Caepio is known to us as a *legatus* of Pompey in the war against the pirates as well as later (Flor. 1, 41, 10; Plut. *Pomp.* 34, 8; Dio 37, 3, 3). This explains his activities on behalf of the Triumvirs. Since Pompeia actually married Faustus Sulla (Suet. *Caes.* 27, 1; *b.Afr.* 95, 3), he appears to have died young. It was probably according to a provision of his will that Caesar's future murderer, M. Brutus, adopted his name, calling himself Q. Caepio Brutus. The name first appears as early as 59 in Cic. *Att.* 2, 24, 2; then in the inscription *IG*, 7, 338=Dessau, *ILS*, 9460, with note 2. See *Neue Jahrb.* 45 (1920), 440; Münzer, *RE*, 2A, 1779.

[2] Suet. *Caes.* 21.

[3] Dio 38, 9, 1; Suet. *Caes.* 21; Plut. *Caes.* 14, 8; *Cat. Min.* 33, 7; *Pomp.* 47, 10; App. *b.c.* 2, 51.

[4] Cic. *Att.* 2, 15, 1; 16, 1–2; 17, 1; 18, 2; Vell. 2, 44, 4

absolutely no move to meet Caesar half-way which would have allowed him to be released, Caesar instructed a tribune to use his veto.[1] After this incident the law was passed in May 59: it provided that, outside the framework of the allotment originally intended, the 200 square miles which had remained the property of the Roman state on the destruction of the Capuan community in 211, should be distributed, in the first instance, to 20,000 Roman citizens with three or more children, among whom there were of course many veterans and leaseholders previously resident in Campania: Capua itself was restored to independence as a colony of Roman citizens.[2] Pompey personally conducted the refoundation and Marcus Terentius Varro took part: in the year 58 Lucius Piso became one of its first *duoviri* [magistrates holding a similar position in municipal towns and colonies to that of the consuls in Rome].[3]

This settlement policy brought Caesar a direct profit, because according to Roman concepts the colonists were bound to follow his political leadership. This is why on one occasion Cicero describes them as 'Caesar's army', with which the partners intended to hold the opposition in check.[4] In his *Civil War* Caesar regards it as an impertinence that Pompey recruited troops in Capua[5] to oppose him: the obvious reply to this is that Pompey was just as much a patron of the colony, since the law expressly laid down that, in the first instance, the members of the commission of twenty should be elected patrons.[6] It was just this connection between the foundation of colonies and political followings that up till now had kept the oligarchy from entering on this path, although sensible members recognized its necessity.

Caesar's two agrarian laws show him as a politician with an outstanding talent for dealing with social problems. Admittedly, the idea of renewing the Italian race by fresh colonization comes from the

---

[1] Plut. *Cat. Min.* 33, 1–4; *Caes.* 14, 11–12, with a different arrangement.

[2] Cic. *Att.* 2, 16, 1, according to which the territory of Capua was sufficient for only 5,000 settlers; Suet. *Caes.* 20, 3; Vell. 2, 44, 2; Dio 38, 7, 3; Cic. *Pis.* 25 (in 55, of Capua): *splendidissimorum hominum, fortissimorum virorum, optimorum civium mihique amicissimorum multitudine redundat*; cf. *Phil.* 2, 101 (briefly: *milites*).

[3] Cic. *Att.* 2, 19, 3; Plin. *n.h.* 7, 176; Cic. *Sest.* 19; *Pis.* 24.

[4] Cic. *Att.* 2, 162, 2 (Pompey): *oppressos vos tenebo exercitu Caesaris*; cf. *Hermes* 63, 115–117.

[5] Caes. *b.c.* 1, 14, 4: *Capuae primum sese confirmant et colligunt dilectumque colonorum, qui lege Iulia Capuam deducti erant, instituunt.*

[6] In the foundation charter of the Colonia Genetiva Iulia, founded in the town of Urso in southern Spain in 44 (Dessau, *ILS*, 6087, c. 97): *neve d(ecurionum) d(ecretum) facito (sc. duovir) fiat, quo quis colon(is) colon(iae) patron(us) sit atopteturve praeter eum cui c(olonis) a(grorum) d(andorum) a(tsignandorum) i(us) ex lege Iulia est, eumque, qui eam colon(iam) deduxerit liberos posterosque eorum.*

Scipionic circle, but so far all attempts to attain this end had been combined with a serious disruption of existing property conditions. Already in 63 Caesar had sought to avoid this snag by laying down that the necessary land where it was not the direct property of the state, should be bought only with the owners' consent. In 59 he took the same line. The further regulation that the properties of the colonists were to be inalienable for twenty years[1] was to ensure that they really settled down. Tiberius Gracchus had declared the land allotments distributed by him to be inalienable, Sulla had repeated this clause for his veteran colonies and a similar provision was made in the bill of 63. The limitation of the period within which the properties might not be sold to twenty years gave the occupiers a tenure as near to full ownership as was possible, and this will have made the restriction more palatable. For experience showed that it was regarded as very irksome, and so was first evaded and eventually set aside. The protection extended to large families as a means of keeping up the population deserves our special attention: it was surely more fruitful than fine words condemning the childless.

We have no reference to the total number provided for during Caesar's consulship. However, in addition to the accommodation of the 20,000 in the territory of Capua, the settlement of veterans, provided for by the first law, was being carried out and continued unceasingly. For in the years 57 and 56 attempts were again made to bring the distribution of the Campanian domains to a halt, and in 51 there was more talk of this.[2] On the other hand a popular decree of the year 55, when the unity of the three allies had been restored, testifies to the vigorous progress of the settlement policy. The three surviving chapters[3] contain regulations about the exact demarcation of the boundaries between the new communities founded in the course of the colonization drive. The number of veterans alone

---

[1] App. b.c. 3, 5; Ernst Muttelsee, *Untersuchungen über die Lex Iulia Municipalis* (Diss. Freiburg i. B., 1913), 54, n. 3.

[2] Cic. Q. fr. 2, 1, 1; 5, 1; 6, 2; fam. 1, 9, 8; 8, 10, 4.

[3] The three chapters of the *Lex Mamilia Roscia Peducaea Alliena Fabia* are to be found in the works of the Roman land-surveyors (*Gromatici veteres*, ed. Lachmann (1848), 1, 263–266), reproduced by Riccobono, *Fontes iuris Romani anteiustiniani*, 1², No. 12. For the date, see Hans Rudolph, *Stadt und Staat im römischen Italien* (1935), 196. The right explanation was advanced by L. R. Taylor (*Studies in Roman Economic History in Honor of A. C. Johnson*, 76 ff.); cf. H. Schaefer, *RE*, 8A, 2585. That this law supplements the *Lex Iulia agraria* of 59 is proved by the fact that chapter 4 was also embodied in the regulation for the Colonia Genetiva Iulia, chapter 104.

ran to about 40,000. We can form some idea of the size of this socio-political achievement from the fact that in the year 46 Caesar still recognized the right of 150,000 adult citizens resident in Rome to the free public distributions of corn, and thereby reduced the list of recipients by 170,000 names.[1] This reduction was achieved principally by colonization on a large scale. A regulation put into effect in the year 44 expressly excluded from the corn distributions participants in the land distribution and those enriched by the sale of land in connection with it, in the event of their moving to take up residence in Rome.[2] This far-sighted policy was introduced in the year 59.

We have seen that Caesar's agrarian law to a large extent realized the intentions of Rullus' proposal in 63. But the readoption of certain sections was carefully avoided, namely everything concerned with the granting of the unusual five-yearly praetorian power to the commission of ten provided for in the bill. Caesar had invented this power at the time in order to counterbalance Pompey's position, but this transparent plan had failed. Since then the political situation had completely changed, and in 59 he dropped the connection of the agrarian law with the five-yearly extraordinary power, which was the main object of the bill in 63. He was now pursuing his end under more favourable circumstances and by different means than before. Cicero revealed his fine sense of intuitive political judgment, when he wrote at the beginning of May 59,[3] 'What is the signifi-cance of this sudden family connection, the Campanian land and the outpouring of money? If this were their last move it would still be bad enough, but in the nature of the case it cannot be the last. For by itself it can surely give them (Pompey and Caesar) no satisfaction! They would never have gone as far as this, if they did not wish to make the way clear for other abominable deeds.' But at this time Caesar so cleverly kept himself in the background that it was in Pompey that Cicero saw the future autocrat.[4] In fact, during these weeks secret preparations were being made for the political action which was to bring Caesar the extraordinary command that he desired, with its enormous prospects.

[1] Suet. *Caes.* 41, 3; Dio 43, 21, 4.

[2] *Tabula Heracleensis* (Riccobono, *FIRA* 1², No. 13), lines 1–19. The decrees collected on this tablet were put into effect by Antony after Caesar's death, on the strength of the *lex de actis Caesaris confirmandis* (Cic. *Phil.* 5, 10; cf. Kornemann, *RE*, 16, 611). This explanation was first advanced by Ernst Muttelsee, a pupil of E. Fabricius, op. cit. (p. 82, n. 1, above), 52 ff.

[3] Cic. *Att.* 2, 17, 1.   [4] Cic. *Att.* 2, 17, 1.

From the alternately frivolous and vulgar farce that was being made of the venerable organs and institutions of the old constitution, all men of insight could see that the Roman state had come to a crisis. Big political decisions could no longer be taken either in the Senate or in the popular assembly: the political future rested with the comprehensive long-term military commands, such as it had been necessary to grant on several occasions since Sulla. This fact, Caesar, to judge by his policies to date, had long recognized. But to attain such a position was more difficult for Caesar than for anyone else since he was mistrusted by all from the outset.

His opponents had already sought to make his consulship as harmless as possible in the year 60: in accordance with the relevant Sempronian law they had assigned to the future consuls of 59 two offensively insignificant administrative tasks for their proconsulship in 58. Under no circumstances could Caesar stand for this, particularly as all possibility of an understanding with his enemies had disappeared during his consulship. They argued that all his acts to date were illegal, since they had been carried out in an unconstitutional manner.[1] The only question was whether they would be strong enough at the end of Caesar's consulship to put their ideas into practice. If possible they surely intended to bring him before a criminal court and at least to destroy him as a politician and citizen. Caesar could only avoid this fate if he secured a position of special power: here the blind and immoderate hatred of his opponents turned out to his advantage, because it at least kept him his allies. For they (and Pompey in particular) had every interest in preventing Caesar's consulship from being declared invalid,[2] since this would hit them just as hard as Caesar, even though the expansion of his power did not in itself serve their interests.

At this time conditions in Gaul offered Caesar his best opportunity. In connection with Catiline's rebellion the Allobroges (in Dauphiné) had in 62 risen against Rome and were pacified by the propraetor Gaius Pomptinus in 61 and 60.[3] But the neighbouring Gallic states were also stirred by serious unrest, and various parties had already appealed to Rome, among them her old allies the Aedui. Diviciacus, one of their princes, had come to Rome in person in 61 in order to

---

[1] Cic. prov. cons. 45: Iulias leges et ceteras illo consule rogatas iure latas negant; 46: cum ab illis aliquotiens condicio C. Caesari lata sit, ut easdem res alio modo ferret, qua condicione auspicia requirebant, leges conprobabant.

[2] Cic. Att. 2, 16, 2.

[3] Dio 37; 47, 1–48, 2; Cic. prov. cons. 32; Caes. b.G. 1, 31, 3–11.

beg for help against the Sequani. Thereupon the Senate commended the Aedui and other friends of Rome to the protection of whoever might be governor of Gallia Narbonensis, but without giving him authority to conduct warlike operations.[1]

The Sequani and Arverni had enlisted the Suebian prince Ariovistus in their service. He crossed the Rhine, and helped the Sequani, but made them cede a third of their land (lower Alsace) to him in payment and prepared to set up a German kingdom on Gallic soil.[2] This upheaval in the territories on the left bank of the Rhine now again aroused the Helvetii, who only a few decades previously had migrated to Switzerland[3] from their original home between the Main and the Rhine. They wished to look for new homes in Central Gaul: preparations began in the year 61 and at the beginning of 60 the first Helvetii appeared in the Roman province.[4]

In Rome, where memories of the Cimbri and Teutones stirred, these events were not taken lightly. In March the Senate decreed that the consuls Quintus Caecilius Metellus Celer and Lucius Afranius should immediately draw lots for the two Gallic provinces and that troops should be recruited without regard for claims to exemption. Furthermore three senators were immediately appointed as ambassadors to the Celtic communities in order to warn them against an alliance with the Helvetii. However, in May the news sounded better—to the displeasure of Celer, whose hopes of a triumph were dashed.[5] He was also prevented by the tribune Lucius Flavius from leaving for Narbonensis.[6] Although he received the province for his proconsulship in the following year he never reached it, being carried away by sudden death in April.[7]

Celer's death cleared the way for Caesar. Afranius and Celer had taken possession of the allotted commands during their consulship. Accordingly, Caesar regarded it as his immediate task to show that the dangerous state of affairs in Gaul had not yet improved. A report from the propraetor Pomptinus, who continued to administer Narbonensis, had just arrived announcing his defeat of the

[1] Caes. b.G. 1, 31, 9; 35, 4; 6, 12, 5; Cic. div. 1, 90.

[2] Caes. b.G. 1, 31, 3–11.

[3] Tac. Germ. 28.2; Ptolem. geogr. 2, 11, 6: ἡ τῶν Ἐλουητίων ἔρημος—according to E. Fabricius, Die Besitznahme Badens durch die Römer (1905), 13, on the north side of the Swabian Jura. See Ed. Norden, Alt-Germanien (1934), 170.

[4] Cic. Att. 1, 19, 2. [5] Cic. Att. 1, 20, 5; 2, 1, 11. [6] Dio 37, 50, 4.

[7] Cic. Att. 2, 5, 2; Cael. 59; Vat. 19; Att. 2, 9, 2.

Allobroges, whereupon the Senate decreed a thanksgiving despite Caesar's opposition.[1] No doubt Caesar questioned the factual justification for the celebration, just as Pomptinus' triumph was later denied him for several years. To secure the greatest publicity, Publius Vatinius with other supporters of Caesar attended a funeral banquet on the public holiday in working clothes. This was provided with great pageantry in the temple of Castor by Quintus Arrius in honour of his father. Since thousands participated, the event attracted all the attention desired.[2]

When the ground had been prepared in this way and the new family ties had strengthened Caesar's rear, in May Vatinius brought the following proposal before the plebs: Caesar was immediately to receive Cisalpine Gaul together with Illyricum, as well as three legions and the necessary means for their maintenance. No other arrangements for this province were to be allowed before March 1, 54.[3] The Senate was entirely excluded from this transaction: the bill left even the appointment of *legati* (of whom at least one had magisterial authority) entirely in Caesar's hands. It was supported by Pompey and Lucius Piso, and carried.

This *lex Vatinia* was a success of incalculable importance. As we have remarked, Caesar had already fixed his eyes on Transalpine Gaul and was later to make it the centre of his activity. I have no doubt that even at this stage he was already reckoning with this possibility. But if in addition to Cisalpine Gaul he also had Illyricum, the Roman coastal strip on the east of the Adriatic from Istria to Lissus (Leshja in Albania) assigned to him, he clearly wished to secure for himself another theatre of operations in the North Balkans, should

---

[1] Cic. *Vat.* 30 with *Schol. Bob.*; *Pis.* 58; cf. H. Gundel, *RE*, 21, 2422.

[2] Cic. *Vat.* 31; *Att.* 2, 7, 3 (April 59).

[3] Suet. *Caes.* 21; Cic. *Vat.* 35–36; *Sest.* 135; *prov. cons.* 36–37; Dio 38, 8, 5; *Hermes* 63, 124. According to the *Lex Sempronia de provinciis consularibus* of C. Gracchus (Cic. *prov. cons.* 3; 17), the Senate had to determine the future consular provinces before the consuls were elected. The elections normally took place in July. If March 1, 54 was mentioned in the Lex Vatinia, this meant that Cisalpine Gaul with Illyricum could not be declared a consular province until the provinces for the consuls to be elected for 53 came under discussion. Another possibility was to make the province praetorian; it could then be assigned to a praetor of 55 immediately after March 1. But as Cicero (*prov. cons.* 17; 36; 39) remarks, the veto could be used against such a decree, whereas according to the Lex Sempronia its use was impermissible against the decree on the consular provinces. For the same reason no veto was used against the senatorial decree of September 29, 51, providing for discussion of the consular provinces on and after March 1, 50 (Cic. *fam.* 8, 8, 5). On March 15, 61, Cicero (*Att.* 1, 15, 1) writes that his brother Quintus, who was praetor in 62, has obtained the province of Asia. On the *Lex Vatinia*, see P. J. Cuff, *Historia* 7 (1958), 454 ff.

occasion arise. The Dacian Burebista was then beginning to found an empire in this area, and its expansion would sooner or later have to lead to a clash with Rome.[1] But whether he found his opportunity to rival Pompey as *imperator* in the north or the east, he could not have wished for a better mainstay for large military operations than Cisalpine Gaul with its large and Romanized population. But it also had a special immediate value for the continuation of the policies of the triumvirate.

For he now, while still consul, possessed a strong military power in Italy: for the next four years he was unassailable and, for his part, ready to intervene if politics at Rome took a turn which he found disagreeable.[2] Furthermore, at the next opportunity Pompey proposed in the Senate that Caesar should also be granted Transalpine Gaul with one legion.[3] Cato opposed the proposal with his usual fearlessness, inveighed against the bargaining with daughters and provinces and coined the expression that 'the Senate was itself placing the tyrant in its citadel'. But realizing that, if the motion were rejected, there was the threat of a further popular decree, the Senate gave way to Pompey and added the province, with one legion, to Caesar's administrative sphere, but with the difference that this governorship, being subject to the Sempronian law, dated from January 1, 58 and had to be renewed annually.[4]

Caesar's irreconcilable opponents of course declared the *lex Vatinia* invalid because it had been passed without regard for the omens announced by Bibulus, a view that proved difficult to maintain in face of the later senatorial decree.[5] Caesar now had no hesitation in threatening them in the Senate with his mailed fist: despite all their howling, he said, he had achieved what he wanted and

---

[1] Strab. 7, 298 and 303–304: Βυρεβίστας or Βοιρεβίστας; Dittenberger, *Syll.*[3] 762, 34 (48 B.C.): Βυραβείστας; Jordan. 11: Burbistas. On the date see Brandis, *RE* 4, 1959; E. Swoboda, *Carnuntum* (1958), 201. When Caesar took over the supreme command in 58, the three legions of Cisalpine Gaul were in winter quarters near Aquileia on the border of Illyricum (*b.G.* 1, 10, 3).

[2] Cic. *dom.* 131 (on the year 58): *absentis exercitus terrore*; *Sest.* 40: Clodius appealed to the three allies, *ex quibus unum habere exercitum in Italia maximum . . . dicebat*; 41: *Caesar . . . erat ad portas, erat cum imperio, erat in Italia eius exercitus*; *p. red. in sen.* 32 : *erat alius ad portas cum imperio in multos annos magnoque exercitu.*

[3] Suet. *Caes.* 22, 1 : *mox per senatum Comatam quoque veritis patribus ne, si ipsi negassent, populus et hanc daret*; Cic. *Att.* 8, 3, 3 (of Pompey): *ille Galliae ulterioris adiunctor.*

[4] Cic. *prov. cons.* 36; *fam.* 1, 7, 10; Dio 38, 8, 3; App. *b.c.* 2, 49; *Ill.* 34; Plut. *Caes.* 14, 10; *Pomp.* 48, 4; *Cat. Min.* 33, 5; Vell. 2, 44, 5; Oros. 6, 7, 1. The Senate could freely dispose of this province, as it was not affected by the *Lex Vatinia.*

[5] Cic. *prov. cons.* 26–28; 36.

would use his position to jump on their heads.[1] However, the enemy were far from suppressed. Their spokesman, the younger Curio, not Pompey or Caesar, was the most popular man in Rome.[2] The edicts of Bibulus still found a ready circulation—on one occasion Cicero relates that the crowd at the place where they were displayed brought the traffic to a halt.[3] While Caesar's friend and helper, the praetor Quintus Fufius Calenus, was booed,[4] at the games of Apollo at the beginning of July, allusions to Pompey's change for the worse met with boundless approval. Caesar was given a feeble welcome, while immediately afterwards thousands greeted Curio with tumultuous applause such as only Pompey had experienced previously.[5] The despots could not afford to ignore such incidents, because they based their constitutional position on popular decrees. These decisions were made by only a small fraction of the electorate, generally by residents in the city, and for this reason such disaffection on the part of the Roman public could have unpleasant consequences.

Pompey and Caesar therefore attached great importance to strengthening their ranks with respected and influential senators. Cicero, in particular, seemed worth winning over. When a member of the commission of twenty died, they wished to have him elected in his place.[6] Caesar repeatedly invited him to become his *legatus* in the following year. Although this would have given Cicero protection from Clodius, he regarded the bad impression that his defection would make on decent people as the greater evil.[7] By an

---

[1] Suet. *Caes.* 22, 2: *quo gaudio elatus non temperavit, quin paucos dies frequenti curia iactaret, invitis et gementibus adversariis adeptum se quae concupisset, proinde ex eo insultaturum omnium capitibus.* I regard this remark as historical. When one considers the volume of filthy abuse heaped on Caesar, it can even be regarded as moderate. In *Sest.* 42 Cicero recalls the circumstances which drove him into exile in 58: *intenta signa legionum existimari cervicibus ac bonis vestris falso, sed putari tamen.* Suetonius further records an obscene interruption, to which Caesar replied: *in Suria quoque regnasse Sameramin magnamque Asiae partem Amazonas tenuisse quondam.* Suspicion had already been thrown on his guest-friendship with King Nicomedes IV of Bithynia by Cn. Dolabella when he was on trial in 77 (Suet. *Caes.* 49, 1), and it had been brought up continually ever since (Suet. *Caes.* 49, 2–4). It is not impossible that Cicero made such an imputation in a (lost) letter, to judge by Cic. *Att.* 2, 24, 3, with its allusion to Caesar's affair with Servilia. It is worth mentioning that Bibulus also launched forth in his 'Archilochian edicts' (Cic. *Att.* 2, 20, 6; 21, 4; *Brut.* 267) with the words (Suet. *Caes.* 49, 2): *collegam suam Bithynicam reginam, eique antea regem fuisse cordi, nunc esse regnum.* In this context Caesar's answer is to be interpreted ironically. Where his soldiers were concerned, at his triumph in 46, he made a serious protest against the allegation (Dio 43, 20, 4).

[2] Cic. *Att.* 2, 18, 1.
[3] Cic. *Att.* 2, 21 4.
[4] Cic. *Att.* 2, 18, 1.
[5] Cic. *Att.* 2, 19, 3.
[6] Cic. *Att.* 2, 19, 4; *prov. cons.* 41 (more precisely): *quinqueviratus.*
[7] Cic. *Att.* 2, 18, 3; 19, 5; *prov. cons.* 41; *Pis.* 79.

edict Bibulus postponed the consular elections to October 18,[1] much
against the wishes of the three allies, who wished to bring the matter
to an early conclusion. For, with the contrast between the parties
becoming continually sharper, every delay improved the prospects
of Gabinius' and Piso's rivals. In a *contio* on July 25 Pompey
spoke against the edict and generally against the deeply wounding
attacks of Bibulus on himself. Cicero's judgment on the speech
was that the total failure to make an impression of a man once so
celebrated was lamentable and perhaps only pleasing to Crassus.[2]
Caesar fared no better, when he wished to lead the popular assembly
to Bibulus' house in order to persuade him to withdraw the edict.[3]
Cicero's only complaint about this state of affairs was that it was a
provocation to fresh acts of violence, and things had come to such a
pass that even Clodius was toying with the idea of joining battle
against the allies.[4] Meetings of the Senate were badly attended, and
the stout-hearted Quintus Considius told Caesar to his face that this
was caused by fear of his soldiers. Asked by Caesar why he was not
then himself afraid, he replied that he was now too old to worry
about death.[5]

This universal mood of deep bitterness eventually became a real
danger for Caesar since, as had already been the case some months
earlier, it was not without effect on Pompey. He began to break
down under the flood of hatred, ridicule and contempt that was
daily poured over his head. He loathed his present condition and
wished to escape from his humiliation.[6]

The most striking indication of the critical position in which
the allies found themselves at this time is that they had to accept
the postponement of the consular elections ordained by Bibulus.
The election of tribunes took place as usual in July, and Clodius
reached the goal at which he had long been aiming,[7] but, as we
have remarked, he was not reliable. This made it all the more important that Gabinius and Piso should secure the consulships for which
they were intended. At this point Bibulus interrupted their plans
with his edict. This defeat may be explained by the fact that in

[1] Cic. *Att.* 2, 20, 6.   [2] Cic. *Att.* 2, 21, 3.
[3] Cic. *Att.* 2, 21, 5.   [4] Cic. *Att.* 2, 21, 1.
[5] Cic. *Att.* 2, 24, 4; *Brut.* 219; Plut. *Caes.* 14, 13–15.
[6] Cic. *Att.* 2, 21, 4.
[7] Cic. *Att.* 2, 22, 1 (end of July, according to L. R. Taylor, *Historia* 1, 48, 10).

G

July a manœuvre of the allies directed against the optimates failed miserably.[1]

On about July 17[2] Cicero wrote to tell his friend Atticus, who was staying in Epirus at the time, that the notorious Lucius Vettius, whom Caesar had imprisoned during his praetorship in 62, was making approaches to young Curio and seeking to persuade him to take part in an attempt on Pompey's life. Curio, however, was not to be caught, but told his father, the consular, who passed the information on to Pompey. The matter now came before the Senate, and Vettius was summoned to appear. After initial denials, when guaranteed his life, he soon volunteered further disclosures. He named a number of distinguished men, both young and old, who he alleged were members of the conspiracy. Its author was Bibulus, whose secretary handed him a dagger. Here he made a big mistake, since Bibulus had already warned Pompey of an attack on May 13 and been thanked by him for this service. The Senate therefore decreed that Vettius should be taken into custody for carrying arms without authority. On the following day, however, Caesar made him repeat his allegations before the assembled people, of course with considerable variations. Thus Lucius Lucullus and Lucius Domitius Ahenobarbus were accused for the first time; he did not mention Cicero, but, questioned by Vatinius, produced the name of Gaius Piso, who was engaged to Cicero's daughter Tullia. But the biggest blow to his credibility was that he now omitted Quintus Caepio Brutus—the name of Caesar's famous murderer since his adoption by a relative of his mother Servilia—to whom he had assigned a leading role on the previous day. For the relationship between the consul and the young man's mother was a matter of common knowledge throughout the city: allegedly he had just made her a present of a pearl worth $1\frac{1}{2}$ million denarii. As Cicero wittily remarked, a night had passed between the two meetings.[3]

In writing to Atticus at this time, Cicero was convinced that Vettius was an agent in Caesar's service. Three years later, in

---

[1] I now subscribe to the interpretation of L. R. Taylor in her very acute essay 'The Date and Meaning of the Vettius Affair', *Historia* 1 (1950), 45–51. In my opinion she has shown convincingly that the letters *Att.* 2, 23 and 24 are to be dated earlier than their position in the collection would suggest. The new dates are tabulated in op. cit., 48, n. 14, and again defended in *CQ* n.s. 4 (1954), 181.

[2] Cic. *Att.* 2, 24, 2 ff.; L. R. Taylor, op. cit., 47.

[3] Cic. *Att.* 2, 24, 3: *ut appareret noctem et nocturnam deprecationem intercessisse.* This, of course, is only a suspicion. Suet. *Caes.* 50, 2: *ante alias dilexit Marci Bruti matrem Serviliam, cui et proximo suo consulatu sexagiens sestertium margaritam mercatus est.*

published speeches, he assigned full responsibility to Vatinius.[1] The truth will have been that Caesar used Vatinius for this as for other dirty business. His main target was young Curio,[2] who had shown himself so successful and dangerous as spokesman for the opposition: next in importance were Lucius Cornelius Lentulus Niger, then a candidate for the consulship,[3] and Domitius Aheno-barbus, who was standing for the praetorship. Cicero's last piece of news for Atticus was that Vettius was to appear before the court dealing with crimes of violence and intended to save himself from condemnation by further disclosures.[4] Those whom he accused were then to be put on trial. In his invective against Vatinius, Cicero maintains that Vatinius had prepared a popular decree establishing a special court to pass judgment on those denounced by Vettius and paying him a large reward. But this plan met with such opposition that Vatinius preferred to have done with the informer and had him strangled in prison.[5] It is a fact that Vettius was found dead, and since the fellow's death was convenient for Caesar, people were ready to believe that he had instigated it.[6]

There can be no doubt that young Curio had brilliantly parried the blow meant for him. Under these circumstances the wisest thing that Caesar could do was to reconcile himself to the edict of Bibulus

---

[1] Cic. Sest. 132; Vat. 24–26.

[2] In Vat. 24 Cicero says of Curio, father and son: C. Curionem, perpetuum hostem impro-borum omnium, auctorem publici consilii in libertate communi tuenda maxime liberum, cum filio prin-cipe iuventutis, cum re publica coniunctiore etiam quam ab illa aetate postulandum fuit, delere voluisti. About 55 the consular Curio composed a sharp invective against Caesar, set as a dialogue between the author, his son, and C. Vibius Pansa, after a meeting of the Senate held by Caesar as consul in 59. In this pamphlet he committed the faux pas ridiculed by Cicero (Brut. 218–219), launching out against Caesar's administration in Gaul in 58–55. We know some of the details through Suetonius (Caes. 9, 2; 49, 1; 50, 1; 52, 3; Münzer, RE, 2A, 867). I do not think that John H. Collins (Propaganda, Ethics and Psychological Assumptions in Caesar's Writings (Diss. Frankfurt a. Main (1952)), 23) is right in not attributing to this work the speeches of Curio quoted by Suetonius.

[3] Cic. Att. 2, 24, 2 on the first statement of Vettius: exposuit manum fuisse iuventutis duce Curione, in qua Paullus initio fuisset et Q. Caepio hic Brutus et Lentulus, flaminis filius, conscio patre, clarified by Vat. 25: L. Lentulum . . . flaminem Martialem, quod erat eo tempore Gabini tui competitor, eiusdem Vetti indicio opprimere voluisti : qui si tum illam labem pestemque (sc. Gabinium) vicisset, quod ei tuo scelere non licuit, res publica (in 58) victa non esset. This is the passage with which L. R. Taylor, op. cit., 48, justifies her thesis that the whole Vettius scandal was connected with the elections.

[4] Cic. Att. 2, 24, 4; Mommsen, Röm. Strafr. 504, n. 2.

[5] Cic. Vat. 26.

[6] Suet. Caes. 20, 5: Caesar is said to have got rid of him by means of poison; Plut. Luc. 42, 8 (allegedly suicide, but traces of strangulation); Cass. Dio 38, 9, 4 and App. b.c. 2, 44 give the variant that Caesar accused the Optimates. See also Cordula Brutscher, Analysen zu Suetons Divus Julius und der Parallelüberlieferung (Noctes Romanae 8, 1958), 62–66.

and to concentrate on ensuring that the result of the consular elections on October 18 was favourable to himself. On this point he was in agreement with Pompey.

In August[1] Cicero spoke in an extortion trial on behalf of Lucius Flaccus, who had rendered him good service in 63 in the fight against Catiline: in concluding, he impressed on the jury that the popular line taken by the present dynasts was endangering the order so happily established in 63 by the union of the two upper orders. The Vettius scandal (he said) showed the threats menacing the defenders of this order; they could consider themselves lucky if they were left alive.[2]

It is understandable that Cicero only viewed the events of this year in the light of his own consular policy which was now being called in question. On the other hand we have also noticed the violent threats which Caesar could on occasion be provoked to utter when riled by insults and abuse. Sallust, who took pains to form a correct judgment, summarizes his impression of Caesar as follows: 'He passionately desired a great command, an army and an unprecedented war, which would give his ability the chance to shine forth.'[3] We may also quote a piece of evidence from Caesar himself: 'For him *dignitas* had always come first: he valued it more highly than his life.' *Dignitas* is the position of honour accorded to a senator in political life. Shortly before this passage he states what value he set on himself: Pompey had (since the year 50) become estranged from him 'because he (Pompey) wished no one to equal him in *dignitas*'. *Dignitas* was based on achievements, and in his particular case it was the Gallic War that had raised him so high.[4] But his claim was more deeply rooted in his certainty that he was the intellectual

---

[1] For the date, see L. R. Taylor, *Historia* 1, 48, following Cic. *Att.* 2, 25, 1.

[2] Cic. *Flacc.* 94–105.

[3] Sall. *Cat.* 54, 4: *sibi magnum imperium, exercitum, bellum novum exoptabat, ubi virtus enitescere posset.* Cf. *Pis.* 59 (in the year 55): *fertur ille gloria, flagrat, ardet cupiditate iusti et magni triumphi.* 'Ability' is not a satisfactory translation of *virtus*. The context reveals Sallust's meaning. First (53, 4), the great achievements of Rome's past had been accomplished by the outstanding *virtus* of a few citizens; then (53, 6), in his own time there were two men 'of surpassing *virtus*', Marcus Cato and Gaius Caesar. If he attributes *virtus* to these two totally different contemporaries, he must have meant more in Caesar's case than an insatiable ambition. W. Steidle, *Sallusts historische Monographien* (*Historia, Einzelschriften* 3 (1958)), 27, says: 'Of course we must not interpret these words to mean that this trait of Caesar's is being assessed entirely in negative terms, or that Sallust was actually seeking to stigmatize his egoism.'

[4] *b.c.* 1, 9, 2: *sibi semper primam fuisse dignitatem vitaque potiorem*; 1, 4, 4 : *ipse Pompeius, ab inimicis Caesaris incitatus et quod neminem dignitate secum exaequari volebat, totum se ab eius amicitia averterat et cum communibus inimicis in gratiam redierat.* Cf., on Caesar's *dignitas*, Cic. *Vat.* 13; 15; 39 (56 B.C.).

superior of his political opponents. We can sympathize with their horror, when they experienced the lack of scruple with which he trampled over the constitutional obstruction practised by them. But we saw that at first Caesar was perfectly ready to win the Senate's approval for his first colonization law. The optimates rejected this only because it came from Caesar. It was a political necessity that the veterans of Pompey should obtain the provision that had been promised them. Further, the law had been carefully thought out, and similarly the supplementary law, which brought in the *ager Campanus*, did great credit to Caesar's statesmanlike foresight.

If in August[1] he now produced further legislation of lasting importance, we cannot fail to recognize that his intention was to quell unintelligent obstruction by measures unexceptionable in content.

Just as his agrarian law showed a way out of Italy's social crisis, so he now attacked another cancerous growth in the oligarchic administration of empire, the gradual destruction of the provinces through the depredations of Roman governors. On one point all Romans were more or less agreed: the provinces existed to be exploited for the benefit of the Roman people. But under the prevailing system the goose that laid the golden eggs would not last for ever. The members of the oligarchy regarded it as their prerogative to cover the enormously increased financial demands of political life with their takings as provincial governors. Strict control could prevent this activity from becoming intolerable, but mutual connivance happens to be the traditional weakness of oligarchy. Popular policies, which had emerged with the Gracchi, only worsened the situation with the one-sided favouritism shown to the knights— the public tax-farming companies and Roman financiers sucked the blood from the provinces no less than the senators—and with the senseless increase in electoral expenditure, not to mention the fact

---

[1] I conclude from Cic. *Flacc.* 13 (*lege hac recenti ac nova certus est inquisitioni comitum numerus constitutus*) that the law had been promulgated by the time of this speech. The *Schol. Bob.* suggest that the reference is to the *lex Vatinia de alternis consiliis reiciendis* (Cic. *Vat.* 27; Mommsen, *Röm. Strafr.*, 216) or to the *lex iudiciaria* of the praetor Q. Fufius Calenus, providing that the three orders should vote separately in the jury-courts (Dio 38, 8, 1; Mommsen, *Röm. Strafr.*, 445, n. 5). But a stipulation about the number of attendants that a plaintiff might take with him to a province in order to find witnesses is appropriate only to the *lex repetundarum*, which, according to Val. Max. 8, 1, 10, also fixed the number of witnesses to be summoned at a maximum of 120. Cicero mentions the new law because the plaintiff D. Laelius is alleged to have taken a whole 'army of attendants' to Asia. The trial was still held under the *Lex Cornelia* (*Rab. Post.* 9). But Cicero already knows of the law promulgated by Caesar.

that the senatorial representatives of this party behaved not a whit better in the provinces. There were, however, some honourable members of the nobility, from whose ranks there came in 149 the first law against the taking of money by magistrates, which provided for the trial of this offence before a special court. This was followed by two laws with stricter regulations, passed in the interests of the equestrian order. Next Sulla's law was effective until 59. Caesar now produced a careful and very comprehensive revision of the whole subject, the *lex Iulia repetundarum*, which remained in force from then on throughout the whole Imperial period.[1]

The law contained exact definitions of the offences[2] and the classes of persons that came within its scope. In addition to the magistrates, the senatorial members of their staff, in particular their *legati*, were included; further also senatorial jurymen, plaintiffs and witnesses who took bribes. The law went on to lay down a new procedure for the conduct of trials and, in connection with its main theme, provided a mass of regulations for provincial administration. The *lex Iulia* contained nothing new in principle, but it was drafted more precisely and strictly than its predecessors and so formed an excellent instrument for the supervision of the senatorial order. Seen from the standpoint of the Empire as a whole, a *lex repetundarum* which ignored the knights[3] was decidedly a half-measure, however much it demonstrated its author's mastery in the administrative field. Even at the time, it met with the approval of the experts—and of Cato[4]—and, as far as we know, was adopted by the people without opposition.

As already mentioned, Caesar's administration of Cisalpine Gaul and Illyricum started in the current year. Here he immediately took up the threads where he had left off as quaestor in 67. By the law of

---

[1] According to Cic. *fam.* 8, 8, 3 over a hundred chapters; *Rab. Post.* 8 : *multa sunt severius scripta quam in antiquis et sanctius*; *Sest.* 135: *optima lex*; *Vat.* 29: *acerrima*; *Pis.* 37: *iustissima atque optima*. Its titles, in *Dig.* 48, 11 (*de lege Iulia repetundarum*); *Cod. Iust.* 9, 27 (*ad legem Iuliam repetundarum*).

[2] Among them, Cic. *Pis.* 50: *exire de provincia, educere exercitum, bellum sua sponte gerere, in regnum iniussu populi ac senatus accedere, quae cum plurimae leges veteres, tum lex Cornelia maiestatis, Iulia de pecuniis repetundis planissime vetat; prov. cons.* 7: Clodius' law had given Piso authority *ut tibi de pecuniis creditis ius in liberos populos contra senatus consulta et contra legem generi tui dicere liceret.* Similarly Cic. *dom.* 23 about *populos liberos multis senatus consultis, etiam recenti lege generi ipsius liberatos.*

[3] Cic. *Rab. Post.* 12: *iste ordo lege ea non tenetur*; 13: in 55 the senatorial majority decided against the views of several strict senators, who demanded *ut tribuni, ut praefecti, ut scribae, ut comites omnes magistratuum lege hac tenerentur.* Complete references in B. Kübler's edition of Caesar, 3, 2 (1897), 172–175.

[4] Dio 38, 7, 5.

Gnaeus Pompeius Strabo, the father of Magnus, the Gallic communities north of the Po, except for those (such as Cremona and Aquileia) which as Latin colonies received Roman citizenship, had acquired Latin rights. This meant that their citizens were equal to the Latins, and those who attained local magistracies thereby gained Roman citizenship for themselves and their descendants.[1] But the Transpadanes now wished for full municipal rights as enjoyed by all independent communities south of the Po since 89. In 67 Caesar had promised them his support in this, and in 65 his ally Marcus Crassus had attempted as censor to enrol them in the census lists. But in the same year all non-citizens were expelled from Rome by a popular decree of the tribune Gaius Papius,[2] which was aimed at the Transpadanes.

Caesar now had Vatinius sponsor a popular decree providing for the strengthening of the Latin colony of Comum by new settlers, and himself took over its implementation. In the course of the next year he settled 5,000 citizens there. According to strict constitutional law, these became Latins, but Caesar continued to regard them as Roman citizens, although this was not expressly stated in the law, and he even went so far as to grant Roman citizenship to 500 men of Greek origin by including them in the list of settlers.[3] In line with this, during his provincial administration he quietly treated all the Transpadane townships as colonies of Roman citizens. This was a step of the greatest importance for his political future. For it was from this area in particular that he drew his reinforcements for the Gallic War and created the devoted army of the Civil War. It remains unclear how far he was systematically pursuing this aim in 59: he certainly recruited two legions from this area in 58.[4] Originally he was probably more interested in the political support of these new citizens at elections and legislative assemblies. But it is certainly remarkable to observe how Caesar's political ventures, while always admirably serving the needs of the moment, at the same time contained still greater possibilities for the future. In constructing his policies he never laid a stone on which he could not build further: as a result, a retrospective view gives the impression that everything was actually planned in advance in full detail, as if by an architect.

[1] Ascon. on Cic. *Pis.* frag. 9; Plin. *n.h.* 3, 138.
[2] Cic. *off.* 3, 47; *leg. agr.* 1, 13; Dio 37, 9, 3–5.
[3] Suet. *Caes.* 28, 3; Plut. *Caes.* 29, 2; App. *b.c.* 2, 98; Strab. 5, 213; Catull. 35, 3.
[4] Caes. *b.G.* 1, 10, 3.

For the foreign policy of his proconsulship Caesar prepared by negotiations with Ariovistus. He wanted events in Gaul to hang fire and so secured senatorial recognition as king and friend of the Roman people for the Suebian prince. The message was accompanied by expensive presents and fully achieved its purpose. Ariovistus felt himself secure and kept the peace until he was attacked in the summer of 58.[1]

The allies were victorious in the consular elections on October 18. Gabinius and Piso were elected. Gaius Cato attempted to bring an action against Gabinius for the use of illegal methods in his canvass, but no praetor dared to accept the case; when he continued to complain on this score in a popular assembly and called Pompey a dictator with no legal authority, he was nearly killed. Clodius too had secured the tribunate which he desired. On the other hand some energetic optimates were elected to the praetorship, in particular Lucius Domitius Ahenobarbus and Gaius Memmius.[2]

As was to be expected, from December 10 Clodius proved himself a demagogue of the wildest kind by a series of bills. Of these the new lex frumentaria was of far-reaching importance. For the cheap corn guaranteed by the state, he substituted a completely free distribution. So many were deemed eligible for this that their numbers had swollen to 320,000 by 46. By 56, these corn distributions were devouring a fifth of the state's revenue.[3] At this stage we must also mention the law which lifted the ban on clubs in the city, imposed in 64, and allowed new ones to be formed without restriction. Its main intention was to facilitate the organization of the rabble of the streets for electoral purposes.[4] Clodius naturally omitted to ask the Senate's advice on this question. So these laws were passed on January 3, 58.[5] Shortly before this, on the last day of December, Bibulus wanted to use the occasion of his oath on laying down office for another address to the people, but was immediately silenced by Clodius.[6] As dictator, Caesar afterwards modified the effect of these Clodian laws,[7] but in his life-and-death struggle there was no room

[1] Caes. b.G. 1, 35, 2; 40, 2; 42, 3; 43, 4; 44, 5; Dio 38, 34, 3; Plut. Caes. 19, 2; App. Celt. 16.
[2] Cic. Q. fr. 1, 2, 15–16; on C. Cato, see Miltner, RE 22, 106.
[3] Dio 38, 13, 1; Cic. Sest. 55; dom. 25; Suet. Caes. 41, 3; Rostovtzeff, RE, 7, 175. But he here misunderstands Dio 39, 24, 1, where it is stated that many slaves were freed by their masters in order to make them eligible for the corn dole.
[4] Dio 38, 13, 2; Cic. Pis. 9 (with Ascon.); Sest. 34, 55; p. red. in sen. 33; Att. 3, 15, 4.
[5] Cic. Pis. 9.   [6] Dio 38, 12, 3.
[7] Suet. Caes. 41, 3; Dio 43, 21, 4; Plut. Caes. 55, 5; App. b.c. 2, 425, misunderstood.

for scruples.[1] For, Clodius notwithstanding, as soon as he was no longer consul, the attacks of his enemies burst forth in their full fury.

The two praetors Lucius Domitius and Gaius Memmius succeeded in having Caesar's consulship discussed in the Senate.[2] All his acts as consul were to be invalidated as unconstitutional. Since Caesar declared himself ready to submit to the judgment of the Senate,[3] three days were spent in argument principally over the agrarian laws. Eventually he decided that it would be better not to wait for the verdict, crossed the *pomerium* and so assumed his proconsular *imperium*. He was accompanied by Vatinius as his *legatus*.[4] However the tribune Lucius Antistius now summoned him before the people's court. He did not appear, but covered himself with the judgment of the other tribunes that he was not liable to prosecution while absent from Rome in an official capacity. On the other hand his former quaestor was prosecuted in the normal way; it is not known with what success.[5]

Since the situation was completely unclear, Caesar waited outside the city to see how effective his counter-measures were. He himself published his 'three speeches against Domitius and Memmius',[6] while Clodius mounted the attack. He now gave notice of the following bills: by the precedent of the *lex Vatinia* on Caesar's provinces, the two consuls of 58 were also to receive their pro-consular provinces by popular decree with unusually large financial allowances.[7] Another proposal provided the penalty of outlawry for any magistrate who executed or had executed a citizen without due process of law. In content it repeated the law of Gaius Gracchus already in existence. We may recall the important part this law had played in Caesar's speech on December 6, 63, and for this reason all men appreciated the significance of its renewal by Clodius. Nevertheless we saw that at the time Caesar did not go so far as to quote the law as evidence against the senatorial decree granting

---

[1] Before December 10, 59, he, like Pompey, promised Cicero that he would protect him from Clodius (Q. fr. 1, 2, 16. Cf. Dio 38, 16, 1).

[2] Suet. Caes. 23, 1; Ner. 2, 2; Cic. Sest. 40.

[3] Cic. Vat. 15. In support of the legality of the lex agraria, Caesar could make the valid point that all the senators, Cato included, had bound themselves by oath to abide by it. This is already admitted in Cic. Sest. 61.

[4] Cic. Vat. 35.   [5] Suet. Caes. 23, 1.

[6] Suet. Caes. 73; Schol. Bob. on Cic. Sest. 40; Cic. Vat. 15. How much one would give to be able to read these speeches as well as the military commentaries!

[7] Cic. dom. 24; 55; 60; 70; 124; Sest. 24; 53; 55; p. red. in sen. 18; Pis. 37; 57; prov. cons. 3–12; Att. 3, 1; Plut. Cic. 30, 2; v. ill. 81, 4.

dictatorial authority. He only issued a warning in view of its provisions. Cicero was right, therefore, when he later said that he had
been a fool not to take this stand himself, but rather to let it appear
from his behaviour that his very existence depended on the
acceptance or rejection of Clodius' bill. For he immediately put on
mourning, removed his senatorial insignia and launched a campaign
against it. Knights and senators organized demonstrations, and the
tribune Lucius Ninnius Quadratus undertook to represent his interests. However, the two consuls were not inclined to support him;
on the contrary, they forbade the wearing of mourning, and Clodius
had little difficulty in breaking up with his gangs the assemblies
called by Ninnius.[1]

Clodius himself held a large meeting of the people in the Circus
Flaminius. He had selected this spot because it was outside the
pomerium, and so Caesar could appear in person.[2] Piso spoke first
about the execution of the Catilinarians: he had always had a leaning
towards compassion, and the cruelty shown in the killing of citizens
without trial filled him with displeasure. Gabinius spoke to the same
effect.[3] After the consuls Clodius called on Caesar to speak. He
referred back to his speech of December 5, 63: it was well known
that he had not approved of the conduct of the consul and Senate
on that occasion, but he did not now consider it right to pass a law
with retrospective effect. This speech was another brilliant demonstration of his statesmanlike discretion. As in 63, he was an adept at
making it appear that he, whom his enemies pursued with pointless
fury, was the only one to view the situation with proper objectivity.
Dignified as ever, he was adverse to brutal violations of justice; in
63 he had of course prophesied to his opponents that it would
come to this. Only a short while before December 10, 59, he had
assured Cicero of his protection. He honoured this promise as far as
was still possible, and Cicero would certainly have acted more
sensibly if he had accepted the post of *legatus* which he was offered.[4]

Pompey went still further when several respected senators visited
him at his Alban country-house in order to beg for his help on
Cicero's behalf. He replied that, as a private citizen, he was unable
to stop the tribune. That was the consuls' business: they should report

---

[1] Dio 38, 14, 4–7, 16, 4; Cic. *Att.* 3, 8, 4; 9, 2; 14, 1; 15, 5; 4, 1, 1; Q. *fr.* 1, 3, 6; *fam.*
14, 3, 1; *Sest.* 25–32; *dom.* 5, 54.
[2] Cic. *p. red. in sen.* 13; *Sest.* 33.
[3] Cic. *p. red. in sen.* 17; *Pis.* 14; Dio 38, 16, 6.
[4] Dio 38, 17, 1–2; Plut. *Cic.* 39, 3–5; Cic. *prov. cons.* 41; *Pis.* 79.

the matter to the Senate. If the Senate then declared a state of emergency, he would take up arms. All the same he avoided receiving Cicero personally and excused himself out of regard for Caesar.[1] Crassus likewise put him off with talk of the consuls.[2] Clodius on the other hand declared daily that he was acting in full agreement with the three allies, a claim which they for their part did not deny. The most they would do was to let it be known that, at a time when their own political achievements stood in great danger, they could not afford to estrange the popular tribune.[3]

Under these circumstances Cicero did not even wait for the vote on the bill, and went into voluntary exile before the middle of March. The law and sentence of outlawry on Cicero personally were passed immediately afterwards.[4] Just at that time serious news from Gaul called Caesar away to his province,[5] but he had stayed near Rome long enough to witness the first defeat of his enemies. That Cicero happened to become their symbol resulted from the person of his henchman at the time: Caesar would certainly have preferred to win the eloquent consular to his own side. His sole aim was to show the senatorial majority, which wished to destroy him, that it had no power.

The final act in this policy—the removal of Cato, his most dangerous enemy, from Italy—was not completed until Caesar had left Rome. Since Clodius had transferred the money allocated for the Julian settlement law to the proconsulships of Gabinius and Piso, means had to be made available from other sources for this purpose and for the new corn law.[6] To this end Clodius introduced a bill providing for the annexation of the kingdom of Cyprus which was then ruled by Ptolemy, the brother of the Egyptian king. The justification for this move bore the genuine Clodian stamp. Years earlier Clodius had fallen into the hands of Cilician pirates and had demanded the price of his ransom from the king of Cyprus. However, the sum he sent was too small. For this reason he was now to be deposed as an accomplice of the pirates. This seemed a particularly gross breach of international law, since his Egyptian brother

---

[1] Cic. *Pis.* 77; *Att.* 10, 4, 3; Dio 38, 17, 3.

[2] Cic. *Sest.* 41; Dio 38, 17, 3.   [3] Cic. *Sest.* 39–40.

[4] Cic. *Att.* 3, 1 (middle of March); Vell. 2, 45, 1; Plut. *Cic.* 31, 5–32, 1; Dio 38, 17, 4–7; Cic. *dom.* 47; 50; 95; 129; *har. resp.* 11. The many other passages in which Cicero refers to these— for him—exceedingly painful events are listed in *RE,* 7A, 916–917; cf. my *Pompeius*², 142–143.

[5] Caes. *b.G.* 1, 6, 4.

[6] Cic. *dom.* 23; *har. resp.* 58; *Pis.* 86; Ammian. Marc. 14, 8, 15.

had at long last just been recognized, and so the pretext of their cousin's notorious testament could no longer be used.[1] When Clodius' gangs had passed the law, by another popular decree he had its execution entrusted to Cato, who was to go on an extraordinary mission as a quaestor with praetorian powers. This was particularly malicious, as Cato was the principal enemy of all extraordinary powers. He was now in a difficult position; if he refused to go, he would have been sharply attacked for insulting the majesty of the Roman people. So he gave way and soon afterwards Clodius could read out a letter in the popular assembly in which the busy pro-consul of Gaul expressed his deep satisfaction that in future Cato would no longer be able to agitate against the granting of extra-ordinary powers.[2]

Caesar's consular year would mark a milestone in Roman history, even if it had not created the indispensable conditions for his own rise to absolute power. For apart from Cinna's permanent consul-ship, remarkable more for its intention than for the success with which it was crowned, the old senior magistracy of the Roman state had long since been reduced to the post of chief executive for the senatorial government, while legislative initiative for constitutional changes was usually left to the tribunes. In particular the big attempts at reform of the last century had come from tribunes, in whose ranks, next to the big popular names of the Gracchi, Saturninus and Sulpicius, we also find the optimate Livius Drusus. After the restoration of the tribunate in 70, there were no more personalities of this calibre, but the popular decree again became the decisive means for settling the urgent political problems of the Empire through the granting of special commands. As a patrician Caesar was ineligible for the tribunate, but he showed what a resolute will could achieve with the consulship. Although he succeeded in carry-ing out the big schemes, which despite their urgency had stagnated previously, we have seen that he was forced to adopt popular or downright revolutionary means in the process by allowing the *comitia* to be prompted by shows of strength when it came for them to express their opinion. In fairness we must admit that the Roman constitution with its innumerable devices for obstruction left no alternative. Caesar himself had made it sufficiently clear that only the cause mattered for him and not the adoption of popular methods. It

---

[1] Cic. *dom.* 20; 52; *Sest.* 57; 59 with *Schol. Bob.*; Dio 38, 30, 5. Cf. Volkmann, *RE* 23, 1748.
[2] Plut. *Cat. Min.* 34, 4–5; Strab. 14, 684; Liv. *per.* 104; Vell. 2, 45, 4; App. *b.c.* 2, 85 (with wrong dating); Cic. *dom.* 22; *Sest.* 60–63.

is the tragic fault of the optimates that they so stubbornly rejected this offer, and our judgment is only tempered by a realization of the overwhelming influence that old customs had on Roman minds, because they were thought to have served Rome well in the past. In the obstinacy with which the optimates now defended their supremacy, there remained after all something of the spirit of their ancestors of the time of the Hannibalic war. Caesar, himself a Roman to the core, was as sensible as any of them to the greatness of the past and to the special responsibility of the aristocracy for its preservation, but his genius spurred him on to deeds with which he intended to round off the construction of the empire, as yet only half achieved. His consulship shows us the first powerful steps in this direction, but at the same time also the enormous boldness of the undertaking. For the old world of the optimate *principes* rose united in opposition, and in fact Caesar faced it alone. Assistants such as Vatinius, Fufius Calenus and Cornelius Balbus have no significance of their own, while his allies Pompey and Crassus were fighting for their own principate.

For the time being Clodius provided a rearguard for his enterprises in the north. But what he wanted to achieve there would still have to be done under the most difficult conditions imaginable. The whole position he had so far won for himself could not stand up to constitutional examination, and the optimate nobility with its followers had given him notice of a fight to the death. He was sustained by his common interests with Pompey and Crassus, which only held good under quite special conditions. His affairs were being managed by Clodius, whose moods were incalculable, and whose very tenure of office was grounded in illegality. The performance of great deeds in Gaul was, therefore, not just a matter of ambition but a question of self-preservation. On the path on which he had entered inactivity meant ruin. Only if he returned much stronger would he be able to win through. But he could only devote half his energies to this end. He was forced to make equally strenuous efforts to ensure that the ground from which he was fighting the Celts was not cut from under his feet in Rome.

CHAPTER FOUR

THE PROCONSULSHIP

WITHOUT doubt Caesar's agents kept him informed about what was going on in the independent part of Gaul. Thus he learned that the Helvetii had fixed a meeting of their whole people, reinforced by some neighbouring cantons, to be held on the banks of the Rhone on March 28, 58. Their homes were in ruins, and they planned to resettle beyond the Jura and the Rhone. The most convenient route ran through the territory of the Allobroges in the Roman province (modern Savoy). Since the Allobroges had just been in revolt against Rome, it was reasonable to assume that the tribesmen would not meet with great difficulty here.[1]

By covering about 90 miles a day, Caesar reached Genava (Geneva) in eight days, and had the bridge over the Rhone there

---

[1] Caes. *b.G.* 1, 5–6. Caesar explains (1, 3–4) that the emigration plan had been strongly supported in 61 by Orgetorix, the most powerful man of the Helvetii, who, it was believed, had committed suicide in 60 (4, 4). As we know from Cic. *Att.* 1, 19, 2, it was for this reason that Rome was filled with *Gallici belli metus* in March 60: the Senate sent three ambassadors to Gaul. As early as May it was believed that the danger was over (*Att.* 1, 20, 5; 2, 1, 11), presumably because of the death of Orgetorix. It therefore came as a surprise when, in 59, the Helvetii nevertheless carried out their plan (Caes. *b.G.* 1, 5, 1). The instructions to the ambassadors in March 60 read: *qui adirent Galliae civitates darentque operam ne eae se cum Helvetiis coniungerent.* As soon became apparent (Caes. *b.G.* 9, 2), the connection formed by Orgetorix with the Aeduan Dumnorix (*b.G.* 1, 3, 5; 18, 3–9) still existed in 59. Thus the information that Caesar provides is directed against the false general view of conditions in Gaul. G. Walser, *Caesar und die Germanen (Historia, Einzelschriften* 1 (1956), 2 ff.), rightly says that one can form no clear picture from Caesar of what happened among the Helvetii. But Caesar was writing for Roman senators and against the talk spread by his enemies that his campaigns in Gaul were useless adventures (Dio 38, 31, 1). Mommsen, *R.G.* 3, 615–616 (English tr., 5, 499 ff.), gives an excellent appreciation of the work. Only his definition 'the military report of the democratic general to the People from whom he had received his commission' is unfortunate, because the 'Roman People', the *plebs urbana*, read no books. In *Vom röm. Staat* (= *Kl. Schr.*, 2, 9 f.) and my Introduction to a selection from Caesar's works (*Heidelberger Texte, Lat. Reihe*, 1 (1957), 18) I referred to Hirtius, *b.G.* 8, 52, 4, where he says of Caesar: *iudicabat enim liberis sententiis patrum conscriptorum causam suam facile obtineri.* Caesar himself (*b.c.* 1, 9, 5) says : *discedant in Italia omnes ab armis, metus civitate tollatur, libera comitia atque omnis res publica senatui populoque Romano permittatur.* The whole problem has been treated thoroughly, with analogies from recent and very recent history, by John H. Collins in *Propaganda, Ethics and Psychological Assumptions in Caesar's Writings* (Diss. Frankfurt a. M. (1952)). As its title suggests, this book deals only briefly with military history. The basic works on this are T. Rice Holmes, *Caesar's Conquest of Gaul*[2] (1911); *Ancient Britain*[2] (1911); *The Roman Republic and the Founder of the Empire*, 2 and 3 (1923); Camille Jullian, *Histoire de la Gaule*, 3 (1920).

demolished. The legion stationed in Transalpine Gaul and the provincial militia were sent to join him. Helvetian representatives demanded permission for the migrants to cross the province. These allegedly numbered 368,000, of whom 92,000 were fit to bear arms. Caesar gives these figures on the strength of evidence discovered later, while modern critics have reduced them to a sum total of 150,000, a quarter of these of military age.[1] He promised to give them a reply on April 13. This gave him time to block the Rhone crossings between the lake of Geneva and the Jura Mountains by means of field fortifications, and he now roundly rejected their demand as incompatible with the practice and principles of the Roman people. When an attempt to force a crossing failed, the Helvetii took the route through the territory of the Sequani (Franche-Comté). Permission to do so was secured through the good offices of the Aeduan chief Dumnorix, brother of Diviciacus, and in this way they were able to proceed towards their goal, the land of the Santones (between Gironde and Charente) without touching Roman soil.[2]

This territory did not border on the Roman province. What was now going on was a matter that concerned independent Celtic tribes, and a proconsul not intent, as Caesar was, on clutching at every opportunity of winning military glory could have allowed events to take their course. Yet Caesar foresaw that these restless migrants might soon endanger the western part of the Roman province near Tolosa, and according to long-standing Roman tradition it was his duty to anticipate this danger.[3] He therefore entrusted the protection of the Rhone frontier to Titus Labienus, his *legatus* with praetorian power, and himself hurried to Cisalpine

[1] Caes. *b.G.* 1, 29, 3; Julius Beloch, *Die Bevölkerung der griechisch-römischen Welt* (1886), 229; E. Kirsten, *Raum und Bevölkerung in der Weltgeschichte*, 1 (1956), 229, writes: 'Despite many doubts and the difficulty of moving and feeding such a mass of men, the numbers can be considered reliable and corresponding to the capacity of the area. The population density would then have been 26 per square mile'.

[2] Caes. *b.G.* 1, 7, 1–10; Dio 38, 31, 2–32, 3.

[3] Caes. *b.G.* 1, 10, 1–2. In Dio 38, 32, 3 Caesar's duty to intervene is further justified by the remark that otherwise the Aedui and Sequani would have allied themselves with the Helvetii. The principle of the 'dangerous neighbours' is first found in Polyb. 1, 10, 6, who, in my opinion, follows Fabius Pictor (*Hermes* 68 (1933), 137 and 163 (=*Kl. Schr.* 3, 59 f., 88 f.)). The further evidence is given in *Vom röm. Staat*, 1 (1943), 45 (=*Kl. Schr.*, 2, 16 f.) : Augustine, *civ. dei* 4, 15 : *sed procul dubio felicitas maior est vicinum bonum habere concordem quam vicinum malum subiugare bellantem.* In Livy, 42, 52, 15 (presumably following Polybius) Perseus says: *cum patre suo gerentis bellum Romanos speciosum Graeciae liberandae praetulisse titulum, nunc propalam Macedoniam in servitutem petere, ne rex vicinus imperio sit Romano, ne quis bello nobilis arma habeat.* Plut. *Caes.* 19, 2.

Gaul. Here he took over the three legions encamped near Aquileia and also recruited two more by the device of treating the young men of the area as if they were all Roman citizens.[1] Caesar had already conducted a similar recruiting campaign on his own initiative while propraetor in Spain; in times of crisis others had surely done the same, but according to traditional practice it was the Senate's business to give orders for the raising of fresh forces.[2]

Caesar knew that his opponents in Rome were watching his every step with suspicion, and that it was just such arbitrary actions that would supply them with most welcome material for a prosecution. For this reason, when he came to publish his military commentaries in the year 51, he had taken particular care to work out how the campaign against the Helvetii, from which all the others necessarily followed, was fully compatible with the established principles of Roman policy: the Helvetii were old enemies of the Roman people, in 107 they had defeated a Roman consul and made his army pass under the yoke, In addition, Caesar had an entirely personal reason for revenge, since the great-grandfather of his wife Calpurnia had lost his life in that battle. In their intended new settlements they would therefore prove most dangerous neighbours for the fertile district of Tolosa.[3] His work *On the Gallic War*, and in particular the first book, is a most valuable source for an understanding of 'Caesar the Politician'. With the same majesty with

[1] Caes. *b.G.* 1, 10, 3; cf. 5, 24, 4 (presumably in 55).

[2] *Gnomon* 1 (1925), 272; Suet. *Caes.* 24, 2 : *qua fiducia* (trust in Pompey and Crassus) *ad legiones, quas a re publica accepisset, alias privato sumptu addidit*; Cic. *Pis.* 37 : *habebas exercitum tantum quantum tibi non senatus aut populus Romanus dederat, sed quantum tua libido conscripserat; aerarium exhauseras. Quas res gessisti imperio, exercitu, provincia consulari?*

[3] Caes. *b.G.* 1, 8, 3; 12, 5–7. I cannot agree with Collins (op. cit., 27) when he denies (arguing against A. Klotz) that Caesar gives his motives for the two campaigns of the year 58 so fully for the above-mentioned reason. Collins (37) rightly emphasizes that the Romans did not consider questions of 'war guilt' in their campaigns against barbarians. But he does not appreciate the fact that Caesar was invalidating in advance the points of the indictment for high treason which his enemies were preparing against him. It was this trial to which his words on the field of Pharsalus referred: *hoc voluerunt; tantis rebus gestis Gaius Caesar condemnatus essem, nisi ab exercitu auxilium petissem* (Suet. *Caes.* 30, 4; Plut. *Caes.* 46,1). What was planned is shown by Suet. *Caes.* 24, 3 : *nec deinde ulla belli occasione, ne iniusti quidem ac periculosi abstinuit, tam foederatis quam infestis ac feris gentibus ultro lacessitis, adeo ut senatus quondam legatos ad explorandum statum Galliarum mittendos decreverit ac nonnulli dedendum eum hostibus censuissent* (the last part, according to Plut. *Caes.* 22, 4, comes from Tanusius Geminus: cf. App. *Celt.* 18, 2; Münzer, *RE*, 4A, 2231). Of particular importance are the offences against the *Lex Cornelia maiestatis* and the *Lex Iulia repetundarum* with which Gabinius was charged, Cic. *Pis.* 49–50: *in Aegyptum venit, signa contulit cum Alexandrinis. quando hoc bellum aut hic ordo aut populus susceperat? . . . mitto exire de provincia, educere exercitum, bellum sua sponte gerere, in regnum iniussu populi ac senatus accedere, quae cum plurimae leges veteres, tum lex Cornelia maiestatis, Iulia de pecuniis repetundis planissime vetat.*

which he had refuted his yelping enemies during his consulship
by means of his excellent laws, he here takes no notice of all the
accusations they had gathered against him, contenting himself with
a bare statement of his exemplary devotion to duty as a Roman
provincial governor and continuing in factual and objective tones
with a particularly impressive record of his own great achievements
and those of his army—as he put it himself, the *tantae res gestae*
which had won him an unassailable *dignitas*.[1]

Caesar had already left his province and crossed to the north
of the Rhone, when a better ground for war presented itself.
As he reports, the Helvetii had caused great damage in the areas
through which they had passed, and consequently the Aedui, the
Ambarri (their southern neighbours), and the Allobroges, living on
the left bank of the Rhone, asked for his protection. He was now
able to say that concern for the welfare of these allies, which the
Senate had enjoined by its resolution of 61,[2] had decided him to
make an immediate attack on the Helvetii. The actual facts of the
situation were that an Aeduan faction led by Diviciacus and the then
vergobretus (elected chieftain) Liscus, who had already appealed for
Roman help in 61, called in Caesar and concerted arrangements for

---

[1] Caes. *b.c.* 1, 13, 1 : the town council of Auximum declares *neque se neque reliquos municipes
pati posse C. Caesarem imperatorem bene de re publica meritum tantis rebus gestis oppido moenibusque prohiberi*; 9, 2: *sibi semper primam fuisse dignitatem vitaque potiorem : doluisse se quod
populi Romani beneficium sibi per contumeliam ab inimicis extorqueretur.* Cf. Cic. *Pis.* 81 : *cum
tantas res gessisset gereretque cotidie* (in 55). Cicero (*Brut.* 262), in line with his own view of
commentarii rerum suarum (*fam.* 5, 12, 10), probably over-emphasizes Caesar's historiographical
intention. Of course, this intention was present, and his book has had this effect on posterity.
Caesar, unlike Pompey, had no need of a Theophanes. But, in the first instance, it was political
journalism directed at his contemporaries. We must regard his reports in the same light as the
narratio of the speeches which were delivered before the Senate, People and courts at the time:
no one expected impartial truth in these. Of course, there is no reason for the modern historian
not to test for 'credibility', but one should not speak in accusing tones of 'déformation historique', as does M. Rambaud in *L'art de la déformation historique dans les Commentaires de
César* (1953). Cf. J. H. Collins, *Gnomon* 26 (1954), 537 ff. and J. P. V. D. Balsdon, *JRS* 45
(1955), 161 ff. I remarked in *HZ* 178 (1954), 453 (=*Kl. Schr.* 2, 290) that the 'easy and speedy'
composition, to which Hirtius (*b.G.* 8, *praef.* 6) testifies, precludes such artful refinement, and
that contemporaries certainly had sources of information about events in Gaul other than
Caesar himself. According to Cicero (*Pis.* 38–40), Piso sent no reports to the Senate, yet
Cicero was in a position to give a full account of his failures and crimes (83–93).

[2] Caes. *b.G.* 1, 10, 5–11, 6; Dio 38, 32, 2–3 differs. Caesar was now acting on the principle,
which Cic. *rep.* 3, 35 states thus: *noster autem populus sociis defendendis terrarum iam omnium
potitus est.* Cf. *Vom röm. Staat*, 1, 33–35 (=*Kl. Schr.* 2, 6–8); 145–147. In addition to the
passages there cited, see also Plaut. *Cistell.* 199–200: *servate vostros socios, vostros socios, veteres et
novos, augete auxilia vostris iustis legibus.* Dio too uses the principle: 38, 36, 5; 39, 5. The s.c.
of 61 is not mentioned until 1, 35, 4. Cf. 43, 7 and 8: *populi Romani hanc esse consuetudinem, ut
socios atque amicos non modo sui nihil deperdere, sed gratia, dignitate, honore auctiores vellet esse.*

H

military assistance with him. On the other hand Dumnorix, the most powerful man in the land, and opposed to the magistrates and his own brother Diviciacus, wished rather to use the Helvetii to restore the old kingship. Still, the official government had come to an agreement with Caesar and so placed a valuable card in his hand.[1]

He soon caught up with the migrants on the Saone. A quarter of them had not yet crossed the river and were smashed by the Romans' surprise attack. As Caesar observes, these were the very people from the canton of the Tigurini, who had once joined the Cimbri and Teutones in defeating the Romans. He immediately crossed to the other bank in pursuit of the remainder. At this stage a Helvetian embassy under the leadership of Divico, the victor in that battle of 107, began negotiations and declared itself willing to settle in any area allotted by Caesar. According to Caesar he concluded his offer with the arrogant remark that it was now up to Caesar to prevent this region from becoming famous for another Roman defeat. The latter replied that even if the Roman people forgot its old disgrace, it could not overlook these new excesses, the attempt to cross the province without permission and the outrages committed in the territory of the Aedui, Ambarri and Allobroges. The Helvetii should not rely on the good fortune that had so far attended them, since it was the practice of the immortal gods to delay the punishment of the wicked in order that their destruction might be the more complete. Nevertheless he would be satisfied with the reparation of the damage which they had caused in the land of the Aedui and the Allobroges, and the delivery of hostages, and would then make peace with them. Divico declared these conditions unworthy of the Helvetii, and on the next day he and his people continued their northward march.[2] For two weeks the Roman army followed at a distance of about five miles. As a result of the accession of the Aeduan cavalry, Caesar now had 41,000 horsemen at his disposal, and his allies had also taken over the commissariat. But the cavalry allowed themselves to be put to flight by the enemy in a disgraceful fashion, and the corn deliveries failed to materialize. Clearly treason was at work, and on making serious remonstrances to the leaders who were with him, Caesar learned that Dumnorix was behind it. Out of consideration for Diviciacus and, in particular, for his extensive connections in

[1] Caes. b.G. 1, 16, 5-18, 10.   [2] Op. cit., 1, 12-14.

Gaul, the proconsul confined himself to rendering him harmless by means of strict supervision.[1]

In order to secure his food supply, he found himself forced to call a temporary halt to his pursuit of the Helvetii and to turn aside northwards to Bibracte (Mont Beuvray), the well-stocked capital of the Aedui.[2] The Helvetii misinterpreted this movement as being dictated by fear, themselves changed direction to pursue the Romans, and soon paid for their presumption with a decisive defeat. During the night after the battle the stream of fugitives rolled northward into the land of the Lingones (in the vicinity of Dijon). Caesar had to grant his troops three days' rest, but threatened the Lingones with immediate war in the event of their rendering any assistance to the Helvetii. His command was obeyed, and the remaining Helvetii were forced to surrender when he marched up. The terms imposed were the delivery of hostages, disarmament and the handing over of Roman deserters. A group of 6,000 who tried to break out were captured on his orders by the surrounding Celts, presumably the Sequani, and fell victim to the harsh rules of war. The remainder, numbering 110,000, had to return to their country and rebuild their homes in order to prevent the Germans from settling there and becoming neighbours of the Roman province. By a treaty of alliance they entered into regular relations with Rome. Its terms included a clause based on earlier treaties with Celtic states guaranteeing that they would lose none of their people by enfranchisement as Roman citizens. The Allobroges were ordered to supply them with corn to meet their immediate needs. The surviving Boii, who had joined the Helvetian migration, were allowed by Caesar to remain in the territory of the Aedui.[3]

This successful war was soon followed by the campaign against Ariovistus.[4] Since the latter had only recently secured the status of a king in alliance with the Roman people, Caesar takes particular pains to show why he had to intervene against him too. According to his narrative, after his victory a number of Celtic chiefs arrived at his camp in order to thank him in the name of their communities for ridding them of the Helvetian danger, and to ask him to grant them a joint audience.[5]

---

[1] Op. cit., 1, 15–20.   [2] Op. cit., 1, 23–26,5.

[3] Op. cit., 1, 26, 5–29. Cic. Balb. 32 (in 56): etenim quaedam foedera exstant, ut Cenomanorum Insubrium Helvetiorum Iapydum, nonnullorum item ex Gallia barbarorum, quorum in foederibus exceptum est, ne quis eorum a nobis civis recipiatur. According to this, Caesar had taken over the conditions of the old treaties of the third century.

[4] On this, see Walser, Caesar und die Germanen, 8 ff.   [5] Caes. b.G. 1, 30.

The actual negotiations were secret, but on their conclusion Diviciacus made the following disclosures to the proconsul on behalf of the assembled chiefs: in 61, when he had asked for the help of the Senate in Rome, the Aedui and their allies had just been defeated by their rivals, the Arverni and the Sequani. Their enemies had won this success through the services of Ariovistus, the Suebian leader, and he had forced the Aedui to give hostages to the Sequani and to himself, to recognize the supremacy of the Sequani and to pay him tribute. As a reward the Suebi received a third of the territory of the Sequani, but were now demanding a further third as new arrivals forced their way in. The only way to stem this flood was a ruling from Rome, and it was this that the assembled representatives of the Gallic states requested.[1] About fifteen years previously[2] strong bands of Germanic nomads, generally described as Suebi by ancient writers, had moved into the part of South Germany between the Main and the Rhine which had been abandoned by its Celtic population at the time of the Cimbrian migrations: these had now also begun to cross the Rhine in the neighbourhood of Mainz. The appearance of these martial peoples gave the Sequani the idea of employing them as mercenaries—a step which they soon regretted bitterly, since the German leader Ariovistus intended to settle permanently in their fertile country, and in negotiations with Rome secured recognition as an independent sovereign.[3]

It was actually on Caesar's initiative that the Senate had proclaimed him king and friend of the Roman people in 59, and so he had no fear as regards Rome. Otherwise he would presumably have supported the Helvetii.[4] However, the attitude of protector of the Aedui adopted by the proconsul since his advance into independent Gaul was in contradiction to his former policy. Caesar may not have realized this until now, but he did not hesitate one moment before changing course. He could not have found a better pretext for further military operations than a request for help from an assembly of Celtic chiefs. But the political reasons which he gives himself were doubtless in full accord with traditional Roman practice: the honour of Rome demanded that she should deliver the Aedui, whom the Senate had repeatedly described as blood

---

[1] Op. cit., 1, 31.

[2] Op. cit., 1, 36, 7. I see no reason to follow Walser (op. cit., 27, 6) in rejecting this statement as fictitious.

[3] Op. cit., 1, 402.   [4] Cf. op. cit., 1, 44, 10.

brothers, from their straits. Above all the dreaded Germans, especially under a leader with the ambitious plans of Ariovistus, had to be kept as far away as possible from the borders of the Roman Empire, in order to prevent them from breaking into Italy as the Cimbri and Teutones had done. Accordingly, Caesar promised the Gallic representatives his protection and declared that he was confident that, in view of the good treatment he had received, Ariovistus would voluntarily obey his instructions and content himself with his previous frontiers.[1]

However, Ariovistus refused to meet Caesar personally at a place midway between their present positions. If Caesar wanted anything, let him come to him. Anyway, he continued, he was astonished that his Gaul, which he had conquered, should be any concern of Caesar's or of the Roman people. Thereupon Caesar sent ambassadors to face him with the following conditions for the continuance of friendly relations: German immigration into the territory on the left bank of the Rhine was to stop; the hostages which he or the Sequani had taken from the Aedui were to be returned; the Aedui were not to be molested in any way, and he was to renounce the use of force against them and their allies. Unless these demands were accepted, Caesar would assume the defence of the friends of the Roman people in accordance with the senatorial decree of 61. Ariovistus bluntly rejected such interference in his affairs. Simultaneously Caesar received news from the Aedui and Treveri of a fresh German invasion.[2]

He now set off towards the north-east and had the good fortune to occupy Vesontio (Besançon), the capital of the Sequani, before Ariovistus could reach the place.[3] Here horrific tales about the irresistibility of the Germans told to his troops by the Celts caused such a serious panic in the army that he was warned that they would refuse to advance farther. He immediately summoned all his senior officers and commanders, and a vigorous speech produced a complete change of mood. Although he only reproduces it in indirect speech, the ideas he expresses are no doubt typical of his attitude in such crises. In a manner very reminiscent of December 5, 63,

---

[1] Op. cit., 1, 33; Dio 38, 34, 1–4.

[2] Caes. b.G., 1, 34–37; Dio 38, 34, 5–6. I regard Walser's view (op. cit. 27), that the answer put into the mouth of Ariovistus in 1, 36 is 'unhistoric', 'Caesar's invention' and 'a pure fabrication of Roman rhetoric', as exaggerated. All internal probability speaks for its authenticity. The variant of Dio, rightly recognized by Walser (28) as genuine, states that Caesar had provoked him.

[3] Caes. b.G. 1, 38.

he faced an agitated meeting with a modest statement of his considered views, which formed a chain of reasoning that led to an inescapable conclusion. He did not demand blind trust even from his subordinates; rather, they were to assure themselves that what seemed a foolhardy adventure was based on a well-thought-out plan. For a start, it was still by no means certain that Ariovistus would not accept his reasonable terms. If he were mad enough to attack, a Roman army had nothing to fear from Germans. That was clear from the victories over the Cimbri and Teutones, and over the Germans in the slave army of Spartacus. Even the Helvetii had often defeated Germans. Ariovistus may have been able to outwit Celts with his strategy in the recent war; he would not succeed in this against a Roman army. However far their advance led them into pathless enemy territory, provisions were assured them by deliveries from the Sequani, the Leuci (around Toul) and the Lingones (around Langres). It was a piece of unseemly impudence to cloak their cowardice by expressing doubts on the score of such elementary planning. A general with Caesar's unblemished reputation was not left in the lurch by his soldiers. Others, who had suffered this fate, had lost the confidence of their men either through their defeats or through their greed, whereas his luck had been proved in the campaign against the Helvetii. He therefore proposed to start during the following night, earlier than he had intended, in order to test whether their sense of honour and duty was not stronger than their fear. If no one else came, he would set out with the tenth legion alone, on which he could rely as on his bodyguard. For the benefit of the reader he adds: 'Caesar had treated this legion with particular distinction and because of its bravery he had most confidence in it.' He himself describes the success of the speech as remarkable. First the tenth legion thanked him through its tribunes for his good opinion of it, and assured him of its readiness to fight under all conditions. Then the other legions through their officers asked for forgiveness.[1] At such decisive moments an overwhelming

[1] Op. cit., 1, 39–41, 3; Dio 38, 35–46. According to Caes. *b.G.* 1, 39, 2 the panic started *a tribunis militum, praefectis reliquisque, qui ex urbe amicitiae causa Caesarem secuti non magnum in re militari usum habebant.* Their excuses follow. Dio (35, 2) offers a variant: the soldiers (37, 1) started to say that they did not wish to take part in a war that was neither just nor sanctioned by the Senate or People (41, 1), but only served Caesar's ambition. Like Caesar (*b.G.* 1, 40, 1) he makes Caesar call all his officers and centurions to a *consilium* (35, 3); but Caesar's big speech, with its many imitations of Thucydides, is a lecture to his officers (37, 3; 46, 2) on how to convince the soldiers of the necessity of the war. Only 46, 3, the appeal to the tenth legion, agrees with Caes. *b.G.* 1, 40, 15. Ed. Schwartz (*RE*, 3, 1707) traces the variants of Dio unfavourable to Caesar back to Livy. These can only be regarded as genuine if Livy

power radiated from his deliberate calm and unshakable confidence. Six days later he was in Upper Alsace (probably in the vicinity of Ribeauvillé),[1] twenty miles from Ariovistus' camp. The latter now agreed to a personal meeting. Caesar repeated his demands orally, and at the same time drew Ariovistus' attention to the distinguished treatment he had hitherto experienced in Rome and to the principle of Roman policy of promoting the power and authority of her allies. Rome could not admit that her old friends the Aedui, from time immemorial the first people in Gaul, should now suffer injury.

Ariovistus replied that he had crossed the Rhine at the request of the Celts: his present position rested on the right of conquest and was no concern of the Romans. Caesar's attempt to base his case on the Aedui did not ring true. Recently, in 61 and 60, Rome's 'blood brothers' had not helped to put down the rebellion of the Allobroges, nor had they asked for Roman help in their war against the Sequani. If Caesar did not evacuate the area, he would treat him as an enemy. He was fully aware that many eminent men in Rome would be grateful for Caesar's removal. Of that he had been expressly assured—a telling blow by Caesar this, at his optimate opponents! On the other hand, if Caesar recognized his right to Gaul, he was at his service in any war he cared to undertake.

Thereupon Caesar again stressed that under no circumstances would he or the Roman people surrender allies who had deserved well of them. Furthermore, Ariovistus' claim to Gaul was no better than Rome's, since after the heavy defeats inflicted on the Arverni and Ruteni in the year 121, it had been in Rome's power to make a tributary province of the country beyond the Cevennes. At that time this had not been done, but the Roman people had a perfectly just claim to mastery over Gaul, and it would not do for Ariovistus to lord it over a country which the Senate had recognized as independent.[2]

was following an earlier source. (Walser (op. cit., 28, n. 2) conjectures Asinius Pollio.) If, as I should like to assume, they include echoes of news which Caesar's enemies in Rome received from their relations or friends at his headquarters, Caesar has described these correspondents in a typically malicious fashion, exposing them to ridicule as cowards without mentioning their 'constitutional' worries; on the same lines is 44, 12, where *principes populi Romani* were in contact with Ariovistus. There was no doubt a speech in Livy as well, and Dio may have drawn something from it.

[1] Thus Kromayer-Veith, *Schlachtenatlas zur antiken Kriegsgeschichte* (1922), 70, map 15. Caesar's statements leave room for much conjecture. On the older suggestions, see C. Jullian, *Hist. de la Gaule*, 3, 231, n. 4. Recently R. Schmittlein (*La première campagne de César contre les Germains* (1956)) has transferred the battle to Belfort. (My only acquaintance with this work is through the discussion by J. H. Collins in *Gnomon* 30 (1958), 300 ff.)

[2] Caes. *b.G.* 1, 42, 45; Dio 38, 47, 3-4.

In his detailed account of these negotiations Caesar reveals the real point of his Gallic campaigns: Ariovistus was trespassing on Rome's sphere of influence, and, as her representative, he would have been guilty of criminal dereliction of duty if he had submitted passively to such provocation. When he published his military commentaries in the year 51, unprejudiced readers were meant to recognize that all that followed was the natural consequence of this position. The conference had to be broken off because the followers of Ariovistus attacked Caesar's soldiers. Two days later, when Ariovistus proposed to resume the talks, Caesar confined himself to sending two envoys, who were promptly arrested by Ariovistus as spies.[1] Then he marched along the edge of the Vosges past Caesar's camp, and took up a position to the south of it (probably on the Zellenberg to the south of Ribeauvillé), from which he threatened Caesar's lines of communication. Caesar countered this danger by fortifying a second camp still farther to the south.[2]

After a week of such manœuvring Caesar was victorious in a bloody battle at the beginning of September. The great warrior race was scattered.[3] The only tribes who succeeded in maintaining themselves on the left bank of the Rhine were the Triboci (to the north of Strasbourg), Nemetes (around Speyer) and Vangiones (around Worms and Mainz).[4] Thus, in two short campaigns, by the beginning of autumn, Caesar had overcome two opponents who had long been regarded with justified apprehension in Rome.

To secure his gains, he could hardly do otherwise than choose the land of the Sequani as winter quarters for his army under the command of Labienus. He himself left for Cisalpine Gaul in order to administer justice on circuit there: above all, he could there take a closer look at the situation in Rome and take steps accordingly. During the winter months there was a continuous coming and going between Caesar and Rome.[5] We know details of the matters under consideration only in so far as they concerned Cicero.

Soon after Caesar's departure in March, 58, the situation in Rome began to change. The insolence of Clodius now knew no bounds, and as early as April Pompey and Gabinius became the object of

[1] Caes. b.G. 1, 46–47.

[2] Op. cit., 1, 48–49; Dio 38, 48, 1–3, with small variants.

[3] Caes. b.G. 1, 50–53; Dio 38, 47, 4–50. Frontin. strat. 2, 6, 3 is perhaps alluding to the battle around the laager, mentioned in Dio 50, 4, and can on no account be interpreted (with Walser, op. cit., 26, n. 6) as contradicting Caesar. Cf. Oros. 6, 7, 8–10.

[4] Caes. b.G. 1, 51, 2; 4, 10, 3; Strab. 4, 193; Plin. n.h. 4, 106; Tac. Germ. 28, 5; Ptol. geogr. 2, 9, 9.

[5] Plut. Caes. 20, 1–3.

his attacks.[1] As a result Pompey found himself forced on to the optimate side and began to concern himself with Cicero's recall. After the elections in July, he discussed the question with the tribune Quintus Terentius Culleo. Caesar's position is made sufficiently clear by the fact that his embittered enemy, the praetor Lucius Domitius Ahenobarbus, was also ready to take up the matter. In view of this, Culleo proposed to Pompey that he should divorce Julia and break off his friendship with Caesar.[2] But Pompey did not waver; rather, he asked for Caesar's agreement before undertaking anything.[3] Clodius now went from bad to worse. On August 11 an attempt on Pompey's life instigated by him was discovered, and on the succeeding days he had a gang blockade Pompey's house, with the result that the latter decided not to go out any more during the current tribunician year.[4] Enraged at the failure of his plans, Clodius suddenly threw himself into the arms of the optimates and declared Caesar's legislation of the previous year illegal.[5]

On October 29, with the approval of Pompey, eight tribunes brought forward a proposal for Cicero's recall: it was, of course, vetoed before it could be put to the vote.[6] Nevertheless, Publius Sestius, one of the tribunes elect and a loyal supporter of Cicero, travelled to northern Italy to secure Caesar's consent. The latter appears to have given a cautious reply;[7] it was certainly to be anticipated that Cicero's presence, in so far as he was allowed to give free rein to his consuming passion for revenge, would not improve Caesar's relations with Pompey. In fact, Cicero had to wait until August, 57, for the recall he so ardently longed for,[8] Caesar intervening in his favour as soon as he realized the inevitability of an event which he did not really desire.[9]

As well as the political scene in the capital, developments in Gaul demanded Caesar's full attention. As was to be expected, the winter quarters of the six legions in the territory of the Sequani aroused widespread concern. During the winter Caesar learned that the powerful Belgic tribes (France north of the Marne and Seine, Belgium and the Netherlands) were combining to resist further Roman penetration.[10]

[1] Cic. Att. 3, 8, 3; dom. 66; Ascon. on Cic. Mil. 37; Dio 38, 30, 1–3.

[2] Cic. Att. 3, 15, 4–5; Plut. Pomp. 49, 4.   [3] Cic. Att. 3, 18, 1.

[4] Cic. Mil. 37 with Ascon.; Sest. 69; Plut. Pomp. 49, 2–3.

[5] Cic. dom. 40; har. resp. 48.   [6] Cic. Att. 3, 23, 1; p. red. in sen. 8.

[7] Cic. Sest. 71.   [8] Cic. Att. 4, 1, 4.

[9] Cic. prov. cons. 43; har. resp. 46; Balb. 59; Pis. 80; fam. 1, 9, 9; Dio 39, 10, 1; Klio 30 (1937), 7 (= Kl. Schr. 2, 234 f.).

[10] Caes. b.G. 2, 1, 1; Dio 39, 1, 2.

At the beginning of 57 he enlisted two new legions in Cisalpine Gaul,[1] thus quietly bringing his army to twice the strength authorized by the Senate and People.[2] These recruits crossed the Alps at the end of March. Caesar himself reached his headquarters at the beginning of summer and instructed the Senones (the people around Sens) and other neighbours of the Belgae to keep him informed of developments in the north.[3] Since the Belgae were massing their troops, he soon advanced with his eight legions into Champagne. The first Belgic people he encountered were the Remi (around Rheims). Their representatives greeted him at the frontier and announced their submission, evidently because the experience of their Celtic neighbours in the previous year suggested that such a step was likely to pay good dividends. Caesar received them with delight and ensured their loyalty by asking for hostages—the chief men of the country had to hand over their children. The submission of the Remi proved to be quite genuine, and it provided Caesar with the same advantage—a firm support for the power of Rome— in the north as was supplied by the Aedui in the south.[4]

After crossing the Aisne he came into contact with the united Belgae and relieved a town of the Remi which was under siege by the Belgic forces. The enormous Belgic levy could not long be held together because of a shortage of food. When Caesar had beaten off an attack on his lines of communication, and let the Aedui advance into the territory of the Bellovaci (Beauvais), it disintegrated within a few days.[5] Caesar pressed on speedily towards the west and, without fighting, was able to accept the *deditio* (unconditional surrender) of the Suessiones (around Soissons), Bellovaci and Ambiani (around Amiens). On the intercession of the Remi the Suessiones received assurances that their state would be preserved, naturally for the duration of Rome's pleasure. Diviciacus intervened on behalf of the Bellovaci as old allies of the Aedui and secured their inclusion among the clients of Rome. However, they had to hand over 600 hostages.[6] In accordance with the long-standing principle of Roman policy, separate arrangements were made with each individual state, the garrisons of the towns on the route of the Roman advance were disarmed, and there can be no doubt that tribute or rather (as Rome called it) reparations (*stipendium*) were at once imposed on all the

[1] Caes., loc. cit.　　　　　　　　　　[2] Suet. *Caes.* 24, 2.
[3] Caes. *b.G.* 2, 2, 2–4.　　　　　　　[4] Op. cit., 2, 3, 1–5, 1; 6, 12, 7–9; Dio 39, 2, 3.
[5] Caes., *b.G.* 2, 5, 2–11, 6; Dio 39, 1, 3—2, 2; Plut. *Caes.* 20, 5.
[6] Caes. *b.G.* 2, 13, 1–15, 2.

states which had come into Rome's power as the result of military operations.[1]

Leaving Amiens Caesar pushed on towards the north-east into the territory of the Nervii (Hainault-Brabant), a people feared for their ancient valour. He learned that their army, reinforced by the Atrebates (Arras) and Viromandui (Vermandois), was awaiting him behind the Sambre (in the area of Maubeugé). The Atuatuci, descendants of an outpost left behind by the Cimbri and Teutones in the neighbourhood of Namur, were expected soon to join them. While Caesar's troops were pitching camp on the near side of the river, the entire enemy army suddenly launched a brilliant assault from the woods in which they had concealed themselves. For a long time it looked as if the fierce engagement would result in defeat for the surprised Romans. Caesar himself assumed personal command of his men at a particularly threatened point, encouraging individual officers by name[2]—a characteristic touch, not to be taken for granted in an army of 40,000 men. Thanks to the intelligent action of his subordinate commanders total victory was eventually achieved, followed immediately by the *deditio* of the Nervii. With calculated leniency Caesar allowed this state too to continue its existence.[3]

Next he advanced up to the town of the Atuatuci. When the siege-engines had been erected, even these doughty opponents capitulated, but asked to keep the weapons which they urgently needed against their neighbours. Caesar explained to them the principles which he used in cases of *deditio*: he was ready to preserve their communal identity because they had surrendered before the battering-ram had touched their walls, but their weapons must definitely be handed over. The Atuatuci pretended to acquiesce, but made a sortie during the following night. It was repelled with much bloodshed. The town was occupied, and to punish this breach of faith the whole population and their property were put up for sale. Fifty-three thousand people are alleged to have been enslaved.[4]

While the siege was still in progress, Caesar had sent off one of his legions under his young friend Publius Licinius Crassus, the son

---

[1] Suet. *Caes.* 25, 1; Caes. *b.G.* 7, 76, 1.

[2] Caes. *b.G.* 2, 25, 2; Plut. *Caes.* 20, 8; Flor. 1, 45, 4; Oros. 6, 7, 16; Val. Max. 3, 2, 19.

[3] Caes. *b.G.* 2, 15, 3–28, 3. According to 28, 2, the ambassadors of the Nervii asserted that of 600 councillors only 3, and of 60,000 men fit to bear arms only 500, survived. According to 5, 38, 4 ff. this was exaggerated; according to 7, 75, 3 ff. they were to provide 6,000 men in 52.

[4] Caes. *b.G.* 2, 29, 1–33, 7. The Atuataci were again militarily effective in 54. Cf. Dio 39, 4.

of his ally, towards the states in modern Normandy and Brittany. The impression made by Caesar's successes can be seen from the fact that all without hesitation recognized the hegemony of Rome. Crassus moved into winter quarters in the country of the Andes (Angers, Anjou), two legions were posted immediately to the east, among the Turones (Tours) and Carnutes (Chartres, Orleans), four more in Belgic territory and the last one, under Servius Sulpicius Galba, in Canton Valais to secure the Great St. Bernard. In the event, this legion had to withdraw into the land of the Allobroges in face of the attacks of the courageous inhabitants.[1]

When Caesar journeyed to Illyricum in the autumn of 57 in order to acquaint himself with that part of his province,[2] he regarded the great war in Gaul as over. The battle of the Sambre had apparently taught all the Celts that it was wiser to bow to their fate. It was now up to him to convert these military and political achievements in distant theatres of war into the currency of the political arena at Rome. On the conclusion of operations he sent a report to the Senate; his account of the unprecedented achievements of the Roman army in this previously quite unknown and very dangerous theatre of war aroused enormous enthusiasm among the public of Rome. Even the Senate, the majority of whose members were not at all well disposed towards Caesar, could not resist the general upsurge of national pride and, under the leadership of Pompey and the recently returned Cicero, ordained a thanksgiving of fifteen days to celebrate these events. The normal length of a thanksgiving had been five days at the most: only Pompey in 63 had been granted ten.[3] In this way Caesar, who since January 58 had broken completely with the optimate majority in the Senate, won a political success of great significance. For this extraordinary honour paid to the proconsul of Gaul cut the ground from under the feet of the strong senatorial party, who maintained that since 58 Caesar had held his position illegally. By it the Senate recognized that Caesar's subsequent military achievements had cancelled out his earlier unconstitutional behaviour—the view expressed by Cicero early in March 56.[4]

In fact this recognition was only the result of a peculiar combination of circumstances, which was forgotten again a few days later. For since Caesar's departure from the city in March 58, the coalition,

---

[1] Caes. *b.G.* 2, 34–3, 6, 5; Dio 39, 5, 2–4.   [2] Caes. *b.G.* 3, 7, 1.

[3] Op. cit., 2, 35, 4; Cic. *prov. cons.* 27; *Balb.* 61; *Pis.* 45 and 59; Dio 39, 5, 1; Plut. *Caes.* 21, 1–2.   [4] Cic. *Vat.* 15. Cf. *dom.* 39–40.

created and directed by himself, of the three great *principes* and the tribune Clodius had long ago collapsed. The recall of Cicero in August 57 marked a complete change in the situation; moreover, the movement for his recall had actually been led by Pompey! For when Clodius' disastrous tribunate came to an end on December 9, 58, the witches' sabbath began in earnest. With his gangs he terrorized the whole of public life and, thanks to his connections, was able to block energetic action on the part of the magistrates by constitutional obstruction. In the absence of a satisfactory police force the two courageous optimate tribunes, Titus Annius Milo and Publius Sestius, found themselves forced—with Pompey's approval—to raise an armed bodyguard of clients, freedmen and slaves. After many weeks of street fighting involving numerous dead and wounded, they managed to break the terror.[1] When the dirty work had been done, Pompey appeared on the scene and completed the rout by lifting the sentence of outlawry on Cicero which Clodius had imposed.[2] While Cicero, in his extravagant delight at victory, deluded himself that in his person the old optimate republic in all its glory was being restored, in the form which he imagined had once been realized during his consulship by the union of all the forces of law and order,[3] Pompey was quietly steering his course towards a dictatorial authority which was to offset Caesar's splendid military successes. He saw his opportunity in the need for a post to look after the corn supply, which was becoming ever more urgent in view of the great demands of the Clodian law providing free distributions. Finally the famine produced a riot on September 5, 57. This settled the matter, and even the Senate gave its consent to a consular law granting Pompey proconsular power to administer the corn supply of the whole Empire for five years as well as fifteen *legati* to assist him. Cicero put the motion to the Senate out of gratitude, but alleges that Pompey really wanted still more than this. At any rate, his agents supported a much more far-reaching tribunician proposal whereby the *curatio annonae* (administration of the corn supply) would have been combined with complete control over the treasury, navy and army, together with an *imperium* in all provinces superior to that exercised there by all regular officials.[4]

---

[1] Cic. *p. red. in sen.* 19–20; *p. red. ad Quir.* 15; *Sest.* 84, 90 and 102; Dio 39, 8, 1.

[2] Cic. *dom.* 25; Vell. 2, 45, 3.

[3] Cic. *p. red. ad Quir.* 17–18; *Sest.* 143; cf. *RE*, 7A, 933.

[4] Cic. *Att.* 4, 1, 6–7; *dom.* 3 and 16–19; Dio 39, 9, 1–10, 1. J. Béranger (*Recherches sur l'aspect idéologique du principat* (1953), 189 and 191, n. 135) remarks that *cura annonae* is not a concept of the republican constitution; for *curatio* see Cic. *dom.* 14; *leg. agr.* 2, 17; Augustus, *r.g.* 5.

That the grant of such sweeping powers could be avoided was certainly to Caesar's advantage as well. Even as it was, the tendency to play son-in-law off against father-in-law was again becoming apparent. It was said that Pompey was displeased at the news of the victories in Gaul and had even let word get round that a successor to Caesar would have to be sent before his term expired.[1] In December 57 Publius Rutilius Rufus, one of the new tribunes, who had just taken office on the 10th, launched an attack on Caesar's second agrarian law. As he later proved to be a partisan of Pompey, it may be assumed that already on this occasion he was not acting against the wishes of Pompey and his circle. Similarly on April 5, 56, Cicero believed that such an attack would not offend Pompey. The latter, in accordance with his normal practice of using men of straw, did not attend the December meeting in person. For this reason the Senate, whose optimate leaders still had no confidence in him, would not commit itself to a debate on the question.[2]

On the other hand the Egyptian problem turned up again and led to a bitter quarrel between Pompey and Crassus. In the year 57 King Ptolemy, the royal oboist, faced by a revolt of the Alexandrians, fled to his benefactor Pompey, who protected him from all attacks. His stay in Rome was marked by a series of scandals: envoys from Alexandria wishing to explain the situation to the Senate were assassinated, while Roman senators were shamelessly bribed.

The Senate became the scene of wild intrigues for and against his restoration, and over the choice of the lucky man to be entrusted with this profitable task. With the help of a Sibylline oracle the Senate decreed early in 56 that no army might be used in the enterprise. Even under these less favourable conditions, Pompey would

[1] Dio 39, 25, 1–2.

[2] Cic. Q. fr. 2, 1, 1: *fuerunt nonnulli aculei in Caesarem, contumeliae in Gellium, expostulationes cum absente Pompeio*. We do not know why Lupus abused the almost eighty-year-old consular L. Gellius Poplicola. According to Plut. *Cic*. 26, 4, he was said to have remarked in 59 that the *ager Campanus* would not be distributed in his lifetime. Nor can the kinds of complaint that he raised against Pompey be clearly explained. It is possible that he wished to make Pompey reveal how he now stood. For on January 13, 56, he proposed in the Senate that the restoration of King Ptolemy should be entrusted to Pompey, a move welcomed by Pompey's *familiares* (*fam*. 1, 1, 3; cf. Q. *fr*. 2, 2, 3). Justinus Klass (*Cicero und Caesar* (1939), 91, n. 52; 92, n. 58) did not take this into consideration. For this reason his judgment (op. cit., 125 ff.) on Cicero's proposal of April 5, 56 (*fam*. 1, 9, 8) is also at fault. Pompey was a master in the art of concealing his real wishes. On January 14, 56, Cicero dined with him after the meeting of the Senate, and reported to P. Lentulus Spinther, the proconsul of Cilicia, who was himself eager for the commission: *quem ego ipsum cum audio, prorsus eum libero omni suspicione cupiditatis; cum autem eius familiares omnium ordinum video, perspicio, id quod iam omnibus est apertum, totam rem istam iam pridem a certis hominibus non invito rege ipso consiliariisque eius esse corruptam* (*fam*. 1, 2, 3). Cf. J. P. V. D. Balsdon, *Historia* 1 (1950), 298.

have been pleased to receive the commission.[1] But the extreme optimates and Clodius—an unnatural alliance behind which he could only suspect that Crassus was lurking—combined to oppose him. It looked as if there was a general conspiracy against him: he went in serious fear of his life, and for his personal protection summoned reliable followers from his native Picenum and the communities of Cisalpine Gaul whose patronship he had inherited from his father. In March 56 the confidence of the Senate and People, which he had enjoyed a few months previously, had vanished.[2]

As a result of these upheavals Caesar's position again became more critical. As consul and since then in the two years of his proconsulship, he had shown himself a statesman with an unparalleled grasp of the domestic and foreign politics of the Empire. His indomitable will to power was ennobled by his knowledge of the remedies needed to cure the political defects of the age. In order to bring this about, he had, however, first to win himself freedom of movement against the prevailing oligarchy—a battle he ingeniously fought with his opponents' own weapons. For in combining with two other senators, who also wished to escape from the restraints imposed by the oligarchy, he made use of the same system of followers and cliques on which the rule of the nobility had so far been based. This, then, was his master strategy, and he used it to achieve his immediate aim, freedom of movement in Gaul. He found that the way to cripple the opposition of the senatorial government was to fill as many magistracies as possible with his own followers and political friends. In the process it became clear that he was continuously dependent on his alliance with Pompey and Crassus; otherwise he would not be able to dispose of a sufficient number of candidates, although he personally did his uttermost to bind ambitious people to himself. His last campaign had brought a vast amount of booty into his hands, and this wealth was at the disposal of anyone who needed it to secure his election or to give games during his term of office, provided that he guaranteed to defend the interests of the absent proconsul against his opponents. Where it seemed necessary, such arrangements were confirmed on oath or in writing. Nor did Caesar neglect to win over the ladies of the relevant circles by paying his

---

[1] The continuous account in Dio 39, 12, 1–16, 3 is confirmed by information in Cic. *fam.* 1, 1; 2; 4; 5a; 5b; 7, 2–6; Q. *fr.* 2, 2, 3; 3, 2. For a specially vivid account of the general atmosphere, see Cic. *Cael.* 23–24; 51–55; Q. *fr.* 2, 8, 2. Cf. Strab. 17, 796; Plut. *Cat. Min.* 35, 4–7; *Pomp.* 49, 9–14; Fenestella, frag. 21 (Peter); Dio Prus. 32, 70.

[2] Cic. Q. *fr.* 2, 3, 3–4; 4, 5–6; Plut. *Pomp.* 48, 11–12; Dio 39 19, 1–2.

respects to them.[1] Naturally the loyal Balbus also received a reward at this time, and became a much envied figure.[2]

But Caesar's unaided efforts were not enough for complete security. At the beginning of 56, after spending the first part of the winter in Illyricum, he moved to Aquileia,[3] and there learned that at the aedilician elections, which had been postponed until January 20 as a result of the unrest at Rome, two of his best-known followers— one of them Publius Vatinius—had been defeated.[4] Nor was Gnaeus Domitius Calvinus, a bitter opponent of his as tribune in 59 and now praetor, to his liking.[5] Yet all this was of little significance compared with the prospect of Lucius Domitius Ahenobarbus, one of the most uncompromising champions of the oligarchy, becoming consul in 55. He was now canvassing on the programme of dismissing Caesar from his illegal command.[6] A few months earlier it had looked as if this issue, on which Caesar's very existence depended, had been disposed of, but it was now revived with a vengeance, not least because Cicero in his speeches on his unconstitutional exile kept reverting to it. He went furthest at the beginning of March, when, in a speech against Vatinius, he described the latter's law on Caesar's province as murder of the ancestral constitution.[7]

Caesar now attempted to have his position ratified through a fresh bill introduced by a number of tribunes. But these simply left him in the lurch, when the consul Lentulus Marcellinus advised them

---

[1] Suet. *Caes.* 23, 2; Plut. *Caes.* 20, 2; *Pomp.* 51, 3.

[2] Cic. *Balb.* 56; 63: *est fortasse nunc nonnullorum particeps commodorum*; *Att.* 7, 7, 6.

[3] We also have information about this visit from fragments of an inscription in Salona, last published by D. Rendić-Miočević in *Studi Aquileiesi offerti a Giovanni Brusin* (Aquileia 1953), 67 ff. This shows that on March 2, 56 B.C., envoys from the island city of Issa (Vis, Lissa), which belonged to Illyricum, negotiated with the Imperator C. Caesar about their freedom, friendship and alliance with the Roman people. Their spokesman was C. Gavenius (Gabinius ?). The first lines read: ἐπὶ ὑπάτων Γν[αίο]υ Λέντυλου Μ[αρ]κελλείνου καὶ Λ[ευκ]ίου Μαρκίου Φι[λίπ]που, πρὸ ἡμερ[ῶν πέ]ντε Νωνῶν [Μαρ]τίων, [ἐν Δὲ Ἴσση] ἐπὶ ἱερομνάμο[νος] Ζωπύ[ρου. . . . After the names of the envoys, line 10 continues: ἐν Ἀκολῃία ἐπὶ Γαίου Ἰουλί[ου] Καί[σαρος] αὐτοκράτορος Γαῖος Γαυένι[ος Γαίου (?) υἱ]ὸς Φαβία λόγους ἐποήσα[το περὶ τῆς τε] ἐλευ[θε]ρίας τῶν Ἰσσαίω[ν καὶ τῆς φιλίάς] τ[ῶν Ῥωμαί]ων καὶ Ἰσσαί[ων. . . .]; frag. B, line 5 . . . . φ]ιλίαν καὶ συμμα[χίαν. . . .

On Issa, see Fluss, *RE Suppl.* 5, 349. Caesar states (*b.c.* 3, 9, 1, 49 B.C.) that 'the commander of Pompey's navy, M. Octavius, came to Salona, *ibi concitatis Dalmatis reliquisque barbaris Issam a Caesaris amicitia avertit*'. In *b. Alex.* 47, 4 Vatinius defeats Octavius in 47 and sails to Issa: *quo ut venit, oppidani supplices se Vatinio dediderunt*. R. Syme (*Historia* 7 (1958), 178, n. 3) comments that the inscription gives Caesar the title 'Imperator', which Caesar did not think worth mentioning in *b.G.* Cicero (*fam.* 7, 5) naturally addresses him by it in 54 B.C.

[4] Cic. *Vat.* 38.

[5] Ibid.

[6] Suet. *Caes.* 24, 1; Plut. *Cat. Min.* 41, 3; he was Cato's brother-in-law.

[7] Cic. *Vat.* 16–18, 23; 35 (*esne igitur patriae certissimus parricida?*), 36; 39.

against the move.[1] Further, on April 5, when the Senate found itself obliged to authorize ten million denarii for Pompey's *curatio annonae*, fierce attacks were immediately launched on the second agrarian law, which had robbed the state of the profitable Campanian domains. Cicero's proposal that the matter should be considered in the Senate on May 15 won unusually loud applause.[2] The well-meaning champion of the good old days had no inkling of the fact that Caesar's preparations for a crushing counter-stroke were already well advanced. In the course of his winter tour of the provinces, the latter had reached Ravenna, where in secret conference he renewed his alliance with Crassus.[3] Then he quietly moved to Luca at the beginning of April. On April 7 Cicero paid a farewell call on Pompey, who was about to leave for Sardinia on April 11 to give his orders for the purchase of the corn supplies on the island. On April 8 Cicero innocently wrote to his brother, who had already been busy in Sardinia for some time as *legatus* to the *curator annonae*, to say that his superior was not yet certain whether he would make the crossing from Pisa or another port.[4]

A few days later Pompey appeared at Caesar's quarters in Luca.[5] The agreements made with Crassus were now expanded and ratified by the adhesion of the third of the allies. Caesar must have shown masterful tact in composing the differences between Crassus and Pompey, since the decisions taken were of such unambiguous clarity and wide impact as to leave no trace of laborious negotiations: the great danger presented by Domitius' candidature for the consulship was to be removed by Crassus' and Pompey's themselves assuming the consulship for 55.[6] Their election was to be secured by the detailing of men on leave from Caesar's army for the purpose, and so had to be postponed until the winter, when these would be available.[7] As consuls they were both to provide themselves with

---

[1] Cic. Q. fr. 2, 4, 5. [2] Op. cit., 2, 5, 1; fam. 1, 9, 8.
[3] Cic. fam. 1, 9, 9. [4] Cic. Q. fr. 2, 5, 3.
[5] Cic. fam. 1, 9, 9; Plut. Crass. 14, 6 is surely right in stressing that the three allies negotiated without witnesses. On the other hand, Plut. Caes. 21, 5; Pomp. 51, 4; App. b.c. 2, 62 know of hordes of other visitors: so many governors that 120 lictors were counted, and more than 200 senators. Plut. Caes. 21, 5 mentions Ap. Claudius Pulcher, proconsul of Sardinia, and Q. Metellus Nepos, proconsul of Hispania Citerior (Dio 39, 54, 1–2). Of Ap. Claudius, Cic. Q. fr. 2, 4, 6 reports in March: *Appius a Caesare nondum redierat*. At that time Caesar was certainly not yet in Luca. So the simultaneous arrival of so many senators, and particularly the 120 lictors, appears to be a gross exaggeration (cf. Mommsen, RStR, 1³, 382 ff.). Surprisingly, the fact that Pompey came to an agreement with Caesar completely escaped Dio (39, 26, 3) He asserts that Pompey combined with Crassus against Caesar.
[6] Suet. Caes. 24, 1. [7] Plut. Pomp. 51, 5; Dio 39, 31, 2.

I

great commands corresponding to Caesar's present position[1] and thus to remove the disparity by which Caesar's partners of the year 59 were obviously feeling themselves increasingly handicapped. Originally they had regarded him as a 'young man' who could be used to refloat their stranded ships, but they were soon forced to recognize that in his consulship, he was going far further than they had ever dreamed. Now he put the tiller in their hands and, in addition to the consulship, granted them an *imperium* which corresponded to his own, in being secured from senatorial interference by a clause forbidding its discussion before March 1, 50. To maintain full equality they, for their part, promised to see that Caesar's *imperium* in the two Gauls was secured until the same date by a similar provision. Then in the year 48, on the expiration of the ten-year interval prescribed by law, he was also to receive a second consulship corresponding to the second term of Crassus and Pompey. By virtue of the provisions of the Sempronian law dealing with the allocation of the consular provinces, he could also expect to remain in possession of his provinces in the years 50 and 49, because the Senate would have to decide in 51 before the election of the consuls for 50 which provinces were to be allotted to them. In view of the clause forbidding discussion of his provinces these would on no account be available for this purpose: furthermore, according to the *lex Cornelia* the consuls of 50 could not normally take over the administration of their proconsular provinces before the year 49. This part of the agreement was of decisive importance for Caesar, as it obviated the danger that the proconsuls would take over the Gallic provinces as early as 49 and leave him a private citizen exposed to the vengeance of his enemies.[2]

These were the main points of the arrangements—for the time being wrapped in deep secrecy—made at Luca. Through them three individual politicians intended for a period of years utterly to subordinate Roman politics to their personal interests without regard for the organs provided by the constitution. This represented, as an

---

[1] Plut. *Caes.* 21, 6; *Pomp.* 51, 1; App. *b.c.* 2, 63.

[2] I attempted to give reasons for this interpretation of the conflicting evidence of the sources in my article in *Hermes* 63 (1928), 125 ff. (=*Kl. Schr.* 2, 216 f.). Cf. *Pompeius*², 152. A sensible discussion of the copious scholarly literature on this disputed topic is offered by J. van Ooteghem in *Pompée le Grand, Bâtisseur d'Empire* (1954), 470 ff. See, recently, the detailed article by P. J. Cuff (*Historia* 7 (1958), 445 ff.). He does not appear to me to have produced anything new and convincing. As to his p. 451, I refer to my essay 'Das erste Consulat des Pompeius und die Übertragung der grossen Imperien' (*Abh. Berlin* (1943), 1), 38 ff. (=*Kl. Schr.* 2, 184 f.) Cf. L. Wickert, *RE*, 22, 2276 to 2278.

ancient writer[1] puts it, 'a conspiracy to share the sovereignty and destroy the constitution'. In addition many points of detail were settled. Since the tribunes detailed to confirm Caesar's position had defected, it was to be given fresh recognition within a few weeks by senatorial decrees. Cicero was to be reprimanded and drawn into service; presumably the other political figures were also passed under review. Some of their political friends and followers appeared in person; among them, Appius Claudius, the brother of Clodius, on his way to Sardinia as propraetor, and Quintus Caecilius Metellus Nepos, *en route* for Nearer Spain as proconsul, had been there since March.

One would not be far wrong in describing these arrangements as entirely characterized by the stamp of Caesar's genius.[2] From whatever angle they are viewed, the same thorough exploitation of the possible appears. Every link in the chain fitted into another. Caesar subordinated his own egotism to a minute regard for equality among the confederates and yet was successful in protecting his own special advantages. How carefully he weighed up how far one could go for the time being in brutal disregard for the constitution! Yet all was permeated by the clear conviction that a fatal blow was being struck against the structure of the optimate oligarchy. Nothing was said of further plans, they would have to emerge as the situation developed.

At all events Pompey and Crassus were highly satisfied. While Caesar returned to the scene of operations, they, visibly invigorated, took the steps agreed upon for Caesar's security at Rome. Admittedly Pompey operated from a distance, since he was next occupied by his journey to Sardinia, Africa and Sicily.[3] Before the end of April he met Quintus Cicero in Sardinia and made him responsible for his brother's future good conduct. He also sent his agent, Lucius Vibullius Rufus, to Cicero personally with instructions to take no steps in the matter of the agrarian law until Pompey's return. Consequently Cicero did not attend the session on May 15.[4] Moreover, a few days later the Senate agreed to a number of decrees which could not have been more favourable to Caesar: firstly, the cost of payment for the four legions raised by him on his own initiative was in future to be met by the treasury; secondly, he was

[1] Plut. *Cat. Min.* 41, 2. Cf. Flor. 2, 13, 11–12; 15.

[2] Suet. *Caes.* 24, 1: *Crassum Pompeiumque in urbem provinciae suae Lucam extractos compulit* etc. Cf. W. Steidle, *Sueton und die antike Biographie* (1951), 41.

[3] Plut. *Pomp.* 50, 1.   [4] Cic. *Q. fr.* 2, 6; *fam.* 1, 9, 9–10.

to have ten *legati*.[1] This meant not only that fresh recognition was to be given to the Vatinian law of 59, but also that all Caesar's actions in Gaul since 58 were given full legal validity. For even the significance of the grant of funds was purely political. All knew that Caesar was perfectly capable of paying the four legions from his own resources, whereas the treasury was continually short of money.[2]

In accordance with the Sempronian law, at the beginning of June the Senate discussed what provinces were to be allocated in 54 to the consuls to be elected for 55. Inevitably Caesar's enemies now made special efforts: Caesar's *imperium* over Cisalpine Gaul and Illyricum was valid by the Vatinian law until at least March 1, 54, whereas Transalpine Gaul was available for disposal from January 1.[3] Furthermore, at the head of the consular candidates stood Lucius Domitius Ahenobarbus, who had inherited the patronship of Transalpine Gaul from his grandfather and intended, if elected, to deprive Caesar of his command.[4] Thus the suggestion was made that the two Gauls should be assigned to the consuls of 55. Others for reasons of expediency wished only to deprive Caesar of one of his provinces, either of Transalpine Gaul because it was at the free disposal of the Senate, or of Cisalpine Gaul with effect from March 1, to prevent its being the subject of another popular decree.[5]

Caesar's representatives enlisted Cicero's oratory to counter this attack and were completely successful. By the publication of this important speech, which, as it contradicted his previous political position—he himself calls it his παλινῳδία[6]—he of course found bitter to deliver, the line taken by Cicero has been preserved for all time. The burden of his case is that Caesar was the right man to complete the work which he had started in Gaul, and that this

---

[1] Cic. *fam.* 1, 7, 10; *prov. cons.* 28; *Balb.* 61. Dio 39, 25, 1 regards the ten *legati* as a senatorial commission to regulate the affairs of the newly conquered province; *Balb.* 61 (*imperatori decem legatos decrevit*) could at a pinch be understood in this way; but in view of *prov. cons.* 28, it is more natural to think of the ratification of Caesar's power to nominate *legati*, which incidentally remedied the violation of the constitution by the *Lex Vatinia*, severely criticized in Cic. *Vat.* 35.

[2] Cic. *Balb.* 61; Plut. *Caes.* 21, 7. On the question of the *acta Caesaris*, see Cic. *prov. cons.* 43–45; *fam.* 1, 9, 14.

[3] Cic. *prov. cons.* 36–37.

[4] Suet. *Caes.* 24, 1; Plut. *Cat. Min.* 41, 3. His grandfather was Cn. Domitius Ahenobarbus, who, as proconsul in 121 B.C., together with the consul Q. Fabius Maximus Allobrogicus, won victories over the Allobroges and Arverni. Cf. Münzer, *RE*, 5, 1323.

[5] Cic. *prov. cons.* 17; 36; 39.

[6] Cic. *Att.* 4, 5, 1; *RE*, 7A, 943. *Contra* J. P. V. D. Balsdon, *JRS* 52 (1962), 139.

could be accomplished within the next two years: as this represented Caesar's own wishes, he should not be prevented from so doing. The conquest of this country, of which Rome had previously possessed only a strip, was of great importance for the security of Italy, as it advanced the frontier from the Alps to the Ocean; and Caesar's good fortune offered the best guarantee that its subjugation would be speedy and complete.[1] If the Senate now left Caesar's provinces out of the reckoning for the year 54, this temporarily confirmed him in his command for this period and gave him room to develop his further secret plans.

While Caesar conducted his important negotiations with Crassus and Pompey, and, as the subsequent senatorial decrees revealed, displayed a very confident attitude as far as Gaul was concerned, in reality he was receiving most disquieting news from beyond the Alps.

As mentioned above, seven legions had gone into winter-quarters in the north of Gaul at the end of the campaigning season of 57: farthest to the west were those under young Crassus in the Anjou area. The surrounding tribes of Brittany and Normandy had all submitted to the supremacy of Rome. But during the winter there was a sudden change in their attitude. The Roman officers who entered their territory to requisition corn found themselves prisoners, to be released only in exchange for the Celtic hostages in the hands of Crassus, and the communities joined together for a common defence of their ancestral freedom. The movement originated with the Veneti, a warlike maritime tribe from the south of Brittany, and soon spread towards the east and south. Kinsfolk even crossed over from Britain.[2]

To prepare for an advance against the seat of the rebellion, Caesar gave instructions, while he was still in north Italy, for the building of a Roman fleet on the Loire and the recruitment of crews from the old province.[3] At the beginning of May he arrived there himself and boldly decided to divide his forces into five groups in order to hold down simultaneously the tribes from Brittany to the Rhine and on the other side to the Pyrenees. He personally led the land attack on the Veneti, but it was not until the late summer that the arrival of the fleet under Decimus Brutus, a most talented young

---

[1] Cic. prov. cons. 29, 32; 33: semitam tantum Galliae tenebamus antea, patres conscripti; ceterae partes a gentibus aut inimicis huic imperio aut infidis aut certe inmanibus et barbaris et bellicosis tenebantur; quas nationes nemo umquam fuit quin frangi domarique cuperet; cf. 34–35.

[2] Caes. b.G. 3, 9, 10.   [3] Ibid., 3, 9, 1; Dio 39, 4, 3.

subordinate, brought a decision. Although he was not yet a senator—incidentally, through his mother Sempronia he may have been a grandson of Gaius Gracchus—Caesar's keen eyes had picked him out for this responsible post.[1] He succeeded in destroying the entire fleet of the Veneti and thus forced the tribe to submit. On this occasion Caesar was ruthless: he had all the councillors executed, and the rest of the population were sold on the slave market. He alleged that he did this to impress on the barbarians the sacrosanctity of ambassadors—as if Roman requisitioning officers had ambassadorial status.[2]

At the same time the *legatus* Quintus Titurius Sabinus defeated the rebels in Normandy and brought them back under Roman rule. The young Crassus did splendidly: with only twelve Roman cohorts, beside some Celtic cavalry, he advanced into Aquitania and there, in a victorious battle, shattered a force of Aquitani many times larger than his own and reinforced by their Spanish neighbours under experienced leaders from the time of Sertorius. As a result a series of Aquitanian tribes (between the Garonne and the Pyrenees) submitted to Rome and furnished hostages.[3]

Labienus maintained peace in the territory of the Belgae up to the Rhine with his Celtic cavalry.[4] In the autumn Caesar himself undertook a campaign in Flanders against the Morini who lived there, but their land was so thickly wooded that he could make no great impression on them. The Roman army took up winter-quarters in the newly-pacified area between the Seine and the Loire.[5]

As usual Caesar made his way back over the Alps.[6] In Rome things had developed as planned. As Crassus and Pompey had failed to give the correct legal notice of their candidature, the energetic consul, Gnaeus Cornelius Lentulus Marcellinus, made it clear to them that there could be no question of their election while he was in office. Thereupon, despite the strongest opposition from the Senate, they got the tribune Gaius Cato to paralyse all electoral activity in the year 56, so that they would be able to secure their own election during an interregnum early in 55. Whatever steps the opposition took, it could not prevail against the combined front of

---

[1] Caes. *b.G.* 3, 11, 5; Münzer, *RE*, 2A, 1446; *Suppl.* 5, 370; *Röm. Adelsp.* (1920), 273.

[2] Caes. *b.G.* 3, 7, 4–16, 4; Dio 39, 40, 1–43, 5; Cic. *Balb.* 64; P. Merlet, *RE*, 8A, 742–752. The *civitas* continued to exist under the Empire: cf. Plin. *n.h.* 4, 107.

[3] Caes. *b.G.* 3, 17, 1–27, 2; Dio 39, 45, 1–46, 4.

[4] Caes. *b.G.* 3, 11, 1–2.   [5] Caes. *b.G.* 3, 28, 1–29, 3.

[6] Caes. *b.G.* 4, 6, 1; 5, 1, 1.

the three dynasts.[1] This was most impressively demonstrated, when
in September 56 Lucius Cornelius Balbus, Caesar's trusted agent,
was—on purely political grounds—brought to trial for usurping
Roman citizenship. The advocacy of no lesser men than Pompey,
Crassus and Cicero secured his acquittal.[2]

Then in January 55 the consular elections were completed. Of
the rival candidates only Lucius Domitius Ahenobarbus, tirelessly
encouraged by his brother-in-law Marcus Porcius Cato, remained
in the field. With Caesar's approval the young Publius Crassus
brought a thousand men on leave from over the Alps in solid ranks.
These sufficed to make certain of the election result.[3] Nevertheless,
during the night before the poll Domitius ventured to go to the
Campus Martius with his friends. Cato hoped that at the last moment
a majority might after all be found, even if hitherto intimidation
had been fairly general. Since Crassus and Pompey wished to avoid a
surprise of this kind, they had their opponent and his followers
forcibly removed. Cato's torch-bearer was killed and Cato himself
wounded in the arm, while Domitius took refuge in his house.
On the next day Crassus and Pompey became consuls, and immediately manipulated the election of the remaining magistrates as
suited them.[4] Their most important action was that at the first
electoral assembly they blocked Cato's election to the praetorship
by the disbursement of vast sums and the well-known obstructive
device of announcing that they had heard thunder. In his place they
secured this post for Publius Vatinius.[5]

In the following weeks the tribune Gaius Trebonius promoted the
bill granting the two consuls the provinces of Spain and Syria for
five years with unlimited powers to raise troops, declare war and
make peace. Supported by two tribunes, Cato battled against it

[1] Dio 39, 27, 1–30, 4; Plut. *Pomp.* 51, 6–8; Cic. *Att.* 4, 5, 2 (June 56): *quoniam qui nihil
possunt, ii me nolunt amare, demus operam ut ab iis qui possunt diligamur; fam.* 1, 7, 10 (July 56):
*nam, qui plus opibus, armis, potentia valent, perfecisse tamen mihi videntur stultitia et inconstantia
adversariorum, ut etiam auctoritate iam plus valerent; har. resp.* 55 (August 56): *qui sine contro-
versia plus possunt; fam.* 1, 8, 1 (January 55): *sunt quidem (res communes) certe in amicorum no-
strorum potestate atque ita, ut nullam mutationem umquam hac hominum aetate habitura res esse
videatur; Q. fr.* 2, 7, 3 (February 55): *tenent omnia idque ita omnis intellegere volunt.*
[2] Cic. *Balb.* 17.
[3] Dio 39, 31, 2. He also mentions such leave in 39, 5, 3—perhaps independent evidence to
be taken with Caes. *b.G.* 3, 2, 2: *compluribus singillatim qui commeatus petendi causa missi erant
absentibus.* In Cic. *Q. fr.* 2, 7, 2 (February 55), Cicero meets P. Crassus at his father's house in
Rome: *fuit huic sermoni P. Crassus adulescens nostri, ut scis, studiosissimus* (cf. *Brut.* 281).
[4] Dio 39, 31; Plut. *Cat. Min.* 41, 3–42, 1; *Pomp.* 52, 1–2; *Crass.* 15, 4–7; App. *b.c.* 2, 64;
Cic. *Att.* 4, 8a, 2 (presumably in November 56, because of the reference to *ludi (plebei ?)*).
[5] Cic. *Q. fr.* 2, 7, 3; Dio 39, 32; Plut. *Cat. Min.* 42, 2–6; *Pomp.* 52, 3.

with great courage, but could not succeed against the campaign of violence. The bill was pushed through at the cost of four dead and many wounded. Crassus personally drew a senator's blood.[1]

Next the two consuls together sponsored a law which fulfilled their obligations towards Caesar.[2] In April they drew lots for their provinces, Pompey receiving the two Spains,[3] as he wished, and Crassus Syria. They both immediately enlisted troops and sent *legati* to take over their territories. While Crassus left Rome as early as the middle of November, Pompey despite his proconsulship remained in the vicinity of the city for the purpose, as it was euphemistically put in the dynasts' circles, of maintaining order there. His *curatio annonae* could provide him with a legal pretext for so doing.[4] In fact, the elections for the following year had shown that the party of the constitution was not yet defenceless. For on this occasion, as colleague of Appius Claudius Pulcher, Lucius Domitius Ahenobarbus succeeded in reaching the consulship, and Cato became praetor.[5]

After the agreed division of power had been legally ratified, Caesar left to rejoin his army earlier in the year than usual.[6] News had come that under pressure from the Suebian migration two Germanic peoples, the Usipetes and Tencteri, had crossed the Rhine in the north of what is now the state of North Rhine-Westphalia. Several Celtic states showed readiness to take them into their service, and the Germans moved first southwards and then to the east towards the lower Moselle.[7] As soon as Caesar had summoned

---

[1] Dio 39, 33, 2; 34; Plut. *Pomp.* 52, 4; *Cat. Min.* 43, 1–7; *Crass.* 35, 3.

[2] Dio 39, 36, 2. Earlier (in 33, 3–4) he asserts, in line with his omission of the meeting at Luca, that Caesar's friends were unpleasantly surprised by the *Lex Trebonia*; and, just as erroneously, that the consuls could only appease them by also renewing Caesar's *imperium* for three years (!). If Dio found this in a source, a contemporary must deliberately have distorted the truth in favour of Pompey. Cf. Plut. *Pomp.* 52, 4; *Cat. Min.* 43, 8; App. *b.c.* 2, 65; Vell. 2, 46, 2.

[3] Cic. *Att.* 4, 9, 1 (April 27, 55), of Pompey: *Syriam spernens, Hispaniam iactans.*

[4] Dio 39, 39, 1–7; *fam.* 7, 5, 1; Caes. *b.G.* 6, 1, 2 (on 53 B.C.) of Pompey: *quoniam ipse ad urbem cum imperio rei publicae causa remaneret*; Cic. *fam.* 1, 9, 20; *Att.* 4, 13, 2 (November 55); Plut. *Cic.* 26, 1; Vell. 2, 48, 1.

[5] Caes. *b.G.* 5, 1, 1; Plut. *Cat. Min.* 44, 1.

[6] Caes. *b.G.* 4, 6, 1.

[7] Caes. *b.G.* 4, 9, 3; 10, 1; 12, 1; 15, 2: *ad confluentem Mosae et Rheni*; 16, 2. With Holmes, *Caesar's Conquest of Gaul*[2], 74 f.; 691–697, I am of the opinion that, at least in the last two passages, the Moselle, not the Meuse, is meant. Cf. Flor. 1, 45, 14: *hic vero iam Caesar ultro Mosellam navali ponte transgreditur ipsumque Rhenum et Hercyniis hostem quaerit in silvis.* The Ubii, for whose protection Caesar crossed the Rhine, lived north of the lower Main (L. Schmidt, *Die Westgermanen*, 2 (1940), 209). Caesar (*b.G.* 6, 9, 3) says of the second Rhine bridge: *paulo supra eum locum quo ante exercitum traduxerat.* Dio 39, 47, 1 speaks of the land of the Treveri.

the Celtic cavalry contingents, he followed after the Germans in the direction of Coblenz, and soon met with a delegation from the two peoples. They requested him either to allot them land on the left bank of the Rhine or to allow them to conquer some for themselves, arguing that the Romans would find them useful friends. Caesar explained that there was no room for them in Gaul, but said that they could settle among the Ubii on the right bank, since these had approached him for protection against the Suebi. At this stage the delegation asked for three days' grace during which Caesar was to halt his advance, while they went to fetch their people's answer. Caesar asserts that they intended to use this time to collect their cavalry, which was away looking for corn. For this reason he continued to move forward to within twelve miles from where the Germans were encamped. Here the delegation again asked him to halt his troops and to give them three days' grace to allow them to come to an agreement with the Ubii. Caesar promised to advance only another four miles to a watering place, and to order his cavalry, who formed the advance guard, to avoid hostilities. However, it came to a cavalry engagement, and the Germans ignominiously routed the Celts who outnumbered them by six to one. On the next day all the German princes and leading men appeared in Caesar's camp and begged his forgiveness for the events of the day before and for a fresh armistice. Instead of this Caesar ordered their arrest and pushed on in military formation to the unsuspecting German camp. Since no organized resistance was offered, the soldiers forced their way in and the migrants scattered. Caesar later asserted that they suffered 430,000 fatalities in all, for the most part through his pursuit, without the loss of a single man on the Roman side. After their peoples had been destroyed, he released the arrested princes.[1]

He used the next month to advance across the Rhine. A section of the German cavalry, who had not been present when Caesar made his surprise attack, escaped to the Sugambri (on the right bank of the Rhine to the north of the Ubii, as far as the region of the Lippe). When these scornfully rejected his demand that they should surrender the fugitives, on the ground that he had no authority on the far side of the Rhine, Caesar felt himself forced to make a demonstration of Roman power for their benefit. At

[1] Caes. b.G. 4, 4–15; Dio 39, 47, 1–48, 2; Plut. Caes. 22, 1–5; App. Celt. 18, 1–4.

the same time the Ubii requested him to put in an appearance and so give them peace from the Suebi. Within ten days a firm bridge was built in the Neuwied basin. Caesar spent eighteen days on the right bank of the Rhine without seeing an enemy, and then returned and had the bridge demolished.[1]

If he was here only concerned for the military security of the Rhine frontier, by contrast the reconnaissance in strength of Britain, which he undertook with two legions in the autumn of 55, was to serve as a prelude to the permanent annexation of the country.

There were close political ties between the Celts on either side of the Channel; at times they had formed a unified kingdom, and in the recent battles, particularly during the war with the Veneti in the previous year, British Celts had actually fought against Caesar. In addition, Britain was held to be a rich country. It was supposed to contain corn, cattle, gold, silver and iron.[2] Diplomatic negotiations with representatives from several British states, who arrived as soon as Caesar's intentions became known, prepared the ground for the expedition. With them on their return journey he sent Commius the Atrebate, whom in return for his good services he had made king over his state and who presumably had connections with the British Atrebates. In the event, the Britons arrested him, and only released him after Caesar had landed.[3] Nothing was achieved in the military sphere, since it proved impossible to bring over the ships containing the cavalry.[4] However, Caesar maintained his camp intact, and after storms had caused considerable damage to his fleet, the expeditionary force regained the continent without suffering too heavy casualties. But for two exceptions, the hostages which Caesar had demanded from all the communities with whom he had come into contact naturally failed to materialize.[5]

[1] Caes. *b.G.* 4, 16–19; Dio 39, 48, 3–49, 2; Plut. *Caes.* 22, 6–23, 1; Cic. *Pis.* 81 (September 55) of Caesar: *ei, cum tantas res gessisset gereretque cotidie, non amicus esse non possem, cuius ego imperium, non Alpinum vallum contra ascensum transgressionemque Gallorum, non Rheni fossam gurgitibus illis redundantem Germanorum inmanissimis gentibus obicio et oppono. perfecit ille, ut si montes resedissent, amnes exaruissent, non naturae praesidio, sed victoria sua rebusque gestis Italiam munitam haberemus.* The reference to the Rhine makes it possible that at the time news of the Rhine crossing or of preparation for it had reached Rome.

[2] Caes. *b.G.* 5, 12, 3–5; Strab. 4, 199. Cf. Cic. *fam.* 7, 7, 1; Suet. *Caes.* 47: *Britanniam petisse spe margaritarum.*

[3] Caes. *b.G.* 4, 20, 1–21; 9; 27, 2–5.   [4] Op. cit., 4, 26, 5; 28, 2–3.

[5] Op. cit., 4, 22, 3–38, 4; Dio 39, 51, 1–53, 1; Plut. *Caes.* 23, 2–3.

However, in Rome this journey to the fabled island made a tremendous impression, and an obliging Senate—attendance at different meetings varied considerably—responded to Caesar's report on the completed year of operations with a thanksgiving of twenty days.[1] By contrast the refusal of the small group of convinced optimates to have anything to do with the admired *imperator* was all the more blunt. At the same meeting Cato, the praetor designate, without more ado made the counter-proposal that Caesar should be handed over to the Germans to atone for his infamous breach of faith so that the curse might fall not on Rome but on the guilty party. However seriously this was intended, it remained only a demonstration; meanwhile the Senate decided to appoint a delegation to investigate the manifold charges raised against the light-hearted way in which Caesar was continually involving the state in new wars without any regard for the principles of legality. When the target of this attack countered with a letter, couched in the sharpest terms, protesting against Cato's behaviour, Cato justified his attitude so convincingly that Caesar's agents regretted that they had read out the letter. We then hear no more about the upshot of this business or even whether the senatorial commission was ever sent off.[2] But Caesar's military commentaries show that he wished to justify his behaviour by asserting that the treacherous surprise

---

[1] Caes. *b.G.* 4, 38, 5; Dio 39, 53, 2; Cicero (*Att.* 4, 13, 1, of November 15, 55=end of October, Jul.) was not present at this meeting of the Senate; Caesar began his return from Britain before September 21 (Jul.); cf. *b.G.* 4, 36, 2. Consequently, the report of his campaign could already be dealt with by the Senate: *ego . . . afuisse me in altercationibus quas in senatu factas audio fero non moleste. nam aut defendissem quod non placeret aut defuissem cui non oporteret.*

[2] Plut. *Cat. Min.* 51, 1–5; Caes. *b.G.* 22, 4, with the assertion that this was reported by Tanusius, in line with App. *Celt.* 18, 2 (τῶν τις συγγραφέων). On Tanusius Geminus, see Münzer, *RE*, 4A, 2231, who conjectures that he was a senator. Suet. *Caes.* 24, 3: *nec deinde ulla belli occasione, ne iniusti quidem ac periculosi abstinuit, tam foederatis quam infestis ac feris gentibus ultro lacessitis, adeo ut senatus quondam legatos ad explorandum statum Galliarum mittendos decreverit ac nonnulli dedendum eum hostibus censuerint.* Cf. W. Steidle, *Sueton u. d. antike Biographie* (1951), 42, 1. Plut. *Caes.* 22, 2 and App. *Celt.* 18, 3 point to a common source in that they both refer to Caesar's contradictory statement in the remarkable terms Καῖσαρ ἐν ταῖς ἐφημερίσι and Καῖσαρ ἐν ταῖς Ἰδίαις ἀναγραφαῖς τῶν ἐφημέρων ἔργων. This leads to the conclusion that it has been transmitted through a Greek writer, e.g. Asinius Pollio of Tralles (*FgrHist* no. 193). Another question is whether Plut. *Cat. Min.* and Suetonius go back only to Tanusius. It may be assumed that Cato's friend Munatius Rufus (Plut. *Cat. Min.* 37, 1; cf. Peter, *HRF*, p. 83) reported this attack by Cato. See the previous note, where I should like to relate the *altercationes* mentioned by Cicero to this incident (*RE*, 7A, 953). Cato's religious motivation was nothing unusual for the senators. Two months earlier Cicero had argued on the same lines against Caesar's father-in-law L. Piso (*Pis.* 84–85): as proconsul of Macedonia, *Denseletis* (on the upper reaches of the Strymon) . . . *nefarium bellum et crudele intulisti . . . tua scelera di immortales in nostros milites expiaverunt. qui cum novo genere morbi affligerentur neque se recreare quisquam posset qui semel incidisset, dubitabat nemo quin violati hospites, legati necati, pacati atque socii nefario bello lacessiti, fana vexata hanc tantam efficerent vastitatem.*

attack of the German cavalry had forced his hand, and the point of the vast numbers which he gives is to emphasize the enormity of the danger which he averted from what was now Roman Gaul, without the sacrifice of a single Roman life. As was his custom, he refuted his critics by a plain statement which, by reference to the facts themselves, demonstrated how brilliantly he was fulfilling his duty as a Roman proconsul.[1]

He remained in Gaul until after the start of the new official year of 54 (until the middle of November 55 according to the later improved Julian calendar) in order to prepare for his great expedition to Britain.[2] On this occasion he was accompanied by Marcus, the elder of the two sons of his ally Crassus, as quaestor.[3] During the winter he had a fleet built on a carefully thought-out plan; it was to be capable of transporting five legions and 2,000 cavalry. But the political safeguards for an enterprise, which was to proceed with a large country in its rear which had just been subdued and whose powers of resistance were not yet sufficiently broken, demanded no less care than the military preparations. Roman domination was not yet a fate to which the Gallic nation was reconciled. It could only be maintained with the willing help of parties friendly to Rome in each state. Everywhere conditions were

---

[1] As has been stressed, especially by Ed. Norden (*Die germanische Urgeschichte in Tacitus Germania* (1920), 87 ff.), Caesar's *commentarii* are based on the dispatches sent to the Senate. But it seems to me that on publication in January 51 Caesar strengthened the allusions to the malicious breaches of faith by the Germans in view of the charges made against him: already during their infiltration into the land of the Menapii on the left bank of the Rhine *simulaverunt* (4, 4, 5); their boast during the first negotiations with Caesar (7, 5) that apart from the Suebi *in terris esse neminem quem non superare possint*; in 9, 3 Caesar notices that their request for an armistice of three days is merely an excuse to call back their cavalry; likewise (11, 2-4) their second request; nevertheless (11, 6) he orders his cavalry commanders not to attack; (12 1) *nihil timentibus nostris, quod legati eorum paulo ante a Caesare discesserant atque is dies indutiis erat ab his petitus*, they are treacherously attacked by the Germans; (3-6) on the Roman side seventy-four dead, among them a distinguished Aquitanian; for this reason Caesar wishes to have nothing more to do with negotiations (13, 1) *ab iis qui per dolum atque insidias petita pace ultro bellum intulissent*; (13, 2) to wait until they were reinforced by their cavalry *summae dementiae esse iudicabat*; (13, 4) *consilio cum legatis et quaestore communicato* given particular prominence to show that his subordinates are united with him; of the return of the German envoys in large numbers *eadem et simulatione et perfidia usi*; (13, 5) *ut si quid possent, de indutiis fallendo impetrarent*; (13, 6) for this reason *sibi Caesar oblatos gavisus illos retineri iussit*; (14, 3) *milites nostri pristini diei perfidia incitati*; Caesar's demand to the Sugambri (16, 3) *qui sibi Galliaeque bellum intulissent, sibi dederent*. A settlement of Germans in the newly pacified Gaul would have incited the Gauls to revolt: 5, 1; 6, 1; 8, 2; 13, 3. The irony of the closing sentence deserves special attention (15, 4): *Caesar iis, quos in castris retinuerat, discedendi potestatem fecit. illi supplicia cruciatusque Gallorum veriti, quorum agros vexaverant, remanere se apud eum velle dixerunt. his Caesar libertatem concessit.*

[2] Caes. *b.G.* 5. 1, 1.   [3] Op. cit., 5, 24, 3; 46, 1.

different. In some cases—as in those of the Atrebates, Carnutes and
Senones—Caesar installed as kings nobles loyal to himself,[1] or—as
was the case with the Eburones—he recognized existing principalities.[2] Elsewhere, however, he thought it to his advantage to
support the aristocracy against attempts at autocracy; this was the
case with the Aedui, Sequani and Suessiones.[3] Caesar had to keep
all these circumstances continually before his eyes and to bind his
followers to himself by plying them with fresh rewards. Thus
he reports in passing how he secured the senior magistracy in their
state for two distinguished Allobroges, arranged for them to become
members of their council before their turn, made them presents of
confiscated goods and money seized as booty and treated them as
trusted friends.[4] This is only one example out of hundreds not
recorded. In his overall policy he used the same principles as he
did towards each individual state. The Celts were used to small
neighbours grouping themselves as clients around the leading states.
Caesar now recognized the Aedui and Remi as leading states,[5] and
the communities who became their clients were favoured by him.
On the other side he could hope most easily to bind his followers to
himself by giving them positions of honour of this kind; Commius,
the Atrebate prince who had served Caesar very well, was rewarded
by his state's being exempted from tribute, while he also received
sovereignty over the Morini.[6]

The same man devised the daring plans of campaign and thought
out all the details of their execution. When he was with his army
he was to be seen tirelessly riding or travelling around its positions.
He often even spent the night in his carriage or litter so as to waste
no time. On the march he shared the hardships of the common
soldier, striding on in front and not caring whether he exposed his
bare head to rain or sun.[7] But this covers only one side of his restless
activity. All Roman senators who were temporarily governing a
distant province continued to regard the Senate House and Forum
as the centre of political life and felt themselves affected by every
detail of what went on there; accordingly they strove to keep in
continuous contact with them through a brisk exchange of correspondence. Caesar had already grown far above the ordinary
consulars and he could only maintain his position by persistently

---

[1] Op. cit., 4, 21, 7; 5, 25, 1; 54, 2.   [2] Op. cit., 5, 26, 2; 27, 2.
[3] Op. cit., 1, 3, 4; 18, 9; 20, 6; 2. 13, 1.   [4] Caes. b.c. 3, 59, 1–2.
[5] Caes. b.G. 6, 12, 7.   [6] Op. cit., 7, 76, 1.
[7] Suet. Caes. 57; Plut. Caes. 17, 2–7.

influencing the course of events at Rome. Fortunately Cicero's correspondence for the year 54 gives us an opportunity to follow his achievements in this field.[1]

He had detailed reports sent to him about all political business, great and small, and based his decisions on them. Gaius Oppius,[2] who from 54 appears next to the experienced Cornelius Balbus as his most important agent, directed this news service. Balbus himself, who had hitherto been the general's personal adjutant (*praefectus fabrum*),[3] transferred completely to the diplomatic service at the end of 55 and was replaced by Mamurra, a knight from Formiae well-known as a voluptuary, who also tried his hand at verses. He had been immortalized by the hate-ridden lampoons of Catullus.[4] The poet from Verona had gone out to Bithynia in 57 on the staff of Gaius Memmius, and returned home thoroughly disgruntled.[5] Things were different with Caesar; all who enlisted in his service soon became very rich. Labienus and Balbus provided the best examples of this.[6] The thought that the stuck-up *bon viveur* Mamurra would in future be squandering the wealth of Gaul and Britain roused Catullus to such a pitch of fury—not only against Mamurra, but also against his important benefactor—that without more ado he designated Caesar as a libertine of the same order who shared the vices of his notorious companion. The poet's father was one of the notables of Verona, at whose house the proconsul regularly stayed when on circuit, and so was considerably worried by the shocking impertinence of his son's verses. For Caesar left no room for doubt that he was seriously offended at being stigmatized in this way. In the spring of 54, while Caesar was residing in North Italy, the young Catullus had to agree to beg for the great man's forgiveness. As further revenge could bring Caesar no political advantage, that was the end of the matter as far as he was

---

[1] From 54 to 52 B.C. Cicero's brother Quintus was with Caesar as a *legatus*. We learn of this from Cic. Q. *fr.* 2, 10–3, 9 (all letters of the year 54) and from a letter from Quintus (*fam*. 16, 16) of 53 B.C. In addition we have in the collection (*fam*. 7, 6–18) the letters that Cicero wrote in the years 54 and 53 to his young friend C. Trebatius Testa, who was later to become a famous lawyer. They are preceded by the characteristic letter of recommendation to Caesar. Trebatius was not a military tribune (8, 1). Caesar consulted him as an adviser on the administration of justice (10, 1; 11, 2; 13, 1; Q. *fr.* 2, 13, 3). Cf. Sonnet, *RE*, 6A, 2257; W. Kunkel, *Herkunft und soziale Stellung der römischen Juristen* (1952), 28; the juristic fragments in O. Lenel, *Palingenesia iuris civilis* (1889), 2, 343 ff.

[2] Q. *fr.* 3, 1, 8; 10; 13; 18; *Att.* 4, 17, 7.   [3] Cic. *Balb.* 64.

[4] Plin. *n.h.* 36, 48; Catull. 29; 41; 43; 57; presumably also 94; 105; 114; 115; cf. Münzer, *RE*, 14, 966.

[5] Catull. 10, 7; 28, 9.   [6] Cic. *Att.* 6. 7, 7.

concerned, and on the very same day he invited his host's son to dinner.[1].

Even now Balbus remained for some time at headquarters. After he had spent the beginning of the year in Rome, we find him in northern Italy in the spring of 54, and also with Caesar during his expedition to Britain. But immediately on its return he was sent back to Rome and was to stay there until May 15, 53. In fact, in a letter dated April 8, Cicero refers to his continued presence there.[2] His chief task must have been to keep intact the connection with Pompey. For the same purpose Pompey sent his adjutant Lucius Vibullius Rufus to Gaul as occasion offered.[3] There was also plenty of other diplomatic business which could not be settled in writing. In general, all correspondence and personal contact with Caesar went through Balbus. When Cicero wishes to recommend a young friend to the general, he does so after consultation with Balbus; when he writes to Caesar he encloses a letter for Balbus; and when he does not dare to bother Caesar, he puts his request before Balbus. The friendly reception which met Quintus Cicero on his arrival at Caesar's camp in the summer of 54 is ascribed largely to the influence of Balbus.[4]

There was a special office at headquarters for political correspondence.[5] In the first years of Caesar's proconsulship this was run by Gnaeus Pompeius Trogus, a Roman citizen of Celtic origin. At all events he was above all Caesar's adviser and helper in Celtic affairs.[6] We do not know how long he held this post, as he is not mentioned by Caesar. In any case, the office seems later to have been run by Aulus Hirtius, to whom we are indebted for the eighth book of the Gallic War and very probably for other continuations of Caesarian military history.[7] Caesar showed how highly

[1] Suet. *Caes.* 73; cf. Catull. 54, 6: *irascere iterum meis iambis inmerentibus, unice imperator.*
[2] Cic. *Q. fr.* 2, 10, 4; 3, 1, 9; 12; *fam.* 7, 5, 2; 6, 1; 9, 1; 18, 3.
[3] Cic. *Q. fr.* 3, 1, 18.   [4] *fam.* 7, 5, 2; 6, 1; 7, 1; 9, 1; *Q. fr.* 3, 1, 9.
[5] Caes. *b.G.* 5, 47, 2: *litterae publicae.*
[6] Iustin. 43, 11–12: *in postremo libro Trogus: maiores suos a Vocontiis* (in Dauphiné) *originem ducere; avum suum Trogum Pompeium Sertoriano bello civitatem a Cn. Pompeio percepisse, patruum Mithridatico bello turmas equitum sub eodem Pompeio duxisse; patrem quoque sub C. Caesare militasse epistularumque et legationum, simul et annuli curam habuisse.* On the Vocontii, see O. Hirschfeld, *Kl. Schr.* 62 ff.
[7] *b.G.* 8, *praef.* 6. In a letter of Q. Cicero of 44 B.C. (*fam.* 16, 27, 2) he is described as a crony of Mark Antony. The latter joined Caesar in 54 (Cic. *Phil.* 2, 49) and was his quaestor in 52 (Caes. *b.G.* 8, 2, 1; Cic. *Att.* 6, 6, 4; *fam.* 2, 15, 4). Hirtius probably became tribune in 48 (Dio 42, 20, 1; Cic. *Phil.* 13, 32). A *rog(atio) Hirtia* is mentioned in a fragment of an inscription (*CIL,* 1², 2, 604). Cf. Broughton, *MRR,* 2, 274. Vonder Mühll, *RE,* 8, 1957, prefers 46, the year of his praetorship.

he valued him by later nominating him for the consulship for the year 43.

In return, these men were filled with unbounded admiration for their general. Despite the significant role which they played on the political stage, they knew very well that they were no more than tools in the master's hand. A large part of Caesar's greatness lies in this ability to imbue others with his own intentions and with their help to increase the effectiveness of his own personality. He radiated a personal magic against which only his toughest political opponents—at times perhaps only Cato—were proof. The longer the Gallic War lasted, the more tense the military as well as the general political situation became. Every day there was the possibility of a new development somewhere that could undo everything. Yet notwithstanding this, Caesar could, when he wanted, at any hour of the day display the most fascinating charm, tender consideration and hilarious good humour. Cicero experienced this in full measure—so we can judge incidentally how highly experts rated his political significance.[1]

In his heart of hearts he always found Caesar's demonic power over men unnatural. Furthermore, in his exile he had learned the painful lesson that it trampled without mercy upon all who dared to stand in its way. On his return he felt himself called to give new substance to the old optimate concept by making the union of all men of good will his watchword,[2] and again found himself faced by the wounding aversion to the *homo novus* of the very nobility whose supremacy he wished to save; he had imagined that his services and sufferings had made this a thing of the past. In this mood he was not insusceptible to the call which went out to him from Pompey and Caesar to represent their interests. The change in his relationship with them not only protected him from Clodius, but also gave him a new standing *vis-à-vis* the arrogant men who still regarded themselves as the only true optimates. For a time in 56 he even fondly imagined that his change of front pointed a way by which the two 'dynasts' could combine with the other *principes* to oppose the revolutionary conduct of Clodius.[3] Naturally this hope was short-lived, as it was too obviously contradicted by facts, and from 55 he absorbed himself more and more in the task of portraying in masterfully composed dialogues his ideal of the perfect

[1] *RE*, 7A, 956.
[2] In the speech for P. Sestius at the beginning of March 56 (*RE*, 7A, 932–933).
[3] In the speech on the verdict of the *haruspices*, August 56 (*RE*, 7A, 945–947).

orator and statesman. This was high above everyday politics and, on the other hand, worlds removed from Caesar's vigorous activity. For, as emerged ever more clearly from his proconsulship, this was dictated by the needs of imperial policy, while Cicero still looked for Rome's salvation to a renewal of her old constitution understood in its true sense. He had never grasped this essential contrast, but, following the concepts of Greek constitutional theory, was forced to include Caesar's struggle for power in the category of tyranny— which at once implied the severest judgment which he could pass.[1] This makes it all the more significant that in this year, despite all their differences, Cicero came to have friendly dealings with Caesar. Clearly the latter's very absence helped to bring this about. The Senate was the scene of Cicero's political activity and, whereas (one might say) all its other members irritated him, he did not meet Caesar there. On the contrary, in his isolation the high regard in which he was held by Caesar gave him a double pleasure. While the optimates by birth never recognized him as their equal, and Pompey with his cold and scheming egoism kept rejecting his over-tures, Caesar treated him with incomparable graciousness as his intellectual equal, with a natural right to corresponding political rank.[2]

At the beginning of 54 Caesar used the chronic financial embar-rassment of the consular living above his means to help him out with a considerable loan—apparently 200,000 denarii—in so far as his own 'straitened circumstances' allowed, as he wrote in jest.[3] This favour

---

[1] It was generally recognized that Roman rule over the provinces had to be continually defended and secured anew by force of arms. In the speech on the consular provinces in June 56, Cicero himself had admirably developed this theme (RE, 7A, 941–943), and Caesar takes this point of view for granted when he briefly explains the necessity for crossing the Rhine or sailing to Britain (b.G. 4, 16, 1; 20, 1). But the optimates refused to admit that in an era of extensive provincial empire the annually changing magistrates no longer satisfied its require-ments, although in the military sphere they already saw themselves forced to replace the citizen levies, called up for a limited period, by long-service professional soldiers. Pompey and Caesar tacitly allowed for this revolutionary change. But it is characteristic that in political journalism it was never, as far as I know, discussed. Men felt the approach of a military monarchy; however, this concept seemed so incompatible with the traditional res publica that, recalling Sulla, they spoke with abhorrence of tyranny (dominatio), but no one dared openly to recommend such a change in the constitution. At the most, in these years, men began to speak of the necessity of a dictatorship (Cic. Q. fr. 2, 13, 5; 3, 4, 1; 7, 2; 8, 4; Att. 4, 18, 3; against this background rep. 1, 63; 6, 12). Even this was suspect; but the dictator-ship was an institution sanctioned by Roman constitutional law and, according to republican notions, it was regarded as a temporary stage. The real question, however, was whether the old res publica with its principles of yearly office, collegiate power and the veto could be maintained.

[2] Demonstrated in fam. 1, 9, 11–18.

[3] Q. fr. 2, 10, 5; Att. 5, 1, 2; 4, 3; 5, 2; 6, 2; 7, 3, 11; 8, 5; cf. RE, 7A, 977.

K

did not fail to make its impression on Cicero; he now felt obliged
to show sincere gratitude to the great man, and did his utmost to
comply with his wish that he should not withdraw from political
business at Rome.[1] For the summer campaign Quintus Cicero
entered the proconsul's service as *legatus* and became a new means
of tying his brother to him. The most insignificant action or utterance by Cicero in Caesar's favour was repaid in the Gallic headquarters by some favour or other shown to the *legatus*. In autumn
54 Cicero writes that Quintus is being treated as if his brother were
the general: Caesar had allowed him to choose his own winter-
quarters.[2] But on other occasions also Cicero always found ears
ready to hear his requests. In the spring, when he had recommended
a man to Caesar, the reply came back that he was to become king
of Gaul or something equally splendid, and Cicero was asked to
send a second man at once. Cicero now requested a post for the
young lawyer Trebatius;[3] whereupon Caesar immediately expressed
his warmest thanks with a witty double-edged remark to the effect
that among his many officers there had hitherto been no one who
could draw up a deed of security.[4] Nor did he later neglect to give
Cicero personal information about his protégé's progress, and Balbus
assured him in conversation that Trebatius would make his fortune.
Soon afterwards Cicero used his influence on behalf of a young man
who wanted a military tribunate for the year 53. Caesar replied
that he would keep one open, and that Cicero was not to make his
requests so timidly.[5]

During the campaign in Britain Caesar wrote to Cicero, as we
hear by chance, on August 23, September 1 and September 25.[6] And
Cicero was, of course, not the only senator with whom he exchanged
letters. To judge by what Cicero reveals of their contents, the witty
points and friendly courtesies in each letter were directed specifically
at the recipient. Caesar spent every free minute on dictation. When

---

[1] Q. *fr.* 2, 11, 1 (February 54): *nam ut scis, iam pridem istum canto Caesarem. mihi crede, in
sinu est neque ego discingor;* 3, 1, 18: *ille mihi secundum te et liberos nostros ita est, ut sit paene par.
videor id iudicio facere; iam enim debeo, sed tamen amore sum incensus; fam.* 1, 9, 21: *Quintus frater
meus legatus est Caesaris et nullum minimum dictum, non modo factum pro Caesare intercessit, quod
ille non ita inlustri gratia excepit, ut ego eum mihi devinctum putarem. itaque eius omni et gratia,
quae summa est, et opibus, quas intellegis esse maximas, sic fruor ut meis, nec mihi aliter potuisse
videor hominum perditorum de me consilia frangere, nisi cum praesidiis iis, quae semper habui, nunc
etiam potentium benevolentiam coniunxissem.* Further evidence in *RE*, 7A, 956. See further
F. Adami, *Hermes* 78 (1943), 282 ff.
[2] Cic. *Att.* 4, 19, 2.   [3] Cic. *fam.* 7, 5, 2.   [4] Cic. Q. *fr.* 2, 13, 3.
[5] Cic. *fam.* 7, 8, 1; 16, 3; Q. *fr.* 2, 13,3; 3, 1, 10.
[6] Cic. Q. *fr.* 3, 1, 17; 25; *Att.* 4, 18, 5.

he was travelling by carriage or litter through his province, a secretary sat by him; on other occasions he was accustomed to employ two at once, and Oppius actually relates that there were often still more.[1]

In the early summer of 54 he used the journey from North Italy to the scene of operations to compose a weighty grammatical work, in which he recommended that the forms of grammatical inflection should be chosen according to reason, in contrast to the customary careless mode of expression. It is a great pity that these two books *de analogia* have been lost. For one suspects that the principle of style which he there champions was derived from his own method of aiming at perfect clarity of expression. Thus the introduction includes the characteristic warning: 'As the sailor avoids the rock, so should you the obsolete and rare word.'[2] The same motto could just as well be applied to his policies, which shunned all display of 'clever' originality, but appeared in their monumental simplicity as the fulfilment of the duties of a true Roman statesman. This work too is dedicated to Cicero, with a flattering preface on the great orator as the creator and master of Latin prose style.[3] Cicero took great pains to show his gratitude with an epic on the expedition to Britain. As a specimen of his skill as a poet he had previously sent him his work *de temporibus suis*, describing in three books his exile and the glories of his recall and return.[4] We may assume that these contained passages which did not correspond to Caesar's view of these events. The fact that Cicero, through his brother's agency, submitted this work to Caesar's judgment serves to underline the new relationship between them. As soon as he had read the first book, Caesar wrote to say that he knew of nothing better even in Greek literature than the opening section, but that later there were parts which had been composed with less care. Cicero asked his

---

[1] Plut. *Caes.* 17, 4–7; Plin. *n.h.* 7, 91: *scribere aut legere, simul dictare et audire solitum accepimus, epistulas vero tantarum rerum quaternas pariter dictare librariis aut, si nihil aliud ageret, septenas.*

[2] Suet. *Caes.* 56, 5; Gell, *n.A.* 1, 10, 4 (the philosopher Favorinus): *vive ergo moribus praeteritis, loquere verbis praesentibus atque id quod a C. Caesare, excellentis ingenii ac prudentiae viro, in primo de analogia libro scriptum est habe semper in memoria atque in pectore, 'ut tamquam scopulum, sic fugias inauditum atque insolens verbum'*. Details in 19, 8, 3–10; Macr. *Sat.* 1, 5, 2; Caes. frag. (Kübler), pp. 140–145.

[3] Cic. *Brut.* 253: '*ac, si cogitata praeclare eloqui ut possent, non nulli studio et usu elaboraverunt, cuius te paene principem copiae atque inventorem bene de nomine ac dignitate populi Romani meritum esse existumare debemus: hunc facilem et cotidianum novisse sermonem num pro relicto est habendum?*' Earlier Cicero makes Atticus say: *qui etiam in maximis occupationibus ad te ipsum (inquit in me intuens) de ratione Latine loquendi accuratissume scripsit primoque in libro dixerit verborum dilectum originem eloquentiae.*

[4] Cic. *Q.fr.* 2, 13, 2; 15, 4; 3, 1, 11; 8, 3; 9, 6; cf. Büchner, *RE*, 7A, 1256.

brother whether this referred to content or style, adding that no
criticism could affect his own satisfaction with the work. Unfortunately we have no answer.[1]

In order visibly to impress the populace of Rome with the greatness of his Gallic victories and conquests, in 54 Caesar began to
construct vast buildings out of the booty, the Basilica Julia on the
south side of the Forum, as well as a new forum and, on the Campus
Martius, an enormous building for the holding of elections. The
immediate problem was the purchase of the site for the new forum
which was still covered with dwelling-houses. Caesar again asked
Cicero to give Oppius his advice, in this complicated matter.[2] It
appears that he lost no opportunity to make use of the services of
the distinguished consular for his own political purposes. And just
as he treated Cicero, so he behaved towards all with whom he came
into contact. 'Caesar was reckoned a great man on the score of the
favours he did and of his generosity', was the judgment of Sallust[3]—
and he had reason to know.

[1] Cic. Q. fr. 2, 15, 5 : *quomodonam, mi frater, de nostris versibus Caesar? nam primum librum
se legisse scripsit ad me ante et prima sic ut neget se ne Graeca quidem meliora legisse; reliqua ad
quendam locum* ῥᾳθυμότερα; *hoc enim utitur verbo. dic mihi verum, num aut res eum aut* χαρακτήρ
non delectat? nihil est quod vereare; ego enim ne pilo quidem minus me amabo. (Cf. Büchner, *RE*,
7A, 1252; Cic. *fam.* 1, 9, 23.) I would conjecture that Caesar's criticism was not political but
directed, as before, at the work's poetical quality. On December 19, 45, when he was
Cicero's guest, he also said nothing about politics, but φιλόλογα *multa* (Cic. *Att.* 13, 52, 2). In
this context, one may perhaps ask, with Wolfgang Schmid (*RhM* (1952), 269), whether the
only surviving verses of Caesar, in which he addresses Terence as *dimidiate Menander* and bases
his judgment on his lack of *vis*, do not belong to this period of frequent and friendly correspondence with Cicero. For, in the *Life* of P. Terentius Afer, taken over by Donatus from the *de
poetis* of Suetonius, they follow four lines from Cicero's *Limon*, and everything speaks for
Caesar having answered Cicero. (See Büchner, *RE*, 7A, 1258, who, as it seems to me, rightly
contests the view that Cicero's verses are to be dated to his youth.) For the verses, see C. *Suetoni
Tranquilli reliquiae*, ed. Reifferscheid (1860), p. 34; *Frag. Poet. Lat.*, ed. W. Morel (1927),
pp. 66 and 91; and F. Leo, *Gesch. der röm. Lit.* (1913), 253. G. Jachmann, in his thorough
appraisal of the poetical achievement of Terence (*RE*, 5A, 627) finds Caesar's judgment
entirely correct: 'For what it amounts to in the end is precisely the lack of force in his artistic
view and of intensity in his feeling and grasp of things. The prevailing lack of equivalence, that
is what profoundly characterizes his kind of reproduction' (in greater detail, pp. 613 ff.).
(Similarly Ed. Norden, *Die röm. Lit.* (1952), 20.) In contrast to the above, W. Schmid, op. cit.,
225 ff., wishes to understand *vis comica* and to place the comma after '*comica*'. I do not feel
myself competent to decide this old problem. Caesar writes:

> *Tu quoque, tu in summis, o dimidiate Menander,*
> *Poneris, et merito, puri sermonis amator.*
> *Lenibus atque utinam scriptis adiuncta foret vis,*
> *Comica ut aequato virtus polleret honore*
> *Cum Graecis neve hac despectus parte iaceres!*
> *Unum hoc maceror ac doleo tibi desse, Terenti.*

[2] Cic. *Att.* 4, 17, 7; Suet. *Caes.* 26, 2; Plin. *n.h.* 36, 103.
[3] Sall. *Cat.* 54, 2.

After this digression we return to the main stream of events. While Caesar was administering justice in Cisalpine Gaul in the early months of 54, he received news that the marauding Pirustae had broken into Roman Illyricum, and was forced to make his way there. He immediately called up the militia of the local communities—a sufficient threat for the Pirustae to declare themselves ready for peace. This was granted on condition that they supplied hostages and recognized an arbitrator appointed by Caesar who was to assess the damage caused by them and the reparations to be paid for it. At the end of May (according to the calendar then in force) he started his northward journey.[1] When he had assured himself on a visit to the winter quarters that the construction of the ships was proceeding satisfactorily, he ordered the fleet to assemble at the port of Boulogne.[2] He employed the time available before the embarkation of the expeditionary force in marching with four legions into the land of the Treveri. This powerful state, led by the prince Indutiomarus, had repudiated its ties with Rome. It sent no representatives to the Gallic diets called by Caesar, and disregarded his summonses to supply troops, while its relations with the Germans across the Rhine were correspondingly more active. Caesar did not intend to leave such a power in his rear. Here, too, the Roman army had only to appear in order to bring the opposition party to the helm. Its leader Cingetorix immediately put himself at Caesar's service. Indutiomarus, who had hoped to mobilize resistance in the Ardennes, was forced to give up the attempt and to come to the Roman camp with 300 hostages. Since Caesar had no time to lose, he forebore to punish him, but proclaimed Cingetorix as the leader recognized by Rome before the assembled nobility of the Treveri.[3]

There were further difficulties when he returned to the port. Caesar had ordered 4,000 Celtic cavalry to assemble there, and had laid particular stress on as complete a turn-out as possible by the heads of all the states. For these were to accompany him across the Channel as hostages. The well-known Aeduan prince Dumnorix stubbornly resisted this plan. He wished to remain in Gaul in order, as Caesar suspected, to set up the kingdom to which he had long

---

[1] Caes. *b.G.* 5, 1, 5–9. The home of the Pirustae is perhaps to be sought in the area of the Boka Kotorska (Polaschek, *RE*, 20, 1731). Presumably one has to think of the towns with partly Roman populations—such as Lissus, Narona, Salona and Iader—as included among the *civitates* (Caes. *b.c.* 3, 9, 1; 29, 1; *b.Alex.* 42, 3; 43, 2; Cic. *fam.* 13, 77, 3; 5, 9, 2; 10b). Cf. Fluss, *RE*, 16, 1749; W. Schmitthenner, *Historia* 7 (1958), 224.

[2] Caes. *b.G.* 5, 2, 3. On Portus Itius, see Haverfield, *RE*, 9, 2368.

[3] Caes. *b.G.* 5, 2, 4–4, 4.

aspired in Caesar's absence. According to information reaching the proconsul from the land of the Aedui, Dumnorix was actually making use of Caesar's name and alleged that he was about to give him the throne; this was the best possible way of raising doubts about Caesar in the minds of the republicans on whose support he depended. Since adverse winds delayed the departure for more than three weeks, Dumnorix found an opportunity to form a conspiracy among the nobles present. Caesar thought it inadvisable to take action against this highly esteemed figure without a clear-cut case; but when a favourable wind came and he ordered the five previously detailed legions and 2,000 cavalry to embark, Dumnorix failed to comply and rode off home with his men. Caesar immediately halted the embarkation and sent his entire cavalry in pursuit of the traitor. A fight developed in which Dumnorix was killed; his followers returned to Caesar.[1]

The expedition to Britain which roughly occupied the months of August and September (according to the calendar then in force)[2] in no way lived up to its great expectations. The threatened British tribes had placed themselves under the supreme command of the powerful king Cassivellaunus whose kingdom lay to the north of the Thames. Although Caesar succeeded in crossing this river, Cassivellaunus showed himself a master of guerrilla warfare. Here, too, Caesar was fortunate in that some of the states subject to Cassivellaunus came over to him; quite some time before, one of their princes had taken refuge with him from Cassivellaunus. This enabled Caesar to capture a strong citadel (perhaps Verulamium, St. Albans, north-west of London), and after an unsuccessful attack on the Roman naval camp Cassivellaunus agreed to negotiations. Caesar took hostages from him and imposed a yearly tribute for the future, but he decided against a permanent occupation of the country, and led his whole army back to Gaul. Of the rich booty, so freely talked about in Rome before the expedition, there was no sign.[3]

---

[1] Op. cit., 5, 5–7.

[2] Cic. Q.fr. 2, 15, 4; 3, 1, 10; 13; 25, 3, 4; Att. 4, 15, 10; 17, 6; 18, 5 (according to the letter of Quintus of September 25, on his return to the coast of Gaul): *confecta Britannia, obsidibus acceptis, nulla praeda, imperata tamen pecunia exercitum ex Britannia reportabant; fam.* 7, 7, 1; 17, 3; 16, 1; Caes. *b.G.* 5, 23, 5.

[3] Caes. *b.G.* 5, 8–23; Dio 40, 1–4; here (1, 2) it is stressed, in a tone unfriendly to Caesar, that he wanted to have Britain at any price; Oros. 6, 9, 4–9; Plut. *Caes.* 23, 4; Suet. *Caes.* 25, 2; Polyaen. *strat.* 8, 23, 5; Cic. Q.fr. 3, 1, 10 (October 1, 54 B.C.); Att. 4, 17, 6: *Britannici belli exitus exspectatur; constat enim aditus insulae esse muratos mirificis molibus. etiam illud iam cognitum est neque argenti scripulum esse ullum in illa insula neque ullam spem praedae nisi ex mancipiis;* Q. fr. 3, 9, 4: Quintus promises his brother slaves.

Meanwhile the situation in Gaul was also deteriorating. A poor harvest came on top of the political discontent.[1] The Carnutes (around Chartres) killed Tasgetius,[2] the king appointed by Caesar. Despite this, Caesar found himself forced by the corn shortage to place his winter-quarters exceptionally far from each other with the result that some legions were left entirely to their own resources. Accordingly, he intended on this occasion to wait at his head-quarters in Samarobriva (Amiens) until the camps were fortified. In the event, it soon became apparent that he would have to spend the whole winter there.[3] Indutiomarus had not been inactive. On his instigation the Eburones near the Meuse, north of Liège, under their cunning and audacious chieftain Ambiorix attacked the most easterly winter-quarters and completely annihilated the 15 cohorts ($1\frac{1}{2}$ legions) encamped there. This Roman defeat—on a scale un-precedented for years—immediately roused the Nervii to take up arms as well, and the camp in their territory (in the area of Namur) commanded by Quintus Cicero had to stand a fearful siege before Caesar succeeded in relieving it with only two under-strength legions.[4]

This victory also gave a breathing space to Labienus who was in the area of Sedan and himself faced by the Treveri under Indutio-marus.[5] But as soon as Caesar had retired with Quintus Cicero to Samarobriva, the indefatigable Gaul prepared a new attack. Although he did not succeed in enticing any Germans over the Rhine, he found a large measure of support in Gaul and so could rely on an influx of volunteers.[6] Just as the Carnutes had murdered their king, their eastern neighbours, the Senones (around Sens), now expelled theirs, another protégé of Caesar. Caesar's summons to their whole council to come to him was disregarded.[7] At an armed meeting of the tribal assembly Indutiomarus declared Cingetorix a public enemy, and again led his people against Labienus. However, the latter had collected a large force of Celtic cavalry, and in

---

[1] Caes. b.G. 5, 24, 1.   [2] Op. cit., 5, 25.
[3] Op. cit., 5, 24, 8; 53, 3; Dio 40, 4, 2; 9, 1.
[4] Caes. b.G. 5, 26–52; Dio 40, 5–10; Plut. Caes. 24; Suet. Caes. 25, 2; Polyaen. strat. 8, 23, 6; Cic. Q.fr. 3, 8, 2 : ubi enim isti sint Nervii et quam longe absint nescio. It was the winter-camp that Quintus was allowed to choose for himself (Att. 4, 19, 2); Q.fr. 3, 1, 17; Rab. Post. 42 (cf. RE, 7A, 965).
[5] Caes. b.G. 5, 53, 1–2.   [6] Op. cit., 5, 55, 1–56, 1.
[7] Op. cit., 5, 54.

accordance with their instructions, these brought the dangerous rebel's head back from a pursuit.[1]

This blow again temporarily prevented the fire of rebellion, which was smouldering everywhere, from flaring up: but it was now perfectly clear to Caesar that he could trust none of the Gallic tribes except the Aedui and the Remi. Throughout the winter he kept summoning the chieftains to himself, and issuing serious warnings to them;[2] but the formation of three new legions in Cisalpine Gaul will have been more effective. One of these had taken the oath of allegiance to Pompey in 55, and was now on Caesar's request loaned to him 'for the sake of the state and of their friendship'. The legion destroyed by the Eburones had also been a newly formed one. Thus Caesar supplied himself with 30 new cohorts in place of the 15 he had lost, so that the army now consisted of 10 full legions.[3]

In the year 53, even before the winter was over, he used four legions to punish the Nervii. The vast booty in men and cattle won on this expedition was handed over in its entirety to the soldiers. The unhappy people submitted anew to the Roman yoke and provided the hostages demanded of them.[4] Altogether Caesar intended this year to spread terror through the land by fearful punishment of all rebels. Since hearing about the destruction of the fifteen cohorts he had let his hair and beard grow; only when his comrades were avenged, so he declared, did he intend to let himself be shorn or shaved. Every man in the army could understand what this meant.[5]

At the spring meeting of the diet not only the eastern tribes allied to the Treveri were missing; no Senones or Carnutes appeared either. This was open rebellion, and in order to demonstrate that he would not tolerate it, Caesar transferred both headquarters and diet from Samarobriva (Amiens) to Lutecia (Paris) as close as possible to the area in revolt.[6] Then he led his army southward into the territory of the Senones. Terrified and taken by surprise, both the

[1] Op. cit., 5, 56, 2–58; Dio 40, 11, 1–2. Trebatius was at the winter-quarters of Samarobriva. Cic. fam. 7, 10, 2, after a joke about the cold winter-camp; *quamquam vos nunc istic satis calere audio; quo quidem nuntio valde mehercule de te timueram;* 11, 2; 12, 1; 16, 3; 18, 4; 13, 2: *Treviros vites censeo.*

[2] Caes. b.G. 5, 54, 1; 4.

[3] Op. cit., 6, 1; 32, 5–33, 4; 8, 54, 2; Plut. *Caes.* 25, 1–2 (incorrectly: two legions of Pompey's; similarly Plut. *Pomp.* 52, 4; but see *Cat. Min.* 45, 6 (one legion)).

[4] Caes. b.G. 6, 3, 1–3.

[5] Suet. *Caes.* 67, 2; Polyaen. *strat.* 8, 23, 23.

[6] Caes. b.G. 6, 3, 4–6.

tribes immediately notified their submission through the agency of the Aedui and Remi.[1] Caesar willingly accepted it, because he was principally interested in destroying the Eburones and over-powering the Treveri. These aims were fully realized. Labienus won a splendid victory over the Treveri as a result of which the clan of Indutiomarus left the country, and in their place Cingetorix again took over as the recognized head of the tribe.[2] Caesar first isolated the Eburones by overrunning the Menapii (in the area around the mouths of the Rhine and Scheldt) in a large-scale marauding expedition; as a result these handed over hostages.[3] Then he crossed the Rhine again to deter the Suebi from having anything further to do with Ambiorix and the Treveri.[4] And now vengeance caught up with the Eburones. For a period of several weeks their whole country was so systematically plundered and laid waste—and, as a matter of fact, the Celts summoned by Caesar developed an enormous enthusiasm for this work—that the name of the tribe henceforth vanishes from history. The Tungri (from around Tongeren) came to take their place. Only the hunt for Ambiorix, pursued by all available means, remained unsuccessful. But he, too, no longer had any role to play.[5]

In the autumn Caesar summoned another diet, this time to Duro-cortorum (Reims), the capital of the loyal Remi. Here before the assembled Celtic nobility he tried Acco, the leader of the rebellious Senones. In accordance with Roman practice the death sentence was carried out after a preliminary flogging. Those of his followers who had escaped were exiled. Agedincum (Sens), the capital of the Senones, had six legions quartered on it for the winter. There was now absolute peace in Gaul, and Caesar could again spend the winter in Northern Italy.[6]

The turn of events in Rome made it vitally important that, after a long interval, Caesar should give them his principal attention for a time. In the early months of 54 the system which he had arranged with his partners for holding down their political opponents had proved its efficiency. The consul Lucius Domitius Ahenobarbus angrily quipped that he could not even nominate a military tribune: his colleague Appius Claudius had run off to Caesar expressly to

[1] Op. cit., 6, 4.   [2] Op. cit., 6, 7–8; Dio 40, 31, 2–6.
[3] Caes. b.G. 6, 5–6.
[4] Op. cit., 6, 9–10; 29, 1–3; Dio 40, 32, 1–2, with the unfriendly comment that Caesar withdrew through fear of the Suebi.
[5] Caes. b.G. 6, 29, 4–43, 6; 8, 24, 4; Dio 40, 32, 3–5.
[6] Caes. b.G. 6, 44.

. secure his approval for appointing one.[1] However, Caesar and Pompey could not agree on the question of who were to be elected consuls for 53. Their common candidate was Gaius Memmius, Caesar's bitter opponent in 58; for his election campaign Pompey now placed at the disposal of Memmius the influence of his patronage in Cisalpine Gaul, and Caesar his soldiers. Rumour had it that if there was any doubt about the prospective outcome of the election, it was to be postponed until the winter, when Caesar's soldiers would again be able to vote.[2] In addition, however, Memmius made sure of his election by agreements which shed an even harsher light on the prevailing corruption of political life. On the advice of the two consuls he combined with Gnaeus Domitius Calvinus, who had also opposed Caesar as tribune in the year 59. Together they now promised the electors of the century which was to cast its vote first[3] a total of 10 million sesterces ($2\frac{1}{2}$ million denarii): further, both the consuls of 54 were to receive 3 million sesterces (1 million denarii) each if Memmius and Calvinus were elected to the consulship for 53 and then found that they were unable to obtain for their predecessors the provinces which they desired. The consul Appius Claudius secured Caesar's approval for this arrangement; for he would be only too happy to place the dangerous Lucius Domitius Ahenobarbus under an obligation in this way. On the other hand Pompey was anxious that a candidate other than Gnaeus Domitius Calvinus should be successful (if possible his former quaestor, Marcus Aemilius Scaurus) and so in September prevailed on Memmius to read out the secret electoral compact in the Senate. In so doing Memmius dug his own grave, since Caesar withdrew his support from him. In his place Marcus Valerius Messalla Rufus joined Calvinus as the candidate with the best prospects. However, they were not elected until July 53.[4]

The fact that Caesar was detained in Gaul this winter increasingly gave Pompey the upper hand as far as politics in Rome were concerned. Since the closing months of the year 54 he had been busying himself with the corn supply.[5] During this period the idea that a dictatorship was necessary, first mooted by his circle in June, was able to gain ground steadily.[6] Nevertheless, on the surface the

[1] Cic. Q.fr. 2, 13, 3.

[2] Cic. Att. 4, 16, 6; Q.fr. 3, 2, 3; 8, 3; fam. 7, 16, 3; Suet. Caes. 73.

[3] On the influence of the praerogativa centuria, see Chr. Meier, RE Suppl. 8, 593.

[4] Cic. Q.fr. 2, 14, 4; 3, 1, 16; 8, 3; 9, 3; Att. 4, 17, 2–3; Dio 40, 45, 1; App. b.c. 2, 69–71.

[5] Cic. Q.fr. 3, 9, 3; Att. 4, 19, 2; Dio 39, 63, 3.

[6] Cic. Q.fr. 3, 8, 4; 6, 9, 3; Att. 4, 18, 3; 19, 1; App. b.c. 2, 72–73; Plut. Pomp. 54, 3–5.

understanding between the two partners continued unimpaired. On their joint instructions in August 54 Cicero defended his old enemy Publius Vatinius,[1] and in December he had to serve his two powerful friends by making the most painful renunciation of his past by representing Aulus Gabinius, on trial for extortion. Pompey made a special journey to Rome and, since a proconsul was not allowed to enter the city, delivered a speech outside the *pomerium* in which he also read out a letter from Caesar. The fact that despite these efforts Gabinius, one of the most distinguished followers of the dynasts, was not acquitted shows the extent to which political life was not yet completely muzzled.[2] The gradual estrangement between Pompey and Caesar sprang from the changed balance of power: but nothing was more important for the way in which it developed than Julia's death, in childbirth, in August 54. Both her father and her husband were sincerely, even tenderly, devoted to her. One may assume that it was precisely her father's amiable characteristics that she had inherited, and one can then imagine the importance of her role as an intermediary. During her funeral procession the people carried off her corpse and, despite the protests of the consul Domitius and the tribunes, buried her on the Campus Martius, thus demonstrating how great an impression her death immediately made on the public. By so doing they intended primarily to honour her father, at the time far away in Britain; and he, despite his sorrow, did not forget to show his gratitude

[1] Cic. *Q.fr.* 2, 15, 3; *fam.* 1, 9, 4; 19; 5, 9, 1; cf. *RE*, 7A, 958.

[2] Dio 39, 63, 3–5; Cic. *Rab. Post.* 19; 32–33. The Roman knight C. Rabirius Postumus in 59 B.C. had lent King Ptolemy XII the money he needed (Cic. op. cit., 25; 38; 39) to buy his recognition as king from Pompey and Caesar (allegedly about 36 million denarii: see Suet. *Caes.* 54, 3 and above, p. 76). In order to recover this sum, he joined the expedition of the proconsul Gabinius, which was to restore the king to Alexandria in 55 B.C., and there assumed the post of finance minister (*dioiketes*); see Cic. *Rab. Post.* 22; 28; *fam.* 7, 17, 1; Suet. *Claud.* 16, 2. When Gabinius, sentenced in a *repetundae* trial to pay into the Roman exchequer the sum allegedly promised by the king as a bribe, had to go into exile through lack of funds, another *repetundae* case was brought against Rabirius, either in December 54 or in January 53, with the object of making him pay the debt, as he had enriched himself through the extortions of Gabinius. Cicero defended him, successfully, it seems (*Rab. Post.* 8; 30; 36–37). In his speech he maintained that Rabirius had gained nothing in Egypt and was totally dependent on Caesar's generosity (39; 41–43): the trial (he claimed) was intended only to shake Caesar's *dignitas* (43: *equitem Romanum veterem amicum suum studiosum, amantem, observantem sui non libidine, non turpibus impensis cupiditatum atque iacturis, sed experientia patrimonii amplificandi labentem excepit, corruere non sivit, fulsit et sustinuit re, fortuna, fide hodieque sustinet nec amicum pendentem corruere patitur*). Here we have evidence for Sallust's testimony (*Cat.* 54, 2) : *Caesar beneficiis ac munificentia magnus habebatur*. But of course Caesar's *fides* was here particularly involved because the money lent to the King had passed into his hands. Cf. F. Vonder Mühll, *RE*, 1A, 26; 7, 429; 7A, 963–966.

in an appropriate fashion. Contrary to all precedent he gave notice of gladiatorial games to be followed by a banquet in honour of his daughter.[1]

For the time being Pompey had plentiful opportunities to follow his own inclinations. Since Caesar's consulship, violation of the constitution and the frivolous misuse of its ancestral practices had become a habit, and political life gradually sank into a state of anarchy. If magistrates were elected at all, they were obstructed by illegal acts of violence and unable to govern. Since there was no adequate police, the abuse by which politicians fought their battles with armed gangs got progressively out of hand. Money and gangs were more or less the only means to political success. The popular assemblies, meetings of the senate, and judicial proceedings all showed the same openly repulsive aspect. In such a world the figure of Cato shines all the more brightly, a man who not only kept his moral character untarnished, but, by fighting tirelessly and fearlessly, in not a few cases actually defeated the prevalent corruption. The ruling nobility of Rome, which could still produce a politician of his stamp, did not die entirely unworthy of its great past.

Even Pompey had to learn this man's political significance: for, in the first half of the year 53, he obstinately opposed all attempts to secure the dictatorship for Pompey.[2] At last, in July, the Senate granted the proconsul who was still in Italy authority to maintain order. Thereupon he returned to the neighbourhood of the city, and in his circle a vigorous propaganda campaign was conducted in favour of a dictatorship, although he himself pretended that he did not want the position. As soon as his personal attitude was made known in the Senate, Cato pinned him down, praising him for it, and begging him to work for the restoration of law and order. Pompey was forced to content himself with the conduct of the consular elections. But in return he took no further action when, with the new election campaigns, the old practices continued. This time they were worse than ever before, for the owners of the

[1] The time of her death is to be deduced from Cic. Q.fr. 3, 1, 17; 25, 8, 3 (end of November): de virtute et gravitate Caesaris, quam in summo dolore adhibuisset, magnam ex epistula tua accepi voluptatem; fam. 7, 9, 1; Suet. Caes. 26, 2; 84, 1; Plut. Caes. 23, 5–7; Pomp. 53, 2–7; App.b.c. 2, 68; Dio 39, 64; 40, 44, 3; Lucan 1, 111–120; 5, 473 f.; 9, 1049; Vell. 2, 47, 2; Liv. per. 106; Flor. 2, 13, 13; Senec. dial. 6, 14, 3: intra tertium diem imperatoris obit munia et tam cito dolorem vicit quam omnia solebat; Tiberius ap. Tac. ann. 3, 6, 2: referendum iam animum ad firmitudinem, ut quoudam divus Iulius amissa unica filia.

[2] Plut. Cat. Min. 45, 5–7. This is certainly based on the biography of Cato's friend Munatius Rufus (37, 1). Cf. Cic. Q.fr. 2, 14, 4.

largest gangs, Titus Annius Milo and Publius Clodius, were themselves candidates for the consulate and praetorship of 52 respectively.[1]
On New Year's Day, 52, there were once again neither consuls
nor praetors.[2] According to the constitution the consular elections
were now to be held by an *interrex*, who was to be selected from
the patrician senators and to be changed every five days.[3] Milo
had hopes of being elected in this way. Pompey, however, preferred
Quintus Metellus Scipio, Rome's most aristocratic citizen, of the
house of the Scipiones Nasicae and the adopted son of the *pontifex
maximus*, Metellus Pius, and, in order further to postpone the
election, on his instigation one of the tribunes vetoed the meeting
of the patricians.[4] Then on January 18 Milo and Clodius met on the
Appian Way: blows were struck and Milo's armed followers cut
down Clodius.[5] Out of this affray dangerous rioting by the mob and
gangs developed in the city. It had long been predictable that Clodius
would come to such an end. But the sudden death of the man who
for years had made the city hold its breath with his insolent pranks,
who as a member of the highest aristocratic society could allow
himself any piece of effrontery and was beloved by the impoverished
masses as their greatest benefactor and tireless champion, struck
like lightning; and when his followers set on fire the meeting-house
of the Senate, the Curia Hostilia near the Forum, all realized that
the last semblance of public order would collapse unless this anarchic
behaviour was immediately suppressed. The Senate at once decreed
the election of an *interrex* on January 19, and entrusted *interrex*,
tribunes and (again) the proconsul Pompey with the protection of
the state. Since, despite this, the unrest continued, it soon issued
instructions that throughout Italy all men of military age should
register for service: Pompey was to recruit the necessary troops.
The latter quickly collected these forces outside the *pomerium*, but
then watched the further course of events from there. In Rome
no elections were held, because the candidates' gangs obstructed
the conduct of state business, and the call for Pompey as dictator
was heard anew.[6]

Meanwhile, also, on January 18 (December 8, Jul.), Caesar had
arrived in Ravenna and, in conformity with the senatorial decree,

[1] Plut. *Pomp.* 54, 4–5; *Cat. Min.* 47, 1; App. *b.c.* 2, 73; Dio 40, 46, 1 (confused in his dating);
Cic. *Mil.* 24–26; *fam.* 2, 4, 1; 5, 2; 6, 3–5.

[2] Dio 40, 46, 3.   [3] Mommsen, *RStR*, 1³, 654 ff.

[4] Ascon. *argum.* to Cic. *Mil.* p. 31 (Clark).   [5] Cic. *Mil.* 27; Ascon. loc. cit.

[6] Cic. *Mil.* 70; Ascon. 33–35; Dio 40, 48–50, 1.

immediately started recruiting in his province.[1] The decision on the future fate of the Roman Empire seemed imminent. On June 9, 53, Marcus Crassus had fallen in Mesopotamia,[2] while in Rome things had developed in such a way that it was reasonable to suppose that Pompey had merely to help himself in order to become dictator. Caesar's agents at Rome could only counter the propaganda for Pompey's dictatorship by demanding for Caesar a joint consulship with Pompey.[3] However, events in Gaul made it quite impossible to implement this plan. From Acco's execution the Celtic nobility had concluded that it was now or never, if they wished to rescue Gallic liberty. They followed the political situation at Rome with intense interest, and when the great crisis arose, immediately drew the conclusion that it would keep Caesar in Italy. Thus the vast revolt broke out, of which the Arvernian prince Vercingetorix was soon recognized as leader by the whole nation.[4] Because of events in Rome Caesar was forced to let him alone for several weeks in order to allow himself time to negotiate with Pompey from Ravenna and secure the best possible terms of agreement.[5]

On the other side Pompey did not feel himself as free as one might have expected. Presumably he did not realize how precarious Caesar's position was at this time, and accordingly had to reckon with him as a serious counterweight. And even if for the moment he was able to have the last word at Rome on the strength of his imposing levy of troops, while the constitutional authorities were helpless and at the mercy of the wild antics of the gangs, yet he rightly did not underestimate the optimates' powers of resistance, with their deep roots in the Roman way of life. But the most profound reason for his hesitation lay in his caution: he no longer dared to undertake any enterprise, the success of which could not

---

[1] Caes. b.G. 7, 1, 1.   [2] Ovid. fast. 6, 465.

[3] Dio 40, 50, 3; Suet. Caes. 26, 1.

[4] Caes. b.G. 7, 1, 2–8; Plut. Caes. 26, 1–2. I have discussed the great rebellion of 52 B.C. in the article 'Vercingetorix' in RE, 8A, 981 ff.

[5] Caesar offers as clues to the date only b.G. 7, 6, 1 (cum iam urbanas res virtute Cn. Pompei commodiorem in statum pervenisse intellegeret) and 8, 2, according to which he crossed the Cevennes durissimo tempore anni altissima nive. The first reference is clearly to the election of Pompey as consul sine collega on February 5 (Jul.). Jullian (3, 428, n. 4) assumes that Caesar learnt of the events in Gaul reported in 7, 1, 2–5, 6 about February 10, which seems very late. If we put the advance over the Cevennes at the end of February (Jul.), that leaves us with a period of about two months between December 18 and Caesar's departure from Italy. Cf. G. Ferrero, Grandezza e Decadenza di Roma (1908), 2, 164, n. 5; Ed. Meyer, Caesars Monarchie (1918), 226, n. 1; 233, n. 1, with reference to b.G. 7, 9, 4, according to which Caesar had sent newly recruited cavalry in advance to Vienna multis ante diebus.

be calculated beforehand with the maximum of certainty. For the audacious daring of his youth had long since disappeared.

Thus in several weeks of negotiations he tried to find a position midway between Caesar and the optimates. Caesar at first proposed that they should renew the ties of relationship broken by Julia's death. He himself wished to marry the daughter of Pompey in place of Calpurnia, while Pompey was to marry Caesar's grand-niece Octavia (the sister of the future Augustus, then the wife of Gaius Marcellus, later consul of 50). This plan was rejected by Pompey.[1] On the other hand, he agreed to support a popular decree whereby Caesar was to be granted the right to stand for the consul-ship of 48 *in absentia*; in other words, he was to be allowed to keep his province until the end of 49 and so be immune from prosecution.[2] On Caesar's urgent request Cicero, who was then at Ravenna, undertook to prevent his protégé, the tribune Marcus Caelius, at that time a strong optimate, from vetoing the proposal.[3] This agreement was of great value to Caesar. He could now feel secure even against a dictatorship of Pompey and could concentrate all his powers on crushing the Celtic rebellion.

Pompey's dealings with the senatorial leaders also led to a com-promise. Although Cato for some time opposed the granting of extraordinary power to Pompey, when it became apparent that the state of anarchy would justify a *coup d'état* on his part, he prevailed on the senate to take the initiative. Instead of a dictatorship the extraordinary power was very cleverly given the form of a consul-ship without colleague.[4] This was no mere playing with words, but in contrast to the dictatorship, as understood by Sulla, his office had a definite time limit, and he could be called to account for his actions in the normal way. In fact Pompey was now abandoning his claim to stand above normal political activity, and stepping back into the ranks of the optimate oligarchy. He had no talent at all for creative statesmanship. Although he had often proved his ability at organizing the means available to cope with particular needs of imperial policy, he could not grasp the idea that the basis of politics might be completely reorganized, let alone allow such a concept to guide his actions. Furthermore, he had not even mastered the

---

[1] Suet. *Caes.* 27, 1 calls Pompeia *Fausto Sullae destinatam*. She was presumably married to him already. In 47 B.C. she had two children (*b. Afr.* 95, 3; App. *b.c.* 2, 416).
[2] Suet. *Caes.* 26, 1; Dio 40, 51, 2; Caes. *b.c.* 1, 9, 2; 32, 3.
[3] Cic. *Att.* 7, 1, 4; 3, 4; 6, 2; 8, 3, 3; *fam.* 6, 6, 5.
[4] Plut. *Cat. Min.* 47, 1–3; Cic. *Mil.* 61.

mechanics of politics as managed in the Senate and popular assembly, with the result that the hopes he entertained in 61 of being from then on the first man in the state had been wretchedly frustrated. And now, when for the second time his fortune brought him the greatest of opportunities, he did not have the ability to use it. The nature of his new relationship with Caesar is illustrated by the fact that the decisive proposal in the Senate was made by Marcus Bibulus, warmly supported by Marcus Cato, and that Lucius Domitius Ahenobarbus was appointed to preside over the special court created to pass judgment on Milo.[1] These three were Caesar's mortal enemies.[2]

On the twenty-fifth of the month intercalated between February 24 and March 1 (February 5, Jul.) Pompey was elected consul for the third time and immediately assumed the reins of government.[3] Instead of Octavia, whom Caesar wished him to marry, he now married Cornelia, the daughter of the ardent anti-Caesarian Quintus Metellus Scipio, and in August he had his father-in-law elected to the other consulship.[4]

The fact that he kept his promise, and despite Cato's opposition recommended the law of the ten tribunes allowing Caesar to stand for the consulship *in absentia*,[5] did not outweigh the evidence of unfriendly feelings towards his partner. On the contrary, in the course of the consular year legislation followed which created a legal basis for Caesar's removal. In one of his laws he took up a senatorial decree of 53,[6] according to which the consular and praetorian provinces were no longer to be assigned to magistrates immediately after their year of office in Rome. The object of the decree was to limit the degree of corruption at the polls,[7] but it soon became apparent that the new law could be turned against Caesar. For now the consuls of 49 would no longer be the first available

---

[1] Plut. *Pomp.* 54, 5–8; *Cat. Min.* 47, 3–4; *Caes.* 28, 7; Dio 40, 50, 4–5; App. *b.c.* 2, 84; Vell. 2, 47, 3; Ascon. on Cic. *Mil.*, pp. 36, 38; Cic. *Mil.* 22.

[2] Sall. *ad. Caes.* 2, 9, 1–3.   [3] Ascon. 36.

[4] Plut. *Pomp.* 55, 1–3; 11; Lucan 3, 23; Dio 40, 51, 2–3; App. *b.c.* 2, 95.

[5] Caes. *b.c.* 1, 32, 3; Dio 40, 51, 2.

[6] Dio 40, 46, 2 speaks of an interval of five years. In the *senatusconsultum* of 51 B.C. (in Cic. *fam.* 8, 8, 8) there is no mention of a *quinquennium*. I therefore think it possible that Dio (or his source) inferred it from the Augustan practice (53, 14, 2). See also *Hermes* 63 (1928), 130 (=*Kl. Schr.* 2, 221 f.); *RE*, 7A, 971; and, differently, my *Pompeius*², 179. Mommsen (*RStR*, 2³, 248) thought of these as transitional arrangements.

[7] Dio 40, 30, 1; 56, 1; Caes. *b.c.* 1, 6, 5 (of the two men nominated for proconsulships for 49 B.C., Metellus Scipio had been consul in 52, L. Domitius Ahenobarbus in 54); 85, 9: *in se iura magistratuum commutari, ne ex praetura et consulatu ut semper, sed per paucos probati et electi in provincias mittantur.*

successors to him; a successor could be sent immediately after March 1, 50. He would then hold no official position until assuming the consulship in 48, and would be liable to criminal proceedings.

A further law of Pompey on the rights of magistrates included the provision that a candidate must canvass in person. Caesar's friends immediately drew attention to the fact that this general provision ran counter to the popular decree about Caesar's candidature for the consulship. However, the law was accepted by the people without mention of Caesar's privilege, inscribed on bronze and included in the state archives. It was only later that Pompey added an appendix excepting Caesar, which of course had no constitutional validity.[1]

This meant that legally the ground on which Caesar stood was completely undermined. But in the course of the years his power, based on violation of the constitution, had become autonomous and so strong that it was beyond the reach of political measures of this kind. In Rome things had reached a stage where the validity of constitutional law was based on the military strength of the leading political figures. Realizing this, Pompey had his command in the Spanish provinces renewed for another five years, and so made it probable that the crisis to which the state had come would be settled by arms.[2] However, the big event in current politics was the conquest of anarchy by the forces of law and order; this was accomplished in a series of trials. First, on April 8, Milo was condemned.[3] Cato's plea that he should be acquitted as a man who had deserved well of the state was unsuccessful,[4] and even Cicero, his counsel, could not save him by maintaining that he had acted in self-defence,[5] since he had actually given orders for the wounded Clodius to be killed.[6] Pompey was provoked to take

[1] Suet. *Caes.* 28, 3; Cic. *Att.* 8, 3, 3 on Pompey: *contendit, ut decem tribuni pl(ebis) ferrent ut absentis ratio haberetur, quod idem ipse sanxit lege quadam sua.* In 51 B.C. the consul M. Marcellus took the opposite position (Suet. *Caes.* 28, 2): *ne absentis ratio comitiis haberetur, quando lege* (thus emended by O. Hirschfeld, *Kl. Schr.*, 810) *plebiscito Pompeius postea obrogasset.* See also Dio 40, 56, 1–3; cf. Mommsen, *RStR*, 1³, 504, n. 2. As I remarked in my *Pompeius²*, 178, I do not believe in trickery by Pompey. Syme (*Rom. Rev.* 40) takes a different view.

[2] Dio 40, 44, 2; 56, 2; Plut. *Pomp.* 55, 12; *Caes.* 28, 8; App. *b.c.* 2, 92. With Lange (*R.A.*, 3, 376), I am of the opinion that it was done through a popular decree (see *Pompeius²*, 179, 85). Lange recalls the judgment of Tacitus on Pompey in *ann.* 3, 28, 1: *suarum legum auctor idem ac subversor, quae armis tuebatur armis amisit.* Cf. Caes. *b.c.* 1, 85, 8: *omnia haec iam pridem contra se parari: in se novi generis imperia constitui, ut idem ad portas urbanis praesideat rebus et duas bellicosissimas provincias absens tot annos obtineat.*

[3] Ascon. on Cic. *Mil.*, p. 40.

[4] Ascon. on Cic. *Mil.* 95, pp. 53–54; Vell. 2, 47, 4; Cic. *fam.* 15, 4, 12.

[5] Cic. *Mil.* 9–11; 23; 26–29; 30; 41–46. [6] Ascon. 35, 53.

L

this action by the opposition of Milo and his friends to the measures which he had taken to preserve the peace, and so approved of the verdict.[1] It naturally suited Caesar perfectly. However, the picture then began to change. The leader of the squad that had killed Clodius was acquitted, and for the rest of the year a series of Clodius' men was tried and condemned.[2] We hear of one case in which Pompey himself intervened unsuccessfully on behalf of a defendant.[3] His present father-in-law, with Cato and Domitius Ahenobarbus, was in the forefront of those directing this purge, and thereafter he let it take its course. This 'domination of the law-courts' demonstrated most clearly the optimate victory and the complete change in the political situation. The political group which was so grievously thinned out by the sentences was filled with boundless indignation at Pompey's treachery. There was certainly none among the condemned who did not fully deserve to be exiled, but after all they had hitherto been among the two dynasts' clients and regarded themselves as badly duped. Caesar remained their only hope, and he received them all.[4] But just when the storm was blowing at its hardest, he was least able to help them. For, when he hurried back to Transalpine Gaul in 52 (while it was still winter), he found that everything he had so far achieved there was again called in question.

The fierceness of the hatred which years of despotic rule had aroused among the oppressed Gauls became horribly apparent. The

[1] Cic. *Mil.* 65–71; Ascon. pp. 36, 38; Dio 40, 53, 2–54, 4.

[2] Ascon. 55–56.

[3] Dio 40, 55; Cic. *fam.* 7, 2, 2; *Phil.* 13, 27; Plut. *Pomp.* 55, 8–11; *Cat. Min.* 48, 8–10; Val. Max. 2, 6, 5.

[4] Sall. *ad. Caes.* 2, 3, 1 (in 50 B.C.): *quoniam Cn. Pompeius aut animi pravitate aut quia nihil eo maluit quod tibi obesset ita lapsus est, ut hostibus tela in manus iaceret;* 2: *primum omnium summam potestatem moderandi de vectigalibus sumptibus iudiciis senatoribus paucis tradidit;* 3: *idem illi factiosi regunt, dant adimunt quae lubet, innocentis circumveniunt, suos ad honorem extollunt;* 6: *homines inertissimi, quorum omnis vis virtusque in lingua sita est, forte atque alterius socordia* (Pompey is meant—see W. Steidle, *Hermes* 78 (1944), 82) *dominationem oblatam insolentes agitant;* 4, 1: *L. Sulla, cui omnia in victoria lege belli licuerunt, tametsi supplicio hostium partis suas muniri intellegebat, tamen paucis interfectis ceteros beneficio quam metu retinere maluit. at hercule M. Catoni L. Domitio ceterisque eiusdem factionis quadraginta senatores, multi praeterea cum spe bona adulescentes sicutei hostiae mactati sunt.* This vast exaggeration is the best evidence of the fury of those hit by the purge; cf. Cicero's report on the *contio* of the tribune M. Antonius of December, 50 (*Att.* 7, 8, 5): *accusatio Pompei usque a toga pura, querela de damnatis, terror armorum.* Also App. *b.c.* 2, 96, and Caes. *b.c.* 1, 4, 3 (of Metellus Scipio): *iudiciorum metus atque ostentatio sui et adulatio potentium, qui in re publica iudiciisque tum plurimum pollebant.* In May 51, M. Caelius wrote to Cicero (*fam.* 8, 1, 4): *Plancus quidem tuus Ravennae est et magno congiario donatus a Caesare nec beatus nec bene instructus est.* This is the tribune of 52, T. Munatius Plancus Bursa, who was prosecuted by Cicero and on whose behalf Pompey intervened in vain (*fam.* 7, 2, 2). Atticus later spoke of the νέκυια (*Att.* 9, 10, 7; 11, 2; 18, 2), when those who had fled to Caesar turned up again in the Civil War.

chief heroes of this national war were men whom he thought he had
won over by his favours. Thus, in the territory of the Belgae Commius the Atrebate prince who had previously rendered him such
signal service was from the start the soul of the rebellion,[1] and even
Vercingetorix, the great leader of the Arverni, had once been
honoured by Caesar with the title of friend.[2] This circumstance also
explains how the Celts came to be so well informed about his
position at Rome. Only a short time after hearing of the murder
of Clodius, the Carnutes massacred the Roman traders as well as
Caesar's commissariat officer who were present in their town of
Cenabum (Orleans).[3] Despite the fact that six legions, the bulk of
the Roman army, were quartered in the land of the Senones, the
intrepid Drappes at once formed a guerrilla force here and seriously
disrupted the Roman food-supply.[4] It seems that this was the reason
why Labienus remained inactive apart from attempting to put a
stop to Commius' intrigues by assassination.[5]

Vercingetorix, whose father Celtillus had been put to death years
earlier for aiming at the kingship,[6] first used this time to draw his
state into the war in face of opposition from the other Arvernian
princes. He was proclaimed king and immediately persuaded a
dozen neighbouring peoples to join him and recognize his supreme
command. Soon his ambition gave him ideas of becoming king in a
national Celtic state, an ideal that had only become a possibility
because Caesar had forced the multifarious Celtic states into the
framework of a unified province, thus making the Celts conscious
of their national unity as being no less a political unity.[7] Vercingetorix himself led part of the federal army which had been recruited
to the Bituriges (Berry) and detached them from the Aedui, their
protecting power.[8] With the other part Lucterius pushed towards the
south and carried the rebellion right to the frontier of the old Roman
province.[9] When Caesar finally appeared on that side of the Alps
towards the end of February, he was just preparing to advance
against the Roman colony of Narbo. But Caesar anticipated this
move by occupying the threatened positions with provincial
militia and the legionary recruits whom he had brought with him.

---

[1] Caes. b.G. 7, 76, 1–2; 8, 23, 3.   [2] Dio 40, 41, 1. Cf. RE, 8A, 982.
[3] Caes. b.G. 7, 3, 1: C. Fufium Citam, honestum equitem Romanum, qui rei frumentariae iussu
Caesaris praeerat.
[4] Op. cit., 8, 30, 1.   [5] Op. cit., 8, 23, 4–6.
[6] Op. cit., 7, 4, 1; Plut. Caes. 25, 5; Cf. RE, 8A, 982.
[7] Caes. b.G. 7, 4, 2–10; Plut. Caes. 27, 1; Polyaen. strat. 8, 23, 9; Oros. 6, 11, 7.
[8] Caes. b.G. 7, 5, 2–6.   [9] Op. cit., 7, 5, 1; 8, 30, 1.

Further, he immediately started to recruit troops for the regular army in the Transalpine province as well, irrespective of whether or not they held Roman citizenship. Eventually 22 new cohorts were formed, with a strong Celtic element.[1]

With whatever men, militia and recruits, he now had available he made a surprise crossing of the heavily snow-covered Cevennes, and threatened the Auvergne. By this demonstration he drew off Vercingetorix to his homeland and himself hastened to Vienne: from there he successfully reached Langres, where the two legions stationed farthest to the south were in quarters, not interrupting his journey even at night.[2] While he was collecting his whole army in the region of Agedincum (Sens), Vercingetorix marched to the north and began to besiege Gorgobina, the centre of the Boii, whom Caesar had settled in that area and placed under the sovereignty of the Aedui. If Vercingetorix succeeded in capturing the town, that would be a signal to the whole of Gaul that Caesar was unable to protect his friends.[3] For this reason Caesar resolved to begin campaigning immediately despite great difficulties in providing food at that time of year. At the same time he intended by smashing the rebels to make others lose their appetite for revolt. He therefore turned first against Cenabum. *En route* he forced a citadel of the Senones to surrender after only a two-day siege. Nor was Cenabum prepared for his attack. The inhabitants intended to escape by night over the Loire bridge, but the Romans got wind of this, forced their way into the town, and captured most of the enemy. The town, where the revolt had originated, was plundered and set on fire, the booty given by Caesar to his soldiers.[4] Then he crossed the Loire and reached the land of the Bituriges. Vercingetorix immediately came to their defence, abandoning Gorgobina. The Roman army was in front of a town called Noviodunum (south of Cenabum), which had just surrendered, when the Celtic vanguard appeared. Thereupon the town again shut its gates, an act that it was soon to regret, as thanks to 400 German horsemen whom Caesar had hired the Celtic cavalry were thrown into flight. He now

---

[1] Op. cit., 7, 7, 1–18, 1; 9, 1; 65, 1. Possibly it was from such steps that the later *legio V Alaudae* was formed; see Suet. *Caes.* 24, 2: *unam etiam ex Transalpinis conscriptam vocabulo quoque Gallico — Alauda enim appellabatur — quam disciplina cultuque Romano institutam et ornatam postea universam civitate donavit*; and Plin. *n.h.* 11, 121: *postea Gallico vocabulo etiam legioni nomen dederat alaudae.* Also Cic. *Phil.* 1, 20; 5, 12; 13, 3; 22; *fam.* 10, 34, 1: *legio.* Cf. *b. Afr.* 1, 5; 28, 2. Cf. Ritterling, *RE*, 12, 1564.

[2] Caes. *b.G.* 7, 8, 2–9, 4.

[3] Op. cit., 7, 9, 6; 10, 1.

[4] Op. cit., 7, 10, 2–11, 9.

advanced (in about April, Jul.) to Avaricum (Bourges), the wealthy and extremely strong capital of the Bituriges. He hoped for much from its conquest, as the winning over of the Bituriges had been one of Vercingetorix's main achievements.[1] For this very reason the latter felt inclined to abandon the town voluntarily, since he could hardly hope to defeat the Romans in a pitched battle. His strategic plain aimed at wearing them right down by denying them provisions. To this end all localities where supplies were stored and which were not thoroughly protected against attack had to be ruthlessly destroyed. Vercingetorix had his fellow-countrymen so well in hand that the Bituriges alone burned twenty towns. They only balked at the destruction of Avaricum, and so it was decided to defend the place.[2] Vercingetorix remained in the neighbourhood with his field force and made strenuous efforts to prevent the Romans from bringing up supplies. For a time they suffered great hunger, and Caesar only dared to continue the siege after he had given his troops the opportunity to withdraw and they had expressly begged him not to give up. This persistence was eventually rewarded by the capture of the fortress with its rich supplies. In their fury the soldiers massacred the whole population of allegedly 40,000 people including women and children.[3] Caesar could now hope that the power of his enemy would crumble. But in this he was completely mistaken. His military success at Avaricum brought him no political profit. For Vercingetorix pointed out to his people that he had been utterly opposed to holding Avaricum and that otherwise the Roman situation had not improved. Supported by universal confidence, he gave orders that the losses should be made good by new levies and successfully sent ambassadors to work on the states that had so far stood aloof. Just at this moment Teotomatus, king of the Nitiobriges (from the middle Garonne) arrived to join him with a strong mounted retinue, despite the fact that his father had been included on the Senate's list of friends of Rome.[4]

Most critical for Caesar was the fact that the Aedui were becoming less and less reliable. They had already been negligent in providing corn for his siege troops.[5] Now he was told that as a result of a divided vote there were two occupants of the supreme magistracy and that civil war was imminent. Some nobles appealed to Caesar to arbitrate. Since it was clear that in the event of a recourse to

---

[1] Op. cit., 7, 12–13; cf. RE, 8A, 985.   [2] Caes. b.G. 7, 14–15.
[3] Op. cit., 7, 16–28; Dio 40, 34; Oros. 6, 11, 1–4.
[4] Caes. b.G. 7, 29–31.   [5] Op. cit., 7, 17, 3.

arms the weaker party would ask Vercingetorix for help, he interrupted his campaign and summoned the council of the Aedui to meet him at Decetia (Decize on the Loire). Caesar's decision upheld the hitherto valid custom and recognized Convictolitavis, who had been elected by the Druids according to long-established practice, as the legal vergobret. Then he expressed the hope that they would now bury their quarrels, participate in the war with enthusiasm and so earn the rich rewards that would follow victory. Accordingly, he gave orders for the entire cavalry and 10,000 infantry to join him in the field.[1]

As the land of the Aedui was to form the base for his further operations, he had his corn supplies moved bodily to Noviodunum (Nevers, somewhat to the south of Decetia and also on the Loire), where the hostages of the Gallic tribes, the governor's treasury, a large portion of the army's baggage and the spare horses bought up in Italy and Spain also stayed behind, protected by a small garrison. For the continuation of the war he divided his forces: while he himself led six legions up the valley of the Allier in the direction of Gergovia, the main stronghold of the Arverni (four miles to the south of Clermont-Ferrand), Labienus was again to march with four legions into the land of the Senones and the Parisii (Paris) situated still farther to the north.[2]

As soon as Caesar arrived before Gergovia it became apparent that he had considerably underestimated the difficulty of an attack on this extensive and naturally very strong position, particularly as it was held by Vercingetorix with superior forces. It could not be captured by blockade but only by storm, and that only in exceptionally favourable circumstances.[3] Meanwhile Vercingetorix's envoys at last succeeded in producing the political change of front among the Aedui which had been preparing for a long time. Even in this state, which owed its present position of power to Caesar, there had always been strong anti-Roman elements—we need only mention Dumnorix. Now even those who had hitherto been friendly to Rome thought that the moment had come to change sides; while their change of allegiance still had some significance, they could hope to play a big role in the new Gallic empire. Thus Convictolitavis actually placed himself at the head of the national movement. At the time their cavalry under Eporedorix and Viridomarus were already in the Roman camp before Gergovia,

---

[1] Op. cit., 7, 32–34, 1.   [2] Op. cit., 7, 34, 2; 2, 55, 1–3; Dio 40, 38, 2.
[3] Caes. b.G. 7, 36.

but the infantry was still to come. Litaviccus, who was of the same mind as the vergobret, was put in command of them. While they were still about two days' march from Gergovia, he roused his 10,000 to revolt against the Romans by telling them that Caesar had executed the two cavalry leaders without trial as traitors. The Romans who were conveying a large supply train to Gergovia under the protection of the Aeduan column were immediately massacred, the supplies were plundered and the homeland called upon to follow this example. It did so at once: throughout the country, with the vergobret's approval, the Romans present were murdered or enslaved and their property plundered. In Cabillonum (Chalon-sur-Saône), where there was a sizeable number of resident Roman merchants, these were ordered out of the town and then attacked, plundered and held prisoner.[1]

As soon as the Aedui before Gergovia learned what had happened to the infantry, Eporedorix informed Caesar and begged him to take immediate counter-measures. This he resolved to do on the spot: he withdrew from Gergovia with four legions and all his cavalry in order to catch the 10,000 and to prevent their treason from spreading any further. Faced with this force, the rebels surrendered without delay and followed Caesar, who did not punish them at all, to Gergovia; Litaviccus, the instigator of the trouble, escaped to Vercingetorix. When this news reached the territory of the Aedui they released the imprisoned Romans and declared themselves ready to pay reparations; envoys were sent to Caesar to apologize for the excesses that had been committed. Caesar made their task easy by declaring that the actions of an ignorant mob in no way influenced his attitude towards the community.[2]

However, such leniency would no longer be of any use, unless it was backed by military successes against the Arverni, and of these there was no sign. Already during Caesar's short absence the enemy had fallen upon the two legions which he had left behind and reduced them to great straits.[3] Caesar realized that he would have to abandon the whole venture; but then, on a tour of his lines, he thought he could still find an opportunity for a surprise attack, and he ordered his troops to assault an unoccupied portion of the enemy fortifications. After an initial success the battle ended in a

[1] Op. cit., 7, 37–38; 42; Dio 40, 37; App. *Celt.* 21.
[2] Caes. *b.G.* 7, 39–41, 1; 43, 1–4.   [3] Op. cit., 7, 41, 2–5.

signal defeat: 46 centurions and 700 legionaries were left dead on the field.[1]

Although he managed to disengage himself from the enemy two days later without further casualties, it looked as if the breakdown of Caesar's strategy was now in sight. Litaviccus immediately moved with the entire cavalry of the federal army to Bibracte (Mont Beuvray), the capital of the Aedui. Viridomarus and Eporedorix demanded to be sent home to deal with him, and Caesar, although he did not trust them, let them go in order to demonstrate his confidence. When the pair reached Noviodunum they learned that the Aeduan state had officially gone over to the Celtic federation and that envoys were already on their way to Vercingetorix. So they had the Roman guard at Noviodunum and the merchants at the storehouses massacred. They took the money and horses as their booty and gave orders that such of the corn as could not be put on board ship should be tipped into the Loire or burnt, while the Celtic hostages were to be taken to Bibracte. Noviodunum itself was set on fire to prevent its being of further use to Caesar. The local militia occupied the Loire crossings, and Celtic horsemen were on patrol everywhere in order to cut the Romans off from provisions. Caesar was either to starve to death or at least to be forced to withdraw into the old province.[2]

Even in the midst of these dangers the general who had won so many victories did not abandon the plan of linking up with Labienus which he had formed for his retreat. In forced marches by day and night he reached the Loire, successfully brought his whole army across a ford, procured the necessary supplies in the country and again marched into the land of the Senones. Here, somewhat to the south of Agedincum, he duly managed to link up with Labienus, who for his part had crossed the Seine, but on news of Caesar's retreat had likewise turned back, and after defeating the levies of the northern tribes forced his way through to Agedincum.[3]

The defection of the Aedui and the capture of the Celtic hostages in Noviodunum were events of the greatest significance. A Gallic assembly was now called in Bibracte and, apart from the Aquitani,

[1] Op. cit., 7, 43, 5–51; Suet. *Caes.* 25, 2: *ad Gergoviam legione fusa;* Oros. 6, 11, 6: *Caesar erumpentibus desuper hostibus pressus multa exercitus sui parte perdita victus aufugit.* The emphasis given to the defeat proably goes back to the source (Livy?), so that a glimmer of the contemporary hostility to Caesar may be detected. Caesar contradicts such exaggerated assertions in his own fashion (7, 52) by reporting the *contio* addressed to his soldiers, in which he attributes the misfortune to their lack of discipline.

[2] Caes. *b.G.* 7, 54–55; Dio 40, 38, 1–3.   [3] Caes. *b.G.* 7, 56–62; Dio 40, 38, 4.

only a few Celtic tribes held aloof, namely the Remi and Lingones, who remained loyal to Rome, and the Treveri who were busy fighting the Germans.[1] By a vote of all present Vercingetorix was confirmed as commander of the federal forces.[2] He persisted in his plan of starving out the Roman forces without a battle, but at the same time the Aedui and other neighbours of the old province were urged to make another attack on it. He hoped that the Allobroges, who had again been crushed with much bloodshed ten years previously, would join the great liberation movement and in return promised them the leading position in the whole Transalpine region.[3] This hope was disappointed, because Caesar had absolutely loyal followers among their nobility. Thus the Allobroges allowed no one to cross the Rhone. Yet in other respects the situation was serious enough. The enemy advance over the Cevennes was successful; the 22 newly recruited cohorts were scattered along the length of the frontier, and Caesar had to come to the rescue in person.[4]

While his opponent was making new preparations, he had granted his stout legions in the land of the Lingones a few weeks of wellearned rest.[5] Since there were no reinforcements available in the province (not to mention Italy), and since the enemy had a far larger cavalry force at their disposal, Caesar had some more German cavalry fetched from across the Rhine; he had learned to respect their incomparable value in the first engagement of the war.[6] Meanwhile, the armed forces of Vercingetorix were collecting further to the south, where he organized Alesia, the citadel of the Mandubii, as his base.[7] In order to be nearer to the old province, Caesar started with his whole army towards the land of the Sequani. When he had reached the neighbourhood of Dijon on his journey,[8] Vercingetorix

[1] Caes. b.G. 7, 63, 7; Plut. Caes. 26, 5.   [2] Caes. b.G. 7, 63, 6.
[3] Op. cit., 7, 64.   [4] Op. cit., 7, 65, 1–3; b.c. 3, 59, 1–3.
[5] Jullian, 3, 483, n. 1; RE, 8A, 995.   [6] Caes. b.G. 7, 65, 4–5.
[7] Op. cit., 7, 69, 5; 71, 7. On Alesia (Mont Auxois with the village of Alise-Sainte-Reine in Burgundy), see RE, 8A, 995 f., 2418–19; J. Carcopino, Alésia et les ruses de César (1958), 1–184.
[8] Thus Jullian and Holmes (RE, 8A, 997) adopting the views of Napoleon III. In 7, 66, 2 Caesar names as his objective the land of the Sequani to the east of the Saône (b.G. 1, 12, 1; Strab. 4, 186; 192). Dio (40, 39, 1) states that Vercingetorix marched against the Allobroges and clashed with Caesar in the land of the Sequani. He has unskilfully abbreviated his source. The reference to the Allobroges ultimately goes back to Caes. b.G. 7, 64, 5 (bellum inferre Allobrogibus iubet); and he is just as inaccurate in rendering b.G. 66, 2 (cum Caesar in Sequanos per extremos Lingonum fines iter faceret) as 'Vercingetorix caught Caesar among the Sequani'. As Dio relates, he needed ten years to make excerpts from the histories which provided him with information from the origins of Rome down to his own time, and twelve for the subsequent artistic elaboration. It is understandable that with this method of work such errors

decided to attack the column with his numerically far superior cavalry. For he rightly argued that Caesar's retreat in no way meant that he was abandoning Gaul for good, and he hoped to delay the march or even to force the Romans to leave behind their baggage-train in ignominious flight. The Celtic cavalry were delighted with the plan and swore a great oath that no one was to return to his home unless he had twice ridden through the Roman column. They charged simultaneously from the front, right and left, but were successfully repulsed by the Romans. Eventually the German cavalry seized the high ground on the right wing and routed the enemy with heavy casualties, so that the remainder soon dispersed from fear of encirclement.[1]

The moral effect of this quite unexpected defeat was so great that Vercingetorix thought it expedient to retire to Alesia. In a flash Caesar grasped the changed situation and began on the next day to enclose the impregnable fortress with a cordon of siege works over ten miles in length. Vercingetorix was barely able to get his cavalry out, with orders to bring the whole federal army to his relief; then the lines closed for ever. Weeks of enormous tension followed, while the contingents of 43 states gathered in the land of the Aedui and were placed under the joint command of Commius, Viridomarus, Eporedorix and Vercassivellaunus, a cousin of Vercingetorix; and Caesar, for his part, was building a second cordon around the inner blockade line in order to keep them out. At last, after more than thirty days, when the stocks of corn in Alesia had already been consumed and supplies in the Roman camp were steadily decreasing, came the great decision.[2]

It opened on the first day with a cavalry battle, which again ended in a Roman victory thanks to the impetuous valour of the Germans. After a day's rest the Roman fortifications were simultaneously attacked from inside and out, but they were nowhere pierced. Around midday on the fourth day the final storm burst; both besieged and relievers put forth their utmost efforts. On this occasion too, after a fearful battle, the Romans came through

---

crept in. One cannot play Dio off against Caesar, as does Carcopino (op. cit., 122). On this method of work, normal in ancient historiography, see the detailed work of Gert Avenarius, *Lukians Schrift zur Geschichtsschreibung* (1956), 85 ff. Plut. *Caes.* 26, 6 is right. Recently Luigi Pareti (*Storia di Roma e del Mondo Romano*, 4 (1955), 133) has conjectured that the battlefield was in the region of Monbard in the Armançon valley, north-west of Alesia. Dijon lies to the sout-east. Carcopino (op. cit., 188) looks for it still closer to Alesia, but also to the north-west.

[1] Caes. *b.G.* 7, 66, 2–67; Plut. *Caes.* 26, 7–8; Dio 40, 39, 2–3; cf. *RE*, 8A, 997–999.
[2] Caes. *b.G.* 7, 68–76; Plut. *Caes.* 27, 1–4; Dio 40, 40, 1–4; cf. *RE*, 8A, 999–1001.

victorious. The great relieving army scattered after the loss of 74 standards. On the next day Vercingetorix surrendered. Caesar ordered the enemy to lay down their arms and hand over their leaders; he had his tribunal erected on one of the bulwarks in order to await their arrival.[1] Vercingetorix rode up proudly on horseback and fell to his knees in silence before Caesar, hoping as a former friend for the victor's forgiveness. Some of the spectators were touched, but Caesar remained unmoved and reproached him with his crime. The great rebel was to suffer the consequences of his audacity, and the general gave orders that he was to be kept in custody until his triumph and subsequent execution. Since he did not triumph until 46, the unfortunate national hero of the Celts had to wait six years in Roman prisons for his death.[2]

The prisoners were divided among the soldiers as slaves, after the 20,000 Aedui and Arverni had been separated from them. To these two powerful states Caesar restored their subjects.[3] He even granted the Aedui their former status as free allies, a position which apart from themselves only the loyal Remi and Lingones received.[4] He also allowed the Arverni easy terms of surrender in return for a large number of hostages. They were recognized as free, i.e., Rome did not interfere in their internal affairs.[5]

This preferential treatment of the two leading tribes fully achieved its purpose. They abandoned the national cause and rendered Caesar every service that he wished. This was very important as the war was by no means over. Admittedly, the danger of a unified Celtic state had passed and a thanksgiving of twenty days' duration[6] could be celebrated at Rome with more justification than ever before;

[1] Caes. b.G. 7, 77–89, 4. Peculiar deviations in Plut. Caes. 27, 1–4; Polyaen. 8, 23, 11. Cf. RE, 8A, 1005.

[2] Dio 40, 41; 43, 19, 4; Plut. Caes. 27, 8–10; Oros. 6, 11, 11; Flor. 1, 45, 23–26. Cf. RE, 8A, 1006. L. Pareti (Storia di Roma, 4, 139), regards the head of a Gaul on a coin of 48 as Vercingetorix (also reproduced in H. Kähler, Rom und seine Welt (1958), plate 59); in addition Pareti gives enlarged coin portraits (pp. 146, 149) of captured Gauls, which he describes as representations of Vercingetorix. Cf. RE, 8A, 989, and, equally sceptical, K. Christ (Historia 6 (1957), 228).

[3] Caes. b.G. 7, 89, 5–90, 3.

[4] Plin. n.h. 4, 107; 106. Cf. Dessau, ILS, 1380; 6997: civitas Remor(um) foeder(ata). Also Tac. hist. 4, 67 on the Lingones. Cf. O. Hirscheld, Kl. Schr., 192–193.

[5] Plin. n.h. 4, 109; cf. Suet. Caes. 25, 1: omnem Galliam . . . praeter socias ac bene meritas civitates in provinciae formam redegit.

[6] Caes. b.G. 7, 89, 5–90, 3. Caesar's enemies presumably voted for it in order to have a reason for recalling Caesar (Suet. Caes. 28, 2: in April 51 the consul M. Marcellus reported to the Senate ut ei succederetur ante tempus, quoniam bello confecto pax esset ac dimitti deberet victor exercitus). Cf. Dio 40, 44, 1.

but it was debatable whether Caesar would still be able during his governorship to restore the rebellious land to allegiance. The Celtic leaders understood conditions at Rome well enough to know that his command would probably expire in the year 50.[1] Would it not be possible, they asked themselves, at least to carry on guerrilla warfare against the scattered Roman army until then, and after Caesar's departure to secure their freedom? In order to nip such plans in the bud Caesar again spent this winter at his headquarters at Bibracte.[2]

The troops had hardly moved into camp when he found it necessary at the beginning of the official year 51 (early December 52, Jul.) to restore order among the Bituriges and their neighbours with two legions. The speed with which the country was occupied made resistance impossible, and, on asking for mercy, they too received favourable terms: their state also became one of the 'free' communities.[3] The soldiers who had taken part in this winter campaign, before marching back to their winter-quarters, received an extra payment of 200 sesterces (50 denarii) and the centurions 2,000 sesterces

---

[1] b.G. 8, 39, 3: *cum omnibus Gallis notum esse sciret reliquam esse unam aestatem provinciae suae.* A Caesarian like Hirtius cannot have meant the summer of 51, as O. Hirschfeld (*Kl. Schr.*, 318; 325) maintained. He takes it for granted (48, 10) that Caesar would remain in Gaul in 50 B.C. Caesar himself (*b.c.* 3, 1, 1) of the year 48: *is enim erat annus, quo per leges ei consulem fieri liceret.* P. J. Cuff (*Historia* 7 (1958), 469, n. 96) rightly argues for 50. If the proposal was made in 52 that Caesar might perhaps assume the consulship with Pompey, this shows that, in the event of an agreement between the two *principes*, Caesar as well as Pompey could have been released from the interval required before the assumption of a second consulship. On this, see *Hermes* 63, 127; cf. ibid., 125, n. 3 (=*Kl. Schr.*, 2, 217 f.), where it is argued that one cannot calculate the duration of Caesar's and Pompey's extraordinary commands in months and days. Caesar's *imperium* was renewed as early as 55, Pompey's in 52, although, according to the *Lex Vatinia* and *Lex Trebonia*, the Senate could reach no decision on the provinces concerned before March 1, 54, and March 1, 50, respectively. Cuff (op. cit., 464) has not noticed this fact.

[2] Caes. *b.G.* 7, 90, 8; cf. 8, 4, 2 (*ibi cum ius diceret*). One should certainly think first of the magisterial jurisdiction in cases between Roman citizens and between Roman citizens and foreigners (*peregrini*). Caesar himself only mentions his *conventus* in Gallia Citerior (1, 54, 3; 5, 1, 5; 2, 1; 6, 44, 3; 7, 1, 1=8, 23, 3: *Caesare in Gallia citeriore ius dicente*). But in his letters to Trebatius, Cicero frequently alludes to the administration of justice in the winter-camp at Samarobriva, in which Trebatius took part as *iuris consultus* (*fam.* 7, 10, 1; 13, 1; 14, 2; 16, 3). It is gratifying for the modern historian that A. Hirtius, the author of Book 8, keeps more closely to the records made in Caesar's office, the *commentarii* in the true sense (F. Bömer, *Hermes* 81 (1953), 214), while his general used the documents with greater freedom and omitted what he thought unimportant.

[3] b.G. 8, 1–4, 1; 3, 5: *Bituriges, cum sibi viderent clementia Caesaris reditum patere in eius amicitiam finitimasque civitates sine ulla poena dedisse obsides atque in fidem receptas esse, idem fecerunt*; Plin. *n.h.* 4, 109: *Bituriges liberi qui Cubi appellantur;* Strab. 4, 190; the Cubi are never mentioned by Caesar (Ihm, *RE*, 3, 548). The *Bituriges cognomine Vivisci* (Plin. *n.h.* 4, 108), with their capital at Burdigala, lived on the lower Garonne.

(500 denarii).[1] After an absence of forty days Caesar returned to Bibracte (at the beginning of January, Jul.); eighteen days later he was called from the administration of justice to help the Bituriges against the Carnutes. By the transfer of two legions to Cenabum this movement too was immediately crushed: the population was forced to flee to the surrounding states.[2]

Next, learning through the Remi that the Bellovaci and some other Belgic states were preparing for war, he immediately concentrated four legions against them. Since they conducted operations very skilfully under the leadership of Correus and Commius, he was soon forced to send for another two legions, but even so suffered some serious reverses, with the result that by the end of April (Jul.) his enemies at Rome, such as Lucius Domitius Ahenobarbus, were actually entertaining secret hopes of a major disaster.[3] However, these came to a sudden end after a successful engagement in which Correus was killed. Envoys from the Bellovaci now humbly begged for forgiveness and put all the blame on their fallen leader. Caesar told them that such excuses were of no avail with him, but did not punish them any further, with the result that the remaining rebellious Belgae immediately surrendered. However, these states were not only required to furnish hostages, but also to pay a tribute proportionate to their previous unreliability.[4] With the pacification of

---

[1] b.G. 8, 4, 1. According to G. R. Watson (Historia 7 (1958), 117) a soldier's annual pay at that time (Plin. n.h. 33, 45) amounted to 112½ denarii. Suet. Caes. 26, 3 states: legionibus stipendium in perpetuum duplicavit. We do not know whether this was done as early as the Gallic War.

[2] b.G. 8, 4, 2–5.

[3] Caelius to Cicero (fam. 8, 1, 4, shortly after May 24, 51): quod ad Caesarem, crebri et non belli de eo rumores, sed susurratores dumtaxat, veniunt. alius equitem perdidisse, quod opinor certe factum est, alius septimam legionem vapulasse, ipsum apud Bellovacos circumsederi interclusum ab reliquo exercitu; neque adhuc certi quicquam est, neque haec incerta tamen vulgo iactantur, sed inter paucos quos tu nosti palam secreto narrantur; at Domitius, cum manus ad os opposuit. The news of which Caelius seems certain is confirmed by Hirtius (12, 3–7), where the cavalry contingent of the Remi suffers heavy casualties. The seventh legion was with Caesar (8, 2), but Hirtius says nothing of a set-back, except (16, 4) in general terms: magna detrimenta Romanis in pabulationibus inferebant. There could be no question of Caesar's being encircled. But Caelius' amusing communication is important because it shows the extent to which Caesar's enemies in Rome were also kept continually informed about events in the Gallic theatre of operations. The false news presumably goes back to rumours circulating in the winter-camps far from Caesar. In April 53 Cicero wrote to Trebatius (fam. 7, 18, 1): tu me velim de ratione Gallici belli certiorem facias; ego enim ignavissimo cuique maximam fidem habeo.

[4] b.G. 8, 6–23, 2; Dio 40, 42–43, 1. On tribute, Suet. Caes. 25, 1; Dio 40, 43, 3. In Hirtius' account of the negotiations with the Bellovaci, it is remarkable that they maintained (21, 4) numquam enim senatum tantum in civitate illo vivo quantum imperitam plebem potuisse. Thereupon Caesar replied (22, 2): neminem tantum pollere ut invitis principibus, resistente senatu, omnibus bonis repugnantibus infirma manu plebis bellum concitare et gerere posset. This is the same social stratification that Caesar (6, 13, 1–2) describes (plebes paene servorum habetur loco). But Hirtius has no

Belgium the most difficult part of the task still remaining was completed. Caesar felt himself strong enough to transfer one legion to northern Italy as a demonstration of how things stood in Gaul.[1] He himself now directed a further devastation of the land of the Eburones, in order to make a return of the hated Ambiorix quite impossible, while his lieutenants brought back to allegiance the peoples of the Loire area, Normandy, Brittany and, in the east, the Treveri. He then visited many of the newly-subjugated districts in person and was everywhere able to reassure the inhabitants by his politic clemency. Even among the Carnutes, who had gone so badly astray, he contented himself with the execution of one solitary leader.[2]

The last serious battle developed for the fortress of Uxellodunum (Puy d'Issolu on the Dordogne) where Drappes and Lucterius hoped to hold out until Caesar's departure. He was very keen that this should not happen, and so in the middle of summer himself made for this theatre of operations, where he soon forced the town to surrender by cutting off its water supply.[3] On this occasion he thought that cruelty would pay him better than clemency; though sparing their lives, he had the hands of all prisoners who had carried arms cut off. The whole of Gaul was not only to hear but also to see how he would treat any further rebellion. Drappes committed suicide in captivity. Lucterius at first escaped, but was later handed over to Caesar by a pro-Roman Arvernian for execution.[4] The only one to fight on in his Belgic homeland until the winter was Commius who eventually surrendered to the quaestor Mark Antony on promise of his life.[5] When Caesar had at last acquainted himself personally with Aquitania, he sent his army into winter-quarters.

hesitation in making him speak of the upper class, which Caesar (13, 3) describes as *equites*, as *omnes boni*, just as Cicero (*p. red. in sen.* 17; *Sest.* 1; 11; 53) speaks of *senatus atque omnes boni*. On this see H. Strasburger, *Concordia ordinum* (Diss. Frankfurt (1931)), 60, who also quotes Cic. *dom.* 94: *ex auctoritate senatus consensu bonorum omnium*; *fam.* 1, 9, 12; 5, 2, 8. Cf. J. Vogt, *Hermes* 68 (1933), 91. In his war books Caesar does not use *bonus* in this political sense, but in his letter to Cicero on April 16, 49 (*Att.* 10, 8b, 2) he says: *quid viro bono et quieto et bono civi magis convenit quam abesse a civilibus controversiis?*

[1] *b.G.* 8, 24, 3. The military reason was protection against barbarian attacks.

[2] *b.G.* 8, 24, 4–31; 38; 45. On the execution of Gutruatus, Hirtius (38, 5) comments: *cogitur in eius supplicium contra naturam suam Caesar maximo militum concursu qui ei omnia pericula et detrimenta belli accepta referebant, adeo ut verberibus exanimatum corpus securi feriretur.* Also Oros. 6, 11, 15–19.

[3] *b.G.* 8, 30; 32–37; 39–43; Oros. 6, 11, 20–28.

[4] *b.G.* 8, 44; Oros. 6, 11, 29–30. Hirtius (44, 1) also comments on this punishment: *Caesar, cum suam lenitatem cognitam omnibus sciret neque vereretur, ne quid crudelitate naturae videretur asperius fecisse . . .*

[5] *b.G.* 8, 47–48.

This year once again he did not cross the Alps, but contented himself with a tour of Narbonensis lasting several days, during which he liberally rewarded all those who had proved loyal in the hard times of the previous year and had thus contributed so much to the final victory. These could have whatever they wanted: money, the confiscated property of rebels, positions of honour in local government.[1]

He spent the rest of the winter at headquarters at Nemetocenna (Arras) and now gave the country its definitive organization. The war in the independent Celtic territory, which he had at first justified as undertaken to protect the Aedui, Rome's blood-brothers, had developed in the course of the years into the conquest of an area of 200,000 square miles. Just as he had fought the war, so he now gave Gaul its constitution on his own authority: the relationship between each state and Rome was settled, and those who—unlike the Aedui, Remi and Lingones—were not recognized as equal allies had their tribute finally assessed. The total sum to be paid annually by Gallia Comata came to 40 million sesterces (10 million denarii): the explanation for this remarkably small figure is to be found in the terrible exhaustion of the country.[2] It was estimated that during the war a third of the men able to bear arms fell before the Roman sword, while another third became prisoners or slaves. Over 800 localities were captured by force, a large part of these destroyed in the process, and wide tracts were thoroughly plundered and laid waste.[3] The wealth which Caesar took from the country in booty, confiscations and war contributions cannot be calculated, but must have been quite enormous. The restoration of his own shattered fortune was the least important factor, but his extravagant generosity towards all who served him knew no bounds. The enthusiastic support of the soldiers for their general rested partly on the splendid rewards with which he recognized the services of

[1] b.C. 8, 46; b.c. 3, 59, 2.

[2] Suet. Caes. 25, 1: omnem Galliam . . . in provinciae formam redegit eique quadringenties centena milium in singulos annos stipendii nomine imposuit.

[3] Plut. Caes. 15, 5; App. Celt. 1, 6 goes back to the same source, but puts the total conquered at four million men and four hundred ἔθνη instead of Plutarch's three million men and three hundred ἔθνη. According to Plin. n.h. 7, 92, Caesar's figures in his Gallic triumph in 46 (Suet. Caes. 37, 1; Dio 43, 19, 1) ran to 1,192,000 dead. Pliny comments on this: non equidem in gloria posuerim tantam etiam coactam humani generis iniuriam; Caesar (he adds) recognized this himself, and did not give the total of those killed in the Civil War. Presumably the number is just as exaggerated as the statements about the size of the enemy armies. Cf. RE, 8A, 999; 1001–1003. The number of 300 or 400 ἔθνη, by which only the pagi of the civitates can be meant, also supports this view. According to Caes. b.G. 1, 12, 4, the civitas of the Helvetii consisted of four pagi; in 1, 37, 3 and 4, 1, 3 the Suebi are given 100 pagi; cf. 4, 22, 5: in eos pagos Morinorum, a quibus ad eum legati non venerunt.

his army. But the largest sums must have been swallowed up by his
political connections. Cicero was only one of the numerous senators
kept afloat by sizeable fortunes from Caesar.[1] His agents and senior
officers all attained ostentatious and much-loathed wealth, and the
number of young men at his Gallic headquarters recovering from
a loose or notorious life at Rome was always considerable.[2] When,
at the end of 52, Titus Munatius Plancus was condemned in the great
purge for the prominent part which he had taken in the anarchy
as tribune of that year, he travelled to Ravenna and lived there
on a pension granted by Caesar.[3] In addition, each year there was
increasing expenditure, fabulous in extent, aimed at winning
popularity in Rome and the provinces. The land alone for the new
Forum Iulium cost 100 million sesterces.[4] He donated buildings to
several cities in Italy, the old Gallic provinces, Spain, Greece and
Asia Minor; to allied kings he sent slaves from his booty or supplied
them with (presumably Celtic) mercenaries.[5] These enormous sums
were raised mainly by the plundering of Celtic shrines, where
valuable treasures had piled up over the centuries as the result of
pious dedications. Italy was flooded with this gold, so that a Roman
pound (320 grammes) was now offered for sale at 3,000 sesterces
(750 denarii), while the same amount in gold coins fetched 4,000
sesterces (1,000 denarii).[6]

   Thus Caesar had reduced the population of Gaul to such a state
that, with the exception of the Bellovaci, who roused themselves
once more in 46,[7] they were incapable of any resistance for more
than a decade.[8] That in every state the reins of government were
held only by well-paid partisans almost goes without saying. As a

   [1] With a loan. At the end of December, 50, Cicero was worried that he was not yet in a
position to pay it back (*Att.* 7, 3, 11; 8, 5). See above, pp. 137 f.
   [2] Cicero to Trebatius (*fam.* 7, 13, 1): *audi, Testa mi: utrum superiorem te pecunia facit an quod
te imperator consulit? moriar ni, quae tua gloria est, puto te malle a Caesare consuli quam inaurari.*
But he can jest that Trebatius is in such a hurry to return home as soon as he has got some
money that it looks as if he had brought the general not Cicero's letter of recommendation
but a promissory note (*fam.* 7, 17, 1). In general, see Dio 40, 60, 3–4; Cic. *Phil.* 2, 50 of Antony.
   [3] M. Caelius to Cicero (*fam.* 8, 1, 4). See above, p. 154, n. 4; p. 147, n. 2.
   [4] Suet. *Caes.* 26, 2; Plin. *n.h.* 36, 103; see p. 140, above.
   [5] Suet. *Caes.* 28, 1.
   [6] Suet. *Caes.* 54, 2. An *aureus* weighed 126 grains, and was worth 100 sesterces. Cf. Becker,
RE, 19, 1474; Hultsch, *RE*, 5, 209.
   [7] Liv. *per.* 114: *Brutus legatus Caesaris in Gallia Bellovacos rebellantes proelio vicit*; App. *b.c.*
2, 465.
   [8] Oros. 6, 12, 1. He follows this with a consideration of the fate of Gaul and makes the
country say, with reference to his own time (12, 7): 'ita me Romani inclinaverunt, ut nec ad
Gothos surgam'—an astonishingly apt verdict on the Roman imperial period. Cf. *Aufstieg
und Untergang der Grossreiche des Altertums* (1958), 125.

Roman statesman he could point out that the *imperium populi Romani* over the new province was at last secure. This achievement received official recognition in the repeated decrees ordaining thanksgivings of many days' duration. As early as 56 Cicero had praised it eloquently: hitherto we only possessed a footpath in Gaul—he is thinking of the land connection with Spain—and yet the country is full of hostile, malevolent, barbarous and warlike peoples, a standing menace to the Roman Empire. But so far no one, not even Gaius Marius, has dared to challenge them all at once. The Romans have so far merely warded off isolated attacks. Caesar, however, is of the opinion that the whole of Gaul must come under the Roman sway. That was why he was pushing into areas, the names of which were previously unknown, and moving the Roman frontier to the ocean.[1] And in 55 he again extols Caesar's military leadership, saying that the Alps no longer formed the barricade against the Celts nor did the Rhine keep the Germans at bay: Italy would be protected by Caesar's victories even if the mountains were to subside or the rivers to dry up.[2] Caesar himself in his military commentaries does not adopt this tone. He always, of course, justifies his campaigns with the necessity of countering most dangerous plans of aggression and conquest. But his victories and the consequent strengthening of Roman dominion over the conquered only represented the fulfilment of duties entrusted to him by popular decrees. The ability thus to portray his actions as the only right and proper ones appears as an important part of his genius. And yet the conquest of Gaul did not mean for him the attainment of an end after which he could rest. His political position in Rome was far too precarious, and the most serious battle was yet to be fought. With this in view he had forged his Gallic army into an instrument the like of which no Roman statesman had ever possessed, and his ability to finance his policies was likewise without precedent. From the autumn of 51 he was again able to concentrate entirely on politics at Rome.

There his opponents continued to work steadfastly for his downfall. Admittedly Marcus Cato, the most dangerous of these, had failed to secure election to the consulship for this year.[3] But Marcus Claudius Marcellus,[4] one of the most distinguished optimates from the point of view of ability and morality, was elected instead and

---

[1] Cic. *prov. cons.* 32–34.   [2] Cic. *Pis.* 81–82.
[3] Plut. *Cat. Min.* 49–50; Dio 40, 58.
[4] Cic. *Brut.* 250. There is a letter from Marcellus in Cic. *fam.* 4, 11.

M

pursued the same programme: Caesar was to be relieved of his command as soon as possible and then as a private citizen to be rendered harmless by condemnation. At every opportunity Cato declared that he would impeach him as soon as his army was dismissed, and then like Milo he was to be called to account before a court heavily guarded by troops.[1]

Caesar had only partly been able to protect himself against this danger by the popular decree of 52 which allowed him to stand for the consulship for 48 without appearing in person. For as a result of Pompey's new law on the administration of the provinces it had become doubtful whether he would remain in possession of his provinces from March 1, 50, to December 29, 49, as could implicitly be taken for granted in the year 55 when only the Sempronian and Cornelian laws were in force. Meanwhile, the Senate had extended Pompey's proconsulship over the two Spanish provinces, while at the same time he held his third consulship. Although the agreements of Luca were entirely of a private nature, we can see from Cicero's speeches of 56 the extent to which the arrangements then made had thereafter to be reckoned with in politics. But one of their main points had been that there was to be complete equality among the partners. So far Pompey had not dropped the mask of friendship, however little his recent behaviour matched his earlier trustworthiness. Thus an attempt to surmount the crisis in the same way as in 56 was worth making, and at the beginning of 51 Caesar proposed to the Senate that his proconsulship should be renewed in the same way in recognition of his prospective consulship for 48.[2] Without doubt his ties with Pompey had been loosened to such an extent since Julia's death and Pompey's marriage to Cornelia that he could scarcely hope for support from this quarter. But he was resolved under no circumstances to allow himself to be subordinated to Pompey. By his deeds in Gaul he had won for himself such a position (*dignitas*) in Roman politics that this demand signified an unbearable insult (*contumelia*).[3] It is said that he repeatedly declared that as *princeps civitatis* it was harder to push him from the first rank to the second than from the second to the last rank,[4] and in his opinion it was only the clique of his stubborn

---

[1] Suet. *Caes.* 30, 3.

[2] Plut. *Caes.* 29, 1 (which confuses the consuls of 51 with those of 49); App. *b.c.* 2, 97.

[3] Caes. *b.c.* 1, 4, 4; 9, 2; 22, 5.

[4] Suet. *Caes.* 29, 1: *difficilius se principem civitatis a primo ordine in secundum quam ex secundo in novissimum detrudi.* He claimed the same pre-eminence for himself as Pompey, of whom he says (*b.c.* 1, 4, 4): *neminem dignitate secum exaequari volebat.*

enemies that refused to recognize his legitimate right. That they controlled the Senate was unconstitutional oligarchy (*factio paucorum*).[1] If only the senators were free to decide for themselves, he would be sure of a majority![2] In order to provide them with the necessary evidence to do so, he published the seven books *de bello Gallico* simultaneously with his proposal.

This work consisted of an impressive and comprehensive edition of the campaign reports, which Caesar had previously sent to the Senate, and ended with the senatorial decree celebrating the glorious suppression of the last great revolt with a thanksgiving of twenty days' duration.[3] Strictly objective in tone and limited to the seven years of war, which won for the Roman Empire a new province in the extensive and rich land of the dreaded Celts, it forces the unprejudiced reader to see things as the author wishes. Even Cicero, to whom this monumentally simple style was alien, has nothing but praise for it: 'In the writing of history nothing is more pleasing than unaffected and lucid brevity.'[4] In our account reference has on several occasions been made to the intention behind Caesar's objectivity. This was only to be expected.[5] But for this reason to

---

[1] Cic. *b.c.* 1, 22, 5.

[2] Hirtius *b.G.* 8, 52, 4: *iudicabat enim liberis sententiis patrum conscriptorum causam suam facile obtineri.* Cf. *b.c.* 1, 9, 5.　　　　　　　　　[3] Caes. *b.G.* 7, 90, 8.

[4] Cic. *Brut.* 262: *nihil est enim in historia pura et illustri brevitate dulcius.* Of course such a factual account by a general could not be history in the strict sense. For this reason M. Rambaud's book *L'art et la déformation historique dans les commentaires de César* (1953) starts from entirely false premises. On this, see J. H. Collins, *Gnomon* 26 (1954), 527 ff.; J. P. V. D. Balsdon, *JRS* 45 (1955), 161 ff. The ridicule directed by A. N. Sherwin-White (*JRS* 48 (1958), 191) at this now fashionable form of Caesar criticism is well deserved.

[5] Cicero (*Brut.* 218) jokes about a dialogue of the consular C. Curio in which, although it is set in 59 B.C., *reprehendit eas res, quas idem Caesar anno post et deinceps reliquis annis administravisset in Gallia.* Suet. *Caes.* 9, 2; 49, 1; 50, 1; 52, 3 give some examples of its muck-raking, from which we can form an impression of how Caesar's activities in Gaul were treated (cf. Suet. *Caes.* 24, 3). Other examples are to be found in the poems of Catullus mentioned above (pp. 134 f.). From Cicero's letters to his brother and Trebatius we get a good picture of the lively correspondence between the politicians at Rome and Caesar's officers and staff (*contubernales*) about all that occurred in the theatres of war and the winter-camps. Tiro has also preserved a letter of Q. Cicero dated December 44 (*fam.* 16, 27) in which he says of A. Hirtius and C. Vibius Pansa, the consuls designate for 43, that even during the campaigns their riotous living was not restrained (*quos ego penitus novi libidinum et languoris effeminatissimi animi plenos*) and for that reason they were sure to join up again with their crony, the *latro* Mark Antony (*incredibile est, quae ego illos scio oppositis Gallorum castris in aestivis fecisse, quos ille latro, nisi aliquid firmius fuerit, societate vitiorum deleniet*). I regard it as possible that it was precisely these correspondents whom Caesar wished to hit in his descriptions of the panic at Vesontio (see above, p. 110) with his malicious comment on the young gentlemen (*b.G.* 1, 39, 2: *qui ex urbe amicitiae causa Caesarem secuti non magnum in re militari usum habebant*). Cf. p. 165, n. 3, above. Those in a position to form an impression of the hate-ridden gossip which for years circulated around Caesar will only be the more impressed by the 'lucid brevity' with which he majestically portrays his campaigns.

call it a work of self-justification is to miss the point. It was directed at Romans who were to marvel at, and in imagination live through, the enormous difficulties which their proconsul's burning sense of duty had mastered for the honour of Rome, and the deeds of heroism performed by his legions against dangerous and numerically always far superior enemies. Vivid descriptions of the country and its inhabitants and exact reproductions of the mighty plans of daring enemy leaders put the reader in a position where he can accurately assess the fearful danger threatening the Empire and Caesar's great service in surmounting it: only the malevolent or stupid could criticize. The vileness of the intrigues at Rome is revealed only once, when the unbearably arrogant Ariovistus dared to question Rome's long-standing claim to Gaul and remarked scornfully that there were men of great distinction in Rome who would be grateful to him for Caesar's removal.[1] If we recall how little rest Caesar was able to grant himself, particularly after the defeat of Vercingetorix, we shall all the better understand the surprise of Aulus Hirtius at the speedy completion of the work. Presumably it had been planned previously, and the earlier books will already have been sketched out, but the composition of Book VII alone with its wealth of dramatic events is sufficiently astonishing. The intellectual vigour of this genius appears to have known no bounds.

However, his enemies at Rome did not allow themselves to be diverted from their plans. After Caesar's death Cicero once gave it as his opinion that all his gifts were directed to only one end—the subjugation of the free state to his lust for power.[2] Caesar was certainly not the *princeps* whom he had called for in his books on the true state and the true statesman,[3] and the living optimate *principes* were even more conscious that his claim threatened the mainspring of their existence.

In April (March, Jul.) when it was his turn to preside over meetings of the Senate, Marcellus issued an edict summoning the Senate in order to report on the general condition of the country in conjunction with Caesar's demand. He took advantage—most maliciously in view of the actual situation (see pp. 166 ff.)—of the news

---

[1] Caes. *b.G.* 1, 44, 12.

[2] Cic. *Phil.* 5, 49: *omnem vim ingenii, quae summa fuit in illo, in populari levitate consumpsit. itaque cum respectum ad senatum et ad bonos non haberet, eam sibi viam patefecit ad opes suas amplificandas, quam virtus liberi populi ferre non posset.*

[3] On the other hand he writes to M. Marcellus in 46 B.C. (*fam.* 4, 8, 2): *quod ego facio, tu quoque animum inducas, si sit aliqua res publica, in ea te esse oportere iudicio hominum reque principem, necessitate cedentem tempori.*

of the victory at Alesia, which had brought Caesar the thanksgiving lasting twenty days: he declared that as the war was now over, the army should be dismissed, and further, that the popular decree about Caesar's candidature had been superseded by the later law of Pompey, so that a successor could be appointed at once.[1] He was opposed by his colleague, the celebrated jurist Servius Sulpicius Rufus, who held before the Senate's eyes the horrors of civil war: the potentates of previous revolutions had been mere novices and their cruelties would be far surpassed by those to come.[2] But above all the proposal violated the clause contained in the law of Pompey and Crassus of the year 55, prohibiting discussion of this matter. So the tribunes working for Caesar gave notice of veto, and the majority of senators would not commit themselves to the formulation of a decree.[3] On the other hand Caesar's request was rejected at the same time, and the Senate also approved of a declaration by Marcellus that Caesar's colonists in Novum Comum did not have Roman citizenship; this was a heavy blow against Caesar's authority in his own province. For he had always treated the Latins of the communities north of the Po as Roman citizens, recruiting them for his legions, and also regarded the 5,000 colonists, whom he had gradually settled in Comum or included in the list of settlers, as Roman citizens, The tribunes in his service therefore vetoed this decree and accordingly, despite its publication by Marcellus, it had no constitutional validity.[4]

This move aroused great excitement in Italy. In Campania it was being said that Caesar would not stand for such treatment; to make sure of the Transpadanes he had given instructions to all the Latin communities to reconstitute themselves as Roman

---

[1] Suet. *Caes.* 28, 2. The date is to be deduced from Cic. *Att.* 5, 2, 3, where Cicero enquires on May 10, 51, *quomodo Caesar ferret de auctoritate perscripta.*

[2] Cic. *fam.* 4, 3, 1 (46 B.C.), according to his own recollection. When, in September 46, Caesar let himself be moved by the request of the Senate to pardon Marcellus, he did so, as Cicero writes to Sulpicius: *accusata 'acerbitate' Marcelli (sic enim appellabat) laudataque honorificentissime et aequitate tua et prudentia* (4, 4, 3).

[3] Hirtius *b.G.* 8, 53, 1: *nam M. Marcello proximo anno* (51 B.C.), *cum impugnaret Caesaris dignitatem, contra legem Pompei et Crassi rettulerat ante tempus* (March 1, 50) *ad senatum de Caesaris provinciis, sententiisque dictis discessionem faciente Marcello, qui sibi omnem dignitatem ex Caesaris invidia quaerebat, senatus frequens in alia omnia transiit.* Dio 40, 59, 1 mentions the tribunes as well as Sulpicius. Suet. *Caes.* 29, 1: *(Caesar) summa ope restitit partim per intercessores tribunos, partim per Servium Sulpicium alterum consulem.* From the senatorial decrees of September 29, 51, preserved in Cic. *fam.* 8, 8, 5–8, we know of four tribunes who used their veto in favour of Caesar. One was C. Vibius Pansa, the future consul of 43.

[4] Suet. *Caes.* 28, 3; Cic. *Att.* 5, 2, 3; Plut. *Caes.* 29, 2; App. *b.c.* 2, 98.

municipia.[1] This rumour was, of course, entirely without foundation, since at the time Caesar was far too busy with the war against the Bellovaci, but even the consul Sulpicius declared that under the circumstances it was impossible for Bibulus and Cicero, the newly appointed proconsuls of Syria and Cilicia respectively, to recruit troops in Italy for their provinces which were threatened by the Parthians. The Senate persisted in the view throughout the year, despite the fact that, since the defeat of Crassus, Rome was not powerful enough in the East to cope with a serious attack on the part of the victors, and the dignity of the Empire required a strong presence there.[2]

Pompey was at Tarentum[3] and appeared to take no part in the proceedings at Rome; it was said that he shortly intended to go to Spain. He promised that, in the event of the danger threatening from Caesar's camp being realized, he was fully prepared to help, but refrained from open acts of hostility towards him.[4] In consequence Marcellus for the time being dropped his main offensive.[5] But when, in June, an event about which we are imperfectly informed gave him the opportunity to exercise his power of *coercitio* against a citizen of Comum, he used it for a drastic demonstration that, despite the vote, he would allow no change in the constitution, and notwithstanding the fact that the man had actually held a magistracy in his community, had him beaten with rods. This represented a most blatant challenge to Caesar because, according to the prevailing view, the Latins were certainly to be distinguished *de facto* (if not *de iure*) from the other *peregrini* in this respect. Cicero, who heard about the incident while in Athens, wrote disapprovingly that it would also displease Pompey as patron of the Transpadanes.[6] Caesar countered by transferring a legion to northern Italy 'in order to protect the Roman colonies from barbarian invasion', as the semi-official explanation read.[7] The attitude of the two parties to the Transpadane question was very characteristic: on one side,

---

[1] Cic. *Att.* 5, 2, 3: *eratque rumor de Transpadanis, eos iussos IVviros creare; fam.* 8, 1, 2. Just as incredible is Appian's report (*b.c.* 2, 97) that Caesar, on learning of the Senate's rejection of his proposal, tapped his sword with the words, 'This will get it for me.' According to Plut. *Pomp.* 58, 3; *Caes.* 29, 7, this remark was made by a centurion.

[2] Cic. *fam.* 3, 3, 1; 8, 5, 1; 10, 2–3. For Cicero's numerous pronouncements about the Parthians, see *RE*, 7A, 978–981; 985, 986.

[3] Cic. *Att.* 5, 5, 2; 6, 1.

[4] Cic. *Att.* 5, 7; 5, 11, 3; *fam.* 2, 8, 2; 3, 8, 10; Dio 40, 59, 2.

[5] Caelius to Cicero, *fam.* 8, 1, 2.

[6] Cic. *Att.* 5, 11, 2; Plut. *Caes.* 29, 2; App. *b.c.* 2, 98.

[7] Hirtius *b.G.* 8, 24, 3.

there was unprofitable insistence on a legal standpoint appropriate to the conditions of the past; on the other, a sure sense of the forces that would count in the political life of the future.

On July 22 Pompey arrived in the neighbourhood of Rome on his way to Ariminum, from where he intended to take a detachment to Spain, and attended a meeting of the Senate. The payment of his troops was just under discussion, and he was immediately asked for information about the legion which he had lent to Caesar at the beginning of 53. He promised to ask for its return, but let it be known that he was not doing this at the wish of Caesar's opponents. As far as the succession in Gaul was concerned, he gave it as his opinion, in conversation, that all must obey the Senate. The Senate expressed the wish that after an interval the matter be discussed in Pompey's presence.[1] However, intrigues and poor attendances at meetings prevented anything from happening in August and September, though it became known that Pompey was against Caesar's reaching the consulship while in possession of his province and army, and his father-in-law Scipio delivered his vote in the Senate in favour of a report on the Gallic provinces on March 1, 50.[2]

On the last day of September the Senate was finally ready for discussions and Pompey's wishes were clear: according to the wording of the consular law of 55 no decision could be taken about Caesar's provinces before March 1, 50, but thereafter there was nothing to prevent his recall.[3] Accordingly the Senate decreed that, from March 1, at first only the consular provinces should be discussed, i.e. which two provinces of the eleven available should be assigned to consulars;[4] the use of the veto against the execution of the decree would be deemed against the public interest.[5] Further, the competent magistrates received instructions to make a report to the Senate about the discharge of Caesar's time-expired soldiers,[6] and finally it was laid down how the nine remaining provinces were to be filled by ex-praetors in the year 50.[7] Thereby it was tacitly settled in a manner incontestable by constitutional means that in the following year the two Gauls were again to be separated

---

[1] Caelius to Cicero (fam. 8, 4, 4).　　　　[2] Caelius (fam. 8, 5, 2–3; 9, 5).

[3] Caelius (fam. 8, 8, 4; 9).

[4] Cic. fam. 8, 8, 5. If one subtracts the two Spains entrusted to Pompey, this leaves Gallia Cisalpina with Illyricum, Gallia Transalpina, Syria, Cilicia, Asia, Bithynia and Pontus, Macedonia, Crete and Cyrene, Africa, Sicilia, Sardinia.

[5] Cic. fam. 8, 8, 6.　　　　[6] Cic. fam. 8, 8, 7.

[7] Cic. fam. 8, 8, 8. Since the hitherto consular province of Cilicia was expressly mentioned only Syria and the two Gauls remained of the consular provinces; one of these, however, was also to become praetorian.

and assigned to new governors (presumably, as happened in 49, Transalpine to a consular and Cisalpine with Illyricum to a man of praetorian rank).

The veto could not be used against the first decree,[1] but the other three were immediately vetoed by some Caesarian tribunes and so remained without legal force. But this had little significance, since Pompey declared that, if the veto were used again after March 1, this would be tantamount to Caesar's rebelling against the Senate, and in this event he had long promised to support the Senate's authority. When he was asked again what would happen if Caesar wished both to be consul and to keep his army, he replied, 'What if my son were to attack me with a cudgel?', pretending confidence in Caesar's loyalty and considering such an eventuality quite impossible. However, his hearers concluded from the remark that the tie

---

[1] According to the Lex Sempronia of 123 B.C. (Cic. prov. cons. 3; 17; 36), cf. P. J. Cuff, Historia 7 (1958), 448. The Lex Sempronia would have required the Senate to decide on the provinces of the consuls to be elected for 49 before the consular elections of 50. The law of Pompey of 52 nullified this expectation because from March 1, 50, it allowed provinces to be assigned to consuls of previous years. Thus, in 51 Cilicia went to Cicero (consul 63) and Syria to Bibulus (consul 59). Cuff (469, n. 96) rightly emphasizes that in Hirtius b.G. 8, 39, 3 (Caesar in possession of his province in 50) the continued validity of the Lex Sempronia is taken for granted. Caesar himself saw in the Lex Pompeia a move directed against him (b.c. 1, 85, 9): *in se iura magistratuum commutari, ne ex praetura et consulatu, ut semper, sed per paucos probati et electi in provincias mittantur.* On the same lines 1, 6, 5: in January, 49, *provinciae privatis decernuntur, duae consulares, reliquae praetoriae.* Caesar justifies the continuance of the Lex Sempronia by the law of the ten tribunes of 52, which allowed him to stand for his second consulship without coming to Rome. Since successors were now nominated as early as January 49, for the half-year until his prospective election he was cheated of the *imperium* taken for granted in the tribunician law (b.c. 1, 9, 2: *doluisse se, quod populi Romani beneficium* (the tribunician law) *sibi per contumeliam ab inimicis extorqueretur ereptoque semenstri imperio in urbem retraheretur, cuius absentis rationem haberi proximis comitiis* (49) *populus iussisset* (52)). In the summer of 49 he expected to be elected consul for 48 (b.c. 3, 1, 1). On April 1, 49, in the Senate (b.c. 1, 32, 2), *docet se nullum extraordinarium honorem adpetisse, sed exspectato legitimo tempore consulatus eo fuisse contentum, quod omnibus civibus pateret. latum ab X tribunis plebis contra dicentibus inimicis . . ., ut sui ratio absentis haberetur;* and later in Spain (b.c. 1, 85, 10): *in se uno non servari, quod sit omnibus datum semper imperatoribus, ut rebus feliciter gestis aut cum honore aliquo aut certe sine ignominia domum revertantur exercitumque dimittant.* Actually no greater *ignominia* than the third senatorial decree of September 29, 51, can be imagined (*fam.* 8, 8, 7): *item senatui placere de militibus, qui in exercitu C. Caesaris sunt, qui eorum stipendia emerita aut causas, quibus de causis missi fieri debeant, habeant, ad hunc ordinem referri, ut eorum ratio habeatur causaeque cognoscantur. si quis huic s(enatus) c(onsulto) intercessisset, senatui placere auctoritatem perscribi et de ea re p(rimo) q(uoque) t(empore) ad hunc ordinem referri. huic s(enatus) c(onsulto) intercessit C. Caelius, C. Pansa tr(ibuni) pl(ebis).* Cuff (op. cit., 468) is right on b.c. 1, 9, 2. But he might have seen (for example from my *Pompeius*², 198, n. 137) that his discovery is not new. As remarked there, I think it possible that the tribunician law referred back to the decision of the tribunes of 58 (Suet. *Caes.* 23, 1) *cum rei publicae causa abesset.* If the tribunes of 51 did not veto a discussion starting on March 1 about the provinces of the future consuls of 49, we may conclude that they were following instructions from Caesar in recognizing the continued validity of the Lex Sempronia.

between Pompey and Caesar, now in its tenth year, was really broken.[1] The war against Parthia seemed the only way to avoid a clash between the two over-powerful proconsuls, and so those who wished to maintain peace began to canvass the view that either Pompey or Caesar should be entrusted with this task. Pompey, the conqueror of Syria, was in fact the obvious choice and himself wrote in this vein to Cicero in Cilicia. However, Caesar's opponents in the Senate on no account wished to allow their champion to leave Italy, and consequently this solution became far less practicable.[2]

From September 29, 51, the position was quite clear to Caesar: if he was not ready to submit, he would have to prepare for the unequal struggle with Pompey and the oligarchy allied with him. We now see him using every possible means to strengthen his position. A particularly dangerous move on the part of his enemies was that the Senate was to decide on the discharge of his soldiers. He drew the teeth of this by doubling the pay of his legions once and for all and by granting ○ them allowances and extra rewards at every opportunity.[3] Although the war in Gaul was over, recruiting and the preparation of war materials continued.[4] The populace of Rome was kept in good spirits by the buildings mentioned above (page 140), but even more by the preparations for the great festivities in honour of his late daughter that were to be held on his return. Stories got around about the contracts he had made with the high-class grocers and of the preparations at his house: also of the letters that his agents, senators and knights, had received with exact instructions as to how the gladiators were to be trained for the sword-fights. But he also donated buildings to the municipalities and colonies of Italy and Gaul and the native city states of Spain, Asia and Greece; and he showed all possible favour to the allied kings, offering a present of 1,000 prisoners to one, and helping another out with troops. That he was the refuge of all whom, for any reason, Rome had become too hot to hold has been repeatedly mentioned already. He was said to have been quite frank with people who were hopelessly in debt in telling them that a civil war was necessary to set them back on their feet.[5]

[1] Caelius to Cicero, *fam.* 8, 8, 9.
[2] Cic. *Att.* 5, 18, 1; 6, 1, 14; Caelius to Cicero, *fam.* 8, 10, 2; 14, 4.
[3] Suet. *Caes.* 26, 3; see above, p. 165, n. 1.   [4] Dio 40, 60, 1.
[5] Suet. *Caes.* 26, 2–3; 27, 1–28, 2; see above, p. 168, n. 4. It is very valuable that Suetonius has preserved for us so much of the contemporary political journalism for and against Caesar. The useful efforts of W. Steidle (*Sueton u. d. ant. Biogr.* (1951), 41 ff.) and Cordula Brutscher (*Analysen zu Suetons Divus Iulius und der Parallelüberlieferung* (1958), 105) to assess Suetonius' personal achievement should not lead to an underestimation of his reliability in reproducing contemporary sources.

However, it is very doubtful whether Caesar really spoke in this way. For, with the existing division of power, war would be a most dubious venture; a diplomatic and political solution, if at all possible, was preferable. Since this could only be achieved if the alliance between the oligarchy and Pompey, on which their present superiority over Caesar rested, could be broken, the interests of the opposing party naturally pushed in the other direction. Between the two extremes, however, there were still considerable forces active which wished to keep the peace and were working at a compromise designed to postpone a decision. This was also indirectly to Caesar's advantage and gave some chance of success to his attempts to avoid war.

For the important political battles impending in the following year he succeeded in winning one of the consuls designate, Lucius Aemilius Paullus, with a sum of nine million denarii, which enabled him to complete the rebuilding of the Basilica Aemilia in the Forum.[1] The other consul designate, Gaius Marcellus, despite his marriage to Octavia, Caesar's grand-niece,[2] was an outspoken optimate. Much more important than Paullus was the capture of the tribune Gaius Scribonius Curio. This politician, brilliantly talented but utterly lacking in moral scruple, had in his youth joined in his father's vigorous attack on Caesar. Nevertheless, he was ready in the summer of 51, when campaigning for the tribunate, to take service with Caesar, but finding that he was offered too little prepared to champion the cause of the oligarchy. Caesar now made another attempt—this time with greater success, since he offered without further ado to settle all Curio's debts, rumoured to be in the region of two and a half million denarii.[3] In him he found an assistant who managed

---

[1] Suet. *Caes.* 29, 1; Plut. *Caes.* 29, 3; *Pomp.* 58, 2; App. *b.c.* 2, 102; Dio 40, 63, 2. Paullus was the brother of the later triumvir M. Lepidus and a son of the revolutionary consul of 78 (Vell. 2, 67, 2; Cic. *Phil.* 13, 8).

[2] Cic. *Phil.* 3, 17; Suet. *Caes.* 27, 1; Nicol. Dam. *FgrHist* 90, F 128, 28; Plut. *Ant.* 31, 2. Cf. Hammond, *RE*, 17, 1859.

[3] Caelius to Cicero, *fam.* 8, 4, 2: on August 1, 51, he hopes *ut spero et volo et ut se fert ipse, bonos et senatum malet; totus, ut nunc est, hoc scaturit, huius autem voluntatis initium et causa est, quod eum non mediocriter Caesar, qui solet infimorum hominum amicitiam sibi qualibet impensa adiungere, valde contempsit.* Vell. 2, 48, 4: *hic primo pro Pompei partibus, id est, ut tunc habebatur, pro re publica, mox simulatione contra Pompeium et Caesarem sed animo pro Caesare stetit; id gratis an accepto centies sestertio fecerit, ut accepimus, in medio relinquam.* This is preceded (3) by the character study: *vir nobilis, eloquens, audax, suae alienaeque et fortunae et pudicitiae prodigus, homo ingeniosissime nequam et facundus malo publico, cuius animo neque opes ullae neque cupiditates sufficere possent.* Val. Max. 9, 1, 6 puts his debts at 15,000,000 denarii. To give an example, for the funeral games of his father, who died in 53 B.C. (see above, p. 171, n. 5), he had built a

his affairs most efficiently. Until the end of February 50 Curio continued to pose as an optimate; but then a disagreement with their leaders gave him an opportunity publicly to justify his transfer to Caesar.[1]

When the discussions on the consular provinces began on March 1, the most violent battles developed, which lasted until a temporary lull at the end of May, with Curio successfully maintaining his veto throughout.[2] At first the consul Gaius Marcellus put the motion that successors should be sent immediately to Caesar's provinces. Curio expressed his agreement, but demanded that Pompey should give up his provinces and army at the same time. This demand was without legal foundation, since Pompey's proconsulship had been regularly prolonged for five years in 52; but it appeared all the more firmly based on equity and republican tradition, which knew nothing of a standing army to protect the government, and it won Curio great popularity.[3] He was, of course, acting on Caesar's instructions. The latter was hereby withdrawing his hopeless demand to be made the equal of Pompey by being left in Gaul, but did not budge from

twin wooden theatre on the stages of which simultaneous performances could be held, but which by the turning of two enormous shafts could also be combined into an amphitheatre (Plin. *n.h.* 36, 177). See also Suet. *Caes.* 29, 1; Plut. *Ant.* 5, 2; *Caes.* 29, 3; *Pomp.* 58, 2; App. *b.c.* 2, 101; Dio 40, 60, 2–3.

[1] Caelius to Cicero, *fam.* 8, 10, 3–4; 6, 4–5; Cicero to Caelius, *fam.* 2, 13, 3; *Att.* 6, 1, 25; 3, 4; Caes. *b.c.* 2, 25, 4; Lucan 4, 688–692; App. *b.c.* 2, 102; Dio 40, 61, 1–62, 2.

[2] Cic. *Att.* 6, 2, 6 (Cicero has at his disposal the *acta urbana* up to March 7, 50); Caelius to Cicero, *fam.* 8, 11, 1. On this, see my *Pompeius*[2], 276, 55: 'Curio will not consent to losing *dies comitiales* as the result of a celebration of thanksgiving for Cicero's achievements in Cilicia' *ne quod furore Paulli adeptus esset boni sua culpa videretur amisisse.* According to Cic. *Att.* 6, 3, 4: *huc enim odiosa adferebantur de Curione, de Paullo,* Curio and Paullus collaborated on Caesar's behalf, which is described by Caelius, then still a thoroughgoing optimate, as *furor Paulli.* Caelius (op. cit., § 3) says: *nostri porro, quos tu bene nosti, ad extremum certamen rem deducere non audebant.* Caelius again in May 50 (*fam.* 8, 13, 2): *voles, Cicero, Curionem nostrum lautum intercessionis de provinciis exitum habuisse; nam cum de intercessione referretur* (cf. the *senatus consultum, fam.* 8, 8, 6), *quae relatio fiebat ex senatus consulto, primaque M. Marcelli sententia pronuntiata esset, qui agendum cum tribunis pl. censebat, frequens senatus in alia omnia it.* On this, see Cic. *Att.* 7, 7, 5 (December 50): *numquam enim Curio sustinuisset, si cum eo agi coeptum esset; quam sententiam senatus sequi noluit; ex quo factum est, ut Caesari non succederetur.* According to Hirtius (*b.G.* 8, 52, 4–5) Curio demanded a vote: *nam C. Curio, tribunus plebis, cum Caesaris causam dignitatemque defendendam suscepisset, saepe erat senatui pollicitus, si quem timor armorum Caesaris laederet et quoniam Pompei dominatio atque arma non minimum terrorem foro inferrent, discederet uterque ab armis exercitusque dimittant. fore eo facto liberam et sui iuris civitatem. neque hoc tantum pollicitus est, sed etiam s.c. per discessionem facere coepit; quod ne fieret consules amicique Pompei evicerunt atque ita rem morando discusserunt.* This is explained in *Hermes* 63 (1928), 132 (=*Kl. Schr.*, 2, 223). On the attacks on Pompey's *dominatio,* see Caelius, in *fam.* 8, 11, 3: *totus eius secundus consulatus exagitur.* This surely refers to the third consulship of 52 (cf. *Pompeius*[2], 277, 65). Sallust (*ad Caes.* 2, 3, 2–3) paints the *dominatio* of Pompey and the *pauci* in harsh colours, see above, p. 154, n. 4.

[3] App. *b.c.* 2, 103–106; Dio 40, 62, 3–4.

his principle of equality.[1] His legal position rested on the decree of
the ten tribunes, freeing him from the need to canvass in person for
his future consulship.[2] If this was recognized, his *imperium* would
formally continue until he entered the city, even after he had given
up his army and provinces. He could be elected to the consulship *in
absentia*, as consul would be beyond the reach of the law,[3] and could
reasonably expect to find ways and means to maintain his position
thereafter, provided that Pompey did not remain in possession of
his army. Now the legality of the popular decree was precisely what
his opponents were questioning. But the decision on whether it
had been invalidated by Pompey's law on magistracies depended
ultimately on the balance of power,[4] and it was therefore important
that Pompey should give up his army and provinces at the same
time as Caesar. There was no need to fear a disarmed Pompey,
as Caesar knew from long experience. His optimate opponents
knew this as well as Caesar, and they only saw a cunning trap in his
proposal.[5] But it was designed to appeal to all those who shuddered
at the prospect of a new civil war,[6] and it became increasingly
obvious that this was the view of the majority of senators. Caesar
was quite correct in describing his enemies as a minority trying to
force their wishes on the others,[7] and, while peace lasted, it was

---

[1] Caes. *b.c.* 1, 4, 4: *Pompeius ab inimicis Caesaris incitatus et quod neminem dignitate secum
exaequari volebat, totum se ab eius amicitia averterat et cum communibus inimicis in gratiam redierat.*

[2] Caes. *b.c.* 1, 9, 2; 32, 3–5; Cic. *Att.* 7, 3, 4; Sall. *ad Caes.* 2, 2, 3: *beneficia populi;* Suet.
Caes. 29, 2: *beneficium populi.*

[3] See above, p. 176, n. 1. *Dig.* 2, 4, 2 (*Ulpianus libro quinto ad edictum*): *in ius vocari non oportet
neque consulem neque praefectum neque praetorem neque proconsulem neque ceteros magistratus,
qui imperium habent;* 4, 6, 26, 2: *ait praetor: 'aut cum eum invitum in ius vocare non liceret neque
defenderetur'. haec clausula ad eos pertinet, quos more maiorum sine fraude in ius vocare non licet,
ut consulem, praetorem ceterosque, qui imperium potestatemve habent.* Cf. Mommsen, *RStR*, 1³,
706, on this, showing that it also applied to criminal trials.

[4] Cic. *Att.* 7, 3, 4 (December 9, 50): *de sua potentia dimicant homines hoc tempore periculo
civitatis; fam.* 4, 4, 3 (46 B.C., to Ser. Sulpicius Rufus): *postquam armis disceptari coeptum sit de
iure publico.*

[5] Suet. *Caes.* 29, 2 (on Caesar's letter to the Senate at the end of 50): *confisus, ut putant, facilius
se, simul atque libuisset, veteranos convocaturum quam Pompeium novos milites.* Above all, Cic.
Att. 7, 9, 3 (at the end of 50): *dices profecto persuaderi illi* (sc. *Caesari*) *ut tradat exercitum et ita
consul fiat. est omnino id eius modi ut, si ille eo descendat, contra dici nihil possit idque eum, si non
obtinet ut ratio habeatur retinentis exercitum, non facere miror. nobis autem, ut quidam putant,
nihil est timendum magis quam ille consul.* Cicero reminds Atticus of Caesar's first consulship
in 59: *vide consulem illum iterum quem vidisti consulatu priore. 'at tum imbecillus plus',* inquit
(perhaps Pompey, with whom Cicero had spoken on December 25: *Att.* 7, 8, 4 and cf. *RE*,
7A, 990), *'valuit quam tota res publica'.* On the other hand Caesar himself (January 49; *b.c.*
1, 9, 5): *proficiscatur Pompeius in suas provincias, ipsi* (Caesar and Pompey) *exercitus dimittant,
discedant in Italia omnes ab armis, metus e civitate tollatur, libera comitia atque omnis res publica
senatui populoque Romano permittatur.*

[6] Cic. *Att*, 7, 5, 4.   [7] Caes. *b.c.* 1, 22, 5.

still possible that they would after all not dare to push things to extremes. For Caesar left no room for doubt that his honour was more important to him than his life, a fact of which he reminded Pompey even after the outbreak of war.[1]

In this position Pompey and the Senate, in order to weaken the charge of unfairness, made Caesar the concession that he need not give up his provinces before November 13—well knowing that this was of no help to him, since it would leave him disarmed throughout the year 49. For this reason Curio did not relax his grip in the slightest.[2]

Meanwhile disquietening news about the Parthians had again arrived from the East, and the Senate decided to send two legions as reinforcements to Syria. Pompey enlarged on this by suggesting that it would be simplest for Caesar and himself each to contribute one legion, and the Senate decreed accordingly. Pompey now designated as his legion the one which he had lent to Caesar in 53 (p. 144) so that the latter was actually weakened by the loss of two legions. Caesar complied, but gave each legionary a parting present of 250 denarii. He was at once able to fill the gap in his ranks with recruits, and one legion continued to be stationed in northern Italy.[3] The care with which he followed all proceedings at Rome at this time and personally kept hold of the threads of his policies is illustrated by an insignificant episode concerning Cicero. At about this time, somewhere near the end of April, the report of Cicero's victory in Cilicia came up for discussion in the Senate, and with it his wish for a celebration of a thanksgiving. Curio was afraid that his enterprises might be disturbed thereby and so opposed it. But Balbus pointed out to him that Caesar would be offended if his friend was treated in this way. And after the thanksgiving had been decreed Caesar immediately wrote a letter of congratulation, in which he emphasized that Cato in mean ingratitude had voted against the celebration.[4]

While the question of the consular provinces was being further debated, Pompey was taken seriously ill and could take no further part in the discussions.[5] Under these circumstances Curio was able at the end of May to bring the debate to a favourable conclusion.

---

[1] Op. cit., 1, 9, 2; Sall. *ad Caes.* 2, 2, 3.

[2] Caelius in *fam.* 8, 11, 3.

[3] Hirtius *b.G.* 8, 54, 2; Caes. *b.c.* 1, 4, 5; 32, 6; Cic. *fam.* 2, 15, 4; Dio 40, 65; App. *b.c.* 2, 114–115; Plut. *Caes.* 29, 4.

[4] Caelius in *fam.* 8, 11, 2; *fam.* 2, 15, 1; *Att.* 7, 1, 7.

[5] Caelius in *fam.* 8, 13, 2; App. *b.c.* 2, 107.

Marcus Marcellus had proposed in the Senate that negotiations should be started in order to make the tribunes give way. Those present rejected the proposal by a large majority and Curio's vote remained intact. In other words, the Senate consented to Caesar's standing for the consulship without giving up his provinces and army.[1]

The current political interest now shifted to the elections. In the election of censors Caesar had the satisfaction of seeing his father-in-law Lucius Piso appointed as colleague of Appius Claudius, now an avowed Pompeian: this would probably put a stop to effective acts of hostility.[2] In the future tribunician college he secured suitable successors to Curio in his trusted proquaestor Mark Antony and Quintus Cassius Longinus.[3] On the other hand, in the consular elections his candidate, the *legatus* Servius Sulpicius Galba, was defeated by Gaius Marcellus and Lucius Lentulus Crus, a result greeted with delight by the oligarchy, although the vast debts of the last-mentioned raised doubts whether he might not eventually be bought by Caesar.[4] Lucius Piso was also too much of an Epicurean to fulfil the expectations held of him and allowed his colleague to purge the senate and equestrian order at his own discretion. This mainly affected Caesarians. Only when he went so far as to attack the tribune Curio while still in office, did Piso and the consul Aemilius Paullus intervene. Nevertheless, Claudius at least read out his judgment in the Senate; this produced a fierce brawl in which Curio tore the censor's toga. On the other hand, Gaius Sallustius Crispus, later to win fame as a historian, who as tribune in 52 had been prominent in the battles against Milo, now lost his seat in the Senate.[5] He thereupon sent a substantial memorandum to

---

[1] See above, p. 179, n. 2.

[2] Cic. *fam.* 3, 10, 1; 11, 4–5; 13, 2; 8, 6, 3; Dio 40, 63, 1–3.

[3] Plut. *Ant.* 5, 2; Cic. *Att.* 6, 8, 2; Caes. *b.c.* 1, 2, 7.

[4] Hirtius *b.G.* 8, 50, 4; Cic. *Att.* 6, 8, 2 (October 1, 50) thinks him capable of supporting Caesar. See Caes. *b.c.* 1, 1, 3; 4, 2; Balbus to Cicero in *Att.* 8, 15a, 2: Balbus received from him the *gentilicium* Cornelius (R. Syme, *Rom. Rev.*, 44, n. 2; 72, n. 2).

[5] Dio 40, 63, 3–64, 1. The time can be calculated from the fact that on October 15 Cicero writes from Athens to ask Atticus for news about the censors (*Att.* 6, 9, 5). O. E. Schmidt, *Der Briefwechsel des M. Tullius Cicero* (1893), 88, assigns Caelius' letter with news about Ap. Claudius (*fam.* 8, 14, 4) to about September 24. Caelius seems not yet to know about the clash with Curio. Dio connects it with the conflict with the consul C. Marcellus, which probably did not happen until December. On the tribunate of Sallust, see Ascon. *argum.* to Cic. *Mil.*, p. 37 (Clark), and on *Mil.* 14; 45; 46. Presumably the adultery scandal mentioned by Varro in his logistoricus *Pius, aut de pace* (ap. Gell. *n.A.* 17, 18: *in adulterio deprehensus ab Annio Milone loris bene caesum dicit et, cum dedisset pecuniam, dimissum*) was taken into account in removing his name from the list of senators. H. Dahlmann (*Varronische Studien*, 1 (*Abh. Ak. Mainz* (1957), 4), 159 ff.) has interpreted this work correctly. The Pius referred to is Metellus Pius Scipio,

Caesar,[1] in which he painted in harsh colours the unbearable reign of terror of the oligarchic clique around Pompey and requested the *imperator* to intervene at once in this desperate situation: in so doing he was not to rest content with protecting his honour, but by sweeping reforms should again enable the people and Senate to fulfil their constitutional roles: otherwise he would bear the fearful responsibility of consigning the power of the Roman people to destruction; on the other hand, were he to complete this task, there would be no greater or more famous man on earth.[2] This document is of particular interest to us since, in contrast to Cicero's works of political philosophy, it offers practical suggestions: the unjustified power of the present nobility and the rule of money must be broken in order to recreate the dignity of the old Roman state.[3] The corruption of the people was to be eliminated by the admission of new citizens:

the consul of 52 and father-in-law of Pompey, who committed suicide in 46. Dahlmann (146) plausibly conjectures that Varro wrote the *Pius* soon afterwards; for the introductory comment *C. Sallustium scriptorem seriae illius et severae orationis, in cuius historia notiones censorias fieri atque exerceri videmus* is by Gellius, not by Varro (164).

[1] I argued for this dating of the second *epistula ad Caesarem senem* preserved in the *cod. Vat.* (*Appendix Sallustiana*, ed. Alph. Kurfess, 1, 1955) in *Vierteljahrsschrift für Sozial- und Wirtschaftsgesch.* 15 (1920), 528 (=*Kl. Schr.*, 2, 203 f.), and in greater detail in *DLZ*, 1921, 1986–1989. See also my Introduction to C. Sallustius Crispus (*Heidelberger Texte*, vol. 8 (1953), 9–10). Here (13), to refute the view propounded by Ed. Fraenkel (*JRS* 41 (1951), 192), that the imitation of Thucydides was an argument against Sallust's authorship, I recalled Cic. *or.* 32, where Cicero, in 46 B.C. (30–32), is thinking of orators, not historians, who used Thucydides as their model. He had already criticized these in *Brut.* 287–288 and *opt. gen. or.* 15–16; likewise Dionys. Hal. *de Thuc.* 2; 50. Reference can now be made above all to W. Steidle, *Sallusts historische Monographien* (*Historia, Einzelschr.* 3, (1958), 95 ff.). He raises the telling objection (96) that the philologists who refuse to allow Sallust the style which he chose for his letters have no qualms about letting their supposed *declamator* of the Imperial period imitate Sallust. This had been pointed out a little earlier by Günter Dietz in *Sallusts Briefe an Caesar* (Diss. Freiburg i. Br. (1956), 138–179). He has also shown (43–99) why these letters cannot be the work of a later rhetorician. Against this, R. Syme's attempt (*Mus. Helv.* 15 (1958)), to support the philological authorities whom he respects (55, 70) is of no avail. He criticizes the author (52) for not naming more and different politicians; but that is evidence for Sallust's authorship. In a memorandum *de summa re publica* (*ep.* 2, 2, 4) the latter had no need to enumerate all his *inimici* for Caesar's benefit. Incidentally he alludes in 2, 3 to the *adversus consul* (C. Marcellus). In 9, 4 he dismisses them as *inertissimi nobiles*. As H. Dahlmann (*Gnomon* 14 (1938), 142) has observed, this reminds one of the verdict of Caelius (*fam.* 8, 10, 3) on M. Marcellus. To this should be added the passage cited above (p. 181, n. 2) about his incompetence towards Curio in 50. In 9, 4 men like L. Postumius and M. Favonius are distinguished from the *nobiles* (*contra* Syme, 53). The note by R. G. M. Nisbet (*JRS* 48 (1958), 30) does not prove anything against Sallust since he, too, may have known of the speech of Lycurgus from his rhetorical training. Cf. W. Avenarius, *Symbolae Osloens.* 33 (1957), 80. I am grateful to Egon Maróti for letting me have a copy of his special publication: 'Der zweite Sallustbrief und Cicero' (*Acta sessionis Ciceronianae diebus* 3–5 *mensis Decembris a.* 1957 *Varsoviae habitae*, Warsaw (1960), 123–141), where the attacks on the authenticity of the letter are again soundly refuted.

[2] Sall. *ad Caes.* 2, 13, 5.　　　　　　　　[3] Op. cit., 7, 3.

combined in colonies with the old citizens, these were to form a healthy citizen body, ready for armed service.[1] In the popular assemblies, the votes of the five census classes were to have equal weight; jurors for the courts were to be chosen from the entire first class; the membership of the Senate was to be increased and secret ballot introduced.[2]

We do not know what Caesar thought on receipt of this exhortation couched in archaic language.[3] Its basic tenets could only be to his liking. But Sallust, like Cicero, is quite oblivious of the fact that the point at issue was no longer only the constitution of the Roman city-state; above all, the question of the government of the Empire (for which the old organs were inadequate) had to be settled. Caesar noted this talented man for future employment, but at present he had not reached the stage of concerning himself with such long-term plans.

The next important electoral battle centred on the augurate of the famous orator Hortensius for which Lucius Domitius Ahenobarbus and Mark Antony were rivals. Towards the end of September Antony was again victorious; Caesar's fanatical enemy was filled with fury at his own defeat.[4]

At about this time Caesar visited northern Italy. As he put it, he wished to commend Mark Antony to the Roman citizens in the municipalities and colonies of his province. This was now no longer necessary. Instead, on his tour through the towns he called on these citizens to remember, when it came to the consular elections of the next year, all that their proconsul had done for them. The indescribable enthusiasm with which all the communities honoured the highest official in their country with brilliant receptions, left no doubt about the attitude of the province.[5] In Rome it was said that he would under no circumstances dismiss his army, and rumour had it that on October 15 four legions would arrive at Placentia.[6] This was of course not true; only one legion was stationed in northern Italy. At this very time Caesar was reviewing the other eight in the land of the Treveri, before dismissing them to winter-quarters in Belgium

---

[1] Op. cit., 5, 8.   [2] Op. cit., 7, 11; 8, 1; 11, 5.

[3] I believe that Sallust wished to impress Caesar by writing as an 'old Roman'. It is underestimating Caesar's intellectual calibre to assume with A. Dihle (*Gnomon* 29 (1957), 598) that he would not have approved of such an attempt because it ran counter to his own stylistic ideal. Cicero also took particular pains over the surviving letters of recommendation to Caesar (*fam.* 7, 5; 13, 15; 16).

[4] Cic. *Brut.* 324; Caelius in *fam.* 8, 14, 1; Hirtius *b.G.* 8, 50, 1; Plut. *Ant.* 5, 2.

[5] Hirtius *b.G.* 8, 50–51.

[6] Cic. *Att.* 6, 9, 5; 7, 1, 1.

and the land of the Aedui. In addition he had the twenty-two newly recruited cohorts, which were presumably stationed in the old province.[1] This rumour completely mistook Caesar's intentions, which were not served by a military threat in northern Italy. The more agitated his opponents became, the more self-restraint he showed in order to win over public opinion by his moderate and irreproachable attitude.[2]

On the other side, Pompey recovered from his illness at Naples, an occasion for thanksgiving throughout Italy: on a journey he was personally greeted with enthusiastic demonstrations.[3] Relying on this attitude he sent a letter to the Senate, in which he reckoned up his own and Caesar's services and stated that nothing could suit his former friend and father-in-law better after his long campaigns than to enjoy his well-deserved honours in Rome. He himself had received his power in the year 52 through no wish of his own; but, if the Senate so desired, he was ready to give it up now before his time had expired. However, this friendly tone did not go down well with Curio, who launched into a spiteful invective against the hypocrisy of Pompey, and offered Caesar's proposal as the only fair solution of the quarrel: the two proconsuls should give up their armies simultaneously, since only then would the state be free and master of its own destiny.[4]

In the eyes of the majority of citizens, who were concerned that peace should be maintained, this continually repeated formula pushed the constitutional conflict—a proconsul with the help of the tribunate was opposing the declared will of the legitimate government—into the background. Nor did Caesar fail to emphasize that, by the cancellation of the favours granted to him by the decree of the ten tribunes, he was being robbed of 'the people's gift'. Cicero, who in December travelled from Brundisium to Rome, wrote on the seventeenth of that month that he had so far found no one who did not prefer a concession to Caesar to war.[5] The formula also had the quality of corresponding to Caesar's actual wishes: for, if his opponents no longer controlled an army, the master of 'popular'

---

[1] Hirtius b.G. 8, 52, 1; 54, 3–5; Caes. b.c. 1, 18, 5.

[2] Hirtius b.G. 8, 55, 2; see above, p. 78.

[3] Cic. Tusc. 1, 86; Vell. 2, 48, 2; Dio 41, 6, 3–4; see my Pompeius[2], 191.

[4] App. b.c. 2, 107–110; Caelius in fam. 8, 14, 2 (September 50): propositum hoc est de quo qui rerum potiuntur sunt dimicaturi, quod Cn. Pompeius constituit non pati C. Caesarem consulem aliter fieri nisi exercitum et provincias tradiderit, Caesari autem persuasum est se salvum esse non posse, si ab exercitu recesserit; fert illam tamen condicionem, ut ambo exercitus tradant. sic illi amores et invidiosa coniunctio (the former triumvirate) non ad occultam recidit obtrectationem, sed ad bellum se erumpit.　　　　　　　　　　　　　　　　[5] Cic. Att. 7, 6, 2.

N

tactics, sure of his veterans, could confidently hope for victory. His second consulship would put him in a position to order the state according to his will.[1]

Pompey, however, was less inclined than ever to make concessions. For Appius Claudius (nephew of the censor), who on the Senate's instructions was bringing the two legions detailed for the Parthian campaign to Italy, reported that morale in Caesar's army was very bad.[2] What was of even greater significance was that Caesar's senior officer, his *legatus pro praetore* Titus Labienus, whom the *imperator* had just placed in command of Cisalpine Gaul in order that he might conveniently conduct his campaign for the consulship from there, was already negotiating with the leaders of the oligarchy about a change of sides. He had recently become very demanding, and could not get over the fact that since then Caesar had been treating him noticeably more coldly.[3] In expectation of the approaching decision Pompey now again took up residence in his palace just outside the city.[4]

In view of the growing movement for peace, Caesar's opponents thought it necessary to force events in their own direction. In December, when it was the turn of the consul Gaius Marcellus to preside over meetings of the Senate, he took advantage of the quarrel between the censor Appius Claudius and Curio to ask the Senate to pass judgment on the latter. But, thanks to Curio's clever handling of the peace-loving majority in the Senate, the discussion took a turn different from what the consul had expected. When Curio finally succeeded in securing a division on the simultaneous retirement of the two proconsuls, 370 senators were in favour and only twenty-two against. While Curio was loudly cheered by the people for this success, Marcellus adjourned the session and on the next day demanded, on the strength of the rumours in circulation, that the Senate should take steps against Caesar's advance.[5] As this was again successfully refuted by Curio, he went out to Pompey with the two consuls designate and his remaining supporters and, without having been authorized to do so by the Senate, granted him authority to defend the state; he

---

[1] See above, p. 180, n. 5.

[2] Plut. *Pomp.* 57, 7–9; *Caes.* 29, 5–6; App. *b.c.* 2, 116–117.

[3] Hirtius *b.G.* 8, 52, 2–3. This consulship can only be that of 48 B.C. Thus at one time Caesar wished to have him as his colleague. According to Dio 41, 4, 4 he regarded himself as Caesar's equal. Since, like Pompey, he came from Picenum, we may infer old ties with the latter, and this could lead to unpleasant consequences for Caesar. Cf. R. Syme, *Rom. Rev.* 67, n. 7.

[4] App. *b.c.* 2, 11.

[5] Dio 40, 64, 1–4; Plut. *Pomp.* 58, 6–10; *Caes.* 30, 1–2; App. *b.c.* 2, 118–121. In dating I follow Ed. Meyer, *Caesars Mon.*, 269, 2. See above, p. 182, n. 5.

was given the command of the two legions destined for the Parthian war, which were in camp near Capua at the time, together with power to recruit more troops. Pompey did as he was instructed.[1] Cicero met him on the way to Capua on December 10 and was told that war was now inevitable, since Caesar was completely estranged from him; Hirtius had visited Rome on the evening of December 6 without calling on him; Balbus had promised to discuss the unresolved problems with Metellus Scipio (the father-in-law of Pompey) early on December 7, but Hirtius had travelled back during the previous night. Cicero ends his letter to his close friend Atticus with the words: 'I do not believe that Caesar has lost his reason to the extent of forcing these issues to a decision. For if he lets himself be carried away, I fear much that I dare not write.' So he was still hoping for a compromise.[2] However, the situation had become very serious through the arbitrary action of the consul and his followers. Curio protested most sharply against it and, on December 10, when his tribunate expired, immediately left to join Caesar.[3]

The latter had returned to Cisalpine Gaul. To cope with the new situation, he concentrated the legion stationed there in Ravenna, and gave secret orders to two legions from Transalpine Gaul and the twenty-two cohorts to march to Italy; he stationed three further legions in Narbonensis to secure himself against the Spanish army of Pompey.[4] But at the same time he left no means untried in order to achieve his aim without resort to war.[5] For his strength seemed to depend more and more on taking this position: the policies which he had hitherto adopted had brought it about that, if it came to a choice of parties in a civil war, he could hardly count on the support of a single respectable man. At this point his political career becomes enmeshed in the toils of a tragic problem. Engaged from his youth in the struggle against the optimates, he had never been able to win real confidence within the ranks of the old ruling class. The few *legati* from the nobility who served under him were insignificant figures. He had no friends from his own class who supported him and were ready to fight for his cause from inner conviction. And this is not to be attributed merely to their selfishness or lack of understanding; the unbridgeable gulf between him and them was

[1] Hirtius *b.G.* 8, 55, 1; Caes. *b.c.* 1, 2, 3; 4, 5; 9, 4; 6, 2—the alleged unreliability of Caesar's soldiers. See also Dio 60, 64, 4; 66, 1–3; App. *b.c.* 2, 121–123; Plut. *Pomp.* 59, 1–2; Oros. 6, 15, 1.   [2] Cic. *Att.* 7, 4, 2–3.
[3] App. *b.c.* 2, 123; Dio 40, 66, 5.
[4] Hirtius *b.G.* 8, 55, 1; Caes. *b.c.* 1, 7, 7; 8, 1; 15, 3; 18, 5; 37, 1–2; App. *b.c.* 2, 124–125; Suet. *Caes.* 30, 1.   [5] Hirtius *b.G.* 8, 55, 2.

due to the moral taint which his past carried in their eyes. They found
something unnatural and impenetrable in his overpowering character, against which all their instincts rose up, as they felt that, unlike
themselves, he did not inevitably regard the conservation of their
inherited supremacy in the state as the be-all and end-all of his life.
The same instinct had for a long time made them mistrust Pompey,
until he eventually abandoned his claim to be more than the other
principes. As a former partisan of Sulla he had always—despite
temporary estrangements—maintained some personal connections
even when he was allied to Caesar, and the latter remarks with
bitterness in his first book on the civil war: 'Pompey, incited by
Caesar's enemies and because he did not wish anyone to rival his own
position, had completely abandoned his friendship with him and
been reconciled with their common enemies, whose hostility he
had for the most part himself brought on Caesar at the time of their
alliance by marriage.'[1] In this he was right in that for him the bridges to
the optimate *principes* had been broken since the time of his consulship.

To be sure, Caesar's army with its centurions formed a reliable
following, the like of which no previous Roman statesman had been
able to employ in a political battle. In addition there were the senior
officers who had been taught in his school to render efficient
service, as well as members of the equestrian order who served him
with absolute loyalty and could be fully relied upon to carry out
his political instructions. But he found no such helpers among the
old ruling class, the nobility and senatorial order. If a man of Curio's
ability let himself be bought, he wished not to serve Caesar but
eventually to imitate him. As early as September, Marcus Caelius,
the optimate tribune of 52, expressed the calculations of these people
in a frank letter to Cicero: 'I am sure that it has not escaped you
that in a domestic quarrel people must support the more decent side
so long as the battle is being fought without weapons, but as soon
as it comes to war and armed camps, they must support the stronger
and regard the more certain cause as the better. In this quarrel I see
that Pompey will have on his side the Senate and members of the
jury-courts; that Caesar will have the support of all who live
in fear and with bad prospects, and that his army is above all comparison with that of Pompey. Anyway, there is still sufficient time
to weigh up the strength of the two sides and choose one's position.'[2]
Caesar, of course, could see this as well for himself, but he was by no
means indifferent to the division of forces between the two camps.

[1] Caes. *b.c.* 1, 4, 4.   [2] Cic. *fam.* 8, 14, 3.

Just as he had been ready to collaborate with the Senate as consul, so he fought for its support now. He knew what it signified at Rome to be opposed by its authority. For this reason he wished to avoid war if only he could maintain his *dignitas*. For it was true that there gathered at his camp only those whose previous political careers had suffered shipwreck: bankrupts, those heavily in debt, exiles, men compromised, unreliable careerists who wished to climb quickly through him, in short those not inappropriately described as the 'wicked' (*improbi*) in the optimate jargon or as the 'kingdom of the dead' in the bitter jest of Cicero's friend Atticus. Accordingly, men expected of his victory the massacre of the leading men of the state as under Cinna, the proscription of the rich as under Sulla, a complete cancellation of debts and the return of all criminals who had fled the country.[1] Even Pompey declared that his former father-in-law wished to throw everything into disorder, since he would neither be able to complete the undertakings which he had begun nor to fulfil the expectations that his arrival had aroused among the people from his private means.[2] The propertied classes, disquieted by these terrifying images, saw their salvation in Pompey. But above all they desired peace. The latest proceedings in the Senate were severely criticized by senators and knights; in general they demanded the acceptance of Caesar's conditions. The majority of the Senate, holders of state leases, financiers and landowners were, in Cicero's judgment, quite ready to endure Caesar's domination, so long as the normal course of business was not disturbed.[3]

We see Caesar's agents remaining in touch with his opponents until December 6, and when he had heard the report of Hirtius, he had new confidential proposals put to them: he was ready to give up his Transalpine province and to keep only two legions until assuming his consulship. This would protect his special position as a candidate and deprive the oligarchy of its pretext for mobilization. But it was precisely his consulship that his enemies feared, and so he received a reply after the manner of Cato, that the state could not be made the subject of a private bargain.[4] At the same time Antony, who had entered on his tribunate on December 10, remorselessly

[1] Cic. *Att.* 7, 3, 5; 7, 7; 11, 1; 12, 2. See above, p. 154, n. 4.
[2] Suet. *Caes.* 30, 2.   [3] Cic. *Att.* 7, 7, 5.
[4] Suet. *Caes.* 29, 2; Plut. *Caes.* 31, 1; Vell. 2, 49, 3; App. *b.c.* 2, 126. Unfortunately this is just the point at which the work of Hirtius, who had in part been in charge of these negotiations, breaks off. They were still in progress on January 4, 49 (*fam.* 16, 11, 2) after Cicero had arrived before Rome. He too then worked hard for an agreement, and so it appears in Plut. *Pomp.* 59, 5 as if he had actually been the first to pass on Caesar's offers. Cicero discussed the possibility of preserving peace with Pompey at Formiae on December 25, 50 (*Att.* 7, 8, 4).

pilloried the conduct of the senatorial minority and of Pompey. He issued an edict in which he demanded the immediate departure of the two legions for Syria and forbade obedience to Pompey's recruiting drive.[1] In a great speech delivered on December 21 he portrayed Pompey as the suppressor of civic freedom, especially during his third consulship.[2] In general, Caesar's propaganda now tirelessly repeated that the state was being enslaved by a small group obstinate in its hatred towards him, while he himself stood for the free expression of their will by the Senate and the popular assembly.[3] Thus he hoped to be able to discredit his opponents in the eyes of public opinion, and so to drive them into a corner and force them to make concessions.

For the next meeting of the Senate, which was to take place on January 1, 49, under the presidency of the new consul Lucius Lentulus, he again summarized his proposal in an official despatch brought over by Curio:[4] after enumerating his services to the state he demanded either that he should—as had been granted to him by the people—keep his provinces, at least until the elections were over, or that all holders of military commands should simultaneously resign their authority.[5] The tribunes Antony and Cassius had difficulty in even reading out the letter. Nor did Lentulus put up the proposals for discussion, but rather the general position of the state. Thereupon the Senate voted by an overwhelming majority for the motion of Scipio that Caesar was to dismiss his army by a fixed date on pain of being regarded a public enemy. The special law in his favour was no longer recognized as valid. He would thus have had to appear in Rome in person during the summer in order to stand for the consulship and would have lost his *imperium* on

---

[1] Plut. *Ant.* 5, 4.　　　　　　　　　　[2] Cic. *Att.* 7, 8, 5.

[3] Caes. *b.c.* 1, 9, 5; 22, 5; Hirtius *b.G.* 8, 52, 4. See above, p. 179, n. 2.

[4] App. *b.c.* 2, 127; Dio 41, 1, 1; Cic. *fam.* 16, 11, 2.

[5] Unfortunately the beginning of Caesar's *bellum civile* as preserved in our manuscripts is defective, and the end of Hirtius' *b.G.* 8 is also missing. In Suet. *Caes.* 29, 2 there is a brief mention of its contents: *ne sibi beneficium populi adimeretur, aut ut ceteri quoque imperatores ab exercitibus discederent.* In Dio 41, 1, 4 only Pompey is mentioned. I am inclined to assume that the general wording goes back to the original because Caesar wished to avoid mentioning Pompey by name. In *b.c.* 1, 9, 3: *cum litteras ad senatum miserit, ut omnes ab exercitibus discederent, ne id quidem impetravisse*; in 1, 5, 5, he speaks of *suis lenissimis postulatis.* On the other hand, see Cic. *fam.* 16, 11, 2 (on January 12, 49): *omnino et ipse Caesar, amicus noster, minacis ad senatum et acerbas litteras miserat et erat adhuc impudens qui exercitum et provinciam invito senatu teneret, et Curio meus illum incitabat.* According to App. *b.c.* 2, 128 he had declared that, in the event of its rejection, τιμωρὸς αὐτίκα τῇ τε πατρίδι καὶ ἑαυτῷ κατὰ τάχος ἀφίξεσθαι. He will not have threatened so bluntly. On the other hand the thought of 1, 9, 3 (*sibi semper primam fuisse dignitatem vitaque potiorem*) will have been present, with which the words quoted in p. 170, n. 4, above are in agreement. This explains Cicero's mode of expression.

crossing the *pomerium*. Consequently, for the next half year, he would have been available for his enemies to instigate the criminal proceedings for which they longed so ardently.[1] Since the two tribunes immediately vetoed this motion, the situation created thereby was discussed on January 2, 5, 6 and 7.[2] On January 4 Cicero arrived before the city: as an *imperator* hoping for a triumph he did not cross the *pomerium*, but took part in important unofficial consultations in Pompey's country-house. He supported a peaceful compromise with the utmost zeal, again advising the acceptance of Caesar's confidential proposals and suggesting to Pompey that he should leave for Spain. Since this was not good enough for Pompey,

[1] Caes. *b.c.* 1, 1, 2–2, 7; 2, 6 (*uti ante certam diem Caesar exercitum dimittat*) certainly reproduces the wording of the proposal. The actual day remained to be fixed. First of all it was decided as a matter of principle that contrary to the latest (unofficial) proposals Caesar was not to retain a single soldier. This fact is correctly recorded in Vell. 2, 49, 4: Caesar declared war *ut deinde spretis omnibus, quae Caesar postulaverat, tantummodo contentus cum una legione titulum retinere provinciae, privatus ut in urbem veniret et se in petitione consulatus suffragiis populi Romani committeret, decrevere*. Karl Barwick (*Caesars Bellum Civile (Tendenz, Auffassung und Stil*), Berlin-Leipzig 99, 1 (1951), 18, 3) propounds a view which, contrary to *RE*, 7A, 991, I no longer regard as correct. I am happy to recognize Barwick's work as a solid contribution to source criticism, but my judgment on his basic interpretation agrees with that of F. Lossmann (*Gnomon* 28 (1956), 355 ff.). Barwick starts with the assumption (14) that Caesar was in the wrong, and attempts to show that he persistently distorted the truth. He also believes (124) that Books 1 and 2 were published at the end of 49, Book 3 at the end of 48. The intention ascribed to him of seeking to influence public opinion in Italy (129) I regard as an unjustified hypothesis. For the readership of which Barwick is thinking (135), the 'large mass of educated men in Rome and Italy', did not exist. As Cicero's collected letters show, the circles interested in politics knew from the start, through pronouncements by the two sides, of what they were accusing each other. Furthermore, Lossmann (*Hermes* 85 (1957), 47 ff.) has demonstrated that nothing can be inferred from the quotation of Asinius Pollio in Suet. *Caes.* 56, 4 about the date of composition. I regard it as most probable that Caesar drafted his *bellum civile* in 47 while staying in Egypt before the final battle in Africa. At this point he wished to make it quite clear that it was his enemies who forced the war on him. Since Book 3 breaks off with the beginning of the Alexandrine War, I conclude that the work remained uncompleted because it was no longer necessary after the victory at Thapsus. Since after Caesar's death Hirtius (*b.G.* 8, *praef.* 2) speaks of it as well known, it seems to have been published at that time. That a politician who takes up the pen represents his own point of view is so natural as not to be worth mentioning. The carping Asinius Pollio maintains (loc. cit.) that Caesar, *vel consulto vel etiam memoria lapsus*, has made many misstatements (*perperam*—see Lossmann, 57, 1), and the historian of today will act on the principle '*audiatur et altera pars*'. But petty references to misrepresentations of the truth do not do justice to Caesar because they presuppose a pettiness foreign to his character. His consciousness of his superiority over his contemporaries led naturally to a feeling that his way of interpreting events was the correct one. If in his hasty dictation he sometimes got his facts awry, this does not make it necessary to look for recherché falsification. As even Pollio admits, he may sometimes not have remembered details exactly. That he should make mistakes in his own favour is only human. But we also know enough from the other side to be able to say that on the whole events occurred as Caesar reports them. See further *HZ* 178 (1954), 453. On the date of composition of the *bellum civile*, see the most recent treatment by J. H. Collins (*AJP* 80 (1959), 113 ff.), who argues (especially p. 126) for the time of the Alexandrine War.

[2] Caes. *b.c.* 1, 2, 8; 5, 4; Dio 41, 3, 4; Plut. *Caes.* 30, 4.

Cicero eventually succeeded in persuading Caesar's friends to reduce their demands to Illyricum without Cisalpine Gaul, together with one legion; and, as he asserts, Pompey was now not disinclined to accept this. But the consul Lentulus and more particularly Cato, who loudly exclaimed that he was not to allow himself to be deceived by Caesar again, restrained him from accepting. So Cicero's attempt at arbitration came to nothing,[1] and on January 7 the Senate followed the example set a month earlier by the consul Gaius Marcellus by granting authority to protect the state to the consuls, praetors, tribunes and proconsuls in the vicinity of the city. Since the decree was passed to protect the interests of the state against the veto of the two tribunes, these declared that their inviolability was threatened and immediately left with Curio and Caelius to join Caesar. In contrast to the arbitrary action of the consul Marcellus, this use of the *senatus consultum ultimum* was fully in accordance with the constitutional law of the time: the regular government of Rome was granting its instruments dictatorial powers in order to force a recalcitrant proconsul to obey its orders. The two tribunes had not had a hair touched; Caesar himself in his *Civil War* does not question the Senate's competence to pass the decree, but denies that there was sufficient cause for it at this time.[2]

News of this event was borne to Ravenna with the speed of lightning, and Caesar will have received it on January 10.[3] The

[1] Cic. *fam.* 16, 12, 2 (January 23, 49); 4, 1, 1 (April 49); 6, 21, 1 (April 45). Retrospectively he thinks (*fam.* 6, 6, 5—October 46): *ea me suasisse Pompeio, quibus ille* (Pompey) *si paruisset, esset hic* (Caesar) *quidem clarus in toga et princeps, sed tantas opes, quantas nunc habet, non haberet. Att.* 8, 11d, 7 (February 27, 49, to Pompey): *primum enim prae me tuli malle quam pacem, non quin eadem timerem quam illi* (the radical enemies of Caesar), *sed ea bello civili leviora ducebam. Att.* 9, 11a, 2 (March 19, 49, to Caesar) of himself: *qui et illi* (Pompey) *semper et senatui cum primum potui pacis auctor fui nec sumptis armis belli ullam partem attigi iudicavique eo bello te violari, contra cuius honorem populi Romani beneficio concessum inimici atque invidi niterentur.* Plut. *Caes.* 31, 1–2; *Pomp.* 59, 5–6; Suet. *Caes.* 29, 2–30, 1; Vell. 2, 49, 4.

[2] Caes. *b.c.* 1, 5, 2–5; 7, 2–5; Cic. *fam.* 16, 11, 2; *Att.* 10, 8, 8; *Deiot.* 11; *Phil.* 2, 51. In the interesting letter of December 27, 50 (*Att.* 7, 9, 2), where Cicero in connection with his conversation with Pompey discusses the various possible developments of the conflict, the following eventuality (which had now occurred) is also considered: that Caesar might start a war simply because the law of the ten tribunes was being disregarded *aut addita causa, si forte tribunus pl. senatum impediens aut populum incitans notatus aut senatus consulto circumscriptus aut sublatus aut expulsus sit dicensve se expulsum ad illum* (Caesar) *confugerit . . .*; Dio 41, 1–3 (contradicting Cic. *fam.* 16, 11, 2); App. *b.c.* 2, 129–133 (dramatizing), similarly Plut. *Ant.* 5, 8–9; *Caes.* 39, 4–6; Liv. *per.* 109.

[3] Caes. *b.c.* 1, 5, 5. The date is to be inferred from the fact that Pompey left Rome on January 17, when news had arrived of Caesar's occupation of Ariminum (Cic. *Att.* 7, 10; 9, 10, 2; 8, 11b, 3; *fam.* 16, 12, 2; Plut. *Pomp.* 60, 1. Cf. O. E. Schmidt, *Briefwechsel*, 104; 106; 114; T. Rice Holmes, *The Rom. Rep. and the Founder of the Empire* (1928), 3, 377). Max Binder (*Studien z. Gesch. des zweiten Bürgerkriegs* (Diss. Freiburg i. Br. (1928), 16; 45)) puts the crossing of the Rubicon as late as January 14.

political situation had changed completely: previously he had been able to adopt a peace-loving role with the approval of a majority in the Senate, but now the senatorial majority was placing the greatest possible legal power in the hands of his opponents. It was clear to him that these would make use of their power to deploy the resources of the whole Empire against him.[1] He had to show that he was not afraid of their superior strength and to anticipate their preparations by a speedy attack. Further diplomatic moves could only be successful if he showed that his military prospects were not hopeless.

For this reason he immediately launched five cohorts towards Ariminum and the other five towards Arretium in Etruria.[2] 'Let the dice fly high', he said (quoting a half-line of his favourite Greek poet, Menander), as he crossed the Rubicon, the frontier river of his province,[3] on the way to Ariminum with his staff. The great

[1] Cic. *Att.* 8, 11, 2; 9, 9, 2; 10, 3; 6: *hoc turpe Gnaeus noster biennio ante cogitavit. ita sullaturit animus eius et proscripturit iam diu.*

[2] Caes. *b.c.* 1, 8, 1; 11, 4. Cf. O. E. Schmidt, op. cit., 105, 1; 115. Binder is certainly right in arguing that Caesar did not, as he says, order Antony to march against Arretium only after he had reached Ariminum.

[3] Caesar does not mention the Rubicon. The decisive significance of the crossing of this frontier is, however, stressed all the more in Vell. 2, 49, 4; Suet. *Caes.* 31, 2; Plut. *Caes.* 32, 5; *Pomp.* 60, 3; App. *b.c.* 2, 139. Since Plut. *Caes.* 32, 7 mentions Asinius Pollio among Caesar's followers, the famous exclamation ἀνερρίφθω κύβος may ultimately be traced back to his history. Plut. *Pomp.* 60, 4 expressly states that Caesar quoted in Greek. The whole verse in Athen. 13, 559e reads: Δεδογμένον τὸ πρᾶγμ' ἀνερρίφθω κύβος. As Caesar reports (1, 6) what happened in Rome on January 7 after the flight of the tribunes, continues (7, 1) *quibus rebus cognitis Caesar apud milites contionatur* (in Ravenna) and claims (8, 1) that it was only in Ariminum that he met the tribunes, he has certainly misrepresented the sequence of events (there is a full discussion of this in Barwick, op. cit., 26 ff.). Dio (41, 4, 1) shifts the address to the soldiers to Ariminum, and the accounts of the advance from Ravenna in Suet. *Caes.* 31, 1–33; Plut. *Caes.* 32, 3–9; App. *b.c.* 2, 137–141 agree with this. According to App. *b.c.* 2, 133 Caesar is said to have presented the tribunes to the soldiers earlier. Suet. *Caes.* 32 adds the story of a miracle, and changes the exclamation to *alea iacta est.* On this, see E. Hohl, *Hermes* 80 (1952), 246 ff.; cf. Petron. 122, 174–176. However, it is noticeable that Caesar, in reporting his *contio* to the thirteenth legion, only mentions the violence done to the tribunes, and so the only remaining deviation from the truth is that he shifts the *contio* to Ravenna, which produces the contradiction that he first meets the tribunes in Ariminum. It appears that Caesar was less worried about this than his critics. He was solely concerned to give the impression that he was marching to Ariminum with the soldiers' consent: (7, 8) *conclamant legionis XIII quae aderat milites . . . sese paratos esse imperatoris sui tribunorumque plebis iniurias defendere;* (8, 1) *cognita militum voluntate Ariminum cum ea legione proficiscitur.* But the whole speech, and in particular the pronouncedly factual explanation of why the s.c. *'darent operam magistratus, ne quid res publica detrimenti caperet'* (7, 5) was not justified in this case, is intended to make clear to the readers that Caesar had to appeal to his soldiers against the injustice that he had suffered. Cicero (*Phil.* 2, 53) charges Antony with having supplied Caesar with this *causa belli contra patriam inferendi: quid enim aliud ille dicebat, quam causam sui dementissimi consili et facti adferebat, nisi quod intercessio neglecta, ius tribunicium sublatum, circumscriptus a senatu esset Antonius? omitto quam haec falsa, quam levia, praesertim cum omnino nulla causa iusta cuiquam esse possit contra patriam arma capiendi.* Caesar's *bellum civile* is directed principally against this condemnation of his course of action. As we can see from the letter to Caesar (*Att.* 9, 11a; p. 192, n. 1,

gamble could now begin; for he was starting a civil war, and, according to the view occasionally expressed in his works, 'Luck is the greatest power in all things and especially in war'.[1] Admittedly, in another passage he adds that human endeavour could lend luck a helping hand, and the knowledge that he would not be found wanting in this respect will have filled him with confidence.[2]

above), Cicero too was capable of putting himself in Caesar's place; similarly, in December 45 (*Deiot.* 11) Lucan makes Caesar deliver the speech (1, 299–351) in Ariminum (1, 231); the hint (340–345) that Caesar's dismissal endangered the provision for his veterans may have represented a real consideration on the soldiers' part. Suet. *Caes.* 33 gives a dramatized account which I am less ready to credit than Ed. Meyer, *Caesars Mon.* (1918), 291: Caesar is said to have worked on the soldiers with tears and rending of his clothes, and to have repeatedly pointed to the gold ring on his left hand, saying that he would sacrifice even that, in order to reward the soldiers for defending his *dignitas*; this is said to have been misinterpreted by the men in the rear ranks as a promise of equestrian status. It is disputed which stream is the Rubicon. Philipp (*RE*, 1A, 1165, map 1163) supports the Uso; J. van Ooteghem (*Pompée le Grand* (1954), illustr. 37 following p. 514) says that recently the Fiumicino has been preferred.

[1] Caes. *b.G.* 6, 30, 2; 35, 2; 42, 1; *b.c.* 3, 10, 6; similarly 1, 21, 2: *magni casus.*

[2] Caes. *b.c.* 3, 73, 4: *si non omnia caderent secunda, fortunam esse industria sublevandam.* With respect to the Menander quotation it is worth noticing that the same sentiment occurs in Terence, *adelph.* 739 ff.:

> *ita vitast hominum, quasi quom ludas tesseris:*
> *si illud quod maxume opus est iactu non cadit,*
> *illud quod cecidit forte, id arte ut corrigas.*

It is an important characteristic of Caesar that he spoke and wrote in a language intelligible to the common man (*ap.* Cic. *Brut.* 253). He was no philosopher, and there is no need to delve deeply into his sayings about *fortuna*. In this I agree with C. (Gigon-) Brutscher, *Mus. Helv.* 15 (1958), 75. But they suggest that his audacity was lent wings by the notion that *fortis fortuna adiuvat* (Ter. *Phormio* 203). 'Mysticism' is quite irrelevant. Demosthenes had said something very like this in the *Second Olynthiac* (22): μεγάλη γὰρ ῥοπή, μᾶλλον δ' ὅλον ἡ τύχη παρὰ πάντ' ἐστὶ τὰ τῶν ἀνθρώπων πράγματα. If Caesar was fond of speaking of *fortuna*, we may assume that he liked quoting proverbs (see also Ennius *ann.* 257; Verg. *Aen.* 10, 284). On the other hand he may equally well have agreed with the sentence in the *Tusculan Disputations* (2, 11): *fortis enim non modo fortuna adiuvat, ut est in vetere proverbio, sed multo magis ratio, quae quibusdam quasi praeceptis confirmat vim fortitudinis.* Cic. *Att.* 7, 11, 1 (January 20, 49): *sibi habeat suam fortunam!* Asinius Pollio (*ap.* Cic. *fam.* 10, 31, 3): *Caesar in tanta fortuna.* Horace (*c.* 2, 1, 2) expects of the work of Asinius that he will discuss *bellique causas et vitia et modos ludumque fortunae gravisque principum amicitias et arma.* On *fortuna* in Caesar, see Harry Erkell, *Augustus, Felicitas, Fortuna, Lateinische Wortstudien* (1952), 160–162. He also discusses (p. 52) the fragment of a letter from Cicero to Cornelius Nepos preserved in Ammian. 21, 16, 13 (frag. 2, 5, ed. Purser): *neque enim quicquam aliud est felicitas, inquit, nisi honestarum rerum prosperitas; vel ut alio modo definiam, felicitas est fortuna adiutrix consiliorum bonorum, quibus qui non utitur felix esse nullo pacto potest. ergo in perditis impiisque consiliis quibus Caesar usus est, nulla potuit esse felicitas; feliciorque meo iudicio Camillus exsulans quam temporibus isdem Manlius, etiam si — id quod cupierat — regnare potuisset.* This is clearly Cicero's judgment after Caesar's murder; *off.* 1, 26 is similar. Erkell also draws attention to *Phil.* 2, 64: *Caesar Alexandria se recepit felix, ut sibi quidem videbatur; mea autem sententia, qui rei publicae sit hostis, felix esse nemo potest.* In fact Caesar (*b.c.* 3, 73, 3) uses *felicitas* as a synonym for *fortuna.* On the other hand, Cicero does grant Caesar *felicitas* (*Marc.* 19) in the year 46, because he had shown himself *sapiens* by pardoning M. Marcellus: *tantus est enim splendor in laude vera, tanta in magnitudine animi et consili dignitas.* Here too (16; 19) he distinguishes *fortuna* from *felicitas.*

CHAPTER FIVE

THE CIVIL WAR

ON the morning of January 11, 49 (November 24, 50, Jul.) Ariminum was in Caesar's hands; here he was able to present the two fugitive tribunes to his soldiers and received the reply that they were ready to avenge the wrong that had been done their general and the sacrosanct officials. The advance continued, and by January 14 Ancona and Arretium were occupied. News of this reached Rome on January 17, causing extreme depression.[1] In the days following January 7 the Senate had decreed a series of further measures implementing the *senatus consultum ultimum*, in particular the levying of troops throughout Italy and the distribution of the governorships to which no appointment had yet been made among consulars and praetorians. Lucius Domitius received Transalpine and the praetorian Marcus Considius Nonianus Cisalpine Gaul.[2] The news of Caesar's advance brought these discussions to a sudden end. To the optimates' fury and disappointment Pompey declared that the city must be abandoned and made it the duty of every patriot to follow him. He retired with the consuls and a large part of the Senate to Campania; in informed circles there was already talk of a further withdrawal to Epirus.[3] As early as December Pompey had told all who were prepared to listen that in the event of an attack by Caesar it might prove necessary to evacuate Rome in order to cut off his supplies and connections with his remaining troops.[4] On the other hand, during the deliberations early in January his pronouncements were full of confidence: he controlled ten legions ready for war, and was sure that Caesar's soldiers would not fight for him in this enterprise.[5] Still earlier he had once laughingly assured some worried questioners: 'I have only to stamp on the soil of Italy for cavalry and infantry to rise from the ground.'[6] Thus

[1] See above, p. 192, note 3.
[2] Caes. *b.c.* 1, 6, 3; 5; Cic. *fam.* 16, 11, 3; 12, 3.
[3] Cic. *Att.* 7, 10; 11, 1; 3; 12, 2; 4; 8, 1, 4; 9, 10, 2 and 4; *fam.* 14, 18, 1; Caes. *b.c.* 1, 14, 1–3; 33, 2; App. *b.c.* 2, 148; Plut. *Pomp.* 61, 6; *Caes.* 33, 6; Suet. *Caes.* 35, 6; Dio 41, 6, 2.
[4] Cic. *Att.* 7, 8, 5; 9, 2; 8, 11d, 6.
[5] Caes. *b.c.* 1, 6, 2.
[6] Plut. *Pomp.* 57, 8–9; 60, 7; *Caes.* 33, 5.

the Senate had reason for confidence that Caesar would not dare to invade with his solitary legion, and this explains their extreme disillusionment.[1]

But Caesar did not overestimate his success. He, if anyone, understood the political and strategic trains of thought of his former son-in-law, namely that he would follow Sulla's example and attempt to recover Italy from the east. His position was incomparably more favourable than Sulla's. The latter had been the outlawed leader of a small army, while Pompey was the celebrated organizer of the eastern half of the empire, the entire forces of which he controlled as a duly authorized proconsul; further, in Spain, of which country he was also the leading patron, he possessed a considerable and fully mobilized army.[2] The disadvantage of a method of waging war which was old-fashioned in comparison with Caesar's was to a large extent made good by the defection of Labienus, Caesar's best *legatus*, who had proved himself often enough as an independent commander.[3]

Caesar's invasion of Italy was a military success, but it also had the (for him) undesirable consequence that the legitimate government fled before him.[4] The man who had previously done everything to put his opponents in the wrong before public opinion now appeared as the revolutionary: his intention to carry out his plans at least formally by constitutional means was thwarted. At one blow he lost the sympathy of peace-loving citizens which his previous willingness to compromise had won him:[5] the more so since he was bringing the horrors of civil war to Italy, and the terror which preceded him was increased by the rumour that there were numerous Celtic troops in his train.[6] For two years he had struggled to obtain without resort to force what he regarded as his rights.[7] No wonder

[1] Caes. *b.c.* 1, 30, 5; Cic. *Att.* 7, 11, 3; 13, 2.

[2] Cic. *Att.* 8, 11, 2; 9, 1, 3; 9, 2; 10, 2 and 3–6; Caes. *b.c.* 1, 38, 1; 39, 1; Cic. *fam.* 16, 12, 4; *Att.* 7, 26, 1; 8, 2, 3; 3, 7.

[3] Cic. *Att.* 7, 12, 5; 13, 1; 13a, 3; 15, 3; 16, 2; *fam.* 14, 14, 2; 16, 12, 4; Dio 41, 3, 3; Plut. *Caes.* 34, 5.

[4] Cic. *Att.* 7, 13, 1: *quid autem sit acturus aut quo modo nescio, sine senatu, sine magistratibus. ne simulare quidem poterit quicquam* πολιτικῶς; 17, 3.

[5] Cic. *Att.* 7, 11, 4.

[6] Cic. *Att.* 7, 11, 3; 13, 3; 9, 13, 4. From this comes the *amplificatio* of Lucan (1, 394–465).

[7] In his own words: the recognition of his *dignitas* (*b.c.* 1, 4, 4; 7, 7; 9, 2). See Cicero's outcry (*Att.* 7, 11, 1): *o hominem amentem et miserum qui ne umbram quidem umquam* τοῦ καλοῦ *viderit! atque haec ait omnia facere se dignitatis causa. ubi est autem dignitas nisi ub ihonestas?* Caesar regards the Civil War as a personal quarrel forced on him by his enemies (1, 22, 5): *se non maleficii*

that at the beginning of his work on the Civil War he is still shaking
with the overpowering fury which flared up in him when these
attempts failed. His short factual account of the first days of January
resounds with lashes that beat down on the heads of the guilty: on
the consul Lentulus, who treats his offer as so much empty air,
shouts down the few voices that counsel reason, and like a second
Sulla wishes to rid himself of his debts; on Cato, whose long-
standing hatred is mingled with resentment over the consulship
which has eluded him; on Metellus Scipio, promising himself a share
in the supreme command with his son-in-law and fawned upon on
all sides as the great man in the law courts; and finally on Pompey
himself who, incited by Caesar's enemies and filled with the ambition
not to allow anyone to rival his own position, has set himself up
as absolute ruler with the help of the two legions disgracefully
stolen from Caesar and is seeking a decision by arms.[1] These so-
called guardians of the constitution are trampling on all divine and
human law.[2] On the other side, Cicero was of the opinion that at
the last Curio in particular poured oil on the flames of Caesar's

causa ex provincia egressum, sed uti se a contumeliis inimicorum defenderet, ut tribunos plebis nefarie
ex civitate expulsos in suam dignitatem restitueret, ut se et populum Romanum factione paucorum
oppressum in libertatem vindicaret. How naturally he mentions himself before the tribunes and
People! By their violation of the tribunician right of veto his enemies gave him a plausible
constitutional pretext, and as a popularis he mentioned the People. But the 'liberation' in reality
meant no more to him than that the oligarchs (the pauci) wished to prevent the realization
of the potentialities due to his dignitas. Even Cicero recognizes this when writing to Caesar
(Att. 9, 11a, 2; see above, p. 192, note 1): iudicavi eo bello te violari contra cuius honorem
populi Romani beneficio concessum inimici atque invidi niterentur. But already on February 2
(Att. 7, 17, 4) he wrote: totam enim Italiam flagraturam bello intellego. tantum mali est excitatum
partim ex improbis, partim ex invidis civibus. As early as December, 50, he had also dissociated
himself from the political group described by Atticus as boni (Att. 7, 7, 5): ego quos tu bonos esse
dicas non intellego. ipse nullos novi, sed ita, si ordines bonorum quaerimus; nam singulares sunt boni
viri. verum in dissensionibus ordines bonorum et genera quaerenda sunt. Yet he knows that with his
great political past he cannot avoid making a decision, and accordingly concludes (7): adsentior
Cn. Pompeio, id est T. Pomponio.

[1] Caes. b.c. 1, 4.

[2] Caes. b.c. 1, 6, 8: omnia divina humanaque iura permiscentur. Cicero (off. 1, 26) makes the
same criticism of him after his death in explanation of the words of Ennius (scaen. 404 Vahlen)
'nulla sancta societas nec fides regni est'. declaravit id modo temeritas C. Caesaris, qui omnia iura
divina et humana pervertit propter eum, quem sibi ipse opinionis errore finxerat, principatum. This
principatus was the conclusion which Caesar drew from his dignitas. Already in January 49
Cicero (Att. 7, 11, 1) called this τυραννίς, quoting Eurip. Phoen. 507 (7, 20, 2; 8, 2, 4 are on
the same lines) and in off. 3, 82 he states that Caesar constantly had lines 525 and 526 on his
lips:

εἴπερ γὰρ ἀδικεῖν χρὴ τυραννίδος πέρι
κάλλιστον ἀδικεῖν τἆλλα δ'εὐσεβεῖν χρεών.

Suet. Caes. 30, 5 follows this. It is worth noting that Cicero twice quotes the same speech of
Euripides. Perhaps it was part of the school curriculum (cf. Quintil. 10, 1, 67) and hence also

anger,[1] and when Cicero met Pompey at the end of December, they had just received the *contio* of Antony in which Pompey was so remorselessly criticized. He commented on this: 'What do you think he will do himself if he gets control of the state, when his weak and bankrupt quaestor dares to speak like this?' Cicero was still on good terms with both sides and would have liked to evade a decision.[2] But he always eventually came round to the conclusion that, if the break was inevitable, Caesar's victory would be the greater evil, because one could expect no better from him than from Cinna or Sulla.[3] As future events were to show, this apprehension was unjustified. But in this lies the tragedy of the situation: no one believed that Caesar was capable of better things.

Certainly his aim, as defined by Pompey, was to gain control of the state. This was the direction in which he had been moving for several years, and there was now no going back for him. But what dangers and obstacles still lay before him! Just now they towered higher than ever. On the other hand, he enjoyed the enormous advantage that he was both politician and general in one person; he could husband his forces as he wished, considerably weaker than his opponents' though they were, and his military operations were no more than a weapon in his political struggle. This was most evident at the start, before there had been any decisive turns to demonstrate the possibility of his final victory.

Controlling his anger, he at once used the official intimation of the senatorial decree of January 7 to send through the messengers who had brought it new assurances of his peaceable intentions to the Senate and to invite Pompey to personal discussions.[4] The latter ignored the invitation, but Caesar had the satisfaction that the Senate, whose peace party was indignant about Pompey's inadequate military preparations, dispatched another delegation. On January 23 Caesar's new conditions reached Teanum Sidicinum where Pompey

---

familiar to Caesar. In addition, he wrote a tragedy *Oedipus* in his youth (Suet. *Caes.* 56, 7). Doubtless Caesar occasionally spoke frankly among his intimates, and Cicero's statement could, like others, go back to someone who had actually heard him speak thus. However, as early as February 27, 49, Cicero writes of Pompey and Caesar (*Att.* 8, 11, 2): *dominatio quaesita ab utroque est, non id actum beata et honesta civitas ut esset.* Neither was Pompey the *princeps* demanded by Cicero in *de republica.* (See op. cit., 9, 7, 1 and 3–4; 9, 2; 10, 2 and 6.)

[1] Cic. *fam.* 16, 11, 2.   [2] Cic. *Att.* 7, 8, 5.

[3] Cic. *Att.* 7, 11, 1; 12, 2; 13, 1; 20, 2; 22, 2; 26, 2.

[4] Dio 41, 5, 3. Caesar himself (*b.c.* 1, 8, 2), though, speaks only of one embassy. Perhaps Dio has not reproduced his source correctly. Thus my *Pompeius*[2], 280, 153.

discussed the reply with the consuls.[1] They meant no less than that Caesar was ready to submit to the Senate's decree of January 1: he was prepared to give up his provinces to the new governors and to forgo his privilege and appear in Rome in person for the elections. In return, however, he demanded the lifting of the *senatus consultum ultimum* passed against him. All troops in Italy were to return to their homes: Pompey, like Caesar, was to dismiss his army and go to Spain. This would secure a free electoral meeting, and the state would be in the constitutional power of the Senate and People. Both parties were to swear on oath to keep the conditions on which they had agreed.[2]

Caesar was thus indubitably taking up a constitutional position, but at headquarters in Teanum they were only concerned with the political significance of these words. The answer, which was immediately published, told him that his splendid achievements merited a second consulship and triumph; if he evacuated the occupied areas of Italy, the Senate would return to Rome to take further decisions and, as soon as Caesar had dismissed his army, Pompey would leave for Spain. The point to which he attached the greatest importance, the disarmament of Italy and Spain, was not so much as mentioned.[3] His opponents had no intention of delivering themselves up to the irresistible demagogue.[4] Thereupon Caesar broke off the negotiations.[5]

He had not ceased military operations during these days and now again made rapid progress. During the first days of February he

---

[1] Cic. *Att.* 7, 14, 1. [2] Caes. *b.c.* 1, 9, 5–6; Cic. *fam.* 16, 12, 3.

[3] Caes. *b.c.* 1, 10–11, 3; Cic. *Att.* 7, 14, 1; 15, 2; 16, 2; 17, 2; 18, 1; 19: C. Furnius (tribune in 50; cf. Kappelmacher, *RE*, 7, 376) informed Cicero of a letter from Curio in which the latter *inridet L. Caesaris legationem*. Thus Curio maintained that Caesar's embassy was not seriously intended. Against this (21, 3): *ipse me Caesar ad pacem hortatur;* (7, 26, 2): *plane eum quoi noster* (Pompey) *alterum consulatum deferret et triumphum (at quibus verbis! 'pro tuis rebus gestis amplissimis') inimicum habere nolueram*; 7, 18, 2; 8, 9, 2; 11d, 7 (Cicero to Pompey) 12, 2.

[4] Cicero, who thought on January 26 that Caesar would withdraw from the occupied towns, notes (*Att.* 7, 15, 3): *vicerit enim, si consul factus erit, et minore scelere vicerit quam quo ingressus est.*

[5] Caes. *b.c.* 1, 11, 4. Here he, in fact, makes it look as if this had occurred in Ariminum and as if only then did he send Antony to Arretium and occupy Pisaurum, Fanum and Ancona, whereas Cicero (*Att.* 7, 11, 1) knew as early as January 20 that he had reached Ancona. A false rumour appears in 7, 18, 2. On January 27 (*fam.* 16, 12, 2) he even writes inaccurately that the senators had left Rome after Caesar's occupation of Ariminum, Pisaurum, Ancona and Arretium. But just as Cicero makes a mistake here after a few days, Caesar did not imagine in 47 B.C. that later readers would be able to check his inaccuracies.

gained control of the whole of Picenum.[1] This success was particularly surprising as this area was decidedly under the patronage of
Pompey. Caesar's narrative duly emphasizes that as he advanced
towards Auximum, its most northerly town, the *decuriones* requested
the praetorian Attius Varus to withdraw with his cohorts. Although
they were not competent to pass judgment about the matter in
dispute, they and their fellow-citizens could not tolerate that the
imperator Caesar, who through his great achievements had deserved
well of the state, should be barred from entry to their town. For
this reason Attius was asked to consider posterity and the risk which
he himself was running.[2] These unpretentious people had grasped
what the narrow-minded optimates refused to admit. He received
a similar enthusiastic welcome at Cingulum, although Labienus
had granted the town its municipal constitution and had constructed
public buildings there at his own expense.[3] Several cohorts recruited
by the optimate senators dispersed or went over to Caesar,[4] nineteen
others succeeded in retreating to the fortified Corfinium in the
Abruzzi, where the proconsul of Transalpine Gaul, Lucius Domitius
Ahenobarbus, had already assembled twelve cohorts.[5] The latter
was himself a large landowner, his troops farmers on the land, whose
loyalty he hoped to buy by promises of a large-scale distribution
of his property.[6] For this reason he could not and would not obey
Pompey's summons to follow him to Brundisium; but on February 14
he was surrounded by Caesar and forced to capitulate a week later.[7]
On the morning of February 21 Caesar had the fifty prisoners
belonging to the senatorial and equestrian orders brought before
him—among them was Publius Lentulus Spinther, the consul of 57—
and for the first time in nine years saw his deadly enemy Domitius
face to face.[8] Although he knew very well what would have been
his fate had their roles been reversed, Caesar, who after more than
two years was still letting Vercingetorix await execution, restrained
himself and, sacrificing personal revenge to a higher political
objective, granted all these prisoners their freedom while their

[1] Cic. *Att.* 7, 16, 2; 21, 2; Caes. *b.c.* 1, 15, 1.
[2] Caes. *b.c.* 1, 13, 1.   [3] Caes. *b.c.* 1, 15, 2.
[4] Caes. *b.c.* 1, 12, 2; 13, 4; 15, 3.
[5] Cic. *Att.* 8, 11a (letter of Pompey to Cicero); Caes. *b.c.* 1, 15, 4–7 (counting 'approximately'
thirty-three cohorts); 17, 2.
[6] Caes. *b.c.* 1, 17, 4; *Att.* 8, 12b, 2 (letter of Pompey to Domitius): Dio 41, 11, 1–2.
[7] Caes. *b.c.* 1, 23, 5; Cic. *Att.* 8, 14, 1; 8, 12c, 1 (letter of Pompey to Domitius).
[8] Caes. *b.c.* 1, 23, 1–2.

troops were incorporated in his own army. All those released continued to fight against him. Caesar does not say that he imposed any conditions upon them, but in other respects they are sufficiently exposed in his narrative: Domitius wishes to escape secretly, whereupon his soldiers arrest him and decide to surrender and hand him over alive to Caesar.[1] He does not allow an immediate occupation of Corfinium because it is night and he wishes to save the town from plunder. However, he encloses the town completely, and he remarks that his entire army waited with interest to see how he would treat the besieged.[2] Towards the end of the night Lentulus requests permission to speak to him and begs for his life, reminding Caesar of their old friendship and of all the help that he had received in his career up to the consulship. But Caesar interrupts him: he had not left his province to do injury but to protect himself against humiliation from his enemies, to restore to their position the tribunes illegally driven from the city and to free the Roman people from oppression by a small clique.[3] Then, when the fifty men of rank are brought before him, he protects them from their own followers, contenting himself with a few words of reproach that some of them should be so ungrateful for the great benefits which they had received.[4]

This 'clemency of Corfinium'[5] did not fail to make the great impression intended by Caesar. Cicero, who at the time was staying on his estate near Formiae on the coast of Latium and had many

[1] Op. cit., 1, 19–20.

[2] Op. cit., 1, 21. The way in which Caesar makes the first far-reaching announcement of his political aims is masterly. Its crucial importance is characterized only by the tense curiosity of his whole army as to what would happen after the capitulation (21, 5–6): *neque vero tam remisso ac languido animo quisquam omnium fuit, qui ea nocte conquieverit: tanta erat summae rerum exspectatio, ut alius in aliam partem mente atque animo traheretur, quid ipsis Corfiniensibus, quid Domitio, quid Lentulo, quid reliquis accideret, qui quosque eventus exciperent.* Many were still alive who remembered with horror how Sulla had behaved in 82 B.C. after the capitulation of Praeneste in executing all non-Romans among the garrison—12,000 in all (Plut. *Sull.* 32, 1), Praenestians and Samnites (App. *b.c.* 1, 437/8), as well as all the officers (Oros. 5, 21, 10: *omnes Marianae militiae principes, hoc est legatos quaestores praefectos et tribunos iussit occidi*). Even Cicero at first expected something of this sort (*Att.* 7, 11, 1; 12, 2; 13, 3). On February 10 (23, 1): *persequi Caesar Pompeium? quid? ut interficiat?* Again on March 10 (9, 5, 3): *sed video plane nihil aliud agi, nihil actum ab initio, nisi ut hunc occideret.* On March 6 (9, 1, 4): the Marcelli, consuls in 51 and 50, would remain in Italy, *nisi gladium Caesaris timuissent. Appius* (the censor of 50) *est eodem in timore et inimicitiarum recentium etiam.*

[3] Caes. *b.c.* 1, 22, 1–5. 　　[4] Op. cit., 1, 23, 3.

[5] Cic. *Att.* 9, 16, 1; 8, 9, 3: *alterum* (Caesar) *existimari conservatorem inimicorum, alterum* (Pompey) *desertorem amicorum;* 4: the younger Balbus told him that Caesar wished for nothing more than a reconciliation with Pompey, on which he comments *id non credo et metuo omnis haec clementia ad Cinneam illam crudelitatem conligatur.*

O

occasions for conversation with the inhabitants of town and country, wrote on March 1 that since it had become clear that Caesar was putting no one to death and confiscating no property opinion was veering right round in his favour.[1] Numerous optimates returned to Rome and prepared to receive the victor.[2] Cicero's friend, Pomponius Atticus, a man of sober judgment, also thought that Caesar might continue along the path that he had once chosen.[3] At about this time Caesar himself sent a letter intended for further distribution to Oppius and Balbus at Rome,[4] saying that he was pleased that they approved of his conduct before Corfinium: 'I shall be glad of your advice, and all the more so because I had already decided on my own to show as much clemency as possible and to attempt a reconciliation with Pompey. Let us do our utmost to win back public opinion in this way and to enjoy a lasting victory; for the others could not escape hatred for their cruelty and, with the exception of Sulla, whom I have no wish to imitate, were unable to maintain their victories for any length of time. Let this be the new way to be victorious, to secure ourselves by mercy and generosity. I have some ideas on how to bring this about and much more can be discovered. Please give the matter your consideration.'[5] He further reports that Numerius Magius, an adjutant of Pompey, had fallen into his hands and that he had immediately sent him to Pompey with an invitation to a personal discussion in Brundisium in order

---

[1] Cic. *Att.* 8, 13; 9, 13, 4; 15, 3.

[2] Cic. *Att.* 8, 16, 1–2; 9, 1, 2; 5, 4; 8, 1; 12, 3. Cicero had already foreseen on February 16 (8, 1, 3): *prope diem video bonorum, id est lautorum et locupletum, urbem refertam fore, municipiis vero his relictis* (if Pompey evacuates Italy) *refertissimam.* Most emphatically (*Att.* 8, 16, 1): *municipia vero deum, nec simulant, ut cum de illo aegroto* (Pompey in 50) *vota faciebant.* Caesar is now their god, and they are just as sincere as in 50 B.C. because they think that the danger is over.

[3] Cic. *Att.* 8, 9, 4; 9, 10, 9: Cicero quotes from a letter from Atticus of March 5, *hoc ita dico, si hic* (Caesar) *qua ratione initium fecit eadem cetera aget, sincere, temperate, prudenter.* On March 9 Atticus (10) wrote that Sex. Peducaeus (Münzer, *RE*, 19, 50—Münzer thought that it was more probably the father, but this is very improbable, to judge by *Att.* 10, 1, 1; Nep. *Att.* 21, 4)—also approved of Cicero's staying in Italy. A few days after March 19 (the date of Cicero's letter to Caesar, *Att.* 9, 11a) Cicero writes that Atticus and one other (*vos duo tales*) intended to meet Caesar at the fifth milestone from Rome: *quanto autem ferocius ille* (Caesar) *causae suae confidet, cum vos, cum vestri similis non modo frequentis sed lauto vultu gratulantis viderit* (*Att.* 8, 9, 2). I suspect that the other was Peducaeus. He is also mentioned in 9, 7, 2; 13, 6.

[4] *Ap.* Cic. *Att.* 9, 7c; cf. Dio 41, 10, 2, where Caesar had letters distributed throughout Italy before the attack on Corfinium.

[5] From Cicero's letters we know how the memory of the horrors of the first civil war affected the older generation. Caesar does his best to suppress this comparison.

to remove the misunderstandings sown between them by their common foes and to restore the country to peace.[1]

He also tried to use the ties binding Lucius Cornelius Balbus to his patron, the consul Lucius Cornelius Lentulus, to induce the latter to return to Rome. He gave Balbus permission to look after his protector's interests in Rome,[2] and on February 23 Balbus' nephew travelled after the consul with instructions from Caesar. But he did not reach him in Brundisium, since on March 4 the two consuls had put out to sea with part of the troops. This was a most vexatious disappointment for Caesar,[3] since the absence of both the consuls deprived the measures which he intended to bring before the Senate of their constitutional façade and, in particular, his election to the consulship was made more difficult.[4]

On March 9 he arrived with six legions before Brundisium to find Pompey still there.[5] The latter immediately sent Magius back to negotiate, but would not consent to the meeting desired by Caesar.[6] Caesar now made use of the good offices of his *legatus* Gaius Caninius Rebilus who was on friendly terms with Lucius Scribonius Libo, then the chief confidant of Pompey and the father-in-law of his son Sextus. Libo granted him an audience and gave Pompey Caesar's message to the effect that in personal discussion they could easily find acceptable conditions, which would allow them both to dismiss their armies. Pompey replied that, in the absence of the consuls, he was unable to negotiate about the settlement of the dispute, and on March 17 succeeded in escaping from the blockade with slight losses and crossed the Adriatic.[7]

This marked the final breakdown of Caesar's plan to detach Pompey from the optimates, as he had been able to do several times in the past ten years. Pompey would not let himself be

---

[1] The same in Caes. *b.c.* 1, 24, 4–6, with the addition that what mattered to him was the meeting with Pompey. In the letter he also mentions the other *praefectus fabrum* L. Vibullius Rufus (*b.c.* 1, 34, 1; Cic. *Att.* 8, 15, 1); he had given instructions to them both *Pompeium hortari, ut malit mihi esse amicus quam iis qui et illi et mihi semper fuerunt inimicissimi, quorum artificiis effectum est, ut res publica in hunc statum perveniret* (cf. *b.c.* 1, 4, 4).

[2] Cic. *Att.* 9, 7b, 2 (letter of Balbus to Cicero).

[3] Cic. *Att.* 8, 9, 4; 11, 5; 15a, 2–3 (Balbus to Cicero); 9, 6, 1 and 3; Caes. *b.c.* 1, 25, 2; 3, 4, 1; Plut. *Pomp.* 62, 3; Caes. *b.c.* 35, 2; App. *b.c.* 2, 152; Dio 41, 12, 1.

[4] Cic. *Att.* 9, 9, 3; 15, 2.

[5] Op. cit., 9, 13a, 1 (Caesar to Oppius and Balbus).

[6] In the same letter: *misit ad me N. Magium de pace. quae visa sunt respondi.* Caes. *b.c.* 1, 26, 2 only emphasizes that Magius was not sent back (a second time). Cf. Plut. *Pomp.* 62, 3. The indignation of Barwick (op. cit., 57) is unjustified.

[7] Caes. *b.c.* 1, 26, 3–6; Cic. *Att.* 9, 15, 6 (letter from Matius and Trebatius to Cicero); Dio 41, 12, 3.

deceived by the words of Caesar then in circulation, that he wished for nothing more than to live without fear while recognizing the supremacy of Pompey:[1] his opponent's whole character contradicted the possibility of such a relationship. Thus Caesar was faced with the necessity of risking a real war against the far stronger coalition. Since he had insufficient ships to pursue Pompey, he had first to turn against Spain from where he was at the moment faced by the greatest military danger. Just as important was the frustration of Pompey's plan to starve him out. For this purpose detachments were at once sent across to Sicily and Sardinia.[2]

On the way to Spain he intended to stop for a few days in Rome and to attempt by means of negotiations in the Senate to create for himself a more or less legitimate position.[3] He possessed the constitutional prerequisite for this in the persons of the two tribunes Antony and Cassius and several praetors, who had returned to Rome together with a considerable number of senators.[4] But the intended decrees would only have political authority if they were supported by some respected leading figures, and accordingly Caesar strained every nerve to secure this end. Several consulars were related to him: Lucius Piso, his father-in-law, Lucius Cotta, his mother's cousin, Lucius Philippus, the husband of his niece Atia and the stepfather of the future Augustus and of his sister Octavia. Of these Piso had offered his services as mediator on January 1 and Cotta and Philippus had been excluded from drawing

---

[1] Cic. *Att.* 8, 9, 4: *Balbus quidem maior ad me scribit nihil malle Caesarem quam principe Pompeio sine metu vivere*; 7, 20, 1 (February 5): Caesar's intention *ut fugam intercludat.*

[2] Caes. *b.c.* 1, 29–30, 2; Cic. *Att.* 7, 26, 1; 8, 2, 3 (February 17): *Afranium exspectabimus et Petreium;* 3, 7. Starvation plan: 9, 7, 3–4; 9, 2 and 4. Lack of ships: 9, 3, 2. M. Curtius Postumus on Caesar's plans: *Att.* 9, 2a, 3 (March 8). This Curtius had already become a military tribune under Caesar in 54 (Münzer, *RE*, 4, 1869, no. 26): *venit nihil nisi classis loquens et exercitus. eripiebat Hispanias, tenebat Asiam, Siciliam, Africam, Sardiniam, confestim in Graeciam persequebatur.* This is the kind of news that tends to be peddled from headquarters. Caesar's saying before the Spanish campaign also belongs in this context (*ap.* Suet. *Caes.* 34, 2: *professus ante inter suos, ire se ad exercitum sine duce et inde reversurum ad ducem sine exercitu*). There is no reason to dispute its authenticity. However, the great efforts made by Caesar to prevent Pompey from getting away speak against his having taken his failure so lightly. For this very reason he had to appear confident before his entourage. On the same lines M. Caelius (Cic. *fam.* 8, 16, 3, on April 16 to Cicero): *Hispanias tibi nuntio adventu Caesaris fore nostras. quam isti* (Pompey and company) *spem habeant amissis Hispaniis nescio.* Similarly Curio *ap.* Cic. *Att.* 10, 4, 8. Yet Cicero did not believe it (*Att.* 10, 8, 2 and 4; Dio 41, 15, 1; Plut. *Caes.* 35, 3).

[3] Caesar informed Cicero of his intention early in March (Cic. *Att.* 9, 6a); *Att.* 9, 8, 2; 15, 6.

[4] Cic. *Att.* 9, 8, 1; 12, 3. Of the praetors, we know M. Aemilius Lepidus (Caes. *b.c.* 2, 21, 5; App. *b.c.* 2, 165) and L. Roscius Fabatus (Caes. *b.c.* 1, 3, 6; Cic. *Att.* 8, 12, 2). Cf. Broughton, *MRR*, 2, 257.

lots, when the provinces were distributed, as unreliable.[1] But after
January 17 they all left the city and contented themselves with a
more or less neutral position with which Caesar eventually declared
himself satisfied, as we know for certain at least where Philippus
was concerned.[2] We do not know the attitude at this time of Lucius
Julius Caesar, who had become his *legatus* in the year 52 and later
appears on his side, or of Gnaeus Domitius Calvinus, his *legatus*
since 48. From Cicero's silence we may perhaps deduce that they
were not working for Caesar. The two consuls of 66, Manius
Lepidus and Lucius Volcacius Tullus, had left Rome but were
disinclined to follow Pompey overseas; as things were, they had
decided to place themselves at Caesar's disposal.[3]

However, Cicero and Servius Sulpicius Rufus were of greater
importance than all those mentioned. Since these men had hitherto
been working for peace with sincere enthusiasm, Caesar hoped to
win them over to his side and thus to secure the moral authority
which he needed so badly. Thanks to Cicero's surviving correspondence we are able to follow with some accuracy how he went
about this. As early as January 22 he gave instructions to his agent
Gaius Trebatius, whom Cicero had originally recommended to him,
to invite the orator to Rome.[4] A few days later he wrote to him
himself. He had learned that his enemies were promising freedom
to the gladiators, whom he was having trained in a barracks at
Capua for the games which he planned to celebrate, on condition
that they took the field against him, and now appealed to his friend
Cicero for help against this infringement of his property, at the
same time asking him to intervene for peace. Further letters from
Caesar's entourage continued to repeat that he was thoroughly
satisfied with Cicero's attitude.[5] Cicero's reply sent early in February
was friendly, full of admiration for Caesar and understanding for his
point of view, but it also spoke up warmly for Pompey. In order
to commit the changeable consular, Caesar immediately made this
document available to a wider circle of readers and in a second letter,
followed by one from Balbus similar in tone, he again assured him
of his friendship, thanked him for remaining neutral so far and
begged him to continue thus. Cicero answered this on February 17,

---

[1] Cic. *Att.* 8, 3; 6, 26, 5. On the praetor Philippus see Münzer, *RE*, 14, 1568–9; Cic. *Att.*
7, 17, 3.
[2] Cic. *Att.* 9, 15, 4; 10, 4, 10.   [3] Op. cit., 8, 1, 3; 9, 3; 15, 2.
[4] Op. cit., 7, 17, 3.
[5] Op. cit., 7, 21, 3; 23, 3; 8, 2, 1; Caes. *b.c.* 1, 14, 4–5; Cic. *Att.* 7, 14, 2.

and on February 25 he mentions a letter of Balbus which contained the not very convincing statement that Caesar only wished to live without fear under the supremacy of Pompey.[1] About this time news came of what had occurred at the surrender of Corfinium, and Cicero expressed his thanks that his former helper Lentulus Spinther had been spared. The further tone of his letter seems to have been that Caesar's clemency, a firm feature of his character, offered hope for a peaceful settlement of the dispute.[2]

Meanwhile a letter from Balbus, written in Rome about March 1, reached Cicero. Pompey was at Brundisium at the time, and Caesar on the march there from Corfinium. Balbus now urgently requested Cicero to bring about a reconciliation between Pompey and Caesar, to urge the consul Lentulus to return to Rome and then himself to lead the Senate in passing a decree in settlement of the dispute.[3] Early in March, while heading for Brundisium, Caesar sent the following message:[4] 'Imperator Caesar sends greetings to Imperator Cicero. Although I merely caught a glimpse of our friend Furnius and was unable to have a quiet word with him or to hear what he had to say, yet, despite the fact that I have done so often before and shall presumably do so again, I could not miss this opportunity to write and send him to you with my thanks. You have deserved that from me. Since I intend soon to come to the city, I ask especially to see you there, that I may make use of your advice, popularity, position and help in all matters. But to return to my request: please forgive my haste and the shortness of this letter. The rest you will learn from Furnius.' This was followed immediately by a letter from Balbus and Oppius in Rome,[5] stating that to the best of their knowledge Caesar wished for a reconciliation with Pompey, but that, if he were forced to continue the war, he asked for no more from Cicero than his neutrality.

After several days of deliberation, on March 19 Cicero answered Caesar's message.[6] He interpreted the words quoted above as an invitation to mediate, as he was equally friendly with both parties, and felt inclined to help on condition that Caesar allowed him appropriate freedom in both directions. When he wrote thus, he did not know that on March 17 Pompey had already evacuated Brundisium and that a mediator no longer had any role to play.

[1] Cic. *Att.* 8, 2, 1; 9, 3–4; 11, 5. See above, p. 204, n. 1.
[2] Op. cit., 9, 11a, 3; 16, 1.　　　　[3] Op. cit., 8, 15a.
[4] Op. cit., 9, 6a; 9, 11, 2. Cicero was hailed as Imperator in 51 while proconsul of Cilicia (cf. *RE*, 7A, 981).
[5] Cic. *Att.* 9, 7a.　　　　[6] Op. cit., 9, 11a.

He received no further letter until March 26,[1] when Caesar referred to Cicero's gratitude for 'the clemency of Corfinium'. He swore to continue in this disposition, although he had learned that Domitius and Spinther were again taking up arms against him, since it was just through this that the difference in character between the two sides was demonstrated: 'Imperator Caesar sends greetings to Imperator Cicero. You are right in supposing—for you know me well—that nothing is further from my thoughts than cruelty. Since I already feel great pleasure in the quality of mercy itself, it makes me quite triumphant that you approve of my case. I am also unmoved by the news that the men whom I released have gone off to fight against me again. For there is nothing that I wish for more than that they and I should remain true each to himself. Where you are concerned, I wish that you could join me near the city so that I might enjoy your advice and help as usual. I can tell you that there is no one dearer to me than your son-in-law Dolabella. There is no other way for me to thank him, for he is incapable of behaving otherwise: he is so kind, gracious and well-disposed to me.' This Dolabella, a young patrician of the stamp of Clodius, had recently married Tullia, a union which was bringing his father-in-law nothing but disappointment and sorrow.[2] So these closing remarks did not achieve their object. But in other respects too, this letter only made Cicero conscious of his unfortunate predicament. For since he had missed the connection with Pompey, he was wholly within Caesar's sphere of control.[3]

At the time he was living on his country estate near Formiae which lay on Caesar's route. A notice published in all the munici-palities invited senators to a meeting on April 1.[4] Thus Cicero was unable to avoid a personal discussion with the victorious imperator. This took place in Formiae on March 28. Caesar demanded Cicero's presence at the meeting: his absence would be tantamount to a condemnation of Caesar's policy and a bad example to the other senators; it was his duty to come and mediate for peace as he saw fit. Thereupon Cicero gave notice that he intended to move that the Senate should decree that Caesar should neither go to Spain nor take troops over to Greece; he also proposed to deplore the situation in which Pompey found himself. This was roundly rejected by Caesar, who asked Cicero to reconsider the matter; if he made it impossible for him to use his advice, he would stick to those who

---

[1] Op. cit., 9, 16, 2–3.   [2] Münzer, RE, 4, 1301.
[3] Cic. Att. 9, 12, 4; 15, 3.   [4] Op. cit., 9, 17, 1.

offered their services, and then anything would be permissible.[1] This threat was intended to lay the responsibility for coming events on Cicero, and he imagined that he knew what was meant. As early as March 25 he reports some occasional remarks from Caesar to his followers from an allegedly reliable source:[2] he would punish Pompey for the death of Gnaeus Carbo and Marcus Brutus and for all the atrocities perpetrated by Sulla with his help;[3] Curio would have as free a hand under him as Pompey had had under Sulla; Caesar was going to recall all those driven into exile by the more stringent penalties of the *leges Pompeiae* of 52,[4] passed while Pompey had been recalling traitors: he was even lamenting Milo as one of the most distinguished victims; yet he would not injure anyone who did not take up arms against him. And now Cicero could see with his own eyes Caesar's entourage, the realm of the shades; he had never seen such a collection of the dregs of Italy![5] This confirmed what had been admitted to him on March 19 by Gaius Matius, one of Caesar's confidants but at the same time of spotless reputation.[6] These unpleasant impressions strengthened Cicero in his brave resolve to remain true to his principles and not to go to Rome.[7]

The rump of the Senate which met on April 1 at Caesar's bidding looked a sorry gathering, since of the consulars only Sulpicius Rufus and Volcacius Tullus attended.[8] Still, it had been legally summoned by the tribunes Antonius and Cassius,[9] and a decree recognizing Caesar was sure to have a certain effect. In a long speech Caesar again set forth his claim against his enemies and enumerated the proofs of his desire for peace. He turned from this theme to invite the Senate to share with him the business of the state and first to

[1] Op. cit., 9, 18; *fam.* 4, 1, 1.

[2] Op. cit., 9, 14, 2. An otherwise unknown Baebius is given as the authority, and he had it from Curio. So the reliability of the story is not as strongly guaranteed as Cicero assumed.

[3] Brutus (the father of Caesar's assassin, and tribune in 83) and Carbo (consul in 85, 84 and 82). Cf. my *Pompeius*[2], 37; 44; also Sall. *ad Caes.* 1, 4, 1.

[4] Rotondi, *Leges publicae p. R.* (1912), 410; *Pompeius*[2], 175. See Cic. *Att.* 7, 11, 1; 10, 4, 8; 8, 2.

[5] Cic. *Att.* 9, 18, 2; 19, 1. They are the Catilinarians brought back to life (10, 8, 8). In 46 B.C. the judgment of Sallust, himself a victim of the optimate reign of terror (*ad Caes.* 2, 4, 2) was no more favourable to these followers (*ad Caes.* 1, 2, 5; 4, 2; 6, 1). But in contrast to Sallust's advice to keep them on a tight rein Caesar is alleged to have said (Suet. *Caes.* 72): *si grassa-torum et sicariorum ope in tuenda sua dignitate usus esset, talibus quoque se parem gratiam relaturum.*

[6] Cic. *Att.* 9, 11, 2. Cf. Münzer, *RE*, 14, 2206.

[7] Cic. *Att.* 9, 18, 3; 19, 2; 10, 1, 1.

[8] Op. cit., 9, 19, 2; 10, 3a, 2; *fam.* 4, 1, 1 (April 49, to Sulpicius—only a *conventus senatorum*); *Att.* 10, 1, 2: *consessus senatorum.*

[9] Dio 41, 15, 2. Since Caesar as proconsul was not allowed to enter the city, the Senate met outside the *pomerium*. On the *contio*, see 16, 1.

undertake official peace negotiations with Pompey: for he was not ashamed to offer the hand of peace, although Pompey had earlier declared in the Senate that this was an admission of defeat and of fear. This, he said, was a narrow view: he, Caesar, not only wished to set an example by his actions but also to lead the way in justice and equity.[1]

He next spoke in similar terms before a popular assembly, underlining his speech by the promise of a corn distribution and a present of 75 denarii per man.[2] The Senate had no choice but to decree the despatch of a peace delegation, but no one was found ready to undertake the task—understandably, since Pompey had even equated staying behind in the city with desertion to Caesar's camp. For three days the negotiations made absolutely no progress.[3] The tribune Lucius Metellus vetoed further proposals from Caesar. Above all Caesar wished to be granted full authority over the *aerarium sanctius*, the reserve treasure in the temple of Saturn, which his opponents had been unable to take away,[4] and so found himself in the awkward position where he, who professed to be fighting for the rights of the people oppressed by the oligarchy and who made so much of the flight of the tribunes on January 7, was himself obliged to use force against a sacrosanct tribune—a fact which he, of course, omits from his narrative. Since Metellus was guarding the locked gate of the temple with his person, Caesar himself went to the temple with a detachment of soldiers to advertise that martial law was now in force.[5] When Metellus nonetheless refused to let himself be intimidated, Caesar threatened to kill him. The tribune now gave in;[6] the

[1] Caes. *b.c.* 1, 32; Vell. 2, 50, 1; Dio 41, 15, 3 emphasizes that he wished to reassure the anxious senators.

[2] Dio 41, 16, 1; App. *b.c.* 2, 163.

[3] Caes. *b.c.* 1, 33. According to Cic. *fam.* 4, 1, 1, Ser. Sulpicius Rufus spoke for peace. See Plut. *Caes.* 35, 4–5.

[4] Caes. *b.c.* 1, 33, 3; 14, 1. Here Caesar's account is proved wrong by Cic. *Att.* 7, 21, 2. The consuls did not go to Rome and could not leave the door to the *aerarium sanctius* open. Caesar put an end to the painful scene by having this door broken open. Cf. Barwick, op. cit., 37, 1. According to Dio 41, 17, 1 the Senate had voted him the money, as it previously had to Pompey (Caes. *b.c.* 1, 6, 3). This, chiefly, was vetoed by L. Metellus (Dio 41, 17, 2).

[5] In so doing he now crossed the *pomerium* after all! Cf. O. E. Schmidt, *Briefwechsel*, 167. See Plut. *Caes.* 35, 6–11.

[6] Cic. *Att.* 10, 4, 8. According to Curio's story Caesar wanted to kill him. According to Lucan 3, 143, he gave way on the advice of a certain Cotta. If this is not just invention, the Cotta concerned was presumably not the consular and ex-censor L. Aurelius Cotta, the cousin of Caesar's mother, but an otherwise unknown tribune (Broughton, *MRR*, 2, 258). See Plut. *Pomp.* 62, 2 (chronologically wrong). According to App. *b.c.* 2, 164, Metellus argued that the *aerarium sanctius* might only be used for a Gallic war, to which Caesar replied that he had pacified Gaul. See Flor. 2, 13, 21.

soldiers broke down the gates and removed 15,000 bars of gold and 30,000 of silver, as well as 30 million sesterces in coin.[1] However, Caesar paid for this profit by the total loss of his popularity with the plebs, who valued above all the inviolability of their champion. In order to avoid unpleasantness, he was even forced to abandon the farewell speech to the people which he had planned.[2]

His visit to Rome had proved wholly ineffectual. What embittered him most was the Senate's silent opposition. 'Everything will originate from me', he was heard to say.[3] But behind this proud self-sufficiency and self-glorification lay concealed his displeasure at having failed to secure any sort of officially recognized legal basis for himself. He took the greatest pains to hold Cicero at least to the formal neutrality that he had so far professed, getting Curio to work on him orally and Caelius in writing, and himself wrote

[1] Plin. *n.h.* 33, 56; Oros. 6, 15, 5.

[2] Cic. *Att.* 10, 4, 8 (according to a report from Curio); 8, 6.

[3] Op. cit., 10, 4, 9: *at ille* (Caesar) *impendio magis odit senatum. 'a me' inquit 'omnia proficiscentur'* (the words of Curio). Caesar himself (*b.c.* 1, 32, 7) writes that if the senators were unwilling from fear to join him in looking after the business of the *res publica, illis se oneri non futurum et per se rem publicam administraturum.* Curio visited Cicero in his villa near Cumae while on the way to Sicily, after he had spoken to the citizens of Puteoli. His friendship with the consular dated from his optimate period. On May 2, Cicero believes that, given the right opportunity, he might switch back to Pompey again (*Att.* 10, 8, 2). Caesar describes him as loyal to himself (*b.c.* 2, 32, 14; 42, 4). Among the optimates he was regarded as the chief instigator of the civil war (Vell. 2, 48, 3: *homo ingeniosissime nequam et facundus malo publico*; Lucan 4, 810 ff.; Petron. 124, 288). Cicero gave Atticus a full account of the conversation and was of the opinion that Curio had expressed himself with sincerity (10, 4, 8). He first aimed to make Cicero terrified of Caesar by saying that his clemency was not honestly intended; if this policy had no success with the people, he would be cruel, *ipsum non voluntate aut natura non esse crudelem.* When Cicero asked what would happen to the *res publica,* he held out no hope (9). However, in the course of further conversation he gave Cicero a favourable report on Caesar's feelings towards him: he was at liberty to withdraw to some quiet spot, even to Greece, if he so wished. Finally, he went so far as to assure him on oath that Dolabella had written to him (Curio) assuring him on oath that Caesar was Cicero's best friend. Caesar's behaviour up to the time of his death refuted the cynical words about his *clementia.* But that Caesar was very angry at the end of his stay in Rome was soon confirmed by M. Caelius (Cic. *Att.* 10, 9a; *fam.* 8, 16, 1): *nihil nisi atrox et severum cogitat atque etiam loquitur; iratus senatui exiit, his intercessionibus plane incitatus est.* That such opposition dared to come into the open shows how little men believed in Caesar's final victory. The last we hear of L. Metellus is that he wished to return to Rome after the battle of Pharsalus, whereupon Caesar wrote to Antony that he was to keep away from Italy until further notice: *prohiberique omnis Italia nisi quorum ipse causam cognovisset; deque eo vehementius erat scriptum* (Cic. *Att.* 11, 7, 2). Typical of Cicero's shifting mood is his letter of April 7 after he had learnt that Atticus had paid his respects to Caesar at Rome (*Att.* 10, 3a, 1): *visum te aiunt in regia, nec reprehendo, quippe cum ipse istam reprehensionem non fugerim.* Then on April 14 we hear again (*Att.* 10, 4, 2): *alter ardet furore et scelere nec remittit aliquid sed in dies ingravescit; modo Italia expulit, nunc alia ex parte persequi, ex alia provincia exspoliare conatur nec iam recusat sed quodam modo postulat ut, quem ad modum est, sic etiam appelletur tyrannus.*

another letter on April 16:[1] 'Imperator Caesar sends greetings to Imperator Cicero. Though I do not believe that you would ever act rashly or imprudently, yet I am sufficiently impressed by the rumours in some quarters to think it my duty to write to you, and ask it as a favour due to our mutual regard that you will not take any step, now that the balance has tipped so decisively, which you thought it right to avoid as long as it still stood even. For that will do our friendship more harm and your own interests a greater disservice: it will appear, not as if you were bowing to success (for success has consistently attended our side and failure theirs) or as if you were joining their cause from conviction (for their cause is the same as it was when you decided to have nothing to do with it)—no, it will look as if there were some action of mine of which you disapproved; and nothing you could do could hurt me more than that. I claim the right of our friendship to entreat you not to take this course. Finally, what more suitable part is there for an upright man and a good peace-loving citizen than to keep aloof from civil dissensions? There were some who approved of this course, but could not adopt it by reason of its danger; you, since you have duly weighed both the evidence of my life and the conclusions of friendship, will find that there is no safer nor more honourable course than to keep entirely aloof from the whole struggle. I am writing this on April 16 while on the march.'

It was all in vain. Political means failed because Pompey's military superiority seemed too overwhelming. The confident gestures of Caesar and his partisans and the fact that they took the conquest of Spain for granted were not regarded as decisive. 'Pompey's plan is entirely Themistoclean. For he holds that whoever is master of the sea must inevitably win the war. Accordingly, he had never made a point of holding the two Spains for their own sake; his first care has always been the mobilization of his fleet. When the time comes, therefore, he will put to sea with an enormous fleet and head for Italy.' This reflection by Cicero on May 2[2] corresponded to the general view. Furthermore, the consuls and the proconsul Pompey had by edict summoned the senators to Thessalonica with the explanation that since Rome was occupied by the enemy, the legitimate government was to be found where the consuls and

---

[1] Cic. *Att.* 10, 8b. But Cicero had already received a letter on April 7 (10, 3a, 2): *Caesar mihi ignoscit per litteras quod non venerim seseque in optimam partem id accipere dicit.*

[2] Cic. *Att.* 10, 8, 4; 12a, 3. Cf. App. *b.c.* 2, 205.

Senate were in residence.[1] In this dispute between legitimacy and revolution only a conclusive decision by arms could effect a change. Admittedly Cicero also had grave reservations about Pompey. 'He is playing at being Sulla', he said of him, but from what he heard from Curio, there was no prospect of a continuation of the *res publica*, as he understood the term, under Caesar. Accordingly he left from Caieta for the east on June 7.[2]

Caesar secured his Spanish campaign by the following measures: in Rome he left the praetor Marcus Antonius Lepidus to look after his interests; he entrusted the command of the troops left in Italy to the tribune Mark Antony, for which task he granted him— on his own authority—the title *pro praetore*; Cisalpine Gaul was governed by Marcus Licinius Crassus, the son of his former ally, who had been Caesar's quaestor in 54. To repel an attack by sea, war-ships were to be assembled by Publius Cornelius Dolabella in the Adriatic and by Quintus Hortensius in the Tyrrhenian Sea. To counter an advance over land, two legions under Gaius Antonius, the younger brother of the tribune, were moved forward to Illyricum. Since Rome and Italy could not in the long run be held without the provinces which supplied them with corn, Gaius Curio was sent with four legions to occupy Sicily and Africa, and Quintus Valerius Orca received one legion in order to go to Sardinia for the same purpose.[3] Caesar was now again in good spirits and on his departure joked to his close friends that he was taking the field against the army without a leader, and on his return would deal with the leader without an army.[4]

On about April 19 (February 28, Jul.) he arrived before Massilia.[5] The judgment of this free state, an ally of long standing, was the same as that of all others; it felt no confidence in Caesar's prospects. Moreover, Lucius Domitius Ahenobarbus, the proconsul of Trans-alpine Gaul appointed by the Senate, had already given notice of his arrival, and a delegation from the city had recently been received by Pompey. The governing board of fifteen therefore declared to Caesar that as their state was equally indebted to Pompey and Caesar for services rendered, it intended to remain neutral in the present war and to close its gates to both parties. From the start, however,

[1] Cic. *Phil.* 13, 26 and 28; Dio 41, 18, 4–5; 43, 2–4; Plut. *Pomp.* 64, 4; Lucan 5, 9–14; 22.

[2] Cic. *Att.* 9, 10, 2 and 6; 11, 3; 14, 1; *fam.* 14, 7, 3; cf. *RE*, 7A, 1001.

[3] Caes. *b.c.* 1, 30, 2; 31, 1; App. *b.c.* 2, 165–166; Flor. 2, 13, 22; Dio 41, 18, 3; Cic. *Att.* 10, 6, 3; 7, 3.

[4] See above, p. 204, n. 2.

[5] The date is deduced by O. E. Schmidt (*Briefwechsel*, 176) from Cic. *Att.* 10, 12a, 3 (May 6).

this promise of neutrality was fulfilled quite unilaterally, since Domitius was admitted to the harbour and was immediately put in charge of defence measures against armed attack.[1]

The attitude of this powerful community was of great importance for the Spanish campaign. For in Further Spain, where through his quaestorship and propraetorship Caesar had become one of the best-known patrons of the country, there was a strong feeling in his favour (as opposed to Hither Spain, whose chief patron Pompey had been since the war against Sertorius). This feeling, however, did not dare to come into the open in view of the hopelessness of his position. He thus staked everything on speedily breaking the resistance of Massilia and immediately began to besiege it with three legions; in order to impose a blockade twelve warships were built on the Rhone. But as the defence was just as well organized and heroically carried out, he was denied a speedy victory. After several weeks he was forced to hand over the siege to his *legatus* Gaius Trebonius and on June 22 (May 1, Jul.) he reached his army in Spain.[2]

There, at the beginning of spring, the *legatus* Gaius Fabius[3] had succeeded in driving the enemy outposts from the passes of the Pyrenees. He now stood with six legions near the fortified town of Ilerda on the Sicoris (Segre) facing the combined five legions of the legates Lucius Afranius and Marcus Petreius.[4] These two were among the most experienced of the enemy generals—Afranius the ex-consul of 60 and Petreius the conqueror of Catiline—and had greatly strengthened their regular forces by a general levy of native contingents.[5] However, Caesar was superior to them in his splendid cavalry, half of whom were 3,000 Celtic nobles individually called up by himself—the usual method of keeping Gaul quiet.[6]

---

[1] Caes. *b.c.* 1, 33, 4–36, 3; Dio 41, 19; Vell. 2, 50, 2; Lucan 3, 300–452 (hostile to Caesar). Ilona Opelt, *Hermes* 85 (1957), 445; cf. *Gnomon* 30 (1958), 450. See Flor. 2, 13, 23.

[2] Caes. *b.c.* 1, 36, 4–5; Dio 41, 19, 3. The date can be calculated from the fact that according to Caes. *b.c.* 2, 32, 5 the Spanish campaign lasted for forty days, and according to Dessau, *ILS*, 8744, the capitulation at Ilerda took place on August 2. Cf. T. Rice Holmes, *Rom. Rep.*, 3, 408.

[3] If he is identical with the tribune of 55 B.C. (Broughton, *MRR*, 2, 220, n. 2), certainly not a patrician. According to Münzer, *RE*, 5, 1745, he could also be the praetor of 58 (Broughton, *MRR*, 2, 194).

[4] Caes. *b.c.* 1, 37; 38, 1 and 4; 39, 2; Dio 41, 20, 1.

[5] Caes. *b.c.* 1, 38, 3; Lucan, 4, 5–10.

[6] Caes. *b.c.* 1, 39, 2. In Spain the rumour spread that Pompey proposed to cross from Mauretania to Spain (39, 3; 60, 5). Caesar (39, 3–4) further mentions that he borrowed money from his military tribunes and centurions, and distributed it to the soldiers. He thus both bound the centurions to him as his creditors and bought the goodwill of the soldiers by his prodigality. Cf. Holmes, *Rom. Rep.*, 3, 390.

After a period of indecisive positional warfare, he suddenly found himself in the greatest difficulty as the result of a flood disaster. The bridges over the Sicoris, on which he was dependent for fodder and reinforcements, were torn away and their reconstruction prevented by the watchful enemy. It looked as if within a few days his destiny would inevitably be fulfilled. For his army lacked the most essential supplies, while the enemy was well provided with everything.[1] In Rome enthusiastic demonstrations took place in front of Afranius' house. Many senators, as well as other respectable citizens, now took the opportunity, even at the eleventh hour, to report to Pompey, and Antony did not stop them.[2] About 200 senators could now be counted at Thessalonica.[3]

Eventually Caesar managed to construct a bridge unnoticed by the enemy twenty miles behind his position and thus secured his supplies. At the same time Decimus Brutus, the commander of the blockading fleet at Massilia, repelled a vigorous attempt by the besieged to break out, with great losses for the latter. This turn of events made several important Spanish communities north of the Ebro come over to Caesar.[4] It is presumably no coincidence that Osca, the town which had for so long been the headquarters of Sertorius, led the way; in general, these were the areas in which he had been able to maintain himself longest.[5] And it was Afranius who at the time had had the task, as Pompey's *legatus*, of cutting down the offshoots of the general insurrection here.[6] Caesar, however, had a good name, since as propraetor of Further Spain he had secured the remission of the tribute imposed by Metellus Pius.[7] So old political contrasts had their after-effects even here.

For this reason, and at the same time because they were under pressure from Caesar's military ventures, Afranius and Petreius decided to shift the scene of operations to the Celtiberian highlands south of the Ebro, where since the war against Sertorius the name of Pompey had been in particularly high repute, while Caesar was little known. Here they hoped to be able to draw on considerable reinforcements, especially cavalry, and imagined that in that familiar country they

---

[1] Caes. *b.c.* 1, 40–52; Lucan 4, 24–120; Dio 41, 20, 2–21, 2; App. *b.c.* 2, 168; Cic. *Att.* 10, 12a, 3; 13, 3; 14, 2; 18, 2. Maps of the theatre of war are to be found in Holmes, *Rom. Rep.*, 3, facing p. 51. Cf. Kromayer-Veith, *Schlachtenatlas, Röm. Abt.*, map 19.

[2] Caes. *b.c.* 1, 53; Dio 41, 21, 2. [3] Dio 41, 43, 2.

[4] Caes. *b.c.* 1, 54–60; Dio 41, 21, 2–4.

[5] Caes. *b.c.* 1, 60, 1; Strab. 3, 161; Plut. *Sert.* 14, 3; 25, 6.

[6] Caes. *b.c.* 1, 61, 3; Oros. 5, 23, 14; Val. Max. 7, 6, ext. 3.

[7] Caes. *b.c.* 2, 17, 2; 18, 6; *b. Hisp.* 42, 2.

could maintain themselves until winter.[1] Meanwhile Caesar received immediate news of their intentions through his scouts, and early in the morning, while they were crossing from Ilerda to the eastern bank of the Sicoris, he at once led his army over the fast-flowing river a little way upstream. For his soldiers implored him not to let the enemy escape, in order that the campaign might soon be over. Thus he succeeded in catching up with the enemy column by the afternoon; Afranius was trying to reach the mountainous area between the Sicoris and Ebro, where he hoped to ward off Caesar's pursuit with a small body of troops until his main force reached the bridge of boats which had already been laid over the Ebro. However, Caesar did not slacken his pace, and so Afranius was forced to pitch camp in the evening on a hill five miles from the safety of the defile. He did not dare to march farther during the night, since he was afraid that in a civil war the discipline of his troops might break down in face of a night attack. But this delay now gave Caesar time to reconnoitre the terrain, and next morning, at the time fixed by Afranius for his departure, he was able amid great exertions to lead his army eastward past the enemy over rocks and gullies, and despite this big detour to win the race and block the entry to the mountains.[2] Again Afranius halted; an attempt to reach the Ebro over the mountains was frustrated by Caesar as soon as it began, and Caesar's soldiers fiercely clamoured for orders to attack a foe whose morale already seemed deeply shaken. But he realized that a battle was no longer necessary, since the enemy could not remain in their present position through shortage of food. Why, then, should he tempt fortune again? Why risk the lives of his good soldiers? And were there not citizens on the other side as well, whom he wished to spare when he could be victorious without a battle? Such considerations, as he reports, found scant favour with his soldiers, who actually threatened that if such an opportunity for victory were let slip they would not fight when Caesar wanted them to.[3]

This disagreement was soon forgotten as events developed. Afranius and Petreius resolved to withdraw and had only to decide whether to head for Ilerda or eastward to Tarraco. Their immediate problem was to secure access to watering places for their camp by means of a fortified line. While they were personally giving instructions for this, their soldiers were temporarily left to their own devices and began to chat with Caesar's outposts. Urged by these

[1] Caes. b.c. 1, 61, 1–3; Lucan 4, 143–147.
[2] Caes. b.c. 1, 61, 4–70, 3; Lucan 4, 167.   [3] Caes. b.c. 1, 70, 4–72, 4.

to capitulate, they sent the senior centurions of the legions to Caesar
as intermediaries, and these were joined by a considerable number
of military tribunes, centurions and Spanish nobles, all of whom
wished to look up their acquaintances in Caesar's camp and to be
introduced by them to him. Even Afranius' son applied to the *legatus*
Publius Sulpicius Rufus concerning a pardon for himself and his
father. Conversely, Caesarians also visited the other camp. The elder
Afranius would have let events take their course, had not Petreius
intervened with his Spanish bodyguard, put a bloody end to the
scenes of fraternization and made the whole army swear a new oath
of allegiance. Any Caesarians whom he caught in the camp he put
to death, whereas Caesar released unharmed those of the enemy
whom he found, if they did not wish to stay with him. He further
comments that these latter were afterwards enrolled in his own army
on honourable terms.[1]

Not long afterwards the enemy started their retreat towards
Ilerda. Caesar harried them unceasingly, and, when they next encamped, cut their water supply by means of field fortifications,
so that the two enemy leaders had no choice but to appeal for negotiations on August 2 (June 10, Jul.).[2] Caesar granted these only on
condition that they were held publicly in the hearing of the two
armies and so secured an opportunity of stating his case clearly
before a large audience. He explained that his only aim had been
to spare the lives of the opposing soldiers, and to make peace with
them as soon as possible. The soldiers had already started negotiations on their own initiative, but their leaders had opposed this
course. Yet he did not want to use their present difficulties to force
the troops to come over and enrol in his service; his one wish was
that the armies, which for years had been stationed in Spain only to
oppose him, should now be disbanded. He would continue to bear
with patience the unjust treatment meted out to him by his political
opponents, but he had to deprive them of the means to injure him.
For this reason the provinces were to be evacuated and the army
dismissed.[3]

Detailed provisions followed: the soldiers domiciled in Spain
were to be released immediately, the remainder on the Var, the
river which marked the boundary between Gaul and Italy. It was
also expressly laid down that no one was to be forced against his

[1] Op. cit., 1, 72, 5–77, 2; App. *b.c.* 2, 168–171; Lucan 4, 174–262.
[2] Dessau, *ILS*, 8744; Caes. *b.c.* 1, 78, 1–84, 1; Lucan 4, 337–340.
[3] Caes. *b.c.* 1, 84, 2–85, 12; App. *b.c.* 2, 172; Lucan 4, 363.

will to take an oath of allegiance.[1] While this business was being concluded, Caesar sent off two legions under the tribune Quintus Cassius to Further Spain, and by an edict summoned all the officials and notables of the province to a meeting at Corduba.[2]

In a campaign of forty days the best army controlled by the enemy had been put out of action.[3] The two experienced legates of Pompey proved unable to cope with Caesar's strategic genius, which could meet all difficulties with such bold decisions because his soldiers surmounted every obstacle. His own account has been reproduced here as accurately as possible, because it gives particularly clear expression to his political objectives. In this theatre, as had also been the case in Italy, he was not fighting to annihilate his enemies, but to reconcile their differences with as little bloodshed as possible, and so to pave the way for a final pacification of a Roman world that had been convulsed by a series of violent crises. We shall see later[4] that in his work On the Civil War, written to present his case, he states this as his sole war aim, and in the only passage where he mentions it, he takes it for granted that his opponents too must recognize it as correct and desirable. As with all political programmes everything depended on its realization, but one may say that it was genuinely Roman in its formulation and intention to maintain existing institutions, and I believe that Caesar spoke in this way not only to win over the Romans, but also because he saw his vocation as a statesman in this light.[5]

Originally Petreius had shared the administration of the further province with Marcus Terentius Varro.[6] On the departure of Petreius

---

[1] Caes. b.c. 1, 86. [2] Op. cit., 2, 19, 1.
[3] Op. cit., 2, 32, 5. [4] See p. 232 below; Caes. b.c. 3, 57, 4.
[5] In a letter (Att. 8, 11, 1) Cicero measures Pompey against the ideal moderator rei publicae, as formulated by himself in rep. 5, 8: ut enim gubernatori cursus secundus, medico salus, imperatori victoria, sic huic moderatori rei publicae beata civium vita proposita est, ut opibus firma, copiis locuples, gloria ampla, virtute honesta sit. huius enim operis maximi inter homines atque optimi illum esse perfectorem volo. Caesar might well have agreed with this. But whereas Cicero, thinking in terms of the city-state—like his model Plato (W. Jaeger, Paideia, 2, 329)—was concerned only with the citizens of his res publica, Caesar looked at the whole Empire: quietem Italiae, pacem provinciarum, salutem imperii. In his excerpt, Appian (b.c. 2, 170) has preserved the malicious comment: Caesar Δημοκοπῶν ἐς τοὺς πολεμίους πανταχοῦ like Curio in Cic. Att. 10, 4, 8. Appian perhaps goes back ultimately to Asinius Pollio, who as early as 43 claimed that he had loved Caesar only with republican reservations (ap. Cic. fam. 10, 31, 3). The candid elder Seneca relates (suas. 6, 15) with justified indignation that in a speech delivered during the triumviral period he set the slander in circulation that Cicero had been ready to deny the authorship of his Philippics and to refute them publicly; though (Seneca says) he had added this lie only to the published version of the speech. Such behaviour should warn us against taking Pollio's judgments too seriously.
[6] Caes. b.c. 1, 38, 1–2. On Varro, H. Dahlmann, RE Suppl. 6, 1172 ff.

P

this task became the sole responsibility of the universal historian, famous also as a poet, and its difficulty was increased by the fact that he had hitherto enjoyed good relations with Caesar.[1] For this reason, if we may believe Caesar's sarcastic account, he only began serious preparations for war when it looked as if luck was deserting Caesar, taking sharp action against the communities well-disposed to him, on which he imposed higher taxes, and against unreliable individuals whom he punished by confiscation of their property. After Caesar's victory he hoped to be able to maintain himself at Gades with his troops, ships and military supplies.[2] But before he reached the town, the whole province had already gone over to Caesar. Even one of his legions mutinied. Thereupon he himself handed over the other to an officer appointed by Caesar and in Corduba placed his province at the victor's disposal.[3]

Caesar made a point of rewarding and honouring all those who had suffered in his cause. Thus he promised Gades a law which was to grant Roman citizenship to the members of that community:[4] however, it goes without saying that he also asked for vast sums to be paid to himself.[5] He placed the country in the charge of the tribune Q. Cassius as *legatus* with praetorian powers, regarding him as particularly suitable for the post because he had been quaestor there a few years earlier; in reality, this was quite a fatal choice since he was already hated there for his insatiable avarice during his previous term, and his renewed activities soon produced a complete change of mood and open rebellion in this province so friendly to Caesar.[6] Cicero's utterance,[7] with which he once characterized the leading Caesarians in general, is very appropriate to Cassius: 'What colleagues or helpers is Caesar to make use of? Are people, none of whom can keep their inheritances in order for two months on end, to rule the provinces and the state?'

On his return journey Caesar also thanked his supporters in Tarraco and then made for Massilia.[8] After a year's intensive siege he received the capitulation of this powerful fortress. The conquered state had to surrender all its military and naval equipment as well as its treasury; it also lost a great part of its territory together with the revenue derived therefrom. Two legions remained as occupation

[1] Caes. *b.c.* 2, 17, 2. [2] Op. cit., 2, 17, 3–18, 6.
[3] Op. cit., 2, 18, 7–20, 8; Dio. 41, 23, 2. [4] Dio 41, 24, 1; Liv. *per.* 110.
[5] Caesar himself (*b.c.* 2, 21, 1–3) mentions only the rewards; Dio 41, 24, 1.
[6] Caes. *b.c.* 2, 21, 4; *b. Alex.* 48–49; Dio 41, 24, 2; 42, 15–16.
[7] Cic. *Att.* 10, 8, 6. [8] Caes. *b.c.* 2, 21, 4–5.

troops.[1] In outward appearance, however, Caesar left Massilia as a formally independent ally because the complete destruction of so ancient and respected a Greek community would have created too unfavourable an impression.[2] At this time Caesar received the news that the praetor Marcus Aemilius Lepidus had nominated him dictator by order of the people. This was the best solution to the problem of securing constitutional conditions in the following year, since as dictator he acquired the authority to hold consular elections. The appointment of a dictator by a praetor was unusual, but had a precedent in 217 and was further provided for by a special popular law.[3]

As the army was returning, for the first time since he had assumed command, a mutiny, originating in the ninth legion, broke out near Placentia. It was said that he was prolonging the war deliberately in order not to have to pay the promised reward, and discontent was prevalent because there had been nothing to plunder.[4] Already in Spain the soldiers had ventured on demonstrations which showed that they were well aware that the rebel Caesar was dependent on their good will and that his habit of sparing the enemy was little to their taste.[5] It now had to be settled whether he was still the *imperator*. Although he was in fact unable to spare a single soldier, he declared to the assembled troops that according to ancient military usage he would decimate the ninth legion and then dismiss the remainder as unfit for service. This courageous inflexibility was so effective that the legion begged to be allowed to remain in his service. This he granted on condition that he was furnished with the names of 120 ringleaders; twelve of these, selected by lot, he inexorably had led to their death. When it became known that an innocent man had been accused by his centurion, without more ado he commanded the centurion to be put to death in his place.[6]

The general military, and consequently also the political, situation had improved as a result of the brilliant Spanish campaign, but had not changed decisively. For in other theatres of war the opposition could also point to significant successes. Off the Dalmatian coast

[1] Op. cit., 2, 22, 5–6; Dio 41, 25, 3; Flor. 2, 13, 25; Oros. 6, 15, 7.

[2] Cic. *Phil.* 8, 19; 13, 32; *off.* 2, 28; *Att.* 14, 14, 6; Strab. 4, 181; Plin. *n.h.* 3, 34; Cf. O. Hirschfeld, *Kl. Schr.*, 57; Holmes, *Rom. Rep.*, 3, 420.

[3] Caes. *b.c.* 2, 21, 5; Liv. 22, 31, 8 (according to 22, 8, 6 from Coelius Antipater); 27, 5, 16. Cf. Mommsen, *RStR*, 2³, 147, n. 4; Cic. *Att.* 9, 15, 2; 10, 4, 11; Dio 41, 36, 1.

[4] Suet. *Caes.* 69; App. *b.c.* 2, 191; Dio 41, 26, 1; Lucan 5, 246.

[5] Caes. *b.c.* 1, 64, 3; 68, 3; 71, 2; 72, 4; 82, 2.

[6] App. *b.c.* 2, 194–195; Dio 41, 35, 5.

Pompey's fleet deprived Dolabella of forty ships; Gaius Antonius, who had come to his help, was forced to surrender with his whole army after suffering heavy losses.[1] By a swift grab Curio had managed to occupy Sicily without any fighting early in May, and had then successfully landed with two legions in Africa. But in a battle against Juba, the king of Numidia, who by joining the side of the oligarchs took his revenge on Caesar for old insults, he and his troops were destroyed.[2] Furthermore, Pompey, as he always preferred to do, was able to take his time in deploying his forces. A fleet of several hundred warships was assembling on the west coast of Greece and nine legions were being trained near Beroea (west of Thessalonica) in Macedonia. 3,000 archers, 1,200 slingers and 7,000 cavalry were provided by the allied states of the east. Quintus Metellus Scipio, the proconsul of Syria, was on his way with the two legions from his province. Secured by the fleet, Pompey planned to put his army into winter-quarters on the Illyrian coast (Albania) in the neighbourhood of Dyrrhachium and Apollonia in order to launch an overwhelming offensive against Italy in the spring.[3]

While Caesar's troops (twelve legions) were marching to Brundisium for the crossing, the dictator spent eleven busy days in Rome.[4] In possession of Rome he could hold legitimate elections and produce a constitutional situation where, as the Romans said, 'the state was on his side'.[5] Hitherto he had been a rebellious proconsul while his opponents represented the legitimate government. Now he was the lawful dictator and in the electoral *comitia* conducted by himself he was lawfully elected to the consulship together with Publius Servilius Isauricus, the son of his former superior. According to the existing laws he could hold the consulship for a second time in 48, as had already been contemplated in 56. In this election, as he emphasizes, the whole Roman people resident in Italy gave its verdict on his personality.[6] The other officials were also elected and vacant priesthoods filled. Nor did he omit to see belatedly to the

---

[1] Caes. *b.c.* 3, 10, 5; 67, 5. The account has been lost after 3, 8, 4. Liv. *per.* 110; Flor. 2, 13, 31–33; Oros. 6, 15, 8–9; App. *b.c.* 2, 191; Dio 41, 40; Lucan 4, 406 ff.

[2] Caes. *b.c.* 1, 30, 5; 2, 23–44; App. *b.c.* 2, 175–190; Dio 41, 41–42; Liv. *per.* 110; Lucan 4, 581–824.

[3] Caes. *b.c.* 3, 3–5; App. *b.c.* 2, 201–204; Vell. 2, 51, 1. Cf. my *Pompeius*[2], 214.

[4] Caes. *b.c.* 5, 2, 1; Plut. *Caes.* 37, 2; App. *b.c.* 2, 196.

[5] Dolabella in Cic. *fam.* 9, 9, 3; *b. Alex.* 68, 1; Dio 41, 43, 2; Lucan 5, 385–398, which maliciously misrepresents the legal position.

[6] Caes. *b.c.* 3, 1, 1.

celebration of the festival of Jupiter Latiaris on the Alban hill, which the consuls of 49 had been unable to hold.[1]

The most pressing and difficult problem of government was posed by the utterly disrupted economy, the chronic unhealthiness of which had done much to create the atmosphere of the civil war. Since its outbreak financial transactions had come to a complete standstill. Debts remained unpaid and the needy could not receive any money.[2] All eyes were turned on Caesar in anticipation. With his past and his entourage of dissolute aristocrats and other adventurers, notwithstanding the clemency which he had shown hitherto, men still feared or hoped for a general cancellation of debts. However, he could not as a statesman humour his followers on this point. Instead of a short-sighted and brutal plunder of the propertied classes in favour of a dubious collection of debtors he issued a well-considered dictatorial edict with force of law (a *lex data* as opposed to a *lex rogata* carried by the people) with directions about loans and property within Italy.[3] By its provisions creditors were obliged to accept in settlement land at its pre-war value as assessed by arbitrators appointed by the urban praetor. In the repayment of capital, paid-up interest to a maximum of about a quarter of the capital sum (i.e. approximately two years' interest at an interest rate of 12 per cent) could be deducted.[4] In order to promote the liquidity of the money market he had resort to an old law whereby no one might hold more than 15,000 denarii in cash.[5] Regulations were also made about the level of the interest rate. To reassure the capitalists he rejected with the utmost emphasis the demand that slaves who denounced their masters for transgressing the law should be rewarded. Even if this attack on private property was severely criticized among the injured creditors,[6] brisk use was made of the concession and it proved of service to a large section of the community, creditors as well as debtors.

---

[1] Op. cit., 3, 2, 1; Dio 41, 36, 2–3; Lucan 5, 400–403; Dio 41, 14, 4.

[2] Cic. *Att.* 7, 18, 4; 9, 9, 4; 10, 11, 2.

[3] Caes. *b.c.* 3, 1, 2 (*constituit*); 20, 1 and 2 (*decretum*).

[4] Op. cit., 3, 1, 2–3; 20, 1; Suet. *Caes.* 42, 2; Dio 41, 57, 3; 42, 22, 3; Plut. *Caes.* 37, 2; App. *b.c.* 2, 198.

[5] Dio 41, 38; Tac. *ann.* 6, 16, 1.

[6] Cic. *off.* 2, 84 (after Caesar's murder): *at vero hic nunc victor* (Caesar since 49) *tum quidem victus* (63 B.C., as a 'Catilinarian'), *quae cogitarat, cum ipsius intererat* (63), *tum* (49) *ea perfecit, cum eius iam nihil interesset. tanta in eo peccandi libido fuit ut hoc ipsum eum delectaret peccare, etiam si causa non esset.* This outburst of hatred is of value only as a symptom. Caesar himself says (*b.c.* 3, 20, 2 and 4) that the debtors recognized the fairness of the procedure.

For less delicate subjects he allowed the legislative machinery to function in the regular fashion through praetors and tribunes. Thus as early as March 11 the Latin communities of Transpadana had been granted their long-promised citizen rights on the proposal of the praetor Lucius Roscius.[1] The tribune Rubrius now secured popular ratification for the unified legal procedure which had in consequence become necessary for the municipalities and other localities of Cisalpine Gaul.[2] The people of Gades likewise received their promised citizenship.[3] True to his past Caesar also instigated a popular decree whereby the right to stand for office was restored to the sons of those proscribed by Sulla.[4] Furthermore, special laws were passed allowing a number of politicians, whom condemnation in the courts had driven into exile and who had then joined Caesar, to return to Rome. Among these was Aulus Gabinius. But the laws applied principally to the victims of the trials held in 52 as a result of Pompey's law on electoral malpractice. At the time Caesar had been unable to stand up for his supporters. For their satisfaction he now had it stated by the people that these proceedings had been a violation of justice.[5] Juba was declared an enemy of the Roman people, while his two Mauretanian neighbours Bocchus and Bogud were recognized as kings.[6]

Senatorial meetings were now also being attended by Caesar's father-in-law Lucius Piso. The situation is characterized by the fact that he dared to revert to the peace offer to Pompey which had been discussed in April. But since Caesar now hoped that he would be able to assume the offensive in Illyria under favourable conditions and that he would not need the collaboration of the Senate in any negotiations that might ensue, he rejected the suggestion by getting Servilius, his fellow consul designate, to vote against it.[7] He made a corn distribution to the populace which was suffering from the increased cost of living;[8] on the other hand the last remaining votive

[1] Mentioned in the fragment of a *lex data* discovered in Ateste (Este): *CIL* 1², 600=Riccobono, *FIRA*, 1², 20, 13: *ante legem seive illud pl(ebei) sc(itum) est, quod L. Roscius a. d. V eid. Mart. populum plebemve rogavit.* See Dio 41, 36, 3.

[2] Mentioned in the fragment of a *lex data* discovered in Veleia (near Piacenza), *CIL*, 1², 592=Riccobono, *FIRA*, 1², 19, 29; 39: *ex lege Rubria seive id pl(ebei) sc(itum) est.* The two fragments show that Roman plebiscites were applied in the individual municipalities by special officials.

[3] Dio 41, 24, 1.

[4] Dio 41, 18, 2; 44, 47, 4; Suet. *Caes.* 41, 2; Plut. *Caes.* 37, 2; Vell. 2, 28, 4.

[5] Cic. *Phil.* 2, 56; 98; *Att.* 10, 8, 3; *fam.* 11, 22, 1; *b. Alex.* 42, 4. Mark Antony was tribune until December 9, 49. Caes. *b.c.* 3, 1, 4; Suet. *Caes.* 41, 1; Dio 41, 36, 2; Plut. *Caes.* 37, 2; App. *b.c.* 2, 198.

[6] Dio 41, 42, 7.　　　　[7] Plut. *Caes.* 37, 1.　　　　[8] App. *b.c.* 2, 198.

offerings, even those on the Capitol, fell victim to his need for money, when he left the city at the end of December 49 after laying down the dictatorship. Even the people escorting him on his way called to him that he should come to an agreement with Pompey. It was a fact that broad sections of the community did not relish the prospect of a decisive victory by either party.[1]

At Brundisium he found his legions tired out by marching and the climate. The number of ships was in normal circumstances sufficient only to carry 15,000 legionaries and 600 cavalry.[2] This was a painful disappointment. For, as he remarks, only this lack of shipping space prevented him from bringing the war to a speedy end. Nevertheless on January 4, 48 (November 6, 49, Jul.), trusting in his luck, he risked the crossing with about 20,000 men and on the following day landed on the coast of Epirus unobserved by the enemy fleet.[3] Pompey was still on the march to the west of Lake Ohrid,[4] so that Caesar by a quick advance northward as far as Apollonia could win a number of weakly defended Epirot towns. The population immediately joined the temporarily stronger side.[5] In this situation he sent Lucius Vibullius Rufus, the former adjutant of Pompey, who—released at Corfinium—had again fallen into his hands in Spain, to the enemy commander with a new offer of peace couched in the following terms:[6] both of them must put an end to their obstinate conflict and not tempt Fortune any further. Heavy losses had been suffered on both sides and these should serve as a lesson. For this reason they should spare themselves and the state. Now was the time to make peace, while both sides still had confidence in themselves and both appeared to be equal. As soon as Fortune inclined ever so slightly to either side, the one with the advantage would no longer be ready to negotiate on equal terms. Since they had previously proved unable to agree on conditions for peace, these should be left to be formulated by the Senate and People in Rome. This would serve the public interest and must be acceptable to themselves. If they both immediately swore an oath before

---

[1] App. *b.c.* 2, 199; Dio 41, 39, 1; ibid. 2–4, omens favourable to Caesar, maliciously misrepresented in Lucan 5, 395.

[2] Caes. *b.c.* 3, 2, 2.

[3] Op. cit., 3, 6, 2–3; App. *b.c.* 2, 214; 221–223; Dio 41, 44, 2–3; Plut. *Caes.* 37, 3; Suet. *Caes.* 58, 2; Vell. 2, 51, 1: *sua celeritate et fortuna C. Caesar usus*; App. *b.c.* 2, 227. According to his own statement, Caesar took seven legions with him. Since in *b.c.* 3, 89, 2 he speaks of 80 cohorts and 22,000 men at the battle of Pharsalus, one can estimate the total number transported at 20,000; cf. Holmes, *Rom. Rep.*, 3, 434.

[4] Caes. *b.c.* 3, 11, 2.   [5] Op. cit., 3 11, 3–12, 4; Dio 41, 45, 1.

[6] Caes. *b.c.* 3, 10, 3.

their assembled armies to dismiss their troops within the next three days, after laying down their arms and renouncing the means in which they now put their trust, they would have no choice but to be content with the decision of the People and Senate.

This manœuvre was again most cleverly planned: it corresponded exactly with Caesar's wish to transfer the political struggle against his opponents from the battlefield back to the Forum. To this end he had long since proposed that both sides should disarm. Being in possession of the city of Rome and all its regular magistrates, and having eliminated the armies in Spain, he could have no doubts about his political victory. That is why Caesar emphasizes that the fortune of war has not yet decided for either side. Since Pompey had, as described above, let himself be surprised by Caesar's landing so that a dangerous panic broke out in the army,[1] he could at this moment be expected to feel particularly inclined to agree to these seemingly reasonable conditions. Admittedly, this would have meant that he would have had no further part to play, as against both Caesar and the oligarchy. Even if, for this very reason, the plan miscarried, it was not useless. Caesar's stay in Rome had demonstrated anew the extent to which Italy longed for peace and that nothing could strengthen his position more than the impression that he wished to procure this blessing for the state. He had rejected the mediation of the Senate, since the radical optimates among his opponents were quite insusceptible to such an approach. On the other hand he might still be successful in separating Pompey from his present allies. If he refused, he would bear the blame for the prolongation of the war, and in any case such an attempt would feed the embers of distrust which were always glowing in the enemy camp.

Vibullius did not make this proposal known to Pompey until the panic of the army had been brought under control. His trusted advisers Lucius Scribonius Libo, Lucius Lucceius and Gnaeus Pompeius Theophanes of Mytilene, then Pompey's adjutant and formerly his historian, were also called in.[2] But as Caesar learned later from bystanders, Vibullius was not even able to finish his speech since Pompey, seeing through Caesar's intentions, prevented him from

---

[1] Op. cit., 3, 13, 2–4; App. *b.c.* 2, 230, toning it down; Cic. *Att.* 11, 1, dated by O. E. Schmidt (*Briefwechsel*, 184) to the beginning of January 48.

[2] *FgrHist*, no. 188.

saying anything else by declaring that it was impossible for him to live his life by the grace of Caesar.[1]

Furthermore, within the next few days the favourable military prerequisites, on the strength of which Caesar wished to open negotiations, melted away. For Marcus Bibulus, the supreme commander of the enemy fleet, did not allow himself to be taken by surprise a second time, but by relentless exposure of his own person organized a very effective blockade, by which he secured the whole coast of Epirus-Illyricum as far as Istria against any attempt at a landing.[2] Caesar, instead of being able to unite his whole army by quickly ferrying across the rest of the troops, had to wait for three months until about April 10 (February 8, Jul.) before the other half of his troops put out to sea.[3] Pompey also succeeded in reaching Dyrrhachium before Caesar and so prevented the loss of this important place, well provided with all materials, which was to serve as the base for his future operations against Italy. Caesar now withdrew behind the Apsus near Apollonia, while Pompey advanced after him as far as the river, and thus the two armies lay facing each other for several weeks.[4] Pompey, true to his nature, refrained from an active conduct of the war since he hoped that as a result of the blockade the enemy would be worn down without a battle. Caesar, cut off from all reinforcements from Italy, was forced, in order to maintain himself, to widen as far as possible the area under his military control from which he could draw sustenance. Accordingly, with one legion he personally pushed southward as far as Buthrotum, on the coast facing Corcyra.[5]

Here he was pleased to receive a message from his commander at Oricum (south of Valona) that the leaders of the enemy fleet, Bibulus and Libo, were asking to speak to him on an important matter. He immediately hurried to Oricum and met Libo for a conference; Bibulus asked to be excused since he did not want to jeopardize the negotiations by an outburst of temper such as might occur if he came too close to his hated enemy. Caesar hoped that he would receive a reply to the offer which he had made through

[1] Caes. b.c. 3, 18, 3–5; Plut. Pomp. 65, 5. Cf. my Pompeius², 220. There is a comprehensive account of the unsuccessful peace negotiations in Dio 41, 53, 2–54, 3.

[2] Caes. b.c. 3, 8, 3–4; Dio 41, 44, 4.

[3] Caes. b.c. 3, 25, 1; Plin. n.h. 2, 122; 18, 239. February 8 was reckoned as the beginning of spring; cf. Groebe in Drumann, 3², 741; O. E. Schmidt, Briefwechsel, 190. See Suet. Caes. 35, 1; cf. Holmes, Rom. Rep., 3, 478.

[4] Caes. b.c. 3, 13, 5–6; App. b.c. 2, 231–232; Dio 41, 47, 1–2.

[5] Caes. b.c. 3, 16, 1.

Vibullius.[1] But Libo[2] explained that, however eagerly he himself wished for peace, he could only arrange the despatch of negotiators and encourage Pompey to accept Caesar's proposals. For the moment it was only a question of arranging an armistice in order to allow negotiations to start. Caesar expressed his agreement to this on condition that the armistice included the lifting of the blockade as well as the cessation of hostilities by land. Since, however, Libo stated that he was not authorized to let the negotiators through nor would he guarantee their safe conduct, Caesar gained the impression that his opponents were only looking for an opportunity in the armistice to provision themselves on the coast occupied by himself and hitherto blocked to all attempts at landing. For the closing of a large stretch of coast was causing great difficulty to the blockading fleet which was forced to obtain all its supplies by sea. Caesar naturally did not wish to abandon his only means of pressure and the discussions failed to achieve any result.[3]

Since this prospect of peace had proved delusive, the *de facto* truce on the Apsus seemed to offer another opportunity for the demoralization of the enemy army by the demagogic methods which had been so successfully practised in Spain. Through frequent conversations of individual soldiers with comrades on the other side, a mood was created which eventually allowed Caesar to send his trusted follower Publius Vatinius to the bank to deliver a loud harangue. In moving language he described the treatment meted out in the past to runaway slaves and pirates, and said that citizens should not now be allowed to use citizens in the same way. Thereupon a shout arose from the audience that on the next day Aulus Terentius Varro Murena,[4] a well-known character also familiar to us from Cicero's letters, would arrive to prepare the way for negotiations. At the appointed hour soldiers from both sides came flocking in; among Caesar's intimates Lucius Cornelius Balbus the younger, who already in the previous year had travelled to Brundisium with Caesar's instructions, was to be seen in the front rank. But from the opposing side Titus Labienus began a haughty altercation with Vatinius and suddenly a volley of missiles, one of which struck Balbus, rained down on Caesar's men. Labienus brought the scene to an end with

[1] Caes. *b.c.* 3, 15, 8.

[2] He was the father-in-law of Pompey's younger son Sextus; Münzer, *RE*, 2A, 881, no. 20.

[3] Caes. *b.c.* 3, 16, 3–17, 6.

[4] Op. cit., 3, 19, 4. Münzer, *RE*, 5A, 705, no. 91. His daughter married Maecenas.

the words: 'Stop this talk of an agreement; peace is impossible for us without the delivery of Caesar's head.'[1]

For Caesar this blunt refusal was a heavy blow. Though Bibulus fell victim to his exertions since he would not leave his post despite a serious illness,[2] the blockade continued as before. Libo even attempted to block the harbour of Brundisium; his attack was brilliantly repelled by Antony,[3] but the desired reinforcements still did not appear. For a time even his news service was interrupted, so that Caesar began to have doubts about the reliability of his legates in Italy.[4] Such doubts suggested themselves all the more readily because just at that time the praetor Marcus Caelius Rufus, a highly regarded partisan of his, had originated a movement completely hostile to the dictatorial edict on the repayment of debts. He eventually went so far as to give notice of bills remitting one year's rent and totally cancelling all indebtedness, and did not even stop at offering violence to his colleague Gaius Trebonius, the *praetor urbanus*, and to the consul Publius Servilius. Fortunately for Caesar, the latter was an energetic character. He stopped a detachment of soldiers who were just marching through on the way to Gaul, had the Senate pass the familiar decree granting him full authority, and so forced the turbulent praetor to cease from exercising his office. It is not without its humorous side to note that on this occasion the same weapons were employed in Caesar's interest which, when used by the oligarchy against him, had made him so indignant. To complete the analogy of this case with the situation on January 7, 49, here too tribunes were found to use their veto in the praetor's favour. Caelius escaped from the city and joined up with Titus Annius Milo, who had come hurrying back from exile. With the help of the latter's gladiatorial bands and freed slaves they intended to unleash an armed revolt against Caesar. But a legion under the praetor Quintus Pedius (Caesar's nephew)[5]

---

[1] Caes. *b.c.* 3, 19. Dio (41, 47, 2–3) also tells of an unsuccessful attack by Pompey, and Appian (*b.c.* 2, 241) comments that on this occasion Pompey missed his best opportunity for victory. Cf. my *Pompeius*[2], 284, 54. Dio's basically optimate narrative seems to presuppose a knowledge of Caesar's account.

[2] Caes. *b.c.* 3, 18, 1; Dio 41, 48, 1; Oros. 6, 15, 10.

[3] Caes. *b.c.* 3, 23–24; Dio 41, 48, 2–3.

[4] Caes. *b.c.* 3, 25, 1 and 4; Dio 41, 46, 1. More in Appian (*b.c.* 2, 238–240), clearly resting on a sound tradition (ultimately Asinius Pollio?). Münzer (*RE*, 22, 896) astutely conjectures that the Postumius mentioned here (239; 240; 242) is none other than the well-known C. Rabirius Postumus; see above, p. 147, n. 2.

[5] Thus Münzer (*RE* 19, 38), as against Suet. *Caes.* 83, 2, where he is described as Caesar's grand-nephew, like C. Octavius and L. Pinarius.

immediately marched against Milo and the rebel fell in battle. Soon afterwards the same fate overtook Caelius.[1]

In general, therefore, the men to whom Caesar had entrusted Italy proved completely reliable; but they offered no greater moral security than Caelius, and the military situation in Epirus gradually became so desperate for Caesar that on one occasion he tried to cross to Italy in disguise in a small boat in order to fetch his troops in person. When the helmsman was on the point of abandoning the journey owing to the high waves, he made himself known and with the cry, 'You carry Caesar and Caesar's fortune!'[2] encouraged him

---

[1] Caes. *b.c.* 3, 20–22; Dio 42, 22–25. Here (23, 1) the use of soldiers and (23, 2) the *s.c. de defendenda re publica* are expressly mentioned, whereas Caesar (21, 3) only says *de quibus rebus Servilius consul ad senatum rettulit senatusque Caelium ab re publica removendum censuit*. See Vell. 2, 68, 1–2; Plin. *n.h.* 2, 147; Oros. 6, 15, 10. M. Caelius was Cicero's talented young friend to whom we owe the interesting letters in *fam.* 8 and who in 50 B.C. propounded the cynical maxim that in a civil war the stronger party should be supported; see above, p. 188, n. 2. He now, at about the end of January, 48 (O. E. Schmidt, *Briefwechsel*, 196), wrote to Cicero that he had let himself be led astray by Curio, but could not stand Caesar's followers any longer (*sed, crede mihi, perire satius est quam hos videre* (*fam.* 8, 17, 1)). Only fear of Pompeian atrocities was preventing a reaction at Rome—*eiecti iam pridem hinc* (from Rome) *essemus; nam hic* (in Rome) *nunc praeter faenatores paucos nec homo nec ordo quisquam est nisi Pompeianus*. He was then engaged in bringing the people round; the Pompeians were asleep and did not know where Caesar's weak spots were (*vos dormitis nec haec adhuc mihi videmini intellegere, qua nos pateamus et qua simus imbecilli*). Nevertheless, his tone has changed; now it is a case of *atque hoc nullius praemi spe faciam sed, quod apud me plurimum solet valere, doloris atque indignitatis causa*. Finally, however, he again admits with reference to the situation in Illyricum that Caesar has the better soldiers: *vestras copias non novi; nostri valde depugnare et facile algere et esurire consuerunt*. As early as March, 49, while under the impression of Caesar's veterans, he had written (*fam.* 8, 15, 1): *num tibi nostri milites, qui durissimis et frigidissimis locis, taeterrima hieme bellum ambulando confecerunt, malis orbiculatis* (=dessert-apples) *esse pasti videntur?* These hurriedly dashed-off lines are invaluable evidence for the state of mind of their author, the ambitious ex-optimate who had gone over to Caesar, but during his absence quarrelled with the old Caesarians, and now wishes to rehabilitate himself by unscrupulous demagogic methods while still not believing in a Pompeian victory. On the other hand, they also illustrate the difficult position of Caesar, whose moderation in victory had not altered the fact that he could only win the war by military means. The law cancelling debts can rightly be regarded as a truly statesmanlike measure. Thus it filled him with anger when a praetor promised the debtors his protection against it (*b.c.* 3, 20, 3: *nam fortasse inopiam excusare et calamitatem aut propriam suam aut temporum et difficultates auctionandi proponere etiam mediocris est animi; integras vero tenere possessiones qui se debere fateantur, cuius animi aut cuius impudentiae est!*)

[2] Thus Plut. *Caes.* 38, 5; App. *b.c.* 2, 236. In Dio 41, 46, 4, 'Have courage, for you carry Caesar'; Flor. 2, 13, 37: *Caesarem vehis*. See also Lucan 5, 585. The original authority for Plutarch and Appian is probably Asinius Pollio, who in a letter to Cicero (*fam.* 10, 31, 3) mentions Caesar's *tanta fortuna: Caesarem vero, quod me in tanta fortuna modo cognitum* (when Pollio joined him at the end of 50 B.C.) *vetustissimorum familiarium loco habuit, dilexi summa cum pietate et fide*. See above, p. 227, n. 4. After Pollio had escaped Curio's disaster in Africa (App. *b.c.* 2, 186) he returned to Caesar (App. *b.c.* 2, 346; Plut. *Caes.* 46, 2; *Pomp.* 72, 4; Suet. *Caes.* 30, 4). Plut. *Caes.* 46, 2 makes it highly probable that the statements of the Greeks go back directly or indirectly to the Greek work of the rhetorician Asinius Pollio of Tralles (*FgrHist*, no. 193).

to try again. But insurmountable storms prevented him from carrying out his intention. However, he finally succeeded in getting a letter across with strict orders to Antony and Fufius Calenus to cross at the first favourable opportunity.[1] The two legates acted on his instructions, and on April 10 from his camp Caesar observed the longed-for troop transports sailing along the Illyrian coast. The wind drove them northward as far as the region of Lissus (Leshja, some thirty-five miles north of Dyrrhachium), but here the ships were able to land safely, unharmed either by the pursuing enemy or by the storm. The corporation of Roman citizens in Lissus had received important help from Caesar during his pro-consulship of Gaul and Illyricum and now welcomed Antony with open arms, so that the Pompeian commander withdrew with all speed. Sixteen Rhodian ships from the enemy fleet ran aground and part of their crews fell into Caesar's hands, but were generously dismissed by him to their homes.[2]

A few days later the two armies were successfully united.[3] Caesar's forces now totalled about 34,000 infantry and 1,400 cavalry,[4] but even so Pompey's troops may have outnumbered his by a quarter. Since the blockade continued and Pompey secured as much of the country's food as possible, Caesar's difficulties in obtaining provisions grew; there was only an improvement in the military situation in so far as he now felt himself strong enough for a decisive battle. For this he could not, of course, count on his whole army: for at the same time he had first to create the necessary basis for the conduct of the war. This circumstance illustrates most clearly the extent to which he found himself at a disadvantage compared with his opponent. His first instructions after the union with Antony were for the detachment of about 12,000 men whom he needed in Macedonia, Thessaly and Aetolia to cover his rear and to relieve his shortage of food. Politically this enterprise was dependent on the opposition parties of the country, with some of whom Caesar had long-standing ties dating from the cases which he had conducted for

---

[1] Caes. b.c. 3, 25, 3. Of course he had no reason to report his own unsuccessful attempt. The account of it seems to go back to Asinius Pollio. See Suet. Caes. 58, 2; App. b.c. 2, 234–240 (see above, p. 227. n. 4.); Plut. Caes. 38; Dio 41, 46, 2–4; Lucan 5, 476–702; Flor. 2, 13, 37. I fail to understand how W. H. Friedrich (Thesaurismata, Festschrift für Ida Kapp (1954), 23) can regard the story as a tendentious invention of the Pompeians.

[2] Caes. b.c. 3, 26–29; App. b.c. 2, 243–245; Dio 41, 48, 4.

[3] Caes. b.c. 3, 30. Cf. my Pompeius², 222–223.

[4] Caes. b.c. 3, 29, 2: Antony brought three veteran legions, one legion of recruits and 800 cavalry. Cf. Holmes, Rom. Rep. 3, 434.

Greeks almost thirty years earlier against the outrages of Sullan oligarchs. As intermediary between the officers and the Greek communities, Callistus, a citizen of Cnidus, rendered particularly outstanding service.[1] The legates Lucius Cassius Longinus and Gaius Calvisius Sabinus were successful in winning Aetolia, Acarnania and Amphilochia for Caesar; later he also sent the trusted Quintus Fufius Calenus to join them, and under his leadership Delphi, Thebes, Orchomenus and other communities of Central Greece were induced to come over. The other important task of holding up the advance of the proconsul of Syria, Quintus Caecilius Metellus Pius Scipio, was entrusted by Caesar to Gnaeus Domitius Calvinus, the only consular in his service beside the exiled Aulus Gabinius. This aim was also satisfactorily achieved, but Thessaly could not be held, as Caesar had hoped.[2]

After Caesar and Antony had joined forces, Pompey took up a position on the Genusus, a river immediately north of the Apsus, still a good day's journey (twenty-four miles) from Dyrrhachium. Here Caesar offered battle to an enemy twice as strong as himself, but the latter was as disinclined as before to let himself be lured into facing the unnecessary hazard of a bloody decision. In order to force the issue Caesar detached himself from the enemy, made a detour around him and suddenly pushed his army into a position between Dyrrhachium and Pompey, so that the latter could only maintain his connection with this important place by sea. He had recognized Caesar's intention too late and had to be content with moving his camp to the rocky plateau of Petra to the south of the enemy. However, this position had the advantage that it afforded protection for all his reinforcements to be brought up in complete security in the innermost part of the bay of Dyrrhachium, which lay behind it. Nevertheless, Caesar boldly resolved to surround it completely by field fortifications.[3] Militarily he wished thereby to put a stop to the disruption of his own food supplies by the far superior enemy cavalry and at the same time, by cutting them off from the possibility of foraging, to weaken their fighting strength. But above all he hoped to make a great impression on the whole Roman world

---

[1] Dittenberger, *Syll.*[3] 761, A, 3; B, 4 and 8.

[2] Caes. *b.c.* 3, 33, 2–38, 4; 56; Dio 41, 51, 2–3.

[3] Caes. *b.c.* 3, 41–43; Dio 41, 49–50, 1; App. *b.c.* 2, 246. Cf. my *Pompeius*[2], 223–226. Maps of the theatre of war are to be found in *RE*, 5, 1882; Kromayer-Veith, *Schlachtenatlas*, map 20; see Holmes, *Rom. Rep.* 3, 135; van Ooteghem, *Pompée*, 594; 607, 610.

by this unusual spectacle of the weaker party encircling an enemy twice as strong without the latter daring to offer battle.[1]

Pompey countered this move by building fortifications himself in a semi-circle of fourteen miles and thus forced Caesar to expand his lines over sixteen miles—the area enclosed is calculated at twenty-two square miles—which, despite the difficulty of the terrain, presented his small army with a formidable task. But Caesar's veterans achieved the incredible.[2] They remembered the hardships which they had survived in Spain and before Alesia and Avaricum.[3] When Pompey was brought a specimen of the bread baked by them from roots for want of corn, he declared that they were fighting against animals and forbade the spreading of such news so as not to demoralize his troops.[4] Thus from the end of April right into July the war of position developed, and eventually the unhealthy state of affairs in Pompey's camp resulting from its complete isolation by land became more and more noticeable. Deserters came over to Caesar almost daily. There was a shortage of water and fodder. Pompey sought to ease the situation by having the cavalry shipped over to Dyrrhachium; on the other hand the ripening harvest improved Caesar's food position.[5]

Once again he immediately used this favourable turn of events in order to secure a negotiated peace. All our knowledge of this matter leads to the conclusion that Caesar regarded Pompey's personal prestige as sufficiently shattered for him to turn on this occasion to some of the oligarchic leaders, apparently in the hope of splitting the opposition in this way. As soon as his troops in Macedonia came into contact with Metellus Scipio, he despatched his agent Aulus Clodius.[6] Originally he had admitted him to his circle on Scipio's recommendation, and thus he was immediately well received by his old patron. Caesar explained[7] that hitherto no

---

[1] Caes. *b.c.* 3, 43, 2–4.　　　　　　[2] Op. cit., 3, 44, 3; 63, 4.

[3] Op. cit., 3, 47, 6.

[4] Op. cit., 3, 47, 6–48, 2; Suet. *Caes.* 68, 2; App. *b.c.* 2, 252; Plut. *Caes.* 39, 2–3; Plin. *n.h.* 19, 144; Lucan 6, 106–117. For the dating, see Cicero's letters *Att.* 11, 3 (June 13) and 11, 4a (a few days later); cf. my *Pompeius*[2], 226–227.

[5] Caes. *b.c.* 3, 49; 58, 1–2; 61, 2.

[6] Known only through the reference in Caes. *b.c.* 3, 57, 1; 90, 1.

[7] Caes. *b.c.* 3, 57, 2–5. As H. Dahlmann (*Varronische Studien*, 1, *Abh. Akad. Mainz* (1957), no. 4, 159 ff.) recognized, against the improbable conjectures of C. Cichorius (*Röm. Studien* (1922), 228 ff.), the *logisticorus* of Varro *Pius aut de pace* mentioned in Gell. *n. A.* 17, 18 is connected with these peace negotiations. H. Fuchs (*Augustin und der antike Friedensgedanke, Neue philol. Unters.* 3 (1926), 151 ff.) believes that the philosophical treatise from which Augustine (*civ. dei* 19, 12–17) took his exposition of ancient concepts of peace was this same

one had dared to make his proposals known to Pompey. Scipio, he continued, occupied a position which not only allowed him to express his views openly, but from which he could also exercise a salutary influence on the deluded one. Indeed, as the holder of an independent command he possessed a real means of exerting pressure. If he made use of his powers, he alone would deserve the thanks of all for the peace of Italy and the preservation of the state.[1] For a few days these declarations seemed to be not without effect, but eventually Marcus Favonius, a convinced adherent of Cato, prevailed and Clodius had to return with a negative answer.

A similar but much more dangerous mission was undertaken by the younger Balbus. Already in February 49 he had tried to use in Caesar's service the ties linking him with the then consul Lucius Lentulus Crus—without success, because he was too late to meet his patron in Brundisium. He now ventured on a long stay in the enemy camp, but these negotiations also failed since Lentulus, luxuriating

work by Varro. Dahlmann's doubts (op. cit., 168) do not seem to me to be justified. If Varro started with Caesar's unsuccessful attempt to negotiate, the *Pius* will not have been written until after Caesar's death, since in my view Caesar did not himself publish the incomplete draft of the *bellum civile* (see above, p. 191, n. 1). In it Varro showed—polemically against Caesar—the prerequisites and character of true peace. According to App. *b.c.* 4, 202–203 he was proscribed by Antony as an 'enemy of the monarchy' but was saved by Fufius Calenus. In dating the *Pius* as early as 46 B.C., Dahlmann (op. cit., 166) overlooks how hated Scipio had made himself in the eyes of the Caesarians and of Caesar by his conduct of operations in Africa (*b. Afr.* 44, 3–46, 4; 48, 2). If the hypothesis of H. Fuchs is correct, we have in Varro's work an important piece of evidence for the significance that is to be attached to Caesar's formulation of his peace aim. Cf. above, p. 182, n. 5.

[1] See above, p. 217, n. 5. H. Strasburger (*HZ* 175 (1953), 256) has described this formulation as an 'isolated and unemphatic turn of phrase', not to be regarded as the propounding of a programme. Further to my arguments against this view (*HZ* 178 (1954), 464), I would add that in composing the *bellum civile* Caesar's main theme, apart from the military narrative, was (3, 90, 1) *quanto studio pacem petisset.* Caesar speaks of Metellus Scipio with particular scorn and bitterness (1, 1, 4; 4, 3; 3, 31–33; 37, 4; 83, 1). In our passage he calls the reader's attention to the chance that Scipio had missed by rejecting his appeal for peace, and so his emphatic choice of words seems to me very significant. He does not speak of Rome and *res publica*, but of the real problems. These are also mentioned by Sallust in his memorandum of 46 B.C., where he discusses the task of producing a *pax quam iustissima et diuturna* in contrast to *imperia crudelia magis acerba quam diuturna* (*ad Caes.* 1, 3, 1). Of Caesar he says (1, 7, 1): *tibi terrae et maria simul omnia componenda sunt.* After speaking of the moral improvement of the Roman people (7, 2–8, 3) he continues (8, 4): *ad hoc providendum est tibi, quonam modo Italia atque provinciae tutiores sint.* Thus the Caesarian. The agreement with Caesar becomes even more evident if we look at the contemporaneous utterances of Cicero, who in his speech of thanks for the pardon granted to M. Marcellus alludes to the statesmanlike tasks still to be mastered by Caesar (*Marc.* 23–29). Here there is talk only of the *res publica*, and in 29 *haec urbs* is expressly mentioned as his crucial sphere of activity. See further below, p. 259, n. 2.

in an insatiable wish for enrichment, feared that he might not do well enough out of the transaction.[1]

Finally, a letter has survived which Publius Cornelius Dolabella wrote around June on Caesar's instructions to his father-in-law Cicero, who was with Pompey at the time.[2] This document may be regarded as typifying the point of view then being spread by Caesar's headquarters: victory has inclined to his side; Pompey is being protected neither by the fame of his name nor by that of his deeds, nor by the following of kings and peoples of which he used to boast; he is not even successful in beating a decent retreat—something of which even the humblest is usually capable. He has been driven from Italy, lost Spain, his veteran army is trapped, and he is now surrounded in a way that has never before befallen a Roman general. Perhaps he will be able to escape disaster once more and hide himself away on his fleet. But Cicero must not follow him there. He too should prefer to be where the state now was rather than to follow the old state and so find himself in none. Therefore, in the event of Pompey's being defeated and forced to turn elsewhere, Cicero was to retire to Athens or some other peaceful community. Caesar with his well-known generosity[3] would be sure to grant him all the privileges appropriate to his rank. It is clear that Caesar was assuming that Pompey would no longer be able to maintain his position. Admittedly the sea route was still open for a withdrawal, but in that event, so Caesar hoped and wished, a large part of his optimate allies would prove disloyal and prefer to make their peace with himself. It was particularly desirable that men of Cicero's rank should leave the sinking ship because of the far-reaching effect that this would have. Such a crumbling away coming on top of a fresh defeat would inevitably mark the beginning of the end for Pompey's cause.

However, as had happened on previous occasions, the progress of his military operations did not fulfil these expectations. On about July 8[4] Caesar hoped to be able to deliver a decisive blow, in that

---

[1] Vell. 2, 51, 2. In 43 Balbus was quaestor in *Hispania ulterior*, and during games that he celebrated in his native city of Gades he put on a play: *de suo itinere ad L. Lentulum proconsulem sollicitandum*. During the performance he is said to have wept with emotion (Asinius Pollio to Cicero in *fam.* 10, 32, 3). Lentulus: see Caes. *b.c.* 1, 4, 2; 3, 96, 1.

[2] Cic. *fam.* 9, 9. He fulfilled this task in a manner so skilful and courteous that it reminds one of Caesar himself. The latter was clearly fond of him, and on his return in 47 B.C. treated him very leniently, although as tribune for that year he had revived the demagogic escapades of Caelius. Like Caesar himself, he surpassed Curio, Antony and Caelius by his patrician birth. On him, see O. Seel, *Cicero* (1953), 299 ff.; see above, p. 207.

[3] *qua est humanitate Caesar.*   [4] Holmes, *Rom. Rep.*, 3, 480.

Q

traitors were to help him to take Dyrrhachium.[1] But the coup failed, and at the same time Pompey made his first—unsuccessful—attempt to break out.[2] According to Caesar's testimony he lost about 2,000 men in the process, while on his own side only twenty were killed but very many wounded. The garrison of one fort is said to have counted 30,000 arrows shot at them. Caesar was brought the shield of the centurion Cassius Scaeva pierced by 120. Caesar expressed his appreciation of this feat, rewarded him with 200,000 sesterces and promoted him to *primus pilus* (the senior centurion in the legion). The whole cohort received double pay and other distinctions.[3]

Nevertheless, on about July 17 (May 15, Jul.) Pompey succeeded in piercing Caesar's line at its southernmost point where it came to an end at the sea seven miles from the main camp as the crow flies; he fortified a new camp there, and thus frustrated the whole of Caesar's plan of investment.[4] In order to weaken the impression of this decisive defeat, Caesar attacked an isolated legion of Pompey with thirty-three of the thirty-five cohorts in all which he had been able to muster there. But the legion received support in time and, gripped by panic terror, the Caesarians fled with heavy losses and outwardly too they now presented the appearance of a defeated army.[5] Caesar lost about 1,000 men and thirty-two standards;[6]

---

[1] Dio 41, 50, 3–4; App. *b.c.* 2, 250. In Caesar (*b.c.* 3, 50, 2) the start of these battles, fought simultaneously in six places (3, 52, 1; 53, 1), is lost.

[2] Caes. *b.c.* 3, 54, 2.

[3] Op. cit., 3, 53, 1–5; Suet. *Caes.* 68, 3–4. App. *b.c.* 2, 249 in his careless excerpt confuses the centurion Cassius Scaeva with the legate L. Minucius Basilus (Münzer, *RE*, 15, 1948). Lucan 6, 126 mentions Minucius, 140–262 Scaeva. Cf. my *Pompeius*[2], 229–230.

[4] Caes. *b.c.* 3, 58, 5–65, 3. Caesar explains (59–61) in detail how Pompey was kept informed of the situation at the point of the breakthrough by the treachery of the two sons of an Allobrogan chieftain who had been in high favour with Caesar since the Gallic War. They had been *instructi liberaliter* (61, 1), which presumably refers to their mastery of the Latin language, but *stulta ac barbara arrogantia* (59, 3) led them astray. On the other hand, their followers told Domitius Calvinus of Pompey's approach (79, 6).

[5] Caes. *b.c.* 3, 66–70; Dio 41, 50, 4–51, 1; App. *b.c.* 2, 256–260; Lucan 6, 263–313; Oros. 6, 15, 19–21. Caesar says (3, 69, 4) that his attempt to bring the standard-bearers to a halt by seizing hold of them did nothing to stop the panic. Plut. *Caes.* 39, 7 adds that a fugitive whom Caesar stopped lifted his sword against him; Caesar would have fallen had not a bodyguard lopped off the arm holding the sword. This stems from the (presumably reliable) tradition preserved in Appian (*b.c.* 2, 258–259) in which a standard-bearer raised the bottom of his standard against Caesar and was cut down by his bodyguard. While Caesar passes over the case of mutiny, he singles out for mention (3, 64, 3–4) the way in which the dying *aquilifer* of the ninth legion saved his eagle. This is also in Appian (2, 256)—though in a different version. On the bodyguards, see A. Alföldi, 'Hasta Summa Imperii', *ASA* 63 (1959), 7; ibid., 12 ff.: the *signa* of the Roman army are spears as symbols of the *imperium*.

[6] Caes. *b.c.* 3, 71, 1–2. According to Oros. 6, 15, 21, 4,000 soldiers fell; according to Plut. *Pomp.* 65, 8, 2,000, yet Caesar (71, 1) gives only 1,000.

the several months of positional warfare to which Caesar had day
and night devoted all the powers of his resourceful spirit ended with
a brilliant victory on Pompey's part, and soon the whole Roman
world again resounded with the new achievement of the old
master of strategy.[1] At that time Caesar's fate was poised for a
moment on the razor's edge, but Pompey did not immediately
appreciate the gravity of the enemy defeat and delayed in following
it up. Thus Caesar remained a free agent, and with a sigh of relief
could say to his comrades, 'To-day the war would have been won
by the enemy if they had a man who knew how to conquer'.[2]
He raised the morale of his soldiers by an address, the gist of which
he reports as follows:[3] 'You must not dwell on what has happened
or let yourselves be deterred by comparing your many successful
battles with one unfavourable one, and that not a particularly heavy
defeat. You must be thankful to fortune because you have conquered
Italy without the slightest loss, because you have pacified the two
Spains where you met the most efficient troops under the most tried
and trusted leaders, and because you have brought the neighbouring
corn-producing provinces into your power. Then you must recall
the happy circumstances in which you reached the opposite shore,
passing through the midst of the enemy fleet which had occupied
not only all the harbours but also all the coasts. If everything does
not go as one wishes, fortune must be supplemented by effort.
The setback which we have suffered can be ascribed to any other
cause rather than to a fault on my part. I gave you a good site for
the battle, captured the enemy camp and scattered and defeated
the enemy. But if your own panic or some mistake or even bad
luck deprived you of the victory that was already yours, you
must all strive to make good this reverse by bravery. If that
happens, the present loss will be turned into profit, as occurred at
Gergovia.'

Without doubt the significance of this speech goes beyond the
immediate circumstances that gave rise to it. Presented in one of the

---

[1] Caes. *b.c.* 3, 72, 4; 79, 4; 80, 2; 81, 1; App. *b.c.* 2, 261; Plut. *Pomp.* 66, 1 and 3; 74, 2;
82, 1. Cf. Dittenberger, *Syll.*[3] 762, 33 ff. See Dio 41, 52, with qualifications favourable to
Pompey.

[2] Suet. *Caes.* 36; App. *b.c.* 2, 260; Plut. *Caes.* 39, 8; *Pomp.* 65, 9. Caesar does not conceal the
tremendous gravity of the defeat (3, 70, 1): *his tantis malis haec subsidia succurrebant, quo minus
omnis deleretur exercitus, quod Pompeius insidias timens, credo . . . munitionibus adpropinquare
aliquamdiu non audebat.*

[3] Caes. *b.c.* 3, 73. Instead of explaining how Caesar mastered the panic, Plut. *Caes.* 39, 9–10
merely tells of a sleepless night.

great crises of his life, it is intended to serve as an example of Caesar's conduct in such situations. One can sense the persuasive assurance that radiates from it on to his listeners, as he lets them share his thoughts, in particular by his reference to the mysterious workings of *fortuna*. Although incalculable, it is still the most important factor in all that happens. Shortly before this he says that 'it has the greatest power in all things and most especially in war'.[1] For this reason it must always be reckoned with. But there follows the factual observation that hitherto it has on the whole been definitely on his side, and that, taken together with the consciousness of personal achievement, it obviously favours the man of efficiency. It is just for this reason that false compassion finds no place here. After the speech the defaulting standard-bearers were dishonourably reduced in rank, which at one blow restored discipline, so that some officers were actually of the opinion that Caesar should at once give battle again.[2]

But after Pompey's cavalry, which outnumbered Caesar's by six to one, had again secured freedom of movement, the provisioning of Caesar's army in the present theatre of operations was no longer possible. The obvious area to which to withdraw was Thessaly, with its plentiful sources of assistance, where he could also link up with his detached troops. If Pompey followed him there, he intended to force him to a decisive battle; if Pompey crossed over to Italy, he intended to march there overland together with Domitius Calvinus; if Pompey besieged Apollonia and Oricum, he intended to attack Metellus Scipio and thus force Pompey to come to his help.[3] The

---

[1] Caes. *b.c.* 3, 68, 1. See above, p. 194, n. 2. Also, in the criticism which he aims at Pompey's report of victory he emphasizes (3, 72, 4): *non denique communes belli casus recordabantur, quam parvulae saepe causae vel falsae suspicionis vel terroris repentini vel obiectae religionis magna detrimenta intulissent, quotiens vel ducis vitio vel culpa tribuni in exercitu esset offensum.* For this reason he disputes that Pompey's victory was won *virtute*. The *parvae res* also worked in Caesar's favour (3, 70, 2).

[2] Caes. *b.c.* 3, 74. Appian (*b.c.* 2, 261–266) claims that Pompey hoped that Caesar's army would come over to him; but God brought it about that the soldiers became ashamed of their failure, and as Caesar only criticized them mildly and forgave them, there was a change of mood. They actually asked to be decimated, and when Caesar refused this, they demanded the execution of the standard-bearers, which Caesar likewise rejected. The resort to the deity makes it clear that in this version Caesar's achievement was to be denigrated. Similarly in 259 we are told that Labienus, misled by God, advised Pompey to pursue the fugitives and so prevented a complete victory. Caesar reports (3, 71, 4) that Labienus requested the prisoners from Pompey, addressed them as comrades, then asked them with curses whether it was customary for veterans to flee, and had them publicly executed.

[3] Caes. *b.c.* 3, 78, 2–4.

army was quickly assembled, and on the very night after the battle he set off on the march. Thanks to the veterans' incomparable capacity for effort, the disengagement from the enemy was completely successful. After a short stay in Apollonia, the march continued through Epirus. At Aeginium, the first town in Thessaly, Domitius Calvinus joined him; his last move had been to return to Heraclea (Monastir), but he was able at the last moment to escape the envelopment threatened by Pompey and Scipio.[1] On the other hand, as a result of the defeat the attitude of the population of the territory through which they passed was hostile, and Androsthenes, the general of the Thessalian League, officially declared for the victor. About July 31, when Caesar arrived before Gomphi, he found the city ready for armed resistance. Here an example had to be made in order to restore his fallen prestige, and he gave orders for immediate preparations to storm the place. The soldiers were all the more eager because he informed them that after its capture the well-stocked town was to be plundered. The assault began in the afternoon, and before the sun set the booty was already theirs as a well-deserved reward for months of deprivation. As a deterrent the dreadful fate of Gomphi was also completely effective: from now on no Thessalian town ignored Caesar's orders, with the exception of Larissa, which was occupied by Scipio's army.[2]

A few days after he had pitched camp in the plain of Pharsalus, probably to the north-west of the town on the north bank of the Enipeus, Pompey, who had marched by the Egnatian Way from Dyrrhachium to Heraclea, joined forces with Scipio and then occupied an excellent position on the heights to the west of Caesar's camp.[3] His army now totalled over 50,000 and outnumbered

---

[1] Op. cit., 3, 75–79.

[2] Op. cit., 3, 80–81; Plut. Caes. 41, 6–8; App. b.c. 2, 267–269; Dio 41, 51, 4–5.

[3] It is disputed whether the battle was fought north or south of the Enipeus, and whether Pompey stood to the east or west of Caesar. The different views have most recently been discussed by van Ooteghem, in Pompée, 624 (with maps), and M. Rambaud, Historia 3 (1955), 346 ff. Caesar himself mentions no place by name, but b. Alex. 48, 1 has Palaepharsali rem feliciter gerebat and 42, 3 Pharsalicum proelium. Palaepharsalus is also given in Strab. 17, 796; Frontin. 2, 3, 22; Eutrop. 6, 20, 4; Oros. 6, 15, 27. Pharsalus is in Suet. Caes. 35, 1 (Pharsalicum proelium); Lucan 6, 313; 7, 61; 175; 204; 407; Plut. Caes. 52, 1; Pomp. 68, 1; Cat. Min. 55, 4; 56, 7; Brut. 6, 1; Cic. 39, 1; Ant. 8, 3; 62, 4. Palaepharsalus is probably the more accurate. Yet its situation is not certain. Appian's statement (2, 313) that it is in the area between Pharsalus and the Enipeus, i.e. south of the Enipeus, seems to be a misunderstanding, presumably taken from the source he used. I concur with the investigation of Holmes (Rom. Rep., 3, 452–467; 569). Decisive in my view is the destination of the march, Scotussa, north of the Enipeus valley and east of the battlefield (Plut. Caes. 43, 7). See Plut. Pomp. 68, 5 for the move ordered by Caesar in b.c. 3, 85, 2.

Caesar's by more than two to one.[1] But whereas the Caesarians had quite recovered from the demoralizing effects of the defeat, their victory had unhappy consequences for the victors. The leaders of the oligarchy, who had only entered the alliance with Pompey out of necessity, wished to get rid of their leader, their 'Agamemnon' or 'King of Kings', as Lucius Domitius Ahenobarbus called him,[2] as soon as possible, and now pressed very forcibly for the decisive battle, as its result seemed certain and would allow them to dispense with a supreme commander. Pompey himself remained convinced that, faced with an opponent like Caesar whose veterans actually desired a pitched battle, a strategy of attrition was the only correct one. But in view of the triumphant mood prevalent throughout his army and the misinterpretation of his conduct of the war by the oligarchs, he was unable to persist in his view without entirely abandoning the reins of control.[3] In his description of these events in the enemy camp Caesar presents a counterpart to the senatorial debates at the outbreak of war:[4] according to the optimates, Pompey was putting off the battle in order that he might continue to treat consulars and praetorians as slaves. Among themselves they were squabbling about praetorships and priesthoods and disposing of

---

[1] Caes. b.c. 3, 84, 4; 88, 3–5; 89, 2; Plut. Caes. 42, 3–4. In Oros. 6, 15, 23 and Eutrop. 6, 20, 4, following the tradition favourable to Pompey which goes back to Livy, Pompey is given 40,000 infantry and 1,100 cavalry, Caesar about 30,000 infantry and 1,000 cavalry. In Dio 41, 55, 2–4, Caesar has the better troops, Pompey great numerical superiority. In App. b.c. 2, 289–290 there are a number of differing statements next to each other. In 291–295 the auxiliaries of the allies and subjects are distinguished from the Italians. According to 290 the maximum number of participants in the battle was 400,000; in Flor. 2, 13, 44 more than 300,000.

[2] Plut. Caes. 41, 2; Pomp. 67, 5; App. b.c. 2, 278.

[3] Plut. Caes. 41, 5; Pomp. 67; App. b.c. 2, 275, 281; Lucan 7, 45 ff. According to Cicero's evidence (fam. 7, 3, 2—August, 46) he eventually let himself be talked round and became confident too. See Caes. b.c. 3, 86, 1.

[4] Caes. b.c. 3, 82, 2–83, 4; 96, 1; Plut. Caes. 42, 2; Pomp. 67, 9; App. b.c. 2, 285. Caesar several times (3, 18, 5; 57, 5; 60, 4; 86, 1) notes that he received news about happenings on the other side after his victory. Plut. Brut. 6, 3–5, following a trustworthy source, reports that Caesar had a conversation about the intentions of Pompey with Brutus, to whom he gave a friendly welcome immediately after the battle. Cicero did not take part in the battle, but had stayed with Varro at Dyrrhachium (fam. 9, 18 2; divin. 1, 68; 2, 114; Plut. Cic. 39, 1). However, his previous experiences at headquarters fully confirm Caesar's account (Att. 11, 4, 1; 6, 2 and 6; fam. 4, 14, 2; 6, 6, 6; 7, 3, 2; 9, 6, 3; Marc. 18). Contrary to the truth, Lucan 7, 62–84 puts the speech demanding that Pompey should offer battle in the mouth of Cicero. As early as March 49 Cicero had foreseen that an optimate victory would mean a repetition of the Sullan reign of terror (Att. 9, 7, 5; 9, 2; 10, 6); retrospectively he is similarly resigned in a letter to M. Marcellus (fam. 4, 9, 2–3 (September 46)): an tu non videbas mecum simul, quam illa crudelis esset futura victoria? In Dio 41, 54, 1; 55,1; 57, 2; 59, 4 there is an apt comment, quite in the spirit of Cicero and presumably stemming from Dio's source, that neither Pompey nor Caesar intended to restore the old freedom. Plut. Pomp. 70, 1 is similar.

the consulship for years in advance. Others were more concerned with the palaces and property of the Caesarians.[1] A major quarrel developed in the council of war over the question whether Lucilius Hirrus, who had left on an embassy to the king of Parthia, would be eligible for the praetorship at the next election despite his absence. This was what Pompey had promised, but others regarded it as unfair favouritism. A serious disagreement broke out among Domitius, Scipio and Lentulus Spinther over the question of Caesar's supreme pontificate, and they abused each other in public. Acutius Rufus accused Afranius before Pompey as a traitor to his army.[2] Domitius proposed that after victory a court should be formed from the senatorial participants in the war to try all those who had remained in Rome or who, though present with Pompey's army, had taken no part in the fighting. Each judge would receive three voting tablets, one for acquittal, a second for the death penalty, and a third for a fine.[3] We also know from Cicero that there was much talk at headquarters of revenge and proscriptions. Caesar had given Domitius and Lentulus Spinther their freedom and attempted to negotiate with Scipio, but time and again the reply was irreconcilable hatred. The readers of the *Civil War* were meant to understand what they would have had to expect from *principes* of this stamp. Scornfully he ends his account with the words: 'they all thought only of offices, financial rewards, vengeance on their personal enemies and of how to exploit their victory instead of how to win it'.

Thus on August 9 (June 7, Jul.)[4] Pompey offered battle in the plain to the north of the Enipeus according to a well-prepared plan. He proclaimed with great confidence that his sevenfold superiority would decide the issue with trifling losses, and Labienus added that Caesar's dreaded veterans had shrunk to a small remnant. They were faced only with the recruits last raised in Cisalpine Gaul. Finally the whole council of war swore that they would only return to camp as victors.[5] Caesar, who on previous days had vainly deployed for battle, was delighted at this development and immediately moved to

---

[1] Cic. *Att.* 11, 6, 6: *de Fannio (RE*, 6, 1991, no. 9) *consoler te? perniciosa loquebatur de mansione tua. L. vero Lentulus* (consul of 49) *Hortensi domum sibi et Caesaris hortos et Baias desponderat.*

[2] According to Plut. *Caes.* 41, 4–5; *Pomp.* 67, 6, he was said to have been bribed by Caesar.

[3] Cic. *Marc.* 18: *quidam non modo armatis sed interdum etiam otiosis minabantur, nec quid quisque sensisset sed ubi fuisset, cogitandum esse dicebant; Att.* 11, 6, 2 and 6: *omnes enim qui in Italia manserunt hostium numero habebantur.*

[4] *Inscr. It.* 13, 2, 190–1 (*Fasti Amiternini*): *Fer(iae) q(uod) e(o) die C. Caes(ar) C. f. Pharsali devicit*; ibid., 208 (*Fasti Antiates*): *Divus Iul(ius) Phars(ali) vicit.*

[5] Caes. *b.c.* 3, 86, 1–87, 7; Plut. *Pomp.* 68, 1.

meet the enemy. As soon as he was close enough to their formation, he recognized with the acuteness of genius that Pompey intended to aim a fatal blow at his right flank with the cavalry massed on his left wing.[1] To counter this he placed a special reserve behind the third line on his right wing[2] and then delivered the usual address to his soldiers. In this he again emphasized that he had always been ready to make peace, as they themselves had witnessed. He had never wished to squander his soldiers' lives or to make their country poorer by the loss of one of its armies.[3] The order to attack followed and all his measures were completely successful. Pompey's attacking wing was routed and put out of action, the legions whose flank was thereby laid bare were rolled up from the left, their camp captured, and on the morning of August 10 the mass of the army (23,000 men) surrendered to the victor about six miles behind the battlefield.[4] Caesar estimated the fallen at 15,000,[5] of whom 6,000 are said to have been Roman citizens.[6] Among them lay Lucius Domitius Ahenobarbus who had commanded the left wing,[7] while Pompey and the other leaders were able to get away to safety in time. Caesar himself suffered the loss of only 200 soldiers, among them thirty centurions,[8] but since he did not view the fate of the empire from a narrow party standpoint, he was equally grieved that the victory had been bought at the cost of so much precious citizen blood. As he inspected the corpses he said: 'They would have it so. I, Gaius Caesar, should have been condemned despite all my achievements, had I not appealed to my army for help.'[9] Of those who

---

[1] Caes. b.c. 3, 86, 3–4; 88, 5.   [2] Op. cit., 3, 89, 4.

[3] Op. cit., 3, 90. Similarly in 1, 72, 3 (in Spain): *movebatur etiam misericordia civium, quos interficiendos videbat: quibus salvis atque incolumibus rem obtinere malebat*. See above, p. 216.

[4] Caes. b.c. 3, 91–98. Plut. Caes. 46, 4 adds that Caesar received most of these prisoners-of-war into his own army, similarly Dio 41, 62, 1, and Caesar himself, b.c. 3, 107, 1.

[5] Caes. b.c. 3, 99, 4; Oros. 6, 15, 27.

[6] Thus Asinius Pollio (Plut. Pomp. 72, 4; Caes. 46, 3; cf. App. b.c. 2, 345–346). Caesar (b.c. 3, 93, 7) mentions the annihilation of the *sagittarii funditoresque* (88, 6).

[7] Caes. b.c. 3, 99, 5; Plut. Caes. 44, 4; Pomp. 69, 1; App. b.c. 2, 316; 346; Cic. Brut. 267; Phil. 2, 71; Tac. ann. 4, 44, 2; Suet. Ner. 2, 3; Lucan 7, 600.

[8] Caes. b.c. 3, 99, 1; App. b.c. 2, 345 adds the variant 1, 200, which is hostile to Caesar.

[9] Suet. Caes. 30, 4: *hoc voluerunt. tantis rebus gestis Gaius Caesar condemnatus essem, nisi ab exercitu auxilium petissem.* 'tantis rebus gestis' recalls b.c. 1, 13, 1: *decuriones Auximi ... docent ... neque se neque reliquos municipes pati posse C. Caesarem imperatorem bene de re publica meritum tantis rebus gestis oppido moenibusque prohiberi.* See above, p. 200, n. 2. Suet. Caes. 30, 4 refers this saying to the testimony of Asinius Pollio. Plut. Caes. 46, 2 offers it as coming from the Greek work of Asinius Pollio of Tralles (FgrHist, no. 193), who continued Timagenes' school of rhetoric and was presumably a freedman of the Roman. Perhaps particular stress is laid on Caesar's having spoken Latin on this occasion because, according to Plut. Pomp. 60, 4 (probably going back to C. Asinius Pollio), he had quoted the line of Menander in

died for him he marks out for honourable mention in his account the former *primipilus* of the tenth legion who had come out of retirement, and with 120 volunteers had opened the attack on the right wing. As he advanced he called to his comrades: 'With this stroke we shall win back for our general the rank (*dignitas*) that is his due as well as freedom for ourselves.'[1] We are to understand that Caesar's veterans were no mercenaries, but Roman citizens fighting for a just system of government.

As can be imagined, victory tasted sweet, not least because of the arrogant spirit that had reigned in the enemy headquarters before the battle.[2] However, the war was by no means over if an energetic enemy leadership made proper use of the plentiful means of resistance still available.[3] Their unimpaired fleet still held the mastery of the sea. Decimus Laelius was engaged on a new blockade of Brundisium.[4] Gaius Cassius (Caesar's future assassin, whose brother Lucius was commanding one of Caesar's legions in Greece) burnt thirty-five Caesarian ships during an attack on Messina, although he was less successful in an attack on Caesar's squadron patrolling the west coast of Italy near Vibo.[5] The opposition had a very secure strongpoint in Africa.[6] Some time previously Caesar had given orders to Quintus Cassius Longinus, his propraetorian legate in southern Spain, to enter Numidia with his army.[7] This movement could not, however, be carried out because the two former Pompeian

Greek when he crossed the Rubicon. See Jacoby, *Commentary*, p. 622. Unlike W. Aly. *Strabon von Amaseia, Untersuchungen über Text, Aufbau und Quellen der Geographika* (1957) 289, I suspect that the Trallian offered more than a mere translation of his patron's work, Suet. *Caes.* 30, 3 recalls the threat of his enemies: *ut si privatus redisset, Milonis exemplo circumpositis armatis causam apud iudices diceret.* Lucan 7, 303 makes Caesar say in his speech before the battle:

> *aut merces hodie bellorum aut poena parata.*
> *Caesareas spectate cruces, spectate catenas*
> *et caput hoc positum rostris effusaque membra*
> *saeptorumque nefas et clausi proelia Campi.*
> *cum duce Sullano gerimus civilia bella.*

Line 3 refers to the punishment with which Caesar was threatened, line 4 to the suppression of the rights of the people.

[1] Caes. *b.c.* 3, 91; 99, 1–2; Plut. *Caes.* 44, 9–12; *Pomp.* 71, 1–4; App. *b.c.* 2, 347–348; Flor. 2, 13, 46. Lucan 7, 470–474 is malicious.

[2] Caes. *b.c.* 96, 1–2. In the camp everything was found ready for a banquet to celebrate the victory. Caesar mentions above all the decorated tent of L. Lentulus Crus, adding bitterly: *at hi miserrimo ac patientissimo exercitui Caesaris luxuriam obiciebant, cui semper omnia ad necessarium usum defuissent.*

[3] In App. *b.c.* 2, 297 Pompey is criticized for not making use of his fleet.

[4] Caes. *b.c.* 3, 100.   [5] Caes. *b.c.* 3, 101.

[6] Cic. *Att.* 11, 7, 3; 10, 2; 12, 3; 14, 1; 15, 1.

[7] *b. Alex.* 51, 1.

legions mutinied, and with them the assize district of Corduba
renounced its allegiance to a governor universally hated for his
unprecedentedly brutal greed.[1] The rebellion was at first openly
Pompeian in character and even when the quaestor Marcus Marcellus took over the command, the attitude of the rebels remained
ambiguous.[2]

Caesar rightly set a great value on the moral effect of Pompey's
defeat. He believed that at that moment he could without danger
move to any part of the Mediterranean world,[3] however small the
forces that accompanied him, and as his next task he took up the
restless pursuit of his former son-in-law in order to deal a final blow
to his shattered prestige. But not only the general had now to take
firm decisions; the politician's were perhaps even more difficult.
The enormous body of the empire had everywhere been shaken
to its foundations by the nineteen months of civil war. However,
Caesar had long since ceased to belong to those politicians who let
themselves be carried along by circumstances. He felt himself
called to master them. 'Repose for Italy, peace for the provinces,
maintenance of the Empire': what the old powers could no longer
achieve he intended to bring about.[4] This programme rose well
above all previous party politics and made the greatest demands on
the statesman who undertook it. The senators with whose aid he
had hitherto conducted the civil war were politically inadequate
for this great task, if they were not actually opposed to it. With
helpers of the stamp of Mark Antony, Quintus Cassius, Publius
Dolabella, Marcus Lepidus, Publius Servilius Isauricus, Aulus
Gabinius, Publius Cornelius Sulla, Gnaeus Domitius Calvinus,
Gaius Sallustius Crispus, Decimus Brutus Albinus, Publius Vatinius,
Quintus Fufius Calenus, Gaius Trebonius and Gaius Vibius Pansa,
however valuable the services some of these rendered, even the
greatest genius could hardly carry out his gigantic plans. Much
depended on whether he was now successful in winning the collaboration of recognized 'heads of the state', famous names of the

---

[1] b. Alex. 53, 4–5; Cic. Att. 11, 10, 2; 12, 3; 16, 1.

[2] b. Alex. 57, 5–63, 2; Dio 42, 15, 3–16, 1.

[3] Caes. b.c. 3, 102, 1; 106, 3.

[4] Hence the frequently repeated attempts at negotiation. Even Cicero, impressed by
Caesar's magnitudo animi (fam. 4, 4, 4), was honestly convinced of this in September, 46
(Marc. 15): nemo erit tam iniustus rerum existimator, qui dubitet quae Caesaris de bello voluntas
fuerit, cum pacis auctores conservandos statim censuerit (among them Cicero), ceteris fuerit iratior.
atque id minus mirum fortasse tum cum esset incertus exitus et anceps fortuna belli; qui vero pacis
auctores diligit, is profecto declarat maluisse se non dimicare quam vincere.

nobility, hitherto in the opposing camp.[1] For this reason he developed the 'clemency' which he had practised hitherto into a fundamental and extensive policy of reconciliation towards the vanquished.[2] Immediately after the battle he had the captured correspondence of Pompey burnt[3] and let it be known that all who approached him could count on pardon and complete freedom. Only those whom he had already spared once, such as Lucius Afranius and Marcus Petreius, were in general excluded.[4] The first bearer of a great name to take advantage of Caesar's favour was Cato's nephew, Quintus Caepio Brutus (his future assassin), a young senator who had already won general respect for a way of life consonant with his high educational ideals. On a personal level Caesar was particularly pleased at this because Brutus was Servilia's son; politically his adherence was invaluable, since not only was he Cato's nephew by birth, but his views also openly emulated those of his uncle. If a man of such convictions placed himself at Caesar's service, this was the best possible recommendation for the policies which he planned. He therefore received him at once in Larissa and admitted him to his circle as a particularly valuable member.[5]

Yet while he was pondering over the future government of the Empire he did not for a moment neglect the military demands of the hour. At the head of his cavalry he pursued the fleeing Pompey to Amphipolis and, not finding him there, went on to the Hellespont. About the middle of September (the beginning of July, Jul.) the two legions he had detailed for the task also arrived there and were ferried across in the available transport. While Caesar himself was on board one of these skiffs, he was surprised by the

---

[1] Cic. fam. 4, 8, 2 (August, 46, to M. Marcellus): *is qui omnia tenet, favet ingeniis, nobilitatem vero et dignitates hominum quantum ei res et ipsius causa concedit, amplectitur.*

[2] Cic. fam. 15, 15, 3 (August, 47, to C. Cassius): *multis honestissimis viris conservatis,* among them C. Cassius (Att. 11, 13, 1; 15, 2). Caes. b.c. 3, 98, 2 says of the army which surrendered after the battle: *pauca apud eos de lenitate sua locutus, quo minore essent timore, omnes conservavit militibusque suis commendavit, ne qui eorum violaretur neu quid sui desiderent.* See App. b.c. 2, 309; 336; 340. In Lucan 7, 312 Caesar begs the gods: *vincat, quicumque necesse non putat in victos saevum destringere ferrum quique suos cives, quod signa adversa tulerunt, non credit fecisse nefas;* and in 319: *civis, qui fugerit, esto.* In Flor. 2, 13, 50 Caesar called out during the battle, now *miles faciem feri,* now *parce civibus.* By a misunderstanding Oros. 6 15, 26 ascribes *parce civibus* to Pompey, as is also shown by Vell. 2, 52, 3 and Polyaen. 8, 23, 27. In Plut. Caes. 45, 2; Pomp. 71, 1; App. b.c. 2, 318; Polyaen. 8, 23, 25; Frontin. 4, 7, 32 *faciem feri* forms part of the orders for the fourth rank in parrying the cavalry attack.

[3] Dio 41, 63, 5.

[4] Dio 41, 62, 2–3. He adds that Caesar allowed each of his friends to beg off one senator or knight who had already been pardoned once. He further declared that the friends of Pompey had committed no crime against himself.

[5] Plut. Brut. 6, 1–4; Caes. 46, 4; 62, 3; App. b.c. 2, 464; Dio 41, 63, 6; Vell. 2, 52, 5.

sudden arrival of a Pompeian squadron. His life's work hung by a thread (as it had done before) and he would have been lost if the enemy commander had appreciated the situation. But his presence of mind did not desert him and he gave orders to steer towards the enemy and demanded the immediate surrender of the ten warships. The foolhardy daring of the victor of Pharsalus was again justified on this occasion and Lucius Cassius (not the brother of Caesar's murderer) humbly begged for pardon.[1]

While information was being gathered about Pompey's further flight, Caesar could, in keeping with his policy for the empire, give some time to the problems of the province of Asia. He first visited Ilium, the city of his heroic ancestor Aeneas, son of Aphrodite —the censor Lucius Caesar, a fellow member of his *gens*, had shown favour to this town forty years earlier for the same reason[2]—and granted the community political autonomy and freedom from taxes. With this gesture he was also imitating Alexander the Great who had honoured Ilium in similar fashion after the battle of the Granicus.[3] This visit was also an unmistakable demonstration of the significance of recent events. The divine descent of this member of the Julii was most intimately connected with his victory and the mastery over the Empire that had fallen to him as its prize. For this reason he did not scorn to report the miracles[4] that had occurred in different localities on August 9: in the temple of Athene at Elis the statue of Victory had turned round, in Antioch and Ptolemaïs the sounds of war were heard, in the inner sanctum of a temple at Pergamum drums rolled and in the temple of Victory at Tralles a palm sprang up out of the stone floor in front of the statue of Caesar that had been dedicated there. The impression all this made on the Greeks of Asia Minor, whose embassies received a friendly welcome from him, was enormous. Shortly afterwards all the communities of the province joined in erecting a monument at Ephesus[5] to 'Gaius Julius Caesar, son of Gaius, high priest, imperator and consul for the second time, descended from Ares and Aphrodite, god made manifest and

---

[1] Caes. *b.c.* 3, 102, 1 and 4; 105, 1; Dio 42, 6, 1–3; Suet. *Caes.* 63. App. *b.c.* 2, 370–372 gives Cassius 70 triremes instead of 10, like Suetonius, and confuses him with C. Cassius; similarly in 464. This L. Cassius (Münzer, *RE*, 3, 1680, no. 14) is otherwise unknown. L. Cassius Longinus, the brother of Gaius, was Caesar's legate (Münzer, *RE*, 3, 1784, no. 65).

[2] Dittenberger, *OGIS*, 440. App. *b.c.* 2, 281 reports a nocturnal sacrifice to Mars and Venus Victrix before the battle of Pharsalus, Plut. *Caes.* 43, 2—perhaps more accurately—a sacrifice two days before the battle.

[3] Strab. 13, 593; 594–595. Cf. Lucan 9, 964–999.

[4] Caes. *b.c.* 3, 105, 2–5.

[5] Dittenberger, *Syll.*[3], 760; T. Taeger, *Charisma*, 2 (1960), 5.

common saviour of mankind'. However cheap divine honours might have become in the area of Hellenistic culture since the death of Alexander, with this universal exuberance and the calculated description of the descendant of Aeneas as also the progeny of Mars, by which he is recognized as the living representative of the Roman people, a new monarchical conception of the Roman government appears.

For the last twenty years Pompey had personified Roman authority throughout the East. He was the great patron of the newly-won provinces and of the allied communities and princes. It was Pompey whom they had furnished with contingents and ships for the great struggle: they had just heard of his brilliant victory at Dyrrhachium and were confident that it would soon be all over with the foolhardy rebel. Pharsalus shattered these illusions like a bolt from the blue, and now the victor had already set foot in Asia Minor. Surely this was an event that demanded a religious explanation.

Caesar omits this homage from his account and altogether makes little of his stay in Asia,[1] because he wanted to portray his actions as self-defence in the spirit of republican traditions. In his own mind he must have been exercised by the problem of the form in which he could give permanence to his victory, and this Hellenistic initiative may have made an important contribution towards its solution.[2] However, the communities had another special reason to be grateful to him. For, as Caesar learned,[3] Metellus Scipio, when on his way to join Pompey with the troops from his province of Syria, had spent

[1] Caes. b.c. 3, 106, 1: *paucos dies in Asia moratus.*

[2] C. Koch (*Hermes* 83 (1955), 43–47) recalls that at Pharsalus Caesar's battle-cry was *Venus Victrix* (App. b.c. 2, 281; 319), that he vowed a temple to her and in 46 dedicated the temple of Venus Genetrix (Dio 43, 22, 2; *Fasti Pinciani* in *Inscr. It.* 13, 2, 48 on September 26; cf. Koch, *RE*, 8A, 865), and interprets these as moves in a dynastic direction.

[3] Caesar (b.c. 3, 31–33) treats Scipio with unsurpassable sarcasm. The collection of documents preserved in Josephus *ant. Iud.* contains a number of decrees (14, 228–232; 234–240) of the Pompeian magistrates of 49 in favour of the Jews concerning exemption from military service and the practice of their cult. Caesar's description (3, 32, 4) suggests that these may not have been granted free of charge. In 49 the community of Pergamum honoured the Imperator Q. Caecilius Metellus Pius Scipio as its 'saviour and benefactor' and also his daughter Cornelia, the wife of the proconsul Cn. Pompeius Magnus (Dittenberger, *Syll.*[3] 757/8). Now, as in 48, they honoured Caesar, Imperator and pontifex maximus, consul for the second time, their patron and benefactor, the saviour and benefactor of all the Greeks, for his piety and justice (*IGRR*, 4, 305). The date of the similar honours, op. cit., 306, 307, is not certain. 303 seems to belong to the period before the Civil War. In 48 he was also honoured as its patron by Chios (*IGRR*, 4, 928). With regard to his earlier relations with the east one may recall Suet. *Caes.* 28, 1: *Asiae quoque et Graeciae potentissimas urbes praecipuis operibus exornans.* The *clementia* shown to Asia in 48 is mentioned by Cicero in his letter to Cassius (*fam.* 15, 15, 2).

the winter of 49 among them and proved ruthless in forcing them
to contribute to the costs of the war. Not only had he raised from
the Roman tax-gatherers the revenue of the last two years together
with an advance on the third, as he had done in Syria, but he
also collected further contributions and requisitions such as a poll
tax from slaves and free citizens, taxes on columns and doors
from houseowners, as well as corn, contingents, weapons, rowers,
artillery and conveyances. The expense of these involved the Roman
citizens and subjects in debts at a high rate of interest. Only urgent
marching orders from Pompey when Caesar landed in Epirus
prevented Scipio from removing also the treasures deposited in the
temple of Artemis at Ephesus. Later when Caesar appeared in Asia,
he was just in time to frustrate a second attempt on the shrine by
the legate Titus Ampius Balbus, so that, as he says, he twice saved
the Ephesians' money.[1] Although he of course urgently needed the
money which he found on his arrival, he abolished the levying of
tithes and tolls by the hated Roman tax-farming companies,
reduced the total taxation by a third and allowed the communities
to collect it themselves.[2] As he had granted their freedom to the
communities of Thessaly to commemorate his victory, so he now
made a present of the freedom of his native city of Cnidus to his
learned friend Theopompus.[3]

However, as soon as news came of Pompey's journey to Egypt,
he left Asia to his legate Gnaeus Domitius Calvinus, set sail from
Rhodes with a fleet of thirty-five ships and 3,200 legionaries and
800 cavalry on board, and arrived before Alexandria on October 2
(July 28, Jul.).[4] While he was taking soundings before landing there,
he learned that Pompey had been murdered, and presently was
brought his head and signet-ring in confirmation. More than eight
years had passed since he had last seen him alive, and it is understandable that the sight brought tears to his eyes. He took the signet-
ring in order to send it as evidence to Rome, the head he had buried
and also sought to save such friends of Pompey as were still alive—
the consular Lucius Lentulus Crus had likewise been put to death.
His greatest pleasure in victory, he wrote to his faithful followers in

[1] Caes. b.c. 3, 105, 1.
[2] Dio 42, 6, 3; App. b.c. 5, 19; Plut. Caes. 48, 1.
[3] Plut. Caes. 48, 1; App. b.c. 2, 368; Strab. 14, 656. Cf. Dittenberger, Syll.³ 761 C with
notes; FgrHist, no. 21. Later he also granted Roman citizenship to Theopompus.
[4] Caes. b.c. 3, 106, 1–3; b. Alex. 34, 1; Liv. per. 112. Pompey died on September 28 (Vell.
2, 53, 4).

Rome, was constantly to spare the lives of fellow citizens who had fought against him.[1]

Since the murder showed that the leading ministers of the young king Ptolemy XIII regarded Pompey's cause as hopeless,[2] he confidently set foot in the Hellenistic capital and took up residence in the royal palace, although from the start the population gave his Roman soldiers an unfriendly reception.[3] It is unlikely that he intended to stay long in Egypt. But the government of the country had fought against him with fifty warships which had only just returned,[4] and this gave him a welcome pretext to levy contributions here as well.[5] He formally based his demand on a claim for $17\frac{1}{2}$ million denarii which was still owing to him from the time of the previous king.[6] One may recall the enormous sums which the latter had to raise in the year 59 in order to be recognized as king (page 76). At the time the money had been procured for him mainly by the Roman financier Gaius Rabirius Postumus. But when this creditor was brought to the brink of bankruptcy by the king's limitless indebtedness, Caesar, the helpful proconsul of Gaul, intervened on his behalf. It seems that in return he had his agent's outstanding Egyptian claims tranferred to himself and that in 48 it was this money with which he was concerned.[7] Caesar was now demanding 10 million.[8] The eunuch Pothinus, head of the government at Alexandria, put every conceivable obstacle in the way of this payment, and by using the temple treasures and the royal plate for the purpose, he was able to display Caesar in an unfavourable light.[9]

---

[1] Caes. *b.c.* 3, 106, 4; Plut. *Caes.* 48, 2–4; *Pomp.* 80, 6–7: Dio 42, 8, 1–3 with a malicious observation; Val. Max. 5, 1, 10; Eutrop. 6, 21, 3; Oros. 6, 15, 29; Lucan 9, 1010–1108.

[2] Caes. *b.c.* 3, 104, 1.

[3] Op. cit., 3, 106, 4–5; 112, 8; Dio 42, 34, 6; Lucan 10, 55.

[4] Caes. *b.c.* 3, 111, 3.

[5] Dio 42, 9, 1; 34, 1. Caesar of course is silent about this. As he says in 3, 106, 1, it was clear to him that Pompey turned to Egypt in the hope of finding a base for operations there (*coniectans eum in Aegyptum iter habere propter necessitudines regni reliquasque eius loci opportunitates*), and so in 3, 104, 1 he makes the royal ministers justify the murder *ne Pompeius Alexandriam Aegyptumque occuparet*, but as an alternative adds *sive despecta eius fortuna, ut plerumque in calamitate ex amicis inimici exsistunt*. In line with this, he explains (3, 106, 2) his boldness in landing at Alexandria with so few troops by the sentence: *sed confisus fama rerum gestarum infirmis auxiliis proficisci non dubitaverat aeque omnem sibi locum tutum fore existimans*. The order to Cn. Domitius Calvinus to send two legions formed from Pompeians (3, 107, 1; *b. Alex.* 34, 3) shows how he proposed to hold Egypt (*b. Alex.* 3, 4). That he himself did not intend to stay any longer is apparent from the sentence *ipse enim necessario etesiis tenebatur, qui navigantibus Alexandria flant adversissimi venti*. These are the north winds that blow from July to September (G. Schmidt, *RE*, 8A, 2212), which agrees with the Julian calendar.

[6] Plut. *Caes.* 48, 8. Cf. Suet. *Caes.* 54, 3.   [7] See above, p. 147, n. 2.

[8] Plut. *Caes.* 48, 8.   [9] Plut. *Caes.* 48, 7; Oros. 6, 15, 29.

Only now did Caesar get a more exact insight into the disorganization of the country. This had recently reached such a pitch that Cleopatra, the king's sister-wife and joint ruler with him, who was loathed by the Alexandrians, had been driven out by Pothinus and was now at Pelusium with an army, intent on forcing her restoration to the throne.[1] Caesar obviously hoped to place the country or at least one party in the kingdom in his debt by settling this dispute, and as consul of the Roman people, who in 59 had concluded the alliance with their father, he invited brother and sister to appear before his judgment seat.[2] In view of his antagonism to Pothinus, this from the start signified an intervention in favour of Cleopatra, and as soon as this unusually shrewd, intellectually and physically attractive girl of twenty-one appreciated the point, she had herself cunningly smuggled through the hostile town into the palace about the end of October (mid-August, Jul.) and at once captivated Caesar with her irresistible feminine charm.[3]

This development infuriated her brother, and he hurried down into the crowd shouting that he had been betrayed and tore the diadem from his head. At this the fires of resentment that had long been smouldering among the populace flared forth. The masses surged towards the palace. Although the Roman soldiers managed to seize the king, Caesar, as his troops were insufficient and taken completely by surprise, attempted to humour the mob by saying that he was ready to fall in completely with the wishes of the Alexandrians. Under these circumstances only the most serious concessions would be of use, and thus it came about that Caesar had to settle the question of the inheritance before the popular assembly. On the basis of their father's will, he decided that the two elder children should reign as joint sovereigns (with completely equal rights); but he went further than this and recognized the younger brother and sister Arsinoe and Ptolemy XIV as joint rulers

---

[1] Caes. *b.c.* 3, 103, 2; Plut. *Caes.* 48, 5; Strab. 17, 796; Pomp. Trog. *prol.* 40. On Cleopatra VII Philopator, see F. Stähelin, *RE*, 11, 750 ff. Cf. H. Volkmann, *Kleopatra, Politik und Propaganda* (1953), 55 ff. (English translation: *Cleopatra* (1958), 59 ff.)

[2] Caes. *b.c.* 3, 107, 2.

[3] Dio 42, 34, 2–35, 1; 51, 5, 4; Plut. *Caes.* 48, 9–49, 3; Flor. 2, 13, 56; *v. ill.* 86, 1; Lucan 10, 53–106; Fronto *fer. Als.* 3, 5 (Haines, 2, 10): *nihil de Gaio Caesare dico acerrimo Cleopatrae hoste, post moecho.* According to Plut. *Ant.* 25, 4 she had already charmed Cn. Pompeius the Younger in 49. Her skill in capturing her lovers is expertly portrayed by G. Ferrero, *Grandezza e decadenza di Roma* (1908), 2, 430. In this connection one may also mention Thornton Wilder's 'fantasy' on the Ides of March. This novel was enthusiastically reviewed by Ludwig Curtius in the periodical *Merkur* 4 (1950), 676–690; the best passages on Cleopatra are reproduced on pp. 682–685. Its distinguished author sent me a copy on July 6, 1950, 'with sincere greetings'.

of Cyprus.[1] We can judge how dangerous his position was from the fact that he, who had just received news from Rome that he had again been nominated dictator,[2] saw himself forced, while in a foreign capital, to renounce a piece of imperial territory which had been formally annexed ten years previously. This could not be regarded as a permanent settlement, but it had to be tolerated until the two legions that Calvinus had been asked to send arrived.[3] For the time being strenuous sightseeing in the city and sumptuous banquets, given in his honour by his royal mistress, helped him over the embarrassment.[4]

Pothinus, however, who had the worst to fear from Cleopatra, did not admit that all was lost, but summoned the royal army under General Achillas from Pelusium into the city.[5] This army of 20,000 veteran mercenaries enormously increased Caesar's danger. Orders from the king which he had sent to them were of no avail; Achillas began a full-scale attack on the palace quarter.[6] Caesar held his own in heavy fighting during the course of which the famous Alexandrian library among other buildings fell victim to the flames.[7] By occupying the Pharos lighthouse he also maintained his connection with the sea. But, outnumbered many times over by the enemy, he could only be saved by reinforcements from outside, and so sent Mithridates

[1] Dio 42, 35; Plut. Caes. 49, 3; Flor. 2, 13, 58. There is no need to explain why Caesar passes over these very painful events in silence. He only mentions (3, 107, 2) his summons to the royal brother and sister, and (108, 4) the will of their father Ptolemy XII Neos Dionysos 'Auletes', but not his decision. In this way he neatly gets round the appearance of Cleopatra. According to 108, 2, Pothinus called for Achillas immediately after the summons. These troops, the core of which was formed by the men left behind by Gabinius in 55 after their restoration of Auletes (110, 2), were approaching (109, 1) while Caesar was trying to bring about a reconciliation on the basis of the will. The tradition preserved in Dio and Plutarch presumably goes back to Asinius Pollio.

[2] Thus Liv. per. 112; Dio 42, 35, 5. Caesar describes himself as consul. According to Dio 42, 18, 2; 20, 3 he was nominated dictator for a year after Pompey's signet-ring had arrived in Rome. According to Plut. Caes. 51, 1 the year seems to have expired in October 47.

[3] Caes. b.c. 3, 107, 1; b. Alex. 9, 3; 34, 3.

[4] Plut. Caes. 49, 4; App. b.c. 2, 376; Lucan 10, 107 ff.; 332; Suet. Caes. 52, 1.

[5] Caes. b.c. 108, 2; 109, 1; Dio 42, 36, 1-3; Plut. Caes. 49, 4; Lucan 10, 333 ff.; 361. The planned assassination reported in Plutarch is expanded by Lucan.

[6] Caes. b.c. 3, 109, 2-6; Dio 42, 36, 4-37, 2.

[7] Caes. b.c. 3, 111, 6 only reports that he was successful in setting fire to the royal fleet. The burning of the library is reported in Plut. Caes. 49, 6; Dio 42, 38, 2. Oros. 6, 15, 31 speaks of 400,000 books. Sen. dial. 9, 9, 5 mentions the same number, citing Livy as his authority. Gell. n.A. 7, 17, 3 has 700,000 scrolls; followed presumably by Amm. Marcell. 22, 16, 13. On the question of where the books were kept, see Dziatzko, RE, 3, 411; Holmes, Rom. Rep., 3, 487 ff. The information in Plut. Ant. 58, 9, that Antony made Cleopatra a present—clearly in compensation—of the 200,000 scrolls of the library of Pergamum, seems credible.

R

of Pergamum, the son of a Galatian princess,[1] to summon the
land and sea forces of the allies and subjects in Syria and Asia Minor
to come to his help with all speed. Until these arrived he would
have to hold out.[2] He regarded the continued detention of the king
as a political asset, although he was disappointed in the hope that an
address from their legitimate master would induce the enemy
soldiers to cease hostilities.[3] Pothinus he had executed as a traitor.
On the other hand, Arsinoe with her chamberlain Ganymedes
succeeded in escaping. The rebels joyfully saluted her as queen,
and after removing Achillas Ganymedes took over the conduct
of affairs.[4]

The battles continued with unabated violence and varied fortune.
Caesar scored a considerable success in that he received intact a
large convoy from Calvinus, which contained, besides corn and
military equipment, a newly raised legion of Pompeians.[5] Thanks
to the efficiency of his Greek seamen, he was in fact able to frustrate
all attempts by the enemy to cut his communications by sea.[6] But
after he had secured control of the whole of the island of Pharos
and the Heptastadion mole which connected it with the city, at the
beginning of February 47 (the end of November 48, Jul.), he
suffered a serious reverse while attempting to take the southern
bridgehead at the end of the mole. This cost him the lives of 400
legionaries alone. He himself had remained to the end with the assault
troops and had to save himself by swimming from the mole to a
ship, leaving his purple general's cloak behind as a trophy for the
enemy.[7] Meanwhile his troops continued to occupy the positions
which they had held previously, and when the Alexandrians asked
him to hand back their king so that they could negotiate peace
terms, he thought he could safely grant their request. In the event
the royal youth, as soon as he had been set free, merely became a tool

---

[1] Caes. b.c. 3, 112, 6; b. Alex. 1, 1; 26, 1; Dio 42, 37, 3. Rostovtzeff (Social and Economic
History of the Hellenistic World, 3, 1528) is surely right in identifying him with the man mentioned in Cic. Flacc. 17; 41. Cf. Strab. 13, 625. See Geyer, RE, 15, 2205, no. 15.

[2] Caes. b.c. 3, 112, 1–8.

[3] Dio 42, 39, 3–4.

[4] Caes. b.c. 3, 112, 9–11; b. Alex. 4; Dio 42, 39, 1; 40, 1.

[5] b. Alex. 9, 3–4; 11, 6.

[6] b. Alex. 13–16. Dio 42, 40, 2 has shortened this considerably, to Caesar's disadvantage.

[7] b. Alex. 17–21; Dio 42, 40, 3–5; Plut. Caes. 49, 7–8; Suet. Caes. 64 disputes the loss of the
cloak. See also App. b.c. 2, 377; Flor. 2, 13, 59; Oros. 6, 15, 34. O. E. Schmidt (Briefwechsel,
221) deduces the date from Cic. Att. 11, 11, 1.

of the war party without a will of his own.[1] However, this was no longer of much significance; for early in March Mithridates of Pergamum appeared with an army and fleet before Pelusium and secured this important fortress by a powerful attack. His best help came from the Idumaean Antipater, the minister of the Jewish High Priest Hyrcanus, who brought him 3,000 Jews, by this example prompting other Syrian dynasts to support Caesar's cause, and then

[1] *b. Alex.* 22–25; Dio 42, 42. The author of the *bellum Alexandrinum* is concerned to justify the release of the king as a well-thought-out act on Caesar's part. He was, of course, familiar with the wiles of the Alexandrians, but argued that either the king would keep his word or it would be more honourable to fight against a king than against a rabble; the king had begged with tears to be allowed to stay, so that even Caesar was moved. His officers and men were pleased that Caesar's excessive guilelessness had received such a blow from the cunning boy, *quasi vero id Caesar bonitate tantum adductus ac non prudentissimo consilio fecisset* (24, 6). In Dio 42, 3–4, Caesar thought it possible that the enemy were really war-weary, and in any case he did not want to provide any hindrance to peace. If they chose to fight on, the young king did not represent any increase in their strength, and after his defeat Caesar would be all the more justified in handing over Egypt to Cleopatra. We do not know whether this second version is nearer to the truth. It was above all A. Klotz (*Caesarstudien* (1910), 180–204) who supported the view that A. Hirtius was the author of the *b. Alex.* He was followed by Holmes (*Rom. Rep.*, 3, 483) and O. Seel (*Gnomon* 9 (1933), 596 ff.). This is not quite certain, since Suet. *Caes.* 56, 1 says: *Alexandrini Africique et Hispaniensis incertus auctor est.* There were, therefore, no attested names of authors. Of course Hirtius (*b.G.* 8, *praef.* 2) says that apart from *b.G.* 8 *novissimumque imperfectum* (sc. *commentarium) ab rebus gestis Alexandriae confeci usque ad exitum* ... *vitae Caesaris* and 8: *mihi ne illud quidem accidit, ut Alexandrino atque Africano bello interessem; quae quamquam ex parte nobis Caesaris sermone sunt nota, tamen aliter audimus ea quae rerum novitate aut admiratione nos capiunt, aliter quae pro testimonio sumus dicturi.* Since the *b. Afr.* and the *b. Hisp.* should not be attributed to Hirtius on stylistic grounds, the *confeci* in the letter of dedication to L. Cornelius Balbus only signifies his intention of continuing Caesar's work down to his death, just as Thucydides (5, 26, 1) says he has taken his work to the end of the Peloponnesian War, when in fact it breaks off in 411 B.C. (H. Pötter, *Untersuchungen zum Bell. Afr. u. B. Alex.*, Diss. Münster (1932), 6). On the other hand, according to the philologists it is possible on a comparison with *b.G.* 8 that Hirtius was also the author of *b. Alex.* Since Hirtius fell on April 21, 43, as consul in the war against Antony, and had been ill for a considerable time since the summer of 44 (Cic. *Phil.* 1, 37; 7, 12; *fam.* 12, 22, 2), this explains why he could not complete his planned history of the war. Book 8 of the *b.G.* shows that he had the files from headquarters at his disposal, and suggests that he had previously helped Caesar with the composition of his *commentarii*. From Cic. *Att.* 11, 14, 3; 20, 1 we know that in 47 he met Caesar in Syria, apparently as one of those who at that time were bringing him news about events in Rome (*b. Alex.* 65, 1), and he will then have taken part in the campaign against Pharnaces. So it is very unlikely that he wrote the last part of *b. Alex.* 65–78 from his personal experience. When, in *b.G.* 8, *praef.* 8, he speaks of oral information from Caesar about the battles in Alexandria, he may be thinking of conversations held during this time together. For the other theatres of war he had the despatches sent to Caesar. According to Cic. *Att.* 11, 20, 1 Cicero learned of the presence of Hirtius in Antioch through a freedman of C. Trebonius (thus O. E. Schmidt, *Briefwechsel*, 231). Trebonius was the successor of Q. Cassius in Hispania Ulterior (*b. Alex.* 64, 2), and so the freedman will have brought a report on the end of the unrest there. Possibly the whole presentation of *b. Alex.* 48–64 goes back to this. Of course, Trebonius would have used information from eye-witnesses. If we regard Hirtius as the author of the *b. Alex.*, as I think he probably was, sections 23–24 show that he used other participants in the war to supplement Caesar's account. His silence about Cleopatra in this context demonstrates his loyalty to Caesar.

brought the Egyptian Jews over to his side.[1] Mithridates continued his victorious progress to Memphis, and then advanced along the western arm of the Nile towards Alexandria. Not until he reached the area of Mareotis did he again meet strong resistance. Bent on his destruction the king, on March 25 (January 13, Jul.), brought up his main forces on board the Nile fleet. Caesar, however, who had also received news from Mithridates at the same time, landed his troops by night on the coast to the west of Alexandria and after an overland march succeeded in joining forces with the relieving army. On March 26 he advanced up to the royal camp and on the next day he took it by storm with a brilliant assault. The fleeing king met his death in the Nile. The same evening Caesar arrived with his cavalry before Alexandria and accepted the surrender of the city.[2]

Caesar had spent, or rather wasted, over half a year in Egypt in this way; for it was a time during which he was unable to exert any influence on the conduct of the war or imperial politics. Cicero writes on June 14, 47, that since December 13, 48, Caesar had not sent a letter to Rome.[3] If in October 48 there were hopes of any early peace, since then a change had occurred which to a great extent cancelled the result of Pharsalus.

After the defeat, the oligarchic leaders who had not followed Pompey to the East made for Dyrrhachium and Corcyra, the two main bases for army and fleet. Marcus Cato, the commandant at Dyrrhachium, thereupon also moved his fifteen cohorts to the island, and when it became apparent that the Peloponnese could not be held with these forces against Fufius Calenus, at the beginning of October 48 he set sail from Patrae to Cyrenaica with Labienus, Afranius and Petreius, in order to place them at the disposal of Pompey. Here Sextus Pompey brought them the news of his father's murder, but they also learned that Metellus Scipio had succeeded in reaching Africa. Surmounting all difficulties, Cato led the 10,000 men whom he still had by the overland route to join him. By the spring of 47 the influence of his personality had produced order among the incompatible elements in the party. Scipio was recognized as supreme commander, Attius Varus, till then governor

---

[1] Joseph. b. Iud. 1, 187–192; ant. 14, 127–136.
[2] b. Alex. 26–32; Dio 42, 41; 43; Plut. Caes. 49, 9; App. b.c. 2, 378. The date of the battle is in Fasti Caeret., Inscr. It. 13, 2, 66, on March 27: fer(iae) quod eo die C. Caes(ar) vicit Alexand(riae); Fasti Maff., ibid., 74. Maps illustrating the Alexandrine War are to be found in Kromayer-Veith, Schlachtenatlas, Röm. Abt., map 21.
[3] Cic. Att. 11, 17a, 3.

of the province, and King Juba of Numidia subordinating themselves to him. A considerable army came into being, numbering ten Roman and four Numidian legions as well as strong cavalry contingents and 120 elephants.[1] The optimate republic which lived on here also possessed an outstanding military leader in Titus Labienus, and Cicero's correspondence shows how highly its chances were rated in May and June 47 (March and April, Jul.), when there was talk of an attack on Italy.[2] Raids were in fact made on Sicily and Sardinia and ties with the two former Pompeian legions in Spain resumed.[3] The unrest there had only been superficially stilled by the appearance in February of the new governor of Further Spain, Gaius Trebonius. Quintus Cassius, who was mainly responsible for that development, met his death on the journey home, but the embers of the Pompeian movement continued to glow under the ashes.[4]

Even in Italy the situation became precarious. In the middle of September 48 Caesar had been nominated dictator for a year.[5] On his instructions the consul Servilius later proclaimed Mark Antony, who had brought the greater part of the victorious army over to Italy, as *magister equitum*,[6] and since December the latter had been wielding supreme power in Italy.[7] When the fall of Pompey was confirmed, the magistrates began to heap upon the victor extraordinary honours and authority extending beyond the dictatorship. Thus a law formally placed the fate of the Pompeians in his hands.[8] He was given the arbitrament of war and peace without obligation to consult the Senate or People, the right to hold the consulship for five years in succession and a seat on the tribunes' bench together with other tribunician privileges.[9] The magisterial

---

[1] Ibid.; Plut. *Cat. Min.* 55–57; App. *b.c.* 2, 364–367; Dio 42, 13, 2–4; 57, 1–3; Lucan 9, 19–949; *b. Afr.* 1, 4; 3, 2; 20, 2; 48, 1 and 5.

[2] Cic. *Att.* 11, 10, 2 (January 19, 47); 14, 1; 15, 1; 16, 1; 17a, 3; 18, 1.

[3] Dio 42, 56, 3–5.

[4] *b. Alex.* 64; cf. *b. Afr.* 23, 3; Dio 42, 16, 2; 43, 29, 1–3.

[5] O. E. Schmidt, *Briefwechsel*, 211; Broughton, *MRR*, 2, 272; H. Andersen, *Cass. Dio und die Begründung des Principats* (1938), 24. See above, p. 249, n. 2..

[6] Dio 42, 21, 1; Cic. *Phil.* 2, 59.

[7] Cic. *Att.* 11, 7, 2; *Phil.* 2, 62; Dio 42, 27, 2; Plut. *Ant.* 8, 5.

[8] Dio 42, 20, 1. Whether this is the *Lex Hirtia* mentioned in Cic. *Phil.* 13, 32 and *CIL*, 1², 604 is disputed. Hirtius would have had to be tribune in 48; see Broughton, *MRR*, 2, 285, n. 3. The *lex* is mentioned by Cicero (*Att.* 11, 9, 1—January 3, 47). O. E. Schmidt (*Briefwechsel*, 210) wishes to assign it to the tribunes who took office on December 10, 48.

[9] Dio 42, 20, 3. Cf. H. Andersen, op. cit., 25–27. I do not think that he has proved his thesis (16–23) that Dio did not take such lists of decrees from an annalistic source, but from a special collection going back to the senatorial records (cf. H. U. Instinsky, *Gnomon* 15, 583). On the other hand, E. Hohl (*Klio* 32 (1939), 63, 71) seems to me to be wrong in rejecting Dio's whole account of the tribunician honours.

elections with the exception of those held in the plebeian assembly were postponed until his return. Pompey's law laying down new conditions for entering on governorships was repealed and the filling of the praetorian governorships was left in his hands. Finally his triumph over King Juba was prematurely decreed.[1]

While the population suffered increasingly under the brutal despotism of Antony,[2] from the beginning of 47 Publius Dolabella as tribune resumed the agitation of Caelius in favour of debtors. When it came to armed encounters between the parties, the Senate gave full authority to Antony and the remaining tribunes by means of the *senatus consultum ultimum*. Yet in view of the uncertainty about Caesar's fate the discontent spread through Italy; above all the veteran legions quartered in Campania became disaffected, so that Antony had to leave Rome in order to reassure them. Consequently the city was left completely to the anarchy of Dolabella and his opponent Trebellius.[3]

During the winter the situation in Illyricum also assumed a threatening aspect. In 48 Caesar had this important piece of coastland secured by Cornificius, his *quaestor pro praetore*, as it lay on the route of a land invasion of Italy, and in the autumn sent Aulus Gabinius to reinforce him with recruits raised in Italy. But contrary to all expectations this experienced leader suffered a severe defeat and died a little later at Salona. Consequently the Pompeian admiral Marcus Octavius was able to make considerable progress in this theatre in collaboration with the native rebels. Thus, in view of the circumstances in Italy, it was of great significance that Publius Vatinius, the courageous commander of Brundisium, succeeded in finally driving the enemy fleet from the Adriatic by a daring attack with inferior ships.[4]

On the other hand Caesar's cause suffered a severe blow in Asia Minor through Pharnaces, the king of the Cimmerian Bosporus

---

[1] Dio 42, 20.

[2] Cic. *Phil.* 2, 62–63; Dio 42, 27, 3–28, 4; 45, 28, 1–2; Plut. *Ant.* 9, 5–9; Plin. *n.h.* 8, 55.

[3] Dio 42, 29, 1–30, 2; Plut. *Ant.* 9, 1–4; *b. Alex.* 65, 1–2; Cic. *Att.* 11, 10, 2 (January 19, 47): *accedit Hispania et alienata Italia, legionum nec vis eadem nec voluntas, urbanae res perditae*; 12, 4; 14, 2; 15, 3; 23, 3; *Phil.* 6, 11; 10, 22; 11, 14. Dolabella himself wished to be rid of his debts. To assume the tribunate, he had, like Clodius, to become a plebeian (Dio 42, 29, 1). As heir to a certain Livia, he should have taken her name; but did he make use of it (Cic. *Att.* 7, 8, 3)? Against Schmitthenner, *Oktavian und das Testament Caesars* (1952), 47, this would support the existence of 'testamentary adoption'. Of course, according to Gai. *inst.* 1, 104: *feminae vero nullo modo adoptare possunt.* Cf. Jörs-Kunkel, *Röm. Privatr.* 186, 3, 2. *Dig.* 1, 7, 38 mentions *adoptio non iure facta.* Cf. Schmitthenner, op. cit., 60, 3.

[4] *b. Alex.* 42–47; Dio 42, 11, 4–5—badly abridged.

(Crimea). This son of the great Mithridates, taking advantage of Rome's troubles, had landed on the north coast of Asia Minor soon after Caesar's departure from Rhodes in order to win back his father's empire. His ambition was therefore directed partly at territories which now belonged to the Galatian king Deiotarus and to Ariobarzanes, King of Cappadocia, and partly at the Roman province of Bithynia and Pontus. Caesar's legate Gnaeus Domitius Calvinus had at his disposal only one regular Roman legion, but Deiotarus provided two Galatian legions armed by Rome, and a legion of militia was called up in Pontus. With these forces Calvinus came upon Pharnaces near Nicopolis in Armenia Minor, and there in December 48 offered battle in order to make his troops available to relieve Caesar. However, the king won a decisive victory, and the legate brought back to Asia only the ruins of his army. Pharnaces occupied Pontus, Amisus was captured amid scenes of disgusting cruelty, Sinope fell, and he was pushing through Bithynia towards Asia, when the news that Asander, his deputy in the Bosporus, had risen against him brought him to a halt.[1]

Such was the military situation with which Caesar was made acquainted after the fall of Alexandria. Nevertheless, he remained in Egypt until the beginning of June (the end of March, Jul.).[2] His motives can only be conjectured. We hear that he went on a splendid Nile cruise with Cleopatra to the southern boundary of the kingdom and that his soldiers took exception to this.[3] But it is unlikely that he sacrificed politics to love; more probably this affair contained a considerable political element.[4] The queen's love guaranteed him

[1] b. Alex. 34–41; Dio 42, 9, 2–3; 45–46; App. Mithr. 591; Strab. 12, 547.

[2] App. b.c. 2, 378 puts his stay in Egypt at nine months. Cic. Att. 11, 18, 1 (June 19, in Brundisium): de illius (sc. Caesaris) Alexandrea discessu nihil adhuc rumoris, contraque opinio valde esse impeditum; 25, 2 (July 5, 47): illum discessisse Alexandrea rumor est non firmus ortus ex Sulpici litteris; quas cuncti postea nuntii confirmarunt. Ser. Sulpicius Rufus, the great jurist, was staying on Samos at the time, according to Cic. Brut. 156. According to Cic. Att. 11, 20, 1 the freedman of Trebonius needed twenty-eight days for the journey from Seleucia (the port of Antioch) to Brundisium. Caesar will therefore have landed at one of the Syrian ports early in June (b. Alex. 66, 1; Joseph. b. Iud. 1, 194). Cf. O. E. Schmidt, Briefwechsel, 224; Holmes, Rom. Rep., 3, 509. H. Volkmann (Kleopatra, 70) makes Caesar leave Alexandria as early as April 10. This cannot be reconciled with the statements of Cicero.

[3] Suet. Caes. 52, 1; App. b.c. 2, 379. A satirical song of the soldiers at the Egyptian triumph is mentioned in Dio 43, 20, 2.

[4] We must recall that he was but imperfectly informed about the highly unpleasant developments in the Empire. According to b. Alex. 65, 1 he did not receive an accurate account of the unrest in Rome until he reached Syria. Cicero, who in October, 48, had travelled to Brundisium in the hope that the war would soon be over (RE, 7A, 1004), writes quite desperately on June 3, 47 (Att. 11, 16, 1): neque enim ulla de adventu eius opinio est neque si qui ex Asia veniunt quicquam auditum esse dicunt de pace; cuius ego spe in hanc fraudem incidi.

the possession of Egypt, a land strategically and economically invaluable to the master of Rome, better than an oath from any one
of his followers could do. For this reason he now acted contrary
to the policies of his youth and instead of making Egypt a province
recognized it as an independent kingdom ruled by Cleopatra and
her second brother-husband Ptolemy XIV, then aged eleven. The
younger sister Arsinoe was to be brought to Rome.[1] To protect
the new order he left three legions in the country under Rufio,
an undoubtedly reliable officer, but the son of a freedman. A reluc-
tance to entrust Egypt to one of his distinguished followers will
have influenced his choice. This was the one political idea which
Augustus, after the annexation of the country, later raised to the
status of a basic tenet of the principate. At the beginning of June
Caesar set out for Syria with only his veteran legion.[2] A few weeks
later Cleopatra bore him a son who received the names of Ptolemy

nihil video quod sperandum putem, nunc praesertim cum ea plaga in Asia sit accepta, in Illyrico, in
Cassiano negotio, in ipsa Alexandrea, in urbe, in Italia. ego vero etiam si rediturus ille est qui adhuc
bellum gerere dicitur, tamen ante reditum eius negotium (landing of the optimates from Africa
in Italy) confectum iri puto. On June 19 (Att. 11, 18, 1): sive enim bellum in Italia futurum est
sive classibus utetur, hic (in Brundisium) esse me minime convenit; quorum fortasse utrumque erit,
alterum certe. Atticus is to make inquiries of Antony. On August 6 (Att. 11, 24, 5) he asks
Atticus: quod scribis litteris putare Africanum negotium confici posse, vellem scriberes cur ita putares;
mihi quidem nihil in mentem venit qua re id putem fieri posse. Atticus had presumably wished to
console Cicero on the strength of some optimistic information from the Caesarians in Rome.
On August 12 Cicero received a letter from Caesar written in Alexandria (Lig. 7: ut essem
idem qui fuissem; fam. 14, 23: litterae satis liberales, et ipse opinione celerius venturus esse dicitur).
O. E. Schmidt (Briefwechsel, 227) is surely right in concluding that this is the letter with
which his freedman Philotimus arrived in Rhodes on May 28 (Att. 11, 23, 2), and conjectures
(228) that Caesar wrote it about May 20. On August 11 (fam. 14, 24) Cicero had still reported:
nos neque de Caesaris adventu neque de litteris quas Philotimus habere dicitur quicquam adhuc certi
habemus. Above all, we get from Cicero an impression of how strong the optimates had grown
in Africa during the year that had passed since Pharsalus (fam. 15, 15, 2, in August to C.
Cassius: in bellis civilibus interpositus annus. Alexandrini belli tanta mora). In view of this situation
it was not only important for Caesar to hold Egypt securely (Caes. b.c. 3, 106, 1), but also
to be clear about what forces he had at his disposal and how they could be most usefully
employed. After the nerve-racking battles in Alexandria his soldiers needed a breathing-space.
Caesar's own recreation was his cruise up the Nile. What Cleopatra will have meant to him
is well described by O. Seel (Cicero (1953), 244–248). But his political correspondence must
have been livelier than ever—we know only of the letter to Cicero—and, if I am not completely mistaken, it was at this time that he composed the bellum civile, which, replying to
the optimates in Africa, proved their guilt in the impious bloodshed; see above, p. 191, n 1.

[1] b. Alex. 33, 1–2; Suet. Caes. 35, 1; Dio 42, 44, 1–4; 43, 19, 2; 51, 15, 4; App. b.c. 378;
Porph. FgrHist, 260, F 2, 16; Strab. 17, 796; Oros. 6, 16, 2; Hieronym. chron. on 47 B.C.:
Caesar in Aegypto regnum Cleopatrae confirmat ob stupri gratiam; similarly Eutrop. 6, 22, 3; v. ill.
86, 1.

[2] b. Alex. 33, 3–5; Suet. Caes. 76, 3. According to App. b.c. 3, 318; 4, 256; 263, four legions,
were stationed in Egypt in 43 B.C. Cf. Holmes, Rom. Rep. 3, 503.

and Caesar and was mockingly referred to by the people of Alexandria as Caesarion (Caesar's offspring).[1]

The nine months of the Egyptian intermezzo present the student of Caesar's life with more than one puzzle. His foolhardiness in entering a city burning with hatred for Rome with such weak forces again threw into the balance everything that seemed to have been won by the decisive battle in Thessaly. And what a strange sight it was to see the victor of Pharsalus and dictator of the Roman people owing his rescue to contingents from Asia Minor and Syria under a Mithridates of Pergamum! But most remarkable of all remains the role of Cleopatra, this romantic novel which almost brought the unique career of the hero to a disreputable end. Much of it can be explained in political terms. Yet the actual course of the Egyptian adventure leaves no room for doubt that more attracted him to this demonic woman than the rank and glitter of the last successor dynasty.

Although the news from Rome made a return to Italy pressingly urgent, Caesar was determined to settle the political and military

[1] Plut. Caes. 49, 10; Ant. 54, 6. After the removal of the young Ptolemy (Porph. FgrHist, 260, F 2, 16; Joseph. ant. 15, 89; c. Ap. 2, 58) Cleopatra took him as her co-regent in 44 (Dio 47, 31, 5). He appears as such in the preamble to a decree of the priests of Thebes in 43 (OGIS 194, 1): Π]τολεμαίου τοῦ καὶ Κα[ί]σαρος, [θ]εοῦ Φιλοπάτορος Φιλομή[τορος]. According to a demotic tombstone, his birthday was June 23, 47; see Stähelin, RE, 11, 754; L. R. Taylor, The Divinity of the Roman Emperor (1931), 103–4; Volkmann, RE, 23, 1760. Caesar (Augustus) had him put to death in 30 (Suet. Aug. 17, 5; Plut. Ant. 82, 1; Dio 51, 15, 5). Volkmann, in Kleopatra, 71 (English translation, 75) and Gnomon 31 (1959), 178, rightly stresses that according to Suet. Caes. 52, 2 Antony declared in the Senate that Caesar had recognized the boy as his own son and that C. Matius, C. Oppius and other friends of Caesar knew this. This must have occurred in 44 during his altercations with Octavian. Suetonius adds that Oppius published a pamphlet, non esse Caesaris filium, quem Cleopatra dicat. Since there is no news of Oppius after 44 B.C., Münzer (RE, 18, 734) considers whether it may have been at this time that Oppius at once denied Antony's statement in favour of Octavian. But it may not have happened until 32 B.C. It is clear that the existence of this bastard, who is also mentioned by Cicero (Att. 14, 20, 2 on May 11, 44: de regina velim atque etiam de Caesare illo—perhaps an allusion to the announcement of Antony in the Senate), was utterly hateful to Octavian, and that all doubts about Caesar's fatherhood in the historical literature go back to him. How difficult they are to substantiate can be seen from Nicolaus of Damascus (FgrHist, 90, F 130, 68) where he alleges that Caesar's will attested that he was childless. W. Schmitthenner (Oktavian und das Testament Caesars (1952), 26) has deduced from this that the will mentioned a possible postumus (Gai. inst. 2, 130). In a Roman will only legitimate descendants were regarded as legal heirs (sui heredes, Gai. 3, 2. See Jörs-Kunkel, Röm. Privatr., 196; Schmitthenner, op. cit., 16, 2, 63). I do not understand Schmitthener's objection (15) to 'modern research'. J. P. V. D. Balsdon (Historia 7 (1958), 87) thinks that Caesar lost his power of procreation after the birth of Julia. Yet in A.D. 70 the Lingonian Julius Sabinus boasted of being a descendant of Caesar through his great-grandmother (Tac. hist. 4, 55; 67; Dio 66, 3, 1; 16, 1). At the Gallic triumph the soldiers sang: urbani servate uxores, moechum calvom adducimus (Suet. Caes. 51). On Ptolemy Caesar, see Volkmann, RE, 23, 1760. Suet. Caes. 52, 2: quem quidem nonnulli Graecorum similem quoque Caesari et forma et incessu tradiderunt. See Holmes, Rom. Rep., 3, 506.

problems of the Eastern provinces beforehand, and the fact that this
difficult business was wound up according to plan in the short time
available shows that everything had been well prepared both
politically and strategically during the festive weeks in Alexandria.
We also know that in a letter written to Cicero at this time he
recognized him as Imperator.[1] The behaviour of the communities
and princes during the Alexandrian war and the battle against
Pharnaces naturally formed the basis for his dispositions in Syria,
Cilicia, Bithynia and Asia. All those who had joined in Mithridates'
rescue operation were now rewarded with decrees giving them
freedom and immunity from taxation, frontier adjustments and
grants of land. Of this wealth of activity only documents relating
to the Jews have survived.[2] The Hasmonaean Hyrcanus II was
recognized as their high priest and prince. He was allowed to
rebuild the walls of Jerusalem and his territory was freed from
contributions and the billeting of Roman soldiers. His chief minister
Antipater (the father of Herod the Great) received Roman citizenship and unlimited tax exemption.[3] But as regarded the rest

---

[1] Cic. Lig. 7; Deiot. 38.

[2] b. Alex. 65, 4: commoratus fere in omnibus civitatibus quae maiore sunt dignitate, praemia bene
meritis et viritim et publice tribuit, de controversiis veteribus cognoscit ac statuit; reges, tyrannos,
dynastas provinciae finitimosque (the distinction between dynasts within the province and allies
outside must not be emended) qui omnes ad eum concurrerant, receptos in fidem condicionibus
impositis provinciae tuendae ac defendendae dimittit et sibi et populo Romano amicissimos. Since Hirtius
(see above, p. 251, n. 1) belonged to Caesar's consilium (Jos. ant. 14, 192), his comments on
Caesar's principles are of particular importance (65, 1): existimabat, quas in provincias regionesque
venisset, eas ita relinquere constitutas ut domesticis dissensionibus liberarentur, iura legesque acciperent,
externorum hostium metum deponerent; (78, 1) in Galatia, Bithynia, Asia: omniumque earum
provinciarum de controversiis cognoscit et statuit; iura in tetrarchas, reges, civitates distribuit. Here
Caesar drew reality to what he had described as pacem provinciarum, salutem imperii in the letter
to Metellus Scipio (b.c. 3, 57, 4: see above, p. 232, n. 1). Of course, like Pompey before him, he
kept within the framework of previous Roman policy. But the speed and accuracy of his
decisions showed that the tired routine of the optimate republic was coming to an end.

[3] Joseph. b. Iud. 1, 194–200; ant. 14, 137; 143–144; 190–195 gives a letter from Caesar to
the city of Sidon about the recognition of Hyrcanus with the decree (192: μετὰ συμβουλίου
γνώμης ἐπέκρινα= de consilii sententia decrevi); 202–206 a decision by Caesar (202: ἔστησεν=
constituit (Caes. b.c. 3, 1, 2) or statuit (b. Alex. 65, 4); cognoscit ac statuit (Cic. Att. 16, 16c, 11))
about the revenue of the dynasty, security against interference by Roman magistrates and
the possession of Joppa. Mommsen's interpretation (R.G. 5, 501, 1; English translation: The
Provinces of the Roman Empire, 2, p. 175, note 1) of the corrupt text is that Hyrcanus was
freed from the tribute imposed by Pompey (Joseph. ant. 14, 74). Cf. Otto, RE Suppl. 2, 55.
Exemption from additional demands of Roman magistrates resembles the provisions of the
plebiscitum for Greater Termessus of 68 (Dessau, ILS, 38, II, 7–18). Joseph. ant. 14, 196–198;
207–210 are confirmatory and supplementary senatorial decrees, presumably of 46 B.C.
The decree about the construction of the walls (200–201) belongs to 44, according to the
traditional date; but according to 144 and 156 permission for this was already given in
47 B.C.

Caesar everywhere acted on the principle that all money that had been raised for Pompey was to be handed over to himself. Those who had shown particular enthusiasm in Pompey's cause had to make extra payments, and finally good care was taken to see that the Hellenistic custom of welcoming a victorious ruler with heavy golden wreaths was enthusiastically observed. For Caesar publicly declared that only two things were needed to rule, soldiers and money, and armies could only be held together with money.[1] His former ally Marcus Crassus is alleged to have declared that anyone wishing to be a *princeps* in the state must be rich enough to maintain an army out of his income.[2] Since the Roman citizen force had inevitably changed into an army of professional soldiers, the *imperator* with his veterans took the political place of the patron and his clients. What some had feared and others aspired to, for decades was fully realized in the person of Caesar; the conqueror of Gaul whom the old powers refused to recognize overwhelmed all resistance and on the strength of an authority based solely on the loyalty of his soldiers was reaching for the government of the Empire.

After Syria's problems had been settled in Antioch, he held a diet for Cilicia at Tarsus.[3] As well as the inhabitants of the province he received several distinguished Pompeians, as he had done in Syria. These threw themselves at his mercy with the customary success. Gaius Cassius was the most important of those who introduced themselves on his landing in Cilicia. His brother-in-law Brutus arranged an excellent reception from the dictator for this outstanding opponent.[4] Then the march against Pharnaces continued through Cappadocia. On the Galatian frontier Deiotarus waited on him and asked to be forgiven for his mistake in joining Pompey. Caesar refused to accept this excuse, because it had been clear since 48 that as constitutionally elected consul he represented the legitimate power of the state. But when the Galatian's friends, including Brutus, interceded for him, he left him his title but reserved the right to delimit his territory later. He had to make his legion and entire cavalry available for the campaign. To these were added Calvinus' two legions which had again been brought up to strength. Caesar's own veteran legion had shrunk to less than a thousand men.[5]

[1] Dio 42, 49, 4.   [2] Plin. *n.h.* 33, 134; cf. *RE*, 13, 300.
[3] *b. Alex.* 66, 2.
[4] Cic. *fam.* 15, 15, 3; *Phil.* 2, 26, with the statement—unintelligible to us—that Cassius was already planning Caesar's assassination then. Cf. O. E. Schmidt, *Briefwechsel*, 225; 227.
[5] *b. Alex.* 67–69; Cic. *Deiot.* 13–14; 17–21; 24; Plut. *Brut.* 56, 4.

Pharnaces had started to withdraw because of the rebellion in the Crimea, and was now occupying a position near the Pontic town of Zela. Being fully informed of Caesar's position, he hoped to be able to avoid an armed encounter by diplomacy and to maintain his freedom of action in Asia Minor after the dictator's departure. Accordingly he sent envoys carrying a golden wreath with a request that Caesar should halt his advance, since he was ready to fulfil his every demand and had moreover given no assistance to Pompey. Before his army was ready to march, Caesar twice listened to this message with interest, but the third time demanded the immediate evacuation of Pontus and the restoration of all Roman property. He further declared sharply that the atrocities committed in the Roman provinces were irremediable and that, in failing to support his patron Pompey, Pharnaces was not doing Caesar a service but following his own interests.[1] Thereupon on August 1 (May 20, Jul.) he advanced to within five miles of the royal camp. On the morning of the next day he had a second camp fortified at a distance of only a mile. Arrogantly confident in the efficiency of his army Pharnaces answered this challenge with an immediate attack. But this time Caesar's veterans decided the issue. Within four hours the enemy army was annihilated, their camp captured and the king himself escaped to Sinope with a few horsemen, only to meet his end soon afterwards in his own country at the hand of the rebels.[2] Caesar sent news of his victory to his confidant Gaius Matius at Rome with the words, 'I came, I saw, I conquered', and commented sarcastically that Pompey was lucky to have been regarded as a great general for conquering such enemies.[3] While he left the booty to his soldiers, he hurried on towards the west coast of Asia Minor, everywhere regulating questions of government and sovereignty as he went. Mithridates of Pergamum received, together with the title of king, one of the Galatian principalities and a claim to what had been Pharnaces' kingdom. Amisus was declared free in

---

[1] b. Alex. 69, 2–71, 2; 70, 2: monuit, ut solebat, mitibus verbis legatos; 71, 2: cognita calliditate hominis, quod aliis temporibus natura facere consueverat tunc necessitate fecit adductus, ut celerius omnium opinione manum consereret; Dio 42, 47, 2–4.

[2] b. Alex. 72–76; Dio 42, 47, 5; Suet. Caes. 35, 2; App. b.c. 2, 381–383; Dio 42, 48, 2. The date is shown by Fasti Amit., Inscr. It., 13, 2, 190–1, on August 2. Cf. Holmes, Rom. Rep., 3, 511 ff.

[3] Plut. Caes. 50, 3; the name of Matius was restored by C. Cichorius (R. Stud. (1922), 248). During the Pontic triumph the victory was characterized by the felicitously coined phrase 'veni, vidi, vici'; see Suet. Caes. 37, 2; App. b.c. 2, 384; Suet. Caes. 35, 2.

compensation for the sufferings which it had undergone.[1] The case of Deiotarus was considered at Nicaea and, thanks to a vigorous speech from Marcus Brutus, he secured a favourable verdict. Deiotarus was obliged to give up Armenia Minor to Ariobarzanes of Cappadocia, but kept his remaining territory. In general the importance of Brutus' position with Caesar is illustrated by a letter of the time, in which he restored Cicero's confidence about his fate. Similarly it will have assisted Caesar's policy of reconciliation when on his journey home he visited Sulpicius Rufus in Samos and Marcus Marcellus living in voluntary exile at Mytilene.[2]

Caesar himself travelled via Athens to Patrae, and on September 24 landed at Tarentum.[3] On the road to Brundisium he met Cicero. The latter had dreaded this moment, but Caesar's charm and friendliness spared him all humiliation. The dictator immediately dismounted from his carriage, and for a fair distance conversed alone with the famous consular. At the beginning of October he arrived in Rome.[4]

The great task facing him now was the war in Africa. His stay in Italy was intended only to prepare him for this. Since even after the fall of Alexandria Caesar was long in arriving, the unrest at Rome had broken out again with renewed violence. Dolabella and Trebellius were involved in bloody street-fighting without intervention from Antony, the *magister equitum*. Only when Dolabella brought in proposals for the cancellation of debts and rents and the Senate again armed Antony with the *senatus consultum ultimum* did he bring in strong troop detachments. These stormed the Forum, which had been barricaded by Dolabella, in an operation costing the lives of 800 Roman citizens; the tablets on which the

[1] *b. Alex.* 77, 2–78, 3; Dio 42, 48, 3–4. In 67 B.C. the legate of Lucullus, C. Valerius Triarius, had suffered a disastrous defeat near Zela (*b. Alex.* 72, 2). In Dio's account (48, 2) Caesar did not destroy the victory memorial of Mithridates because it was dedicated to the gods of war, but eclipsed it by his own far larger monument; see Strab. 12, 547; 13, 625; App. *Mithr.* 596.

[2] In the proceedings against Deiotarus the other Galatian tetrarchs appeared as plaintiffs and stated that he had unjustly taken possession of their principalities as well as securing recognition from the Senate as King of Armenia Minor (*b. Alex.* 67, 1; 78, 3; Cic. *div.* 1, 27; 2, 79; Strab. 12, 568). Since a client relationship with Deiotarus existed from earlier times (*b. Alex.* 68, 1), Caesar was angry with him (Cic. *Phil.* 2, 94); however, Brutus was able to win him over. Caesar afterwards said of Brutus: 'A great deal depends on *what* he wants, but whatever he wants, he wants very much.' See Cic. *Att.* 14, 1, 2; *Brut.* 11; 21; 156; 250; 330; *Deiot.* 14; Plut. *Brut.* 6, 7; Sen. *dial.* 12, 9, 4–6; Dio 42, 48, 3–4. In Asia he showed favour to Pergamum (*IGRR*, 4, 304; 306). In Bithynia he gave permission to the quaestorian T. Antistius to return to Rome (Cic. *fam.* 13, 29, 4).

[3] Cic. *Att.* 11, 20, 2; 21, 2; Plut. *Cic.* 39, 4. The date is calculated by O. E. Schmidt, *Briefwechsel*, 226. [4] Plut. *Cic.* 39, 4–5; cf. *RE*, 7A, 1007–8.

law was inscribed were smashed, and a number of ringleaders thrown from the Tarpeian rock.[1]

Antony thereby forfeited all political credit; already regarded as a necessary evil in respectable circles, he now also threw away the favour of the rabble. The dictator would surely have been prepared to overlook his way of life, offensively dissolute even by Roman standards though it was, but he could not ignore the fact that he had been politically compromised by his *magister equitum*. His former favourite was punished by being dropped for two years.[2] On the other hand, he continued to have confidence in Dolabella and even to some extent condoned his behaviour by imposing on house-owners a rent reduction for the current year of up to 500 denarii in Rome and 125 in Italy. But he again decisively rejected a further cancellation of debts and stood by his dictatorial edict of 49,[3] very cleverly tying this up with his own financial operations. Since he had spent his own fortune in the service of the state, he said, he was dependent on loans, and so would himself be one of the main beneficiaries of a cancellation of debts. For at the time he was beginning with good success to draw on Italy for the financing of the war, and in particular for the impending provision for his veterans. Following the example set in the provinces, he held collections for golden wreaths and statues in the municipalities, and written instructions were sent out to communities and individuals to support him with loans. We know that in Rome even the size of the loans was prescribed, as this caused merriment among the soldiers at his triumph. The loans were never repaid.[4] The property of his opponents who had fallen, died or not been pardoned was publicly auctioned. At the sale Antony bought the palace of Pompey together with all its contents including slaves, but to his great surprise was forced by Caesar to pay the full price which he had bid, just like anybody else. Only Servilia, Caesar's mistress of long standing, is said to have secured some more bargains on this occasion.[5]

This time he was faced with the greatest difficulty in forming an army. The veterans who had been mustered in Campania for the crossing to Africa wanted at last to see an end to their service and,

[1] Dio 42, 30, 3–33, 1; Liv. *per.* 113.

[2] Cic. *Phil.* 2, 71; Plut. *Ant.* 10, 2; *Caes.* 51, 3.

[3] Dio 42, 33, 2–3; 51, 1–2; Suet. *Caes.* 38, 2; Cic. *fam.* 9, 18, 4; *off.* 2, 84.

[4] Dio 42, 50, 2–5; Nep. *Att.* 7, 3; *b. Alex.* 64, 2; Suet. *Caes.* 51: *aurum in Gallia effutuisti, hic sumpsisti mutuum.*

[5] Cic. *Phil.* 2, 64–69; 71–73; 13, 10–11; Plut. *Ant.* 10, 3; Dio 45, 28, 3–4; 48, 38, 2; Suet. *Caes.* 50, 2; Macr. *Sat.* 2, 2, 5.

above all, to have their often-promised rewards. Under the leadership of some tribunes and centurions, they began to plunder the places where they were billeted and refused to leave for Sicily. Antony could do nothing, and Publius Sulla was greeted with a shower of stones. Caesar now sent them Gaius Sallustius Crispus, the newly elected praetor and talented political pamphleteer who was to become the great historian, with a promise of a further 1,000 denarii for each man. But he too had to flee, two other senators were put to death, and the entire legion set off for Rome.[1] For the immediate protection of the city Caesar had available the security forces of Antony; but when the veterans reached the *Campus Martius*, he went out in order to answer their demands in person. The appearance of their glorious *imperator* broke the spirit of the mutineers. They pretended that they had only come to beg for their discharge, although they hoped that the rest would follow naturally from Caesar's embarrassing situation. However, he abruptly shattered all their hopes. As soon as he addressed them as 'Quirites' (citizens) instead of 'comrades' their defiance ebbed away. But he went on to pronounce their discharge and declared that he would fulfil the promises which he had made, when he returned from his campaign to triumph with other soldiers. At a blow their roles were reversed. It was now Caesar's turn to yield to the soldiers' persistent entreaties and to agree to take them with him. He then explained his plans for their settlement which fitted in with his earlier agrarian legislation. Unlike Sulla, who had dispossessed entire communities in order to found closed military colonies, every veteran was to receive his personally allocated estate either out of Caesar's own or from the public domains. Although he did not punish the ringleaders, their names were secretly noted for use on lost hopes as occasion arose. Those who survived eventually forfeited a third of their bounty and land settlement.[2] Comparing this case with the earlier mutiny in 49, one can see that on both occasions Caesar acted according to the same psychological and disciplinary principles. He won over the majority and knew how to deal with the instigators.

Although the greater part of the year was already over, he had the missing magistrates elected immediately after his arrival. He rewarded Fufius Calenus and Vatinius with the consulship of 47

---

[1] Cic. *Att.* 11, 20, 2; 21, 2; 22, 2 (August, 47); *b. Afr.* 19, 3; 28, 2; 54; App. *b.c.* 2, 386–387; Dio 42, 52, 1–2.

[2] App. *b.c.* 2, 388–396; Dio 42, 52, 1–55, 3; Plut. *Caes.* 51, 2; Suet. *Caes.* 38, 1; 70; Polyaen. 8, 23, 15. Caesar was merciless towards mutineers; see Suet. *Caes.* 67, 1: *desertorum ac seditiosorum et inquisitor et punitor acerrimus conivebat in ceteris* = Dio 42, 55, 3; *b. Afr.* 28, 2; 46, 4; 54.

and others of his senatorial followers with the remaining offices as well as with priesthoods. He took the next consulship for himself, choosing as his colleague Marcus Lepidus, whom he henceforth liked to push into the limelight as his most distinguished helper: already on his return from Spain as propraetor he had allowed him to triumph, although he had achieved nothing. For 46 he designated ten praetors for election instead of the usual eight, and he also increased the number of priesthoods. The Senate he filled up with followers of lower rank.[1] Apart from Roman knights, some of whom stemmed from Spain and Gaul, these included deserving centurions and people of still humbler origin. Thus he created reliable instruments of government for himself. Yet he resigned the dictatorship, and the question remained open whether the traditional free constitution would not come into force again later. For the conduct of the African war he possessed special authority. Even the triumph over Juba, as we have seen, had already been decreed.[2]

Early in December (middle of September, Jul.) Caesar was again free to leave Rome; he arrived in Lilybaeum on the 17th, and set sail on the 25th with six legions, five of which were composed of recruits, and 2,000 cavalry. The warships were manned by the seven cohorts which Vatinius had formed from convalescent veterans. The other four veteran legions from Campania had not yet arrived.[3] But on this occasion, as when he crossed to Epirus, Caesar wished to take the enemy by surprise. The result of the campaign was by no means a foregone conclusion. Caesar could not attack the enemy with superior forces because he needed a large part of his troops to secure the Empire. Failure in Africa would have had far-reaching consequences everywhere. So once again he had to apply all his talents, but, as his manner was, he also trusted in the luck which had not failed him yet. The officer to whom we owe the account of this war has preserved two characteristic instances of this: at Lilybaeum Caesar had his tent pitched at the farthest extremity of the shore in order to make clear to every soldier his unimpaired will to attack, and as he sailed off he was unable to give his captains any harbour on the African coast as their destination because he did not know himself where a landing would be possible.[4]

---

[1] Dio 42, 51, 3–5; 55, 4; 43, 1–3; b. Afr. 28, 2: Titii, Hispani adulescentes, tribuni legionis V, quorum patrem Caesar in senatum legerat.

[2] Plut. Caes. 51, 1. On the dictatorship see U. Wilcken, Zur Entwicklung der röm. Diktatur, Abh. Berlin (1940, 1), 16–19; Broughton, MRR, 2, 248, n. 1; see above, p. 254, n. 1.

[3] b. Afr. 1, 1 and 5; 2, 1 and 3; 10, 1; 34, 4; 53; 77, 3. Cf. Holmes, Rom. Rep. 3, 534.

[4] b. Afr. 1, 1; 3, 4–5; Plut. Caes. 52, 2.

Since the main enemy force was stationed near Utica, he chose a place for landing in the south of the province. When he put in at Hadrumetum on December 28, he had only 3,000 infantry and 150 cavalry with him, as his other ships had been carried away to the north.[1] This was a bad start, made worse in the eyes of the soldiers by the fact that Caesar stumbled as he disembarked. However, he immediately laid their superstitious fear by grasping the earth with his hands and joyfully calling out: 'I hold you, Africa!' It was this same consideration for his soldiers' way of thinking that made him take a disreputable member of the Cornelian house, a certain Scipio Salvitto, on the campaign because harm had been prophesied from the circumstance that the enemy's supreme commander was called Scipio.[2] Since Hadrumetum was strongly occupied and Gaius Considius, the legate in charge, showed himself proof against the powers of persuasion of Caesar's follower, Lucius Munatius Plancus, Caesar marched farther south, won the free city of Leptis Minor and finally took up a position north of the town on the favourably situated coastal plateau of Ruspina, where he could wait for his remaining troops in safety. On the morning of January 4, 46, the rest of the first convoy landed, and on the same day he started on a requisitioning expedition with thirty cohorts, 400 cavalry and 150 archers, during which he quite unexpectedly came upon a strong force of Labienus' men, consisting of cavalry and light-armed troops. After he had fought his way back in a heavy engagement, Petreius appeared with a second force, and again put him in a critical position. Things went so badly that with his own hands he caught by the shoulder, and turned round, a fleeing standard-bearer, saying, 'That is where the enemy are!' But the genius which never let him down found a way out in a thrust through the enemy line towards a chain of hills, from where he managed to get back to camp under cover of darkness.[3]

[1] b. Afr. 3, 1. Maps of the theatre of war are to be found in Holmes, Rom. Rep., 3, 237; Kromayer-Veith, Schlachtenatlas, Röm. Abt., map 22.

[2] Suet. Caes. 59; Dio 42, 58; Plut. Caes. 52, 4–5; Plin. n.h. 7, 54. On the other hand Caesar set out for Africa without worrying about the warning of his haruspices, which Cicero quotes (divin. 2, 52) among the examples proving that no value should be set on their art of soothsaying.

[3] b. Afr. 3–18; App. b.c. 2, 398–400 ascribes Caesar's rescue to his fortuna; similarly Dio (43, 2, 3–4). Plutarch (Caes. 52, 6–9) mentions that Asinius Pollio was with Caesar, which suggests that this version is from his history. The enthusiastically Caesarian author of the bellum Africanum gives a vivid account (10, 3–4) of the effect Caesar's confidence had on his frightened soldiers (mainly recruits): neque quicquam solatii in praesentia neque auxilii in suorum consilio animum advertebant, nisi in ipsius imperatoris vultu vigore mirabilique hilaritate; animum enim altum et erectum prae se gerebat. huic adquiescebant homines et in eius scientia et consilio omnia sibi proclivia omnes fore sperabant. See Val. Max. 3, 2, 19.

S

But when Scipio united the main enemy forces facing him, Caesar for the time being stayed on the defensive, which involved his troops in further harsh deprivations, as he was dependent on supplies brought by sea.[1] Nor were the political consequences to be expected in the Empire long in coming. Acting on the bad news, Caecilius Bassus, a Roman knight resident in Tyre, who had fought on Pompey's side, instigated a mutiny among the legions of Syria. Caesar's governor, Sextus Caesar, was among its victims, and Bassus took over the government in his place.[2] However, fortunately the policy which Caesar had followed towards Bocchus of Mauretania now paid dividends. His invasion of Numidia and seizure of important localities forced king Juba to part company with Scipio. The heart and soul of this enterprise was the Roman adventurer Publius Sittius, a former Catilinarian who had become a Mauretanian military captain.[3]

Caesar as usual mounted a many-sided propaganda campaign to undermine the enemy's morale. The folly of preferring to be the subjects of the barbarian Juba rather than to live in peace with their fellow citizens was continually impressed on the Romans on the other side. Scipio was portrayed as a lieutenant of Juba without a will of his own or even the courage to wear his purple *imperator*'s cloak in the king's presence.[4] Caesar promised to everyone that came over to him the preservation of his fortune, freedom and even equal treatment with his own soldiers in respect of bounties.[5] In the province itself he let it be spread about that he had come to liberate them from a reign of terror, while he sent word to Italy that no effort must be spared to send reinforcements, as Africa was being completely ruined by his opponents: if help did not arrive quickly, there would soon not be a single roof left in the whole of the territory.[6] In reality, of course, it was only a matter of demolitions being carried out to make Caesar's stay in the country as difficult as possible.[7] To the Numidians and their southern neighbours, the Gaetuli, who had provided the enemy with numerous cavalry, he presented himself as the nephew of their former benefactor Gaius Marius. These efforts had a success that increased noticeably with

---

[1] b. Afr. 19–36.

[2] Liv. per. 114; Dio 47, 26, 3–27, 1; App. b.c. 3, 315; Joseph. b. Iud. 1, 216; ant. 14, 268; Cic. fam. 12, 18, 1; Deiot. 23; 25. Cf. Broughton, MRR, 2, 297 on Q. Cornificius. Strab. 16, 753. Caecilius Bassus maintained his position until 43 B.C. (Münzer, RE, 3, 1199).

[3] Dio 41, 42, 7; 43, 3, 1–5; b. Afr. 25, 2–5; 36, 4; Sall. Cat. 21, 3; App. b.c. 4, 231–232.

[4] b. Afr. 8, 5; 57, 2–6.   [5] Dio 43, 5, 1–2.

[6] b. Afr. 26.   [7] b. Afr. 20, 4; 24, 3–4; 26, 5–6.

the improvement in his military position. Eventually legionaries and natives came over to him in their thousands, and various city states also joined his side.[1] Scipio's attempt at counter-propaganda failed miserably, because, as a source sarcastically assures us, he made no material promises and spoke only of the liberation of Senate and People.[2]

After a three weeks' lull in operations two veteran legions, 800 Celtic cavalry and 1,000 archers and slingers at last arrived; at the same time Sallust seized the well-stocked granaries of the enemy on the island of Cercina in the gulf of the Lesser Syrtis, and on January 25 Caesar again took the initiative by suddenly leaving the position on the Ruspina plateau and offering battle to Scipio at Uzita farther to the south. However, as the latter did not lay himself open to attack, after a few skirmishes Caesar had to resume positional warfare.[3] Scipio was reinforced by Juba who returned with three legions, thirty elephants and many horsemen and light-armed troops, Caesar by his last two legions.[4] When the siege of Uzita also proved unsuccessful, in the middle of March difficulty in obtaining provisions forced Caesar to shift the scene of operations farther to the

---

[1] b. Afr. 31, 2–6; 32, 3–4; 33, 1; 35, 2–6; 36, 2; 43; 51, 3; 52, 5; 56, 3; Dio 43, 4, 2.

[2] Dio 43, 5, 3–4; b. Afr. 44, 3 (addressing captured Caesarians): *non vestra, inquit, sponte vos certo scio, sed illius scelerati vestri imperatoris impulsu et imperio coactos civis et optimum quemque nefarie consectari. quos quoniam fortuna in nostram detulit potestatem, si id quod facere debetis, rem publicam cum optimo quoque defendetis, certum est vobis vitam et pecuniam donare. quapropter quid sentiatis proloquimini.* The prisoners came from two ships of the second convoy which were driven off course by a storm and captured by the enemy fleet. A centurion of the fourteenth legion (in the Gallic army since 57 B.C.), answering in their name, thanked Scipio for assuring them their lives according to the laws of war, but then continued (45, 3): *egone contra Caesarem imperatorem meum, apud quem ordinem duxi eiusque exercitum, pro cuius dignitate victoriaque amplius tricies armis depugnavi, adversus armatusque consistam?* That Scipio might recognize the kind of troops with which he had to deal, he asked permission for himself and ten comrades to fight against a whole cohort: *tunc ex virtute nostra intelleges, quid ex tuis copiis sperare debeas.* Scipio flew into a rage and had all the veterans put to death; the recruits he divided among his legions.

[3] b. Afr. 8, 3; 34, 1–3; 37–47; Dio 43, 4–5.

[4] b. Afr. 48, 1–2; 53; Dio 43, 4, 6; App. b.c. 2, 401. The report on the depressed mood in Caesar's camp because of Juba's approach (b. Afr. 48, 3) is supplemented by Suet. Caes. 66: Caesar is said to have announced in a *contio* that the king was sure to arrive soon with ten legions, 30,000 cavalry, 100,000 light-armed troops and 300 elephants, *proinde desinant quidam quaerere ultra aut opinari mihique, qui compertum habeo, credant; aut quidem vetustissima nave impositus quocumque vento in quascumque terras iubebo avehi.* The author of the b. Afr. also relates (54) how two military tribunes and two centurions were carried off to a ship (cf. 46, 4). Caesar, who was dependent on supplies from Sicily, found himself in just as dangerous a position as two years before at Dyrrhachium. For in addition to their numerical superiority, the enemy also possessed energetic and experienced commanders in Labienus, Afranius and Petreius. In Rome the (false) rumour spread that Caesar's legate L. Statius Murcus (Dessau, ILS, 885) had been drowned while crossing and Asinius Pollio had been taken prisoner (Cic. Att. 12, 2, 1), and in Asia Minor it was being said that Cn. Domitius Calvinus (b. Afr. 86, 3; 93, 1) had also gone down in a shipwreck (Cic. Deiot. 25).

south. This did not produce a change in the general situation. For the enemy would not agree to a decisive battle while making effective use of their superiority in cavalry and light troops.[1] This state of uncertainty was highly undesirable for Caesar, not least for political reasons, and on April 4 he put an end to it by a bold decision to march to the strongly held coastal town of Thapsus, which he had already been blockading for some time by sea.[2] He thus entered an isthmus formed by the sea and an inland lake, the approaches to which could easily be blocked by the enemy—an operation which could very probably be expected to develop into a pitched battle. This daring enterprise was completely successful. While Juba and Afranius barred the southern passage, on the morning of April 6 (February 7, Jul.) Scipio began to blockade the northern end. Caesar immediately gave orders to march out to meet him, and before they were fully deployed his veterans forced him to begin the attack. They saw panic break out among the enemy, and the officers implored Caesar to give the order to advance. He refused and shouted that he did not want the right wing to press on. But then the signal to attack demanded by the soldiers rang out despite the opposition of the centurions. Caesar now gave the battle-cry *Felicitas*, and galloped forward. The enemy soon turned tail and their camp was captured. The survivors withdrew towards the two southern camps, but on arrival found these were already in Caesar's hands. They now wished to surrender, but Caesar's veterans would grant no quarter and altogether over 10,000 of the enemy died. How the political meaning of the civil war was reflected in the minds of the soldiers is illustrated by the fact that they suddenly went on to turn their fury against their own officers of senatorial and equestrian rank as the authors of the war. Nor were their proletarian instincts at fault in this; for this civil war, just as much as its predecessor, was solely a concern of the ruling classes. In fact, the chief blame rested with Caesar, whom no one dared to attack.[3]

Another campaign had been decided by Caesar's daring. Leaving behind five legions to eliminate the enemy garrisons still holding out

---

[1] *b. Afr.* 49–78; Dio 43, 6.

[2] *b. Afr.* 79, 1. Prior to this a convoy had arrived with 4,000 legionaries (previously on leave or sick), 400 cavalry and 1,000 slingers and archers (77, 3).

[3] *b. Afr.* 80–85; Dio 43, 7–9, 1; Plut. *Caes.* 53—with the somewhat doubtful variant that Caesar had to retire to a tower during the battle because of an epileptic fit (s. 6). Plut. (*Caes.* 17, 2) reports another such attack at Corduba in 49 and (60, 7) in Rome in 44 B.C. This last attack was intended to serve as an excuse, and so the excesses of the soldiers may perhaps also have been explained in this way. See *b. Afr.* 85, 9: *itaque ibi omnes Scipionis milites cum fidem*

in the south, he himself led the rest of the army to Utica.[1] The city's defences were in excellent shape, plenty of supplies were available and Cato, its commander, wished to continue the fight, particularly as renewed possibilities of resistance were opening up in Spain. However, the impression left by the defeat was too overwhelming and he had to be content with helping those to escape who did not intend to surrender. He himself committed suicide on the morning of the day when the victor appeared before Utica. There can be no doubt that Caesar would have been very pleased to pardon him, but his great opponent set the seal on his republican principles by his death. 'I do not wish to be indebted to the tyrant for his illegal actions: for he is acting against the laws when he pardons men over whom he has no sovereignty as if he were their master.' At the time Caesar may have underestimated the political importance of the spiritual legacy of this martyr of Roman civic freedom.[2]

Other leaders of the opposition met a less dignified end. Scipio perished on the flight to Spain in a sea-battle against the ships of Sittius. Faustus Sulla and Afranius also fell into Sittius' hands on the march to Spain, and were soon put to death on Caesar's instructions. Petreius fled with Juba to the latter's capital city of Zama. When they were not admitted, Petreius cut down Juba in a duel, and a slave then rendered him the same service. Gaius Considius was killed in flight by the Gaetuli. On the other hand, Labienus, Attius Varus and the two sons of Pompey, Gnaeus and Sextus, successfully reached Spain.[3]

For the rest, even now the lives of most of those who threw themselves on Caesar's mercy were spared.[4] Therefore, it occasioned

---

Caesaris implorarent, inspectante ipso Caesare et a militibus deprecante, eis uti parcerent, ad unum sunt interfecti. Suet. Caes. 45, 1 reports two attacks during battles. 10,000 dead in b. Afr. 86, 1; 50,000 in Plut. Caes. 53, 4. The date is in Fasti Praen., Inscr. It., 13, 2, 126–7, on April 6; Ovid fast. 4, 379–383.

[1] b. Afr. 86, 3.

[2] b. Afr. 87–88; Dio 43, 10–11; Plut. Cat. Min. 58, 13–72, 3 (Cato's saying is in 66, 2); Caes. 54, 1–2; Cic. Att. 12, 4, 2 (June 13, 46): Cato is to be praised quod ea quae nunc sunt et futura viderit et ne fierent contenderit et facta ne videret vitam reliquerit. It is remarkable that the author of the b. Afr. also mentions Cato only with respect: 22, 1–23, 1; 88, 5: quem Uticenses quamquam oderant partium gratia, tamen propter eius singularem integritatem et quod dissimillimus reliquorum ducum fuerat . . . sepultura adficiunt. See also App. b.c. 2, 406–412.

[3] b. Afr. 94–96; Dio 43, 12, 2; 29, 2; 30, 4; App. b.c. 2, 417. On Scipio's suicide, Liv. per. 114; Val. Max. 3, 2, 13.

[4] b. Afr. 89 mentions twelve cases by name and adds (s. 5): pro natura sua et pro instituto, later ex sua consuetudine; 86, 2: Caesar himself suam lenitatem et clementiam commemoravit; 88, 6: Caesaris clementia; 92, 4: de eius lenitate clementiaque. Only those who had once been pardoned and then joined the enemy again could not hope for pardon (64, 1: quem ob periuri perfidiam, Caesar iussit necari); Suet. Caes. 75, 3; Dio 43, 12, 2. Here, in 43, 13, 2 and Plin. n.h. 7, 94

all the more surprise when he suddenly put to death Lucius Caesar, a member of his own *gens*, whose freedom he had granted while reserving the right to conduct further investigations. He was alleged to have committed great atrocities against the dictator's slaves and freedmen and even to have destroyed animals which had been collected for the funeral games planned in honour of Julia.[1] In Utica Caesar thanked the citizens for standing loyally by his side despite enemy occupation. The city was indebted to him for the services which he had rendered it, apparently in the year 59. He also granted their lives to the numerous Roman citizens settled there, although they had declared against him. However, he imposed a fine of 50 million denarii on their committee of 300 members who had taken over the financing of the enemy war-effort: this was to be paid to the Roman people in six instalments within three years.[2]

it is reported that he had the captured correspondence of Metellus Scipio burned unread (as Pompey had once done with that of Sertorius, Plut. *Pomp.* 20, 8), and further (13, 3) that besides the many whom he pardoned at their own request, as after Pharsalus (Dio 41, 62, 2; Suet. *Caes.* 75, 2) he again allowed each of his comrades and *contubernales* to secure the release of one man—clearly this refers to those who could not hope for clemency.

[1] *b. Afr.* 89, 4–5 only mentions the amnesty; Dio 42, 12, 3 gives greater detail: that Caesar had intended to bring him to trial for his persistently hostile attitude, but had then postponed this so as not to have to pronounce a death sentence himself, and in the end had had him put to death secretly. According to Suet. *Caes.* 75, 3 this occurred without Caesar's permission, but here we have the atrocities mentioned above, which are clearly intended to excuse the murder. The events after the battle (*b. Afr.* 85, 7–9) make it seem possible that it happened against Caesar's will. For his father L. Caesar had been Caesar's legate since 52 B.C., and in 48 B.C. was temporarily appointed *praefectus urbi* by his nephew Mark Antony, the *magister equitum* (Dio 42, 30, 1–2). After the dictator's murder he is said to have protested against the *funus publicum* (Lact. *inst. div.* 1, 15, 30). Cf. Münzer, *RE*, 10, 474. Cicero learned about this at the end of May (*fam.* 9, 7, 1 to Varro). He had not dared to leave Rome during the war in order not to arouse the suspicion of the Caesarians (*Att.* 12, 2, 2; *fam.* 9, 3, 1), but had remained with the depressing feeling that an optimate victory would not bring any good either (*fam.* 5, 21, 3, to his former quaestor Mescinius): *quamquam multum intersit inter eorum causas qui dimicant, tamen inter victorias non multum interfuturum putem.* After the victory at Thapsus he wrote to Varro (*fam.* 9, 2, 2): *qui enim victoria se efferunt, quasi victos nos intuentur, qui autem victos nostros* (the optimates) *moleste ferunt, nos dolent vivere.* Thus the death of his acquaintance L. Caesar gave him a shock and he joked bitterly (*fam.* 9, 7, 2): *itaque non desino apud istos, qui nunc dominantur, cenitare* (according to *Att.* 12, 2, 2, above all Hirtius and Balbus). *quid faciam? tempori serviendum est;* yet in reality (he adds) it was no laughing matter. When Cicero, who in 48 had been together with Varro at Dyrrhachium (*divin.*2, 114; *fam.* 9, 6, 3), resumed his ties with him from Rome (*fam.* 9, 1), Varro was living quietly on one of his estates, absorbed in his literary work. As a former Pompeian legate, who had surrendered in Spain in 49 (Caes. *b.c.* 2, 20, 8) and then again made for the east, he certainly had more to answer for than Cicero, and thus Antony had already helped himself to one of his estates. However, Caesar ordered him by letter from Alexandria to hand it back (Cic. *Phil.* 2, 103–104). H. Dahlmann, *RE Suppl.* 6, 1187; 1234, assumes that Varro dedicated his *antiquitates rerum divinarum* to Caesar at this time (Lact. *inst.* 1, 6, 7); of course this need not have occurred as early as 47. On the *logistoricus Pius aut de pace*, see above, p. 231, n. 7.

[2] *b. Afr.* 87, 3; 88, 5; 90; Plut. *Cat. Min.* 58, 1.

Then he went on to Zama, where he had the royal estate and the property of those Roman citizens 'who had carried arms against the Roman people' auctioned. Those responsible for the revolt from the king were rewarded, the royal revenues distributed among new lessees and as much of the kingdom as did not go to the kings of Mauretania and Sittius was placed under the proconsul Gaius Sallustius Crispus as the province of New Africa. However, it must be admitted that as an administrator the talented propagandist did not live up to the high moral standards that one might have expected from his reformist political pamphlets. He plundered the province to such an extent that Caesar later called him to account on the strength of complaints which he had received. The case ended with an acquittal, but it was whispered that this had cost 300,000 denarii.[1]

Meanwhile the last resistance had also been broken in the old province, and Caesar fixed the penalties here as well: the fortunes of Romans who had served under Juba and Petreius as centurions were confiscated, while individual communities and their corporations of Roman citizens were to make contributions in money and kind. Leptis Magna in Tripolitania was to pay a yearly tribute of 220,000 gallons of oil.[2] Furthermore, in order to avoid future difficulties he now removed from his army the troublesome elements among the veterans and settled them in citizen colonies in the coastal towns of Clupea and Curubis.[3] On June 13 he sailed with his fleet to Sardinia, 'the only one of his properties which he has not yet visited', as Cicero wrote in bitter jest to Varro. When he added that however bad it was, Caesar did not turn up his nose at it, he was proved right: for here, too, he imposed a fine of $2\frac{1}{2}$ million denarii on the community of Sulci for supporting the enemy and raised the annual tax on the produce of its soil from a tenth to an eighth. On June 27 he again put out to sea, but because of contrary winds did not reach Rome until July 25 (May 26, Jul.).[4]

---

[1] b. Afr. 97, 1; Dio 43, 9, 2–4; App. b.c. 2, 415; Ps.-Cic. in Sall. 19; Suet. gramm. 15; Lact. inst. 2, 12, 12; Symm. ep. 5, 68, 2; Macr. Sat. 3, 13, 9: Sallustius gravissimus alienae luxuriae obiurgator et censor.

[2] b. Afr. 97, 2–4. [3] Dio 43, 14, 1; Dessau, ILS, 1945; 5320.

[4] b. Afr. 98; Cic. fam. 9, 6, 1; 7, 2; O. E. Schmidt, Briefwechsel, 234.

CHAPTER SIX

VICTORY AND CATASTROPHE

AFTER more than three years of stubborn and varied conflict the Optimate oligarchy had been overthrown in the field, and it was now open to the victor to make a political settlement at his own pleasure.

A lesser man than Caesar might well have been dismayed by the number of problems piling up before him. Italy and all the provinces had been the theatres of civil war. Many men were dead. The survivors had suffered grievously. Ruinous taxes and contributions in kind had been extorted from them; their property had been looted and destroyed. The years 48 and 47 had seen the forcible suppression in Rome and Italy of agitation aiming at social revolution. The victorious soldiery was clamouring for its reward. Caesar had kept reiterating that he would not follow Sulla's example. Yet the damage was far too great to be repaired without further sacrifice. For the prevailing disintegration was not a new phenomenon, to be attributed to the war alone; the war was itself a result of the failure of the Republic and its ruling oligarchy for decades past to cope with the social and political problems of the empire which they had conquered. Augustus later enjoyed over forty-five years of power to confer on the Mediterranean world the blessings of the *pax Romana*. Caesar's assassins, on the other hand, left him only two years, just long enough to give an indication of his plans. The extent of his achievements in so short a time is all the more astounding. For he combined extraordinary speed in decision and action with inexhaustible energy.[1] Two years earlier, in a letter

---

[1] These talents do not only characterize his military activity. His short stay in Rome at the end of 49 B.C. had already borne testimony to them, and then the many decisions in Syria, Asia Minor and Africa, during the few weeks which he allowed himself for them. On the difficulties, see Cicero's letter to Ser. Sulpicius Rufus in September, 46 (*fam.* 4, 4, 2): *quia tanta perturbatio et confusio est rerum, ita perculsa et prostrata foedissimo bello iacent omnia . . .* Also *fam.* 9, 17, 3; see below, p. 283. The speed with which he conducted operations is shown in Cic. *Att.* 7, 22, 1 (February, 49): *o celeritatem incredibilem!*; 8, 9, 4 (February, 49): *hoc τέρας horribili vigilantia, celeritate, diligentia est;* 8, 14, 1 (March, 49): *eo modo autem ambulat Caesar et iis diariis* (food rations) *militum celeritatem incitat, ut timeam, ne citius ad Brundisium quam opus sit acceserit;* 9, 18, 2 (March, 49): *multum vigilat, audet; fam.* 15, 15, 2 (August, 47): Cicero surmised after Pharsalus *ut illo quasi quodam fatali proelio facto et victores communi saluti consuli vellent et victi suae; utrumque autem positum esse arbitrabar in celeritate victoris;* 8, 15, 1 (Caelius to Cicero,

to Metellus Scipio, he had listed his political aims as tranquillity for Italy, peace for the provinces and security for the Empire. As has already been pointed out,[1] this remark—incidental though it is—is the only approximation to a political programme in Caesar's extant writings. In its brevity and conservative style it is typically Roman. Yet it is significant also because of the very fact that Rome herself is not mentioned. This shows that Caesar was unlike other Roman statesmen in that his political activity was not bounded by the city state, but by the Empire: it embraced the length and breadth of Italy and the provinces. For over eleven of the last twelve years he had been away from Rome, and this will have helped him considerably in forming these views.[2] In Gaul, from 58, his power had been absolute: he had made his veterans the sure instrument of his wishes and had formed a staff of assistants from suitable followers. Gaius Vibius Pansa, Aulus Hirtius, Lucius Cornelius Balbus, Gaius Oppius, Gaius Matius, Marcus Curtius Postumus—these were virtually his cabinet ministers, handling and settling all political

---

March, 49): *ecquem autem Caesare nostro acriorem in rebus gerendis, eodem in victoria temperatiorem aut legisti aut audisti?*; *Att.* 16, 10, 1 (November, 44) of Antony: *aiunt enim eum Caesarina uti celeritate.* For his intellectual vigour, see Hirtius *b.G.* 8, *praef.* 6 (of Caesar's *commentarii*): *ceteri enim quam bene atque emendate, nos etiam quam facile atque celeriter eos perfecerit scimus;* Vell. 2, 41, 2: *forma omnium civium excellentissimus, vigore animi acerrimus . . . celeritate bellandi, patientia periculorum Magno illi Alexandro sed sobrio neque iracundo simillimus;* 2, 51, 1 (on the crossing to Epirus): *sua et celeritate et fortuna C. Caesar usus;* Plin. *n.h.* 7, 91: *animi vigore praestantissimum arbitror genitum Caesarem dictatorem nec virtutem constantiamque nunc commemoro nec sublimitatem omnium capacem quae caelo continentur, sed proprium vigorem celeritatemque quodam igne volucrem. scribere aut legere, simul dictare et audire solitum accepimus, epistulas vero tantarum rerum quaternas pariter dictare librariis aut, si nihil aliud ageret, septenas.* Fr. Münzer (*Festschr. z. 49. Vers. deutsch. Phil. u. Schulm.*, Basel (1907), 256) conjectured that for his numerous biographical passages Velleius used works *de viris illustribus.* The same could apply to Pliny. Of the authors mentioned as his sources in Book 1, Varro, Cornelius Nepos and Pomponius Atticus suggest themselves.

[1] See above, p. 217, n. 4 and p. 232, n. 1.

[2] Nicol. Dam. (*FgrHist*, 90) draws such a conclusion from Caesar's long absence (F 130, 67): Caesar was deceived by the extravagant decrees in his honour inspired by his enemies, ἅτε ἁπλοῦς ὢν τὸ ἦθος καὶ ἄπειρος πολιτικῆς τέχνης διὰ τὰς ἐκδήμους στρατείας. According to Jacoby's commentary on the fragments, p. 264, the βίος Καίσαρος is based principally on the autobiography of Augustus (*HRF*, p. 252: *de vita sua;* according to Suet. *Aug.* 85, 1, it goes down to the year 25), and Nicolaus may have published it as early as the twenties. It seems doubtful to me whether the Syrian writer adapted the work at first hand, and I should be inclined to assume that he had an amanuensis with literary ability who may have made other contributions as well. The judgment on Caesar's lack of guile and political inexperience will hardly have been formulated quite so naïvely by Augustus. However, Hirtius (*b. Alex.* 24, 6) also testifies that Caesar's devoted officers and soldiers were amazed at his *nimia bonitas* (see above, p. 251, n. 1), and the second observation contains the grain of truth that after his victory he no longer took seriously the traditional politics of the city of Rome.

business.[1] There grew up at the proconsul's headquarters an unofficial administrative machine—partly military, partly political— which overshadowed the regular government posts existing alongside it, and which in the Civil War was to stand the test even against overwhelming odds. Not that it was free from the prevailing corruption. There is incidental evidence of a widespread sale of Roman citizenship by minor officials. Of these the best known is the 'clerk' Faberius, who could afford a palace on the Aventine. However, no sooner had news of these transactions leaked out than the bronze tablet containing the forged names was removed on the dictator's orders.[2]

During the Civil War Rome saw Caesar only for brief periods. On the other hand, in the course of time he visited all the provinces. Some of his visits were prolonged, and in most cases his presence made a decisive difference to provincial life. It is, therefore, hardly surprising that his view of the provinces was quite different from that of the ordinary senator, for whom politics began and ended in Rome. In fact Caesar had grown increasingly contemptuous of political life in the capital. He had risen to power in the teeth of opposition from the senatorial oligarchy and always remained its avowed enemy. Admittedly no one knew better than he how to make use of the popular machinery: but it was precisely this knowledge which told him that the so-called popular assemblies, which were the instruments of political action, could not be equated with the real Roman people, the sum total of Roman citizens. Master though he was of the language of popular policy, in his heart he believed 'that the *res publica* was nothing—a mere name without form or substance', a credible saying, though recorded by an opponent.[3] In this context *res publica* is not simply a synonym for

---

[1] Listed as Caesar's *familiares* by Cicero (*fam.* 6, 12, 2, November, 46). Curtius Postumus is perhaps identical with Rabirius; see F. Vonder Mühll, *RE*, 1A, 27; Münzer, 22, 896. See above, p. 227, n. 4. Cic. *Att.* 10, 8, 6 (May 49): *iam quibus utatur vel sociis vel ministris? ii provincias, ii rem publicam regent quorum nemo duo menses potuit patrimonium suum gubernare?*

[2] On Faberius see App. *b.c.* 3, 16; Vitruv. 7, 9, 2; cf. Münzer, *RE*, 6, 1736; Cic. *fam.* 13, 36, 1.

[3] Suet. *Caes.* 77, from a pamphlet by the ex-praetor T. Ampius Balbus: *nihil esse rem publicam, appellationem modo sine corpore ac specie.* According to Cicero's letter, *fam.* 6, 12, 3, Caesar (influenced above all by Pansa's intervention) gave him permission to return to Rome, probably in November, 46 (O. E. Schmidt, *Briefwechsel*, 258). Other Caesarians, who called him *tuba belli civilis*, objected. We know from Curio (Cic. *Att.* 10, 4, 9) and Caelius (*fam.* 8, 16, 1) that Caesar sometimes expressed his irritation openly among his confidants and that such utterances of his were spread around. His conversation with Cicero on March 28, 49 (*Att.* 9, 18, 3) also ended with the threat: *si sibi consiliis nostris uti non liceret, usurum quorum posset ad omniaque esse descensurum.* The saying about the *res publica* may have been occasioned by displeasure at exhortations to restore it.

the State: it stands rather for the Roman constitution with its magistrates, Senate and popular assemblies, which had been represented by Cicero, in his famous work published a few years previously, as the best conceivable form of government, provided only it was used in the way their ancestors had intended.[1] On Caesar's return from Africa men as different as Cicero and Sallust had urgently recommended its restoration as the task it was now his duty to undertake. Of course he was himself aware of the emotional significance which this 'name' held for the Romans, and so far he had shown that it was far from his thoughts to abolish Republican institutions. In the political argument of his *Civil War*—the work breaks off at the start of the fighting in Alexandria and so was probably drafted in Egypt in 47—he is at pains to emphasize that his behaviour had been constitutional. Again, in the peace proposals which he made to Pompey through Vibullius[2] he suggested that after both sides had laid down their arms, it should be left to the Senate and People to settle the terms: this was in accordance with his usual tactics up to that time. In 49, just as in 59, he even tried to win the Senate for his plans. True, he rode ruthlessly over all attempts to obstruct them. And on such occasions he used strong language. He records his own remark in a speech to the Senate in January 49, that he would henceforth run the state on his own—a declaration that may well have voiced his real sentiments.[3] Anyone familiar with the history of the last decades of the Republic will agree that in view of the breakdown of the old institutions there was no other solution.

Even Cicero in his *Republic* suggested that a dictatorship was necessary to tide Rome over the crisis,[4] but only as a means of instilling new life into the old constitution. He hoped in this work to provide an intellectual framework for this revived Republic. During the African War he composed the *Brutus*, a history of Roman oratory in dialogue form. Since oratory can only flourish in a free state, this too was in itself a political manifesto. For during the Civil War Republican institutions were as completely eclipsed as they had been in the years of the popular revolution. It was after this that Sulla's restoration of laws and law-courts produced the era in which oratory reached its greatest heights. Since the dialogue

---

[1] Cic. *rep.* 1, 70.　　　　[2] See above, p. 224.

[3] Caes. *b.c.* 1, 32, 7: *sin timore defugiant, illis se oneri non futurum et per se rem publicam administraturum.*

[4] Cic. *rep.* 1, 31; 6, 12.

includes a full and flattering appreciation of Caesar as a man of letters there can be little doubt that he was intended to read it—and note its unmistakable hints.[1]

There is no evidence that he did so, but it seems impossible that he should have ignored this masterpiece on a subject that must have held the greatest interest for him. On the other hand we do know that on his return he treated Cicero with his usual kindness, and that Cicero himself believed that he might now be in a position to do something for his friend, the scholarly ex-praetor Publius Nigidius Figulus, who was still living outside Italy.[2]

It was probably also in 46 that Sallust addressed a second memorandum to him, to advise him how to secure permanent peace for the Republic. His chief demand was that Caesar should stand above the existing factions,[3] and he had no qualms about using the sharpest language to criticize the worthlessness of those of Caesar's followers who were disappointed with the policy of reconciliation.[4] In general, Sallust regarded the wild extravagance practised by young men of aristocratic family as the root cause of Rome's political malady, since it led to the plundering of citizens and subjects and so to internal strife. To stop this process he suggested that the borrowing and lending of money should be forbidden. An end to the largesse

[1] Cic. *Brut.* 2; 4; 6–9; 12; 16; 21; 22; 157; 266; 324; 330–332. On Caesar, 248–262. Cf. *RE*, 7A, 1008 ff.

[2] Cic. *fam.* 4, 13, 2: *nulla me ipsum privatim propulit insignis iniuria nec mihi quicquam tali tempore in mentem venit optare, quod non ultro mihi Caesar detulerit.* Later: *obtinemus ipsius Caesaris summam erga nos humanitatem, sed ea plus non potest quam vis et mutatio omnium rerum atque temporum;* 5: *videor mihi perspicere primum ipsius animum, qui plurimum potest, propensum ad salutem tuam;* Caesar was hesitating only because there were cases where he did not intend to forgive; 6: Cicero claims that so far he has been on good terms with the *familiarissimi*, and *et in ipsius consuetudinem, quam adhuc meus pudor mihi clausit, insinuabo et certe omnis vias persequar, quibus putabo ad id quod volumus pervenire posse.* Hieron. *chron.* on the year 45: *Nigidius Figulus Pythagoricus et magus in exilio moritur.* His good relations with Caesar's *familiares* are attested in Cic. *fam.* 9, 16, 2 (July, 46); they report Cicero's utterances to Caesar (s. 4). Cf. 9, 18, 1; 20, 3.

[3] Sall. *ad Caes.* 1, 3, 1; 5, 1: *ita bonis malisque dimotis patenti via ad verum pergas.* On the labels *boni malique* see Cic. *Att.* 10, 1, 4: *aut enim mihi libere inter malos* (with Caesar) πολιτευτέον *fuit aut vel periculose cum bonis* (with Pompey). In the following sentence instead of *mali* he uses the more familiar *improbi*. The dating to the end of 48 was suggested by E. Wistrand, *Eranos* 60 (1962), 160–73. Earlier opinion put the memorandum in 46, after the victory of Thapsus. Wistrand rests his case above all on the point that only Pompey is mentioned as Caesar's enemy (*ad Caes.* 2, 7; 4, 1). It may be added that the characterization of the depravity and cupidity of Caesar's adherents agrees with Cicero's description of them in spring 49 (*Att.* 9, 18, 2; 19, 1). In 2, 5–7 one may see allusions to the rising of the praetor M. Caelius Rufus against Caesar in 48 (p. 227 above).

[4] Sall. *ad Caes.* 1, 2, 5–7; 4, 3–4. Their unreliability is described by Caelius (with a different assessment) in *fam.* 8, 17, 2.

and corn doles that corrupted the populace would follow. In struggles between individuals as between peoples the party that despised wealth was always victorious. This sentiment had already emerged from his earlier pamphlet: it was to appear again in his historical works. His only other practical proposals were that all citizens should be equally liable for military service, and that the corn previously distributed to the work-shy urban population should be diverted to the veterans settled in municipalities and colonies.[1]

Where Caesar is concerned, it is particularly significant that the Republic is again the central theme of this pamphlet. Sallust assumes that an improvement in the moral standards of the younger generation would be sufficient to restore it to working order: 'So, in the name of Heaven, I entreat you: take the Republic in hand and surmount all difficulties as you always do.'[2] At the same time the hopes expressed by some of Caesar's supporters that they and their leader would 'conquer the state' are stigmatized as criminal.[3] The policy of reconciliation was already sufficiently clear to show that Caesar was not going to grant these elements a free hand. He had, however, lost—if, indeed, he had ever shared—that belief in the Republic which Sallust presupposed in him.

Caesar's most recent experiences in the provinces and in Egypt served to strengthen his contempt for the traditional Roman constitution. Here the Roman power of command (*imperium*) had everywhere a more extensive range than in the capital or in Italy; further, the East was the area of the Hellenistic monarchies. The more remote he came to feel from the traditions of Republican Rome, the greater the attraction of Oriental traditions. We have seen that as early as 48 he allowed himself to be honoured in Asia Minor as divine ruler and saviour of the world.[4] With his political insight he understood that the political loyalty of Hellenistic subjects to their monarchies could only be expressed in terms of a ruler-cult (i.e., in the recognition that the ruler's sovereignty was divinely ordained), since Greeks could only feel patriotism for the city state and the kingdoms of the East had no basis of national unity. A statesman

[1] Sall. *ad Caes.* 1, 7, 2–8, 3 and 6.
[2] Ibid., 6, 3. [3] Ibid., 4, 3.
[4] See above, pp. 244–5. Lily Ross Taylor (*The Divinity of the Roman Emperor* (1931), 60) recalls the visits of the young Caesar to Asia Minor and describes (61/2) the impressions of the Egyptian ruler-cult which he may have received during the journey up the Nile with Cleopatra.

who saw the provinces as part of a single Empire must inevitably have found these arguments even more applicable to the still greater variety embraced by Roman rule. This is not to suggest that Caesar allowed his policy to be dictated by abstract constitutional theory. He had only one unshakable principle—he would not let go the power he had won.

Thus Caesar's personal leaning towards monarchy grew ever stronger: it was reinforced by the failure of the optimate oligarchy and the Republican constitution to cope with the problems of empire. Monarchy then was his inevitable and chosen objective: we pass now to a more detailed consideration of the paths he trod in his attempt to achieve it and where they led him.

On his arrival in Rome, the Senate decreed him new and un-precedented honours: a festival of thanksgiving of forty days' dur-ation for his victory, the dictatorship for ten years, seventy-two lictors for his triumphs, control over morals for three years (an enhancement of one of the powers belonging to the censors), the right of designating even extraordinary magistrates for popular election, and in the Senate the right of sitting on the curule chair between the consuls at all meetings and of speaking first on all questions. Further, he was to give the signal at all games, and his name was to replace that of Catulus on the Capitoline Temple. Inside the temple, a triumphal chariot was set up, on which stood a statue of Caesar with the globe at its feet and an inscription, later removed on the dictator's orders, recalling his descent from Venus and Anchises and describing him as a demigod.[1]

---

[1] Dio 43, 14. Dio says (s. 4) that 'they elected' him *praefectus morum* (Suet. *Caes.* 76, 1; cf. Cic. *fam.* 9, 15, 5: *praefectus moribus*) for three years and dictator for ten years. This suggests popular election (cf. L. Lange, *R.A.*, 3, 445). Accordingly, in 46, Caesar was *dictator tertio, designatus dictator quarto* (*b. Hisp.* 2, 1). In 44, until he assumed the title *dictator perpetuus* or *perpetuo* (according to Cic. *Phil.* 2, 87 on February 15, 44) he called himself *dictator quartum*. A. Alföldi (*Studien über Caesars Monarchie, Bulletin de la Société Royale des Lettres de Lund* (1953, 6), 16) puts the change about March 1. However, R. A. G. Carson (*Gnomon* 28 (1956), 182) denies that the coin reproduced in Alföldi's plates 2, 5 and 6 portrays Caesar with a diadem. See Alföldi's retort in 'The Portrait of Caesar on the denarii of 44 B.C.' (*Centennial Vol. of the American Numismatic Society* (1958), 39–41). K. Kraft ('Der goldene Kranz Caesars', *Jahrbuch für Numismatik u. Geldgeschichte der Bayer. Numism. Ges.* 3/4 (Jahrgang 1952–3), 8; 66) is cautious. On the globe as a symbol of world rule, see Alföldi, *RhM* 50 (1935), 37, 117 ff. L. R. Taylor (*Divinity*, 64, n. 12) recalls Duris' description (*FgrHist* 76, 14) of a painting on the proscenium at Athens portraying Demetrius Poliorcetes on a globe. On p. 63, n. 13 she conjectures (basing herself on Serv. Dan. on Verg. *ecl.* 9, 47) that the inscription was in Greek and that Caesar had it erased because he found the designation insufficient. According to Balsdon (*Historia* 7, (1958), 84), it was perhaps *divo*. Cf. F. Taeger (*Charisma* 2 (1960), 60) ('probably Greek').

The honours and powers he accepted.[1] But, both in the Senate and later before the people, he again pledged himself to a policy of reconciliation, declaring that the very idea of a despotism was repugnant to his character. He refused to follow either Sulla's example or that of Marius and Cinna, respectively his uncle and his one-time father-in-law. At every opportunity he repeated his official line: he had only fought the Civil War to save himself from dishonour. His victorious army had done battle to protect its rights and Caesar's dignity. Further pursuit of his enemies had now become pointless.[2] During the following weeks he made a serious effort to win over the leading members of the party opposing him to active collaboration. Of Pompey he spoke only with respect. Even before his departure for Africa he had appointed Servius Sulpicius (consul 51) as governor of Greece, and Marcus Brutus to Cisalpine Gaul. Gaius Cassius too was employed as a legate;[3] but he laid particular weight on maintaining a constant connection with Cicero. The great orator was giving lessons in rhetoric to Hirtius and Dolabella, who were required to give the dictator an exact account of his witty sayings. Since Caesar's return he had been attending meetings of the Senate. Of course he did not vote at first and so was unable directly to influence the decisions of the dictator. But his lively intercourse with Caesar's confidants noticeably raised Cicero's hopes that the policy of reconciliation was serious and that a far-reaching restoration of the Republic was planned.[4]

[1] Dio remarks (43, 14, 7, as before in 42, 19, 4) that he is mentioning only those honours which Caesar accepted.

[2] The speech in Dio 43, 15, 2–18, 5, besides commonplaces surely contains some ideas based on contemporary tradition, as Caes. *b.c.* shows. That the Civil War is to be regarded as a fate ordained by the deity (17, 4) is the thought also of Cic. *Lig.* 17: *fatalis quaedam calamitas incidisse videtur et improvidas hominum mentes occupavisse, ut nemo mirari debeat humana consilia divina necessitate esse superata.* The statement that large means are necessary to satisfy the veterans and pay the army (18, 1–5), as already explained in 42, 49, 3–5, may also be considered as part of the tradition. According to Plut. *Caes.* 55, 1 he had already mentioned before the people that the tribute in kind paid by Africa guaranteed the corn and oil supplies.

[3] Cic. *fam.* 6, 6, 10. On Ser. Sulpicius see *fam.* 4, 3—which according to Münzer, *RE*, 4A, 855 belongs to the beginning of 46—and the letters of recommendation sent to him (*fam.* 13, 17–28a). Letters of recommendation to Brutus: *fam.* 13, 10–14; cf. *Brut.* 171; *orat.* 34; Plut. *Brut.* 6, 10; App. *b.c.* 2, 465.

[4] Cic. *fam.* 9, 16, 2, 4 and 7; 18, 1. Though Cicero complained during the African War of *communes miseriae* (*fam.* 4, 15, 1; 14, 1), he yet felt himself relieved of an oppressive burden by Caesar's victory. For he had nothing but ill to expect of the Pompeians (*fam.* 9, 6, 3). He prided himself on having foreseen everything correctly when he advised compromise in the early days of January 49 (4, 14, 2). If Pompey had not been jealous of him, *et ipse beatus esset et omnes boni* (5, 21, 2). Writing to Varro, he goes so far as to put the blame for the war on the optimates (*fam.* 9, 6, 2): *vidi enim (nam tu aberas) nostros amicos cupere bellum, hunc* (Caesar)

Cicero then thought himself justified in sending various friends reassuring news about their prospects of pardon, and, when the question arose of encouraging Marcus Marcellus, the most important of the Republicans, to return from exile, he was quite ready to explore the ground. In doing so he was able to inform his friend that—amid a profusion of auction sales[1]—his property was still intact[2] and that Caesar was very well-disposed to men of talent and nobility.[3] Cicero's hopes reached their peak when in mid-September

autem non tam cupere quam non timere; ergo haec consili fuerunt, reliqua necessaria, vincere autem aut hos aut illos necesse. To his old friend M. Marius (fam. 7, 3, 3) he writes: quae acciderunt, omnia dixi futura; further (5) notum tibi omne meum consilium esse volui, ut primum scires me numquam voluisse plus quemquam posse quam universam rem p., postea autem quam alicuius (Pompey) culpa tantum valeret unus (Caesar), ut obsisti non posset, me voluisse pacem. Similarly in August 46 (before Marcellus had been pardoned), writing to Q. Ligarius, whose life Caesar had spared in Africa (b. Afr. 89, 2), he describes his chances of return as favourable (fam. 6, 13, 2): non fore in te Caesarem duriorem; nam et res eum cotidie et dies et opinio hominum et, ut mihi videtur, etiam sua natura mitiorem facit. This is what he hears from the familiarissimi. Even more confident is his letter to A. Caecina (soon after Marcellus' pardon, fam. 6, 6, 5): he had been a friend of both Pompey and Caesar; if Pompey had followed his advice, esset hic (Caesar) quidem clarus in toga et princeps, sed tantas opes quantas nunc habet non haberet. Thus it was only the fault of Pompey that Caesar won such overwhelming power. Even on March 20, 43, in the face of the threats of Antony he admits (Phil. 13, 2): si aliquid de summa gravitate Pompeius, multum de cupiditate Caesar remisisset, et pacem stabilem et aliquam rem publicam nobis habere licuisset. In Phil. 2, 24 Cicero claims that, if in 55 Pompey had followed his advice not to prolong Caesar's imperium, and in 52 had not allowed the law about his consular candidature, in has miserias numquam incidissemus and later even res publica staret. In the letter he does not mention these two pieces of advice, in order not to seem ungrateful to Caesar: nolo enim hunc (Caesar) de me optime meritum existimare ea me suasisse Pompeio quibus ille si paruisset etc. Of Caesar's character only good is to be expected (8): he is mitis clemensque natura and mirifice ingeniis excellentibus quale est tuum delectatur; he is serious about his policy of reconciliation (10): in quo admirari soleo gravitatem et iustitiam et sapientiam Caesaris. According to Suet. Caes. 75, 5 Caecina was the author of a criminosissimus liber against Caesar. Where Cicero's judgments are concerned, one must always pay attention to his mood and political objective in delivering them. When in Phil. 2, 116 he says adversarios clementiae specie devinxerat, in reality he knew that his clementia was not mere pretence; for on May 4, 44, he let slip the admission (Att. 14, 17, 6): ille enim nescio quo pacto ferebat me quidem mirabiliter, and Phil. 13, 18, comparing him with Antony: Caesare dominante veniebamus in senatum, si non libere, at tamen tuto.

[1] Cic. fam. 9, 10, 3; 15, 17, 2; 19, 3; 13, 8, 2; off. 2, 27; 29; 83; Phil. 2, 64; 103; 104, 8, 9.

[2] Cic. fam. 4, 7, 5.

[3] Cic. fam. 4, 8, 2: sed, mihi crede, etiam is qui omnia tenet favet ingeniis, nobilitatem vero et dignitates hominum, quantum ei res et ipsius causa concedit, amplectitur. Cicero had already declared in the Brutus (250) that Marcellus was the contemporary who satisfied his ideal of the orator with an all-round education, and while he otherwise only discussed the dead, he made the same exception in the case of Marcellus as he did in those of himself and of Caesar. He there-fore attached particular importance to bringing this optimate distinguished for his social position, intellect and morality round to his own way of political thought. For this reason he asks him not to scorn the victor's liberalitas (4, 9, 4). Cicero finds remarkably sympathetic words for Caesar (9, 2): omnia enim delata ad unum sunt; is utitur consilio ne suorum quidem sed suo. If Pompey had won, this would have been no different, or rather worse, since in war he always listened to the most ignorant advisers and in victory he would not have called upon Marcellus and Cicero (9, 3): omnia sunt misera in bellis civilibus, quae maiores nostri ne semel

the case of Marcellus was raised in the Senate by Lucius Piso. His cousin Gaius Marcellus (consul 50) fell to his knees and interceded for him, the whole Senate rose to its feet in support, and Caesar, notwithstanding his recollection of the bitter hostility shown him by Marcellus in 51, without hesitation granted their request.[1] This was the moment for Cicero to break his long silence. He paid homage to the victor in a brilliant speech of thanksgiving: here was Caesar's greatest achievement. In this moment he had risen above his victory and had almost become a god.[2] However, the main significance of the speech is that it gives expression to Cicero's own political programme. Caesar had recently alluded to a plot against his life. Cicero took up this point and declared that the welfare of all depended on Caesar's life alone. He delivered a strong protest against the dictator's usual rejoinder in such contexts: 'Whether measured by length of days or by glory my life has been long enough.'[3] If he died now he would leave the state in ruins. It was essential, therefore, that he should enact the comprehensive legislation which was at that time in active preparation, and, above all, he must produce a constitution that would survive him. Then and only then would his life's work be done.[4]

In the most flattering language, but unambiguously, Cicero once more defined it as Caesar's task to establish the republic on

quidem, nostra aetas saepe iam sensit, sed miserius nihil quam ipsa victoria; quae, etiam si ad meliores venit, tamen eos ipsos ferociores impotentioresque reddit, ut etiam si natura tales non sint, necessitate esse cogantur; multa enim victori eorum arbitrio, per quos vicit, etiam invita facienda sunt. This again applies to Pompey, while Caesar did not allow free play to such influences. A few weeks later, however, while under the impression of the games to celebrate the dedication of the temple of Venus Genetrix on September 26 (Fasti Pinc., Inscr. It. 13, 2, 48; Dio 43, 22, 3; Wissowa, Rel. u. Kult. d. Röm.², 292), he writes to Q. Cornificius, at that time presumably quaestor pro praetore in Cilicia (Broughton, MRR, 2, 297), in fam. 12, 18, 2, that the present peace in Rome was such in qua, si adesses, multa te non delectarent, ea tamen quae ne ipsum Caesarem quidem delectant. bellorum enim civilium ii semper exitus sunt, ut non ea solum fiant quae velit victor, sed etiam ut iis mos gerendus sit quibus adiutoribus sit parta victoria; cf. Plut. Caes. 51, 4—and this is also part of the theme of Sallust's memorandum.

[1] Described in the letter to Ser. Sulpicius, who had been consul with him in 51 (see above, pp. 172–3), in fam. 4, 4; here (4) fregit hoc meum consilium et Caesaris magnitudo animi et senatus officium. Cicero was really carried away by this surprising decision on the part of Caesar, who, after again recalling the bitter events of 51, (3) repente praeter spem dixit se senatui roganti de Marcello ne ominis quidem causa negaturum. By his qualifying remark about the bad omen he clearly meant that he had no doubt that Marcellus remained unreconciled. The latter, for his part, wrote to Cicero, saying that he thanked him only for his good offices as a friend (fam. 4, 11, 2): reliqua sunt eius modi, quibus ego, quoniam haec erant tempora, facile et aequo animo carebam. Thus he did not hurry to return, but was eventually murdered on his way back at Athens on May 25, 45 (fam. 4, 12—the report of Ser. Sulpicius; Att. 13, 10, 1 and 3; 22, 2).

[2] Cic. Marc. 7; 8; 12. [3] Ibid. 21–25: satis diu vel naturae vixi vel gloriae.
[4] Ibid. 26.

T

new legal principles and again to make it viable;[1] in other words he was to become the successor of Sulla, and only to regard the dictatorship as a means to an end. For the time being it suited Caesar very well that this view should gain ground, and he gladly developed out of it the idea that if he wished to live on, he did so only for the sake of the state which, if anything were to happen to him, would be plunged into new civil wars under worse conditions.[2] But this did not represent his innermost intentions. For among his intimates he openly declared that Sulla had not known his political alphabet when he laid down the dictatorship.[3] The future depended on the development of this contrast: would the gap be widened or bridged? Would the optimates come to terms with the new situation or would they persist in Cato's point of view that for republicans he was simply an intolerable tyrant? Not only fundamental principles divided him from them: they were also filled with insurmountable mistrust at the memory of his past. How could they be expected to understand his plan of government when even his admirer Sallust was unable to grasp it? And it became even harder to find a satisfactory solution because some of his old partisans were also totally dissatisfied with his policy of reconciliation and restoration of order. The attempted assassination mentioned above seems to have originated from this circle; rumour held Antony responsible.[4] The higher Caesar climbed, the lonelier his position became. However, on his arrival he lost no time in reflection, but immediately began with tireless energy to set in train all that he regarded as necessary in his own and the Empire's interests. As a result of his victory the Empire had at last passed into the hands of a man of genuine political ability, who no longer followed selfish party or class interests, but who intended to shape the Empire as a whole in the way that circumstances required.[5]

---

[1] Cic. Marc. 23: constituenda iudicia, revocanda fides, comprimendae libidines, propaganda suboles, omnia quae dilapsa iam diffluxerunt, severis legibus vincienda sunt; 24: nunc tibi omnia belli vulnera sananda sunt, quibus praeter te mederi nemo potest; 27: haec igitur tibi reliqua pars est, hic restat actus, in hoc elaborandum est, ut rem publicam constituas; 29: nisi haec urbs stabilita tuis consiliis et institutis erit . . . nisi belli civilis incendium salute patriae restinxeris. . . .

[2] Suet. Caes. 86, 2: rem publicam, si quid sibi eveniret, neque quietam fore et aliquanto deteriore condicione civilia bella subituram.

[3] Ibid., 77: Sullam nescisse litteras, qui dictaturam deposuerit. Cf. above, p. 274, n. 3.

[4] Cic. Marc. 21; Phil. 2, 74.

[5] Cicero also admitted this unique genius after Caesar's death (Phil. 2, 116): fuit in illo ingenium, ratio, memoria, litterae, cura, cogitatio, diligentia, res bello gesserat quamvis rei publicae calamitosas, at tamen magnas; multos annos regnare meditatus magno labore, magnis periculis quod cogitarat effecerat. In Phil. 5, 49 he speaks of the vis ingenii, quae summa fuit in illo. Of course, he

Of primary importance was the provision of land in Italy for his veterans according to the principles which he had evolved on the occasion of the great mutiny. He delegated the task of finding land to legates with praetorian authority, but in doubtful cases reserved the final decision for himself. This lengthy task had not been completed at his death, and neither was it possible everywhere to adhere to the plan of not settling the veterans in closed communities, nor had all the dispossessed owners been compensated by then.[1]

believes that he had wasted it on popular policies, then found that he could no longer come to terms with the Senate and the *boni*, and for this reason *eam sibi viam ipse patefecit ad opes suas amplificandas quam virtus liberi populi ferre non posset.* Here Sallust's vision was more penetrating when he recommended (*ep.* 1, 5, 1): *ita bonis malisque dimotis patenti via ad verum perges.* And in the *Histories* (1, 12) he exposed the catch-phrases of party warfare: *bonique et mali cives appellati non ob merita in rem publicam, omnibus pariter corruptis, sed ubi quisque locupletissimus et iniuria validior, quia praesentia defendebat, pro bono ducebatur.*

[1] According to App. *b.c.* 2, 395, Caesar had declared in 47 that to settle the veterans he would use *ager publicus*, then land belonging to himself, and in so far as this was insufficient he would buy more. Against this, it is claimed in a speech by Brutus (2, 586), that Caesar, like Sulla, had paid no compensation and (591) that Caesar's murderers were going to put this right. Many veterans were not provided for at this time, and in the confusion after Caesar's death the winning of the veterans was a matter of paramount importance in the struggle for power. As early as March 17 the Senate recognized the validity of Caesar's *acta* and thereby also the allotment of land to the veterans (*Phil.* 1, 6; 2, 100). Soon a senatorial decree followed, instructing the consuls to implement the measures which had only been planned by Caesar. On June 3 this was confirmed by a law (Cic. *Att.* 16, 16c, 11). By the end of April Antony had gone off to Campania in order to continue the allotment of land to veterans that Caesar had begun there. H. Rudolph (*Stadt und Staat im röm. Italien* (1935), 200) has seen, on the strength of Caelius *ap.* Cic. *fam.* 8, 10, 4, that at the end of 51 the distribution of the *ager Campanus* started by Caesar in 59 had not yet been completed, which explains how in 46 a large number of veterans could receive land there (according to Nicol. Dam. F 130, 132 and 138 those of the Seventh and Eighth Legions; cf. Suet. *Caes.* 81, 1). Cicero (*Phil.* 2, 102) mentions Casilinum as a veteran colony of Caesar thus; also *Att.* 16, 8, 1; App. *b.c.* 3, 165. Nicol. Dam. F 130, 136 likewise mentions Calatia. In addition, Cicero (*Phil.* 2, 102) claims that Antony had founded a new colony at Casilinum with further settlers. In June the consuls had themselves empowered by law to found colonies (Cic. *Phil.* 5, 10; *Att.* 15, 19, 2). Nevertheless, in October of 44, 3,000 of these veterans immediately joined the young Caesar (*Att.* 16, 8, 2; App. *b.c.* 3, 240). Eventually they are said to have numbered 10,000 (App. *b.c.* 3, 165). When in 43 the laws of Antony were declared invalid, the veterans' allotments were recognized by means of a new law (Cic. *Phil.* 13, 31). On January 1 Cicero at once proposed a motion to reward the veterans and legions under the command of the young Caesar (*Phil.* 5, 53). On the veterans it reads: *uti C. Pansa A. Hirtius consules alter ambove si eis videretur cognoscerent, qui ager iis coloniis esset, quo milites veterani deducti essent, qui contra legem Iuliam possideretur, ut is militibus veteranis divideretur; de agro Campano separatim cognoscerent inirentque rationem de commodis militum veteranorum augendis.* From this it can be seen that Caesar the dictator based his provision for the veterans on his law of 59. Now the veterans who had been settled in colonies by Antony *contra legem Iuliam* were to retain their estates. Those settled by Caesar on the *ager Campanus* (in the narrower sense) were to be made equal to the colonists of Antony, who were apparently better placed. The legions were given the expectation: *uti C. Pansa A. Hirtius consules alter ambove si eis videretur rationem agri haberent qui sine iniuria privatorum dividi posset.* According to Cic. *fam.* 9, 17, 2 (August, 46) Caesar also had the *ager Veiens* and *Capenas* measured out for settlement. On Veii in the *liber coloniarum* (*Röm. Feldmesser*, 1, 220):

Concurrently, the first weeks were occupied principally with preparations for the four triumphs which were to be celebrated from September 20 to October 1 (from July 20 to July 30, Jul.).[1] The magnificent representation of his victories and the splendid festivities connected with them were to provide a most impressive demonstration of the power which he had won. The triumphs marked the defeat of Gaul, Egypt and the kings Pharnaces and Juba. The number of enemies killed—excluding the fallen citizens—was given as 1,192,000.[2] As well as the varied and wonderful trappings, there were also remarkable prisoners to be seen: Vercingetorix, Arsinoe, the sister of Cleopatra, and the four-year-old prince Juba. While the last two were afterwards released, the famous Celtic leader was executed as a treacherous rebel.[3] This the Romans found perfectly in order;[4] but the malicious representation in the African triumphal procession of the fall of the heroes of liberty, Cato,

---

ager eius militibus adsignatus ex lege Iulia. Ibid. (216) on Capena: *ubi miles portionem habuit.* In 45 Cicero requests (*fam.* 13, 4) Q. Valerius Orca, who is serving in Etruria as *legatus pro praetore,* to exempt the community of Volaterrae from ceding land on the ground that Caesar himself had not touched it in 59. In any case he was asked to leave the decision to Caesar himself; in 13, 5, 2 Cicero makes a special request on behalf of the local landowner C. Curtius, whom Caesar had admitted to the Senate; after such a loss of property he could not remain a senator, *minimeque convenit ex agro, qui Caesaris iussu dividatur, eum moveri, qui Caesaris beneficio senator sit.* At the same time Cicero appeals to C. Cluvius on behalf of real estate owned by the Campanian city of Atella in Gallia Citerior(*fam.* 13, 7), and cites as a precedent that Rhegium had been exempted in similar circumstances. Here, too, Caesar himself ought to decide; in 13, 8, 2 he commends to a certain M. Rutilius the real estate of a C. Albinius who had had to take over this land from a M. Laberius in lieu of cash payment. The latter had acquired it at an auction of enemy property. Here Cicero argues that, as Caesar recognizes the right of ownership where estates had been acquired in the Sullan proscriptions, it would be illogical *si ea praedia dividentur, quae ipse Caesar vendidit.* It seems to me impossible that Caesar handed private property to veterans without compensation. However, it is certain that a sizeable amount of real estate came into his hands with the property of the opponents who continued the Civil War after Pharsalus. Much of this was sold by auction to private individuals. But it is perfectly possible that some was also used for compensating private owners who had been forced to cede territory for colonization (as provided for in the *lex agraria* of 111; see Riccobono, *FIRA²,* 8, 21). However, such exchanges were understandably unpopular, cf. below, p. 312, n. 4. Further, Caesar attempted to win new land for cultivation by the draining of marshes, which forced even Cicero to admit (*Phil.* 5, 7): *ille* (Caesar) *paludis siccare voluit* (see Dio 44, 5, 1), *hic* (Antony) *omnem Italiam moderato homini L. Antonio dividendam dedit.* Cf. Ed. Meyer, *Caesars Mon.,* 407 ff.; Fr. Vittinghoff, *Röm. Kolonisation (Abh. Mainz* (1951), 14), 53.

[1] *CIL,* 1², p. 322. See above, p. 280, n. 3.
[2] Plin. *n.h.* 7, 92.   [3] Dio 43, 19, 4.
[4] Cic. *Verr.* 2, 5, 77: *qui triumphant eoque diutius vivos hostium duces reservant, ut his per triumphum ductis pulcherrimum spectaculum fructumque victoriae populus Romanus percipere possit, tamen cum de foro in Capitolium currus flectere incipiunt, illos duci in carcerem iubent, idemque dies et victoribus imperi et victis vitae finem facit.* See *RE,* 8A, 1007. For a possible coin portrait of Vercingetorix, see Sydenham, *CRR,* no. 952. A similar Gallic portrait (enlarged) in H. Kähler, *Rom und seine Welt,* plate 59; see above, p. 163.

Scipio and Petreius, aroused universal disapproval.[1] The victory of Pharsalus Caesar passed over in silence,[2] but in the case of Africa, in keeping with his attitude hitherto, he apparently hoped to hit his enemies by branding the last Republicans as traitors in the service of Juba.[3] The soldiers who, according to ancient custom, sang satirical songs about their general at his triumph did not stop at obscenities, but made allusions to his new monarchical affectations. He managed not to show displeasure at this, but—just as he had divorced his wife on the occasion of the Clodius scandal—he immediately denied with the utmost emphasis that there was any truth in the rumour that thirty years earlier he had been the catamite of king Nicomedes.[4]

The vast quantity of precious metals taken as booty or otherwise collected, which had been carried in the procession to the astonishment of the spectators, was to a large extent divided among the veterans and poor citizens entitled to free distributions of corn. Private soldiers each received 5,000 denarii, centurions twice this sum, and military tribunes and cavalry officers four times as much.[5] The citizens concerned—the total eligible numbered 320,000 at this time—were to have 100 denarii each, twenty-five more than he had promised in the year 49, as well as ten pecks of grain and thirty-six pounds of oil.[6] At the same time, in fulfilment of the promise given at Julia's death, a public banquet at 22,000 tables and a distribution of meat took place. The gladiatorial games in honour of his daughter, for which preparations had long since been made, were now also celebrated.[7] Many thousands of prisoners-of-war and condemned criminals had to fight their bloody battles.[8] As an extra attraction Caesar also allowed knights to display their skill as fencers; however, he would not grant a senator permission to do likewise.[9] A greater sensation was caused by the fact that the ruler caused the popular writer of comedies, Decimus Laberius, a sixty-year-old knight, to appear in person in one of his plays. For the victim took his revenge with pointed allusions. Among

---

[1] App. b.c. 2, 420.　　　　　　　　[2] Cic. Phil. 14, 23.

[3] b. Afr. 57, 2–6. On the triumphs, see Suet. Caes. 37; Plut. Caes. 55, 2; App. b.c. 2, 418–419; Dio 43, 19.

[4] Dio 43, 20; Suet. Caes. 49, 4; 51; 80, 2; Plin. n.h. 19, 144; Hor. epist. 1, 1, 59; Isid. etym. 9, 3, 4.

[5] Suet. Caes. 38, 1; App. b.c. 2, 422; Dio 43, 21, 3.

[6] Suet. Caes. 38, 1; 41, 3; Plut. Caes. 55, 5; Dio 43, 21, 3.

[7] Suet. Caes. 26, 2; 38, 2; 39, 1; Dio 43, 22, 3; 23, 4; Plut. Caes. 55, 4.

[8] App. b.c. 2, 423; Dio 43, 23, 3–4; 24, 1.

[9] Dio 43, 23, 5, clearly more accurate than Suet. Caes. 39, 1.

others the following lines occurred: 'Hither, citizens! We have lost our freedom', and 'The man whom many fear must also fear many'· Caesar awarded the prize to a freedman, Publilius Syrus, who appeared in one of his own plays at the same time, but paid the knight a fee of 125,000 denarii, and by granting him a gold ring again recognized him as a member of the equestrian order.[1] The masses were less affected by such attacks on the established social order than the convinced republicans of the upper class. We can see from Cicero's correspondence how these events again estranged him spiritually from Caesar. The hopes of the speech for Marcellus had been disappointed.[2]

On the other hand the soldiers were grumbling about the amount of money that was being squandered on entertaining the people. At a performance the audience did not calm down until Caesar personally led a complainant off to execution. He had two others sacrificed to Mars by the priests on the Campus Martius and their heads displayed outside the Regia, his official residence. He was generally fond of emphasizing his sacred position as *pontifex maximus* and augur, and this quite unusual human sacrifice must have been directed at the religious beliefs of the multitude.[3] Again when the axle-tree of his chariot broke during the first triumphal procession he did not shrink from climbing the steps of the Capitol on his knees to atone for this unfavourable omen.[4] It is, however, explicitly reported that he himself did not believe in such things.[5] It was also for reasons of religious policy that, on September 26, he dedicated the Forum Julium, which had been built since 54, as part of the victory celebrations. In its midst there rose the temple of Venus vowed before the battle of Pharsalus. The deity worshipped in it was Venus Genetrix, Venus the ancestress of the Julii, not Venus Victrix

---

[1] Cic. *fam.* 12, 18, 2; Macrob. *Sat.* 2, 7, 2–9; Suet. *Caes.* 39, 2; Sen. *contr.* 7, 3, 9.

[2] Especially in the letter to Paetus, *fam.* 9, 15, 3: the man who previously sat at the helm of the ship of state can now hardly find room in the bilge-water. Also 9, 26, 1 and 3; 13, 77, 1; *orat.* 34–35; *fam.* 6, 7, 4.

[3] Dio 43, 24, 3–4. Previously (24, 1–2) a general criticism of the waste of money. In 18, 2 Dio (no doubt basing himself on tradition) makes Caesar say that his heavy demands for money are necessary to satisfy the soldiers and to cover his own expenditure and indebtedness to date. On his title of *pontifex maximus*, see A. Alföldi, *Stud. über Caesars Mon.*, 9; 35, 3, with plate 9. A representation of the *lituus* (the augur's staff: see Latte, *RE*, 13, 805), ibid., plate 2 and plate 5; also Alföldi, *The Portrait of Caesar*, plate 1.

[4] Dio 43, 21, 1–2. If (according to Dio 60, 23, 1) this was repeated by Claudius, I do not agree with Ed. Meyer (*Caesars Mon.*, 383, 2) that it was simply a question of 'an old custom'. I should prefer to regard it as a form of *supplicatio* (Wissowa, *Rel. u. Kult. d. Röm.*², 424). On the usual apotropaic ceremonies at a triumph, see Ehlers, *RE*, 7A, 496, 507.

[5] Suet. *Caes.* 77; Cic. *div.* 2, 52; App. *b.c.* 2, 488; Polyaen. 8, 23, 32; 33.

to whom it had been promised.[1] In other words the deity of his clan was to be marked out as the bestower of victory. This tendency was revealed even more clearly when Cleopatra with her husband, son and the rest of her court, appeared in Rome at this time and was billeted by him for a long stay in the gardens on the far side of the Tiber. For it was doubtless of some significance that he now erected a golden statue of the queen next to the image of his divine ancestress.[2]

Thus the great victory celebration had considerable political significance. If it was successful in binding the veterans and population of the city to the person of the ruler,[3] it also gave fresh sustenance to the spirit of the opposition to monarchy.

The following months could be devoted entirely to the enormous task of reform by legislation. Following up his earlier efforts he first of all attacked the social problems of Rome and Italy, and he laid a foundation for this by taking an exact census of the whole population of the city. On the results of this the free distribution of corn was regulated anew, so that the total number of recipients was reduced from 320,000 to a maximum of 150,000, a number not to be exceeded in future. It was to be kept up by an annual drawing of lots from among the registered applicants. It seems that in these regulations he granted special privileges to fathers of large families, which was in the spirit of 59 and particularly appropriate in view of the large number of war casualties.[4] In order to suppress revolutionary intrigues among the inhabitants of the city he again banned all political clubs by edict.[5] But he was preparing a more effective remedy with his plan to settle a considerable portion of the

---

[1] Dio 43, 22, 2; App. b.c. 2, 424. For the date, Fasti Arv., Fasti Pinc., Inscr. It. 13, 2, 34–5; 48. Cf. C. Koch, RE, 8A, 865.

[2] Suet. Caes. 52, 1 is wrong in saying that Caesar himself sent her home. For according to Cic. Att. 14, 8, 1; 20, 2; 15, 1, 5; 4, 4; 15, 2; 17, 2, she was in Rome until April 44. Dio 43, 27, 3: the king and queen were recognized as 'friends and allies' of the Roman people; cf. 51, 22, 3; App. b.c. 2, 424; Hieron. chron. on 46 B.C. Dio mentions that the visit gave offence; this has been expanded by G. Ferrero, Grandezza e Decad. di Roma, 2, 470. Cicero does not mention the queen until after Caesar's murder, and his hatred seems to spring from a personal encounter (Att. 15, 15, 2): superbiam autem ipsius reginae, cum esset trans Tiberim in hortis, commemorare sine magno dolore non possum. J. H. Collins (Historia 4 (1955), 462 ff.) suspects that she exercised a disastrous influence on Caesar.

[3] Cic. Phil. 2, 116: muneribus, monumentis, congiariis, epulis multitudinem imperitam delenierat; suos praemiis, adversarios clementiae specie devinxerat, 3, 3: the beneficia towards the veterans.

[4] Suet. Caes. 41, 3; Plut. Caes. 55, 5–6; Liv. per. 115; App. b.c. 2, 425; Dio 43, 21, 4; 25, 2; Cf. Cic. Marc. 23: propaganda suboles.

[5] Suet. Caes. 42, 3; Joseph. ant. 14, 215: the right of assembly of the Jewish community was expressly recognized. Cf. Philo, leg. ad. Gai. 312.

proletarian populace in citizen colonies overseas. In the period up to his death 80,000 citizens were provided for in this way.[1]

The measures designed to reduce the proletariat were supplemented by others which aimed to increase the bourgeoisie. To doctors and teachers of the liberal arts who settled in Rome he granted citizenship. Nor was he niggardly in this respect where rich provincials were concerned. He only intervened when some of his agents started to sell the citizenship.[2] Further, he forbade citizens domiciled in Italy to be absent from Italy for more than three years at a time except on military service. The sons of senators might leave Italy only on public service.[3] The owners of *latifundia* were obliged to recruit a third of their employees engaged on pasturage from free men.[4] As *praefectus moribus* he attempted to improve the wealthy classes by means of a sumptuary law which limited the use of litters, purple clothes and pearls, and also laid down exact instructions about permissible dishes and funerary memorials. Although lictors and soldiers were detailed to see that it was observed, it could not be enforced, as he himself admitted after a time.[5] Since the time of the Gracchi the control of the jury-courts had been contested. Here, too, in a double law dealing with criminal and civil trials he produced a general ordinance which from then on determined procedure. Politically the fact worth noting was that he now allowed only senators and knights to serve on juries, although since 70 men with a lower property qualification, the so-called *tribuni aerarii*, had shared in the courts. This shows that he rejected popular claims as ruthlessly as he did oligarchic principles. He also stepped up penalties; thus in murder cases he introduced the confiscation of the whole of the criminal's property and in other cases of half, since wealthy criminals in exile had not previously suffered much under their penalties.[6] Finally, an equally important law provided that after their year of office praetors should govern a province for one year,

[1] Suet. *Caes.* 42, 1. Cf. Fr. Vittinghoff, *Röm. Kolon.*, 56.

[2] Suet. *Caes.* 42, 1. Cicero in the autumn of 46, writing to Paetus, says that the appreciation of traditional Roman humour was disappearing (*fam.* 9, 15, 2): *cum in urbem nostram est infusa peregrinitas, nunc vero etiam bracatis* (wearers of trousers) *et Transalpinis nationibus, ut nullum veteris leporis vestigium appareat; cf. fam.* 13, 36, 1.

[3] Suet. *Caes.* 42, 1.

[4] Loc. cit.

[5] Suet. *Caes.* 43, 1–2; Dio 43, 25, 2; Cic. *fam.* 9, 15, 5; 26, 3; *Att.* 12, 13, 2; 35, 2; 36, 1; 13, 6, 1; 7, 1 (June, 45): Caesar has written *ne se absente leges suae neglegerentur sicut esset neglecta sumptuaria; cf. Marc.* 23: *comprimendae libidines.*

[6] Suet. *Caes.* 41, 2; 42, 3; Dio 43, 25, 1; Cic. *Marc.* 23; *Phil.* 1, 19; 24; 5, 12–16; 13, 3.

consuls for two. Longer terms of office were forbidden as a precaution against future revolutionary governors.[1]

Above these political measures there towers as an act of lasting significance the improvement of the Roman calendar by the introduction of the Julian calendar named after Caesar. This he undertook as *pontifex maximus*. In place of the traditional lunar year he introduced, as from January 1, 45, a solar year of $365\frac{1}{4}$ days, and in order to make the transition inserted sixty-seven days between November and December. As a regular intercalary month had already been inserted after February 24, this meant that in the year 46 there was a total of 445 days. It appears that the astronomical calculations were made by the Greek scholar Sosigenes.[2]

To implement his new order, he used normal constitutional devices: the edict, the senatorial decree and the popular law.[3] Unfortunately we are not able properly to appreciate the extent of his activity in this field, since besides some incidental literary references only a few fragments have been preserved in the original.[4] We can only see that they applied to the whole Empire, to the provinces as well as to Rome and Italy. By a remarkable coincidence fragmentary inscriptions of two of Caesar's laws have come down to us in the form in which they were put into force by the consuls Antony and Dolabella a few months after his death, on the strength

---

[1] Dio 43, 25, 3; Cic. *Phil.* 1, 19; 24; 3, 38; 5, 7; 8, 28.

[2] Censor. *de die nat.* 20, 8–12; 21, 7; Macrob. *Sat.* 1, 14, 2–3; Plin. *n.h.* 18, 211; Solin. 1, 45; Suet. *Caes.* 40; Dio 43, 26; Plut. *Caes.* 59, 5–6; App. *b.c.* 2, 648. Cf. W. Sontheimer, *RE*, 16, 61. On Sosigenes, see A. Rehm, *RE*, 3A, 1154; 18 (4), 1357. Klotz (*RE*, 10, 266) is probably right in doubting whether Caesar himself was the author of the work *de astris* ascribed to him. Evidence and fragments in the edition of Caesar by B. Kübler, 3, 2, pp. 150–168. Plutarch reports a joke by Cicero as characteristic of the dissatisfied optimates' mania for carping at even the best of Caesar's reforms: when reminded by an acquaintance that the constellation Lyra was due to rise on the following day, he replied, 'Yes, by edict'.

[3] Cic. *Phil.* 1, 18: if one were to ask Caesar *quidnam egisset in urbe et in toga, leges multas responderet se et praeclaras tulisse*; 1, 19: *quod ad populum centuriatis comitiis tulit;* 24: *quibus latis gloriabatur eisque legibus rem publicam contineri putabat, de provinciis, de indiciis;* 2, 109: *leges Caesaris easque praeclaras.*

[4] Among these are the very badly preserved documents in Joseph. *ant.* 14, 196 ff., relating to the Jewish High Priest Hyrcanus. It seems certain that of these 14, 196–198 and 207–210 belong to a senatorial decree, and that 211–212 is a senatorial decree proposed by Caesar on February 9, 44 (221), the validity of which was recognized on April 11, 44 (219). Their purport is to confirm Caesar's decrees of 47 (see above, p. 258, n. 3). The attempt by Eugen Täubler (*Imperium Romanum*, 1 (1913), 159–176) to arrive at an unambiguous clarification of the confusion caused by Josephus had no chance of success. Above all, he did not appreciate (160) that the senatorial decree of ss. 145–148 belongs to the year 134 (Broughton, *MRR*, 1, 491; Bickermann, *Gnomon*, 6, 360).

of a special authorization.[1] One contains regulations supplementing the *lex frumentaria* and dealing with the maintenance and use of the public streets of Rome and the qualifications of municipal magistrates and town councils, as well as the holding of the census in Italy,[2] the other the law about the foundation of a citizen colony in the town of Urso in southern Spain.[3] In each case we have only the outline of a law which was published in all its roughness in the language of a first draft. From this it appears—as was only to be expected—that the dictator's subordinates composed the first draft of laws on lines laid down by himself.[4] This was why on his sudden death so much remained incomplete. Yet even so the number of decrees which he issued himself was so great that there was not enough time to keep to the usual complicated procedure. In particular he often shortened the transactions in the Senate by merely informing the senior members of his plans and, if he called a meeting of the whole body, he simply announced his decisions to it and without any discussion these were then entered in the archives as senatorial decrees. In this way, particularly, he regulated Rome's relations with her subjects and allies, and it sometimes happened that in the engrossment of such senatorial decrees the names of witnesses were included who knew nothing at all about the document.[5]

Republican circles were deeply offended at this cavalier treatment, and no less at his constant addition to the Senate of followers of

---

[1] As mentioned above p. 283, n.1, soon after March 17, 44, a senatorial decree instructed the consuls to implement Caesar's plans, and on June 3 the *lex Antonia de actis Caesaris confirmandis* (Cic. *Phil*. 5, 10; *Att*. 16, 16a, 6; 16c, 11; App. *b.c*. 3, 81; Dio 44, 53, 2; 45, 23, 5) was passed. This is where the senatorial decree proposed by the consuls Dolabella and Antony on April 11, 44, belongs (Joseph. *ant*. 14, 219–222).

[2] *CIL*, 1², 592; Dessau, *ILS*, 6085; Bruns, *FIR*⁷, no. 18—on the reverse of a bronze tablet which bears on its obverse a Greek inscription of the fourth century from the south Italian city of Heraclea; hence known as the *Tabula Heracleensis*. It used to be wrongly called *lex Iulia municipalis* (on the strength of the reference to such a law in *ILS*, 5406, and *Dig*. 50, 1 (heading); see *frg. Vat*. 237; 243). According to Cic. *fam*. 6, 18, 1; 13, 11, 3 a law of Caesar which laid down the basic principles of municipal constitutions was passed in 46; cf. Lange, *R.A*., 3, 449; H. Rudolph, *Stadt und Staat im röm. Italien* (1935), 113–120; 217. The correct explanation of the *Tabula Heracleensis* was discovered by A. von Premerstein, *Sav Z*. 3, 43 (1922), 45 ff. He was followed by Kornemann, *RE*, 16, 611 ff.

[3] *CIL*, 1², 594; *ILS*, 6087; Bruns, *FIR*⁷, no. 28; Riccobono, *FIRA*², no. 21; Kornemann, *RE*, 16, 613.

[4] Fritz Schulz (*History of Roman Legal Science* (1946), 12; 87–88; 96–97) was—as far as I know—the first to stress that Roman politicians did not themselves formulate the texts of laws they proposed, but left this as routine work for their *scribae*. This explains the pedantically old-fashioned style of the surviving laws. The words of the law of June 3, 44, were: *eae res quas Caesar statuisset, decrevisset, egisset* (Cic. *Att*. 16, 16c, 11); *Phil*. 1, 18; 2, 109: *chirographa*; 2, 35: *commentarii et chirographa*; 3, 30; 5, 11: *commentarii*; 8, 26.

[5] Cic. *fam*. 9, 15, 3–4; 13, 77, 1; Dio 43, 27, 1.

obscure and even of provincial origin. By the time of his death he had gradually increased its membership to 900, and it is clear that such adherents outnumbered the old-style senators.[1] When the undesirability of this debasement of the Senate was pointed out to him he replied that if bandits and cut-throats had helped to defend his honour, he would have shown even them the gratitude they deserved.[2] In fact, people of this kind could always count on his generosity and consideration. In order to satisfy them, as late as 45 he was ready to sell the last available public land (even that belonging to holy places) either to allow himself to make presents of money or to give others the chance to buy land cheaply. At this time he also acquitted a series of his followers—Sallust may have been among them—who had been charged with taking bribes, although their guilt was patent.[3]

Of course, one must not give too much weight to the complaints of the optimates. For, by creating a majority in the Senate for his own followers, he was defeating them with their own weapons. Nor can it be maintained that this influx of fresh blood reduced the intrinsic worth of the distinguished assembly: this was certainly not his intention, as the above-mentioned regulations laying down the necessary qualifications for magistrates and councillors in the municipalities make clear. These excluded—doubtless in agreement with the prevailing social prejudices—those following the career of a public crier, inviter to funerals, grave-digger, fencing master, actor or procurer.[4] But his relationship with the Senate threw into bold relief two aspects of his policy which hardly went down well with the average Roman: he no longer allowed the resolutions of this body the decisive influence which it had claimed hitherto, and in its composition the proportion of members from the city of Rome was decreased in favour of Italians, and even a few Romans from the provinces. He thereby struck at the roots not only of the optimate oligarchy but also of the concept of the *imperium populi Romani* as a city state. For us it is easy to see that he was pioneering a development of which there had been numerous warnings during the previous century. But the strong forces which had just risen to oppose him in the civil war proclaimed how great a hold the

---

[1] Dio 43, 47, 3; Cic. *div.* 2, 23: Caesar murdered *in eo senatu, quem maiore ex parte ipse cooptasset; off.* 2, 29; *fam.* 6, 18, 1; *Phil.* 11, 4 and 12; Macrob. *Sat.* 2, 3, 11; Gell. *n.A.* 15, 4, 3; Suet. *Caes.* 76, 3: *civitate donatos et quosdam e semibarbaris Gallorum recepit in curiam*; 80, 2.

[2] Suet. *Caes.* 72.

[3] Dio 43, 47, 4–6. On Sallust, 43, 9, 3; ps.-Cic. *in Sall.* 19.

[4] *Tab. Heracl.* 94; 104; 113; 123; Cic. *fam.* 6, 18, 1.

old constitution despite all its faults still held over Roman minds, and if Caesar now tried to soften the harsh reality of his victory by a generous policy of reconciliation, this failed to find an answering echo in those very men whom it was particularly designed to win over. By a tragic misfortune his past came between them.[1] The peace was suspect, and there was a general air of depression,[2] especially since the limitless extravagance, as displayed on the triumphal days with money gathered by all forms of coercion, aroused considerable dissatisfaction. This reactionary movement was not concealed from him, but he believed that he could break it by continuing to pardon his enemies. In November he gave permission for the ex-praetor Titus Ampius Balbus to return to Rome. The significance of this can be gauged from the fact that this politician's nickname was 'trumpet of the civil war',[3] and in the following intercalary month (October, Jul.) he even allowed Quintus Ligarius, whom he personally loathed, to return to Rome after he had heard his case expounded by Cicero before a plaintiff in a formal hearing in the Forum.[4]

Meanwhile, the reports coming in about the situation in Spain sounded increasingly serious. After the conclusion of the war in Africa, on the surface things had been quiet there, only the Balearic and Pityusae islands being in the hands of Gnaeus Pompeius.[5]

---

[1] Cic. Phil. 5, 49.

[2] Cic. fam. 9, 15 and 26 to Paetus; 6, 1 to A. Manlius Torquatus (praetor of 70).

[3] Cic. fam. 6, 12, 3.

[4] Cic. fam. 6, 13; 14. According to Plut. Cic. 39, 6, Caesar said as Cicero came forward, 'What is there to stop us once more hearing a speech from Cicero, since the verdict on Ligarius as a wicked man and an enemy is certain?' Before Cicero, C. Vibius Pansa spoke for him (Cic. Lig. 1 and 6). Q. Aelius Tubero, who from personal enmity (Caes. b.c. 1, 31, 3; Quintil. 11, 1, 80) sought to prevent his pardon, himself belonged to the pardoned (Lig. 2; 8–10; 29). Cicero described Caesar's clementia (6; 10; 15; 19; 29; 30), misericordia (1; 15; 29; 37), lenitas (15), humanitas (16; 29) and bonitas (37) with great forcefulness, and concluded with the words: homines ad deos nulla re propius accedunt quam salutem hominibus dando, nihil habet nec fortuna tua maius quam ut possis nec natura melius quam ut velis servare quam plurimos. This takes for granted that Caesar was pleased with the allusions to his fortuna and natura. Hence the speech was successful (Plut. Cic. 39, 7; Brut. 11, 1). With regard to the Civil War he acknowledged that Caesar only took up arms in order to avert contumelia: quid egit tuus invictus exercitus, nisi ut suum ius tueretur et dignitatem tuam? (18). But he also dared to say (19): principum dignitas erat paene par, non par fortasse eorum qui sequebantur, whereby he boldly claimed the greater dignitas for the Pompeians. Thus the Civil War was fatalis quaedam calamitas, whereby humana consilia were overwhelmed divina necessitate (17). Accordingly the better side was now to be reckoned as the one quam etiam di adiuverunt. cognita vero clementia tua quis non eam victoriam probet in qua occiderit nemo nisi armatus? (19). As Caesar's remark shows, he knew what value to set on the rhetoric of such a deprecatio (Quintil. 5, 13, 5) but, spoken in public in the Forum (39), it probably seemed desirable all the same.

[5] Dio 43, 29, 2.

In June (April, Jul.) Caesar sent his fleet against him from Sardinia under Gaius Didius.[1] Its appearance in Spanish waters was viewed with the greatest suspicion by the two Pompeian legions which had risen against Quintus Cassius two years previously, and suddenly two Roman knights placed themselves at their head, drove out the proconsul Gaius Trebonius and recognized Pompey as imperator in Further Spain. Soon Sextus Pompeius, Attius Varus and Labienus arrived with ships and the remains of the African army. Only a small section of the Spanish communities offered effective resistance and Gnaeus Pompeius gradually raised an army of thirteen legions. Of course the bulk of this force consisted of non-citizen natives but, besides the two veteran legions mentioned already, another could be formed from the Roman population of the province—the Roman cities of Italica and Corduba come to mind in this context—and the veterans of Afranius now also enlisted in great numbers.[2] Although Gaius Didius defeated Attius Varus in a sea-battle near Carteia,[3] the legates Quintus Fabius Maximus and Quintus Pedius, to whom Caesar had entrusted the supreme command by land, were not able to make headway against the enemy with their legions composed of recruits, and remained encamped near Obulco (Porcuna), thirty-five miles east of Corduba on the road from Saguntum to the valley of the Guadalquivir.[4]

At the beginning of November Caesar therefore decided to go to the scene of operations in person.[5] The danger of the Pompeian rebellion was not to be underestimated, because the victorious dictator no longer had at his disposal the bulk of his trusted veterans on whom his military superiority had to a large extent depended hitherto. Of his famous legions he was accompanied only by the tenth, presumably composed of volunteers; otherwise only the fifth (raised in Transalpine Gaul with the Celtic cognomen *Alaudae*)

[1] Dio, 43, 14, 2. For the date, see *b. Afr.* 98, 2.

[2] Ibid., 43, 29, 3–30, 5; *b. Hisp.* 7, 4. At the beginning of 45, Cicero had heard of a pronouncement by Caesar that Pompey had eleven legions (*fam.* 6, 18, 2).

[3] Dio 43, 31, 3.

[4] *b. Hisp.* 2, 2; Dio 43, 28, 1; 31, 1; Strab. 3, 160. Cf. also W. Aly, *Strabon v. Amaseia* (1957), 119.

[5] Plut. *Caes.* 56, 1—as consul designate for the fourth time; App. *b.c.* 2, 426—as consul for the fourth time, which he was from January 1, 45; *b. Hisp.* 2, 1: *dictator tertio, designatus dictator quarto.* See above, p. 278, n. 1. The assumption that since 46 the annual dictatorships ran from April to April is probably correct. Cf. Broughton, *MRR*, 2, 305. The wish of Cicero's son to go to Spain (*Att.* 12, 7, 1) suggests, according to O. E. Schmidt (*Briefwechsel*, 262), that Caesar set out in 46 B.C.

is named as a veteran legion.[1] The other available troops were largely tied down in the provinces. Thus to all intents and purposes he had to make do with the forces already in Spain and consequently found himself in scarcely a more favourable position than a year earlier in Africa. The consequences of defeat would once more be incalculable.

His departure was arranged at such short notice that there was not time to appoint the magistrates of the following year in the regular way. For the time being only tribunes and plebeian aediles were elected.[2] At the head of the government was Marcus Lepidus, the consul of 46 as well as *magister equitum*.[3] At his side the dictator placed eight prefects who were to attend to the business of the praetors and urban quaestors.[4] Only after his departure did Lepidus hold consular elections and had the dictator elected consul for 45 without a colleague.[5] The direction of policy in fact lay with Balbus and Oppius, with whom the ruler was in frequent contact by letter.[6]

On the seventeenth day of his journey he reached Saguntum and on the twenty-seventh (at the beginning of December) he reached the camp at Obulco.[7] That he immediately described this journey in a poem entitled *Iter* bears witness to his unique intellectual vigour.[8] Gnaeus Pompeius had for several months been besieging Ulia, eighteen miles south of Corduba; this was a fortified town which had also remained loyal to Caesar in 48,[9] but whose fall now seemed imminent. However, Caesar succeeded in bringing in

---

[1] *b. Hisp.* 23, 3; 30, 7; 31, 4; *b. Afr.* 1, 5; Suet. *Caes.* 24, 2; Plin. *n.h.* 11, 121; Cic. *Phil.* 1, 20; cf. Holmes, *Rom. Rep.* 3, 542.

[2] Suet. *Caes.* 76, 2.

[3] Dio 43, 33, 1; *Inscr. It.* 13, 1, 56–7, on 45 B.C. (*Fasti Capitolini*).

[4] Suet. *Caes.* 76, 2: *qui absente se res urbanas administrarent*; Dio 43, 28, 2; 48, 1–2. Lange (*RA*, 3, 459) explains the authority granted according to Dio 43, 14, 5 as the right to nominate such extraordinary magistrates, going beyond the right already granted in 48 B.C. to designate the non-plebeian magistrates (Dio 42, 20, 4).

[5] *Fasti Cap.*, loc. cit.: *consul sine c(ollega)*; *Fasti Amer.*, *Inscr. It.* 13, 1, 242: *Fasti Colot.*, ibid., p. 273; Dio 43, 33, 1; Eutrop. 6, 24: *se consulem fecit* will be inexact. In the letter (*Att.* 12, 8) Cicero asks whether Atticus' relative Q. Pilius Celer (Münzer, *RE*, 20, 1326) has any idea about Caesar's plans with regard to the candidates for 45—whether he intended to nominate them on the 'fennel-field' or on the Campus Martius. According to Strab. 3, 160, the 'fennel-field' lay in the hinterland of Emporiae in Hispania Citerior. On this, see Aly, op. cit., 121. O. E. Schmidt (*Briefwechsel*, 262–263) puts this letter, correctly in my view, quite a few days after 12, 7. One might conclude from this that the eight *praefecti urbi* were also not appointed until after Caesar's departure.

[6] Cic. *fam.* 6, 8, 1; 18, 1; Tac. *ann.* 12, 60, 4.

[7] Oros. 6, 16, 6; Strab. 3, 160; App. *b.c.* 2, 429. Aly, op. cit., 119, remarks that on a rough estimate the distance from Rome to Obulco was 1,500 miles, so that about 56 miles a day were covered. See Dio 43, 32, 1.

[8] Suet. *Caes.* 56, 5.   [9] *b. Alex.* 61, 2; 63, 1; *b. Hisp.* 3, 3.

considerable reinforcements and, when he began to advance on Corduba with the rest of his army, Pompey, as his opponent had intended, abandoned the siege in order to cover the capital. A detachment in the city under Sextus Pompeius prevented its capture and Gnaeus, again advised on matters of strategy by Labienus, refused to fight a pitched battle. Caesar was therefore forced to conduct a winter campaign with its concomitant difficulty in finding food and shelter.[1]

For this reason he detached himself from the enemy at the beginning of January 45 and began to besiege the town of Ategua, which was well supplied with provisions and situated on the Salsum (Guadajoz, a southern tributary of the Guadalquivir), a day's march distant from Corduba. Since Pompey thought the place impregnable he did not at first grudge his soldiers their pleasant quarters in Corduba. But Caesar did not let himself be deterred by the time of year from investing the town completely. Pompey now followed him, but was unable to bring any more effective help. On February 19 the fortress fell after a heroic defence by its small Roman garrison hampered by the unreliable attitude of the townspeople. On top of the military defeat this represented a great moral setback for Pompey:[2] the Spanish communities began to lose confidence in his cause, desertions increased and the military situation reached such a pass that he could maintain his position only by a decisive battle.

He first withdrew in a southerly direction with Caesar challenging him all the way. On March 5 an engagement took place near Soricaria (probably also on the Guadajoz), the result of which was so unfavourable for Pompey that all the Roman knights in his camp planned to go over to Caesar; although the plan was frustrated by the treachery of a slave, Pompey was now only concerned to offer battle in a favourable position.[3] He found such a position after a few days near Munda (about six miles west of Urso). On the morning of March 17 Caesar received the news that the enemy had marched out to battle, and immediately had the battle flag run up on his tent.[4] He had only eighty cohorts of infantry, but his 8,000 cavalry were far superior to the enemy's, both in number and in quality.[5] The enemy awaited the attack on the heights and especially

[1] Dio 43, 32, 2–7; b. Hisp. 3, 1–6, 1. There are maps of the scene of operations in Kromayer-Veith, *Schlachtenatlas*, *Röm. Abt.*, map 23; Holmes, *Rom. Rep.*, 3, facing p. 229.

[2] Dio 43, 33, 2–35, 2; b. Hisp. 6–19; Frontin. *strat.* 3, 14, 1; Val. Max. 9, 2, 4.

[3] b. Hisp. 23–27, 2. An intercepted letter from Cn. Pompeius to the city of Urso is given in 26, 3–6. On Soricaria and the other localities, see Holmes, *Rom. Rep.* 3, 543.

[4] b. Hisp. 28, 1; 31, 8.   [5] b. Hisp. 7, 5; 30, 1.

the Romans in their ranks fought with the bravery of despair, since Caesar had hitherto executed his prisoners as rebels. Thus the hand-to-hand fighting was exceptionally tough until at last Caesar's men began to give way. Once again he saw his whole life's work in the balance. He jumped from his horse, seized a shield and, forcing his way into the front line, into a hail of missiles, called out that this would be his last day and the last day of soldiering for his army; did his men want to deliver him into the hands of those boys? Let them take a good look at the spot where they were leaving their general in the lurch![1] Once again fortune was on his side. This personal effort brought the waverers to a halt, and gave the cavalry who were assembled on the left wing time to attack the enemy on the right flank and in the rear.[2] Towards evening this blow transformed the battle into a final defeat for the enemy: the bodies of 30,000 Pompeians covered the field, among them those of Labienus and Attius Varus, to whom Caesar afforded burial.[3]

The fugitive remnants of the defeated army attempted to continue their desperate resistance in a number of strongpoints. Caesar left the capture of Munda and Urso (Osuna) to his legate Fabius Maximus, and himself turned back to Corduba.[4] Sextus Pompeius had already fled and the citizens asked Caesar to send in his legions to protect them from the Pompeians. This he did and all armed men present in the town were put to death, while the community had to pay an enormous indemnity. The occupation of Hispalis (Seville) under similar conditions followed at once. From here Caesar went on to Gades. Meanwhile Gnaeus Pompeius had been killed in flight and on April 12 his head was displayed to the crowd in Hispalis.[5]

Caesar remained in the Spanish provinces until about June and sketched out on the spot the lines on which he planned that imperial administration should develop there in future. In Spain where the Roman cities of Italica and Corduba, later joined by the citizen colonies of Valentia and Gades, could already look back on a century of history and where Carteia had been organized as a Latin colony

[1] Plut. *Caes.* 56, 2 and 4; Vell. 2, 55, 3; App. *b.c.* 2, 432–433; Suet. *Caes.* 36; Flor. 2, 13, 82–83; Polyaen. 8, 23, 16. Without Caesar's words: Dio 43, 37, 4–5; Frontin. 2, 8, 13; Eutrop. 6, 24.

[2] The accounts of the last phase of the battle are inadequate. From *b. Hisp.* 30, 7; 31, 5 I assume that the cavalry attack started on Caesar's left wing. Dio 43, 48, 2–3 and Flor. 2, 18, 83 seem to go back to the same source (presumably Livy), but with different rhetorical abridgements. Cf. Holmes, *Rom. Rep.*, 3, 551; and Kromayer-Veith's explanation of map 4, p. 115.

[3] *b. Hisp.* 31, 9; Plut. *Caes.* 56, 3; Oros. 6, 16, 8.

[4] *b. Hisp.* 32, 1–4; 34, 6; 41; Dio 43, 39, 4; Flor. 2, 13, 85; Oros. 6, 16, 9 (erroneous).

[5] *b. Hisp.* 32, 4–39, 3; Dio 43, 39, 1–4; App. *b.c.* 2, 434–439; Plut. *Caes.* 56, 6; Flor. 2, 13, 86.

as far back as 171, Romanization had made great progress during the last fifty years. As early as the Social War, Spanish troops had received Roman citizenship in considerable numbers, and the ten years of war against Sertorius had a decisive influence in spreading Roman civilization and political institutions. In the ensuing civil war we already find that the legions fighting on Spanish soil were to a large extent recruited from native Spaniards.[1]

What had been created by circumstances in the past was built on by Caesar in the furtherance of his own policies. For veterans and proletarians and to reward trusted Spanish communities he founded a large number of new citizen colonies: in the territory of Hispalis on the left bank of the Baetis (Guadalquivir) Colonia Romulensis;[2] Urso was allocated to proletarian settlers as Colonia Genetiva Iulia Urbanorum,[3] while the loyal town of Ulia became Colonia Fidentia,[4] Ucubi (south-east of Corduba) became Claritas Julia[5] and Ituci Virtus Julia.[6] The colonies Hasta Regia[7] and Asido Caesarina[8] also seem to belong to this group of foundations. Castulo received Latin rights.[9] The important harbours of the east coast became colonies, New Carthage as Julia Victrix Nova Carthago[10] and Tarraco as Julia Victrix Triumphalis Tarraco.[11] Roman citizens were also settled in Emporiae,[12] in Lusitania Olisipo (Lisbon) became a *municipium* as Felicitas Julia,[13] and Colonia Norbensis Caesarina, Scallabis Praesidium Julium and the Latin colony of Ebora Liberalitas Julia (all three in Lusitania) are presumably also Caesarian.[14]

This radical transplanting of communities of Roman citizens to territories with no geographical connection with Rome dealt a death blow to the character of the Roman republic as a city

---

[1] On this see Fr. Vittinghoff, *Röm. Kolon.*, 72–3. Legionaries from Spain are mentioned in Caes. *b.c.* 1, 85, 6; 86, 3; 2, 19, 3; 20, 4; *b. Alex.* 53, 5; 56, 4; *b. Hisp.* 3, 4; 7, 4; 10, 3.

[2] Plin. *n.h.* 3, 11; Isid. *etym.* 15, 1, 71; Strab. 3, 141. Cf. *ILS*, 6920; Vittinghoff, op. cit., 74, 4–6.

[3] Plin. *n.h.* 3, 12.

[4] Op. cit., 3, 10. Cf. Vittinghoff, op. cit., 75, 1.

[5] Plin. *n.h.* 3, 12. Cf. *ILS*, 5972; Vittinghoff, op. cit., 75, 2.

[6] Plin. *n.h.* 3, 12. Cf. Vittinghoff, op. cit., 74, 8.

[7] Plin. *n.h.* 3, 11. Cf. Vittinghoff, op. cit., 74, 7.

[8] Plin. loc. cit. *ILS* 6920. According to Hübner (*RE*, 2, 1579) in fact a *municipium*. Cf. Vittinghoff, op. cit., 76, 7.

[9] Plin. *n.h.* 3, 25: *oppidani Lati veteris Castulonenses, qui Caesarii Iuvenales appellantur.* Cf. Hübner, *RE*, 3, 1779.

[10] Hübner, *RE*, 3, 1625. Cf. Vittinghoff, op. cit., 79, 4.

[11] *ILS*, 1952; 6956; Schulten, *RE*, 4A, 1625; Vittinghoff, op. cit., 79, 10.

[12] Liv. 34, 9, 3. Cf. Vittinghoff, op. cit., 80, 2.

[13] Plin. *n.h.* 4, 117. Cf. Schulten, *RE*, 17, 2482; Vittinghoff, op. cit., 78, 2.

[14] Plin. loc. cit. Cf. Vittinghoff, op. cit., 77.

U

state and symbolizes the monarchic imperial policy beside which the assemblies of the sovereign people were merely decorative formalities.

Of the constitutions which were worked out for these communities under Caesar's directions largish fragments of that for Genetiva (not put into effect until after Caesar's death) have been preserved. From these it can be seen that the foundation took place 'on the dictator's orders'.[1] Its name recalls Venus Genetrix and the placing of Venus next to the Capitoline triad of Juppiter, Juno and Minerva as a communal deity presumably serves the same purpose.[2] Furthermore, freedmen were expressly made eligible for membership of the town council.[3] This regulation was particularly appropriate for a proletarian colony. But we also find it in use in the African colonies of Curubis and Clupea[4] and in the later colonies of freedmen at Carthage[5] and Corinth,[6] so that it may be conjectured that this was a matter of principle with Caesar. Further, the citizens are liable to universal military service. The town itself is fortified, and citizens and other residents can be called up by the senior magistrate to armed defence of their territory.[7] This points to the great military importance which in Caesar's view these colonies in the provinces had in holding the Empire together.

He also ordered anew the affairs of the non-Roman communities. Those that were hostile he punished by reducing their territory, imposing indemnities and increasing their tribute assessment; those that had helped him he rewarded by expanding their territory and freeing them from taxes. But as usual he also extracted as much as he could from his friends. He did not even spare the votive offerings in the temple of Hercules, the protecting deity of Gades. After all, in the year 47 he had also cleaned out his temple in Tyre.[8]

On the return journey he stopped for a few weeks in *Gallia Narbonensis* where he also applied his new principles. Through his long proconsulship he was particularly familiar with this province, which had helped him greatly in the conduct of the war, not least by providing him with troops. Since 118 it had contained the Roman citizen colony of Narbo Martius, and Roman businessmen

---

[1] *ILS*, 6087, c. 104; 106; 125.　　　　[2] Op. cit., c. 71.

[3] Op. cit., c. 105.　　　　[4] *ILS*, 5320; 1945.

[5] *ILS*, 1945.

[6] Strab. 8, 381; Crinagoras, *Anthol. Gr.* 9, 284. Cf. Vittinghoff, op. cit., 86.

[7] *ILS*, c. 98; 103. Similarly in 4 B.C. the colony of Berytus founded by Augustus provided Varus, the governor of Syria, with 1,500 men (Joseph. *b. Iud.* 2, 67; *ant.* 17, 287).

[8] Dio 43, 39, 4–5; 42, 49, 2.

and farmers had for decades been playing a large part in the economic life of the country. Caesar strengthened the existing colony by settling veterans of the tenth legion there, established Arelate (Arles)[1] on what had been the territory of Massilia with veterans of the sixth legion, and on the coast he founded the naval port of Forum Julii (Fréjus).[2] These were the only communities of Roman citizens organized by him, but he granted Latin rights to Gallic communities whereby the holders of high office obtained Roman citizenship, and in this way the upper class was eventually Romanized. He thereby gave Narbonensis the same legal standing as Transpadana had enjoyed until 49. More than a dozen such colonies are known to us by name. The remaining localities of the district were assigned to them. Thus twenty-four villages belonged to Nemausus.[3] In this system an extraordinary position was held by Massilia and the land of the Vocontii (between the Rhone and the Alps, the Isère and the Durance), whose relationship with Rome was controlled by treaty (*foedus*), and these two states so different in character were so far recognized as independent allies even by Caesar that the power of the Roman governor did not extend to them.[4]

During Caesar's stay in Narbo Mark Antony arrived and was received with the greatest respect. Caesar regarded their quarrel as over, and promised him the consulship for next year. When he continued his journey to Rome he kept him permanently in his immediate entourage and made him sit with him in his carriage as the only other passenger, while his grandnephew Gaius Octavius, who had been present at headquarters since May, travelled in the second carriage with Decimus Brutus Albinus. But the man who was basking in the light—now more brilliant than ever—of his restoration to favour did not betray by a single syllable that while still in Narbo he had heard and understood hints from another senior follower, Gaius Trebonius, that it was time to put an end to the dictator.[5]

This episode gives a most important insight into Caesar's domestic political position as well as into the ethical concepts of contemporary politicians. For it shows that his leading political helpers

---

[1] Suet. *Tib.* 4, 1; Plin. *n.h.* 3, 32 and 36. Cf. *ILS*, 6965; Gössler, *RE* Suppl. 7, 530; Vittinghoff, op. cit., 66, 4.

[2] Cic. *fam.* 10, 15, 3; 17, 1; Plin. *n.h.* 3, 35.

[3] Plin. *n.h.* 3, 36–37; Strab. 4, 187. The number of rights granted by Caesar is uncertain. Cf. O. Hirschfeld, *Kl. Schr.*, 53; Vittinghoff, op. cit., 65, 1.

[5] Plin. *n.h.* 3, 34 and 37; Strab. 4, 181; 203. Cf. Hirschfeld, *Kl. Schr.*, 55; 66.

[4] Cic. *Phil.* 2, 34; Plut. *Ant.* 11, 2; 13, 2.

with whose aid he had hitherto secured his aims were as yet by no means ready to recognize him as the lawful ruler. They had followed him because he was leading them to victory and offered good pay for services rendered. But as senators they felt themselves his equals and did not wish to be his officials and officers. When their ambition was no longer satisfied as hitherto, in a relationship built up on egotism and political interest, they began to consider whether it would not be more advantageous to remove their all too autocratic leader. Such a plan had been mooted as early as 47—Antony had also been mentioned in connection with this—and since then this feeling had obviously gained ground.[1]

If Caesar's leading adherents felt no awe for his unique genius, he could hardly expect to meet with approval from the former opposition. From Cicero's correspondence we can form a good idea of the tone of conversation among friends in these circles. While accepting pardon and outwardly acquiescing in the present state of affairs, inwardly they utterly rejected it. They were living in a wretched time, as slaves, without a state, law-courts or Senate.[2] So admirable a man as the consular Servius Sulpicius Rufus, who was administering Greece on Caesar's behalf, wrote on the occasion of the death of Cicero's daughter: they had been deprived of country, honour, respect and rank, of everything that ought to be no less dear to men than their children; better to die without pain than to be forced to continue living in a present which offered their sons no future, since they no longer had the power to preserve their ancestral inheritance by their own efforts, of standing for offices of state in the regular way and enjoying freedom of movement in looking after the interests of their friends. In the last few years so many men of distinction had perished, the Roman Empire had suffered such losses and all the provinces were in confusion. Since they were forced by fate to be time-servers, Cicero should avoid giving the impression that he was mourning less for his daughter than for the misfortune of his country and the victory of the enemy.[3] Even if the particular circumstances of this letter encouraged him to draw a gloomy

---

[1] See p. 282, n. 4 above.

[2] Cicero on January 1, 43 (*Phil.* 5, 49): *utinam C. Caesari — patri dico — contigisset adulescenti ut esset senatui atque optimo cuique carissimus! quod cum consequi neglexisset, omnem vim ingenii, quae summa fuit in illo, in populari levitate consumpsit. itaque cum respectum ad senatum et ad bonos non haberet, eam sibi viam ipse patefecit ad opes suas amplificandas, quam virtus liberi populi ferre non posset; fam.* 4, 5, 2; 5, 15, 4; 6, 1, 1; 3, 4; 4, 4; 21, 3; 9, 16, 3; *Att.* 12, 23, 1; 28, 2; *orat.* 35: *tempora inimica virtuti.*

[3] Cic. *fam.* 4, 5, 2–3 and 6.

picture, it is still very significant of the mood of the Roman aristocracy. They regarded Caesar's despotism as a complete break
with all earlier traditions. We can understand what this meant in a
state where aristocratic rule had lasted for centuries and could look
back over splendid achievements which had left their mark on the
history of the world.

Nevertheless, the war in Spain, whose outcome, as viewed from
Rome, seemed quite uncertain for several months, aroused more
fears than hopes. For all who had abandoned the cause of the republic
after Pharsalus could expect the worst from the narrow fanaticism of
Gnaeus Pompeius. The war offers only two possibilities, wrote
Cicero: destruction or slavery.[1] Of Cicero's correspondents only
Lucius Lucceius, the friend of the elder Pompey, and the still exiled
Aulus Manlius Torquatus thought otherwise,[2] while the general
mood is well reflected by Gaius Cassius when he writes in January
45: 'I am exceedingly worried and would prefer to keep our mild
old master than to make trial of the cruel new one. You know
what a fool Gnaeus is; you know how he takes cruelty for bravery;
you know how he always thinks that we are making a fool of him;
I fear that like a peasant he will reply with the sword.'[3] Of course
this only means that Caesar was regarded as the lesser evil.

The attitude of the optimates meant that his policy of reconciliation had failed completely. But he could not understand this
resistance until at the end of 46 he read Cicero's *Cato*, the literary
monument dedicated on the wishes of Brutus by the greatest Roman
writer to the hero of Utica.[4] In this work Cato, who had always
been Caesar's harshest enemy and had gone to his death in order
to brand him as an intolerable tyrant,[5] was extolled as the embodi-
ment of true Roman *virtus*. Among other things it was said that he
was one of the few people who were greater than their reputation.[6]
Here an unbridgeable chasm opened. Caesar had so far not rejected
Cicero's repeated admonitions to restore the republic and clearly
hoped that the optimates would eventually get used to his way of
dealing with this question, and, even if they did not forget their

---

[1] Op. cit., 6, 21, 1.

[2] Op. cit., 5, 13, 3; 14, 1; 6, 1, 2 and 6; 2, 2; 4, 1–2.

[3] Op. cit., 15, 9, 4. Cf. 6, 4, 1: *alteros prope modum iam sumus experti; de altero nemo est quin cogitet quam sit metuendus iratus victor armatus.* Cicero had already been threatened with death by him in Corcyra in 48 for withdrawing from the war (Plut. *Cic.* 39, 2; *Cat. Min.* 55, 6).

[4] Cic. *orat.* 35.

[5] Cic. *off.* 1, 112; Plut. *Cat. Min.* 66, 2.

[6] Cic. *Phil.* 13, 30: *omnium gentium virtute princeps*; Macrob. *Sat.* 6, 2, 33.

difference of opinion about the character of the republic, would at least allow it to fade into the background. However, this tribute to Cato again gave these demands a clearly defined form; it was the old optimate republic within which there was no room for the activities started by Caesar. Cicero had also written about the true statesman in his work *de republica*. But there he was concerned with the qualities which could justify a spiritual authority within the framework of an idealized Roman constitution, not with a new office of state, and the question of the government of the Empire was not even mentioned.[1]

Caesar refused to tolerate the setting up of the narrow-minded optimate Cato, of all people, as the type of the genuine Roman and immediately after the battle of Munda began to write a refutation in two books.[2] So that no time should be lost he also gave Hirtius orders to write one, and the latter produced a book which came into Cicero's hands on May 9. It cannot have been very successful in its object, since Cicero wrote to his friend Atticus asking him to secure as wide a circulation for it as possible so that Cato's glory might shine forth the more.[3] Caesar's *Anti-Cato* began with a few courteous sentences of introduction to the effect that this was the work of a soldier who had neither the ability nor the time to elaborate his theme as the orator had done. Cicero was compared with Pericles as an orator and with Theramenes as a politician.[4] This was already rather two-edged praise, since Theramenes had the reputation of an untrustworthy politician; and Caesar then went on to display a mood of great irritation.[5] For he attempted to attack his great opponent in the moral sphere—just the point where he was generally regarded as unassailable. When he directed on to his private life the full malice of ancient invective, nothing remained of the lauded hero of liberty but an eccentric drunkard and miser, who was finally driven by avarice to sell his wife to Hortensius.[6] We can understand the political motives behind this outburst of uncontrollable fury, but its want of moderation brought about the opposite

---

[1] Cic. *de rep.* 2, 51: compared to the tyrant *bonus et sapiens et peritus utilitatis dignitatisque civilis, quasi tutor et procurator rei publicae; sic enim appelletur quicumque erit rector et gubernator civitatis. quem virum facite ut agnoscatis; iste est enim qui consilio et opera civitatem tueri potest.* Cf. *RE*, 7A, 974–975.

[2] Suet. *Caes.* 56, 5. Cf. H. Drexler, *Hermes* 70 (1935), 203.

[3] Cic. *Att.* 12, 40, 1; 41, 4; 44, 1; 45, 2; 48.

[4] Plut. *Caes.* 3, 4; *Cic.* 39, 5. Cf. Drexler, op. cit., 2. App. *b.c.* 2, 414; Dio 43, 13, 4.

[5] Cic. *top.* 94: *nimis impudenter Caesar contra Catonem meum.*

[6] Plut. *Cat. Min.* 11, 7; 36, 4–5; 52, 5–7 (as an answer to this, Lucan 2, 326–391); Gell. *n.A.* 4, 16, 8; Plin. *ep.* 3, 12, 2–3. Other evidence is given in Kübler, 3, 145–148.

result to that intended. The picture of Cato was too distorted to win approval in any quarter and thus his enemy became much more dangerous in death than he had been in life, because his defenders were now even more inclined to elevate him to the status of the tyrant's equal opponent.[1] At the same time, however, the abuse heaped on the universally admired Cato raised justified doubts about the 'magnanimity' which Caesar advertised with his policy of reconciliation and, as a result, those optimates who had been ready to trust him increasingly lost this confidence.[2] Of course his captivating charm succeeded in keeping alive a glimmer of hope. When he heard of the death of Cicero's daughter, although weighed down with business in Spain, he found time on April 30 to send the deeply afflicted father a letter of sympathy,[3] and on August 12 Balbus showed him a letter from the dictator in which he said that he had learned much stylistically from repeated readings of Cicero's *Cato*, whereas he found himself eloquent by comparison with Brutus' pamphlet on the same subject.[4] Since Cicero had tried in vain a few months earlier to win Brutus for his oratorical ideal in his *Orator*[5] this was a well-calculated compliment. In this emphatically aesthetic appreciation one may perhaps also see a deliberate attempt to turn the discussion away from politics.

---

[1] The author of the *b. Afr.* already calls him *homo gravissimus* (23, 1), and tells us (88, 5) how the citizens of Utica who supported Caesar politically honoured him with a funeral *propter eius singularem integritatem et quod dissimillimus reliquorum ducum fuerat*. Next Sallust (*Cat.* 53, 6 ff.), in the famous comparison with Caesar, made him the representative of *virtus*; 54, 1: *magnitudo animi par, item gloria, sed alia alii. Caesar beneficiis ac munificentia magnus habebatur, integritate vitae Cato.* Liv. frag. 55 (ed. Weissenborn-Müller, from Jerome's *prol. libri II in Hoseam*) on Cicero's and Caesar's pamphlets on Cato: *cuius gloriae neque profuit quisquam laudando nec vituperando nocuit, cum utrumque summis praediti fecerint ingeniis;* Hor. *car.* 1, 12, 35: *Catonis nobile letum;* 2, 1, 23: *cuncta subacta praeter atrocem animum Catonis;* Vell. 2, 35, 2: *homo virtuti simillimus et per omnia ingenio diis quam hominibus propior;* Val. Max. 2, 10 8: *omnibus, numeris perfecta virtus. quae quidem effecit ut quisquis sanctum et egregium civem significare velit, sub nomine Catonis definiat.* In Lucan he is always connected with *virtus*: 2, 243, 258; 263; 287; 9, 371; 445. Petron. *sat.* 119, 41: *venalis populus venalis curia patrum.* That is why Cato is not elected consul (48): *non homo pulsus erat, sed in uno victa potestas Romanumque decus.* Cic. *Lig.* 19: *nunc melior ea* (sc. *causa*) *iudicanda est quam etiam di adiuverunt,* was followed by Lucan 1, 128: *victrix causa deis placuit, sed victa Catoni.* Cato stands above the gods of popular belief and is addressed in 9, 556: *certe vita tibi semper secreta supernas ad leges sequerisque deum.* He is in harmony with the Stoic universal deity (9, 578): *estque dei sedes, nisi terra et pontus et aer et caelum et virtus? superos quid quaerimus ultra? Iuppiter est quodcumque vides quodcumque moveris.*

[2] Thus after the assassination Cicero allowed himself to utter the slander (*off.* 2, 84): *tanta in eo peccandi libido fuit, ut hoc ipsum eum delectaret peccare, etiam si causa non esset.*

[3] Cic. *Att.* 13, 20, 1. Cicero had sent the two letters of recommendation (*fam.* 13, 15 and 16) to him in Spain; of these the first in particular will have given Caesar pleasure, with its numerous quotations from the Greek poets and witty allusions to Cicero's political disappointments.

[4] Cic. *Att.* 13, 46, 2.   [5] Op. cit., 14, 20, 3.

The *Cato* of Brutus, on the other hand, again called to mind that two different political worlds were facing each other. For no Republican had accepted the policy of reconciliation more readily than this nephew of Cato; by the end of 47 Caesar had already given him the very important post of governor of Cisalpine Gaul.[1] At the end of March 45 he handed the province over to Gaius Vibius Pansa, but returned once more at the end of July in order to welcome the dictator.[2] Caesar expressed himself very satisfied with his tenure of the governorship and promised him the urban praetorship for the following year, and the consulship for 41.[3] In this way he succeeded in again keeping Brutus on his side. Yet Brutus, who had just married Porcia, Cato's daughter and the widow of Caesar's equally irreconcilable opponent Bibulus,[4] fondly concluded from these signs of favour that Caesar sincerely intended to restore the republic and, writing to his friends in Rome about his meeting with the dictator, said, 'He supports the men of the right opinion', which in optimate language referred to themselves.

When Cicero received this report early in August he could only mock at such credulity.[5] For, on the prompting of Atticus, who was acting in agreement with Balbus and Oppius in the matter, he had himself sketched a letter to Caesar on May 13, in which he developed some ideas of a 'citizen of the right opinion forced to adapt himself to the times' about the ordering of the state.[6] Surviving allusions showed that Caesar declared that his next task was to settle accounts with the Parthians.[7] He had not been able to undertake anything in this direction during his short stay in Syria in 47, but knew that Pompey had tried to make contact with the Parthian king Orodes. For the time being he had left behind Sextus Caesar, the son of a cousin, presumably as *quaestor pro praetore* with two legions, to protect the province.[8]

---

[1] Plut. *Brut.* 6, 10; App. *b.c.* 2, 465; Cic. *Brut.* 171; *fam.* 6, 6, 10.

[2] Cic. *Att.* 12, 27, 3; 13, 44, 1.

[3] Plut. *Brut.* 6, 6–7, 5; *Caes.* 57, 5; 62, 4; Cic. *fam.* 12, 2, 2; *Phil.* 8, 27; Vell. 2, 56, 3.

[4] Plut. *Brut.* 13, 3; Vell, 2, 56, 3; Cic. *Att.* 13, 10, 3; 11, 1; 17, 1. Cf. *RE*, 10, 986. But *laudatio Porciae* (*Att.* 13, 37, 3; 48, 2) refers to the recently deceased sister of Cato, the widow of L. Domitius Ahenobarbus.

[5] Cic. *Att.* 13, 40, 1.

[6] Op. cit., 13, 26, 2; 12, 51, 2; 52, 2. The correct chronological sequence of the letters on this topic was deduced by O. E. Schmidt (*Briefwechsel*, 285 ff.).

[7] Cic. *Att.* 13, 27, 1; 31, 3.

[8] Caes. *b.c.* 3, 82, 4; Dio 41, 55, 4; 42, 2, 5. Cf. Münzer, *RE*, 10, 477; Broughton, *MRR*, 2, 289. See also *b. Alex.* 66, 1; Dio 47, 26, 3; Joseph. *ant.* 14, 160; 170; App. *b.c.* 3, 312=4, 250 gives him only one legion. See above, p. 266.

But during the war in Africa Quintus Caecilius Bassus, a Roman knight who had fought under Pompey and disappeared in Tyre after Pharsalus, tampered with the soldiers of Sextus, claiming that he had been nominated as governor of Syria by Metellus Scipio, and eventually persuaded them to murder Sextus.[1] Caesar first gave the task of overthrowing Caecilius Bassus to Quintus Cornificius, who had rendered good service as quaestor in Illyricum in 48 and 47 and was now on duty in Cilicia. But soon, as Cicero learned in December 46, danger also threatened from the Parthians. That was why Caesar sent out at least two legions.[2] Yet it was not until 45 that Cornificius' successor Gaius Antistius Vetus was able, with these reinforcements, to start the attack on Apamea, where Bassus had entrenched himself. For some time no decision was reached; finally, towards the end of the year, Pacorus, the son of the king of Parthia, arrived with a large army and drove the besiegers off with heavy losses.[3] Presumably it was his experiences in Spain which showed Caesar that in the East too he would have to put things right in person. If he at first used young men for the task, this was because he did not think any of his old legates capable of mastering it. The disaster of Crassus served as an eloquent warning against underestimating the difficulties, and he owed it to his reputation on this occasion to make suitable preparations before proceeding:[4] he accordingly explained in letters to his intimates that he wished to ensure the maintenance of his reforms in Rome before setting out.[5]

However, when Cicero came to speak in his letter about the ordering of affairs at Rome, it sounded like a protest about the authoritarian régime during the Spanish campaign and as if he were afraid that the same conditions might prevail during the eastern campaign. For this reason Balbus and Oppius recommended that the letter should only be sent after a thorough revision. But Cicero refused to renounce all his own ideas in this way. He preferred to

[1] Dio 47, 26, 3–7; Liv. per. 114; App. b.c. 3, 315; previously, 3, 312=4, 250—an inferior version. Joseph. b. Iud. 1, 216; ant. 14, 268. Cicero heard about this in Rome in September, 46 (fam. 12, 17, 1; cf. O. E. Schmidt, op. cit., 254).

[2] b. Alex. 42, 2; 47, 5; Cic. fam. 12, 19, 1–2.

[3] Cic. Att. 14, 9, 3; Deiot. 23; Dio 47, 27, 2–5; Strab. 16, 752–753.

[4] For this reason Appian (b.c. 2, 459), who makes the campaign appear an improvisation after February 15, 44, is very foolish, especially since we read in the same author (3, 312; 4, 250) that as early as 47 Caesar had envisaged a Parthian War. Dio 43, 51, 1 shows that the war was very popular.

[5] Cic. Att. 13, 31, 3; 7, 1. The Theopompus mentioned here is his highly esteemed guest-friend from Cnidus; see above, p. 246, n. 3. See also Cic. Phil. 13, 33.

preserve 'a semi-independence by silence and self-concealment'.[1] Not until August could he be induced after repeated cajolement at least to write to tell Caesar that he had greatly enjoyed his books about Cato. But in private conversation he simply called him *rex*— a word uttered only with abhorrence since the foundation of the republic.[2]

Caesar was well informed about the mood of traditionalist circles in Rome and for certain purposes even paid attention to it, as is revealed by his relations with Brutus. But although he was already present in northern Italy in July, he did not enter Rome until his triumph at the beginning of October[3] and showed thereby that he was little concerned with the restoration of the state in the spirit of Cicero. In September he spent some time on his estate at Labici (south-east of Rome). Here he wrote his will, in which he named his nearest male relatives as heirs; his grandnephew Gaius Octavius was to receive three-quarters of the inheritance and his grand-nephew Lucius Pinarius and nephew Quintus Pedius the remaining quarter.[4] He had already had Octavius elected pontifex in 47 in place of Lucius Domitius Ahenobarbus, and then during the Spanish war came so to appreciate the talents of this unusually precocious sixteen-year-old that he increasingly hoped to find in him his political heir.[5] On the last page of his will he finally arranged for his adoption.[6] Such care for the continuation of one's family was entirely

---

[1] Cic. *Att.* 13, 27, 1; 31, 3. At the time he wrote to Varro (*fam.* 9, 8, 2): *atque utinam quietis temporibus atque aliquo si non bono at saltem certo statu civitatis haec inter nos studia exercere possemus!*

[2] Cic. *Att.* 13, 50, 1; 51, 1; 37, 2; *fam,* 11, 27, 8.

[3] Vell. 2, 56, 3.

[4] Suet. *Caes.* 83, 1–2. Münzer, *Hermes,* 71 (1936), 228, and *RE,* 19, 39 argues from Pedius' age that he was Caesar's nephew. Less exact on the co-heirs are Liv. *per.* 116; Nicol. Dam. F 128, 30; 130, 48; App. *b.c.* 3, 82; 89; Plin. *n.h.* 35, 21.

[5] Nicol. Dam. F 127, 9; Vell. 2, 59, 3; Cic. *Phil.* 5, 46 and 53. Cf. *ILS,* 75. Suet. *Aug.* 8, 1; Nicol. Dam. F 127, 24; Dio 43, 41, 3.

[6] Walter Schmitthenner, *Oktavian und das Testament Caesars* (*Zetemata* 4 (1952)), 18 and 32, rightly refers Suetonius' *in ima cera* (against my earlier interpretation 'at the bottom of the wax tablet') to the last of the wax tablets which, combined as a codex, contained the will. It seems to me that in the reference to the collection of senatorial decrees in Dittenberger, *Syll.*[3] 747, 58: ἐμ πραγμάτων συμβεβουλευμένων Δέλτωι πρώτηι κηρώματι τεσσαρεσκαιΔεκάτωι, the word Δέλτος (=*tabula*) also means a codex. Similarly in Suet. *Ner.* 17 there is mention of *primae duae cerae* in wills. On the other hand Schmitthenner's attempt (39 ff.) to deny testamentary adoption as a legal institution, and to argue that it was a matter of the *condicio nominis ferendi* mentioned in *Dig.* 36, 1, 65, 10, is rightly rejected by H. Volkmann (*Gnomon* 26 (1954), 43), L. Wickert (*RE,* 22, 2189) and H. Nesselhauf (*Hermes* 83 (1955), 484, n. 1). See Vell. 2, 59, 1: *Caesaris deinde testamentum apertum est, quo C. Octavium, nepotem sororis suae Iuliae, adoptabat.*

in keeping with ancient Roman concepts, but in view of Caesar's position an adoption by him will have meant more than usual.

When on April 20[1] news of the battle of Munda reached Rome, the Senate and People used all their powers of invention in order to offer the victor new honours. April 21 was from now on to be celebrated annually with races in the Circus, and thanks were to be offered to the gods for fifty days on end. He was granted the title of Imperator as a hereditary name, was to appear on all official occasions in triumphal garb and was authorized always to wear a laurel wreath. For his victory over the Pompeians he received the additional name of the 'liberator'. The building of a temple to Freedom was decreed as well as a palace on the Quirinal for Caesar, to be paid for out of public funds. The anniversaries of his previous victories were to be celebrated with annual sacrifices. The celebrations and sacrifices of thanksgiving for every future victory were fixed in advance even if Caesar were to have no personal part in it: this followed naturally from the decree which put the entire management of the army and finance in his hands alone. To the ten-year dictatorship was added the consulship for ten years.[2]

In May it was further decreed that his ivory statue on its special litter, together with the carriage for its trappings, should be carried with the images of the other gods in the procession in the Circus. A statue with the inscription 'To the unconquerable god' was to be erected in the temple of Quirinus and another on the Capitol among the statues of the kings and Lucius Brutus. By these moves the ruler cult was officially introduced to Rome by senatorial and popular decree. On this topic Cicero let slip the remark: 'I'd rather see him sharing the temple of Quirinus than that of Salus.' To understand the point of this one must recall that although Quirinus represented

---

[1] Dio 43, 42, 3.

[2] Dio 43, 42, 2–3; 43, 1; 44, 1–45, 2; Suet. Caes. 45, 2; App. b.c. 2, 440–443 (abridged); Suet. Caes. 76, 1 (praenomen Imperatoris). Dio 44, 2–5 is thinking of the later imperial praenomen. But Caesar never used the praenomen (Wickert, RE, 22, 2279). Coins with Caesar imperator (A. Alföldi, Stud. über Caesars Mon., 29–34; 86, and plates 6–9; Sydenham, CRR, pp. 176–178, nos. 1055, 1056, 1060, 1070; Konrad Kraft, Der goldene Kranz Caesars, 66) do not appear before February, 44. Contrary to Syme (Historia 7 (1958), 179), I conclude, with Alföldi, that Caesar made use of the right which he had been granted, and signified his permanent power of command by means of the title. From Cic. Att. 12, 45, 2 I conjecture that Caesar's palace was on the Quirinal. Caesar thereby became the vicinus of Atticus, whose house, according to 12, 48 rose in value because of its distinguished surroundings. This does not seem to refer only to the statue in the temple of Quirinus (Dio 43, 45, 3), as Wissowa (Rel. u. Kult. d. Röm.² 155, 7) assumes.

the deified Romulus, the latter—so the story went—had been torn to pieces by the senators because he had become a tyrant.[1]

But the busy invention of Caesar's creatures had asked too much at one time even of the susceptibilities of the common people. On July 20 the first repetition of the victory games was held, and when the procession passed by with the innovations described above there was no applause at the appearance of Caesar's statue with that of Victory; the erection of Caesar's image among the statues of the kings caused great dissatisfaction and talk of a tyrant. This was so well known that in November in a debate held in Caesar's presence Cicero spoke quite openly about it.[2]

On one of the first days in October he celebrated the triumph over Spain. The official interpretation that a foreign enemy had been annihilated in this campaign was even less tenable than when applied to the war in Africa, and consequently this celebration also aroused much bitter feeling. Furthermore, an embarrassing scene occurred when the triumphal chariot passed the tribunes' bench and one of the tribunes, Pontius Aquila, failed to rise to greet the *triumphator*. Such behaviour could only be regarded as a tribunician demonstration against the dictator and Caesar quickly countered by calling to him: 'Why don't you make me give up the state, Aquila? After all, you are a tribune!' For several days he was so angry with him that he qualified every promise which he made with the ironic remark: 'Provided that Pontius Aquila gives me permission.' Perhaps it was in connection with these events that Caesar believed that the entertainment of the people after the triumph had not been sufficiently lavish, and ordered another public breakfast to be served four days later. But not satisfied with this, contrary to all

---

[1] Dio 43, 45, 2–4. (This dates Cic. *Att.* 12, 45, 2.) Cf. L. R. Taylor, *Divinity of the Roman Emperor*, 65. App. *b.c.* 2, 476; cf. F. Taeger, *Charisma* 2, 50 ff.

[2] Cic. *Att.* 13, 44, 1; *Deiot.* 33, where the leader of the embassy sent by the Galatian king Deiotarus is said to have reported to Galatia: *ad regem scribere solebat te in invidia esse, tyrannum existimari, statua inter reges posita animos hominum vehementer offensos, plaudi tibi non solere.* Cicero comments (34): *valde enim invidendum est statuis cuius tropeais non invidemus! nam si locus adfert indiviam, nullus est ad statuam quidem rostris clarior. de plausu autem quid respondeam? qui nec desideratus umquam in te est et nonnumquam obstupefactis hominibus ipsa admiratione compressus est, et fortasse eo praetermissus, quia nihil vulgare te dignum videri potest.* But, as Helmut Rahn ('Cicero und die Rhetorik', *Rivista Ciceroniana* 1 (1959), 23) has admirably demonstrated, Cicero's rhetorical mastery is revealed in that 'his personality is not concerned to express "itself" but "something", something suitable to the subject and situation'. Thus Caesar listened to this speech in defence by Cicero. The same also applies to the speech for Ligarius; see above, p. 292.

tradition he also allowed his two legates Fabius and Pedius to triumph on October 13 and December 13 respectively.[1]

Before Fabius' triumph Caesar had retired from the consulship himself, and had Fabius and Gaius Trebonius elected consuls for the last three months of the year.[2] Pedius ranked as proconsul of Nearer Spain.[3] He had fourteen praetors and forty quaestors elected for the current year, and for the following year sixteen praetors, among them Brutus and Cassius.[4] Mark Antony was designated consul; Caesar intended to hold the other consulship himself until his departure for the Parthian campaign and then Publius Dolabella, not yet thirty years old, was to replace him.[5] Governors were appointed by Caesar without drawing lots. On the other hand, he rejected the right to designate all the magistrates which was granted to him at this time: nominally these were elected by the people and plebs,[6] but in practice all elections degenerated more or less to formalities. After December 10 the newly-elected tribune Lucius Antonius (brother of Marcus) passed a law granting Caesar a binding right of recommendation for half the candidates in the election of all magistrates except the consuls.[7] This new law was first used after a popular decree had given Caesar the command of the Parthian expedition and, in connection with this, immediate authority to appoint officials for three years (43 to 41), the presumed duration of the campaign.[8] Hereupon, Aulus Hirtius and Gaius Pansa were first elected consuls for 43; with 16 praetors, 40 quaestors, 2 curule and 4 plebeian aediles (in addition to the regular law, there were two new *aediles plebis Ceriales* to look after the corn supply). At the beginning of March 44 the election of the consuls for 42, Decimus Brutus and Lucius Munatius Plancus, took place, as well as that of the tribunes.[9] For his fifth dictatorship (44) Caesar temporarily retained Marcus Lepidus as *magister equitum*; when he set out for the

[1] Vell. 2, 56, 3; Quintil. 6, 3, 61; Plut. *Caes.* 56, 7–9; 57, 8; Suet. *Caes.* 37, 1; 38, 2; 78, 2; *Acta triumph.*, *Inscr. It.* 13, 1, 86–7; Dio 43, 42, 1.

[2] Dio 43, 46, 2. Cf. *Inscr. It.* 13, 1, 56–7.

[3] *Acta triumph.* (loc. cit.).

[4] Dio 43, 47, 2; 49, 1; Plut. *Caes.* 57, 5; *Brut.* 7, 1–5.

[5] Cic. *Phil.* 2, 79; Vell. 2, 58, 2; Plut. *Ant.* 11, 3; Dio 43, 51, 8; App. *b.c.* 2, 511; 539. Dolabella is said to have been only twenty-five years old—presumably an exaggeration. If it were true he would have been ten years younger than his wife Tullia, which Groebe (*RE*, 7A, 1331) is ready to believe.

[6] Dio 43, 47, 1.

[7] Cic. *Phil.* 7, 16; Suet. *Caes.* 41, 2; Dio 43, 51, 3; Nicol. Dam., *FgrHist* 90, F 130, 67.

[8] Dio 43, 51, 1–2.

[9] Nicol. Dam. F 130, 77; Cic. *Phil.* 3, 37; 39; 12, 20; 13, 26; 5, 36; *fam.* 10, 8; 11, 4 ff.; *ad Brut.* 1, 1, 1; Vell. 2, 58, 1; Dio 43, 51, 3 and 6.

Parthian war Gaius Octavius was to take his place and for 43 he had Gnaeus Domitius Calvinus in mind.[1] It was at the same time that by his new appointments he increased the membership of the senate to 900. Sons of freedmen, centurions and native Celts thereby received their reward, without consideration for Roman ideas.[2] But senior followers were also putting forward their claims. To satisfy them he awarded ten ex-praetors the rank and insignia of consulars, with corresponding promotion for men of lower rank.[3] He was also empowered by the law of the tribune Lucius Cassius to nominate new patricians. On the strength of this, among many others, he raised Gaius Octavius to the status of Rome's ancient aristocracy.[4]

In all this he was chiefly concerned to create a large and devoted imperial civil service.[5] With so many plans awaiting realization there was not enough time for all the formalities prescribed by law. In fact, the constitutional forms only continued to be used very superficially. In Caesar's defence we can argue that from time immemorial elections at Rome had been 'fixed' by powerful politicians (whether in office or not).[6] But all the same the right to vote had always been represented as one of the most treasured possessions of the Roman people. Accordingly the contempt with which he treated these important matters offered a very suitable target for the incitement of the masses. This became immediately apparent when the new consul Fabius Maximus entered the theatre for the first time and his lictor called the audience to order in the usual way. A general cry was raised that he was no consul,[7] but Caesar did not let himself

---

[1] Dio 43, 51, 7; App. b.c. 3, 30; Fast. Cap. on 44 B.C., Inscr. It. 13, 1, 56–7; Plin. n.h. 7, 147.

[2] Dio 43, 47, 3; 48, 22, 3; Suet. Caes. 41, 1; 76, 3; 80, 2; Cic. fam. 6, 18, 1; Phil. 11, 12; 13, 27. As already remarked above (p. 292), Caesar did not intend to do away with the plutocratic order of society. R. Syme shows in his brilliant chapter on 'Caesar's New Senators' (Rom. Rev., 78–96) that the majority of them were Italians whose families had possessed the Roman citizenship since the Social War. He estimates their number at about 400 (p. 90). It is understandable that the old senators were displeased at this flood of homines novi. Syme rightly finds (94) that the appointment of consuls from 48 to 44 was 'not revolutionary'. Five came from the nobility: P. Servilius Isauricus, M. Aemilius Lepidus, Q. Fabius Maximus, M. Antonius, P. Cornelius Dolabella (three patricians); the four homines novi Q. Fufius Calenus, P. Vatinius, C. Trebonius, C. Caninius Rebilus had gone through the lower magistracies and were legati of distinction. But the phantom of noble rule had disappeared.

[3] Suet. Caes. 76, 3; Dio 43, 47, 3; Plut. Caes. 58, 1.

[4] Tac. ann. 11, 25, 2 (speech of Claudius); Dio 43, 47, 3; Suet. Caes. 41, 1. Cf. Broughton, MRR, 2, 324. Q. Cassius was the brother of Caesar's murderer (Cic. Att. 14, 2, 1; fam. 12, 2, 2). See also Suet. Aug. 2, 1; Nicol. Dam. F 128, 35; Dio 45, 2, 7.

[5] See above, p. 273.

[6] L. R. Taylor, Party Politics in the Age of Caesar (1949), especially pp. 62 ff.

[7] Suet. Caes. 80, 2.

be influenced by it. At seven o'clock in the morning on December 31, 45, the people assembled to elect quaestors. When the auspices had been taken for a meeting by tribes, news arrived of the death of the consul Maximus. Caesar now had his chair removed, made the electors group themselves by centuries and at one o'clock in the afternoon Gaius Caninius Rebilus was raised to the consulship for the remaining hours of the day. Republican institutions could not have been more grossly abused and the impression was given that Caesar had used this opportunity to proclaim the new epoch. Cicero indeed jested about the affair: no one, he said, had breakfasted while Caninius was consul, nor had any harm been done, thanks to the watchfulness of a consul who during his whole term of office had not once shut his eyes. But at the same time he confessed that one who had experienced these events could not hold back his tears.[1] The unworthy senators were also greeted with notices posted on walls: 'A fine deed! No one is to show a new senator the way to the Council-house!'

Despite the pain caused to the republicans by these occurrences, for Caesar they were only incidental episodes within his grand design of government. A main item of this continued to be the energetic prosecution of his policy of colonization. To the allotments and settlements in Italy, Spain and Gaul new ones were added in Africa, Greece and Asia Minor. In Africa Carthage was founded as Colonia Julia Concordia Carthago for veterans and proletarians. In Greece, too, he made amends for the destruction of 146 by the foundation, primarily for freedmen, of Laus Julia Corinthus.[2] In Asia Minor Myrlea-Apamea on the Sea of Marmara became Colonia Julia Concordia Apamea. Further colonies were established on the territories of the city states of Lampsacus, Heraclea and Sinope (which continued to exist beside them).[3] A colony was also planned for Buthrotum in Epirus (facing Corcyra) because the city was in arrears with the payment of its tribute. Atticus owned large estates there and, backed by Cicero, he now intervened with the dictator on its behalf. The latter granted their request; in return

[1] Cic. *fam.* 7, 30, 1–2; *Inscr. It.* 13, 1, 56–7; 133; Dio 43, 46, 2–4; Plut. *Caes.* 58, 2–3; Plin. *n.h.* 7, 181; Macrob. *Sat.* 2, 3, 6; Suet. *Caes.* 76, 2.

[2] Dio 43, 50, 3–5; Plut. *Caes.* 57, 8; Diod. 32, 327, 3; Strab. 8, 381; 17, 833; Paus. 2, 1, 2; App. *Lib.* 646. Cf. Kornemann, *RE*, 4, 530; 532; Vittinghoff, *Röm. Kolonis.*, 81; 82, n. 5 (about the other colonies in Africa which should perhaps be ascribed to Caesar); 86.

[3] Plin. *n.h.* 5, 149; App. *b.c.* 5, 570; Plin. *ep.* 10, 47, 1; Strab. 12, 542; 546. Cf. Vittinghoff, op. cit., 88. Rostovtzeff (*Social and Economic History of the Hellenistic World*, 1577, n. 102) takes the view that Caesar intended to create bases for the Parthian War here; cf. 999.

Atticus advanced the sum due and Caesar had his decision drawn up in writing. When the colonists detailed for the venture nonetheless began to assemble, he explained to the worried Atticus that he simply did not wish to give offence to these people by telling them of the change of plan; once they were over on the other side he would allocate them another area. From this information we can see how things went in such cases, but also how Caesar did his best to avoid irritating the colonists so long as they were in Rome;[1] it also serves as evidence that he viewed the disregard of republican institutions as of far less importance. Nor did the distribution of land in Italy proceed without violence, as we again learn from letters by Cicero, who was concerned that some properties which had already been confiscated should be exempt from distribution.[2] The final decision in all these cases rested with Caesar himself. He did not grant Latin rights in the East, since the prerequisite of knowledge of Latin among the upper class was lacking there. On the other hand he granted such rights to all the communities of Sicily.[3]

If one considers as a connected whole the achievements of his policy of settlement and colonization in permeating the empire with Roman elements within the space of a few months, it becomes clear that he intended to produce a degree of fusion between the nationally and (what was felt even more) politically very different peoples of the Empire. The Roman citizenship which no longer had any significance politically (in the sense of a self-governing Roman people) became throughout the Empire the hallmark of the upper class in society which provided the ruler with officials and soldiers. The early stages of such a development now began to be discernible, and it is understandable that Caesar, occupied with such prospects, no longer regarded the susceptibilities of the Roman aristocracy. If these gentlemen refused to understand him despite his strenuous efforts to secure their collaboration, he simply by-passed them as he had done previously during his consulship. His policy of reconciliation was certainly meant sincerely, and it was for this reason that he regarded the break with his peers as tragic. No doubt he would rather have chosen other helpers from the nobility than Antony, Lepidus and Dolabella and must sometimes have felt that among the noblest of his opponents enthusiasm for the *res publica* was more

---

[1] Cic. *Att.* 16, 16a, 4–5. The settlers *qui agrum Buthrotium concupissent* could be people who had had to give up land for colonization in Italy. Cf. Vittinghoff, op. cit., 86.

[2] See above, p. 283, n. 1.

[3] Cic. *Att.* 14, 12, 1. Cf. Vittinghoff, op. cit., 71, 4.

than a mere cover for selfish ends. And this tragic element became ever stronger as he was now under increasing pressure to follow the path leading away from Roman traditions. This was most strikingly illustrated by the ruler cult. That such decrees were possible at all shows that the new senators in their religious attitudes were as ready for them as the people. Nor is this surprising, since for the last century Hellenism had been forcing its way through innumerable channels into every stratum of Roman and Italian society. Apart from intellectual influences, the number of people of oriental origin in the urban population had been growing enormously. Of these the freedmen and their descendants possessed Roman citizenship and to a large extent determined the character of the *plebs urbana*. Men of this kind could express their relationship with a ruler and in particular with Caesar, at whose feet the 'globe' lay, only in terms of worship, while they did not understand the subtleties of the Roman constitution at all.[1] Here he was met by the growth of a loyalty among his subjects, which did not ask what was the legal justification of his rule, but devoutly accepted it as the dispensation of a divinity. One can appreciate how he welcomed this powerful current since he could not reach any understanding with the optimates. In time it would also surely sweep away what opposition there still was among the people! Furthermore, it corresponded exactly with his supranational political tendencies.[2] In the eyes of his opponents, however, he was thus becoming ever more un-Roman and unbearable.

In December 45 he undertook a journey to Campania. Cicero was staying at his estate near Puteoli at the time and so for once had the opportunity to observe the ruler's life at close quarters. In a valuable letter to Atticus he has portrayed his impressions and thereby left us a picture of Caesar's restless activity. On December 18 the dictator put up for the night with Cicero's neighbour, Lucius Marcius Philippus, the stepfather of Gaius Octavius; his retinue of friends, freedmen, slaves and soldiers numbered 2,000. Next morning he worked with Balbus until one o'clock without receiving anyone else. Then he walked across to Cicero's villa, where he took a bath at two o'clock. While in the bath he heard something (probably complaints) about Mamurra, his well-known follower. After he

---

[1] On the composition of the urban population in Rome, see L. Friedländer, *Sittengesch.*, 1, 233 ff. A critical scrutiny of modern research by F. G. Maier is to be found in *Historia* 2 (1954), 328 ff., especially 336 ff. and 344 ff.

[2] On this, see Vittinghoff, op. cit., 91 ff.

X

had been anointed, he dined with Cicero as his guest. He enjoyed his food enormously and, avoiding politics, conversed with animation about literature. After the meal, in order to keep mentally fresh, he relieved himself by means of his customary emetic. Then he continued on his journey towards Puteoli.[1]

His grandiose concept of government is also illustrated by the following plans which, though in serious preparation, remained unfulfilled as a result of his death. To improve sea communications between Italy and the East a canal was to be cut through the Isthmus of Corinth. In Italy a canal was to be dug from the Tiber near Rome to Tarracina in order both to drain the Pontine marshes and to form a new waterway. He also wished to build an imposing extension to the harbour at Ostia. The draining of the Fucine lake was to produce more valuable arable land, while traffic in Italy was to be improved by a new trunk road from the Adriatic over the Apennines to the Tiber valley. As he had increased the Roman Empire, he had won the right to extend the *pomerium*, the sacred boundary of the city. In connection with this he was toying with the idea of building up the Campus Martius and replacing it with the Vatican plain by moving the course of the Tiber to the west. On the Campus Martius the largest temple in the world was to arise, dedicated to Mars, and the largest theatre was to rest against the Tarpeian rock.[2]

Marcus Varro was commissioned to collect the whole of Greek and Roman literature in a vast library. Others were to unify the whole body of valid civil law, which was spread over innumerable enactments, in one synoptic work—a plan that was only realized many centuries later.[3]

His policy of reconciliation was crowned with a general amnesty for all political opponents, allowing them to return from exile and granting them the same rights in public life as were enjoyed by other citizens. The widows of men who had suffered confiscation of property had their dowries paid out and their children were given a share in their inheritance.[4] As outward confirmation of the new state of peace the statues of Sulla and Pompey were re-erected in their

[1] Cic. *Att.* 13, 52.

[2] Plin. *n.h.* 4, 10; Suet. *Caes.* 44, 1–3; Dio 43, 49, 2; 50, 1; 44, 5, 1; Plut. *Caes.* 58, 8–10; Suet. *Claud.* 20, 1; Cic. *Phil.* 5, 7; *Att.* 13, 33a, 1.

[3] Suet. *Caes.* 44, 2–3; Isid. *etym.* 5, 1, 5; 6, 5, 1. Cf. F. Schulz, *Hist. of Rom. Leg. Science* (1946), 61.

[4] Dio 43, 50, 1–2; Suet. *Caes.* 75, 4; App. *b.c.* 2, 448; Nicol. Dam. F 130, 59.

old places. This occasioned a comment from Cicero that by such generosity Caesar was ensuring the stability of his own statues.[1]

The Senate incessantly accompanied all these messages of the dictator, which were sent to it for ratification, with new honours. Since Caesar had refused to sit on the curule chair at theatrical performances, preferring on these occasions to take a seat on the tribunician bench, he was given permission to make use of the triumphal garb and curule chair without limit of time or place, and was to be allowed to dedicate *spolia opima* to Jupiter Feretrius as if he had killed an enemy commander with his own hands. The fasces of his lictors were always to be wreathed with laurel. After the sacrifice on the Alban Hill he was to return to Rome on horseback as if holding an *ovatio* or minor triumph. He was granted the title of *pater patriae*, his birthday was declared a public holiday and statues of him were to be set up in all the temples of Rome and the municipalities as well as two on the platform in the Forum, one with the *corona civica*, the other with the *corona muralis*. The building of a new temple of Concordia and an annual festival of this divinity were decreed, as well as a temple to Felicitas on the site of the old senate-house, in place of which a Curia Julia was to be built. The month of his birth Quinctilis received the name of Julius, and a tribe was to bear his name. His dictatorship and censorial authority (*praefectura morum*) were extended for life. To his honorary tribunician rights inviolability (*sacrosanctitas*) was expressly added. His son or adopted son was to be designated *pontifex maximus*, a veiled recognition of hereditary monarchy, as was also his use of the name Imperator.[2]

On another occasion the use of a gilded chair in place of the usual curule chair for sessions of the Senate and courts was devised for him, and for clothing the all-purple garb of the ancient Roman

---

[1] Suet. *Caes.* 75, 4; Dio 43, 49, 1; Plut. *Caes.* 57, 6; *Cic.* 40, 5; Polyaen. 8, 23, 31.

[2] Dio 44, 4, 2–5; 5, 2–3; Suet. *Caes.* 76, 1; App. *b.c.* 2, 440–443; Liv. *per.* 116. For the coins mentioned in Dio 44, 4, 4 with the legend *parens patriae* see A. Alföldi, *Stud. über Caesars Mon.*, 20; 44; 86, with plates 14 and 15. (According to Sydenham, *CRR*, no. 1069, not until April, 44.) On the pillar erected at this time by the plebs with the inscription *parenti patriae* (Suet. *Caes.* 85), see Alföldi, op. cit., 70. The authenticity of the lost inscription *ILS*, 71 (*C. Iulio Caesari pont. max. patri patriae*) is doubtful. The *sacrosanctitas* mentioned in Dio 44, 5, 3 does not mean that Caesar possessed the *tribunicia potestas* of the later emperors. In this I agree with E. Hohl (*Klio* 32 (1939), 71). But I differ from him (72) in thinking that it was for mere comfort that Caesar preferred to sit on the tribunes' bench in the theatre without his triumphal garb. Hohl recalls the very interesting passage in Suet. *Aug.* 45, 1, according to which Caesar annoyed the public by dealing with his correspondence during performances: *Augustus patrem Caesarem vulgo reprehensum commemorabat, quod inter spectandum epistulis libellisque legendis aut rescribendis vacaret.*

kings. For his protection a bodyguard of senators and knights was to be formed. All the senators swore an oath that they were ready to protect his life. New officials on entering their posts had to swear to abide by the acts of his administration, and his future governmental actions were declared valid in advance. Every four years games were to be held in his honour as for a hero; furthermore, public votive offerings were to be made on his behalf annually. An oath by his *genius* was introduced. In the ancient priesthood of the Luperci ('repellers of wolves') a new college of Luperci Julii was formed to join the traditional Luperci Fabiani and Quinctiales. During all gladiatorial games in Rome and Italy one day was to be dedicated to Caesar.[1]

A final batch of such honours was decreed on one and the same day at the end of 45 in the dictator's absence[2]—this was meant to demonstrate the Senate's independence. He was given a golden chair and golden wreath adorned with jewels for the games. The divine image in his likeness which was carried in the circus procession was to receive a holy resting-place (*pulvinar*) like other deities, and a pediment like that on temples was to be set on his house. The new god was to be honoured as *divus* (meaning the same as *deus*) Julius in a separate temple together with Clementia. Antony was appointed

---

[1] Dio 44, 6, 1–4. Cf. L. R. Taylor, *Divinity of the Roman Emperor*, 67. It is not clear what Dio's expression 'as to a hero' is translating; perhaps *divus*. L. R. Taylor remarks (69) that Cic. *Phil.* 2, 110 describes Antony as *flamen Divi Iuli*. H. Dessau (*Gesch. d. röm. Kaiserz.*, 1, 354, n. 2) has likewise concluded from this passage that Caesar was called thus during his lifetime. L. R. Taylor gives as evidence (268 ff.) the text of the inscriptions in *ILS*, 73; 73a; 72; 6343, which perhaps refer to the decrees before Caesar's murder. Broughton (*MRR*, 2, 360) regards the author of the *lex Rufrena* mentioned in 73 and 73a as a tribune of 42 B.C. 6343 is erected *decurioni* [*be*]*neficio dei Caesaris* in Nola. In *Carm. epigr.* 964, 2 a freedman of Caesar's wife Calpurnia refers to her as *magnifici coniunx Caesaris illa dei*. On Lupercalia and Luperci, see Marbach, *RE*, 13, 1816 ff.; 1834 ff. On the gilded *sella curulis* (Suet. *Caes.* 76, 1: *sedem auream;* Cic. *Phil.* 2, 85: *in sella aurea;* Att. 15, 3, 2: *de sella Caesaris*), see Alföldi, *Stud. über Caesars Mon.*, 22. A representation of the coin is shown in *R.M.* 50, plates 14, 10. Among the ornaments of the ancient kings of Rome (Dio 44, 6, 1) there was also the golden wreath originally worn by the Etruscan kings, which the coins of 44 represent Caesar as wearing. This is the brilliant discovery of K. Kraft, described in 'Der goldene Kranz Caesars und der Kampf um die Entlarvung des "Tyrannen" ' (*Jahrb. f. Numism. der Bayer. Numism. Ges.* (1953)), 20; 35; 73. It can best be seen in the enlarged coin portraits in A. Alföldi, 'The Portrait of Caesar', *Centennial Vol. of the Am. Numism. Soc.* (1958), plates 1–6; and in Sydenham, *CRR*, nos. 1057, 1063, 1089 and 1129A. It is not the laurel wreath mentioned by Dio in 43, 43, 1; Suet. *Caes.* 45, 2 (cf. Kraft, op. cit., 13 ff.). On the other hand we may accept Dio's account in 43, 43, 2: after the triumph of 45 (not 46, as U. Wilcken in 'Z. Entwicklung d. röm. Diktatur', *Abh. Berlin* (1940), 20) he sometimes wore the tall red shoes of the Alban kings on the ground that this was his right as the descendant of Aeneas' son Iulus.

[2] Dio 44, 8, 2.

his priest (*flamen*). In contrast to all other mortals, when the time came, Caesar was to be buried inside the city.[1]

The Senate had these decrees of deification inscribed in letters of gold on silver tablets, to set them up at the feet of Capitoline Jupiter. Only Cassius and some of those who shared his views dared to vote against the proposals.[2] After their acceptance all the magistrates with the consuls at their head,[3] followed by the whole Senate, made their way to Caesar who was on a visit to his newly established forum. They found him sitting in front of the temple of Venus Genetrix, and it was thus, without rising, that he received the most distinguished body in Rome when it appeared before him with its solemn pronouncement. Perhaps he was attempting thereby to express the fact that the sovereign authority with which he had gradually been entrusted, even to the extent of full recognition of the divinity which was manifesting itself in him, extended over all subjects of whatever rank.

But this behaviour was unfavourably received both by the participant senators and by the watching multitude, and he thought it advisable to spread it around that he had been seized by a sudden physical infirmity.[4] He also forbade his followers to bring forward in the Senate a proposal to grant him the title of king since this lay under an ancient curse.[5] A particularly clear indication was that he dismissed the Spanish cohorts whom he had hitherto employed as a personal bodyguard without forming the guard of senators and

---

[1] Dio 44, 6, 3–7, 1; Nicol. Dam. F 130, 78 with deliberate bias moved the date to after February 15, 44. See E. Hohl, *Klio* 34 (1941), 113. According to Dio 45, 6, 5; App. *b.c.* 3, 105; Nicol. Dam. F 130, 108, the decree about the gilded *sella* and the golden wreath meant that the chair was to be set up even when Caesar was not present in person. Cf. Alföldi, *Stud. über Caesars Mon.*, 76; L. R. Taylor, *Divinity of the Roman Emperor*, 87; Kraft, op. cit., 32. I do not understand why Alföldi and Kraft postpone this decree until after February 15. Nor should the *pulvinar* (Cic. *Phil.* 2, 110; Suet. *Caes.* 76, 1) be equated with the *sella*. The expression *sellisternium* is used only for goddesses (Klotz, *RE*, 2A, 1322). Coins of the year 44 (after Caesar's death) with the temple of Clementia: Alföldi, op. cit., 46, plates 15, 5–6; L. R. Taylor, op. cit., 69; Sydenham, *CRR*, no. 1076.

[2] Dio 44, 7, 1; 8, 1.

[3] Plut. *Caes.* 60, 4; App. *b.c.* 2, 445 (which points to 45 b.c.). Against this, Nicol. Dam. F 130, 78 puts Antony in place of the consuls. On the other hand, both Plutarch and Appian mention the Rostra instead of the Forum Julium.

[4] Dio 44, 8, 1–4; Liv. *per.* 116; Eutrop. 6, 25; Suet. *Caes.* 78, 1; Plut. *Caes.* 60, 4–8; App. *b.c.* 2, 445–446. These differ in detail. The tone of Nicol. Dam. F 130, 78–79 is strongly apologetic. According to Plut. *Caes.* 60, 4–6, Caesar is said to have answered that honours should rather be restricted than multiplied; this only angered those present, and they withdrew abashed; disconcerted by this incident, he bared his neck in the presence of his friends and shouted that he was ready to let himself be stabbed to death.

[5] App. *b.c.* 2, 444; Dio 44, 9, 2; Nicol. Dam. F 130, 80, presumably independent of Appian's tradition.

knights for which the Senate had given permission.[1] Thus recurrent doubts about his actual intentions were felt by public opinion. In fact, he was unmistakably aiming at giving his position the short and comprehensive name. The references found in various honours to Romulus-Quirinus and the ancient kings at least show that he felt no embarrassment at repeatedly calling to mind the proscribed kingship. Since 45 he had also on festive occasions been wearing tall red boots distinct from the similar footwear of patrician senators (*mullei*), of which he said that they belonged to the dress of the ancient Alban kings and befitted him as their descendant.[2] Similarly, the newly-created college of Luperci brought him close to the legendary founders of the city, whether one accepted Evander or Romulus as the author of the ancient priesthood.[3] If he did not actually order the honours and did not accept all of them, he doubtless welcomed such ties with the time of the kings and worked actively and ceaselessly[4] in order to stir the people into producing a demonstration in this sense, so impressive that none could ignore it.

One day one of Caesar's statues on the rostra was found adorned with a diadem. Since the time of Alexander the Great this ribbon had been the symbol of Hellenistic monarchy, but was by now so familiar to contemporary Romans that they even represented their

---

[1] Dio 44, 7, 4; App. *b.c.* 2, 444; 455; 498; Suet. *Caes.* 486, 2; Nicol. Dam. F 130, 80; Vell. 2, 57, 1. Cf. Cic. *Phil.* 2, 108, comparing Caesar and Antony: *erant fortasse gladii, sed absconditi nec ita multi;* 5, 17; 13, 18: *Caesare dominante veniebamus in senatum, si non libere, at tamen tuto. hoc archipirata — quid enim dicam tyranno — haec subsellia ab Ityraeis occupabantur.*

[2] See above, p. 316, n. 1. Cf. Mommsen, *RStR,* 3³, 888 ff.

[3] Marbach, *RE,* 13, 1818.

[4] Dio 44, 9, 1 reports that it started among Caesar's enemies. In this case Nicol. Dam. F 130, 67 has probably hit upon a better answer when he says that a majority of the Senate wished to do him a favour with the extravagant honours; only a few intended to make him hated. As Jacoby emphasizes in his *Commentary,* p. 265, Nicolaus' work is based on the autobiography of Augustus. In April, 43, Antony reproached Cicero with having deliberately deceived Caesar (*Phil.* 13, 40; 41). On the other hand, a little later M. Brutus accused the Senate and Cicero of *imbecillitas* and *desperatio* which *Caesarem in cupiditatem regni impulit* (*ap.* Cic. *Brut.* 1, 16, 3). Cicero (no doubt rightly) rejected the reproach of Antony; cf. *RE,* 7A, 1024; Ed. Meyer, *Caesars Mon.,* 510. The passage of Appian cited in p. 317, n. 5 is not in itself completely reliable evidence, and if Caesar thus rejected the title of king, enthusiastic partisans could still think that he was not quite in earnest, since he had already accepted the complete costume of the ancient kings of Rome. Although I previously held a different view (also in *Vom Römischen Staat* (1943), 1, 126), K. Kraft's impressive exposition has convinced me that 'an attempt to win the diadem and title of king on Caesar's part would have been utter political madness' ('Der goldene Kranz', 45). This consideration speaks for the inherent probability of the tradition passed on by Appian. Cf. Mommsen, *R.G.,* 3, 486 (English translation, Vol. 5, pp. 336 f.); L. Pareti, *Stor. di Roma* IV (1955), 344.

own kings as wearing it.[1] However, the tribunes Gaius Epidius Marullus and Lucius Caesetius Flavus immediately had it removed, declaring that Caesar did not need such contrivances.[2] Shortly afterwards, on January 26, when he was returning to Rome on horseback from the Alban Hill,[3] as had been decreed, some of the spectators greeted him as king. He at once replied that his name was not 'Rex' (the cognomen of a branch of the Marcii) but 'Caesar'; but Marullus and Flavus with the consent of the onlookers had the man who had first raised the cry removed by their official servants in order to pass judgment on him before the people's court.[4] Caesar now ceased to conceal his disapproval of their attitude, which he regarded simply as vulgar agitation. They countered with a joint edict to the effect that the exercise of their office was in danger. The dictator could contain himself no longer. He summoned the Senate and explained that he found himself in the wretched position of either having to act against his nature or of suffering a diminution of his dignity.[5] Since he did not insist on the death penalty, the Senate decreed that the two tribunes were to be deposed and removed from the list of senators.[6] Thereupon the tribune Helvius Cinna, the poet known to us as a friend of Catullus,[7] had two substitutes elected, and Caesar erased the two names from the senatorial roll.[8] He even went so far as to demand that Caesetius' father should disinherit his son, but did not press the point when the latter refused.[9]

It is understandable that he should have believed that he owed it to his position to crush the opposition decisively after putting up with its provocations for a considerable time. But the incident throws a harsh light on his relationship with the Roman republic. The

[1] Sydenham, *CRR*, 713B (Numa and Ancus Marcius); 1032 (Numa); Kraft, op. cit., plates 3, 6–8, 15; but cf. plate 3, 7: Numa wearing a golden wreath on a cameo. (On this, see p. 38.)

[2] Dio 44, 9, 1–3; App. *b.c.* 2, 449. The date is given as January 26 in Suet. *Caes.* 79, 1; Plut. *Caes.* 61, 8. According to Dio, Caesar was angry with the tribunes, but said nothing. (A different version in Nicol. Dam. F 130, 69.)

[3] *Acta triumph.* in *Inscr. It.* 13, 1, 86–7: C. *Iulius C.f. C.n. Caesar VI dict. IIII ovans . . . ex monte Albano VII K. Febr.*

[4] Dio 44, 10, 1; Suet. *Caes.* 79, 2; App. *b.c.* 2, 450. The ready answer is not a 'bad joke', as Ed. Meyer (*Caesars Mon.*, 519) thought.

[5] Vell. 2, 68, 3.

[6] Cic. *Phil.* 13, 31; Dio 44, 10, 3.

[7] Plut. *Brut.* 20, 8. There is no reason to delete ποιητικός. Cf. F. Vonder Mühll, *RE*, 8, 226; Broughton, *MRR*, 2, 324; R. Syme, *Rom. Rev.*, 79.

[8] Dio 44, 10, 3; Vell. 2, 68, 3; Suet. *Caes.* 79, 1; Nicol. Dam. F 130, 69; Plut. *Caes.* 61, 10; App. *b.c.* 2, 452; 575; Liv. *per.* 116; *Obseq.* 70.

[9] Val. Max. 5, 7, 2.

man who had embarked on civil war ostensibly in defence of the violated tribunate was forced, as before in 49, to ride roughshod over tribunician inviolability with a brutality which his opponents had never dared to use. When the consular elections for 42 took place a little later, some votes were delivered with the names of the deposed tribunes, a silent but impressive protest against the trampling of the ancient rights of the people.[1]

Caesar continued on his way. He assumed the dictatorship for life. In a document of February 9, 44, he is described as dictator for the fourth time, consul for the fifth time, and designated dictator for life:[2] from this we may draw the conclusion that he hesitated for quite a time after being decreed the dictatorship for life before making use of this authority. On February 15 he officially bore the title of *dictator perpetuus*; this is expressly attested by Cicero.[3] *Dictator perpetuus*, a new concept and one incompatible with the Republican constitution, in essentials amounted to the same as *rex* but avoided this hated word.[4] It finally put an end to the hopes of the Republicans that Caesar might after all retire, as Sulla had done, when his legislative task was complete; Titus Ampius Balbus could report that he had once openly declared that Sulla had shown himself illiterate in laying down the dictatorship.[5] Even if Caesar himself was content with the monarchic position which had been gradually built up by a series of decrees, each more extravagant

---

[1] Suet. *Caes.* 80, 3; Dio 44, 11, 4; Nicol. Dam. F 130, 77.

[2] On April 11, 44, on the motion of the consuls Mark Antony and P. Dolabella, a senatorial decree concerning the High Priest Hyrcanus (Joseph. *ant.* 14, 211–212), which Caesar had submitted on February 9, was confirmed (Joseph. *ant.* 14, 219–222). L. Lange (*R.A.*, 3, 481) had already recognized this. Cf. Hohl, *Klio* 34, 117; Alföldi, *Stud. über Caesars Mon.*, 16. Caesar's magisterial powers are given in the preamble (Joseph. *ant.* 14, 211). The date of February 9 is given only at the end of the confirmatory senatorial decree of April (Joseph. *ant.* 14, 222). See above, p. 289, n. 4. See also *Fasti Cap.* in *Inscr. It.* 13, 1, 56–7 on the year 44: C. Iulius C. f. C. n. Caes[a]r III abd. [dictator]; *Fasti Amit.* ibid., 170–1: [C. Iulius Ca]esar dict. [in p]er[p]etuum.

[3] Cic. *Phil.* 2, 87. As mentioned p. 278, n. 1 above, Alföldi believes that in view of the sequence of four moneyers in the year 44, the date has to be moved down to March 1. Whatever the interpretation of the example of a coin of 44, on which Alföldi recognizes a diadem, I cannot ignore Cicero's evidence. Representations of this coin with *dict. quart.* are to be found in Alföldi, op. cit., 83, and, much enlarged, on plates 2, 5 and 6. The coins with *dict. quart.* and *dict. perpetuo* or *im per.* are in Sydenham, *CRR*, pp. 177–178, plates 28, nos. 1057, 1063.

[4] Cic. *Phil.* 1, 3 on Antony in April, 44 (*RE* 7A, 1033): *dictaturam, quae iam vim regiae potestatis obsederat, funditus ex re publica sustulit*; 4: *propter perpetuae dictaturae recentem memoriam*; 32; 2, 91; App. *b.c.* 2, 463.

[5] Suet. *Caes.* 77; Dio 44, 8, 4 emphasizes how disastrous was Caesar's failure to reject the dictatorship for life. Likewise Flor. 2, 13, 91. Surprisingly, Mommsen (*R.G.*, 3, 479; Eng. trans., Vol. 5, p. 328) does not appreciate the importance of the dictatorship. He is of the opinion (486; Eng. trans., Vol. 5, p. 336) that Caesar wished to appropriate 'the substance of

than its predecessor, the rumour that he desired still more would not be laid. At the feast of the Lupercalia on February 15 he appeared for the first time in public in the ceremonial garb of the ancient Roman kings which he had been granted. Adorned with the purple toga and golden wreath and seated on the gilded chair, he watched from the rostra as the Luperci, naked but for a goatskin around their loins, ran round the Palatine as they had done since ancient times. When the priests reached the Forum, their leader (*magister*), the consul Mark Antony, detached himself from them,[1] climbed up to Caesar on the rostra and placed a diadem on his head. Caesar, however, removed it to the applause of the people and with the words 'Jupiter Optimus Maximus alone is king of the Romans' ordered it to be taken to the Capitoline temple. He also had an entry made in the state calendar under the feast of the Lupercalia that the *dictator perpetuus* Caesar had refused the kingship offered to him at the people's command by the consul Mark Antony.[2]

The background to this scene remains obscure, but it is hard to imagine that it was pure improvisation by Antony. We know what Caesar did and might draw the conclusion that by an official refusal he intended to put an end to speculation. On March 20, 43, Cicero went so far as to say that this scene made Antony his real murderer.[3] The malicious might claim that Caesar only rejected the diadem because the people did not applaud the offer.[4] Cicero is certainly

the kingship under the title of Imperator'. Cic. *Phil.* 2, 86 says *iure interfectum esse* of the *dictator perpetuus*, although he rejected the diadem (*regni insigne, Phil.* 3, 12). In August, 44, M. Brutus warns Antony (*ap.* Cic. *fam.* 11, 3, 4) to recall for how short a time Caesar was king, *quam non diu regnarit fac cogites*.

[1] Dio 46, 5, 2.

[2] This is how Cicero describes the scene of which he was perhaps an eye-witness (*RE*, 7A, 1029) in *Phil.* 2, 85–87; 87: *adscribi iussit* (Antony) *in fastis ad Lupercalia C. Caesari dictatori perpetuo M. Antonium consulem populi iussu regnum detulisse, Caesarem uti noluisse*; also *Phil.* 3, 12; 5, 38; 10, 7; 13, 17; 31 and 41; Caesar's words in Dio 44, 11, 3. In other respects Dio's account (11, 1–3) agrees with Cicero's. Val. Max. 1, 6, 13 especially stresses that he wore the royal costume in order not to offend the Senate which had granted it to him. Cf. Suet. *Caes.* 79, 2. Liv. *per.* 116 (*diadema capite suo impositum in sella reposuit*) was plausibly emended by E. Hohl in *Klio* 34, 104 to: *in cella (Iovis) reposuit*. See also Cic. *divin.* 1, 119: *illo die, quo primum in sella aurea sedit et cum purpura vesti processit*. The remaining accounts, in Plut. *Caes.* 61, 4–7; *Ant.* 12, 1–6; App. *b.c.* 2, 456–458; Flor. 2, 13, 91; Vell. 2, 56, 4, are less exact. A completely divergent version is given in Nicol. Dam. F 130, 71–75, who has depicted the scene in the style of 'tragic' historiography, among other things including in it the future assassins C. Cassius and P. Casca. On this, see Hohl (*Klio* 34, 95 ff.).

[3] Cic. *Phil.* 13, 41: *deceptum autem Caesarem a me dicere audes? tu, tu, inquam, illum occidisti Lupercalibus.* On the other hand Dio (46, 17, 5 and 7; 19, 1 and 4–7) makes Q. Fufius Calenus reply that Antony thereby dissuaded Caesar from his unhappy ambition, which had arisen as a result of the senatorial decree on the royal dress. Cf. K. Kraft, op. cit., 55 ff.

[4] Plut. *Caes.* 61, 6; Dio 44, 11, 3; Nicol. Dam. F 130, 73.

right to the extent that among senators devoted to the optimate republic there now arose the determination to remove the tyrant. Thus rumours which could justify such an undertaking now secured an even wider currency.

The dictator himself was occupied above all by preparations for the Parthian campaign. We may recall that at the turn of the year 45-44 Pacorus, the son of the Parthian king, brought help with a large army to the rebel Caecilius Bassus, who was being besieged in Apamea, and drove back Caesar's legate Antistius Vetus.[1] Caesar planned to assemble a total of sixteen legions and 10,000 cavalry,[2] of which six legions with many auxiliaries had already crossed the Adriatic and were in readiness in the region of Apollonia.[3] He himself intended to follow on March 18[4] and planned to employ his army first in restoring order in the north of the province of Macedonia,[5] where in recent years the Dacian king Burebista, in alliance with the prophet Decaeneus, had extended his dominions far from his homeland (Rumania and Hungary) over Illyrians and Thracians south of the Danube, and had already attacked part of the Roman province. Dionysopolis (Balchik in the Dobruja) was subject to him, and when Pompey was on his way to Thessaly after his victory at Dyrrhachium, the king had sent a citizen of it to pay his respects to him.[6] Caesar knew about this state of affairs from his time in Illyricum. After securing the frontier here he proposed to launch the attack on Parthia from Armenia. For the rest, there were hints that he wished to return by way of southern Russia along the Caspian Sea and around the Caucasus, and then perhaps intended to follow the course of the Danube to Gaul. Since Pompey's war against Mithridates, men had been speaking of Roman dominion over the world. Thus it was not utopian for Caesar, who had advanced as far as Britain, to feel confident that he would also realize this claim in the North.[7] He hoped that he would achieve it within three years.

---

[1] See above, p. 305, n. 3. See further D. Brutus in April, 44, ap. Cic. fam. 11, 1, 4.
[2] App. b.c. 2, 460.
[3] Op. cit., 3, 92; Nicol. Dam. F 130, 41; Suet. Aug. 8, 2.
[4] App. b.c. 2, 462; 476.   [5] Op. cit., 2, 459; 3, 93; Suet. Caes. 44, 3.
[6] Jordan. 11; Pomp. Trog. prol. 32; Strab. 7, 198; 304; 16, 762; Dittenberger, Syll.[3] 762, 21–36; Suet. Caes. 44, 3.
[7] Plut. Caes. 58, 6–7. When Nicol. Dam. F 130, 95 mentions the Indians alongside the Parthians, this is to be taken no more seriously than when Horace (carm. 1, 12, 56) writes of the subjugation of the Seres and the Indians. Cf. carm. 4, 14, 12, or Vergil, Aen. 6, 794: super Garamantas et Indos. I regard it as confusing when Ed. Meyer (Caesars Mon., 466) writes: 'Caesar's monarchy in its conception represents the renewal and complete realization of Alexander's world-monarchy: world conquest in the fullest sense is its prerequisite and

Under the stress of these preparations a rumour won belief that a Sibylline oracle had been discovered, to the effect that the Parthians could only be defeated by a king; Lucius Cotta, a member of the college of fifteen men responsible for preserving and interpreting the oracles, and a cousin of Caesar's mother, would therefore propose in the Senate on March 15 that the dictator should be declared king, with the proviso that this was to apply to the provinces and not to Rome.[1] Gossip was also circulating to the effect that Caesar intended to shift his residence either—for love of Cleopatra—to Alexandria, or—because of his ancestry—to Ilium.[2] No more convincing is the story that the tribune Helvius Cinna let it be known that he had prepared a bill—to be proposed after Caesar's departure—which would have enabled him to marry more than one wife in order to procreate children. It was easy to invent something like this retrospectively as an insult to Cleopatra and her small son,[3] since after the funeral on March 20 the enthusiastic Caesarian Cinna was murdered by the frenzied mob in mistake for the praetor Cornelius Cinna.[4]

The atmosphere was becoming oppressive. Caesar no longer tried to ignore the fact that the gap separating him from Romans of the old school had become unbridgeable. Already in the letter of December 19, 45, mentioned above, Cicero stresses[5] that there had

justification.' Pompey of course wanted to be regarded as a new Alexander (see my *Pompeius*[2], 124 ff.). The *dictator perpetuus* had no need of the diadem. Of him one might well say that he wished to complete the Roman *orbis terrarum*, which had emerged from the previous course of Roman history. Cf. J. Vogt, *Vom Reichsgedanken der Römer* (1942), 65; 178 ff. We do not know how far he wished to push back the Parthians, perhaps as far as Trajan and Septimius Severus after him. The plan for the return journey shows that he did not intend to conquer the Parthian Empire. H. Strasburger (*HZ* 175, 255) is of course right in saying that he had never expressed such a purpose. As I remarked in *Vom. röm. Staat* 1, 37 (=*Kl. Schr.* 2, 10) he left it to Cicero to assess the geopolitical significance of the conquest of Gaul, and certainly did not enter upon his consulship with such a programme. It was his way to act as the situation of the moment in his view required. However, this was done with a sure instinct for Roman tradition and with a result appropriate to his aim of perfecting what had been so far achieved.

[1] Cic. *divin.* 2, 110, of Cotta: *falsa quaedam hominum fama dicturus in senatu putabatur eum, quem re vera regem habebamus, appellandum quoque esse regem, si salvi esse vellemus.* Holmes (*Rom. Rep.*, 336, n. 4) is right on this, as against Ed. Meyer, op. cit., 522, n. 1. See further K. Kraft, op. cit., 56; Dio 44, 15, 3; Suet. *Caes.* 79, 4; Plut. *Caes.* 60, 2; 64, 3; App. *b.c.* 2, 461, with the addition that Caesar declined.

[2] Suet. *Caes.* 79, 4; Nicol. Dam. F 130, 68.

[3] Cf. p. 228, n. 1 above.

[4] Suet. *Caes.* 52, 3, 8; Dio 44, 7, 3; Plut. *Caes.* 68, 3–6; *Brut.* 20, 8–11; App. *b.c.* 2, 613; Dio 44, 50, 4; 46, 49, 2; Val. Max. 9, 9, 1. Shakespeare's *Julius Caesar*, 3, 9 contains an exquisite dramatization of the unhappy end of 'Cinna the Poet'.

[5] Cic. *Att.* 13, 52.

been much literary conversation at table, but not a word about politics. But he prefaces this with the comment: 'Not a guest to whom one says "Please look me up again on your way back"!' Shortly before March 15 Cicero went to the ruler's house in order to present a petition on a friend's behalf, but had to wait a long time before securing admission. Caesar noticed this, and according to Matius remarked: 'Can I doubt that I am utterly loathed when Marcus Cicero has to sit waiting instead of having free access to me? And if anyone is easy to win over it is he. For all that, I have no doubt that he hates me bitterly.'[1]

Such hatred, and deep indignation at the destruction of the old optimate oligarchy and its freedom, at this time brought together about sixty men with the intention of killing the tyrant, as the unwritten constitution of the republic enjoined on every Roman as a civic duty. This ranked above the oath of allegiance which they had sworn to Caesar a short time before, since by accepting the dictatorship for life he had dropped his last mask. In the versions of Roman annals current at the time one could read that Romulus had been put to death by the senators because his rule had degenerated from constitutional monarchy to tyranny;[2] furthermore, that it was because of such degeneration that the monarchy under Tarquinius Superbus was finally overthrown, and that the Roman people of the time had sworn a solemn oath for themselves and their descendants never again to tolerate a king at Rome.[3] The leading figures in the conspiracy were Quintus Caepio Brutus, his brother-in-law Gaius Cassius, Decimus Brutus and Gaius Trebonius. Brutus and Cassius then held the praetorship with the prospect of becoming consuls in the year 41, Decimus was consul designate for 42 and Trebonius the ex-consul of 45. Thus they were all politicians who enjoyed Caesar's highest favour.[4] The other participants were of

---

[1] Cic. *Att.* 14, 1, 2; 2, 3.

[2] Liv. 1, 16, 4; Dionys. Hal. 2, 56; Plut. *Rom.* 27, 6; Val. Max. 5, 3, 1; App. *b.c.* 2, 476.

[3] Cic. *rep.* 1, 62; 2, 45–47; Liv. 2, 1, 9; Dionys. Hal. 4, 73; 5, 1; 11, 41; App. *b.c.* 2, 499; 4, 382. The number of murderers is given in Eutrop. 6, 25 and Oros. 6, 17, 2, presumably following Livy. Sixteen are known by name (see Groebe, *RE*, 10, 255). Since Gérard Walter in his biographical novel on Caesar (p. 33) assigns the poisoning planned by a slave to this period, it should be noted that from its context in Suet. *Caes.* 74, 1, this story will belong to a much earlier period (about 63, 62 or 59 B.C.). The latest contributions to the discussion on Caesar's murder are by John H. Collins ('Caesar and the Corruption of Power', *Historia* 4 (1955), 455 ff.) and J. P. V. D. Balsdon ('The Ides of March', *Historia* 7 (1958), 80 ff.); both give excellent accounts of the vast modern literature: *quot homines tot sententiae.* My *sententia* I deliver in this book.

[4] Cic. *Phil.* 2, 26–27; Nicol. Dam. F 130, 66; Dio 44, 14, 3–4.

lower rank and less importance, but all determined men, not a traitor among them. Like their leaders they came from both camps in the civil war. Caepio Brutus saw to it that by limiting the enterprise to the murder of Caesar alone they elevated it to a strictly defensive measure for the sake of the republic. After other proposals had been rejected, they agreed on the meeting of the Senate fixed for March 15. The planned tyrannicide thus became a repetition of the sentence once executed on Romulus, and there were hopes that the Senate would at once be in a position to resume government.[1]

Although those in the plot gave nothing away directly, it is certain that Caesar was warned. Apart from the omens foreboding evil to which the ancient narrators attach great importance,[2] his few sincerely devoted followers such as Hirtius and Pansa advised him to secure himself again by a bodyguard of Spanish cohorts. However, he refused, with remarks such as 'There is nothing more unfortunate than a permanent guard, which is a sign of ever present fear', or 'It is better to die once than to be always expecting death.'[3] On the evening of March 14 he was the guest of his *magister equitum* Lepidus. There he expressed himself in similar terms: the most pleasant death, he said, was a sudden and unexpected one.[4]

In considering this attitude of his one must bear in mind that he intended on March 18 to set out to join his army. At headquarters, where politics operated under different conditions, the distressing break with the old-style senators ceased to have significance, and this disagreeable episode could be surmounted by new achievements. On the other hand his precarious health prepared men for a sudden end. For a time he had been suffering from more frequent

---

[1] Dio 44, 15, 4 reports that March 15 was chosen because of the rumour that a decision was to be taken on the Sibylline oracle. In fact Caesar wanted to discuss the raising of objections by Antony in his role as augur, when Dolabella was to have been elected as consul for 44 in the place of the dictator (Cic. *Phil.* 2, 83; 88). See Suet. *Caes.* 80, 4; Nicol. Dam. F 130, 81. That Brutus had saved Antony's life was constantly criticized by Cicero (*ad Brut.* 2, 5, 1; 1, 4, 2; especially *Att.* 14, 21, 3, on May 11, 44: *acta enim illa res est animo virili, consilio puerili. qui enim hoc non vidit regni heredem relictum?* 15, 4, 2, on May 24: *animis enim usi sumus virilibus, consiliis, mihi credes, puerilibus. excisa enim est arbor, non evulsa, itaque quam fruticetur vides;* 11, 2; Plut. *Brut.* 18, 4. For further details, see *RE,* 10, 990; 7A, 1032.

[2] Plut. *Caes.* 63, 1–6; Suet. *Caes.* 81, 1–2; Dio 44, 17, 1; 18, 4; App. *b.c.* 2, 619; Val. Max. 1, 6, 13; 8, 11, 2; Vell. 2, 57, 1; Obseq. 67.

[3] Vell. 2, 57, 1; Suet. *Caes.* 86, 2; 87; App. *b.c.* 2, 455.

[4] Suet. *Caes.* 87; Plut. *Caes.* 63, 7, with the comment that Caesar, as was his custom, had been 'signing' letters (i.e. adding a final greeting such as *vale* in his own hand) even on the dining-couch, and when the question was raised had very quickly expressed his opinion. A different version in App. *b.c.* 2, 479.

spells of dizziness; some of the ancient authors speak of epileptic fits.[1] The ceaseless physical and psychological strain to which he had subjected himself since his consulship had left its mark even on his strong constitution. The best coin portraits of the year 44 show an aged man,[2] just as Frederick the Great, at the age of fifty-one, returned from the Seven Years' War as 'old Fritz'. His head was bald, and we are told that he was particularly pleased with the right to wear a laurel wreath because it allowed him to conceal the baldness.[3] Thus his sudden death would not have caused surprise;[4] after all, the words quoted above are closely connected with trains of thought which we meet in Caesar's surviving writings and which generally seem to have had a great influence on his decisions. He personally had no faith in the religion of Rome, and only used it as a political weapon. In the last weeks of his life, when his soothsayer inspecting sacrificial entrails prophesied calamity, he replied that things would turn out well since he wished it so: a sheep without a heart, he added, should not be regarded as a portent, since the same phenomenon had occurred before the battle of Munda.[5] Nor did he hold to any philosophical doctrines, as many of his educated contemporaries did. But he did believe in the secret workings of luck (fortuna, τύχη). He felt himself and all human achievement dependent on the rule of this power: 'Luck is the

---

[1] Plut. *Caes.* 17, 3 first mentions such a fainting fit at Corduba in 49 B.C., then (53, 6) during the battle of Thapsus (see above, p. 268, n. 3); this is confirmed by Suet. *Caes.* 45, 1: *comitiali quoque morbo bis inter res agendas correptus est.* Previously Caesar had enjoyed *valitudine prospera, nisi quod tempore extremo repente animo linqui atque etiam per somnum exterreri solebat;* 86, 1. Dio 43, 32, 7 mentions an illness during the Spanish campaign of 45 B.C. Other references are in Nicol. Dam. F 130, 83; App. *b.c.* 2, 459. A particularly competent modern physician who thoroughly investigated the evidence about Caesar's illness came to the conclusion that it was doubtful whether a diagnosis could be made after 2,000 years. There is nothing in the sources to suggest that illness impaired Caesar's energy, as L. Lange (*R.A.*, 3, 466) concluded. G. Ferrero (*Grandezza e Decadenza di Roma*, 2, 468) exaggerates it to 'decadenza intellettuale'. Against this, see Ed. Meyer, *Caesars Mon.*, 459 ff.; Collins, *Historia* 4, 461.

[2] The six best, reproduced in enlargement and with a commentary by A. Alföldi, are in *Antike Kunst* 2 (1959), 27 ff. There is also the head now in the Turin museum, reproduced as the frontispiece of this book; it was found at Tusculum in 1825, but not rediscovered until 1943 (by M. Borda). On this, see Erika Simon, *Archäol. Anzeiger* (1952), 125 ff., with illustrations on pp. 126 and 127. She argues (p. 134) that, apart from coins, this is the only contemporary likeness. On pp. 183 ff. she further discusses the portrait in the Museo Torlonia (illustrated on p. 134); the expression of pain which characterizes it suggests that it was produced soon after March 15.

[3] Suet. *Caes.* 45, 2; Dio 43, 43, 1.

[4] In his disappointment at the consequences of Caesar's murder, Cicero wrote on May 24, 44 (*Att.* 15, 4, 3): *me Idus Martiae non delectant. ille* (Caesar) *numquam revertisset* (from the Parthian War).

[5] Suet. *Caes.* 77; App. *b.c.* 2, 488; Cic. *divin.* 1, 119; 2, 37; Plin. *n.h.* 11, 186.

sovereign power in all things, but especially in war. By moving small weights in the balance it produces great vicissitudes.' More than once he expresses himself thus in his works.[1] That is why the quotation 'Let the dice fly high!' came to his lips when he crossed the Rubicon. But at the same time he felt himself favoured by fortune and also held the view that, although she should not be wantonly tempted, her favour could be won by grasping her gifts at the right moment.[2]

This belief was widespread among educated men of the time, but in Caesar's case was clearly based mainly on his personal experiences. For without wishing to deny his genius we must admit that he had a remarkable amount of luck in his life: he escaped the Sullan terror, in the following years he repeatedly risked his life against pirates and on military service, his life was in danger during the Catilinarian troubles and in the ensuing years of campaigning the fate of himself and his army was often balanced on a razor's edge. But it was not just a matter of individual crises; until the final victory his political position was permanently under a severe threat. A calculation of the material resources of the two sides would certainly not have suggested Caesar's victory. And even those who made a just assessment of his military and political genius were moved to doubt whether this was sufficient to prevail over the superior forces on the other side. In such cases human wisdom is unable to foretell the outcome; the religious man will see the hand of God in the course of history. Caesar, however, belonged to those who speak of luck or chance (fortuna and τύχη have both these meanings). But true to this belief and to his character he dared and won, and this again strengthened him in his belief.

His contemporaries also regarded him as the favourite of fortune. 'Caesar and his luck' became almost proverbial. From the speeches directed at him by Cicero in 46 and 45 we can see that this view, although it limited the achievement of his genius, was also officially welcome.[3] For it gave to the victor's rule the stamp of the supernatural which called for obedience and which had already found expression in religious worship. He also trusted in his luck where the irreconcilable republican opposition was concerned; for, having no ethical scruples in political life and well knowing the general

---

[1] See above, p. 194, n. 2; p. 236, n. 1.   [2] Caes. *b.c.* 3, 73, 4–6.

[3] Cic. *Lig.* 38: *nihil habet nec fortuna tua maius quam ut possis nec natura melius quam ut velis servare quam plurimos; Deiot.* 19 (words put in the plaintiff's mouth): *tua te eadem quae saepe fortuna servavit.* See above, p. 308, n. 2.

moral corruption, he had to face the fact that no security precautions would be proof against an attempt at assassination. Since his luck had preserved him hitherto—we know of two incidents—had he not every reason to continue to rely on it?

On top of this he was counting on the political insight of his opponents, who would realize that his death would plunge the Empire into limitless confusion.[1] However, just as he himself underestimated the vigour of the republican idea, the pride of the nobility and the spirit of Cato, so his opponents failed to recognize the far-reaching change which his intervention had produced in the structure of the Empire. The rule of the nobility, which for a hundred years had shown itself inadequate, could not pick up the threads where it appeared to have dropped them in the year 49. Yet the feeling that they were having to endure an intolerable servitude prevented them from appreciating this. The reconciliation offered by Caesar meant nothing to the optimates. The former masters of the state did not wish to become the ruler's officials. That men of the moral eminence of Brutus and Cicero saw in Caesar's murder an altogether splendid deed without a trace of any other sentiment is the best illustration of the enormous hatred which inspired them.[2] And yet they were dealing with the greatest man of his time and one with whom they had both actively enjoyed friendly relations!

On the morning of March 15 the Senate assembled in the hall of Pompey's theatre. Caesar did not arrive until about eleven o'clock. He was not feeling well and because of various premonitions his wife Calpurnia had urged him to cancel the meeting. But eventually Decimus Brutus succeeded in persuading him to make a personal appearance. When the ruler had taken his seat and before proceedings began, his enemies surrounded him on the pretext of making personal requests. The consul Antony was detained in the ante-room by Trebonius. As soon as the liberators were sure of

---

[1] Suet. *Caes.* 86, 2: *non tam sua quam rei publicae interesse, uti salvus esset: se iam pridem potentiae gloriaeque abunde adeptum; rem publicam, si quid sibi eveniret, neque quietam fore et aliquanto deteriore condicione civilia bella subituram.*

[2] In the letter mentioned p. 326, n. 4 above (*Att.* 15, 4, 3), in which he recognizes Caesar's murder as superfluous, he couples his name with a curse!—*ita gratiosi eramus apud illum (quem di mortuum perduint!), ut nostrae aetati, quoniam interfecto domino liberi non sumus, non fuerit dominus ille fugiendus.* As here, he admits as early as May 4 (*Att.* 14, 17, 6): *minore periculo existimo contra illas nefarias partis vivo tyranno dici potuisse quam mortuo. ille enim nescio quo pacto ferebat me quidem mirabiliter.*

themselves, the daggers were drawn and Caesar collapsed, silently wrapping himself in his toga, struck twenty-three times.[1]

The deed was so frightful that it is not surprising if events did not develop as its authors had expected. Instead of the Senate's immediately taking over the government, a numbing terror gripped the whole city and temporarily there was a political vacuum. But from it there later developed, with an inner necessity, the new civil war of thirteen years' duration which Caesar had foretold. On April 7 Gaius Matius made a telling comment on the situation. The problems, he said, were insoluble: 'for if Caesar with all his genius could not find a way out, who will find one now?'[2] So long as the defeated oligarchy possessed leaders like Brutus and Cassius, another battle against the new military monarchy was inevitable. Caesar's tragic end merely brought this necessity straight into the limelight.

Yet despite the catastrophe of March 15 Caesar remained the victor. For during the ensuing period political developments entirely followed the lines laid down by him. Even though his immediate successor took account of earlier experiences and contented himself with less harsh forms of dominion, the Roman imperial period still rested on the basis created by Caesar. The oligarchy based on the votes of the people was replaced by a military monarchy in which the will of the ruler supported by a standing army was the only basis of power. For a long time this military monarchy brought 'quiet to Italy, peace to the provinces and welfare to the empire',[3] and for this reason the peoples freed from the horrors of civil war gratefully honoured it as the rule of the deity made manifest.

Caesar, if anyone, deserves to be called a master of politics. He was equally great in understanding general political trends as in directing them. With consummate skill he handled the machinery of political details, without ever sacrificing his major aim of winning decisive power. He felt himself capable of becoming the first citizen (*princeps*). His achievements in Gaul confirmed this rank and the civil war represents the defence of his *dignitas*. His intentions after victory are revealed by his restless activity as ruler. He published no programme; a practical politician through and through, he recognized the problems in every situation and set about mastering them with a will. Our sources—his own narrative and the accounts of contemporaries—give us an insight into individual cases but no certain

---

[1] Cic. *Att.* 14, 4, 4; *divin.* 2, 23; *Phil.* 2, 88–89; Suet. *Caes.* 81, 4–82, 3; Plut. *Caes.* 66; Nicol. Dam. F 130, 82–90; Dio 44, 16–19; App. *b.c.* 2, 490–498.

[2] Cic. *Att.* 14, 1, 1.   [3] Caes. *b.c.* 3, 57, 4.

Y

information about his innermost thoughts. We may go so far as to assert that eventually the dictatorship for life corresponded to his wishes. But it remains obscure when, to use the language of Cicero,[1] he decided on this form for his *principatus*. For it is not possible to determine how far the extravagant senatorial decrees which granted him this vast power were inspired by himself. We must guard against ascribing to him actions, plans and motives for which there is no authority;[2] yet the observer who researches honestly into Caesar's life cannot escape the impression that the unusually varied series of individual acts eventually fits together in a comprehensive whole. Each of his enterprises supported the other. He spun no thread which he could not pick up again at the right time. Aristocratic nonchalance was present in all that he did. He never compromised himself and always jealously guarded his honour. His words bore the stamp of self-evident superiority. He avoided the ordinary quarrels of everyday politics in order to impose his personality with all the more effect at the crucial moment. However difficult the situation, he was never embarrassed. The combination of statesman and general in his person was unique. In the military field he displayed the same characteristics which distinguished him as a politician. He was no less effective as a tactician than as a strategist, and the *esprit de corps* which he instilled in his army became a pillar of his policy. In fact, his strategy was intended only to assist him as a politician.

His family ties and ability made him a 'popular' politician implacably opposed to the Sullan oligarchy. But his policy, like Sulla's, ended with the dictatorship won from his province. This was the fault of circumstances. But the different use which he made of the dictatorship derived from his will. His personal experiences had a decisive effect on him here, since more than ten years' absence from Rome had completely liberated him from the constraint of city-state concepts. His Gallic proconsulship and long sojourn in all the remaining provinces of the Empire had given him the idea of a monarchically governed imperial state, but he had only just started on his task as ruler when the hands of murderers snatched him away. Horrified we see his brilliant figure sink into the darkness of this catastrophe. What a tragedy lies over the life of the greatest

---

[1] Cic. *off.* 1, 26: *quem sibi ipse opinionis errore finxerat principatum.* To appreciate this one should recall the passage in the letter of 46 B.C. (*fam.* 6, 6, 5): if Pompey had avoided civil war, *esset hic quidem clarus in toga et princeps, sed tantas opes quantas nunc habet non haberet.*

[2] This is admirably argued by H. Strasburger in *HZ* 175, 225.

genius produced by Rome—to be snuffed out by Romans who imagined that they were acting on behalf of their *res publica*! His demonic genius raised him in every respect above all his contemporaries—through his spiritual and physical vigour, through the faster tempo of his life, through his free-ranging gaze which, unfettered by traditional concepts, everywhere discovered new possibilities, and through the masterful way in which he overcame difficulties and realized the most daring plans. Thus, although he was a Roman through and through and intended only to use his rule in order to raise the *imperium populi Romani* to the level of perfection required by the circumstances, nevertheless the flights of his genius lifted him to a lonely eminence where others were unable to follow him.

Involved from his youth in the fight against the inadequacy of the optimates, he did not fail to recognize that despite their degeneracy these descendants kept alive the traditions which had once made Rome great, and in the civil war he had become fully acquainted with the tough powers of resistance which they possessed. The policy of reconciliation after victory was therefore seriously intended and its failure was the cause of the catastrophe. Nothing is more moving than this conclusion. For the man proscribed as a tyrant only fell because out of inner conviction he tried to complete the revolution he had set in train without terror and without an appropriate regard for the security of his own person.[1] If his struggle for the support of the optimates remained unsuccessful, this is not to be attributed only to their failure to understand his activity as a statesman or the necessity of absolute rule. Between them and him there lay the fearful hatred that had accumulated in two decades of violent battles, but which in reality went further back, since it arose from a society that had long been unsettled by revolution and still trembled at the memory of the Sullan proscriptions. Caesar's attack on the laboriously restored order was from the start

---

[1] On the policy of reconciliation, see Caesar's utterance of 49 B.C. (above, p. 202, n. 4). When Cicero, in *Lig.* 38 (the passage quoted in p. 327, n. 3, above), ascribes this to his natural disposition, it may be rhetorical. But in the passages of the letters quoted in p. 328, n. 2, above he reluctantly confirms his opinion even after March 15. Dio (in the epitome of Xiphilinus) reports that in 197 he personally heard Septimius Severus read a speech to the Senate in which he demonstrated the advantages of cruelty from the examples of Sulla, Marius and Augustus, while Pompey and Caesar came to grief through their clemency (75, 8, 1). In view of the rosy light in which the Augustan age is still seen even in our own time, it is worth noting that Septimius Severus took Augustus, the man of the Proscriptions, as his model. Cf. Vittinghoff, *Kaiser Augustus* (1959), 44. On the after-effects of Cicero's condemnation of the tyrant Caesar, see the excellent remarks by J. Béranger, *Hermes* 87 (1959), 110; 117.

stigmatized as a criminal act of destruction, and it could not be denied that in the furtherance of his aims he stopped at no act of corruption or violence. Of course he was unsurpassed in the art of putting his enemies in the wrong and of representing their opposition as wicked stubbornness which could only be surmounted by force, but at the same time he displayed the most winning charm in personal relationships, against which even determined opponents were not always proof.

Scintillating and many-sided, his genius was thus displayed to his politically involved contemporaries. And so there was something uncanny in his manner, which made his enemies suspicious of any overture from him and on the other hand impeded genuine friendship. Although he had followers of lower rank, who served him with limitless admiration, and could count on his veterans, among his peers he found no allies who saw in him more than the furtherer of their own selfish ambitions, none who, convinced of the necessity of his political work, became willing pillars of his rule. Here we come to a point that should be carefully noted. Whereas Caesar during his earlier career and until well into the civil war explained and justified his policy by word and pen, he kept silent about his ultimate plans, so that these can only be inferred from actions and occasional utterances more or less well attested. Circumstances had so ordained that an answer was demanded of him to the question of how he conceived the future of the *res publica*, and this question in fact drove him into a corner, since it was posed with a particular expectation which he did not intend to fulfil. He wished to resolve the dilemma by leaving for the war against the Parthians. But already too much had happened which revealed his intentions. He had risen too high always to keep his self-control before the many signs of opposition. One also forms the impression that he eventually lost his patience and would not wait for the new order to grow to maturity. But his most disastrous mistake was the immoderate attack on the dead Cato. For he, if anyone, had been his foe from idealistic motives, and the malicious campaign which Caesar waged against his umblemished figure could therefore only strengthen the judgment that Cato had passed on him in the name of the *res publica*.

History will not repeat this judgment. The universal historian may speculate whether the Roman Empire brought happiness to the peoples united under it. For the Romans this was no problem. Even the optimates found nothing to criticize in this aspect of Roman

policy as it had developed. Their aversion to Caesar was of a different kind. Like all the other optimates Cato was unable to grasp
that the time for oligarchy was now over, although he personally
wore himself out in hopeless efforts to kill the many-headed hydra
of its degeneracy. All regarded *regnum* as the greatest crime against
the spirit of the Roman constitution. But whereas for many this
had sunk to the level of a political catchphrase, for Cato, with his
Roman spirit based on Stoic foundations, tyranny negated the
concept of the state, while the tyrant was identified with the depths
of inhumanity, the beast which denied the dignity of man. As early
as December 5, in the year 63, he had recognized these characteristics in Caesar and from then on worked tirelessly to open the eyes
of others to them. We should fail to sympathize fully with the
tragic element in Caesar's catastrophe, if we did not recognize
that Cato thereby struck the Achilles heel of his opponent. Plutarch[1]
tells the story that in 61, while passing through a poor Alpine village
on the way to Spain, Caesar, jokingly asked by his suite whether
there were electoral battles and struggles for position even there,
promptly replied: 'I would rather be the first among these people
than second at Rome.' Similarly Cicero[2] saw the reason for his
downfall in his passion for power. 'With the army of the Roman
people he oppressed the Roman people itself and forced the citizens
of a state which was not only free itself, but ruled over the peoples
of the world, to be his slaves.'

But this is measuring Caesar's achievement as a statesman with
an inadequate yardstick. His ambition soared so high because he was
conscious of his power to become the master of the Empire. He had
never believed in the ideologies of the optimates and populares
which he had encountered on his entry into political life. A born
enemy of the optimates, he regarded demagogy as no more than
the means to an end. On his way to power he did not meet men who
could impress him. He only saw selfishness and envy, and eventually
emerged from a life of continuous and bitter conflict as a cynic who
assessed all relationships only according to their political value and,
judging the others by himself, could not believe that their *res publica*
could still be to them something other than 'a mere name without
body and form'.[3] This does not lessen the guilt of his murderers,
but we can at least understand that things happened as they did.

---

[1] Plut. *Caes.* 11, 3–4.   [2] Cic. *off.* 3, 84.   [3] Suet. *Caes.* 77.

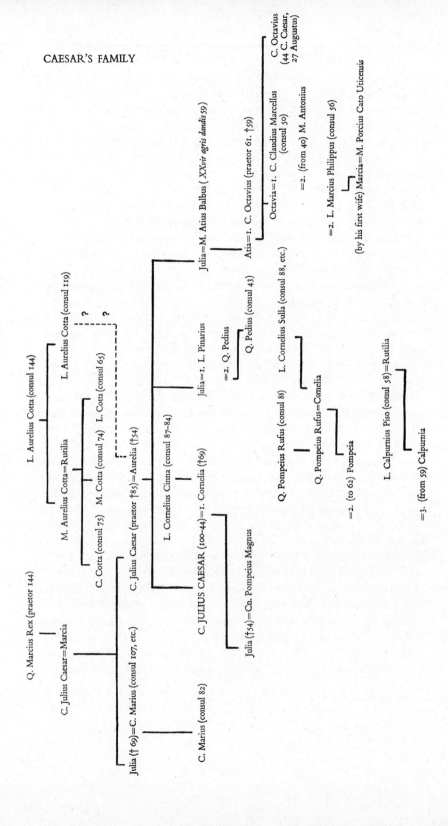

CAESAR'S FAMILY

CHRONOLOGY OF CAESAR'S LIFE

100 Caesar born on July 13.

87 After the victory of C. Marius and L. Cornelius Cinna, designated for the high dignity of *flamen Dialis*.

84 Marries Cornelia, the daughter of Cinna.

81 In danger after Sulla's victory; pardoned, he refuses to divorce Cornelia. His daughter Julia was born of this marriage.

80 Military service with the governor of Asia. At the capture of Mytilene he wins the *corona civica*.

78 Military service under P. Servilius Isauricus in Cilicia. After Sulla's death returns to Rome.

77 Prosecutes the consular Cn. Cornelius Dolabella.

75 Journey to Rhodes. Adventure with the pirates.

74 On the outbreak of the Mithridatic War he fights against a royal detachment in the province of Asia.

73 Pontifex.

72 Military tribune.

69 Quaestor under the governor of Further Spain. Funeral speeches over Julia, the widow of Marius, and over his own wife Cornelia.

67 Marries Pompeia; speaks in favour of the Lex Gabinia; curator of the Appian Way.

66 Speaks in favour of the Lex Manilia.

65 Curule Aedile.

64 Iudex quaestionis.

63 Pontifex Maximus; on December 5 warns the Senate against condemning the arrested Catilinarians to death.

62 Praetor; divorces Pompeia because of the Clodius scandal.

61 Proconsul of the province of Further Spain; victorious campain against the Lusitani.

60 Stands for the consulship; in the teeth of heavy optimate opposition elected with the support of Pompey and Crassus.

59 Consul; despite optimate opposition receives the provinces of Cisalpine Gaul (with Illyricum) and Transalpine Gaul. Pompey marries Julia, Caesar Calpurnia.

58 Proconsul; campaigns against the Helvetii and Ariovistus.

57 Campaign against the Belgae.

56 Renewal of the 'triumvirate' with Pompey and Crassus. Campaigns against rebellious tribes in Brittany and Normandy and against the Aquitani.

55 Pompey and Crassus consuls for second time; they pass a law prolonging Caesar's proconsulship for five years. Caesar against the Usipetes and Tencteri; first Rhine crossing; reconnaissance mission to Britain.

54 Expedition to Britain. Contrary to his usual practice Caesar spends the winter in Gaul. Ambiorix destroys fifteen cohorts. The winter quarters of the legate Q. Cicero besieged; relieved by Caesar. Labienus against the Treveri.   Death of Julia.

53 Punitive expeditions against the rebellious tribes; second Rhine crossing; the Eburones exterminated; Ambiorix escapes. On June 9 battle of Carrhae in Mesopotamia; a few days later Crassus dies.

52 In Rome: on January 18 Clodius is murdered. Pompey is authorized by the Senate to restore order and is elected 'consul without a colleague' on February 25. Caesar negotiates from Ravenna and by the law of the ten tribunes is exempted from a personal canvass in the year 49 for the consulship of 48.
In Gaul: outbreak of the great rebellion led by Vercingetorix. Caesar captures Avaricum, has to abandon the siege of Gergovia, is victorious in the neighbourhood of Dijon, surrounds Vercingetorix in Alesia, repels the attempt of the combined Celtic levies to relieve him; Vercingetorix surrenders.

51 Caesar subdues the tribes still in arms. At Rome the optimates begin attempts to recall Caesar prematurely. Caesar publishes the seven books on the Gallic War.

50 In Rome the optimates continue their efforts to recall Caesar and bring him to trial. The tribune C. Curio prevents the passing of a decree.

49 On January 7 the Senate decrees that Caesar must dismiss his army by an appointed day, and despite tribunician veto grants Pompey and the other magistrates dictatorial authority. During the night of January 10 Caesar crosses the Rubicon; on February 21 Corfinium surrenders; on March 17 Pompey crosses to the Balkan peninsula; on August 2 Pompey's army in Nearer

Spain ceases hostilities; the southern Spanish province follows
suit. Massilia surrenders after six months of siege. Caesar is
elected dictator.

48 2nd Consulship. Caesar resigns the dictatorship, crosses the
Adriatic, in April surrounds Pompey at Dyrrhachium; Pompey
breaks through the siege line in July, Caesar marches to
Thessaly, on August 9 defeats Pompey at Pharsalus; pursues
him to Egypt; on September 28, before Caesar's arrival,
Pompey is murdered. Caesar occupies Alexandria, with his
small force is besieged by the king's party.

47 In March reinforcements arrive from Asia Minor; on March 27
Caesar is victorious on the Nile, installs Cleopatra as queen,
leaves Egypt at the beginning of June, on August 1 defeats
king Pharnaces in Asia Minor. In Rome, on news of the battle
of Pharsalus, he has already been appointed dictator for a
year. At the beginning of October Caesar arrives in Rome,
on December 28 lands on the coast of Africa. Since 48 the
optimates have been collecting a large army in the province
of Africa.

46 3rd Consulship. On April 6 Caesar is victorious at Thapsus;
on July 25 he arrives in Rome. Dictator for ten years. In Spain
the sons of Pompey renew the war. At the beginning of November Caesar leaves Rome.

45 4th Consulship. On March 17 Caesar is victorious at Munda;
in October he is back in Rome. Extravagant decrees in his
honour, including dictatorship for life and divine worship.

44 5th Consulship. On February 15 Caesar appears at the Lupercalia as *dictator perpetuus* in the dress of the ancient kings of
Rome with the golden wreath; he refuses the diadem offered
by the consul Mark Antony and thus the title of king. About
60 Republicans join together to remove the tyrant. On March
15 Caesar is murdered.

ANALYTICAL INDEX OF NAMES

NOTE: C. stands for Caesar, except in conjunction with other names, when it denotes the praenomen Gaius.

References to the notes have not been included when there is already reference to the page on which they occur.

* Main references only given.

* Main references only are given.

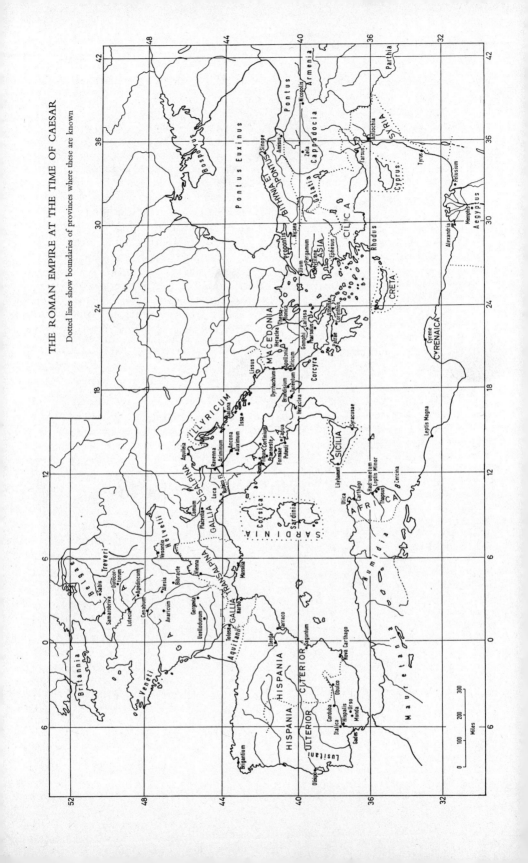

THE ROMAN EMPIRE AT THE TIME OF CAESAR

Dotted lines show boundaries of provinces where these are known